S0-AUN-070

HONOLULU ~WAIKIKI HANDBOOK

THE ISLAND OF OAHU

HONOLULU ~WAIKIKI HANDBOOK

THE ISLAND OF OAHU

THIRD EDITION

J.D. BISIGNANI

**COMPILED AND REVISED BY
ROBERT NILSEN**

MOON
TRAVEL
HANDBOOKS

HONOLULU~WAIKIKI HANDBOOK
THIRD EDITION

Published by
Moon Publications, Inc.
P.O. Box 3040
Chico, California 95927-3040, USA

Printed by
Colorcraft Ltd.

Please send all comments,
corrections, additions,
amendments, and critiques to:

**HONOLULU~WAIKIKI HANDBOOK
MOON TRAVEL HANDBOOKS
P.O. BOX 3040
CHICO, CA 95927-3040, USA
e-mail: travel@moon.com
www.moon.com**

© Text and photographs copyright J.D. Bisignani, 1999.
All rights reserved.

© Illustrations and maps copyright Moon Publications, Inc., 1999.
All rights reserved.

Some photos and illustrations are used by permission
and are the property of the original copyright owners.

Printing History
1st edition—1990
3rd edition—February 1999

ISBN: 1-56691-128-1
ISSN: 1077-288X

Editor: Deana Corbitt Shields
Editorial Assistance: Pauli Galin
Copy Editors: Deana Corbitt Shields, Asha Johnson
Production & Design: David Hurst, Rob Warner
Illustration: Bob Race
Cartography: Eric Allen
Index: Jeannie Trizzino

Front cover photo: Waikiki, HI courtesy of Photo Network

All photos by J.D. Bisignani unless otherwise noted.

Distributed in the United States and Canada by Publishers Group West

Printed in China

All rights reserved. No part of this book may be translated or reproduced in any form, except brief extracts by a reviewer for the purpose of a review, without written permission of the copyright owner.

Although the author and publisher have made every effort to ensure that the information was correct at the time of going to press, the author and publisher do not assume and hereby disclaim any liability to any party for any loss or damage caused by errors, omissions, or any potential travel disruption due to labor or financial difficulty, whether such errors or omissions result from negligence, accident, or any other cause.

ACKNOWLEDGMENTS

Writing the acknowledgments for a book is supercharged with energy. It's a time when you look forward, hopefully, to a bright future for your work, and a time when you reflect on all that has gone into producing it. Mostly it's a time to say thank you. Thank you for the grace necessary to carry out the task, and thank you to all the wonderful people whose efforts have helped so much along the way. To the following people, I offer my most sincere thank you.

Firstly, to the Moon staff, professionals every one. As time has passed, and one book has followed another, they've become amazingly adept at their work, to the point where their mastery is a marvel to watch.

I would also like to thank the following people for their special help and consideration: Dr. Greg Leo, an adventurer and environmentalist who has done remarkable field research and provided me with invaluable information about the unique flora and fauna of Hawaii; Roger Rose of the Bishop Museum; Lee Wild, Hawaiian Mission Houses Museum; Marilyn Nicholson, State Foundation on Culture and the Arts; the Hawaii Visitors Bureau; Donna Jung, Donna Jung and Associates, who has shown confidence in me since day one; Haunani Vieira, Dollar Rent A Car; Keoni Wagner, Hawaiian Airlines; Jim and John Costello; Dr. Terry and Nancy Carolan; Aubrey Hawk, Bozelle Advertising; Constance Wright, Molokai Visitors Assoc.; Barbara Schonley, of Molokai; Elisa Josephsohn, Public Relations; Faith Ogawa, for helping me keep the faith; Joyce Matsumoto, Halekulani Hotel; Bernie Caalim-Polanzi, Hilton Hotels; Nancy Daniels, Outrigger Hotels; Donn Takahashi, Regional Manager Prince Hotels; Alvin Wong, Hawaii Prince Hotel Waikiki; Martin Kahn, Kahn Galleries; Allison Kneubuhl, Kahala Mandarin Oriental; Matt Bailey, Manele Bay Hotel; Kurt Matsumoto, Lodge at Koele; Stephanie Reid, Princeville Hotel; Margy Parker, Poipu Beach Resort Assoc.; Yvonne Landavazo, Ritz-Carlton Kapalua; Catherine Sharpe, Stryker Weiner; Adi Kohler, Percy Higashi, and Jon Fukuda, Mauna Kea Beach Hotel and Hapuna Prince Hotel; Donna Kimura, Orchid at Mauna Lani; Denise Anderson, Hawaiian Regent; Dennis Costa, Maui Hill; Kim Marshall, Grand Wailea Resort; Sheila Donnelly, of Sheila Donnelly and Associates; Sandi Kato-Klutke, Aston Kauai Beach Villa; Barbara Sheehan, Sheraton Moana Surfrider; Aston Hotels; Norm Manzione, Suntrips; Renee Cochran and Will Titus, Colony Resorts; Linda Darling-Mann, a helpful Kauai friend; Sonia Franzel, Public Relations; Alexander Doyle, Aston Wailea Resort. To all of you, my deepest *aloha*.

CONTENTS

MAP SYMBOLS

═══════	Superhighway	○	City	✗	International Airport
═══════	Main Road	○	Town	✗	Airfield/Airstrip
═══════	Other Road	▪	Sight	▲	Mountain
··········	Trail	•	Accommodation	⬎	Waterfall
⬮	US Interstate	⌕	Golf Course	⬌	Swamp/Marsh
◯	State Highway	∧	Campground		Water
⊛	State Capital	🏯	Heiau		Reef

MAPS

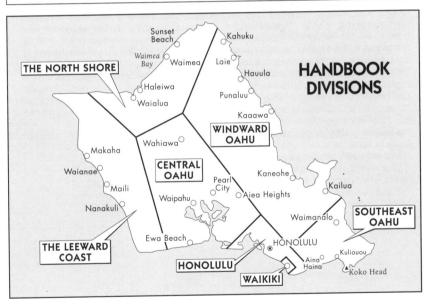

HANDBOOK DIVISIONS

ABBREVIATIONS

A.F.B.—Air Force Base
B.Y.O.—Bring Your Own
4WD—Four-wheel Drive
H-1—Hawaii Interstate Highway 1
HVB—Hawaii Visitors Bureau
NWR—National Wildlife Refuge
OHA—Office of Hawaiian Affairs

PADI—Professional Association of Dive
    Instructors
P.O.—Post Office
Rt.—Route
SASE—Self-addressed, Stamped Envelope
SRA—State Recreation Area
YH—Youth Hostel

HELP MAKE THIS A BETTER BOOK

In today's world, things change so rapidly that it's impossible for one person to keep up with everything happening in any one place. This is particularly true in Hawaii, where situations are always in flux. Travel books are like automobiles: they require fine tuning and frequent overhauls to keep in shape. Help us keep this book in shape! We require input from our readers so that we can continue to provide the best, most current information available. Please write to let us know about any inaccuracies, new information, or misleading suggestions. Although we try to make our maps as accurate as possible, errors do occur. If you have any suggestions for improvement or places that should be included, please let us know about them.

We especially appreciate letters from female travelers, visiting expatriates, local residents, and hikers and outdoor enthusiasts. We also like hearing from experts in the field as well as from local hotel owners and individuals wishing to accommodate visitors from abroad.

If you take a photograph during your trip that you feel might be included in future editions, please send it to us. Send only good slide duplicates or glossy black-and-white prints. Drawings and other artwork are also appreciated. If we use your photo or drawing, you'll be mentioned in the credits and receive a free copy of the book. Keep in mind, however, that the publisher cannot return any materials unless you include a self-addressed, stamped envelope. Moon Publications will own the rights on all material submitted. Address your letter to:

Honolulu-Waikiki Handbook
Moon Travel Handbooks
P.O. Box 3040
Chico, CA 95927-3040 USA
e-mail: travel@moon.com

BOB RACE

INTRODUCTION

It is the destiny of certain places on earth to be imbued with an inexplicable magnetism, a power that draws people whose visions and desires combine at just the right moment to create a dynamism so strong that it becomes history. The result for these "certain places" is greatness . . . and Oahu is one of these.

It is difficult to separate Oahu from its vibrant metropolis, Honolulu, whose massive political, economic, and social muscle dominates the entire state, let alone its home island. But to look at Honolulu *as* Oahu is to look only upon the face of a great sculpture, ignoring the beauty and subtleties of the whole. Just the words "Honolulu, Waikiki, Pearl Harbor" conjure up visions common to people the world over. Immediately imaginations flush with palm trees swaying, a healthy tan, bombs dropping with infamy, and a golden moon rising romantically over coiled lovers on a white-sand beach.

Oahu is called the "Gathering Place," and to itself it has indeed gathered the noble memories of old Hawaii, the vibrancy of a bright-eyed fledgling state, and the brawny power so necessary for the future. On this amazing piece of land

adrift in the great ocean, 885,000 people live; nearly seven times that number visit yearly, and as time passes Oahu remains strong as one of those "certain places."

OVERVIEW

Oahu is partly a tropical garden, bathed by soft showers and sunshine, and swaying with a gentle but firm rhythm. You can experience this feeling all over the island, even in pockets of downtown Honolulu and Waikiki. However, its other side is brash—dominated by the confidence of a major American city perched upon the Pacific Basin whose music is a pounding staccato jackhammer, a droning bulldozer, and the mechanical screech of the ever present building crane. The vast majority of first-time and return visitors land at Honolulu International and spend at least a few days on Oahu, usually in Waikiki.

People are amazed at the diversity of experiences the island has to offer. Besides the obvious (and endless) beach activities are museums, botanical gardens, a fantastic zoo and aquarium, nightclubs, extravagant shows, free entertainment, cultural classes, theaters, sporting events, a major university, historical sights galore, an exotic cosmopolitan atmosphere, backcountry trekking, and an abundance of camping—all easily accessible via terrific public transportation. Finally, to sweeten the pot, Oahu can easily be the least expensive of the Hawaiian Islands to visit.

Waikiki

Loosely, this world-famous beach is a hunk of land bordered by the Ala Wai Canal and running eastward to Diamond Head. Early last century these two golden miles were little more than a string of dirty beaches backed by a mosquito-infested swamp. Until 1901, when the Moana Hotel was built, only Hawaii's few remaining *ali'i* and a handful of wealthy *kama'aina* families had homes here. Now, over 120 hotels, condos, and other lodgings provide more than 31,000 rooms, and if you placed a $20 bill on the ground, it would barely cover the cost of the land beneath it.

This hyperactive area will delight and disgust you, excite and overwhelm you, but never bore you. Waikiki gives you the feeling that you've arrived *someplace*. Besides lolling on the beach and walking the gauntlet of restaurants, hotels, malls, and street merchants, you can visit the **Waikiki Aquarium** or **Honolulu Zoo**. Then, ever present Diamond Head, that monolith of frozen lava so symbolic of Hawaii, is easily reached by a few minutes' drive and a leisurely stroll to its summit.

Downtown Honolulu

Head for downtown and give yourself a full day to catch all the sights. It's as if a huge grappling hook, attached to the heart of a Mainland city, hauled it down to the sea. But don't get the idea that Honolulu is not unique, because it is! You'll find a delightful mixture of quaintly historic and future-shock new, exotic, and ordinary. The center is **Iolani Palace**, the only royal palace in America, heralded by the gilded statue of Kamehameha I. In an easy walking radius is the **State Capitol** and attendant government buildings. Chrome and glass skyscrapers holding the offices of Hawaii's economically mighty shade small stone and wooden structures from last century: **Mission Houses Museum, Kawaiahao Church,** and **St. Andrew's Cathedral.**

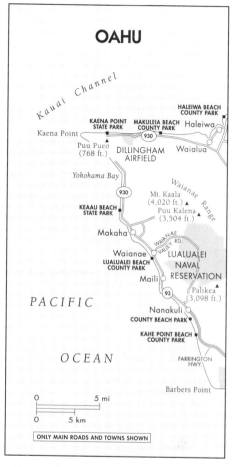

OAHU

Kauai Channel

HALEIWA BEACH COUNTY PARK

KAENA POINT STATE PARK

MAKULEIA BEACH COUNTY PARK

Kaena Point

Haleiwa

930

Puu Pueo (768 ft.)

DILLINGHAM AIRFIELD

Waialua

Yokohama Bay

930

Waianae Range

Mt. Kaala (4,020 ft.)

KEAAU BEACH STATE PARK

Puu Kalena (3,504 ft.)

Makaha

WAIANAE VALLEY RD.

Waianae

LUALUALEI BEACH COUNTY PARK

LUALUALEI NAVAL RESERVATION

Maili

93

Palikea (3,098 ft.)

PACIFIC

Nanakuli

NANAKULI COUNTY BEACH PARK

KAHE POINT BEACH COUNTY PARK

OCEAN

FARRINGTON HWY.

Barbers Point

0   5 mi

0   5 km

ONLY MAIN ROADS AND TOWNS SHOWN

Down at the harbor **Aloha Tower** greets the few passenger ships that still make port; nearby is the floating museum ship, ***Falls of Clyde,*** a nostalgic reminder of simpler times. Hotel Street takes you to old but not always venerable **Chinatown,** filled with alleyways housing tiny temples, herbalists, aromatic markets, inexpensive eateries, rough night spots, dives, and the strong, distinctive flavor of transplanted Asia.

If the hustle and bustle gets to be too much, head for **Foster Botanical Garden.** Or hop a bus for the serenity of the **Bishop Museum,** un-

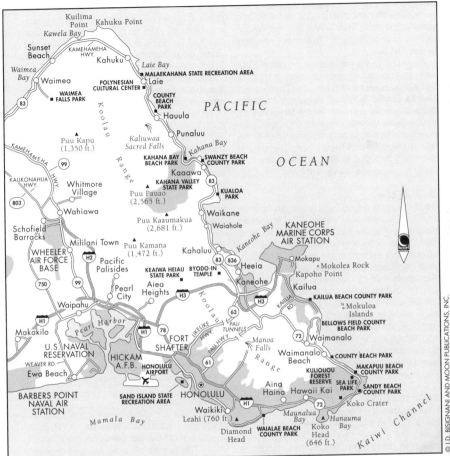

© J.D. BISIGNANI AND MOON PUBLICATIONS, INC.

doubtedly *the* best Polynesian cultural and anthropological museum in the world.

Pearl Harbor

Hawaii's major interstate, H-1, runs west of the city center to Pearl Harbor. You can't help noticing the huge military presence throughout the area, and it becomes clear why Hawaii is considered the most militarized state in the country. The attraction here, which shouldn't be missed, is the **USS *Arizona* Memorial.** The museum, visitor center, and tours, operated jointly by the U.S. Navy and the National Park Service, are both excellent and free. Nearby is the **USS *Bowfin*** Submarine Museum and Park, another worthy stop.

Heading for the Hills

Behind the city is the **Koolau Range.** As you head for these beckoning hills, you can take a sidetrip over to the **University of Hawaii** and the **East-West Center** while passing through Manoa Valley, epitome of the "good life" in Hawaii. Route 61 takes you up and over Nuuanu Pali to Oahu's windward side. En route you'll pass **Punchbowl,** an old crater holding some of the dead from WW II and the Korean and Vietnam Wars in the **National Cemetery of the Pacific.**

As you climb, the road passes the **Royal Mausoleum,** final resting place for some of Hawaii's last kings, queens, and nobility. Then comes **Queen Emma Summer Palace,** a Victorian home of gentility and lace. Next is **Nuuanu Pali,** where Kamehameha drove 16,000 Oahu warriors over the cliff, sealing his dominance of the island kingdom with their blood. The view is hauntingly beautiful, as the mountains drop suddenly to the coast of windward Oahu.

Central Oahu

Pearl Harbor is ringed by rather ordinary communities, suburbs of Honolulu, but farther up the plateau the land has been put to other uses. Early in the 19th century, huge pineapple plantations were started on the rich soil and today vast tracts are still planted in this fruit. The **Pineapple Variety Garden** is a good place to stop for an introduction to the history of pineapple production on the island. Also dominating huge areas of this central plain are the broad and beautiful **Schofield Barracks** Army base and **Wheeler Air Force Base,** two of the island's important military installations and significant players in America's armed conflicts in the Pacific and Asia.

Southeast Oahu

Head eastward around the bulge of Diamond Head, passing exclusive residential areas; you quickly find a string of secluded beaches. Around this tip you pass **Koko Head Crater,** a trekker's haven; **Hanauma Bay,** an underwater conservation park renowned for magnificent family-class snorkeling; **Sea Life Park,** an extravaganza of the deep; and the sleepy village of **Waimanalo Beach.** Nearby at **Bellow's Field Beach Park** is camping, where it's hard to believe the city's just 10 miles back.

Windward Oahu

On the windward side, **Kailua** and **Kaneohe** have become suburban bedroom communities for Honolulu; this entire coast has few tourist accommodations, so it remains relatively uncrowded.

The beaches are excellent, with beach parks and camping spots one after another, and the winds make this side of the island perfect for windsurfing. North of Kaneohe is **Valley of the Temples,** where a Christian cross sits high on a hill, and Buddha rests calmly in **Byodo-In Temple.**

Just up Route 83, the coastal highway, comes **Waiahole,** Oahu's outback, where tiny farms and taro patches dot the valleys and local folks move with the slow beat of bygone days. Then a quick succession of beaches follows, many rarely visited by more than a passing fisherman. **Punaluu** comes next, offering some of the only accommodations along this coast and a lovely walk to **Kaliuwaa,** the Sacred Falls. In **Laie** is the **Polynesian Cultural Center,** operated by the Mormon Church. **Brigham Young University** is here too, along with a solid Mormon temple that's open to visitors.

North Shore

The North Shore is famous for magnificent surf. From **Sunset Beach** to **Haleiwa,** world-class surfers come to be challenged by the liquid thunder of the **Banzai Pipeline** and **Waimea Bay.** Art shops, boutiques, tiny restaurants, and secluded hideaways line these sun-drenched miles. At the far western end is **Dillingham Airfield,** where you can take a glider ride or air tour of the island. The road ends with a very rugged jeep trail leading to **Kaena Point,** renowned for the most monstrous surf on the North Shore.

Leeward Coast

The western end of the island is the **Waianae coast.** The towns of **Maili, Waianae,** and **Makaha** are considered the last domain of the locals of Oahu. This coastal area has escaped development so far, and it's one of the few places on the island where ordinary people can afford to live near the beach. Sometimes an attitude of resentment spills over against tourists; mostly though, lovely people with good hearts live here, who will treat you as nicely as you're willing to treat them.

World-class surfing beaches along this coast are preferred by many of the best-known surfers from Hawaii. Many work as lifeguards in the beach parks, and they all congregate for the annual surfing championships held in Makaha. Here is a perfect chance to mingle with the people and soak up some of the last real *aloha* left on Oahu.

THE LAND

When Papa, the Hawaiian earth mother, returned from vacationing in Tahiti, she was less than pleased. She had learned through a gossiping messenger that her husband, Wakea, had been playing around. Besides simple philandering, he'd been foolish enough to impregnate Hina, a lovely young goddess who bore him island children. Papa, scorned and furious, showed Wakea that two could play the same game by taking a handsome young lover, Lua. Their brief interlude yielded the man-child Oahu, sixth of the great island children. Geologically, Oahu is the second oldest main island after Kauai. It emerged from beneath the waves as hissing lava a few million years after Kauai, and cooled a little quicker than Papa's temper to form Hawaii's third largest island.

The modern geological theory concerning the formation of the Hawaiian Islands is no less fanciful than the Polynesian legends sung about their origins. Science maintains that 30 million years ago, while the great continents were being geologically tortured into their rudimentary shapes, the Hawaiian Islands were a mere ooze of bubbling magma 20,000 feet below the surface of the primordial sea. For millions of years this molten rock flowed up from fissures in the sea floor. Slowly, layer upon layer of lava was deposited until an island rose above the surface of the sea. The great weight then sealed the fissure, whose own colossal forces progressively crept in a southwestern direction, to burst out again and again building the chain of what we now call the Hawaiian Islands. At the same time the entire Pacific plate was afloat on the giant sea of molten magma, and it slowly glided to the northwest, carrying the newly formed islands with it.

In the beginning the spewing crack formed Kure and Midway islands in the extreme northwestern sector of the Hawaiian chain. This process continued for eons, and today 132 islands, islets, and shoals make up the Hawaiian Islands, stretching nearly 1,600 miles across an expanse of the North Pacific. Some geologists maintain that the "hot spot" now primarily under the Big Island remains relatively stationary, and that the 1,600-mile spread of the Hawaiian archipelago is due to a northwest drifting effect of about three to five inches per year. Still, with the center of activity under the Big Island, Mauna Loa and Kilauea volcanoes regularly add more land to the only state in the country that is literally still growing. About 30 miles southeast of the Big Island is Loihi Sea Mount, waiting 3,000 feet below the waves. Frequent eruptions bring it closer and closer to the surface until one day it will emerge and become the newest Hawaiian island.

Land Facts

Oahu has a total land area of 597 square miles, and measured from its farthest points it is 44 miles long by 30 miles wide. The 112-mile coastline holds the two largest harbors in the state, **Honolulu** and **Pearl**. The **Koolau Range** runs north-south for almost the entire length of the island, dramatically creating windward and leeward Oahu. The **Waianae Range** is smaller, confined to the western section of the island. It too runs north-south, dividing the **Waianae coast** from the massive **Leilehua Plateau** of the interior. **Mount Ka'ala**, at 4,020 feet, in the northern portion of the Waianae Range, is Oahu's highest peak. Even with these two mountain ranges, 45% of Oahu is less than 500 feet in elevation, the lowest of the six major islands. The huge Leilehua Plateau is still covered in pineapple and sugarcane. Lying between the two mountain ranges, it runs all the way from Waialua on the North Shore to Ewa, just west of Pearl Harbor. At its widest point, around Schofield Barracks, it's more than six miles across.

Oahu's most impressive natural features were formed after the heavy volcanic activity ceased and erosion began to sculpt the island. The most obvious are the wall-like cliffs of the *pali*—mountain heads eroded by winds from the east, valleys cut by streams from the west. Perfect examples of these eroded valleys are **Nuuanu** and **Kalihi**. Other impressive examples are **Diamond Head, Koko Head,** and **Punchbowl**, three "tuff-cone" volcanoes created after the heavy volcanic activity of early Oahu. A tuff cone is volcanic ash cemented together to form solid rock. Diamond Head is the most dramatic, formed after a minor

Waikiki growing rice, circa 1920

HAWAII STATE ARCHIVES

eruption about 100,000 years ago and rising 760 feet from its base.

Oahu has the state's longest stream, **Kaukonahua,** which begins atop Pu'u Kaaumakua at 2,681 feet in the central Koolau Range and runs westward 33 miles through the Leilehua Plateau. En route, it bypasses the **Wahiawa Reservoir** which, at 302 acres, forms the second largest body of fresh water in Hawaii. Oahu's tallest waterfalls are 80-feet **Kaliuwaa** ("Sacred Falls"), just west of Punaluu, and **Waihee Falls,** in the famous Waimea Park on the North Shore, which have a sheer drop of over 40 feet. Oahu's main water concern is that usage is outstripping supply, and major municipal water shortages are expected by the year 2000 unless conservation measures and new technology are employed.

Island Builders
The Hawaiians worshipped Madame Pele, the fire goddess. Her name translates equally as "volcano," "fire pit," or "eruption of lava." When she was angry, she complained by spitting fire, which cooled and formed land. Volcanologists say that the islands are huge mounds of cooled basaltic lava surrounded by billions of polyp skeletons that have formed coral reefs. The Hawaiian Islands are shield volcanoes that erupt gently and form an elongated dome much like a turtle shell. Oahu, like the rest, is a perfect example of this. Once above the surface of the sea, the tremendous weight of lava seals the fissure below. Eventually the giant tube that car-

ried lava to the surface sinks in on itself and forms a caldera, as evidenced at Hanauma Bay, the famous snorkeling spot on Oahu's southeast coast. More eruptions occur periodically, and they cover the already existing island like frosting on a titanic cake. Wind and water next take over and relentlessly sculpt the raw lava into deep crevices and cuts that become valleys. The once smooth *pali* of windward Oahu are now undulating green monoliths due to this process.

Lava
Lava flows in two distinct types, for which the Hawaiian names have become universal geological terms: a'a and pahoehoe. They're easily distinguished in appearance, but chemically they're the same. A'a is extremely rough and spiny, and will quickly tear up your shoes if you do much hiking over it. Also, if you have the misfortune to fall down, you'll immediately know why they call it a'a. Pahoehoe is billowy, ropy lava that looks like burned pancake batter and can mold itself into fantastic shapes. Examples of both are encountered on various hikes throughout Oahu. Other lava oddities that you may spot on Oahu are peridots, green gemlike stones called "Maui Diamonds"; clear feldspar; and gray lichens covering the older flows known as "Hawaiian snow."

Rivers and Lakes
Oahu has no navigable rivers, but there are hundreds of streams. The two largest are Kaukon-

ahua Stream, which runs through central Oahu, and Waikele Stream, which drains the area around Schofield Barracks. A few reservoirs dot the island; Wahiawa Reservoir and Nuuanu Pali Reservoir are both excellent freshwater fishing spots, but there are no natural bodies of water on Oahu. Hikers should be aware that the uncountable streams and rivulets can quickly turn from trickles to torrents, causing flash floods in valleys that were the height of hospitality only minutes before.

Tsunamis

"Tsunami" is the Japanese word for "tidal wave." It ranks up there with the worst in sparking horror in human beings. But if you were to count up all the people in Hawaii who have been swept away by tidal waves in the last 50 years, the toll wouldn't come close to those killed on bicycles in only a few Mainland cities in just five years.

A Hawaiian tsunami is actually a seismic sea wave generated by an earthquake that could easily have had its origins thousands of miles away in South America or Alaska. Some waves have been clocked at speeds up to 500 miles per hour. The safest place, besides high ground well away from beach areas, is out on the open ocean where even an enormous wave is perceived only as a large swell—a tidal wave is only dangerous when it is opposed by land. The worst tsunami to strike the islands in modern times occurred on April 1, 1946. The Hana Coast of windward east Maui bore the brunt with a tragic loss of many lives as entire villages were swept away. Hilo, on the Big Island, also suffered greatly.

Earthquakes

These rumblings can be a concern in Hawaii, offering a double threat because they can generate tsunamis. If you ever feel a tremor and are close to a beach, get as far away as fast as possible. A few tremors are felt on Oahu, but the Big Island, because of its active volcanoes, experiences hundreds of technical earthquakes, although 99% can only be felt on very delicate equipment. The last major quake occurred on the Big Island in late November 1975, reaching 7.2 on the Richter scale and causing many millions of dollars worth of damage in the island's southern regions. The only loss of life occurred when a beach collapsed and two people from a large camping party were drowned. Oahu, like the rest of the state, has an elaborate warning system against natural disasters. You will notice loudspeakers high atop poles along many beaches and coastal areas; these warn of tsunamis, hurricanes, and earthquakes. They are tested at 11 a.m. on the first working day of each month. All island telephone books contain a civil defense warning and procedures section with which you should acquaint yourself. Note the maps in the telephone books, which show the areas traditionally inundated by tsunamis and what procedures to follow in case an emergency occurs.

THE CLIMATE

"So Good" Weather

The ancient Hawaiians had words to describe climatic specifics such as rain, wind, fog, and even snow, but they didn't have a general word for "weather." The reason is that the weather is just about the same throughout the year and depends more on where you are on any given island than on what season it is. The Hawaiians did distinguish between *kau* (summer, May-Oct.) and *hoo'ilo* (winter, Nov.-April), but this distinction included social, religious, and even navigational factors, far beyond a mere distinction of weather variations.

The average daytime temperature throughout Hawaii is about 80° F (26° C), with the average winter (January) day registering 78°, and the average summer (August) day raising the thermometer only seven degrees to 85°. Nighttime temperatures drop less than 10 degrees. Elevation, however, does drop temperatures about three degrees for every 1,000 feet you climb. The lowest temperature ever recorded in Hawaii was inside the Mauna Kea summit crater on the Big Island of Hawaii in January 1970, when the mercury dropped to a mere 1° F; the hottest day occurred in 1931 at Pahala in the Kau District of the Big Island with a scorching (for Hawaii) 100° F.

Oahu, like all the Hawaiian Islands, has equitable weather year-round with the average daily temperature ranging between 71° and 80° F. The mountainous interior experiences about the same temperatures as the coastal areas because of the small difference in elevation. However, the *pali* are known for strong, cooling winds that rise up the mountainside from the coast. The coldest temperature recorded on the island was 43° in Kaneohe on the windward coast, while the hottest was 96° at Waianae on the leeward coast.

Rainfall

Precipitation is the biggest differentiating factor in the climate of Oahu. Hardly a day goes by that it isn't raining somewhere on the island. Precipitation occurs mostly at and below the 3,000-foot level. Although rain can occur at any time of year, it's more plentiful in winter. Hawaiian rains generally aren't very nasty. Much of the time just a light drizzle, they hardly ever last all day. Mostly localized to a relatively small area, you can oftentimes spot them by looking for the rainbows. An important rain factor is the mountains, which act like water magnets. Moist winds gather around them and eventually build rain clouds. The ancient Hawaiians used these clouds and the reflected green light on their underbellies to spot land from great distances.

Generally, the entire leeward coast, the "rain shadow," from Makaha to Koko Head, is dry. Waianae, Honolulu International Airport, and Waikiki average only 20-25 inches of rain a year. The Leilehua Plateau in the center of the island does a little better at about 40 inches a year. Rain falls much more frequently and heavily in the Koolau Mountains and along the windward coast. The bay town of Kaneohe sees 75-90 inches a year, while the Nuuanu Reservoir in the mountains above Honolulu gets a whopping 120-130 inches yearly, with some years substantially greater than that. The maxim throughout the islands is "don't let rain spoil your day." If it's raining, simply move on to the next beach, or around to the other side of the island where it'll probably be dry. You can most often depend on the beaches of Waikiki and Waianae to be sunny and bright. No matter where you go for that day on the beach, however, the temperature of the ocean water will run 75-80° year-round.

The Trade Winds

One factor that keeps the Hawaiian temperatures both constant and moderate is the trade winds. These breezes are so reliable that the northeast sides of the islands are always referred to as "windward," regardless of where the wind happens to be blowing on any given day. You can count on the trades to be blowing on an average of 300 days per year, hardly missing a day during summer, and occurring half the time in winter. They blow throughout the day but are strongest during the heat of the afternoon, then weaken at night. Just when you need a cooling breeze, there they are, and when the temperature drops at night, it's as if someone turned down the giant fan.

The trade winds are also a factor in keeping down the humidity. They will suddenly disappear, however, usually in winter, and might not resume for a few weeks. The tropic of Cancer runs through the center of Hawaii, yet its famed oppressively hot and muggy weather is joyfully absent. Honolulu, on the same latitude as sweaty Hong Kong and Havana, has only a 50-60% daily humidity factor.

TEMPERATURE AND RAINFALL

TOWN		JAN.	MARCH	MAY	JUNE	SEPT.	NOV.
Honolulu	High	80°	82°	84°	85°	82°	81°
	Low	60°	52°	68°	70°	71°	68°
	Rain	4"	2"	0"	0"	0"	4"
Kaneohe	High	80°	80°	80°	82°	82°	80°
	Low	67°	62°	68°	70°	70°	68°
	Rain	5"	5"	2"	0"	2"	5"
Waialua	High	79°	79°	81°	82°	82°	80°
	Low	60°	60°	61°	63°	62°	61°
	Rain	2"	1"	0"	0"	1"	3"

temp in °F, rainfall in inches

WHAT IS A HURRICANE?

Tropical Depression: low-pressure system or cyclone with winds below 39 mph.

Tropical Storm: cyclone with winds between 39-73 mph.

Hurricane: cyclone with winds over 74 mph. These winds are often accompanied by torrential rains, destructive waves, and storm surges.

The National Weather Service issues a Hurricane Watch if hurricane conditions are expected in the area within 36 hours. A Hurricane Warning is issued when a hurricane is expected to strike within 24 hours. The state of Hawaii has an elaborate warning system against natural disasters. You will notice loudspeakers high atop poles along many beaches and coastal areas; these warn of tsunamis, hurricanes, and earthquakes. As the figures below attest, property damage has been great but the loss of life has, thankfully, been minimal.

MAJOR HURRICANES SINCE 1950

NAME	DATE	ISLANDS AFFECTED	DAMAGES
Hiki	Aug. 1950	Kauai	1 death
Nina	Dec. 1957	Kauai	—
Dot	Aug. 1959	Kauai	$5.5 million
Fico	July 1978	Hawaii	—
Iwa	Nov. 1982	Kauai, Oahu	1 death; $234 million
Estelle	July 1986	Maui, Hawaii	$2 million
Iniki	Sept. 1992	Kauai, Oahu	8 deaths; $1,900 million

Kona Winds

"Kona" means "leeward" in Hawaiian, and when the northeasterly trades stop blowing these southerly winds often take over, bringing in hot sticky air. To anyone from Hawaii, "kona wind" is euphemistic for bad weather. Luckily, they are most common during the cooler months, from October to April, when they appear roughly half the time. The temperatures drop slightly during the winter so these hot winds are tolerable, and even useful for moderating the thermometer. In the summer they are awful, but luckily—again—they hardly ever blow during this season.

A "kona storm" is another matter. These subtropical low-pressure storms develop west of the Hawaiian Islands, and as they move east they draw winds up from the south. Usual only in winter, they can cause considerable damage to crops and real estate. There is no real pattern to kona storms—some years they come every few weeks while in other years they don't appear at all.

Severe Weather

With all this talk of ideal weather it might seem like there isn't any bad. Read on. When a storm does hit an island, conditions can be bleak and miserable. The worst storms occur in the fall and winter and often have the warped sense of humor to drop their heaviest rainfalls on areas that are normally quite dry. It's not unusual for a storm to dump more than three inches of rain an hour; this can go as high as 10, making Hawaiian rainfalls some of the heaviest on earth.

Hawaii has also been hit with some walloping hurricanes in the last few decades. There haven't been many but they've been destructive. The vast majority of hurricanes originate far to the southeast off the coast of Mexico and Latin America. Some, particularly later in the season, start in the midst of the Pacific Ocean near the equator south of Hawaii. Hurricane season is generally considered June to November. Most pass harmlessly south of Hawaii, but some, swept along by kona winds, strike the islands. The most recent and destructive was Hurricane Iniki, which battered the islands in 1992, killing eight people and causing an estimated $2 billion worth of damage. It had its greatest effect on Niihau, the Poipu Beach area of Kauai, and the leeward coast of Oahu.

FLORA AND FAUNA

THE MYSTERY OF MIGRATION

Anyone who loves a mystery will be intrigued by the speculation about how plants and animals first came to Hawaii. Most people's idea of an island paradise includes swaying palms, dense mysterious jungles ablaze with wildflowers, and luscious fruits just waiting to be plucked. In fact, for millions of years the Hawaiian chain consisted of raw and barren islands where no plants grew and no birds sang. Why? Because they are geological orphans that spontaneously popped up in the middle of the Pacific Ocean. The islands, more than 2,000 miles from any continental landfall, were therefore isolated from the normal ecological spread of plants and animals. Even the most tenacious travelers of the fauna and flora kingdoms would be sorely tried in crossing the mighty Pacific. Those that made it by pure chance found a totally foreign ecosystem. They had to adapt or perish. The survivors evolved quickly, and many plants and birds became so specialized that they were not only limited to specific islands in the chain but to habitats that frequently encompassed a single isolated valley. It was as if after traveling so far, and finding a niche, they never budged again. Luckily, the soil of Hawaii was virgin and rich, the competition from other plants or animals was nonexistent, and the climate was sufficiently varied and nearly perfect for most growing things.

The evolution of plants and animals on the isolated islands was astonishingly rapid. A tremendous change in environment, coupled with a limited gene pool, accelerated natural selection. For example, many plants lost their protective thorns and spines because there were no grazing animals or birds to destroy them.

Before settlement, Hawaii had no fruits, vegetables, coconut palms, edible land animals, conifers, mangroves, or banyans. Tropical flowers, wild and vibrant as we know them today, were relatively few. In a land where thousands of orchids now brighten every corner, there were only four native varieties, the least in any of the 50 states. By the beginning of this century, native plants below 1,500 feet were almost completely extinct or totally replaced by introduced species. Today, the indigenous plants and animals of Hawaii have the highest rate of extinction anywhere on earth—more than one-third of the endangered plants and animals in the U.S. are Hawaiian species.

The land and its living things have been greatly transformed by man and his agriculture. This inexorable process began when Hawaii was the domain of its original Polynesian settlers, then greatly accelerated when the land was inundated by Westerners.

The indigenous plants and birds of Oahu have suffered the same fate as those of the other Hawaiian islands and are disappearing at an alarming rate. There are several sanctuaries on Oahu where native species still live, but they must be vigorously protected. Do your bit to save them; enjoy but don't disturb.

FLORA

Hawaii's indigenous and endemic plants, flowers, and trees are both fascinating and beautiful, but unfortunately, like everything else that was native, they are quickly disappearing. The majority of flora found exotic by visitors was either introduced by the original Polynesians or later by white settlers. The Polynesians who colonized Hawaii brought foodstuffs, including coconut, banana, taro, breadfruit, sweet potato, yam, and sugarcane. They also carried along gourds to use as containers, the *awa* plant to make a basic intoxicant, and the ti plant to use for offerings or to string into hula skirts. Non-Hawaiian settlers over the years have brought mangoes, papayas, passion fruit, pineapples, and all the other tropical fruits and vegetables associated with the islands. Also, most of the flowers, including protea, plumeria, anthuriums, orchids, heliconia, ginger, and most hibiscus have come from every continent on earth. Tropical America, Asia, Java, India, and China have all contributed their most beautiful and delicate blooms. Hawaii is blessed with national and state parks, gardens, undisturbed rain-

PUBLIC AND PRIVATE BOTANICAL GARDENS

Honolulu Botanical Gardens are five separate gardens supported and maintained by the county. All are open daily 9 a.m.-4 p.m. No admission fee, except for the Foster Botanical Garden.

1) **Foster Botanical Garden,** 50 N. Vineyard Blvd., tel. (808) 522-7065. Fifteen-acre oasis of exotic trees and rare plants. Guided tours Mon.-Fri. at 1 p.m.

2) **Ho'omaluhia Botanical Garden,** 45-680 Luluku Road, Kaneohe, tel. (808) 233-7323. Some guided hiking tours are offered

3) **Koko Crater Botanical Garden,** in Koko Head Regional Park, tel. (808) 522-7060.

4) **Lili'uokalani Botanical Garden,** between Kuakini and School Streets, Honolulu, tel. (808) 522-7066.

5) **Wahiawa Botanical Garden,** 1396 California Ave., Wahiawa, tel. (808) 621-7321. Twenty-seven acres of cultivated trees, flowers, and ferns from around the world.

Haiku Gardens, 46-336 Haiku Road, Kaneohe. Many acres of flowers, ornamental trees, and ponds. Chart House Restaurant on site.

Lyon Arboretum, 3860 Manoa Road, Honolulu, tel. (808) 988-3177 or (808) 988-7378. Dr. Lyon planted 194 acres of trees and flowers in the late 1800s. Research facility of the University of Hawaii. Open Mon.-Sat. 9 a.m.-3 p.m. Some guided tours offered.

Moanalua Gardens, 1352 Pineapple Place, tel. (808) 833-1944. Former Damon Estate property. Open to public for self-guided walks by reservation only. Guided tours given weekends at 9 a.m.; call (808) 839-5334.

Senator Fong's Plantation and Gardens, 47-285 Pulama Road, Kaneohe, tel. (808) 239-6775. Open daily 10 a.m.-4 p.m., except Christmas and New Year's Day. Offers 725 acres of natural and cultivated flower, tree, palm, and fern gardens. Admission.

Waimea Arboretum and Botanical Garden, at Waimea Falls Park, tel. (808) 638-8511. Collects, grows, and preserves rare Hawaiian flora. Flowers and plants labeled.

---

forests, private reserves, and commercial nurseries that offer an exhaustive botanical survey of the islands. The following is a sampling of common native and introduced flora that add the dazzling colors and exotic tastes to the landscape.

Native Trees

Koa and **ohia** are two indigenous trees still commonly seen on the main islands. Both have been greatly reduced by the foraging of introduced cattle and goats, and through logging and forest fires. The koa, a form of acacia, is Hawaii's finest native tree. It can grow to over 70 feet high and has a strong straight trunk, which can measure more than 10 feet in circumference. The foliage is sickle shaped and produces an inconspicuous pale yellow flower. The koa does best in well-drained soil in deep forest areas, but scruffy specimens will grow in poorer soil. The Hawaiians used koa as the main log for their dugout canoes, and elaborate ceremonies were performed when a log was cut and dragged to a canoe shed. Koa wood was also preferred for paddles, spears, even surfboards. Today it is still consid-

ered an excellent furniture wood, and although fine specimens can be found in reserves, loggers are harvesting the last of the big trees.

The ohia is a survivor and therefore the most abundant of all the native Hawaiian trees. Coming in a variety of shapes and sizes, it grows as miniature trees in wet bogs or as 100-foot giants on the cool dark slopes of higher elevations. This tree is often the first life in new lava flows. The ohia produces a tuftlike flower that resembles a natural pompon—usually red, but occasionally orange, yellow, or white, the latter being very rare and elusive. Considered sacred to Pele, it was said that she would cause a rainstorm if you picked ohia blossoms without the proper prayers. The flowers were fashioned into lei that resembled feather boas. The strong, hard wood was used to make canoes, poi bowls, and especially for temple images. Ohia logs were also shipped to the Mainland as railroad ties. It's believed that the "golden spike" linking rail lines between the U.S. East and West Coasts was driven into an ohia log from the Big Island when the two railroads came together in Ogden, Utah.

Tropical Rainforests

When it comes to pure and diverse natural beauty, the U.S. is one of the finest pieces of real estate on earth. As if purple mountains' majesty and fruited plains weren't enough, it even received a tiny living emerald of tropical rainforest. A tropical rainforest is where the earth itself takes a breath and exhales pure sweet oxygen through its vibrant living green canopy. Located in the territories of Puerto Rico and the Virgin Islands, and in the state of Hawaii, these forests comprise only one-half of one percent of the world's total, and they must be preserved. The U.S. Congress passed two bills in 1986 designed to protect the unique biological diversity of its tropical areas, but their destruction has continued unabated.

The lowland rainforests of Hawaii, composed mostly of native ohia, are being razed. Landowners slash, burn, and bulldoze them to create more land for cattle, agriculture, and—most distressingly—for wood chips to generate electricity! Introduced wild boar gouge the forest floor, exposing sensitive roots and leaving tiny, fetid ponds where mosquito larvae thrive. Feral goats that roam the forests are hoofed locusts that strip all vegetation within reach.

Almost half of the birds classified in the U.S. as endangered are from Hawaii, and almost all of these make their home in the rainforests. For example, Maui's rainforests have yielded the *po'ouli,* a new species of bird discovered only in 1974 and believed to number less than half a dozen. Another forest survey in 1981 rediscovered the **Bishop's 'o'o,** a bird thought to be extinct at the turn of the century. We can only lament the passing of the rainforests that have already fallen to ignorance, but if this ill-fated destruction continues on the global level, we will soon be lamenting our own passing. We must nurture the rainforests that remain with the simple enlightenment to let them be.

Hawaiian stilt

FAUNA

You would think that with Oahu's dense human population, little room would be left for animals. In fact, they are environmentally stressed, but they do survive.

The interior mountain slopes are home to **wild pigs,** and a small population of **feral goats** survives in the Waianae Range. Migrating **whales** pass by, especially along the leeward coast where they can be observed from lookouts ranging from Waikiki to Koko Head. Half a dozen introduced game birds are found around the island, but Oahu's real animal wealth is its indigenous birdlife.

Birds

One of the great tragedies of natural history is the continuing demise of Hawaiian birdlife. Perhaps only 15 original species of birds remain of the more than 70 native families that thrived before the coming of humans. Since the arrival of Captain Cook in 1778, 23 species have become extinct, with 31 more in danger. And what's not known is how many species were wiped out before the coming of white explorers. Experts believe that the Hawaiians annihilated about 40 species, including seven other species of geese besides the *nene,* a rare one-legged owl, ibis, lovebirds, sea eagles, and hunting creepers—all gone before Captain Cook arrived. Hawaii's endangered birds account for 40% of the birds officially listed as endangered or threatened by the U.S. Fish and Wildlife Service. In the last 200 years, more than four times as many birds have become extinct in Hawaii as in all of North America. These figures unfortunately suggest that a full 40% of Hawaii's endemic birds no longer exist. Almost all of Oahu's native birds are gone and few indigenous Hawaiian birds can be found on any island below the 3,000-foot level.

Native birds have been reduced in number because of multiple factors. The original Polynesians helped wipe out many species. They altered large areas for farming and used fire to destroy patches of pristine forests. Also, bird feathers were highly prized for the making of lei, for featherwork in capes and helmets, and for the large *kahili* fans that indicated rank among the *ali'i.* Introduced exotic birds and the new diseases they carried are another major reason for reduction of native bird numbers, along with predation by the mongoose and rat—especially upon ground-nesting birds. Bird malaria and bird pox are also devastating to the native species. Mosquitoes, un-

KAREN McKINLEY

known in Hawaii until a ship named the *Wellington* introduced them at Lahaina in 1826 through larvae carried in its water barrels, infect most native birds, causing a rapid reduction in birdlife. Feral pigs rooting deep in the rainforests knock over ferns and small trees, creating stagnant pools in which mosquito larvae thrive. However, the most damaging factor by far is the assault upon native forests by agriculture and land developers. The vast majority of Hawaiian birds evolved into specialists. They lived in only one small area and ate a very limited number of plants or insects, which once removed or altered resulted in the birds' deaths.

The shores around Oahu, including those off Koko Head and Sand Island, but especially on the tiny islets of Moku Manu and Manana on the windward side, are home to thriving colonies of marine birds. On these diminutive islands it's quite easy to spot a number of birds from the **tern** family, including the white, gray, and sooty tern. All have distinctive screeching voices and approximate wingspans of 30 inches. Part of their problem is that they have little fear of humans. Along with the terns are **shearwaters.** These birds have normal wingspans of about 36 inches and make a series of moans and wails, oftentimes while in flight. For some reason shearwaters are drawn to the bright lights of the city, where they fall prey to house cats and automobiles. Sometimes Moku Manu even attracts an enormous **Laysan albatross** with its seven-foot wingspan. **Tropic birds,** with their lovely streamerlike tails, are often seen along the windward coast.

To catch a glimpse of exotic birds on Oahu you don't have to head for the sea or the hills. The city streets and beach parks are constantly aflutter with wings. Black **myna birds** with their sassy yellow eyes are common mimics around town. **Sparrows,** introduced to Hawaii through Oahu in the 1870s, are everywhere, while **munia,** first introduced as cage birds from Southeast Asia, have escaped and can be found almost anywhere around the island. Another escaped cage bird from Asia is the **bulbul,** a natural clown that perches on any likely city roost and draws attention to itself with loud calls and generally ridiculous behavior.

If you're lucky, you can also catch a glimpse of the *pueo* (Hawaiian owl) in the mountainous areas of Waianae and the Koolau Range. Also, along trails and deep in the forest from Tantalus to the Waianae Range you can sometimes see elusive native birds like the *elepaio, amakihi,* and the fiery red *'i'iwi.*

The **amakihi** and *'i'iwi* are endemic birds not endangered at the moment. The *amakihi* is one of the most common native birds; yellowish green, it frequents the high branches of the ohia, koa, and sandalwood trees looking for insects, nectar, or fruit. It is less specialized than most other Hawaiian birds, the main reason for its continued existence. The *'i'iwi,* a bright red bird with a salmon-colored, hooked bill, is found in the forests above 2,000 feet. It too feeds on a variety of insects and flowers. The *'i'iwi* is known for a harsh voice that sounds like a squeaking hinge, but it's also capable of a melodious song. The feathers of the *'i'iwi* were highly prized by the *ali'i* for clothing decoration. The **elepaio,** with its long tail (often held upright), is a fairly common five-inch brown bird (appearance can vary considerably) that can be coaxed to come within touching distance of the observer. Sometimes it will sit on lower branches above your head and scold you. This bird was the special *amakua* (personal spirit) of canoe builders in ancient lore. The *apapane* is abundant in Hawaii, and being the most common native bird, is the easiest to see. It's a chubby, red-bodied bird about five inches long with a black bill, legs, wingtips, and tail feathers. It's quick and flitty and has a wide variety of calls and songs, from beautiful warbles to mechanical buzzes. Like the *'i'iwi,* its feathers were sought by Hawaiians to produce distinctive capes and helmets for the *ali'i.*

Oahu also is home to a number of game birds mostly found in the dry upland forests. These include three varieties of **dove,** the **Japanese quail,** both the **green** and **ring-necked pheasant,** and **Erkel's francolin.** Hunting of these birds occurs during different periods year-round and information can be had by contacting the Oahu branch of the Division of Forestry and Wildlife.

MARINELIFE

Hawaiian Whales and Dolphins
Perhaps it's their tremendous size and graceful power, coupled with a dancer's delicacy of movement, that render whales so aesthetically and emotionally captivating. In fact, many people claim

that they feel a spirit-bond to these obviously intelligent mammals that at one time shared dry land with us and then re-evolved into creatures of the great seas. Experts often remark that whales exhibit behavior akin to the highest social virtues. For example, whales rely much more on learned behavior than on instinct, one sign of a highly evolved intelligence. Gentle mothers and protective "escort" males join to teach the young to survive. They display loyalty and bravery in times of distress, and innate gentleness and curiosity. Their "songs," especially those of the humpbacks, fascinate scientists and are considered a unique form of communication in the animal kingdom. Humpback whales migrate to Hawaii every year from November to May. Here, they winter, mate, give birth, and nurture their young until returning to food-rich northern waters in the spring. It's hoped that the human race can peacefully share the oceans with these magnificent giants forever. Then, perhaps, we will have taken the first step in saving ourselves.

The role of whales and dolphins in Hawaiian culture seems quite limited. Unlike fish, which were intimately known and individually named, only two generic names described whales: *kohola* (whale) and *palaoa* (sperm whale). Dolphins were all lumped together under one name, *nai'a;* Hawaiians were known to harvest dolphins on occasion by herding them onto a beach. Whale jewelry was worn by the *ali'i.* The most coveted ornament came from a sperm whale's tooth, called a *lei niho palaoa,* which was carved into one large curved pendant. Sperm whales have upward of 50 teeth, which range in size from four to 12 inches and weigh up to two pounds. One whale could provide numerous pendants. The most famous whale in Hawaiian waters is the humpback, but others often sighted include the sperm, killer, false killer, pilot, Cuvier's, Blainsville, and pygmy killer. There are technically no porpoises, but dolphins include the common, bottlenose, spinner, white-sided, broad-beaked, slender-beaked, and rough-toothed.

Whalewatching

If you're in Hawaii from late November to early May, you have an excellent chance of spotting a humpback. You can often see a whale from a vantage point on land (a good spot on Oahu is in the southeast near Koko Head), but this is nowhere near as thrilling as seeing them close-up from a boat. Either way, binoculars are a must. Telephoto and zoom lenses are also useful, and you might even get a nifty photo in the bargain. But don't waste your film unless you have a fairly high-powered zoom: fixed-lens cameras give pictures with a lot of ocean and a tiny black speck. If you're lucky enough to see a whale breach (jump clear of the water), keep watching—they often repeat this a number of times. If a whale dives and lifts its fluke high in the air, expect it to be down for at least 15 minutes and not come up in the same spot. Other times they'll dive shallowly, then bob up and down quite often.

Coral

Whether you're an avid scuba diver or novice snorkeler, you'll become aware of Hawaii's underwater coral gardens and grottoes whenever you peer at the fantastic seascapes below the waves. Although there is plenty of it, the coral in Hawaii doesn't do as well as in other more equatorial areas because the water is too wild and it's not quite as warm. Coral looks like a plant fashioned from colorful stone, but it's the skeleton of tiny animals, zoophytes, which need algae in order to live. Coral grows best in water that is quite still, where the days are sunny, and where the algae can thrive. Many of Hawaii's reefs have been dying in the last 20 years, and no one seems to know why. Pesticides, used in agriculture, have been pointed to as a possible cause.

OAHU WILDLIFE REFUGES, BIRD SANCTUARIES, AND NATURE RESERVES

Two areas at opposite ends of the island have been set aside as national wildlife refuges (NWR): **James Campbell NWR,** above the town of Kahuku on the extreme northern tip, and **Pearl Harbor NWR,** on the West Lock of the harbor. Both were established in the mid-'70s and are managed by the U.S. Fish and Wildlife Service. They serve mainly as wetland habitats for the endangered Hawaiian gallinule *(alae'ula),* stilt *(aeo),* and coot *(alae ke'oke'o).* Clinging to existence, these birds should have a future as long as their nesting grounds remain undisturbed. These refuges also attract a wide variety of other birds, mostly introduced species such as **cattle egrets, herons,** a few species of **doves, munia, cardinals,** and the **common finch.**

Much of the area within the refuges is natural marshland, but ponds, complete with water-regulating pumps and dikes, have been built. The general public is not admitted to these areas without permission from the refuge managers. For more information, and to arrange a visit, contact Refuge Manager, Hawaiian and Pacific Islands NWR, U.S. Fish and Wildlife Service, Federal Bldg., Room 5231, P.O. Box 50167, Honolulu, HI 96850, tel. (808) 541-1201.

The Nature Conservancy of Hawaii maintains two nature preserves in coordination with one public and one private owner. **Honouliuli,** a 3,692-acre tract located on the southeast slope of the Waianae Mountains above Makakilo and Schofield Barracks, is home to more than 60 rare and endangered plants and animals, including a handful found nowhere else on earth. Two guided hikes into the preserve are offered once a month on Saturday or Sunday. Much smaller in size is the 30-acre **Ihi'ihilauakea** preserve. In this shallow crater above Hanauma Bay at the southeastern tip of the island is a totally unique vernal pool and a very rare *marsilea villosa* fern. Because of the nature of this extremely fragile ecosystem, visitation is limited. For more information on hikes or volunteer activities, contact the Nature Conservancy at (808) 537-4508.

Dotting the windward coast from Makapuu Point in the south to Kahuku in the north are over a dozen small islands that compose the Oahu section of the **Hawaii State Seabird Sanctuary.** None more than a half mile offshore, these islands are set aside to help seabirds nest, feed, and propagate, as well as to maintain native vegetation. Frequently seen on these islands are the frigate bird, sooty tern, red-footed booby, wedge-tail shearwater, and red-tail tropic bird, many of which lay their eggs and raise their chicks here. Others, like the wandering tattler and bristle-thighed curlew, migrate south from arctic regions to forage for food and winter over. Landing on Moku Manu and Manana islands is prohibited, but the rest can be visited, if posted regulations are followed.

BOB RACE

pueo

In order to help preserve specific land areas from greater degradation, three natural area reserves have been created on Oahu. Lying on the coast at the western tip of the island is **Kaena Point Natural Area Reserve,** where natural sand dunes and low-lying shore plants predominate. It's also an area where the Laysan albatross mate and the Hawaiian monk seal is starting to return to again after nearly being driven to the point of extinction. In the Waianae Mountains above Kaena is the lowland dry forest **Pahole Natural Area Reserve.** Here, isolated stands of native trees represent what some say is only about 10% of the dryland forests that once swathed these islands. High above Pahole is **Mt. Kahala Natural Area Reserve.** Below the peak on this flat top mountain is a cloud forest and boggy plateau, while down its eastern slope cut deep gorges filled with drier forests. Native trees, ferns, flowers, and birds abound and introduced plants and animals are being eradicated.

ENVIRONMENTAL RESOURCE GROUPS

Anyone interested in Hawaii's environmental issues could contact the following for more information: **Earthjustice Legal Defense Fund** (formerly, Sierra Club Legal Defense Fund), 223 S. King St., 4th Fl., Honolulu, HI 96813, tel. (808) 599-2436, e-mail: eajushi@igc.apc.org; **Greenpeace,** 1807 Waianuenue Ave., Hilo, HI 96720, tel. (808) 969-9910; **The Nature Conservancy,** 1116 Smith St., Suite 201, Honolulu, HI 96817, tel. (808) 537-4508, e-mail: TNCH1@aol.com, Web site: www.tnc.org/hawaii; **Rainforest Action Network,** 221 Pine St., Suite 500, San Francisco, CA 94104, tel. (415) 398-4404, e-mail: rainforest@ran.org, Web site: www.ran.org/ran; **Sierra Club Hawaii Chapter,** 233 Merchant St., 2nd Fl., Honolulu, HI 96813, tel. (808) 538-6616, Web site: www.hi.sierraclub.org; **Earth Trust,** 25 Kaneohe Bay Dr., Suite 205, Kailua, HI 96734, tel. (808) 254-2866, e-mail: earthtrust@aloha.net,

Web site: www.earthtrust.org; and **Conservation Council For Hawaii,** P.O. Box 2923, Honolulu, HI 96804, tel. (808) 236-2234, an affiliate of the National Wildlife Federation.

Environment Hawai'i, 200 Kanoelehua Ave., Suite 103-325, Hilo, HI 96720, tel. (808) 934-0115, fax 934-8321, e-mail: pattum@aloha.net, individual subscription rate $35 per year, is a savvy monthly newsletter that focuses on environmental and political issues facing Hawaii today. The well-re-searched and concisely written newsletter attempts to be fair to all parties concerned, explaining both sides to most controversies. Short on preaching and long on common sense, *Environment Hawai'i* is an excellent resource for anyone interested in sociopolitical and environmental issues.

For organizations offering environment-conscious tours in Hawaii see "Sightseeing Tours" in the "Getting Around" section of the Out and About chapter.

HISTORY

THE ROAD FROM TAHITI

Until the 1820s, when New England missionaries began a phonetic rendering of the Hawaiian language, the past was kept vividly alive only by the sonorous voices of special *kahuna* who chanted the sacred *mele.* The chants were beautiful flowing word pictures that captured the essence of every aspect of life. These *mele* praised the land *(mele aina),* royalty *(mele ali'i),* and life's tender aspects *(mele aloha).* Chants were dedicated to friendship, hardship, and to favorite children. Entire villages sometimes joined together to compose a *mele*—every word was chosen carefully, and the wise old *kapuna* would decide if the words were lucky or unlucky. Some *mele* were bawdy or funny on the surface, but

The canoe hull was a log shaped by masterly stone adze work. The sides were planks that were drilled and sewn together with fiber cord.

LOUISE FOOTE

contained secret meanings, often with biting sarcasm, that ridiculed an inept or cruel leader. But the most important chants took the listeners back into the dim past, even before people lived in Hawaii. From these genealogies *(ko'ihonua)* the *ali'i* derived the right to rule, since these chants went back to the gods Wakea and Papa from whom the *ali'i* were directly descended.

The Kumulipo

The great genealogies, finally compiled in the late 1800s by order of King Kalakaua, were collectively known as *The Kumulipo, A Hawaiian Creation Chant,* basically a Polynesian account of Genesis. Other chants related to the beginning of this world, but *The Kumulipo* sums it all up and is generally considered the best. The chant relates that after the beginning of time, there is a period of darkness. The darkness, however, mysteriously brims with spontaneous life; during this period plants and animals are born, as well as Kumulipo, the man, and Po'ele, the woman. In the eighth chant darkness gives way to light and the gods descend to earth. Wakea is "the sky father" and Papa is "the earth mother," whose union gives birth to the islands of Hawaii. First born is Hawaii, followed by Maui, then Kahoolawe. Apparently, Papa becomes bushed after three consecutive births and decides to vacation in Tahiti. While Papa is away recovering from postpartum depression and working on her tan, Wakea gets lonely, and takes Kaula as his second wife, who bears him the island-child of Lanai. Not fully cheered up, but getting the hang of it, Wakea takes a third wife, Hina, who promptly bears the island of Molokai. Meanwhile, Papa gets wind of these shenanigans, returns from

Polynesia, and retaliates by taking up with Lua, a young and virile god, and soon gives birth to the island of Oahu. Papa and Wakea finally decide that they really are meant for each other and reconcile to conceive Kauai, Niihau, Kaula, and Nihoa. These two progenitors are the source from which all the ali'i ultimately traced their lineage, and from which they derived their god-ordained power to rule.

Basically, there are two major genealogical families: the **Nana'ulu,** who became the royal ali'i of Oahu and Kauai; and the **Ulu,** who provided the royalty of Maui and Hawaii. The best sources of information on Hawaiian myth and legend are Martha Beckwith's Hawaiian Mythology and the monumental three-volume opus An Account of the Polynesian Race compiled by Abraham Fornander 1878-85. Fornander, after settling in Hawaii, married an ali'i from Molokai and had an illustrious career as a newspaper man, Maui circuit judge, and finally Supreme Court justice. For years Fornander sent scribes to every corner of the kingdom to listen to the elder kupuna. They returned with the firsthand accounts, which he dutifully recorded.

The Great Navigators

No one knows exactly when the first Polynesians arrived in Hawaii, but the great "deliberate migrations" from the southern islands seem to have taken place A.D. 500-800, though anthropologists keep pushing the date backward in time as new evidence becomes available. Even before that, however, it's reasonable to assume that the first people to set foot on Hawaii were probably fishermen, or perhaps defeated warriors whose canoes were blown hopelessly northward into unfamiliar waters. They arrived by a combination of extraordinary good luck and an uncanny ability to sail and navigate without instruments, using the sun by day and the moon and rising stars by night. They could feel the water and determine direction by swells, tides, and currents. The movements of fish and cloud formations were also utilized to give direction. Since their arrival was probably an accident, they were unprepared to settle on the fertile but barren lands, having no stock animals, plant cuttings, or women. Forced to return southward, undoubtedly many lost their lives at sea, but a few wild-eyed stragglers must have made it

home to tell tales of a paradise to the north where land was plentiful and the sea bounteous. This is affirmed by ancient navigational chants from Tahiti, Moorea, and Bora Bora, which passing from father to son revealed how to follow the stars to the "heavenly homeland in the north." Possibly a few migrations followed, but it's known that for centuries there was no real reason for a mass exodus, so the chants alone remained and eventually became shadowy legend.

From Where They Came

It's generally agreed that the first planned migrations were from the violent cannibal islands that Spanish explorers called the Marquesas, 11 islands in extreme eastern Polynesia. The islands themselves are harsh and inhospitable, breeding a toughness into these people which enabled them to withstand the hardships of long, unsure ocean voyages and years of resettlement. Marquesans were a fiercely independent people whose chiefs could rise from the ranks because of bravery or intelligence. They must have also been a fierce-looking lot. Both men and women tattooed themselves in complex blue patterns from head to foot. The warriors carried massive, intricately designed ironwood war clubs and wore carved whale teeth in slits in their earlobes, which became stretched to the shoulders. They shaved the sides of their heads with sharks' teeth, tied their hair in two topknots that looked like horns, and rubbed their heavily muscled and tattooed bodies with scented coconut oils. Their religion worshiped mummified ancestors; the bodies of warriors of defeated neighboring tribes were consumed. They were masters at building great double-hulled canoes launched from huge canoe sheds. Two hulls were fastened together to form a catamaran, and a hut in the center provided shelter in bad weather. The average voyaging canoe was 60-80 feet long and could comfortably hold an extended family of about 30 people. These small family bands carried all the staples they would need in the new lands.

The New Lands

For five centuries the Marquesans settled and lived peacefully on the new land, as if Hawaii's aloha spirit overcame most of their fierceness. The tribes coexisted in relative harmony, espe-

POLYNESIAN TRIANGLE

HAWAII

Palmyra

Baker

Christmas

Phoenix   EQUATOR

Tokelau

Marquesas

Society   Tuamoto

Samoa

Niue   Tahiti

Mangareva

Tonga   Cook

Austral

Pitcairn

Rapa

Easter

Kermadec

NEW ZEALAND

Chatham

0   1000 mi

0   1000 km

© J.D. BISIGNANI AND MOON PUBLICATIONS, INC.

cially since there was no competition for land. Cannibalism died out. There was much coming and going between Hawaii and Polynesia and new people came to settle for hundreds of years. Then, it appears that in the 12th century a deliberate exodus of warlike Tahitians arrived and subjugated the settled islanders. They came to conquer. This incursion had a terrific significance on the Hawaiian religious and social system. Oral tradition relates that a Tahitian priest, Paao, found the mana of the Hawaiian chiefs to be low, signifying that their gods were weak. Paao built a *heiau* at Waha'ula on the Big Island, then introduced the warlike god Ku and the rigid *kapu* system through which the new rulers became dominant. Voyages between Tahiti and Hawaii continued for about 100 years and Tahitian customs, legends, and language became the Hawaiian way of life. Then suddenly, for no recorded or apparent reason, the voyages discontinued and Hawaii returned to total isolation.

The islands remained forgotten for almost 500 years until the indomitable English seaman, Capt. James Cook, sighted Oahu on January 18, 1778, and stepped ashore at Waimea on Kauai two days later. At that time Hawaii's isolation was so complete that even the Polynesians had forgotten about it. On an earlier voyage, Tupaia, a high priest from Raiatea, had accompanied Capt. Cook as he sailed throughout Polynesia. Tupaia demonstrated his vast knowledge of existing archipelagoes throughout the South Pacific by naming over 130 islands and drawing a map that included the Tonga group, the Cook Islands, the Marquesas, and even tiny Pitcairn, a rock in far eastern Polynesia where the mutinous crew of the *Bounty* found solace. In mentioning the Marquesas, Tupaia said, *"He ma'a te ka'ata,"* which equals "Food is man" or simply "Cannibals!" But remarkably absent from Tupaia's vast knowledge was the existence of Easter Island, New Zealand, and Hawaii.

The next waves of people to Hawaii would be white men, and the Hawaiian world would be changed quickly and forever.

THE WORLD DISCOVERS HAWAII

The late 18th century was an extraordinary time in Hawaiian history. Monumental changes seemed to happen all at once. First, Capt. James Cook, a Yorkshire farm boy, fulfilling his destiny as the all-time greatest Pacific explorer, found Hawaii for the rest of the world. For better or worse, it could no longer be an isolated Polynesian homeland. For the first time in Hawaiian history, a charismatic leader, named Kamehameha, emerged, and after a long civil war united all the islands into one centralized kingdom. The death of Captain Cook in Hawaii marked the beginning of a long series of tragic misunderstandings between white man and native. When Kamehameha died, the old religious system of *kapu* came to an end, leaving the Hawaiians in a spiritual vortex. Many takers arrived to fill the void: missionaries after souls, whalers after their prey and a good time, traders and planters after profits and a home. The islands were opened and devoured like ripe fruit. Powerful nations, including Russia, Great Britain, France, and the United States, yearned to bring this strategic Pacific jewel under their own influence. The 19th century brought the demise of the Hawaiian people as a dominant political force in their own land and with it the end of Hawaii as a sovereign monarchy. An almost bloodless yet bitter military coup followed by a brief Hawaiian Republic ended in annexation by the United States. As the U.S. became completely entrenched politically and militarily, a new social and economic order was founded on the plantation system. Amazingly rapid population growth occurred with the importation of plantation workers from Asia and Europe, which yielded a unique cosmopolitan blend of races like nowhere else on earth. By the dawning of the 20th century, the face of old Hawaii had been altered forever; the "sacred homeland in the north" was hurled into the modern age. The attack on Pearl Harbor saw a tremendous loss of life and brought Hawaii closer

to the U.S. by a baptism of blood. Finally, on August 21, 1959, after 59 years as a "territory," Hawaii officially became the 50th state of the Union.

Captain Cook Sights Hawaii

In 1776, Capt. James Cook set sail for the Pacific from Plymouth, England, on his third and final expedition into this still vastly unexplored region of the world. On a fruitless quest for the fabled Northwest Passage across the North American continent, he sailed down the coast of Africa, rounded the Cape of Good Hope, crossed the Indian Ocean, and traveled past New Zealand, Tasmania, and the Friendly Islands (where an unsuccessful plot was hatched by the *friendly* natives to murder him). On January 18, 1778, Captain Cook's 100-foot flagship HMS *Resolution* and its 90-foot companion HMS *Discovery* sighted Oahu. Two days later, they sighted Kauai and went ashore at the village of Waimea on January 20, 1778. Though anxious to get on with his mission, Cook decided to make a quick sortie to investigate this new land and reprovision his ships. He did, however, take time to remark in his diary about the close resemblance of these newfound people to others he had encountered as far south as New Zealand, and marveled at their widespread habitation across the Pacific.

The first trade was some brass medals for a mackerel. Cook also stated that he had never before met natives so astonished by a ship, and that they had an amazing fascination for iron, which they called *toe,* Hawaiian for "adze." There is even some conjecture that a Spanish ship under one Captain Gaetano had landed in Hawaii as early as the 16th century, trading a few scraps of iron that the Hawaiians valued even more than the Europeans valued gold. It was also noted that the Hawaiian women gave themselves freely to the sailors with the apparent good wishes of the island men. This was actually a ploy by the *kahuna* to test if the newcomers were gods or men—gods didn't need women. These sailors proved immediately mortal. Cook, who was also a physician, tried valiantly to keep the 66 men (out of 112) who had measurable cases of venereal disease away from the women. The task proved impossible as women literally swarmed the ships; when Cook returned less than a year later, it was logged that signs of VD were already apparent on some natives' faces.

HAWAII STATE ARCHIVES

Capt. James Cook

Cook was impressed with the Hawaiians' swimming ability and with their well-bred manners. They had happy dispositions and sticky fingers, stealing any object made of metal, especially nails. The first item stolen was a butcher's cleaver. An unidentified native grabbed it, plunged overboard, swam to shore, and waved his booty in triumph. The Hawaiians didn't seem to care for beads and were not at all impressed with a mirror. Cook provisioned his ships by trading chisels for hogs, while common sailors gleefully traded nails for sex. Landing parties were sent inland to fill casks with fresh water. On one such excursion a Mr. Williamson, who was eventually drummed out of the Royal Navy for cowardice, unnecessarily shot and killed a native. After a brief stop on Niihau, the ships sailed away, but both groups were indelibly impressed with the memory of each other.

Cook Returns

Almost a year later, when winter weather forced Cook to return from the coast of Alaska, his discovery began to take on far-reaching significance. Cook had named Hawaii the "Sandwich Islands" in honor of one of his patrons, John Montague, the Earl of Sandwich. On this return voyage, he spotted Maui on November 26, 1778.

After eight weeks of seeking a suitable harbor, the ships bypassed it, but not before the coastline was duly drawn by Lt. William Bligh, one of Cook's finest and most trusted officers. (Bligh would find his own drama almost 10 years later as commander of the infamous HMS *Bounty.*) The *Discovery* and *Resolution* finally found a safe anchorage at Kealakekua on the Kona coast of the Big Island. It is very lucky for history that on board was Mr. Anderson, ship's chronicler, who left a handwritten record of the strange and tragic events that followed. Even more important were the drawings of John Webber, ship's artist, who rendered invaluable impressions in superb drawings and etchings. Other noteworthy men aboard were George Vancouver, who would lead the first British return to Hawaii after Cook's death and introduce many fruits, vegetables, cattle, sheep, and goats, and James Burney, who would become a long-standing leading authority on the Pacific.

The Great God Lono Returns

By all accounts Cook was a humane and just captain, greatly admired by his men. Unlike many other supremacists of that time, he was known to have a respectful attitude toward any people he discovered, treating them as equals and recognizing the significance of their cultures. Not known as a violent man, he would use his superior weapons against natives only in an absolute case of self-defense. His hardened crew had been at sea facing untold hardship for almost three years; returning to Hawaii was truly like reentering paradise.

A strange series of coincidences sailed with Cook into Kealakekua Bay on January 16, 1779. It was *makahiki* time, a period of rejoicing and festivity dedicated to the fertility god of the earth, Lono. Normal *kapu* days were suspended, and willing partners freely enjoyed each other sexually, along with dancing, feasting, and the islands' version of Olympic games. It was long held in Hawaiian legend that the great god Lono would return to earth. Lono's image was a small wooden figure perched on a tall mastlike crossbeam; hanging from the crossbeam were long, white sheets of tapa. Who else could Cook be but Lono, and what else could his ships with their masts and white sails be but his sacred floating *heiau?* This explained the Hawaiians' previous fascination with his ships, but to add to the remarkable coincidence, Kealakekua Bay happened to be considered Lono's private sacred harbor. Natives from throughout the land prostrated themselves and paid homage to the returning god. Cook was taken ashore and brought to Lono's sacred temple where he was afforded the highest respect. The ships badly needed fresh supplies and the Hawaiians readily gave all they had, stretching their own provisions to the limit. To the sailors' delight, this included full measures of the *aloha* spirit.

The Fatal Misunderstandings

After an uproarious welcome and generous hospitality for over a month, it became obvious that the newcomers were beginning to overstay their welcome. During the interim a seaman named William Watman died, convincing the Hawaiians that the *haole* were indeed mortals, not gods. Watman was buried at Hikiau Heiau, where a plaque commemorates the event to this day. Incidents of petty theft began to increase dramatically. The lesser chiefs indicated it was time to leave by "rubbing the Englishmen's bellies." Inadvertently, many *kapu* were broken by the Englishmen, and once-friendly relations became strained. Finally, the ships sailed away on February 4, 1779.

After plying terrible seas for only a week, *Resolution's* foremast was badly damaged. Cook sailed back into Kealakekua Bay, dragging the mast ashore on February 13. The natives, now totally hostile, hurled rocks at the sailors. Orders were given to load muskets with ball; firearms had previously only been loaded with shot and a light charge. Confrontations increased when some Hawaiians stole a small boat and Cook's men set after them, capturing the fleeing canoe, which held an *ali'i* named Palea. The Englishmen treated him roughly; to the Hawaiians horror, they even smacked him on the head with a paddle. The Hawaiians then furiously attacked the marines, who abandoned the small boat.

Cook Goes Down

Next the Hawaiians stole a small cutter from the *Discovery* that had been moored to a buoy and partially sunk to protect it from the sun. For the first time Captain Cook became furious. He ordered Captain Clerk of the *Discovery* to sail to the southeast end of the bay and to stop any canoe trying to leave Kealakekua. Cook then made a

fatal error in judgment. He decided to take nine armed marines ashore in an attempt to convince the venerable King Kalaniopuu to accompany him back aboard ship where he would hold him for ransom in exchange for the cutter. The old king agreed, but his wife prevailed upon him not to trust the *haole*. Kalaniopuu sat down on the beach to think while the tension steadily grew.

Meanwhile, a group of marines fired upon a canoe trying to leave the bay and a lesser chief, Nookemai, was killed. The crowd around Cook and his men reached an estimated 20,000, and warriors outraged by the killing of the chief armed themselves with clubs and protective straw-mat armor. One bold warrior advanced on Cook and struck him with his *pahoa* (dagger). In retaliation Cook drew a tiny pistol lightly loaded with shot and fired at the warrior. His bullets spent themselves on the straw armor and fell harmlessly to the ground. The Hawaiians went wild. Lieutenant Molesworth Phillips, in charge of the nine marines, began a withering fire; Cook himself slew two natives.

Overpowered by sheer numbers, the marines headed for boats standing offshore, while Lieutenant Phillips lay wounded. It is believed that Captain Cook, the greatest seaman ever to enter the Pacific, stood helplessly in knee-deep water instead of making for the boats because he could not swim! Hopelessly surrounded, he was knocked on the head, then countless warriors passed a knife around and hacked and mutilated his lifeless body. A sad Lieutenant King lamented in his diary, "Thus fell our great and excellent commander."

The Final Chapter

Captain Clerk, now in charge, settled his men and prevailed upon the Hawaiians to return Cook's body. On the morning of February 16 a grisly piece of charred meat was brought aboard: the Hawaiians, according to their custom, had afforded Cook the highest honor by baking his body in an underground oven to remove the flesh from the bones. On February 17, a group of Hawaiians in a canoe taunted the marines by brandishing Cook's hat. The Englishmen, strained to the limit and thinking that Cook was being desecrated, finally broke. Foaming with blood-lust, they leveled their cannon and muskets on shore and shot anything that moved. It is believed that Kamehameha the Great was wounded in this flurry, along with four *ali'i;* 25 *maka'ainana* (commoners) were killed. Finally, on February 21, 1779, the bones of Capt. James Cook's hands, skull, arms, and legs were returned and tearfully buried at sea. A common seaman, one Mr. Zimmerman, summed up the feelings of all who sailed under Cook when he wrote, ". . . he was our leading star." The English sailed next morning after dropping off their Hawaiian girlfriends who were still aboard.

Captain Clerk, in bad health, carried on with the fruitless search for the Northwest Passage. He died and was buried at the Siberian village of Petropavlovisk. England was at war with upstart colonists in America, so the return of the expedition warranted little fanfare. The *Resolution* was converted into an army transport to fight the pesky Americans; the once proud *Discovery* was reduced to a convict ship ferrying inmates to Botany Bay, Australia. Mrs. Cook, the great captain's steadfast and chaste wife, lived to the age of 93, surviving all her children. She was given a stipend of 200 pounds per year and finished her days surrounded by Cook's mementos, observing the anniversary of his death to the very end by fasting and reading from the Bible.

last for about 100 years, until the independent monarchy of Hawaii forever ceased to be. To add a zing to this brewing political stew, Westerners and their technology were beginning to come in ever increasing numbers. In 1786, Captain LaPerouse and his French exploration party landed in what's now LaPerouse Bay, near Lahaina, foreshadowing European attention to the islands. In 1786 two American captains, Portlock and Dixon, made landfall in Hawaii. Also, it was known that a fortune could be made on the fur trade between the great Northwest and Canton, China; stopping in Hawaii could make it feasible. After this was reported, the fate of Hawaii was sealed.

Hawaii under Kamehameha was ready to enter its "golden age." The social order was medieval, with the *ali'i* as knights, owing their military allegiance to the king, and the serflike *maka'ainana* paying tribute and working the lands. The priesthood of *kahuna* filled the posts of advisors, sorcerers, navigators, doctors, and historians. This was Polynesian Hawaii at its apex. But like the uniquely Hawaiian silversword, the old culture blossomed, and as soon as it did, it began to wither. Ever since, all that was purely Hawaiian has been supplanted by the relentless foreign influences that began bearing down upon it.

THE UNIFICATION OF OLD HAWAII

Hawaii was already in a state of political turmoil and civil war when Cook arrived. In the 1780s the islands were roughly divided into three kingdoms: venerable Kalaniopuu ruled Hawaii and the Hana district of Maui; wily and ruthless warrior-king Kahekili ruled Maui, Kahoolawe, Lanai, and later Oahu; and Kaeo, Kahekili's brother, ruled Kauai. War ravaged the land until a remarkable chief, Kamehameha, rose and subjugated all the islands under one rule. Kamehameha initiated a dynasty that would

Kamehameha I as drawn by Louis Choris, ship's artist for the Otto Von Kotzebue expedition, circa 1816. This was supposedly the only time that Kamehameha sat to have his portrait rendered.

HAWAII STATE ARCHIVES

Young Kamehameha

Kamehameha was a man noticed by everyone; there was no doubt he was a force to be reckoned with. He had met Captain Cook when the *Discovery* unsuccessfully tried to land at Hana on Maui. While aboard, he made a lasting impression, distinguishing himself from the multitude of natives swarming the ships by his royal bearing. Lieutenant James King, in a diary entry, remarked that Kamehameha was a fierce-looking man, almost ugly, but that he was obviously intelligent, observant, and very good-natured. Kamehameha received his early military training from his uncle Kalaniopuu, the great king of Hawaii and Hana, who fought fierce battles against Alapai, the usurper who stole his hereditary lands. After regaining Hawaii, Kalaniopuu returned to his Hana district and turned his attention to conquering all of Maui. During this period young Kamehameha distinguished himself as a ferocious warrior and earned himself the nickname of "the hard-shelled crab," even though old Kahekili, Maui's king, almost annihilated Kalaniopuu's army at the sand hills of Wailuku.

When the old king neared death he passed on the kingdom to his son Kiwalao. He also, however, empowered Kamehameha as the keeper of the family war god, Kukailimoku: Ku of the Bloody Red Mouth, Ku the Destroyer. Oddly enough, Kamehameha had been born not 500 yards from Ku's great *heiau* at Kohala, and had heard the chanting and observed the ceremonies dedicated to this fierce god from his first breath. Soon after Kalaniopuu died, Kamehameha found himself in a bitter war that he did not seek against his two cousins, Kiwalao and his brother Keoua, with the island of Hawaii at stake. The skirmishing lasted nine years until Kamehameha's armies met the two brothers at Mokuohai in an indecisive battle in which Kiwalao was killed. The result was a shaky truce with Keoua, a much embittered enemy. During this fighting, Kahekili of Maui conquered Oahu, where he built a house of the skulls and bones of his adversaries as a reminder of his omnipotence. He also extended his will to Kauai by marrying his half-brother to a high-ranking chieftess of that island. A new factor would resolve this stalemate of power—the coming of the *haole.*

The Olowalu Massacre

In 1790 the American merchant ship *Ella Nora,* commanded by Yankee captain Simon Metcalfe, was looking for a harbor after its long voyage from the Pacific Northwest. Following a day behind was the *Fair American,* a tiny ship manned by Metcalfe's son Thomas and a crew of five. Metcalfe, perhaps by necessity, was a stern and humorless man who would brook no interference. While anchored at Olowalu, a beach area about five miles east of Lahaina, some natives slipped close in their canoes and stole a small boat, killing a seaman in the process. Metcalfe decided to trick the Hawaiians by first negotiating a truce and then unleashing full fury upon them. Signaling

he was willing to trade, he invited canoes of innocent natives to visit his ship. In the meantime, he ordered that all cannon and muskets be readied with scatter shot. When the canoes were within hailing distance, he ordered his crew to fire at will. Over 100 people were slain; the Hawaiians remembered this killing as "the day of spilled brains." Metcalfe then sailed away to Kealakekua Bay and in an unrelated incident succeeded in insulting Kameiamoku, a ruling chief, who vowed to annihilate the next *haole* ship that he saw.

Fate sent him the *Fair American* and young Thomas Metcalfe. The little ship was entirely overrun by superior forces. In the ensuing battle, the mate, Isaac Davis, so distinguished himself by open acts of bravery that his life alone was spared. Kameiamoku later turned over both Davis and the ship to Kamehameha. Meanwhile, while harbored at Kealakekua, Simon Metcalfe sent John Young to reconnoiter. Kamehameha, having learned of the capture of the *Fair American,* detained Young so he could not report, and Metcalfe, losing patience, marooned his own man and sailed off to Canton. (Metcalfe never learned of the fate of his son Thomas and was later killed with another son while trading with the North Americans along the Pacific coast of the Mainland.) Kamehameha quickly realized the significance of his two captives and the *Fair American* with its brace of small cannon. He appropriated the ship and made Davis and Young trusted advisors, eventually raising them to the rank of chief. They would all play a significant role in the unification of Hawaii.

Kamehameha the Great

Later in 1790, supported by the savvy of Davis and Young and the cannon from the *Fair American,* which he mounted on carts, Kamehameha invaded Maui, using Hana as his power base. The island defenders under Kalaniekupule, son of Kahekili who was lingering on Oahu, were totally demoralized, then driven back into the deathtrap of Iao Valley. There, Kamehameha's forces annihilated them. No mercy was expected and none given, although mostly commoners were slain with no significant *ali'i* falling to the victors. So many were killed in this sheer-walled, inescapable valley that the battle was called *"ka pani wai,"* which means "the damming of the waters"—literally with dead bodies.

While Kamehameha was fighting on Maui, his old nemesis Keoua was busy running amok back on Hawaii, again pillaging Kamehameha's lands. The great warrior returned home flushed with victory, but in two battles could not subdue Keoua. Finally, Kamehameha had a prophetic dream in which he was told that Ku would lead him to victory over all the lands of Hawaii if he would build a *heiau* to the war god at Kawaihae. Even before the temple was finished, old Kahekili attempted to invade Waipio, Kamehameha's stronghold. But Kamehameha summoned Davis and Young, and with the *Fair American* and an enormous fleet of war canoes defeated Kahekili at Waimanu. Kahekili had no choice but to accept the indomitable Kamehameha as the king of Maui, although he himself remained the administrative head until his death in 1794.

Now only Keoua remained in the way and he would be defeated not by war, but by the great mana of Ku. While Keoua's armies were crossing the desert on the southern slopes of Kilauea, the fire goddess Pele trumpeted her disapproval and sent a huge cloud of poisonous gas and mud-ash into the air. It descended upon and instantly killed the middle legions of Keoua's armies and their families. The footprints of this ill-fated army remain to this day outlined in the mud-ash as clearly as if they were deliberately encased in wet cement. Keoua's intuition told him that the victorious mana of the gods had swung to Kamehameha and that his own fate was sealed. Kamehameha sent word that he wanted Keoua to meet with him at Ku's newly dedicated temple in Kawaihae. Both knew that Keoua must die. The old nemesis came riding proudly in his canoe, gloriously outfitted in the red and gold feathered cape and helmet signifying his exalted rank. When he stepped ashore he was felled by Kamehameha's warriors and his body was ceremoniously laid upon the altar along with 11 others who were slaughtered and dedicated to Ku, of the Maggot-dripping Mouth.

Increasing Contact

By the time Kamehameha had won the Big Island, Hawaii was becoming a regular stopover for numerous ships seeking the lucrative sandalwood trade with China. In February 1791, Capt. George Vancouver, still seeking the Northwest Passage, returned to Kealakekua where he was greeted by a throng of 30,000. The captain at once recognized Kamehameha, who was wearing a Chinese dressing gown that he had received in tribute from another chief who in turn had received it directly from the hands of Cook himself. The diary of a crew member, Thomas Manby, relates that Kamehameha, missing his front teeth, was more fierce-looking than ever as he approached the ship in an elegant double-hulled canoe sporting 46 rowers. The king invited all to a great feast prepared for them on the beach. Kamehameha's appetite matched his tremendous size. It was noted that he ate two sizable fish, a king-size bowl of poi, a small pig, and an entire baked dog. Kamehameha personally entertained the Englishmen by putting on a mock battle in which he deftly avoided spears by rolling, tumbling, and catching them in midair, all the while hurling his own a great distance. The English reciprocated by firing cannon bursts into the air, creating an impromptu fireworks display. Kamehameha requested from Vancouver a full table setting, with which he was provided, but his request for firearms was prudently denied. Captain Vancouver became a trusted advisor of Kamehameha, and told him about the white man's form of worship. He even interceded for Kamehameha with his headstrong queen, Kaahumanu, and coaxed her from her hiding place under a rock when she sought refuge at Pu'uhonua O Honaunau. The captain gave gifts of beef cattle, fowl, and breeding stock of sheep and goats. The ship's naturalist, Archibald Menzies, was the first *haole* to climb Mauna Kea; he also introduced a large assortment of fruits and vegetables. The Hawaiians were cheerful, outgoing, and showed remorse when they indicated that the remainder of Cook's bones had been buried at a temple close to Kealakekua. John Young, by this time firmly entrenched into Hawaiian society, made no request to sail away with Vancouver. During the next two decades of Kamehameha's rule, the French, Russians, English, and Americans discovered the great whaling waters off Hawaii. Their increasing visits shook and finally tumbled the ancient religion and social order of *kapu*.

Finishing Touches

After Keoua was laid to rest it was only a matter of time till Kamehameha consolidated his power over all of Hawaii. In 1794 the old warrior Kahekili of Maui died and gave Oahu to his son

Kalanikupule, while Kauai and Niihau went to his brother Kaeo. Warring between themselves, Kalanikupule was victorious, though he did not possess the grit of his father nor the great mana of Kamehameha. He had previously murdered a Captain Brown, who had anchored in Honolulu, and seized the ship, the *Jackall*. With the aid of this ship, Kalanikupule now determined to attack Kamehameha. However, while en route the sailors regained control of their ship and cruised to the Big Island to inform and join with Kamehameha. An army of 16,000 was raised and sailed for Maui, where they met only token resistance, destroyed Lahaina, pillaged the countryside, and vanquished Molokai in one bloody battle.

The war canoes next sailed for Oahu and the final showdown. The great army landed at Waikiki, and though defenders fought bravely, giving up Oahu by the inch, they were steadily driven into the surrounding mountains. The beleaguered army made its last stand at Nuuanu Pali, a great precipice in the mountains behind present-day Honolulu. Kamehameha's warriors mercilessly drove the enemy into the great abyss. Kalanikupule, who hid in the mountains, was captured after a few months and sacrificed to Ku, The Snatcher of Lands, thereby ending the struggle for power.

Kamehameha put down a revolt on Hawaii in 1796 and the king of Kauai, Kaumuali, accepting the inevitable, recognized Kamehameha as supreme ruler without suffering the hopeless ravages of a needless war. Kamehameha, for the first time in Hawaiian history, was the undisputed ruler of all the islands of "the heavenly homeland in the north."

Kamehameha's Rule

Kamehameha was as gentle in victory as he was ferocious in battle. Under his rule, which lasted until his death on May 8, 1819, Hawaii enjoyed a peace unlike any the warring islands had ever known. The king moved his royal court to Lahaina, where in 1803 he built the "Brick Palace," the first permanent building of Hawaii. The benevolent tyrant also enacted the "Law of the Splintered Paddle." This law, which protected the weak from the exploitation of the strong, had its origins in an incident of many years before. A brave defender of a small overwhelmed village broke a paddle over Kamehameha's head and taught the chief—literally in one stroke—about the nobility of the commoner.

However, just as Old Hawaii reached its "golden age," its demise was at hand. The relentless waves of *haole* both innocently and determinedly battered the old ways into the ground. With the foreign ships came prosperity and fanciful new goods after which the *ali'i* lusted. The *maka'ainana* were worked mercilessly to provide sandalwood for the China trade. This was the first "boom" economy to hit the islands, but it set the standard of exploitation that would follow. Kamehameha built an observation tower in Lahaina to watch for ships, many of which were his own, returning laden with riches from the world at large. In the last years of his life Kamehameha returned to his beloved Kona coast where he enjoyed the excellent fishing renowned to this day. He had taken Hawaii from the darkness of

the great Queen Kaahumanu, by ship's artist Louis Choris from the Otto Von Kotzebue expedition, circa 1816

warfare into the light of peace. He died true to the religious and moral *kapu* of his youth, the only ones he had ever known, and with him died a unique way of life. Two loyal retainers buried his bones after the baked flesh had been ceremoniously stripped away. A secret burial cave was chosen so that no one could desecrate the remains of the great chief, thereby absorbing his mana. The tomb's whereabouts remains unknown, and disturbing the dead remains one of the strictest *kapu* to this day. "The Lonely One's" kingdom would pass to his son, Liholiho, but true power would be in the hands of his beloved and feisty wife Kaahumanu. As Kamehameha's spirit drifted from this earth, two forces sailing around Cape Horn would forever change Hawaii: the whalers and the missionaries.

MISSIONARIES AND WHALERS

The year 1819 is of the utmost significance in Hawaiian history. It marked the death of Kamehameha, the overthrow of the ancient *kapu* system, the arrival of the first "whaler" in Lahaina, and the departure of Calvinist missionaries from New England determined to convert the heathen islands. Great changes began to rattle the old order to its foundations. With the *kapu* system and all of the ancient gods abandoned (except for the fire goddess Pele of Kilauea), a great void permeated the souls of the Hawaiians. In the coming decades Hawaii, also coveted by Russia, France, and England, was finally consumed by America. The islands had the first American school, printing press, and newspaper west of the Mississippi. Lahaina, in its heyday, became the world's greatest whaling port, accommodating over 500 ships of all types during its peak years.

The Royal Family

Maui's Hana District provided Hawaii with one of its greatest queens, Kaahumanu, born in 1768 in a cave within walking distance of Hana Harbor. At the age of 17 she became the third of Kamehameha's 21 wives and eventually the love of his life. At first she proved to be totally independent and unmanageable, and was known to openly defy her king by taking numerous lovers. Kamehameha placed a *kapu* on her body and even had her attended by horribly deformed hunchbacks to curb her carnal appetites, but she continued to flaunt his authority. Young Kaahumanu had no love for her great, lumbering, unattractive husband, but in time (even Captain Vancouver was pressed into service as a marriage counselor) she learned to love him dearly. She in turn became his favorite wife, although she remained childless throughout her life. Kamehameha's first wife was the supremely royal Keopuolani, who so outranked even him that the king himself had to approach her naked and crawling on his belly. Keopuolani produced the royal children Liholiho and Kauikeaouli, who became King Kamehameha II and III, respectively. Just before Kamehameha I died in 1819 he appointed Liholiho his successor, but he also had the wisdom to make Kaahumanu the *kuhina nui* or queen regent. Initially, Liholiho was weak and became a drunkard. Later he became a good ruler, but he was always supported by his royal mother Keopuolani and by the ever-formidable Kaahumanu.

Kapu Is *Pau*

Kaahumanu was greatly loved and respected by the people. On public occasions, she donned Kamehameha's royal cloak and spear: so attired and infused with the king's mana, she demonstrated that she was the real leader of Hawaii. For six months after Kamehameha's death, Kaahumanu counseled Liholiho on what he must do. The wise *kuhina nui* knew that the old ways were *pau* (finished) and that Hawaii could not hope to function in a rapidly changing world under the *kapu* system. In November 1819, Kaahumanu and Keopuolani prevailed upon Liholiho to break two of the oldest and most sacred *kapu* by eating with women and by allowing women to eat previously forbidden foods, such as bananas and certain fish. Heavily fortified with strong drink and attended by other high-ranking chiefs and a handful of foreigners, Kaahumanu sat with Liholiho to eat in public. This feast became known as Ai Noa ("Free Eating"). As the first morsels passed Kaahumanu's lips the ancient gods of Hawaii tumbled. Throughout the land revered *heiau* were burned and abandoned and the idols knocked to the ground. Now the people had nothing but their own weakened inner selves to rely on. Nothing and no one could answer their prayers; their spiritual lives were empty and in shambles.

Missionaries

Into this spiritual vortex sailed the brig *Thaddeus* on April 4, 1820. It had set sail from Boston on October 23, 1819, lured to the Big Island by Henry Opukahaia, a local boy who had earlier been taken to New England. The ship landed at Kailua, on the Kona coast, where Liholiho had moved the royal court. The Reverends Bingham and Thurston were granted a one-year, trial missionary period by King Liholiho. They established themselves on Hawaii and Oahu and from there began the transformation of Hawaii. The missionaries were men of God, but also practical-minded Yankees. They brought education, enterprise, and most importantly, unlike the transient seafarers, a commitment to stay and build. By 1824 the new faith had such a foothold that Chieftess Keopuolani climbed to the firepit atop Kilauea and defied Pele. This was even more striking than the previous breaking of the food *kapu* because the strength of Pele could actually be seen. Keopuolani ate forbidden *ohelo* berries and cried out, "Jehovah is my God." Over the next decades the governing of Hawaii slipped away from the Big Island and moved to the new port cities of Lahaina and, later, Honolulu.

Rapid Conversions

The year 1824 also marked the death of Keopuolani, who was given a Christian burial. She had set the standard by accepting Christianity, and a number of the *ali'i* followed the queen's lead. Liholiho had sailed off to England, where he and his wife contracted measles and died. Their bodies were returned by the British in 1825, on the HMS *Blonde* captained by Lord Byron, cousin of *the* Lord Byron. During these years, Kaahumanu allied herself with Reverend Richards and together they wrote Hawaii's first code of laws based upon the Ten Commandments. Foremost was the condemnation of murder, theft, brawling, and the desecration of the Sabbath by work or play. The early missionaries had the best of intentions, but, like all zealots, were blinded by the single-mindedness that was also their greatest ally. They were not surgically selective in their destruction of the native beliefs. *Anything* native was felt to be inferior, and they set about to wipe out all traces of the old ways. In their rampage they reduced the Hawaiian culture to ashes, plucking self-will and determination from the hearts of a once proud people. More so than the whalers, they terminated the Hawaiian way of life.

The Early Seamen

A good portion of the common seamen of the early 19th century were the dregs of the Western world. Many a whoremongering drunkard had awoken from a stupor and found himself on the pitching deck of a ship, discovering to his dismay that he had been "pressed into naval service." For the most part these sailors were a filthy, uneducated, lawless rabble. Their present situation was dim, their future hopeless, and they would live to be 30 if they were lucky and didn't die from scurvy or a thousand other miserable fates. They snatched brief pleasure in every port, and jumped ship at every opportunity, especially in an easy berth like Lahaina. They displayed the worst elements of Western culture—which the Hawaiians naively mimicked. In exchange for *aloha* they gave drunkenness, sloth, and insidious death by disease. By the 1850s, the population of native Hawaiians tumbled from the estimated 300,000 reported by Captain Cook in 1778 to barely 60,000. Common conditions such as colds, flu, venereal disease, and sometimes smallpox and cholera decimated the Hawaiians, who had no natural immunities to these foreign ailments. By the time the missionaries arrived, *hapa haole* children were common in Lahaina streets.

The earliest merchant ships to the islands were owned or skippered by lawless opportunists who had come seeking sandalwood after first filling their holds with furs from the Pacific Northwest. Aided by *ali'i* hungry for manufactured goods and Western finery, they raped Hawaiian forests of this fragrant wood so coveted in China. Next, droves of sailors came in search of the whales. The whalers, decent men at home, left their morals back in the Atlantic and lived by the slogan "no conscience east of the Cape." The delights of Hawaii were just too tempting for most.

Two Worlds Tragically Collide

The 1820s were a time of confusion and soul-searching for the Hawaiians. When Kamehameha II died the kingdom passed to Kauikeaouli (Kamehameha III), who made his life-long residence in Lahaina. The young king was only nine years old when the title passed to him, but his power was secure because Kaahumanu was still a vibrant *kuhina nui*. The young prince, more so than any other, was raised in the cultural confusion of the times. His childhood was spent during the very cusp of the change from old ways to new, and he was often pulled in two directions by vastly differing beliefs. Since he was royal born, according to age-old Hawaiian tradition he must mate and produce an heir with the highest ranking *ali'i* in the kingdom. This natural mate happened to be his younger sister, the Princess Nahienaena. To the old Hawaiian advisors, this arrangement was perfectly acceptable and encouraged. To the increasingly influential missionaries, incest was an unimaginable abomination in the eyes of God. The problem was compounded by the fact that Kamehameha III and Nahienaena were drawn to each other and were deeply in love. The young king could not stand the mental pressure imposed by conflicting worlds. He became a teenage alcoholic too royal to be restrained by anyone in the kingdom, and his bouts of drunkenness and womanizing were both legendary and scandalous.

Kamehameha III

Meanwhile, Nahienaena was even more pressured because she was a favorite of the missionaries, baptized into the church at age 12. She too vacillated between the old and the new. At times a pious Christian, at others she drank all night and took numerous lovers. As the prince and princess grew into their late teens, they became even more attached to each other and hardly made an attempt to keep their relationship from the missionaries. Whenever possible, they lived together in a grass house built for the princess by her father.

In 1832, the great Kaahumanu died, leaving the king on his own. In 1833, at the age of 18, Kamehameha III announced that the "regency" was over and that all the lands in Hawaii were his, personally, and that he alone was the ultimate law. Almost immediately, however, he decreed that his half sister Kinau would be "premier," signifying that he would leave the actual running of the kingdom in her hands. Kamehameha III fell into total drunken confusion, until one night he attempted suicide. After this episode he seemed to straighten up a bit and mostly kept a low profile. In 1836, Princess Nahienaena was convinced by the missionaries to take a husband. She married Leleiohoku, a chief from the Big Island, but continued to sleep with her brother. It is uncertain who fathered the child, but Nahienaena gave birth to a baby boy in September 1836. The young prince survived for only a few hours, and Nahienaena never recovered from her convalescence. She died in December 1836 and was laid to rest in the mausoleum next to her mother, Keopuolani, on the royal island in Mokuhina Pond (still in existence in modern-day Lahaina). After the death of his sister, Kamehameha III became a sober and righteous ruler. Oftentimes seen paying his respects at the royal mausoleum, he ruled longer than any other king until his death in 1854.

HAWAII STATE ARCHIVES

The Missionaries Prevail

In 1823, the first mission was established in Lahaina under the pastorate of Reverend Richards and his wife. Within a few years, many of the notable *ali'i* had been, at least in appearance, converted to Christianity. By 1828 the cornerstones for Wainee Church, the first stone church on the island, were laid just behind the palace of Kamehameha III. The struggle between missionaries and whalers centered around public drunkenness and the servicing of sailors by local native girls. The normally god-fearing whalers had signed on for perilous duty that lasted up to three years, and when they anchored in Lahaina they sought their pleasure. The missionaries were instrumental in placing a curfew on sailors and prohibiting native girls from boarding ships, which had become customary. These measures certainly did not stop the liaisons between sailor and *wahine*, but it did impose a modicum of social sanction and tolled the end of the wide-open days. The sailors were outraged; in 1825 the crew from the *Daniel* attacked the home of the meddler, Reverend Richards. A year later a similar incident occurred. In 1827, confined and lonely sailors from the whaler *John Palmer* fired their cannon at Reverend Richards' newly built home.

Slowly the tensions eased, and by 1836 many sailors were regulars at the Seamen's Chapel, adjacent to the Baldwin Home. Unfortunately, even the missionaries couldn't stop the pesky mosquito from entering the islands through the port of Lahaina. The mosquitoes arrived in 1826, from Mexico, aboard the merchant *Wellington*. They were inadvertently carried as larvae in the water barrels and democratically pestered everyone in the islands from that day forward regardless of race, religion, or creed.

Lahaina Becomes a Cultural Center

By 1831, Lahaina was firmly established as a seat of Western influence in Hawaii. That year marked the founding of Lahainaluna School, the first *real* American school west of the Rockies. Virtually a copy of a New England normal school, it attracted the best students, both native and white, from throughout the kingdom. By 1834, Lahainaluna had an operating printing press publishing the islands' first newspaper, *The Torch of Hawaii,* starting a lucrative printing industry centered in Lahaina that dominated not only the islands but also California for many years.

An early native student was David Malo. He was brilliant and well-educated, but more importantly, he remembered the "old ways." One of the first Hawaiians to realize his native land was being swallowed up by the newcomers, Malo compiled the first history of precontact Hawaii and the resulting book, *Hawaiian Antiquities,* became a reference masterpiece which has yet to be eclipsed. David Malo insisted that the printing be done in Hawaiian, not English. Malo is buried in the mountains above Lahainaluna where, by his own request, he is "high above

the tide of foreign invasion." By the 1840s, Lahaina was firmly established as the "whaling capital of the world"; the peak year of 1846 saw 395 whaling ships anchored here. A census in 1846 reported that Lahaina was home to 3,445 natives, 112 permanent *haole,* 600 sailors, and over 500 dogs. The populace was housed in 882 grass houses, 155 adobe houses, and 59 relatively permanent stone and wooden-framed structures. Lahaina would probably have remained the islands' capital, had Kamehameha III not moved the royal capital to the burgeoning port of Honolulu on the island of Oahu.

Foreign Influence

By the 1840s, Honolulu was becoming the center of commerce in the islands; when Kamehameha III moved the royal court there from Lahaina the ascendant fate of the new capital was guaranteed. In 1843, Lord Paulet, commander of the warship *Carysfort,* forced Kamehameha III to sign a treaty ceding Hawaii to the British. London, however, repudiated this act and Hawaii's independence was restored within a few months when Queen Victoria sent Admiral Thomas as her personal agent of good intentions. The king memorialized the turn of events by a speech in which he uttered the phrase, *"Ua mau ke ea o ka aina i ka pono,"* ("The life of the land is preserved in righteousness"), now the Hawaii state motto. The French used similar bullying tactics to force an unfavorable treaty on the Hawaiians in 1839; as part of these heavy-handed negotiations they exacted a payment of $20,000, as well as the right for Catholics to enjoy religious freedom in the islands. In 1842 the U.S. recognized and guaranteed Hawaii's independence without a formal treaty, and by 1860 over 80% of the islands' trade was with the United States.

The Great *Mahele*

In 1840, Kamehameha III ended his autocratic rule and instituted a constitutional monarchy. This brought about the Hawaiian Bill of Rights, but the most far-reaching change was the transition to private ownership of land. Formerly, all land belonged to the ruling chief, who gave wedge-shaped parcels called *ahupua'a* to lesser chiefs to be worked for him. The commoners did all the real labor, their produce heavily taxed by the *ali'i.* The fortunes of war, the death of a chief, or the mere whim of a superior could force a commoner off his land. The Hawaiians, however, could not think in terms of "owning" land. No one could *possess* land, one could only *use* land, and its *ownership* was a strange foreign concept. As a result, naive Hawaiians gave up their lands for a song to unscrupulous traders, which remains an integral, unrectified problem to this day. In 1847 Kamehameha III and his advisers separated the lands of Hawaii into three groupings: crown land (belonging to the king), government land (belonging to the chiefs), and the people's land (the largest parcels). In 1848, 245 *ali'i* entered their land claims in the *Mahele Book,* assuring them ownership. In 1850, the commoners were given title in fee simple to the lands they cultivated and lived on as tenants, not including house lots in towns. Commoners without land could buy small *kuleana* (farms) from the government at 50 cents per acre. In 1850, foreigners were also allowed to purchase land in fee simple, and the ownership of Hawaii from that day forward slipped steadily from the hands of its indigenous people.

KING SUGAR

The sugar industry began at Hana, Maui, in 1849. A whaler named George Wilfong hauled four blubber pots ashore and set them up on a rocky hill in the middle of 60 acres he had planted in sugar. A team of oxen turned "crushing rollers" and the cane juice flowed down an open trough into the pots, under which an attending native kept a roaring fire burning. Wilfong's methods of refining were crude, but the resultant high-quality sugar turned a neat profit in Lahaina. The main problem was labor. The Hawaiians, who had participated willingly as whalers, were basically indentured workers. They became extremely disillusioned with their contracts, which could last up to 10 years. Most of their wages were eaten up by manufactured commodities sold at the company store, and it didn't take long for them to realize that they were little more than slaves. At every opportunity they either left the area or just refused to work.

Imported Labor
The **Masters and Servants Act of 1850,** which allowed importation of laborers under the contract system, ostensibly guaranteed an endless supply of cheap labor for the plantations. Chinese laborers were imported, but were too enterprising to remain in the fields for a meager $3 per month. They left as soon as opportunity permitted and went into business as small merchants and retailers. In the meantime, Wilfong had sold out, releasing most of the Hawaiians previously held under contract, and his plantation fell into disuse. In 1860, two Danish brothers, August and Oscar Unna, bought land at Hana to raise sugar. They solved the labor problem by importing Japanese laborers who were extremely hardworking and easily managed. The workday lasted 10 hours, six days a week, for a salary of $20 per month with housing and medical care thrown in. Plantation life was very structured with stringent rules governing even bedtimes and lights out. A worker could be fined for being late or for smoking on the job. Even the Japanese couldn't function under these circumstances, and improvements in benefits and housing were slowly gained.

Sugar Grows
The demand for "Sandwich Island Sugar" grew as California was populated during the gold rush, and increased dramatically when the American Civil War demanded a constant supply. The only sugar plantations on the Mainland were small plots confined to the Confederate states, whose products could hardly be bought by the Union and whose fields, later in the war, were destroyed. By the 1870s it was clear to the planters, still mainly New Englanders, that the U.S. was their market; they tried often to gain closer ties and favorable tariffs. The Americans also planted rumors that the British were interested in annexing Hawaii; this put pressure on the U.S. Congress to pass the long-desired **Reciprocity Act,** which would exempt sugar from import duty. It finally passed in 1875, in exchange for U.S. long-range rights to the strategic naval port of Pearl Harbor, among other concessions. These agreements gave increased political power to a small group of American planters, whose outlooks were similar to the post-Civil War South where a few powerful whites were the virtual masters of a multitude of dark-skinned laborers. Sugar was now big business and the Hana District alone exported almost 3,000 tons per year. All of Hawaii would have to reckon with the "sugar barons."

Changing Society

The sugar plantation system changed life in Hawaii physically, spiritually, politically, and economically. Now boatloads of workers came not only from Japan, but from Portugal, Germany, and even Russia. The white-skinned workers were most often the field foremen *(luna)*. With the immigrants came new religions, new animals and plants, unique cuisines, and a plantation language known as pidgin, or *da'kine*. Many Asians, and to a lesser extent the other groups, including the white plantation owners, intermarried with Hawaiians. A new class of people properly termed "cosmopolitan" but more familiarly and aptly known as "locals" was emerging. These were the people of multiple race backgrounds who couldn't exactly say *what* they were, but it was clear to all just *who* they were. The plantation owners became the new "chiefs" of Hawaii who would carve up the land and dispense favors. The Hawaiian monarchy was soon eliminated.

A KINGDOM PASSES

The fate of Lahaina's Wainee Church through the years has been a symbol of the political and economic climate of the times. Its construction heralded the beginning of missionary dominance in 1828. It was destroyed by a tornado or "ghost wind" in 1858, just when whaling began to falter and the previously dominant missionaries began losing their control to the merchants and planters. In 1894, Wainee Church was burned to the ground by royalists supporting the besieged Queen Liliuokalani. Rebuilding was begun in 1897—while Hawaii was a republic ruled by the sugar planters—with a grant from H.P. Baldwin. It wasn't until 1947 that the Wainee was finally completed and remodeled.

The Beginning of the End

Like the Hawaiian people themselves, the Kamehameha dynasty in the mid-1800s was dying from within. King Kamehameha IV (Alexander Liholiho) ruled 1854-63; his only child died in 1862. He was succeeded by his older brother Kamehameha V (Lot Kamehameha), who ruled until 1872. With his passing the Kamehameha line ended. William Lunalilo, elected king in 1873 by popular vote, was of royal, but not Kamehameha, lineage. He died after only a year in office, and

being a bachelor left no heirs. He was succeeded by David Kalakaua, known far and wide as "The Merrie Monarch," who made a world tour and was well received wherever he went. He built Iolani Palace in Honolulu and was personally in favor of closer ties with the U.S., helping push through the Reciprocity Act. Kalakaua died in 1891 and was replaced by his sister Lydia Liliuokalani, last of the Hawaiian monarchs.

The Revolution

When Liliuokalani took office in 1891 the native population was at a low of 40,000 and she felt the U.S. had too much influence over her homeland. She was known to personally favor the English over the Americans. She attempted to replace the liberal constitution of 1887 (adopted by her pro-American brother) with an autocratic mandate in which she would have much more political and economic control of the islands. When the McKinley Tariff of 1890 brought a decline in sugar profits, she made no attempt to improve the situation. Thus, the planters saw her as a political obstacle to their economic growth; most of Hawaii's American planters and merchants were in favor

HAWAII STATE ARCHIVES

Queen Liliuokalani

of a rebellion. She would have to go! A central spokesman and firebrand was Lorrin Thurston, a Honolulu publisher who, with a central core of about 30 men, challenged the Hawaiian monarchy. Although Liliuokalani rallied some support and had a small military potential in her personal guard, the coup was ridiculously easy—it took only one casualty. Captain John Good shot a Hawaiian policeman in the arm and that did it. Naturally, the conspirators could not have succeeded without some solid assurances from a secret contingent in the U.S. Congress as well as outgoing President Benjamin Harrison, who favored Hawaii's annexation. Marines from the *Boston* went ashore to "protect American lives," and on January 17, 1893, the Hawaiian monarchy came to an end.

The provisional government was headed by Sanford B. Dole, who became president of the Hawaiian Republic. Liliuokalani actually surrendered not to the conspirators, but to U.S. Ambassador John Stevens. She believed that the U.S. government, which had assured Hawaiian independence, would be outraged by the overthrow and would come to her aid. Incoming President Grover Cleveland *was* outraged and Hawaii wasn't immediately annexed as expected. When queried about what she would do with the conspirators if she were reinstated, Liliuokalani said that they would be hung as traitors. The racist press of the times, which portrayed the Hawaiians as half-civilized, bloodthirsty heathens, publicized this widely. Since the conspirators were the leading citizens of the land, the queen's words proved untimely. In January 1895, a small, ill-fated counterrevolution headed by Liliuokalani failed, and she was placed under house arrest in Iolani Palace. Officials of the Republic insisted that she use her married name (Mrs. John Dominis) to sign the documents forcing her to abdicate her throne. She was also forced to swear allegiance to the new Republic. Liliuokalani went on to write *Hawaii's Story* and also the lyric ballad *Aloha O'e.* She never forgave the conspirators and remained to the Hawaiians "queen" until her death in 1917.

Annexation

The overwhelming majority of Hawaiians opposed annexation and desired to restore the monarchy. But they were prevented from voting by the new Republic because they couldn't meet the imposed property and income qualifications—a transparent ruse by the planters to control the majority. Most *haole* were racist and believed that the "common people" could not be entrusted with the vote because they were childish and incapable of ruling themselves. The fact that the Hawaiians had existed quite well for 1,000 years before the white man even reached Hawaii was never considered. The Philippine theater of the Spanish-American War also prompted annexation. One of the strongest proponents was Alfred Mahon, a brilliant naval strategist who, with support from Theodore Roosevelt, argued that the U.S. military must have Hawaii to be a viable force in the Pacific. In addition, Japan, flushed with victory in its recent war with China, protested the American intention to annex, and in so doing prompted even moderates to support annexation in fear that the Japanese themselves coveted the prize. On July 7, 1898, President McKinley signed the annexation agreement, and this "tropical fruit" was finally put into the U.S.'s basket.

MODERN TIMES

Hawaii entered the 20th century totally transformed from what it had been. The old Hawaiian language, religion, culture, and leadership were all gone. Western dress, values, education, and recreation were the norm. Native Hawaiians were now unseen citizens who lived in dwindling numbers in remote areas. The plantations, new centers of social order, had a strong Asian flavor; more than 75% of their workforce was Asian. There was a small white middle class, an all-powerful white elite, and a single political party ruled by that elite. Education, however, was always highly prized, and by the turn of the century all racial groups were encouraged to attend school. By 1900, almost 90% of Hawaiians were literate (far above the national norm) and schooling was mandatory for all children between ages six and 15. Intermarriage was accepted, and there was a mixing of the races like nowhere else on earth. The military became increasingly important to Hawaii. It brought in money and jobs, dominating the island economy. The Japanese attack on Pearl Harbor, which began U.S. involvement in World War II, bound Hawaii to America forever. Once the islands had been baptized by blood, the average Mainlander felt that Hawaii was American soil. A movement among Hawaiians to become part of the United States began to grow. They wanted a real voice in Washington, not merely a voteless delegate as provided under their territory status. Hawaii became the 50th state in 1959 and the jumbo-jet revolution of the 1960s made it easily accessible to growing numbers of tourists from all over the world.

Military History

A few military strategists realized the importance of Hawaii early in the 19th century, but most didn't recognize the advantages until the Spanish-American War. It was clearly an unsinkable ship in the middle of the Pacific from which the U.S. could launch military operations. Troops were stationed at Camp McKinley, at the foot of Diamond Head, the main military compound until it became obsolete in 1907. Pearl Harbor was first surveyed in 1872 by General Schofield. Later a military base named in his honor, Schofield Barracks, became a main military post in central Oahu. It first housed the U.S. 5th Cavalry in 1909 and was heavily bombed by the Japanese at the outset of WW II. Pearl Harbor, first dredged in 1908, was officially opened on December 11, 1911. The first warship to enter was the cruiser *California*. Ever since, the military has been a mainstay of island economy. Unfortunately, there has been long-standing bad blood between locals and military personnel. Each group has tended to look down upon the other.

Pearl Harbor Attack

On the morning of December 7, 1941, the Japanese carrier *Akagi*, flying the battle flag of the famed Admiral Togo of the Russo-Japanese War, received and broadcast over its PA system island music from Honolulu station KGMB. Deep in the bowels of the ship a radio man listened for a much different message, coming thousands of miles from the Japanese mainland. When the ironic poetic message "east wind rain" was received, the attack was launched. At the end of the day, 2,325 U.S. servicemen and 57 civilians were dead; 188 planes were destroyed; 18 major warships were sunk or heavily damaged; and the U.S. was in the war. Japanese casualties were ludicrously light. The ignited conflict would rage for four years until Japan, through the atomic bombs dropped on Nagasaki and Hiroshima, was vaporized into total submission. At the end of hostilities, Hawaii would never again be considered separate from America.

Statehood

A number of economic and political reasons explain why the ruling elite of Hawaii desired statehood, but simply, the vast majority of people who lived there, especially after WW II, considered themselves Americans. The first serious mention of making "The Sandwich Islands" a state was in the 1850s under President Franklin Pierce, but it wasn't taken seriously until the monarchy was overthrown in the 1890s. For the next 50 years statehood proposals were made repeatedly to Congress, but there was stiff opposition, especially from the southern states. With Hawaii a territory, an import quota system beneficial to Mainland producers could be enacted on produce, especially sugar. Also, there was prejudice against creating a state in a place where the majority of the populace was not white. This situation was illuminated by the infamous Massie Rape case of 1931 (see the "People" section below), which went down as one of the greatest miscarriages of justice in American history.

During WW II, Hawaii was placed under martial law, but no serious attempt to intern the Japanese population was made, as in California. There were simply too many Japanese, who went on to gain the respect of the American people by their outstanding fighting record during the war. Hawaii's own 100th Battalion became the famous 442nd Regimental Combat Team, which gained notoriety by saving the Lost Texas Battalion during the Battle of the Bulge, and went on to be *the* most decorated battalion in all of WW II. When these GIs returned home, *no one* was going to tell them that they were not loyal Americans. Many of these AJAs (Americans of Japanese Ancestry) took advantage of the GI Bill and received higher education. They were from the common people, not the elite, and they rallied grassroots support for statehood. When the vote finally occurred, approximately 132,900 voted in favor of statehood with only 7,800 votes against. Congress passed the Hawaii State Bill on March 12, 1959, and on August 21, 1959, President Eisenhower announced that Hawaii was officially the 50th state.

GOVERNMENT

The only difference between the government of the state of Hawaii and other states is that it's "streamlined," and in theory more efficient. There are only two levels of government: the state and the county. With no town or city governments to deal with, considerable bureaucracy is eliminated.

Hawaii, in anticipation of becoming a state, drafted a constitution in 1950 and was ready to go when statehood came. Politics and government are taken seriously in the Aloha State, which consistently turns in the best national voting record per capita. For example, in the first state elections 173,000 of 180,000 registered voters voted—a whopping 94% of the electorate. In the election to ratify statehood, hardly a ballot went uncast, with 95% of the voters opting for statehood. The bill carried every island of Hawaii except for Niihau, where, coincidentally, most of people (total population 250 or so) are of relatively pure Hawaiian blood. When Hawaii became the 50th state in 1959, Honolulu became the capital. The present governor is Benjamin J. Cayetano, the second Hawaiian governor of the state, and the first with any Filipino heritage. Mr. Cayetano has held this office since 1994.

Oahu has been the center of government for about 150 years, since King Kamehameha III permanently established the royal court there in the 1840s. In 1873-74, King David Kalakaua built Iolani Palace as the central showpiece of the island kingdom. Liliuokalani, the last Hawaiian monarch, lived after her dethronement in the nearby residence Washington Place. While Hawaii was a territory, and for a few years after it became a state, the palace was used as the capitol building, the governor residing in Washington Place. Modern Oahu, besides being the center of state government, governs itself as the City and County of Honolulu. The county not only covers the entire island of Oahu, but all the far-flung Northwestern Islands, except for Midway, which is under federal jurisdiction.

City and County of Honolulu

The island of Oahu has three times as many people as the other islands combined. Nowhere is this more evident than in the representation of

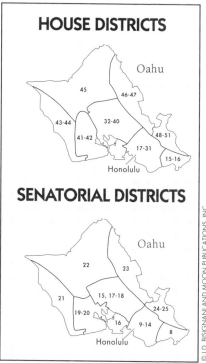

© J.D. BISIGNANI AND MOON PUBLICATIONS, INC.

Oahu in the state House and Senate. Oahu claims 18 of the 25 state senators and 37 of the 51 state representatives. These lopsided figures make it obvious that Oahu has plenty of clout, especially Honolulu urban districts, which elect more than 50% of Oahu's representatives. Frequent political battles ensue, since what's good for the city and county of Honolulu isn't always good for the rest of the state. More often than not, the political moguls of Oahu, backed by huge business interests, prevail.

Like the rest of the state, the voters on the island of Oahu are principally Democratic in orientation, but not in as great a percentage as on the other islands. The current mayor is Jeremy Harris, Democrat. He is assisted by an elected county council consisting of nine members, one from each council district around the island. The Oahu state senators are overwhelmingly Democratic, except for two Republicans from the Koko Head and Kailua Districts. Democratic state representatives also outnumber Republicans, but not by quite as huge a margin. Most of the 10 Republican districts are in urban Honolulu and the suburban communities of Kailua and Kaneohe.

ECONOMY

Hawaii's mid-Pacific location makes it perfect for two primary sources of income: tourism and the military. Tourists come in anticipation of endless golden days on soothing beaches, while the military is provided with the strategic position of an unsinkable battleship. Each economic sector nets Hawaii about $4 billion annually, money which should keep flowing smoothly and even increasingly into the foreseeable future. These revenues mostly remain aloof from the normal ups and downs of the Mainland U.S. economy. Together they make up 60% of the islands' income, and both attract either gung-ho enthusiasts or rabidly negative detractors. The remaining 40% comes in descending proportions from manufacturing, construction, and agriculture (mainly sugar and pineapples). As long as the sun shines and the balance of global power requires a military presence, the economic stability of Hawaii is guaranteed.

Economically, Oahu dwarfs the rest of the islands combined. It generates income from government spending, tourism, and agriculture. A huge military presence, an international airport that receives the lion's share of visitors, and, unbelievably, half of the state's best arable lands keep Oahu in the economic catbird seat. The famous "Big Five" all maintain their corporate offices in downtown Honolulu, from which they oversee vast holdings throughout Hawaii and the Mainland. Located in about the same spots as when their founders helped to overthrow the monarchy, things are about the same as then, except that they're going strong, while the old royalty of Hawaii has vanished.

TOURISM

"The earthly paradise! Don't you want to go to it? Why, of course!" This was the opening line of *The Hawaiian Guide Book* by Henry Whitney, which appeared in 1875. In print for 25 years, it sold for 60 cents during a time when a roundtrip sea voyage between San Francisco and Honolulu cost $125. The technique is a bit dated, but the human desires remain the same: some of us seek paradise, all seek escape, some are drawn to play out a drama in a beautiful setting. Tourists have been coming to Hawaii ever since steamship service began in the 1860s. Until WW II, luxury liners carried the financial elite on exclusive voyages to the islands. By the 1920s 10,000 visitors a year were spending almost $5 million—cementing the bond between Hawaii and tourism.

A $25,000 prize offered by James Dole of pineapple fame sparked a trans-Pacific air race in 1927. The success of the aerial daredevils who answered the challenge proved that commercial air travel to Hawaii was feasible. Two years later, **Hawaiian Air** was offering regularly scheduled flights between all of the major islands. By 1950, airplanes had captured over 50% of the transportation market, and ocean voyages were relegated to "specialty travel," catering to the elite. By 1960 the large airbuses made their debut; 300,000 tourists arrived on eight designated airlines. The Boeing 747 began operating in 1969. These enormous planes could carry hundreds of passengers at reasonable rates, so travel to Hawaii became possible for the average-income person. In 1970, two million arrived, and by 1980 close to six million passengers arrived on 22 international air carriers. The first hotel in Honolulu was the **Hawaiian,** built in 1872. It was predated by **Volcano House,** which overlooked Kilauea Crater on the Big Island and was built in 1866. The coral-pink **Royal Hawaiian,** built in 1927, is Waikiki's graciously aging grande dame, a symbol of days gone by. As late as the 1950s it had Waikiki Beach almost to itself. Only 10,000 hotel units were available in the islands in 1960; today there are nearly 50,000, with more than 20,000 condos as well.

J.D. BISIGNANI

Mainland visitors

The flow of visitors to Oahu has remained unabated ever since tourism outstripped sugar and pineapples in the early 1960s, becoming Hawaii's top moneymaker. Of the more than six million people who visit the state yearly, more than one-half stay on Oahu. This means that on any given day, Oahu plays host to about 80,000 visitors. Waikiki is still many people's idea of paradise. Most all the rest, en route to the Neighbor Islands, at least pass through. The overwhelming number of these tourists are on package tours. Hotels directly employ over 18,000 workers, half the state's total, not including all the shop assistants, waiters and waitresses, taxi drivers, and everyone else needed to ensure a carefree vacation. Of the state's 70,000 accommodation units, Oahu claims 36,000; of those, more than 31,000 are in Waikiki. The Oahu hotels consistently have the highest occupancy rates in the state, hovering around 80%. In contrast, the average daily room rate is the lowest in the state, making accommodations on Oahu slightly more of a bargain than on the other islands. The visitor industry generates over $2 billion of yearly revenue, and this is only the amount that can be directly related to the hotel and restaurant trades. With the flow of visitors seemingly endless, Oahu has a bright economic future.

Tourists: Who, When, and Where

Tourism-based income outstripped pineapples and sugar by the mid-'60s and the boom was on. Long-time residents could even feel a physical change in air temperature: many trees were removed from Honolulu to build parking lots, and reflected sunlight made Honolulu much hotter and at times unbearable. Even the trade winds, known to moderate temperatures, were not up to that task. So many people from the outlying farming communities were attracted to work in the hotels that there was a poi famine in 1967. But for the most part, islanders knew that their economic future was tied to this "nonpolluting industry."

Most visitors (54%) are American, and the largest numbers come from the West Coast. Sun-seeking refugees from frigid Alaska, however, make up the greatest proportional number, according to population figures. The remaining arrivals are, in descending order, from Japan, Canada, Korea, Australia, Germany, England, and Taiwan. Europe, as a whole, sends proportionately fewer visitors than North America or Asia, while the fewest come from South America. The Japanese market is constantly growing, reaching about 2 million visitors per year in 1995. This is particularly beneficial to the tourist market because the average Western tourist spends about $135 per day, while the Japanese counterpart spends $340 per day. The average Japanese tourist, however, stays only about six days as opposed to 10 days for the westbound traveler. Up until very recently the Japanese traveled only in groups and primarily stayed on Oahu. Now the trend is to travel independently, or come with a group and then peel off, with a hefty percentage heading for the "Neighbor Islands" (all islands other than Oahu).

The typical visitor is slightly affluent, and female visitors outnumber males three to two. The average age (35) is a touch higher than in most vacation areas because it reflects an inflated proportion of retirees heading for Hawaii, especially Honolulu, to fulfill lifelong "dream" vacations. A typical stay lasts about 10 days, down from a month in the 1950s; a full 56% are repeat visitors. On any given day there are about 80,000 travelers on Oahu, 35,000 on Maui, 19,000 on Hawaii, and about 8,000 on Kauai. Molokai and Lanai get so few visitors, 1,400 and 1,000, respectively, that the figures are hardly counted. In 1964 only 10% of the islands' hotel rooms were on the Neighbor Islands, but by 1966 the figure jumped to 25%, with more than 70% of tourists opting to visit the Neighbor Islands. Today, nearly half of the state's hotel rooms are on the Neighbor Islands.

Joaquin Miller, the 19th-century poet of the Sierra, said, "I tell you my boy, the man who has not seen the Sandwich Islands, in this one great ocean's warm heart, has not seen the world." The times have certainly changed, but the sentiments of most visitors to Hawaii remain the same.

Tourism-Related Problems

Tourism is both boon and blight to Hawaii. It is the root cause of two problems: one environmental, the other socioeconomic. The environmental impact is obvious and best described in the lament of songstress Joni Mitchell's "Big Yellow Taxi": "They paved paradise and put up a parking lot." Put simply, tourism can draw too many people to an area and overburden it. In the process, it stresses the land and destroys the natural beauty that attracted people in the first place. Tourists come to Hawaii for what has been called its "ambient resource": a balanced collage of indulgent climate, invigorating waters, intoxicating scenery, and exotic people all wrapped up neatly in one area which can both soothe and excite. It is in the best interest of Hawaii to preserve this "resource."

Like the land, humans are stressed by tourism. Local people, who once took the "Hawaiian lifestyle" for granted, become displaced and estranged in their own land. Some areas, predominantly along gorgeous beaches that were average-to-low-income communities, are now overdeveloped with prices going through the roof. The locals are not only forced to move out, but often must come back as service personnel in the tourist industry and cater to the very people who displaced them. At one time the psychological blow was softened because, after all, the newcomers were merely benign tourists who would stay a short time, spend a wad of money, and leave.

Today, condos are being built and a different sort of visitor is arriving. Many condo owners are well-educated businesspeople and professionals in the above-average income bracket. The average condo owner is a Mainlander who purchases one as a second or retirement home. These people are not islanders and have a tough time relating to the locals, who naturally feel resentment. Moreover, since they don't *leave* like normal tourists, they use community facilities, find those special nooks and crannies for shopping or sunbathing that were once exclusively the domain of locals, and have a say as voters in community governments. The islanders become more and more disenfranchised. Many believe that the new order instigated by tourism is similar to what has always existed in Hawaii: a few from the privileged class being catered to by many from the working class. In a way it's an extension of the plantation system, but instead of carrying pineapples, most islanders find themselves carrying luggage, cocktails, or broiled fish. One argument, however, remains undeniable: whether it's people or pineapples, one has to make a living. The days of a little grass shack on a sunny beach aren't gone; it's just that you need a wallet full of credit cards to afford one.

THE MILITARY

Hawaii is the most militarized state in the U.S.: all five services are represented. Camp H.M. Smith, overlooking Pearl Harbor, is the headquarters of CINCPAC (Commander in Chief Pacific), which is responsible for 70% of the earth's surface, from California to the east coast of Africa and to both poles. The U.S. military presence dates back to 1887, when Pearl Harbor was given to the Navy as part of the Sugar Reciprocity Treaty. The sugar planters were given favorable duty-free treatment for their sugar, while the U.S. Navy was allowed exclusive rights to one of the best harbors in the Pacific. In 1894, when the monarchy was being overthrown by the sugar planters, the USS *Boston* sent a contingency of U.S. Marines ashore to "keep order," which really amounted to a show of force, backing the revolution. The Spanish-American War saw U.S. troops billeted at Camp McKinley at the foot of Diamond Head, and Schofield Barracks opened to receive the 5th Cavalry in 1909.

Pearl Harbor's flames ignited WW II, and there has been no looking back since then.

About 44,000 military personnel are stationed in Hawaii (99% on Oahu), with over 54,000 dependents. This number has slowly but steadily been decreasing since 1988, when the military was at its greatest strength in the state, and is now lower than at any time since the mid-'50s. The Army has the largest contingent with nearly 20,000, followed by the Navy at 11,000, Marine Corps at 7,000, Air Force at more than 5,000, and 1,500 or so with the Coast Guard. Besides this, 17,000 civilian support personnel account for 65% of all federal jobs in Hawaii. The combined services are one of the largest landholders with over 242,000 acres, accounting for six percent of Hawaiian land. The two major holdings are the 100,000-acre Pohahuloa Training Area on Hawaii and 100,000 acres on Oahu, which is a full 26% of the entire island. The Army controls 71% of the military lands, followed by the Navy at 25%, and the remainder goes to the Air Force and a few small installations to the Coast Guard.

The Military Has No *Aloha*
Not everyone is thrilled about the strong military presence in Hawaii. Two factions, native Hawaiians and antinuclear groups, are downright angry. Radical contingencies of native Hawaiian-rights groups consider Hawaii an independent country, besieged and "occupied" by the U.S. government. They date their loss of independence to Liliuokalani's overthrow in 1893. The vast majority of ethnic Hawaiians, though they consider themselves Americans, are concerned with loss of their rightful homelands, with no financial reparation, and about continuing destruction of and disregard for their traditional religious and historical sites. A long list of grievances is cited by native Hawaiian action groups, but the best and clearest example was the controversy over the sacred island, Kahoolawe, which, until 1994, was used as a bombing target by the U.S. Navy.

A second controversy raised by the military presence on Hawaii as a nuclear target. The ultimate goal of the antinuclear protesters is to see the Pacific, and the entire world, free from nuclear arms. They see Hawaii as a big target used by the international power merchants on the Mainland as both pawn and watchdog—if war breaks out, they say, the Hawaiian Islands will be reduced to cinders. The military naturally counters that a strong Hawaii is a deterrent to nuclear war and that Hawaii is not only a powerful offensive weapon, but one of the best-defended regions of the world. Unfortunately, when you are on an island there is no place to go: like a boxer in a ring, you can run, but you can't hide. Also, the military has been recently cited for disposing of stockpiles of chemical weapons by incineration on Johnston Island, a military installation southwest of the Big Island. Because there was no environmental impact study, scientists fear that wind and currents could carry the pollutants to the main Hawaiian Islands, destroying delicate coral reefs along the way.

AGRICULTURE

You'd think that with all the people living on Oahu, coupled with the constant land development, there'd hardly be any room left for things to grow. But that's not the case. The land is productive, though definitely stressed. It is startling that in downtown Honolulu and Waikiki, so many trees have been removed to build parking lots that the asphalt becomes overheated from the lack of shade, allowing temperatures, once moderated by the trade winds, to rise demonstrably.

Changing times and attitudes led to a "poi famine" that hit Oahu in 1967 because very few people were interested in the hard work of farming this staple. While Oahu has, by far, the smallest acreage in farms and the smallest average size of farm in the state, it still manages to produce a considerable amount of sugarcane, pineapples, and the many products of diversified agriculture. Sugar lands account for 22,000 acres, most owned by the James Campbell Estate, located around Ewa, north and west of Pearl Harbor, with some acreage around Waimea and Waialua on the North Shore. Pineapples cover 11,500 acres, with the biggest holdings in the Leilehua Plateau belonging to Dole, a subsidiary of Castle and Cooke. In the hills, entrepreneurs raise *pakalolo,* or marijuana, which has become the state's most productive cash crop. Oahu is also a huge agricultural consumer, demanding more than four times as much vegetables, fruits, meats, and poultry to feed its citizens and visitors than the remainder of the state combined.

LAND OWNERSHIP

Oahu
380,800 Acres

STATE

FEDERAL

HAWAIIAN HOMELANDS

SMALL PRIVATE

LARGE PRIVATE

© J.D. BISIGNANI AND MOON PUBLICATIONS, INC.

THE "BIG FIVE"

Until statehood, Hawaii was ruled economically by a consortium of corporations known as "the Big Five": **C. Brewer and Co.,** sugar, ranching, and chemicals, founded 1826; **Theo. H. Davies & Co.,** sugar, investments, insurance, and transportation, founded 1845; **Amfac Inc.** (originally H. Hackfield Inc.—a German firm that changed its name and ownership during the anti-German sentiment of WW I to American Factors), sugar, insurance, and land development, founded 1849; **Castle and Cooke Inc.** (Dole), pineapple, food packing, and land development, founded 1851; and **Alexander and Baldwin Inc.,** shipping, sugar, and pineapple, founded 1895. This economic oligarchy ruled Hawaii with a velvet glove and a steel grip.

With members on all important corporate boards, they controlled all major commerce, including banking, shipping, insurance, hotel development, agriculture, utilities, and wholesale and retail merchandising. Anyone trying to buck the system was ground to dust, finding it suddenly impossible to do business in the islands. The Big Five were made up of the islands' oldest and most well-established *haole* families; all in-

cluded bloodlines from Hawaii's own nobility They looked only among themselves for suitable husbands and wives, so that breaking in from the outside even through marriage was hardly possible. The only time they were successfully challenged prior to statehood was when Sears, Roebuck and Co. opened a store on Oahu. Closing ranks, the Big Five decreed that their steamships would not carry Sears freight. When Sears threatened to buy its own steamship line, the Big Five relented. The original Sears in downtown Honolulu along Beretania Street, managed by W.G. McDermid, is now a temporary police station, but it was renowned as the very first building in Hawaii to be air-conditioned (the entire roof was flooded with water to achieve the result). The Honolulu Sears was also the very first store to sell coordinated aloha wear for the entire family, the very successful brainchild of Sears manager, Morley Theaker, who in 1956 wanted to incorporate the idea of "this is Hawaii" into his store.

Actually, statehood, and more to the point, tourism, broke their oligarchy. After 1960 too much money was at stake for Mainland-based corporations to ignore. Eventually the grip of the Big Five was loosened, but they are still enormously powerful and richer than ever, though unlike before, they don't control everything. Now their power is land.

LAND OWNERSHIP

Landwise, Hawaii is a small pie, and its slices are not at all well divided. Of the state's 6,423 square miles of land, the six main inhabited islands make up 98% of it. (This figure does not include Niihau, which is privately owned by the Robinson family and inhabited by some of the last remaining pure-blooded Hawaiians, nor does it include uninhabited Kahoolawe.) Of the 4,110,966 acres that make up the inhabited islands, 34% is owned by the state, 16% by the federal government, and the remaining 50% is in private hands. But only 40 owners, with 5,000 or more acres each, own 75% of all private lands; the top seven control 40% of it. To be more specific, Castle and Cooke Inc. owns 99% of Lanai, while 40-60% of Maui, Oahu, Molokai, Kauai, and Hawaii are owned by less than a dozen private parties. The largest private landowner, with over 336,000 acres or eight percent of the total land area of the state, is the Kamehameha Schools/Bishop Estate, which recently lost a Supreme Court battle that ended with a ruling allowing the state of Hawaii to acquire privately owned land for "the public good."

More than in any other state, Hawaii's landowners tend to lease land instead of sell it, and many private homes are on rented ground. Many feel that with land prices going up all the time, only the very rich land developers will be able to purchase, and the "people" of Hawaii will become even more land-poor.

> *The land and industries of Hawaii are owned by old families and large corporations, and Hawaii is only so large.*
>
> —*Jack London*

PEOPLE

Nowhere else on earth can you find such a kaleidoscopic mixture of people. Every major race is accounted for, and over 50 ethnic groups are represented throughout the islands, making Hawaii the most racially integrated state in the United States. Its population of 1.2 million includes nearly 100,000 permanently stationed military personnel and their dependents. It's the only state where whites are not the majority. About 56% of the people living in Hawaii were born there; 26% were born on the Mainland U.S., and 18% of the people are foreign-born.

The population of Hawaii has been growing steadily in recent times, but it fluctuated wildly in times past. In 1876 it ebbed to its lowest, with only 55,000 permanent residents in the islands. This was the era of large sugar plantations; their constant demand for labor was the primary cause of the importation of various peoples from around the world, which is what led to Hawaii's racially integrated society. World War II saw Hawaii's population swell from 400,000 just prior to the war to 900,000 during the war. Naturally, 500,000 were military personnel who left at war's end, but many returned to settle after getting a taste of island living.

Of the 1.2 million people in the islands today (1995 est.), 877,000 live on Oahu, with slightly less than half of these living in the Honolulu Metropolitan Area, making Honolulu the 11th largest city in the nation. The rest of the population is distributed as follows: 137,000 on Hawaii, with 47,000 living in Hilo; 115,000 on Maui, with the largest concentration, 53,000, in Wailuku/Kahului; 56,000 on Kauai, including 230 pure-blood Hawaiians on Niihau; 6,700 on Molokai; and just under 3,000 on Lanai. The population density, statewide, is 186 people per square mile, approximately that of California. The population is not at all evenly distributed, with Oahu claiming about 1,430 people per square mile and Hawaii barely 34 residents per square mile. Statewide, city dwellers outnumber those living in the country by nine to one. For the island of Oahu, 96% are urban while only four percent live rurally.

For most visitors, regardless of where they've come from, Oahu (especially Honolulu) will be the first place they've ever encountered such an integrated multiracial society. Various countries may be cosmopolitan, but nowhere will you meet so many individuals from such a diversity of ethnic groups, and mixes of these groups. You could be driven to your hotel by a Chinese-Portuguese cab driver, checked in by a Japanese-Hawaiian clerk, served lunch by a Korean waiter, serenaded by a Hawaiian-Italian-German musician, while an Irish-English-Filipino-French chambermaid tidies your room. This racial symphony is evident throughout Hawaii, but it's more apparent on Oahu, where the large population creates more opportunity for a racial hodgepodge. The warm feeling you get almost immediately upon arrival is that everyone belongs.

Population Figures

Oahu's 877,000 residents account for 73% of the state's population. All these people are on an island comprising only 19% of the state's land total. Sections of Waikiki can have a combined population of permanent residents and visitors as high as 90,000 per square mile, making cities like Tokyo, Hong Kong, and New York seem quite roomy by comparison. The good news is that Oahu *expects* all these people and knows how to accommodate them comfortably.

Over 400,000 people live in greater Honolulu, the built-up area from Aiea to Koko Head. The next most populous urban centers after Honolulu are the Kailua/Kaneohe area with about 100,000 residents, followed by Pearl City and Waipahu with a combined total of about 70,000 or so. On the Leilehua Plateau, 47,000 live in Mililani Town and Wahiawa. The strip of towns on the leeward coast, including Waianae, totals about 33,400 inhabitants. In the last decade, the areas that have had the greatest increase in population are Wahiawa and Ewa.

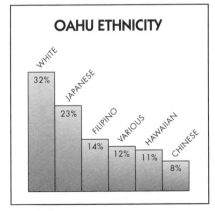

OAHU ETHNICITY

WHITE 32%
JAPANESE 23%
FILIPINO 14%
VARIOUS 12%
HAWAIIAN 11%
CHINESE 8%

With all of these people, and such a finite land resource, real estate on the island is sky-high. The average single-family home on Oahu sells for $375,000 ($50,000 higher than the state average), while a condo averages about $180,000. And for plenty of prime real estate, these figures would barely cover the down payment!

So where is everybody? Of the major ethnic groups you'll find the Hawaiians clustered around Waianae and the windward coast near Waiahole; the whites tend to be in Wahiawa, around Koko Head, in Waikiki, and in Kailua/Kaneohe; those of Japanese ancestry prefer the valleys heading toward the *pali,* including Kalihi, Nuuanu, and Tantalus; Filipinos live just east of the airport, in downtown Honolulu, around Barbers Point, and in Wahiawa; the Chinese are in Chinatown and around the Diamond Head area. Of the minor ethnic groups the highest concentration of blacks is in the Army towns around Schofield Barracks; Samoans live along with the Hawaiians in Waianae and the windward coastal towns, though they are most concentrated in downtown Honolulu not far from Aloha Tower; Koreans and Vietnamese are scattered here and there, but mostly in Honolulu. The ethnic breakdown of Oahu's 877,000 residents is as follows: 32% Caucasian, 23% Japanese, 14% Filipino, 11% Hawaiian, 8% Chinese, and 12% other.

THE HAWAIIANS

The study of the native Hawaiians is ultimately a study in tragedy because it ends in their demise as a viable people: when Captain Cook first sighted Hawaii in 1778, there were an estimated 300,000 natives living in harmony with their ecological surroundings; within 100 years a scant 50,000 demoralized and dejected Hawaiians existed almost as wards of the state. Today, although more than 210,000 people claim varying degrees of Hawaiian blood, experts say that fewer than 1,000 are pure Hawaiian, and this is stretching it.

It's easy to see why people of Hawaiian lineage could be bitter over what they have lost, being strangers in their own land now, much like the American Indians. The overwhelming majority of "Hawaiians" are of mixed heritage, and the wisest take the best from all worlds. From the Hawaiian side comes simplicity, love of the land, and acceptance of people. It is the Hawaiian legacy of *aloha* that remains immortal and adds that special elusive quality that *is* Hawaii.

Polynesian Roots

The Polynesians' original stock is muddled and remains an anthropological mystery, but it's believed that they were nomadic wanderers who migrated from both the Indian subcontinent and Southeast Asia through Indonesia, where they learned to sail and navigate on protected waterways. As they migrated they honed their sailing skills until they could take on the Pacific, and as they moved, they absorbed people from other cultures and races until they had coalesced into what we now know as Polynesians.

Abraham Fornander, still considered a major authority on the subject, wrote in his 1885 *An Account of the Polynesian Race* that he believed the Polynesians started as a white (Aryan) race that was heavily influenced by contact with the Cushite Chaldeo-Arabian civilization. He estimated their arrival in Hawaii at A.D. 600, based on Hawaiian genealogical chants. Modern science seems to bear this date out, although it remains skeptical about his other surmises. According to others, the intrepid Polynesians who actually settled Hawaii are believed to have come from the Marquesas Islands, 1,000 miles southeast of Hawaii. The Marquesans were cannibals known for their tenacity and strength, attributes that would serve them well.

The Caste System

Hawaiian society was divided into rankings by a strict caste system determined by birth, and from which there was no chance of escaping. The highest rank was the *ali'i*, the chiefs and royalty. The impeccable genealogies of the *ali'i* were traced back to the gods themselves, and the chants *(mo'o ali'i)* were memorized and sung by professionals (called *ku'auhau*) who were themselves *ali'i*. Ranking passed from both father and mother and custom dictated that the first mating of an *ali'i* be with a person of equal status.

A *kahuna* was a highly skilled person whose advice was sought before any major project was undertaken, such as building a house, hollowing a canoe log, or even offering a prayer. The *mo'o kahuna* were the priests of Ku and Lono, and they were in charge of praying and following rituals. They were very powerful *ali'i* and kept strict secrets and laws concerning their various functions.

Besides this priesthood of *kahuna,* there were other *kahuna* who were not *ali'i* but commoners. The two most important were the healers *(kahuna lapa'au)* and the black magicians *(kahuna ana'ana)*. The *kahuna lapa'au* had a marvelous pharmacopoeia of herbs and spices that could cure over 230 diseases common to the Hawaiians. The *kahuna ana'ana* could be hired to cast a love spell over a person or cause his untimely death. They seldom had to send out a reminder of payment!

The common people were called the *maka'ainana,* "the people of land"—the farmers, craftsmen, and fishermen. The land that they lived on was owned by the *ali'i,* but they were not bound to it. If the local *ali'i* was cruel or unfair, the *maka'ainana* had the right to leave and reside on another's lands. The *maka'ainana* mostly loved their local *ali'i* much like a child loves a parent, and the feeling was reciprocal. *Maka'ainana* who lived close to the *ali'i* and could be counted on as warriors in times of trouble were called *kanaka no lua kaua,* "a man for the heat of battle." They were treated with greater favor than those who lived in the backcountry, *kanaka no hii kua,* whose lesser standing opened them up to discrimination and cruelty. All *maka'ainana* formed extended families called *ohana* and they usually lived on the same section of land, called *ahupua'a.* Those farmers who lived inland would barter their produce with the fishermen who lived on the shore, and thus all shared equally in the bounty of the land and sea.

A special group called *kauwa* was a landless, untouchable caste confined to living on reservations. Their origins were obviously Polynesian, but they appeared to be descendants of castaways who had survived and become perhaps the aboriginals of Hawaii before the main migrations. It was *kapu* for anyone to go onto *kauwa* lands, and doing so meant instant death. If a human sacrifice was needed, the *kahuna* would simply summon a *kauwa,* who had no recourse but to mutely comply. To this day, to call someone *kauwa,* which now supposedly only means servant, is still considered a fight-provoking insult.

Kapu and Day-to-Day Life

There were occasional horrible wars, but mostly the people lived a quiet and ordered life based on a strict caste society and the *kapu* system. Famine was known but only on a regional level,

HAWAII STATE ARCHIVES

Ship's artist Jacques Arago depicts the harsh verdict delivered to a kapu breaker, circa 1819.

and the population was kept in check by birth control, crude abortions, and the distasteful practice of infanticide, especially of baby girls. The Hawaiians were absolutely loving and nurturing parents under most circumstances, and would even take in an adopted *hanai* (child or oldster), a lovely practice that lingers to this day.

A strict division of labor existed among men and women. Men were the only ones permitted to have anything to do with taro: this foodstuff was so sacred that there were a greater number of *kapu* concerning taro than concerning man himself. Men pounded poi and served it to the women. Men also were the fishermen and the builders of houses, canoes, irrigation ditches, and walls. Women tended to other gardens and shoreline fishing, and were responsible for making tapa cloth. The entire family lived in the common house called the *hale noa*.

Certain things were *kapu* between the sexes. Primarily, women could not enter the *mua* (man's house), nor could they eat with men. Certain foods such as pork and bananas were forbidden to women, and it was *kapu* for a man to have intercourse before going fishing, engaging in battle, or attending a religious ceremony. Young boys lived with the women until they underwent a circumcision rite called *pule ipu*. After this was performed, they were required to keep the *kapu* of men. A true Hawaiian settlement required a min-

imum of five huts: the men's eating hut, women's menstruation hut, women's eating hut, communal sleeping hut, and prayer hut. Without these five separate structures, Hawaiian "society" could not happen, since the *ia kapu* (forbidden eating between men and women) could not be observed.

Ali'i could also declare a *kapu,* and often did so. Certain lands or fishing areas were temporarily made *kapu* so that they could revitalize. Even today, it is *kapu* for anyone to remove all the *opihi* (a type of limpet) from a rock. The great King Kamehameha I even placed a *kapu* on the body of his notoriously unfaithful child bride, Kaahumanu. It didn't work! The greatest *kapu (kapu moe)* was afforded to the highest ranking *ali'i*: anyone coming into their presence had to prostrate themselves. Lesser ranking *ali'i* were afforded the *kapu noho:* lessers had to sit or kneel in their presence. Commoners could not let their shadows fall upon an *ali'i* or enter their houses except through a special door. Breaking a *kapu* meant immediate death.

Fatal Flaws

Less than 100 years after Captain Cook's arrival, King Kalakaua found himself with only 48,000 Hawaiian subjects. Wherever the king went, he would beseech his people, *"Hooulu lahui,"* "Increase the race," but it was already too late. It was as if nature herself had turned her back on these once proud people. Many of their marriages were barren, and in 1874, when only 1,400 children were born, a full 75% died in infancy. The Hawaiians could do little as their race nearly faded from existence.

The Causes of Decline
The ecological system of Hawaii has always been exceptionally fragile and this included its people. When the white man came he found a great people who were large, strong, and virile; however, when it came to fighting off the most minor diseases, the Hawaiians proved as delicate as hothouse flowers. To exacerbate the situation, the Hawaiians were totally uninhibited toward sexual intercourse between willing partners, and they engaged in it openly and with abandon. Unfortunately, the sailors who arrived were full of syphilis and gonorrhea. The Hawaiian women brought these diseases home and, given the nature of Hawaiian society at the time, they spread like wildfire. By the time the missionaries came in 1820 and helped to halt the unbridled fornication, they estimated the native population at only 140,000, less than half of what it had been only 40 years since initial contact! In the next 50 years measles, mumps, influenza, and tuberculosis further ravaged the people. Furthermore, Hawaiian men were excellent sailors and it's estimated that during the whaling years at least 25% of all ablebodied Hawaiian men sailed away, never to return.

But the coup de grace that really ended the Hawaiian race, as such, was that all racial newcomers to the islands were attracted to the Hawaiians and the Hawaiians were in turn attracted to them. With so many interracial marriages, the Hawaiians literally bred themselves nearly out of existence. By 1910, there were still twice as many full-blooded Hawaiians as mixedbloods, but by 1940 mixed-blooded Hawaiians were the fastest-growing group, and full-blooded the fastest declining.

Hawaiians Today
Many of the Hawaiians who moved to the cities became more and more disenfranchised. Their folk society stressed openness and a giving nature, but downplayed the individual and the ownership of private property. These cultural traits made them easy targets for the users and schemers until they finally became either apathetic or angry. Most sur-

Aloha *still shows.*

veys reveal that although Hawaiians number only 13% of the population, they account for almost 50% of the financially destitute families and about half of all arrests and illegitimate births. Niihau, a privately owned island, is home to about 230 pureblood Hawaiians, representing the largest concentration of them, per capita, in the islands. The Robinson family, which owns the island, restricts visitors to invited guests only.

The second largest concentration is on Molokai, where 2,700 Hawaiians, living mostly on 40-acre *kuleana* of Hawaiian Home Lands, make up 40% of that island's population. The majority of mixed-blood Hawaiians, 80,000 or so, live on Oahu, where they are particularly strong in the hotel and entertainment fields. People of Hawaiian extraction are still a delight to meet, and anyone so lucky as to be befriended by one long regards this friendship as the highlight of his travels. The Hawaiians have always given their *aloha* freely to all the people of the world, and it is we who must acknowledge this precious gift.

THE CHINESE

Next to Yankees from New England, the Chinese are the oldest migrant group in Hawaii, and their influence has far outshone their meager numbers. They brought to Hawaii, along with their individuality, Confucianism, Taoism, and Buddhism, although many have long since become Christians. The Chinese population at 68,000 makes up only six percent of the state's total, and the vast majority reside on Oahu. As an ethnic group they account for the least amount of crime, the highest per capita income, and a disproportionate number of professionals.

The First Chinese

No one knows his name, but an unknown Chinese immigrant is credited with being the first person in Hawaii to refine sugar. This Asian wanderer tried his hand at crude refining on Lanai in 1802. Fifty years later the sugar plantations desperately needed workers, and the first Chinese brought to Hawaii under the newly passed Masters and Servants Act were 195 coolies from Amoy who arrived in 1852. These conscripts were contracted for three to five years and given $3 per month plus room and board. This was for 12 hours a day, six days a week, and even in 1852 these wages were the pits. The Chinese almost always left the plantations the minute their contracts expired. They went into business for themselves and promptly monopolized the restaurant and small shop trades.

The Chinese Niche

Although many people in Hawaii considered all Chinese ethnically the same, they were actually quite different. The majority came from Guangdong Province in southern China. They were two distinct ethnic groups: the Punti made up 75% of the immigrants, and the Hakka made up the remainder. In China, they remained separate from each other, never mixing; in Hawaii, they mixed out of necessity. For one, hardly any Chinese women came over at first, and the ones who followed were at a premium and gladly accepted as wives, regardless of ethnic background. The Chinese were also one of the first groups who willingly intermarried with the Hawaiians, from whom they gained a reputation for being exceptionally caring husbands.

The Chinese accepted the social order and kept a low profile. For example, during the turbulent labor movements of the 1930s and '40s in Hawaii, the Chinese community produced not one labor leader, radical intellectual, or left-wing politician. When Hawaii became a state, one of the two senators elected was Hiram Fong, a racially mixed Chinese. Since statehood, the Chinese community has carried on business as usual as they continue to rise both economically and socially.

THE JAPANESE

Most scholars believe that (inevitably) a few Japanese castaways floated to Hawaii long before Captain Cook arrived and might have introduced the iron with which the islanders seemed to be familiar before the white explorers arrived. The first official arrivals from Japan were ambassadors sent by the Japanese shogun to negotiate in Washington; they stopped en route at Honolulu in March 1860. But it was as plantation workers that the Japanese were brought en masse to the islands. A small group arrived in 1868, and mass migration started in 1885.

In 1886, because of famine, the Japanese government allowed farmers, mainly from southern Honshu, Kyushu, and Okinawa, to emigrate. Among these were members of Japan's little-talked-about untouchable caste, called *eta* or *burakumin* in Japan and *chorinbo* in Hawaii. They gratefully seized this opportunity to better their lot, an impossibility in Japan. The first Japanese migrants were almost all men. Between 1897 and 1908 migration was steady, with about 70% of the immigrants being men. Afterward, migration slowed because of a "gentlemen's agreement," a euphemism for racism against the "yellow peril." By 1900 there were over 60,000 Japanese in the islands, constituting the largest ethnic group.

AJAs, Americans of Japanese Ancestry

Parents of most Japanese children born before WW II were *issei* (first generation), who considered themselves apart from other Americans and clung to the notion of "we Japanese." Their children, the *nisei* or second generation, were a different matter altogether. In one generation they had become Americans, and they put into practice the high Japanese virtues of obligation, duty, and loyalty to the homeland; that homeland was now unquestionably America. After Pearl Harbor was bombed, the FBI kept close tabs on the Japanese community, and the men-

indentured Japanese plantation workers and their mounted overseer

HAWAII STATE ARCHIVES

ace of the "enemy within" prompted the decision to place Hawaii under martial law for the duration of the war. It has since been noted that not a single charge of espionage or sabotage was ever reported against the Japanese community in Hawaii during the war.

AJAs as GIs

Although Japanese had formed a battalion during WW I, they were insulted by being considered unacceptable as American soldiers in WW II. Some Japanese-Americans volunteered to serve in labor battalions, and because of their flawless work and loyalty, it was decided to put out a call for a few hundred volunteers to form a combat unit. Over 10,000 signed up! AJAs formed two distinguished units in WW II: the 100th Infantry Battalion, and later the 442nd Regimental Combat Team. They landed in Italy at Salerno and even fought from Guadalcanal to Okinawa. They distinguished themselves by becoming *the* most decorated unit in American military history.

The AJAs Return

Many returning AJAs took advantage of the GI Bill and received college educations. The "Big Five" Corporations for the first time accepted former AJA officers as executives, and the old order was changed. Many Japanese became involved with Hawaiian politics and the first elected to Congress was Daniel Inouye, who had lost an arm

fighting in WW II. Hawaii's past governor, George Ariyoshi, elected in 1974, was the country's first Japanese-American to reach such a high office. Most Japanese, even as they climb the economic ladder, tend to remain Democrats.

Today, one out of every two political offices in Hawaii is held by a Japanese-American. In one of those weird quirks of fate, it is now the Hawaiian Japanese who are accused by other ethnic groups of engaging in unfair political practices—nepotism and reverse discrimination. Many of these accusations against AJAs are undoubtedly motivated by jealousy, but the AJAs' record in social fairness issues is not without blemish; true to their custom of family loyalty, they do stick together.

There are now 250,000 people in Hawaii of Japanese ancestry, nearly one-quarter of the state's population. They are the least likely of any ethnic group in Hawaii to marry outside of their group—especially the men—and they enjoy a higher-than-average standard of living.

CAUCASIANS

White people have a distinction separating them from all other ethnic groups in Hawaii: they are lumped together as one. You can be anything from a Protestant Norwegian dockworker to a Greek Orthodox shipping tycoon, but if your skin is white, in Hawaii, you're a *haole*. What's more, you could have arrived at Waikiki from Missoula, Montana, in the last 24 hours, or your *kama'aina* family can go back five generations, but again, if you're white, you're a *haole*.

The word *haole* has a floating connotation that depends upon the spirit in which it's used. It can mean everything from a derisive "honky" or "cracker" to nothing more than "white person." The exact Hawaiian meaning is clouded, but some say it meant "a man of no background," because white men couldn't chant a genealogical *kanaenae* telling the Hawaiians who they were. The word eventually evolved to mean "foreign white man" and today, simply "white person."

White History

Next to Hawaiians themselves, white people have the oldest stake in Hawaii. They've been there as settlers in earnest since the missionaries of the 1820s, and were established long before any other migrant group. From last century until statehood, old *haole* families owned and controlled everything, and although they were generally benevolent, philanthropic, and paternalistic, they were also racist. They were established *kama'aina* families, many of whom made up the boards of the Big Five Corporations or owned huge plantations and formed an inner social circle that was closed to the outside. Many managed to find mates from among close family acquaintances.

Their paternalism, which they accepted with grave responsibility, at first only extended to the Hawaiians, who saw them as replacing their own *ali'i*. Asians were considered primarily instruments of production. These supremacist attitudes tended to drag on in Hawaii until quite recent times. They are today responsible for the sometimes sour relations between white and nonwhite people in the islands. Today, all individual white people are resented to a certain degree because of these past acts, even though they personally were in no way involved.

White Plantation Workers

In the 1880s the white landowners looked around and felt surrounded and outnumbered by Asians, so they tried to import white people for plantation work. None of their schemes seemed to work out. Europeans were accustomed to a much higher wage scale and better living conditions than were provided on the plantations. Although only workers

and not considered the equals of the ruling elite, they still were expected to act like a special class. They were treated preferentially, which meant higher wages for the same jobs performed by Asians. Some of the imported workers included: 600 Scandinavians in 1881; 1,400 Germans from 1881 to 1885; 400 Poles from 1897 to 1898; and 2,400 Russians from 1909 to 1912. Many proved troublesome, like the Poles and Russians who staged strikes after only months on the job. Many quickly moved to the Mainland. A contingency of Scots, who first came as mule skinners, did become successful plantation managers and supervisors. The Germans and Scandinavians were well received and climbed the social ladder rapidly, becoming professionals and skilled workers.

The Depression years, not as economically bad in Hawaii as in the continental U.S., brought many Mainland whites seeking opportunity, mostly from the South and the West. These new people were even more racist toward brown-skinned people and Asians than the *kama'aina haole*, and they made matters worse. They also competed more intensely for jobs. The racial tension generated during this period came to a head in 1932 with the infamous "Massie Rape Case."

The Massie Rape Case

Thomas Massie, a naval officer, and his young wife, Thalia, attended a party at the Officers Club. After drinking and dancing all evening, they got into a row and Thalia rushed out in a huff. A few hours later, Thalia was at home, confused and hysterical, claiming to have been raped by some local men. On the most circumstantial evidence, Joseph Kahahawai and four friends of mixed ethnic background were accused. In a highly controversial trial rife with racial tensions, the verdict ended in a hung jury.

While a new trial was being set, Kahahawai and his friends were out on bail. Seeking revenge, Thomas Massie and Grace Fortescue, Thalia's mother, kidnapped Joseph Kahahawai with a plan of extracting a confession from him. They were aided by two enlisted men assigned to guard Thalia. While questioning Joseph, they killed him and attempted to dump his body in the sea but were apprehended. Another controversial trial—this time for Mrs. Fortescue, Massie, and the accomplices—followed. Clarence Darrow, the famous lawyer, sailed to Hawaii to defend them. For killing

Kahahawai, these people served *one hour* of imprisonment in the judge's private chambers. The other four, acquitted with Joseph Kahahawai, maintain innocence of the rape to this day. Later, the Massies divorced, and Thalia went on to become a depressed alcoholic who took her own life.

The Portuguese

The last time anyone looked, Portugal was still attached to the European continent, but for some anomalous reason the Portuguese weren't considered *haole* in Hawaii for the longest time. About 12,000 arrived between 1878 and 1887, and another 6,000 came between 1906 and 1913. Accompanied during this period by 8,000 Spanish, they were considered one and the same. Most of the Portuguese were illiterate peasants from Madeira and the Azores, and the Spanish hailed from Andalusia. They were very well received, and because they were white but not *haole* they made a perfect "buffer" ethnic group. Committed to staying in Hawaii, they rose to be skilled workers—the *"luna* class" on the plantations. They, however, de-emphasized education and became very racist toward Asians, regarding them as a threat to their job security.

By 1920 the 27,000 Portuguese made up 11% of the population. After that they tended to blend with the other ethnic groups and weren't counted separately. Portuguese men tended to marry within their ethnic group, but a good portion of Portuguese women married other white men and became closer to the *haole* group, while another large portion chose Hawaiian mates and grew further away. Although they didn't originate pidgin English (see "Language"), the unique melodious quality of their native tongue did give pidgin that certain lilt it has today. Also, the ukulele ("jumping flea") was closely patterned after the *cavaquinho,* a Portuguese stringed folk instrument.

The Caucasian Population

Today Caucasians make up the largest racial group in the islands at 33% (about 370,000) of the population. There are heavy white concentrations throughout Oahu, especially in Waikiki, Kailua/Kaneohe, and around Pearl City. In terms of pure numbers, the white population is the fastest growing in the islands because most people resettling in Hawaii are white Americans predominantly from the West Coast.

FILIPINOS AND OTHERS

The Filipinos who came to Hawaii brought high hopes of amassing personal fortunes and returning home as rich heroes: for most it was a dream that never came true. Filipinos had been American nationals ever since the Spanish-American War of 1898, and as such weren't subject to immigration laws that curtailed the importation of other Asian workers at the turn of this century. The first to arrive were 15 families in 1906, but a large number came in 1924 as strikebreakers. The majority were illiterate peasants called *Ilocanos* from the northern Philippines, with about 10% Visayans from the central cities. The Visayans were not as hard-working or thrifty, but were much more sophisticated. From the first, Filipinos were looked down upon by all the other immigrant groups, and were considered particularly uncouth by the Japanese. The value they placed on education was the least of any group, and even by 1930 only about half could speak rudimentary English, the majority remaining illiterate. They were billeted in the worst housing, performed the most menial jobs, and were the last hired and first fired.

One big difference between Filipinos and other groups was that the men brought no Filipino women to marry, so they clung to the idea of returning home. In 1930 there were 30,000 men and only 360 women. This hopeless situation led to a great deal of prostitution and homosexuality; many of these terribly lonely bachelors would feast and drink on weekends and engage in their gruesome but exciting pastime of cockfighting on Sundays. When some did manage to find wives, their mates were inevitably part Hawaiian. Today, there are still plenty of old Filipino bachelors who never managed to get home, and the Sunday cockfights remain a way of life.

The Filipinos constitute 15% of Hawaii's population (170,000), with almost 70% living on Oahu. Many visitors to Hawaii mistake Filipinos for Hawaiians because of their dark skin, and this is a minor irritant to both groups. Some streetwise Filipinos even claim to be Hawaiians, because being Hawaiian is "in" and goes over well with the tourists, especially the young women tourists. For the most part, these people are hardworking, dependable laborers who do tough work for little recognition. They remain low on the social totem pole and have not yet organized politically to stand up for their rights.

Other Groups

About 10% of Hawaii's population is made up of a conglomerate of small ethnic groups. Of these, one of the largest and fastest growing is Korean, with 25,000 people. About 8,000 Koreans came to Hawaii from 1903 until 1905, when their own government halted emigration. During the same period about 6,000 Puerto Ricans arrived, but they have become so assimilated that only 4,000 people in Hawaii today consider themselves Puerto Rican. There were also two attempts made last century to import other Polynesians to strengthen the dying Hawaiian race, but they were failures. In 1869 only 126 central Polynesian natives could be lured to Hawaii, and from 1878 to 1885 2,500 Gilbert Islanders arrived. Both groups became immediate-

ly disenchanted with Hawaii. They pined away for their own islands and departed for home as soon as possible.

Today, however, 15,000 Samoans have settled in Hawaii, and with more on the way they are the fastest growing minority in the state. For unexplainable reasons, Samoans and native Hawaiians get along extremely poorly and have the worst racial tensions and animosity of any groups. The Samoans ostensibly should represent the archetypal Polynesians that the Hawaiians are seeking, but it doesn't work that way. Samoans are criticized by Hawaiians for their hot tempers, lingering feuds, and petty jealousies. They're clannish and often are the butt of "dumb" jokes. This racism seems especially ridiculous, but that's the way it is.

Just to add a bit more exotic spice to the stew, there are about 27,000 blacks, 5,000 American Indians, and 6,000 Vietnamese refugees living on the islands.

LANGUAGE

Hawaii is part of the U.S. and people speak English there, but that's not the whole story. If you turn on the TV to catch the evening news, you'll hear "Walter Cronkite" English, unless of course you happen to tune in a Japanese-language broadcast designed for tourists from that country. You can easily pick up a Chinese-language newspaper, or groove to the music on a Filipino radio station, but let's not confuse the issue. All your needs and requests at airports, car rental agencies, restaurants, hotels, or wherever you happen to travel will be completely understood, as well as answered, in English. However, when you happen to overhear islanders speaking, what they're saying will sound somewhat familiar, but you won't be able to pick up all the words, and the beat and melody of the language will be noticeably different.

Hawaii—like New England, the deep South, and the Midwest—has its own unmistakable linguistic regionalism. The many ethnic people who make up Hawaii have enriched the English spoken there with words, expressions, and subtle shades of meaning that are commonly used and understood throughout the islands. The greatest influence on English has come from the Hawaiian language itself, and words such as "aloha," "hula," and "muumuu" are familiarly used and understood by most Americans.

Other migrant people, especially the Chinese, Japanese, and Portuguese, influenced the local dialect to such an extent that the simplified plantation lingo they spoke has become known as "pidgin." A fun and enriching part of the "island experience" is picking up a few words of Hawaiian and pidgin. English is the official language of the state, business, education, and perhaps even the mind; but pidgin is the language of the people, the emotions, and life, while Hawaiian remains the language of the heart and the soul.

Note: Many Hawaiian words are commonly used in English, appear in English dictionaries, and therefore would ordinarily be subject to the rules of English grammar. The Hawaiian language, however, does not pluralize nouns by adding an "s"; the singular and plural are differentiated in context. For purposes of this book, and to highlight rather than denigrate the Hawaiian culture, the Hawaiian style of pluralization will be followed for common Hawaiian words. The following are some examples of plural Hawaiian nouns treated this way in this book: *haole* (not haoles), hula, *kahuna,* lei, luau, and *nene.*

PIDGIN

The dictionary definition of pidgin is: a simplified language with a rudimentary grammar used as a means of communication between people speaking different languages. Hawaiian pidgin is a little more complicated than that. It had its roots during the plantation days of last century when white owners and *luna* (foremen) had to communicate with recently arrived Chinese, Japanese, and Portuguese laborers. It was designed as a simple language of the here and now, and was primarily concerned with the necessary functions of working, eating, and sleeping. It has an economical noun-verb-object structure (although not necessarily in that order).

CAPSULE PIDGIN

The following are a few commonly used words and expressions that should give you an idea of pidgin. It really can't be written properly, merely approximated, but for now, "Brah, study da' kine an' bimbye you be hele on, brah! OK? Lesgo."

an' den—and then? big deal; what's next; how boring

bimbye—after a while; bye and bye. "Bimbye, you learn pidgin."

blalah—brother, but actually only refers to a large, heavy-set, good-natured Hawaiian man

brah—all the bros in Hawaii are brahs; brother; pal. Used to call someone's attention. One of the most common words used even among people who are not acquainted. After a fill-up at a gas station, a person would say "Tanks, brah."

cockaroach—steal; rip off. If you really want to find out what *cockaroach* means, just leave your camera on your beach blanket when you take a little dip.

da' kine—a catchall word of many meanings that epitomizes the essence of pidgin. *Da' kine* is easily used as a euphemism for pidgin and is substituted whenever the speaker is at a loss for a word or just wants to generalize. It can mean: you know? watchamacallit; of that type.

geev um—give it to them; give them hell; go for it. Can be used as an encouragement. If a surfer is riding a great wave, the people on the beach might yell, "Geev um, brah!"

hana ho—again. Especially after a concert the audience shouts "hana ho" (one more!).

hele on—right on! hip; with it; groovy

howzit?—as in "howzit brah?" what's happening? how is it going? The most common greeting, used in place of the more formal "How do you do?"

hu hu—angry! "You put the make on the wrong da' kine wahine brah, and you in da' kine trouble, if you get one big Hawaiian blalah plenty hu hu."

kapu—a Hawaiian word meaning forbidden. If *kapu* is written on a gate or posted on a tree it means "No trespassing." *Kapu*-breakers are still very unpopular in the islands.

lesgo—Let's go! Do it!

li'dis an' li'dat—like this or that; a catch-all grouping especially if you want to avoid details; like, ya' know?

lolo buggah—stupid or crazy guy (person). Words to a tropical island song go, "I want to find the lolo who stole my pakalolo."

mo' bettah—real good! great idea. An island sentiment used to be, "mo' bettah you *come* Hawaii." Now it has subtly changed to, "mo' bettah you *visit* Hawaii."

ono—number one! delicious; great; groovy. "Hawaii is ono, brah!"

pakalolo—literally "crazy smoke"; marijuana; grass; reefer. "Hey, brah! Maui-wowie da' kine ono pakalolo."

pakiki head—stubborn; bull-headed

pau—a Hawaiian word meaning finished; done; over and done with. *Pau hana* means end of work or quitting time. Once used by plantation workers, now used by everyone.

stink face—basically frowning at someone; using facial expression to show displeasure. Hard looks. What you'll get if you give local people a hard time.

swell head—burned up; angry

talk story—spinning yarns; shooting the breeze; throwing the bull; a rap session. If you're lucky enough to be around to hear *kapuna* (elders) "talk story," you can hear some fantastic tales in the tradition of old Hawaii.

tita—sister, but only used to describe a fun-loving, down-to-earth country girl

waddascoops—what's the scoop? what's up? what's happening?

Hawaiian words make up most of pidgin's non-English vocabulary. It includes a good smattering of Chinese, Japanese, and Samoan, and the distinctive rising inflection is provided by the melodious Mediterranean lilt of the Portuguese. Pidgin is not a stagnant language. It's kept alive by hip new words introduced by people who are "so radical," or especially by slang words introduced by teenagers. It's a colorful English, like "jive" or "ghettoese" spoken by American blacks, and is as regionally unique as the speech of Cajuns from Louisiana's bayous. *Maka'ainana* of all socioethnic backgrounds can at least understand pidgin. Most islanders are proud of it, while some consider it a low-class jargon. The Hawaiian House of Representatives has given pidgin an official sanction, and most people feel that it adds a real local style and should be preserved.

Pidgin Lives
Pidgin is first learned at school, where all students, regardless of background, are exposed to it. The pidgin spoken by young people today is "fo' real" different from that of their parents. It's no longer only plantation talk, but has moved to the streets and picked up some sophistication. At one time there was an academic movement to exterminate it, but that idea died away with the same thinking that insisted on making left-handed people write with their right hands. It is strange, however, that pidgin has become the unofficial language of Hawaii's grassroots movement, when it actually began as a white owners' language that was used to supplant Hawaiian and all other languages brought to the islands.

Although hip young *haole* use pidgin all the time, it has gained the connotation of being the language of the nonwhite locals, and is part of the "us against them" way of thinking. All local people, *haole* or not, do consider pidgin their own island language, and don't really like it when it's used by *malihini* (newcomers). If you're in the islands long enough, you don't have to bother learning pidgin; it'll learn you. There's a book sold all over the islands called *Pidgin to da Max,* written by (you guessed it) a *haole* from Nebraska named Doug Simonson. You might not be able to understand what's being said by locals speaking pidgin (that's usually the idea), but you should be able to *feel* what's being meant.

HAWAIIAN

The Hawaiian language sways like a palm tree in a gentle wind. Its words are as melodious as a love song. Linguists say that you can learn a lot about people through their language: when you hear Hawaiian you think of gentleness and love, and it's hard to imagine the ferocious side so evident in Hawaii's past. With its many Polynesian root words easily traced to Indonesian and Malay, Hawaiian is obviously from this same stock. The Hawaiian spoken today is very different from old Hawaiian. Its greatest metamorphosis occurred when the missionaries began to write it down in the 1820s. There is a movement to reestablish the Hawaiian language, and courses in it are offered at the University of

THE ALPHABET.

VOWELS.		SOUND.	
	Names.	Ex. in Eng.	Ex. in Hawaii.
A a	a	as in *father*,	la—sun.
E e	e	— *tete*,	hemo—cast off.
I i	e	— *marine*,	marie—quiet.
O o	o	— *over*,	ono—sweet.
U u	oo	—*rule*,	nui—large.

CONSONANTS.	Names.	CONSONANTS.	Names.
B b	be	N n	nu
D d	de	P p	pi
H h	he	R r	ro
K k	ke	T t	ti
L l	la	V v	vi
M m	mu	W w	we

The following are used in spelling foreign words:

F f	fe	S s	se
G g	ge	Y y	yi

1

The cover page of the first Hawaiian primer shows the phonetic rendering of the ancient Hawaiian language before five of the consonants were dropped.

Hawaii. Many scholars have put forth translations of Hawaiian, but there are endless, volatile disagreements in the academic sector about the real meanings of Hawaiian words. Hawaiian is, by and large, no longer spoken as a language except on Niihau and in Hawaiian-language immersion classes, and the closest tourists will come to it is in place-names, street names, and in words that have become part of common usage, such as "aloha" and "mahalo." A few old Hawaiians still speak it at home and there are sermons in Hawaiian at some local churches. Kawaiahao Church in downtown Honolulu is the most famous of these. (See the Glossary for lists of commonly used Hawaiian words.)

Wiki Wiki Hawaiian

Thanks to the missionaries, the Hawaiian language is rendered phonetically using only 12 letters, the five vowels, a-e-i-o-u, sounded as they are in Italian, and seven consonants, h-k-l-m-n-p-w, sounded exactly as they are in English. Sometimes "w" is pronounced as "v," but this only occurs in the middle of a word and always follows a vowel. A consonant is always followed by a vowel, forming two-letter syllables, but vowels are often found in pairs or even triplets. A slight oddity about Hawaiian is the "glottal stop." This is an abrupt break in sound in the middle of a word such as "oh-oh" in English, and is denoted with an apostrophe ('). A good example is ali'i; or even better, the Oahu town of Ha'iku, which actually means "Abrupt Break."

Pronunciation Key

For those unfamiliar with the sounds of Italian or other Romance languages, the vowels are sounded as follows:

A—in stressed syllables, pronounced as in "ah" (that feels good!). For example, Haleakala is pronounced "hah-lay-AH-kah-lah." Unstressed syllables are pronounced "uh" as in "again" or "above." For example, Kamehameha would be "kuh-MAY-huh-MAY-huh."

E—short "e" is "eh," as in "pen" or "dent" (thus hale is "HAH-leh"). Long "e" sounds like "ay" as in "sway" or "day." For example, the Hawaiian goose (nene) is a "nay nay," not a "knee knee."

I—pronounced "ee" as in "see" or "we" (thus pali is pronounced "PAH-lee").

O—pronounced as in "no" or "oh," such as "KOH-uh" (koa) or "OH-noh" (ono).

U—pronounced "oo" as in "do" or "stew"; for example, "KAH-poo" (kapu) or "POO-nuh" (Puna).

Diphthongs

There are also eight vowel pairs known as "diphthongs" (ae-ai-ao-au-ei-eu-oi-ou). These are the sounds made by gliding from one vowel to another within a syllable. The stress is placed on the first vowel. In English, examples would be soil and euphoria. Common examples in Hawaiian are lei and heiau.

Stress

The best way to learn which syllables are stressed in Hawaiian is by listening closely. It becomes obvious after a while. There are also some vowel sounds that are held longer than others and these can occur at the beginning of a word such as the first "a" in aina or in the middle of a word, like the first "a" in lanai. Again, it's a matter of tuning your ear and paying attention. No one is going to give you a hard time if you mispronounce a word. It's good, however, to pay close attention to the pronunciation of street and place-names because many Hawaiian words sound alike and a misplaced vowel here or there could be the difference between getting to where you want to go and getting lost.

RELIGION

The Lord saw fit to keep His island paradise secret from humanity for a few million years, but once we finally arrived we were awfully thankful. Hawaii sometimes seems like a floating tabernacle; everywhere you look there's a church, temple, shrine, or heiau. The islands are either a very holy place, or there's a powerful lot of sinning going on that would require so many houses of prayer. Actually, it's just America's "right to worship" concept fully employed . . . in microcosm. All of the peoples who came to Hawaii brought their own form of devotion. The Polynesian Hawaiians praised the primordial creators, Wakea and Papa, from whom their pantheon of animistically inspired gods sprang. Obviously, to a modern world, these old gods would never do. Unfortunately for the old gods, there were simply too many of them, and belief in them was looked upon as mere superstition, the folly of semicivilized pagans. So the famous missionaries of the 1820s brought Congregational Christianity and the "true path" to heaven.

Inconveniently, the Catholics, Mormons, Reformed Mormons, Adventists, Episcopalians, Unitarians, Christian Scientists, Lutherans, Baptists, Jehovah's Witnesses, Salvation Army, and every other major and minor denomination of Christianity that followed in their wake brought their own brand of enlightenment and never quite agreed with each other. Chinese and Japanese migrants established all the major sects of Buddhism, Confucianism, Taoism, and Shintoism. Allah is praised, the Torah is chanted in Jewish synagogues, and nirvana is available at a variety of Hindu temples. If the spirit moves you, a Hare Krishna devotee will be glad to point you in the right direction and give you a free flower for only a dollar or two. If the world is still too much with you, you might find peace at a Church of Scientology, or meditate at a Kundalini yoga institute, or perhaps find relief at a local assembly of Baha'i. Anyway, rejoice, because in Hawaii you'll not only find paradise, but you might even find salvation.

HAWAIIAN BELIEFS

The Polynesian Hawaiians worshipped nature. They saw its forces manifested in a multiplicity of forms to which they ascribed godlike powers, and based daily life on this animistic philosophy. Handpicked and specially trained storytellers chanted the exploits of the gods. These ancient tales, kept alive in a special oral tradition called *moolelo*, were recited only by day. Entranced listeners encircled the chanter; in respect for the gods and in fear of their wrath, they were forbidden to move once the tale was begun. This was serious business where a person's life could be at stake. It was not like the telling of *kaao*, which were simple fictions, tall tales, and yarns of ancient heroes related for amusement and to pass the long nights. Any object, animate or inanimate, could be a god. All could be infused with mana, especially a dead body, or a respected ancestor.

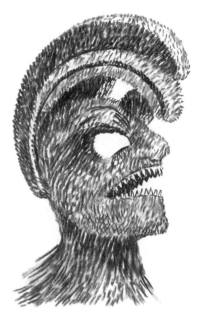

BOB RACE

Kukailimoku, Kamehameha's war god, was 30 inches tall. Fashioned from feathers, it presented a horrible sight with its gaping mouth of dog's teeth and was reputed to utter loud cries while battle was being waged.

Ohana had personal family gods called *amakua* on whom they called in times of danger or strife. There were children of gods called *kupua* who were thought to live among humans and were distinguished either for their beauty and strength or for their ugliness and terror. It was told that processions of dead *ali'i*, called "Marchers of the Night," wandered through the land of the living, and unless you were properly protected it could mean death if they looked upon you. There were simple ghosts known as *akua lapu* who merely frightened people. Forests, waterfalls, trees, springs, and a thousand forms of nature were the manifestations of *akua li'i*, "little spirits" who could be invoked at any time for help or protection. It made no difference who or what you were in old Hawaii; the gods were ever present and they took a direct and active role in your life.

Behind all of these beliefs was an innate sense of natural balance and order. It could be interpreted as positive-negative, yin-yang, plus-minus, life-death, light-dark, whatever, but the main idea was that everything had its opposite. The time of darkness when only the gods lived was *po.* When the great gods descended to the earth and created light, this was *ao* and humanity was born. All of these *moolelo* are part of *The Kumulipo,* the great chant that records the Hawaiian version of creation from the time the gods descended and touched the earth at Ku Moku on Lanai, where genealogies were kept. Unlike the Bible, these included the noble families of female *ali'i* as well as males.

THE STRIFES OF MAUI

Of all the heroes and mythological figures of Polynesia, Maui is the best known. His "strifes" are like the great Greek epics, and they make excellent tales of daring that elders loved to relate to youngsters around the evening fire. Maui was abandoned by his mother, Hina of Fire, when he was an infant. She wrapped him in her hair and cast him upon the sea where she expected him to die; he lived and returned home to become her favorite. She knew then that he was a born hero and had strength far beyond that of ordinary mortals. His first exploit was to lift the sky. In those days the sky hung so low that humans had to crawl around on all fours. A seductive young woman approached Maui and asked him to use his great strength to lift the sky. In fine heroic fashion, the big boy agreed, if the beautiful woman would euphemistically "give him a drink from her gourd." He then obliged her by lifting the sky, and he might even have made the earth move for her once or twice.

More Land
The territory of mankind was small at that time. Maui decided that more land was needed, so he conspired to "fish up islands." He descended into the land of the dead and petitioned an ancestress to fashion him a hook out of her jawbone. She obliged, and created the mythical hook *Manai ikalani.* Maui then secured a sacred *alae* bird that he intended to use for bait and bid his brothers to paddle him far out to sea. When

he arrived at the deepest spot, he lowered *Manai ikalani* baited with the sacred bird, and his sister, Hina of the Sea, placed it into the mouth of "Old One Tooth," who held the land fast to the bottom of the waters. Maui then exhorted his brothers to row, but warned them not to look back. They strained at the oars with all their might and slowly a great landmass arose. One brother, overcome by curiosity, looked back, and when he did so, the land shattered into all of the islands of Polynesia.

Further Exploits
Maui still desired to serve mankind. People were without fire, the secret of which was held by the sacred *alae* birds, who learned it from Maui's far distant mother. Hina of Fire gave Maui her burning fingernails, but he oafishly kept dropping them into streams until all had fizzled out and he had totally irritated his generous progenitor. She pursued him, trying to burn him to a cinder; Maui chanted for rain to put out her scorching fires. When she saw that they were all being quenched she hid her fire in the barks of special trees and informed the mud hens where they could be found, but first made them promise never to tell humans. Maui knew of this and captured a mud hen, threatening to wring its scrawny, traitorous neck unless it gave up the secret. The bird tried trickery and told Maui first to rub together the stems of sugarcane, then banana and even taro. None worked, and Maui's determined rubbing is why these plants have hollow roots today.

Finally, with Maui's hands tightening around the mud hen's gizzard, the bird confessed that fire could be found in the *hau* tree and also the sandalwood, which Maui named *ili aha* (fire bark) in its honor. He then rubbed all the feathers off the mud hen's head for being so deceitful, which is why their crowns are featherless today.

The Sun Is Snared
Maui's greatest deed, however, was in snaring the sun and exacting a promise that it would go slower across the heavens. The people complained that there were not enough daylight hours to fish or farm. Maui's mother could not dry her tapa cloth because the sun rose and set so quickly. She asked her son to help. Maui went to his blind grandmother, who lived on the slopes of Haleakala and was responsible for cooking the

sun's bananas, which he ate every day in passing. She told him to personally weave 16 strong ropes with nooses from his sister's hair. Some say these came from her head, but other versions insist that it was no doubt Hina's pubic hair that had the power to hold the sun-god. Maui positioned himself with the rope, and as each of the 16 rays of the sun came across Haleakala, he snared them until the sun was defenseless and had to bargain for his life. Maui agreed to free him if he promised to go more slowly. From that time forward the sun agreed to move slowly and Haleakala ("The House of the Sun") became his home.

HEIAU AND IDOLS

A *heiau* is a Hawaiian temple. The basic *heiau* was a masterfully built and fitted rectangular stone wall that varied in size from about as big as a basketball court to the size of a football field. Once the restraining outer walls were built, the interior was backfilled with smaller stones and the top dressing was expertly laid and then rolled, perhaps with a log, to form a pavementlike surface. All that remains of Hawaii's many *heiau* are the stone platforms. The buildings upon them, made from perishable wood, leaves, and grass, have long since disappeared.

Some *heiau* were dreaded temples where human sacrifices were made. Tradition says that this barbaric custom began at Waha'ula Heiau on the Big Island in the 13th century and was introduced by a ferocious Tahitian priest named Paao. Other *heiau,* such as Pu'uhonua o Honaunau, also on the Big Island, were temples of refuge where the weak, widowed, orphaned, and vanquished could find safety and sanctuary.

Idols
The Hawaiian people worshipped gods who took the form of idols fashioned from wood, feathers, or stone. The eyes were made from shells, and until these were inlaid, the idol was dormant. The hair used was often human hair, and the arms and legs were usually flexed. The mouth was either gaping or formed a wide figure-eight lying on its side, and more likely than not was lined with glistening dog teeth. Small figures made of woven basketry were expertly covered with feathers. Red and yellow feathers were favorites taken from specific birds by men whose only work was to roam the forests in search of them.

Ghosts
The Hawaiians had countless superstitions and ghost legends, but two of the more interesting involve astral travel of the soul and the "Marchers of the Night." The soul, *uhane,* was considered by Hawaiians to be totally free and independent of its body, *kino.* The soul could separate, leaving the body asleep or very drowsy. This disincorporated soul *(hihi'o)* could visit people and was considered quite different from a *lapu,* an ordinary spir-

Early foreigners inspect Hawaiian amakua

it of a dead person. A *kahuna* could immediately recognize if a person's *uhane* had left his body, and a special wreath was placed upon his head to protect him and to facilitate reentry.

If confronted by an apparition, one could test to see if it was indeed dead or still alive by placing leaves of an *ape* plant upon the ground. If the leaves tore when they were walked upon, the spirit was merely human, but if they remained intact it was a ghost. Or you could sneak up and startle the vision, and if it disappeared it was a ghost. Also, if no reflection of the face appeared when it drank water from an offered calabash, it was a ghost. Unfortunately, there were no instructions to follow once you had determined that you indeed had a ghost on your hands. Maybe it was better not to know! Some people would sprinkle salt and water around their houses, but this kept away evil spirits, not ghosts.

There are also many stories of *kahuna* restoring a soul to a dead body. First they had to catch it and keep it in a gourd. They then placed beautiful tapa and fragrant flowers and herbs about the body to make it more enticing. Slowly, they would coax the soul out of the gourd until it reentered the body through the big toe.

Death Marchers
One inexplicable phenomenon that many people attest to is *ka huakai o ka po,* "Marchers of the Night." This march of the dead is fatal if you gaze upon it, unless one of the marchers happens to be a friendly ancestor who will protect you. The peak time for "the march" is 7:30 p.m.-2 a.m. The marchers can be dead *ali'i* and warriors, the gods themselves, or the lesser *amakua.* When the *amakua* march there is usually chanting and music. *Ali'i* marches are more somber. The entire procession, lit by torches, often stops at the house of a relative and might even carry him or her away. When the gods themselves march, there is often thunder, lightning, and heavy seas. The sky is lit with torches, and they walk six abreast, three gods and three goddesses. If you get in the way of a march, remove your clothing and prostrate yourself. If the marching gods or *amakua* happen to be ones to which you prayed, you might be spared. If it's a march of the *ali'i* you might make it if you lie face upward and feign death. If you *do* see a death march, the last thing that you'll worry about is lying naked on the ground and looking ridiculous.

MISSIONARIES ONE AND ALL

In Hawaii, when you say "missionaries," it's taken for granted you're referring to the small and determined band of Congregationalists who arrived aboard the brig *Thaddeus* in 1820, and the follow-up groups called "companies" or "packets" that reinforced them. They were sent from Boston by the American Board of Commissioners for Foreign Missions (ABCFM), which learned of the supposed sad and godless plight of the Hawaiian people through returning sailors and especially through the few Hawaiians who had come to America to study.

The person most instrumental in bringing the missionaries to Hawaii was a young man named Opukahaia. He was an orphan befriended by a ship's captain and taken to New England, where he studied theology. Obsessed with the desire to return home and save his people from certain damnation, Opukahaia wrote accounts of life in Hawaii that were published and widely read. These accounts were directly responsible for the formation of the Pioneer Company to the Sandwich Islands Missions in 1819. Unfortunately, Opukahaia died in New England from typhus the year before they left.

"Civilizing" Hawaii
The first missionaries had the straightforward task of bringing the Hawaiians out of paganism and into Christianity and civilization. They met with terrible hostility—not from the natives, but from the sea captains and traders who were very happy with the open debauchery and wanton whoremongering that was status quo in the Hawaii of 1820. Many direct confrontations between these two factions even included the cannonading of missionaries' homes by American sea captains, who were denied the customary visits of island women, thanks to meddlesome "do-gooders." The most memorable of these incidents involved "Mad Jack" Percival, the captain of the USS *Dolphin,* who bombed a church in Lahaina to show his rancor. In actuality, the truth of the situation was much closer to the sentiments of James Jarves, who wrote, "The missionary was a far more useful and agreeable man than his Catholicism would indicate; and the trader was not so bad a man as the mis-

sionary would make him out to be." The missionaries' primary aim might have been conversion, but the most fortuitous by-product was education, which raised the consciousness of every Hawaiian, regardless of religious affiliation. In 40 short years Hawaii was considered a civilized nation well on its way into the modern world, and the American Board of Missions officially ended its support in 1863.

Non-Christians

By the turn of the century, both Shintoism and Buddhism, brought by the Japanese and Chinese, were firmly established in Hawaii. The first official Buddhist temple was Hongpa Hongwanji, established on Oahu in 1889. All the denominations of Buddhism account for 17% of the island's religious total, and there are about 50,000 Shintoists. The Hindu religion has perhaps 2,000 adherents, and about the same number of Jewish people live throughout Hawaii, with only one synagogue, Temple Emanuel, on Oahu. The largest number of people in Hawaii (300,000) remain unaffiliated, and about 10,000 people are in new religious movements and lesser-known faiths such as Baha'i and Unitarianism.

ARTS AND MUSIC

Referring to Hawaii as "paradise" is about as hackneyed as you can get, but when you combine it into "artists' paradise" it's the absolute truth. Something about the place evokes art (or at least personal expression) from most people. The islands are like a magnet: they not only draw artists to them, but they draw art *from* the artists.

The inspiration comes from the astounding natural surroundings. The land is so beautiful yet so raw; the ocean's power and rhythm are primal and ever present; the riotous colors of flowers and fruit leap from the deep-green jungle background. Crystal water beads and pale mists turn the mountains into mystic temples, while rainbows ride the crests of waves. The stunning variety of faces begging to be rendered appears as if all the world sent delegations to the islands. And in most cases it did! Inspiration is everywhere, as is art, good or bad.

Sometimes the artwork is overpowering in itself and in its sheer volume. Though geared to the tourist's market of cheap souvenirs, there is hardly a shop in Hawaii that doesn't sell some item that falls into the general category of "art." You can find everything from carved monkey-face coconut shells to true masterpieces. The Polynesian Hawaiians were master craftsmen, and their legacy still lives in a wide variety of woodcarvings, basketry, and weavings. The hula is art in swaying motion, and the true form is rigorously studied and taken very seriously. There is hardly a resort area that doesn't offer the "bump and grind" tourist's hula, and even these revues are accompanied by proficient local musicians. Nightclubs offer "slack key" balladeers and island music made on ukuleles, and Hawaii's own steel guitars spill from many lounges.

Vibrant fabrics, which catch the spirit of the islands, are rendered into muumuu and aloha shirts at countless local factories. They're almost a mandatory purchase! Pottery, heavily influenced by the Japanese, is a well-developed craft at numerous kilns. Local artisans fashion delicate jewelry from coral and olivine, while some ply the whaler's legacy of etching on ivory, called scrimshaw. There is a fine tradition of quilting, flower art in lei, and street artists working in everything from airbrush to glass.

ARTS OF OLD HAWAII

Since everything in old Hawaii had to be fashioned by hand, almost every object was either a work of art or at least a highly refined craft. With the "civilizing" of the natives, most of the "old ways" disappeared, including the old arts and crafts. Most authentic Hawaiian art exists only in museums, but with the resurgence of Hawaiian roots, many old arts are being revitalized, and a few artists are becoming proficient in them.

Magnificent Canoes

The most respected artisans in old Hawaii were the canoe makers. With little more than a stone adze and a pump drill, they built canoes that could carry 200 people and last for generations—sleek, well proportioned, and infinitely seaworthy. The main hull was usually a gigantic koa log, and the gunwale planks were minutely drilled and sewn to the sides with sennit rope. Apprenticeships lasted for years, and a young man knew that he had graduated when one day he was nonchalantly asked to sit down and eat with the master builders. Small family-sized canoes with outriggers were used for fishing, and perhaps carried a spear rack; large oceangoing double-hulled canoes were used for migration and warfare. On these, the giant logs had been adzed to about two inches thick. A mainsail woven from pandanus was mounted on a central platform, and the boat was steered by two long paddles. The hull was dyed with plant juices and charcoal, and the entire village helped launch the canoe in a ceremony called "drinking the sea."

Carving and Weaving

Wood was a primary material used by Hawaiian craftsmen. They almost exclusively used koa because of its density, strength, and natural luster. It was turned into canoes, woodware, calabashes, and furniture used by the *ali'i.* Temple idols were also a major product of woodcarving. Various stone artifacts were turned out, including poi pounders, mirrors, fish sinkers, and small idols.

Hawaiians became the best basket makers and mat weavers in all of Polynesia. *Ulana* (mats) were made from *lau hala* (pandanus) leaves. Once split, the spine was removed and the leaves stored in large rolls. When needed they were soaked, pounded, and then fashioned into various floor coverings and sleeping mats. Intricate geometrical patterns were woven in, and the edges were rolled and well fashioned. Coconut palms were not used to make mats in old Hawaii, but a wide variety of basketry was made from the aerial root *'ie'ie.* The shapes varied according to use. Some baskets were tall and narrow, some were cones, others were flat like trays, while many were woven around gourds and calabashes.

A strong tradition of weaving and carving has survived in Hawaii, and the time-tested material of *lau hala* is still the best, although much is now made from coconut fronds. You can purchase anything from beach mats to a woven hat and all share the desired qualities of strength, lightness, and ventilation.

Featherwork

This highly refined art was only found on the islands of Tahiti, New Zealand, and Hawaii, while the fashioning of feather helmets and idols was unique to Hawaii alone. Favorite colors were red and yellow, which came only in a very limited number on a few birds such as the *'o'o, 'i'iwi, mamo,* and *apapane.* Professional bird hunters in old Hawaii paid their taxes to *ali'i* in prized feathers. The feathers were fastened to a woven net of *olona* cord and made into helmets, idols, and beautiful flowing capes and cloaks. These resplendent garments were made and worn only by men, especially during battle when a fine cloak

LOUISE FOOTE

The ali'i wore magnificent feathered capes that signified their rank. The noblest colors were red and yellow, provided by specialized hunters who snared and plucked just the right birds.

became a great trophy of war. Featherwork was also employed in the making of *kahili* and lei, which were highly prized by the noble *ali'i* women.

Tapa Cloth

Tapa, cloth made from tree bark, was common throughout Polynesia and was a woman's art. A few trees such as the *wauke* (paper mulberry) and *mamaki* produced the best cloth, but a variety of other bark types could be utilized. First the raw bark was pounded into a feltlike pulp and beaten together to form strips (the beaters had distinctive patterns that also helped make the cloth supple). They were then decorated by stamping, using a form of block printing, and dyed with natural colors from plants and sea animals, in shades of gray, purple, pink, and red. They were even painted with natural brushes made from pandanus fruit, with an overall gray color made from charcoal. The tapa cloth was sewn together to make bed coverings, and fragrant flowers and herbs were either sewn or pounded in to produce a permanent fragrance. Tapa cloth is still available today, but the Hawaiian methods have been lost, and most comes from other areas of Polynesia.

First Western Artists

When Captain Cook made first contact in 1778, the ship's artists immediately began recording things Hawaiian. John Webber and James Clevely made etchings and pen-and-ink drawings of Hawaiian people, structures, *heiau* and everyday occurrences that struck them as noteworthy or peculiar. William Ellis, ship's surgeon, also a fair hand at etching, was attracted to portraying native architecture. These three left a priceless and faithful record of what Hawaii was like at the moment of contact. Louis Choris, ship's artist with Otto Von Kotzebue in 1816, painted early portraits of King Kamehameha and Queen Kaahumanu, the two grandest figures in Hawaii's history. Jacques Arago, aboard the *Uranie* with the French Captain de Freycinet in 1819, recorded some gruesome customs of punishment of *kapu* breakers, and made many drawings of island people. Robert Dampier, who sailed on the *Blonde,* the ship that returned King Liholiho's body from England, recorded one of the earliest landscapes of Honolulu, a site which has continued to be depicted on film by more tourists than almost any other city on earth. These early artists merely set a trend

that continues unabated to this day; artists endeavor to "capture" Hawaii, and they do so with every artistic medium available.

Modern Masters

Countless artists working at all levels of accomplishment try to match their skills to the vigor and beauty of the islands. Some have set the standards, and their names have become synonymous with Hawaiian art. Heading this list of luminaries are Huc Luquiens, Madge Tennent, Tadashi Sato, Jean Charlot, and John Kelly. Madge Tennent (1889-1972) was an Englishwoman who came to Hawaii via Samoa after spending years in South Africa and New Zealand. She worked in oils that she applied liberally and in bold strokes. Enamored with the people of Hawaii, her portraits are of a race striking in appearance and noble in character. Her works, along with those of other island artists, are displayed at the Tennent Art Foundation, on the slopes of Punchbowl on Oahu.

Huc Luquiens, former chairman of the Art Department at the University of Hawaii, was a master at etching, and was especially accomplished in dry point. His works, mainly island landscapes, are displayed in the Hawaiiana Collection of the Honolulu Academy of Arts. Maui-born Tadashi Sato, a superbly accomplished muralist, has produced such famous mosaics as the 30-foot *Aquarius* at the State Capitol in Honolulu, and the 60-foot *Portals of Immortality* at the Maui Memorial Gymnasium in Lahaina.

Frenchman Jean Charlot perfected his mural art in Mexico before coming to Hawaii in 1949. He is renowned for his frescoes and became a well-known art critic and the grand old man of Hawaiian art. He died in 1979 at the ripe old age of 90. John M. Kelly was in love with Hawaiian women; his etchings of them are both inspired and technically flawless. Kelly was infinitely patient, rendering his subjects in the minutest detail.

These artists are the "Big Five of Hawaiian Art"; their accomplishments should be seen as an "artistic gauge" of what Hawaii can inspire in an artist. By observing their works you can get an instant "art course" and a comparative view of the state of the arts in Hawaii.

Contemporary Artists

The crop of new artists making their mark always seems to be bounteous, and their works,

MUSEUMS AND GALLERIES OF OAHU

Bishop Museum, 1525 Bernice St., Honolulu, HI 96817, tel. (808) 847-3511, Web site: www.bishop.hawaii.org. Open daily 9 a.m.-5 p.m. The best collection in the world on Polynesia in general and Hawaii specifically. A true cultural treat. Should not be missed.

The Contemporary Museum, 2411 Makiki Heights Dr., Honolulu, HI 96822, tel. (808) 526-1322, open Tues.-Sat. 10 a.m.-4 p.m., Sunday noon-4 p.m., closed Monday. The focus is on exhibitions, not collections, although works by David Hockney are on permanent display. Changing exhibits reflect different themes in contemporary art.

Damien Museum, located at Saint Augustine Catholic Church, 130 Ohua Ave. in Waikiki, tel. (808) 923-2690. Displays photographs, papers, artifacts, and mementos of the legendary Father Damien. Open weekdays only 9 a.m.-3 p.m. Donations gratefully accepted.

Hawaii Maritime Center, at Pier 7, Honolulu Harbor, HI 96813, tel. (808) 536-6373. Open daily 8:30 a.m.-5 p.m. A museum chronicling the exploration and exploitation of Hawaii by the seafarers who have come to its shores. Visit the famous double-hulled canoe *Hokule'a* and the tall-masted *Falls of Clyde.*

Hawaii's Plantation Village, 94-695 Waipahu St., Waipahu, HI 96797, tel. (808) 677-0110. An open-air museum portraying sugar plantation life and the ethnic mix of plantation workers. Restored buildings and memorabilia. Open for guided tours only Mon.-Fri. 9 a.m.-3 p.m. and Saturday 10 a.m.-3 p.m.

Honolulu Academy of Arts, 900 S. Beretania St., Honolulu, HI 96814, tel. (808) 532-8700, Web site: www.honoluluacademy.org. Open Tues.-Sat. 10 a.m.-4:30 p.m., Sunday 1-5 p.m. Collects, preserves, and exhibits works of art, classic and modern, with a strong emphasis on Asian art. Permanent and special exhibitions, with tours, classes, lectures, and films.

Honolulu Art Center, across from the Academy of Arts, displays student artwork. Contemporary Hawaiian works.

Iolani Palace, on the Iolani Palace Grounds, P.O. Box 2259, Honolulu, HI 96804, tel. (808) 522-0832. The only royal palace in the United States. Vintage artwork and antiques. Guided tours. Open Tues.-Sat. 9 a.m.-2:15 p.m.

Mission Houses Museum, 553 S. King St., Honolulu, HI 96813, tel. (808) 531-0481. Open Tues.-Sat. 9 a.m.-4 p.m. Two homes, a printing house, and a library; an early mission compound. Guided tours. Excellent.

---

heavily influenced by the "feeling of Hawaii," continue to be superb. The following list of artists, with a short description of their work, is by no means exhaustive. It merely shows the wide range of artwork available.

Richard Fields, a former Californian, now lives on Maui. The fascinating beauty of the *aina* is his inspiration that he depicts in his supra-realistic paintings of birds, mountains, clouds, flowers, and waterfalls. Richard creates his rich renditions using a mixed media of airbrush, acrylic, India ink, and stencils. His works are as striking and as inspiring as the ever-changing beauty of the islands.

Robert Nelson is a Maui artist who superbly transmits the integrated mystical life of land and sea. His watercolors are often diffused with the strange filtered light found beneath the waves. A conservationist, he has often depicted the gentle frolicking life of the whales that visit Hawaiian waters.

Bill Christian is a master of scrimshaw, which he renders on slate. He also produces fine oil paintings of the sea and old salts. A world-class artist, his works are displayed at art galleries on Maui as well as in the Smithsonian and the New Bedford Massachusetts Whaling Museum.

Pegge Hopper is often compared with Madge Tennent. She works in bold colors and strokes. Her subject matter is islanders, especially the delicacy and inner strength of women. Her works are displayed at various galleries, especially on Maui and Oahu, and are often available in limited-edition serigraphs.

John Costello, an Oahu artist, specializes in pointillism to capture the waves, women, and

Pacific Aerospace Museum, tel. (808) 839-0777, at the Honolulu International Airport, is open daily 9 a.m.-6 p.m. The focus is on aerospace travel and the aviation history of Hawaii, with interactive displays and an interpretive film.

Queen Emma's Summer Palace, 2913 Pali Hwy., Honolulu, HI 96817, tel. (808) 595-3167. Open daily 9 a.m.-4 p.m., except major holidays. Restored historic home, built about 1848. Furniture and mementos of Queen Emma and her family. Some items belong to other members of royal family.

Queen's Medical Center Historical Room, 1301 Punchbowl St., Honolulu, HI 96813, tel. (808) 547-4397. Exhibits display the history of the Queen's Medical Center (founded 1859) and the history of medicine in Hawaii. Open weekdays 8:30 a.m.-3:30 p.m.; no charge.

Tennent Art Foundation Gallery, 201-203 Prospect St., Honolulu, HI 96813, tel. (808) 531-1987. Shows work of Madge Tennent and other, mostly contemporary, works of art.

Tropic Lightning Museum, located directly up from Macomb Gate on Schofield Barracks, Wahiawa. Military museum on the history of Schofield Barracks Army Base and the 25th Infantry Division. Open 10 a.m.-4 p.m. Tues.-Sat., tel. (808) 655-0438.

University of Hawaii Art Gallery, 2535 The Mall, Honolulu, HI 96822, tel. (808) 956-6888. On the third floor of the student center. Showcases faculty, student, and traveling exhibitions. Open Mon.-Fri. 10 a.m.-4 p.m. and Sunday noon-4 p.m. Gallery closed between exhibitions.

U.S. Army Museum of Hawaii, Fort DeRussy, Waikiki, tel. (808) 438-2821. Open Tues.-Sun. 10 a.m.-4:30 p.m. Military history of Hawaii from the time of Kamehameha I to the activities of the U.S. Army in east Asia and the Pacific islands.

USS *Arizona* Memorial, Arizona Memorial Dr., Pearl Harbor, HI 96818, tel. (808) 422-2771 or 422-0561. A free tour of the sleek 184-foot white concrete structure that spans the sunken USS *Arizona.* Free Navy launches take you on the tour of "Battleship Row." Open daily 7:30 a.m.-5 p.m. No reservations—first-come, first-served. Launches every 15 minutes. Visitor center offers graphic materials and film, reflecting events of the Pearl Harbor attack.

USS *Bowfin* Submarine Museum, 11 Arizona Memorial Dr., Honolulu, HI 96818, tel. (808) 432-1341, fax 422-5201, Web site: www.aloha.net /~bowfin, e-mail: bowfin@aloha.net. Open daily 8 a.m.-5 p.m. Fully restored WW II submarine. Insight into the underwater war. Guided tours. Fascinating. Next door to *Arizona* Memorial.

flora of Hawaii in a sensitive and mystical way. He co-owns and operates Ka'ala Art with his brother, Jim, in Haleiwa on North Shore Oahu. John's works as well as local artists' are showcased in their small shop.

Alapai Hanapi is a traditionalist sculptor who tries to recreate the motifs of his Hawaiian ancestors. He works in wood and stone with tools that he fashions himself. His driving force is "cultural awareness," and through his art he tells of the old ways. He lives simply with his wife and three daughters near an old fishpond on eastern Molokai. His work is known for its simplicity and is available at art shows periodically held throughout the islands.

Al Furtado is a freelance artist working in Honolulu. He specializes in capturing the movement of Hawaiian dance. His depictions are often larger than life with a strong sense of vitality and motion.

The following is a potpourri of other distinguished artists displayed at various galleries around the islands. Any work bearing one of their names is authentic island art considered to be superior by fellow artists: William Waterfall, photographer; Satoru Abe, sculptor; Ruthadell Anderson, weaver; Betty Tseng Yu-ho Ecke, *dsui* painter; Claude Horan, sculptor, ceramics; Erica Karawina, stained glass; Ron Kowalke, painter; Ben Norris, painter; Louis Pohl, printmaker; Mamoru Sato, sculptor; Reuben Tam, painter; Jean Williams, weaver; John Wisnosky, painter; John Young, painter.

HULA AND LEI

Hula

The hula is more than an ethnic dance; it is the soul of Hawaii expressed in motion. It began as

hula dancers at Waimea
Falls Park

J.D. BISIGNANI

a form of worship during religious ceremonies and was danced only by highly trained men. It gradually evolved into a form of entertainment, but in no regard was it sexual. The hula was the opera, theater, and lecture hall of the islands all rolled into one. It was history portrayed in the performing arts. In the beginning an androgynous deity named Laka descended to earth and taught men how to dance the hula. In time the male aspect of Laka departed for the heavens, but the female aspect remained. The female Laka set up her own special hula *heiau* at Haena Point on the Na Pali coast of Kauai, where it still exists. As time went on women were allowed to learn the hula. Scholars surmise that men became too busy wresting a living from the land to maintain the art form.

Men did retain a type of hula for themselves called *lua*. This was a form of martial art employed in hand-to-hand combat that evolved into a ritualized warfare dance called *hula kui*. During the 19th century, the hula almost vanished because the missionaries considered it vile and heathen. King Kalakaua is generally regarded as saving it during the 1800s, when he formed his own troupe and encouraged the dancers to learn the old hula. Many of the original dances were forgotten, but some were retained and are performed to this day. Although professional dancers were highly trained, everyone took part in the hula. *Ali'i*, commoners, young, and old all danced.

Today, hula *halau* (schools) are active on every island, teaching hula and keeping the old

ways and culture alive. Performers still spend years perfecting their techniques. They show off their accomplishments during the fierce competition of the Merrie Monarch Festival in Hilo every April. The winning *halau* is praised and recognized throughout the islands.

Hawaiian hula was never performed in grass skirts; tapa or ti-leaf skirts were worn. Grass skirts came to Hawaii from the Gilbert Islands, so if you see grass or cellophane skirts in a "hula revue," it's not traditional. Almost every major resort offering entertainment or a luau also offers a revue. Most times, young island beauties accompanied by local musicians put on a floor show for the tourists. It's fun, but it won't be traditional. Hula, like all art forms, has its own highly specialized techniques. A dancer has to learn how to control every part of his/her body, including the facial expressions, which help set the mood. The hands are extremely important and provide instant background scenery. For example, if the hands are thrust outward in an aggressive manner, this can be a battle; if they sway gently overhead, they refer to the gods or to creation; they can easily symbolize rain, clouds, sun, sea, or moon. Watch the hands to get the gist of the story, though in the words of one wise guy, "You watch the parts you like, and I'll watch the parts I like."

Swaying hips, depending upon their motion, can be a long walk, a canoe ride, or sexual intercourse. The foot motion can portray a battle, a walk, or any kind of movement or conveyance.

The correct chanting of the *mele* is an integral part of the performance. These story chants, accompanied by musical instruments, make the hula very much like opera; it is especially similar in the way the tale unfolds.

Lei Making

Any flower or blossom can be strung into a lei, but the most common are carnations or the lovely smelling plumeria. Lei, like babies, are all beautiful, but special lei are highly prized by those who know what to look for. Of the different stringing styles, the most common is *kui*—stringing the flower through the middle or side. Most "airport-quality" lei are of this type. The *humuhumu* style, reserved for making flat lei, is made by sewing flowers and ferns to a ti, banana, or sometimes *hala* leaf. A *humuhumu* lei makes an excellent hatband. *Wili* is the winding together of greenery, ferns, and flowers into short, bouquet-type lengths. The most traditional form is *hili*, which requires no stringing at all but involves braiding fragrant ferns and leaves such as *maile*. If flowers are interwoven, the *hili* becomes the *haku* style, the most difficult and most beautiful type of lei.

The Lei of the Land

Every major island is symbolized by its own lei made from a distinctive flower, shell, or fern. Each island has its own official color as well, though it doesn't necessarily correspond to the color of the island's lei. Oahu, "The Gathering Place," is symbolized by yellow, the color of the tropical sun. Its flower is the delicate *ilima,* which resembles hibiscus and ranges in color from pastel yellow to a burnt orange. The blooms are about as large as a silver dollar and lei made from *ilima* were at one time reserved only for the *ali'i*, designating them as a royal flower.

THAT GOOD OLD ISLAND MUSIC

The missionaries usually take a beating when it's recounted how much Hawaiian culture they destroyed while "civilizing" the natives. However, they seem to have done one thing right. They introduced the Hawaiians to the diatonic musical scale and immediately opened a door to latent and superbly harmonious talent. Before the mis-

sionaries, the Hawaiians knew little about melody. Though sonorous, their *mele* were repetitive chants in which the emphasis was placed on historical accuracy and not on "making music." The Hawaiians, in short, didn't *sing*. But within a few years of the missionaries' arrival, they were belting out good old Christian hymns and one of their favorite pastimes became group and individual singing.

Early in the 1800s, Spanish *vaqueros* from California were imported to teach the Hawaiians how to be cowboys. With them came guitars and moody ballads. The Hawaiian *paniolos* (cowboys) quickly learned how to punch cows and croon away the long lonely nights on the range. Immigrants that came along a little later in the 19th century, especially from Portugal, helped create a Hawaiian-style music. Their biggest influence was a small four-stringed instrument called a *braga* or *cavaquinho*. One owned by Augusto Dias was the prototype of a homegrown Hawaiian instrument that became known as the ukulele. "Jumping flea," the translation of ukulele, is an appropriate name devised by the Hawaiians when they saw how nimble the fingers were as they "jumped" over the strings.

The Merrie Monarch, King Kalakaua, and Queen Liliuokalani were both patrons of the arts who furthered the Hawaiian musical identity at the turn of the century. Kalakaua revived the hula and was also a gifted lyricist and balladeer. He wrote the words to "Hawaii Pono," which became the national anthem of Hawaii and later the state anthem. Liliuokalani wrote the hauntingly beautiful "Aloha O'e," which is often pointed to as the "spirit of Hawaii" in music. Detractors say that its melody is extremely close to the old Christian hymn, "Rock Beside the Sea," but the lyrics are so beautiful and perfectly fitted that this doesn't matter.

Just prior to Kalakaua's reign a Prussian bandmaster, Capt. Henri Berger, was invited to head the fledgling Royal Hawaiian Band, which he turned into a very respectable orchestra lauded by many visitors to the islands. Berger was open-minded and learned to love Hawaiian music. He collaborated with Kalakaua and other island musicians to incorporate their music into a Western format. He headed the band for 43 years until 1915, and was instrumental in making music a serious pursuit of talented Hawaiians.

Popular Hawaiian Music

Hawaiian music has a unique twang, a special feeling that says the same thing to everyone who hears it: "Relax, sit back in the moonlight, watch the swaying palms as the surf sings a lullaby." This special sound is epitomized by the bouncy ukulele, the falsettos of Hawaiian crooners, and by the smooth ring of the "steel" or "Hawaiian" guitar. The steel guitar is a variation originated by Joseph Kekuku in the 1890s. Stories abound of how Joseph Kekuku devised this instrument; the most popular versions say that Joe dropped his comb or pocketknife on his guitar strings and liked what he heard. Driven by the faint rhythm of an inner sound, he went to the machine shop at the Kamehameha School and turned out a steel bar for sliding over the strings. To complete the sound he changed the cat-gut strings to steel and raised them so they wouldn't hit the frets. Voila!—Hawaiian music as the world knows it today.

The first melodious strains of **slack-key guitar** *(ki ho'alu)* can be traced back to the time of Kamehameha III and the *vaqueros* from California. The Spanish had their way of tuning the guitar, and played difficult and aggressive music that did not sit well with Hawaiians, who were much more gentle and casual in their manners.

Hawaiians soon became adept at making their own music. At first, one person played the melody, but it lacked fullness. There was no body to the sound. So, as one *paniolo* fooled with the melody, another soon learned to play bass, which added depth. But, a player was often alone, and by experimenting learned that he could get the right hand going with the melody, and at the same time could play the bass note with the thumb to improve the sound. Singers also learned that they could "open tune" the guitar to match their rich voices.

Hawaiians believed knowledge was sacred, and what is sacred should be treated with utmost respect—which meant keeping it secret, except from sincere apprentices. Guitar playing became a personal art form whose secrets were closely guarded, handed down only to family members, and only to those who showed ability and determination. When old-time slack-key guitar players were done strumming, they loosened all the strings so no one could figure out how they had them tuned. If they were playing, and some folks came by that were interested and weren't part of the family, the Hawaiians stopped what they were doing, put their guitars down, and put their feet across the strings to wait for the folks to go away. As time went on, more and more Hawaiians began to play slack key, and a common repertoire emerged.

An accomplished musician could easily figure out the simple songs, once they had figured out how the family had tuned the guitar. One of the most popular tunings was the "open G." Old Hawaiian folks called it the "taro patch tune." Different songs came out, and if you were in their family and were interested in the guitar, they took the time to sit down and teach you. The way they taught was straightforward—and a test of your sincerity at the same time. The old master would start to play. He just wanted you to listen and get a feel for the music—nothing more than that. You brought your guitar and *listened*. When you felt it, you played it, and the knowledge was transferred. Today, only a handful of slack-key guitar players know how to play the traditional tunes classically. The best-known and perhaps greatest slack-key player was Gabby Pahinui, with The Sons of Hawaii. When he died he left many recordings behind. A slack-key master still singing and playing is Raymond Kane. Raymond now teaches a handful of students his wonderful and haunting music. Not one of his students are from his own family, and most are *haole* musicians trying to preserve the classical method of playing.

Hawaiian music received its biggest boost from a remarkable radio program known as "Hawaii Calls." This program sent out its music from the Banyan Court of the Moana Hotel from 1935 until 1975. At its peak in the mid-1950s, it was syndicated on over 700 radio stations throughout the world. Ironically, Japanese pilots heading for Pearl Harbor tuned in island music as a signal beam. Some internationally famous classic tunes came out of the '40s and '50s. Jack Pitman composed "Beyond the Reef" in 1948; over 300 artists have recorded it, and it has sold well over 12 million records. Other million-sellers include: "Sweet Leilani," "Lovely Hula Hands," "The Crosseyed Mayor of Kaunakakai," and "The Hawaiian Wedding Song."

By the 1960s, Hawaiian music began to die. Just too corny and light for those turbulent years, it belonged to the older generation and the good times that followed WW II. One man was instrumental in keeping Hawaiian music alive during this period. Don Ho, with his "Tiny Bubbles," became the token Hawaiian musician of the '60s and early '70s. He's persevered long enough to become a legend in his own time, and his Polynesian Extravaganza at the Hilton Hawaiian Village packed visitors in until the early 1990s. He now plays at the Waikiki Beachcomber Hotel five nights a week. Al Harrington, "The South Pacific Man," until his recent retirement had another Honolulu "big revue" that drew large crowds. Of this type of entertainment, perhaps the most Hawaiian is Danny Kaleikini, still performing at the Kahala Hilton, who entertains his audience with dances, Hawaiian anecdotes, and tunes on the traditional Hawaiian nose flute.

The Beat Goes On

Beginning in the mid-'70s islanders began to assert their cultural identity. One of the unifying factors was the coming of age of "Hawaiian"

music. It graduated from the "little grass shack" novelty tune and began to include sophisticated jazz, rock, and contemporary rhythms. Accomplished musicians whose roots were in traditional island music began to highlight their tunes with this distinctive sound. The best embellish their arrangements with ukuleles, steel guitars, and traditional percussion and melodic instruments. Some excellent modern recording artists have become island institutions. The local people say that you know if the Hawaiian harmonies are good if they give you "chicken skin."

Each year special music awards, **Na Hoku Hanohano,** or Hoku for short, are given to distinguished island musicians. The following are recent Hoku winners considered by their contemporaries to be among the best in Hawaii. **Barney Isaacs and George Kuo** won Instrumental Album of the Year for *Hawaiian Touch.* Na Leo Pilimihana ("Flying With Angels") won Song of the Year, Album of the Year, Contemporary Album of the Year, and Group of the Year. **Robi**

THE ARTS IN HAWAII

Following are the names and addresses of organizations that dispense information on Hawaiian arts and crafts.

Both Honolulu daily newspapers, the ***Honolulu Advertiser*** and the ***Star Bulletin,*** run calendars of current and upcoming cultural events for around the island.

Bishop Museum, 1525 Bernice St., Honolulu, HI 96817, tel. (808) 847-3511, Web site: www.bishop.hawaii.org. The world's *best* museum covering Hawaii and Polynesia. Exhibits, galleries, archives, demonstrations of Hawaiian crafts, and a planetarium. On the premises, Shop Pacifica has a complete selection of books and publications on all aspects of Hawaiian art and culture.

Hawaii Craftsmen, P.O. Box 22145, Honolulu, HI 96823, tel. (808) 596-8128. Increases awareness of Hawaiian crafts through programs, exhibitions, workshops, lectures, and demonstrations.

Honolulu Academy of Arts, 900 S. Beretania St., Honolulu, HI 96814, tel. (808) 532-8700, Web site:

www.honoluluacademy.org. Collects, preserves and exhibits works of fine art. Offers public art education programs related to its collections. Also offers tours, classes, lectures, films, and a variety of publications.

Mayor's Office on Culture and the Arts, 530 S. King St., Honolulu, HI 96813, tel. (808) 523-4674, Web site: www.hcc.hawaii.edu/artweb. The City and County of Honolulu's official organ for visual and performing arts information islandwide.

Pacific Handcrafters Guild, P.O. Box 29389, Honolulu, HI 96820-1789, tel. (808) 254-6788. Focuses on developing and preserving handicrafts and fine arts of all mediums. The guild sponsors four major crafts fairs annually.

State Foundation on Culture and the Arts, 44 Merchant St., Honolulu, HI 96813, tel. (808) 586-0300, Web site: hi50.com/sfca, e-mail: sfca@iav.com. Begun by state legislature in 1965 to preserve and promote Hawaii's diverse cultural, artistic, and historical heritage. Manages grants and maintains programs in folk arts and art in public places.

Kahakalau's *Sistah Robi* earned Female Vocalist and Island Contemporary Album of the Year. "Friends in Me" won Single of the Year for **Brothers and Sister. Keali'i Reichel**'s *Lei Hali'a* was voted Popular Hawaiian Album of the Year (and the artist also won Male Vocalist of the Year and Favorite Entertainer of the Year). *Broken Hearts* earned **Darren Benitez** a Most Promising Artist of the Year award; **Sonny Kamahele** received a Lifetime Achievement Award; and **Ledward Ka'apana** is a Slack Key Award winner.

Past Hoku winners who have become renowned performers include: **Brothers Cazimero,** who are blessed with beautiful harmonic voices; **Krush,** who are highly regarded for their contemporary sounds; **The Peter Moon Band,** fantastic performers with a strong traditional sound; **Karen Keawehawai'i,** who has a sparkling voice and can be very funny when the mood strikes her; and **Henry Kapono,** formerly of Cecilio and Kapono, who keeps a low profile but is an incredible performer and excellent songwriter (his shows are noncommercial and very special). **Cecilio** is now teamed up with **Maggie Herron;** they are hot together and have a strong following in Honolulu. **The Beamer Brothers** are excellent performers and can be seen at various nightspots. **Loyal Garner,** who was awarded Female Vocalist of the Year for *I Shall Sing,* is a truly wonderful artist. **Del Beazley** is a talented energized performer. **Makaha Sons Of Niihau** are the best traditional Hawaiian band and shouldn't be missed. **Hawaiian Style Band** is known for *Vanishing Treasures,* a terrific album filled with contemporary music. **Bryan Kessler & Me No Hoa Aloha** perform songs like "Heiau," a haunting melody. **Susan Gillespie** and **Susi Hussong** are first-rate instrumentalists, and **Kealohi,** who recorded *Kealohi,* is very promising.

Other top-notch performers with strong followings are Ledward Kaapana; Mango; Oliver Kelly; Ka'eo; Freitas Brothers; Brickwood Galuteria, who won a double Hoku for Best Male Vocalist and Most Promising Artist; and Third Road Delite.

BOB RACE

ON THE ROAD

SPORTS AND RECREATION

CAMPING

Few people equate visiting Oahu with camping. The two seem mutually exclusive, especially when you focus on the mystique of Waikiki, and the dominance of a major city like Honolulu. But between state, county, and private campgrounds, and even a military reserve or two, you have about 20 spots to choose from all over the island. Camping on Oahu, however, is a little different from camping on the Neighbor Islands, which are simply more amenable to camping. In an island state, they're considered "the woods, the sticks, the backcountry," and camping seems more acceptable there.

Although totally legal to camp, and done by both visitors and residents, Oahu's camping problems are widely divergent, with social and financial implications. When the politically powerful tourist industry thinks of visitors, it imagines people sitting by a hotel pool, drinking mai tais, and dutifully

spending money! Campers just won't cooperate in parting with their quota of dollars, so there's not much impetus to cater to their wants and needs. Moreover, Honolulu is an international city that attracts both the best and worst kinds of people. The tourist industry, supported by the civil authorities, has a mortal dread that low-lifers, loafers, and bums will ensconce themselves on Oahu's beaches. This would be disastrous for Oahu's image! Mainland cities, not so dependent upon tourism, can obviously be more tolerant of their citizens who have fallen through the social net. So in Oahu they keep a close eye on the campgrounds, enforcing the rules, controlling the situation. The campgrounds are patrolled, adding a measure of strictness along with a measure of security. Even decent people can't bend the rules and slide by a little, where they normally might on the Neighbor Islands.

An odd, inherent social situation adds to the problem. Not too long ago, the local people either lived on the beaches or used them extensively, often for their livelihoods. Many, especially fishermen and their families, would set up semipermanent camps for a good part of the year. You can see the remnants of this practice at some of the more remote and ethnically claimed campgrounds. As Oahu, much more than the Neighbor Islands, felt the pressures of growing tourism, beachfront property became astronomically expensive. Local people had to relinquish what they thought of as their beaches. The state and county, in an effort to keep some beaches public and therefore undeveloped, created beach parks. This ensured that all could use the beaches forever, but it also meant that their access would be governed and regulated.

Local people, just like visitors, must follow the rules and apply for camping permits limited by the number of days that you can spend in any one spot. Out went the semipermanent camp and with it, for the local people, the idea of *our* beach. Now, you have the same rights to camp in a spot that may have been used, or even owned, in past generations, by the family of dark-skinned people next to you. They feel dispossessed, infringed upon, and bitter. And you, especially if you have white skin, can be the focus of this bitterness. This situation, although psychologically understandable, can be a monumental drag. Of course, not all island people have this attitude, and chances are very good that nothing negative will happen. But you must be aware of underlying motivations so that you can read the vibes of the people around your camp spot.

If all of these "problems" haven't made you want to pull up your tent stakes and head into a more congenial sunset, you can have a great and inexpensive time camping on Oahu. All of this is just the social climate that you *may* have to face, but most likely, nothing unpleasant will happen, and you'll come home tanned, relaxed, and singing the praises of the great outdoors on Hawaii's capital island.

Note: For private group camps, mostly church-affiliated, see "Camps" in the Yellow Pages.

State Parks

Oahu boasts 22 state parks, recreation areas, waysides, and monuments. A majority offer a beach for day use, walking paths, picnic areas, toilets, showers, and/or pavilions. Included in these state properties are three *heiau*, **Iolani Palace,** the **Royal Mausoleum,** and **Diamond Head.** Of the 22, three are registered National Historical Landmarks and one is a National Natural Landmark.

Oahu state parks close their gates and parking lots at night. Those *not* offering camping are open 7 a.m.-7:45 p.m. from April 1 to Labor Day, closing during the remainder of the year at 6:45 p.m.

Four state parks currently offer tent camping: **Sand Island State Recreation Area,** just a few minutes from downtown Honolulu; **Keaiwa Heiau State Recreation Area,** in the interior on the heights above Aiea; **Malaekahana Bay State Recreation Area,** a mile north of Laie on the windward coast; and **Kahana Valley State Park** between Punaluu and Ka'a'awa on the windward coast.

To camp at Sand Island, Keaiwa Heiau, or Kahana Valley parks, you must acquire a permit (free) from the Department of Land and Natural Resources, Division of State Parks, P.O. Box 621 (1151 Punchbowl St.), Honolulu, HI 96809, tel. (808) 587-0300, open weekdays 8 a.m.-3:30 p.m. Oahu campsite **permit reservations** can be made only 30 days prior to the first day of camping, but *must* be made at least one week in advance. Write for a permit application form. Information needed includes your name, address, phone number, names and identification numbers of all persons over 18 years of age in your party, type of permit requested, duration of your stay, and specific dates requested. The permits can be picked up on arrival with proof of identification.

On Oahu campsites are at a premium and people line up at 8 a.m. on the first-floor breezeway on the Beretania Street side of the issuing office, just outside the double glass doors, where you are given a number on a first-come first-served basis (usually no hassle except on three-day holiday weekends). After this, go to the third floor where the office is located.

Note: Camping is allowed *only* from 8 a.m. Friday to 8 a.m. Wednesday (closed all day Wednesday and Thursday for camping—other activities okay) with the shutdown, supposedly, for regrowth. Camping on Sand Island State Recreation Area only is Friday through Monday. Camping is allowed for only five consecutive days in any one month, and don't forget a parking permit for your vehicle, which must remain within the locked park gates at night. Alooohaaa!

Camping at Malaekahana State Recreation Area is handled by the Friends of Malaekahana, tel. (808) 293-1736, fax 293-2066, P.O. Box 305, Laie, HI 96762. Reservations are taken up to 12 months in advance and at least 14 days before planned arrival; two-night minimum stay required. Check-in is handled 3-5 p.m.; checkout time is noon. The office is open Mon.-Fri. 10 a.m.-3 p.m. Write or call for information and reservation applications. Firearms, fireworks, pets, and drinking of alcoholic beverages are prohibited in the park, and a quiet time is enforced 10:30 p.m.-8 a.m. Half a dozen beach houses, which sleep up to 10, run $66 a night during the week and $80 on weekends. Tent campers pay $5 a night. There also are a few yurts on the property that can be rented when not occupied by students during the school year. The yurts do not have bath or cooking facilities, but they have floors and electricity. Outside hot showers and bathroom facilities are shared. Bring mosquito repellent. The pavilion can be rented for day events or for the day and night ($250)—it sleeps 15. Parking is limited. Make sure to call and make arrangements with the staff if you will be arriving later than office hours. The park gate is locked—for your security—7 a.m.-7 p.m.

The park service offers special culture and arts programs at Kahana Valley State Park and talks and guided tours weekdays at the Royal Mausoleum. Tours and other services at Iolani Palace are provided by the nonprofit Friends of Iolani Palace.

County Parks

There are nearly 300 county parks on the island of Oahu. The city and county of Honolulu has opened 13 (these change periodically) of its 62 beach parks around the island to tent camping, and most allow trailers and RVs. Unfortunately, these are the very parks at which you're more likely to encounter hassles. A free permit is required, and camping is allowed only from Friday at 8 a.m. until the following Wednesday at 8 a.m., at which time your campsite must be vacated (no camping Wednesday and Thursday evenings). A few of these parks have camping only on the weekends and one allows it only during summer months, so be sure to ask for particulars. These campsites are also at a premium, but you can write for reservations and pick up your permits on arrival with proper identification. For information and reservations write or visit City and County of Honolulu, Department of Parks and Recreation, Permit Section, 650 S. King St., Honolulu, HI 96813, tel. (808) 523-4525. Permits are also available from the satellite city halls around the island.

Note: All of the beach parks are closed during designated months (they differ from park to park) throughout the year. This is supposedly for cleaning, but really it's to reduce the possibility of squatters moving in. Make sure, if you're reserving far in advance, that the park will be open when you arrive! Don't count on the Parks and Recreation Department to inform you!

HIKING

The best way to leave the crowds of tourists behind and become intimate with the beauty of Oahu is to hike it. Although the Neighbor Islands receive fewer visitors, a higher percentage of people hike them than Oahu. Don't get the impression that you'll have the island to yourself, but you will be amazed at how open and lovely this crowded island can be. Some cultural and social hikes can be taken without leaving the city, like a stroll through Waikiki and a historical walking tour of downtown Honolulu and Chinatown. But others—some mere jaunts, others quite strenuous—are well worth the time and effort.

Remember that much of Oahu is privately owned, and you must have permission to cross this land, or you may be open to prosecution. Usually private property is marked by signs. Another source that might stomp your hiking plans with their jungle boots is the military. A full 25% of Oahu belongs to Uncle Sam, and he isn't al-

ways thrilled when you decide to play in his back yard. Some of the finest walks (like to the summit of Mt. Ka'ala) require crossing military lands, much of which has been altered by very unfriendly looking installations. Always check and obey any posted signs to avert trouble. The following listings are by no means all-inclusive, but should help you to choose a trail that seems interesting and is within your ability level.

Diamond Head

The most recognized symbol of Hawaii, this is the first place you should head for a strikingly beautiful panorama of Waikiki and greater Honolulu. Called Leahi ("Casting Point") by the Hawaiians, it was named Diamond Head after a group of wild-eyed English sailors espied what they thought to be diamonds glistening in the rocks. Hawaii had fulfilled so many other dreams, why not a mountain of diamonds?! Unfortunately, the glimmer was caused by worthless calcite crystals. No fortune was made, but the name stuck.

To get there, follow Kalakaua Avenue south from Waikiki until it leads into Diamond Head Road, then quickly a sign points you to Diamond Head Crater. Pass through a tunnel and into the heavily militarized section in the center of the crater; the trail starts here. Although the hike is moderate, you should bring along water, a flashlight (a must), and binoculars if you have them. Run by the Division of State Parks, the park is open daily from 6 a.m. to 6 p.m. A sign at the beginning describes the rigors you'll encounter and informs that the trail is seven-tenths of a mile long and was built to the 760-foot summit of Leahi Point in 1908 to serve as a U.S. Coast Artillery Observation Station. It was heavily fortified during WW II, and part of the fun is exploring the old gun emplacements and tunnels built to link and service them.

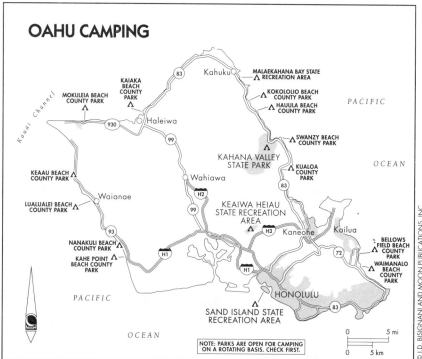

OAHU CAMPING

© J.D. BISIGNANI AND MOON PUBLICATIONS, INC.

NOTE: PARKS ARE OPEN FOR CAMPING ON A ROTATING BASIS. CHECK FIRST.

HAWAII STATE ARCHIVES

engraving of Hawaii's unique pali, *by Barthelme Lauvergue, circa 1836*

Though only 10 minutes from Waikiki, wildflowers and chirping birds create a peaceful setting. When you come to a series of cement and stone steps, walk to a flat area to the left to find an old winch that hauled the heavy building materials to the top. Here's a wide panorama of the sea and Koko Head, and notice too that atop every little hillock is an old gun emplacement. Next comes a short but dark tunnel (bring a flashlight!) and immediately a series of 99 steps. You can avoid the steps by taking the trail to the left, but the footing is slippery and there are no guard rails. Following the steps is a spiral staircase that leads down into a large gun emplacement, through which you walk and come to another tunnel. If you haven't brought a flashlight, give your eyes a few minutes to adjust; there's enough light to make it. Once on top, another stairway and ladder take you to the very summit.

Judd Trail

This is an excellent trail to take to experience Oahu's "jungle" while visiting the historic and picturesque **Nuuanu Pali.** From Honolulu take H-1 and turn onto Rt. 61, the Pali Highway. Turn right onto the Old Pali Highway, then right again onto Nuuanu Pali Drive. Follow it for just under a mile to Reservoir No. 2 spillway. The trail begins on the ocean side of the spillway and leads through fragrant eucalyptus and a dense stand of picture-perfect Norfolk pines. It continues through the forest reserve and makes a loop back to the starting point. En route you pass **Jackass Ginger Pool.** In the immediate area are "mud slides," where you can take a ride on a makeshift toboggan of *pili* grass, ti leaves, or a piece of plastic, if you've brought one. This activity is rough on your clothes, and even rougher on your body. The wet conditions after a rain are perfect. Afterward, a dip in Jackass Pool cleans the mud and refreshes at the same time. Continue down the trail to observe wild ginger, guava, and *kukui,* but don't take any confusing side trails. If you get lost head back to the stream and follow it until it intersects the main trail.

Tantalus and Makiki Valley Trails

Great sightseeing and hiking can be combined when you climb the road atop Tantalus. A range of trails in this area offer magnificent views. A few roads lead up Tantalus, but a good one heads past Punchbowl along Puowaina Drive; just keep going until it turns into Tantalus Drive. The road switchbacks past some incredible homes and views until it reaches the 2,013-foot summit, where it changes its name to Round Top Drive, then heads down the other side.

The best place to start is at the top of Tantalus at the **Manoa Cliff Trailhead,** where a number of intersecting trails give you a selection of adventure. Once on Round Top Drive, pass a brick wall with the name Kalaiopua Road imbedded in the stonework, and continue until you pass Forest Ridge Way, right after which is a large turnout on both sides of the road near telephone pole no. 56. To the right is the beginning of half-mile-long **Moleka Trail,** which offers some excellent views and an opportunity to experience the trails in this area without an all-day commitment. The trails are excellently maintained by the State Division of Forestry and Wildlife. Your greatest hazard here is mud, but in a moment you're in a handsome stand of bamboo, and in 10 minutes the foliage parts onto a lovely panorama of Makiki Valley and Honolulu in the background. These views are captivating, but remember to have "small eyes"—check out the variety of colored mosses and fungi, and don't forget the flowers and fruit growing around you.

A branch trail to the left leads to Round Top Drive, and if you continue the trail splits into three: the right is the **Makiki Valley Trail,** which cuts across the valley starting at a Boy Scout camp on Round Top Drive and ending atop Tantalus; **Ualakaa Trail** branches left and goes for another half mile, connecting the Makiki Valley Trail with Pu'u Ualakaa State Park; straight ahead is the **Makiki Branch A Trail,** which descends for one-half mile, ending at the Division of Forestry Baseyard at the bottom of the valley.

On the mountainside of the Manoa Cliffs Trailhead is the **Connector Trail.** This pragmatic-sounding trail does indeed connect the lower trails with **Manoa Cliffs Trail,** skirting around the backside of Tantalus and intersecting the **Puu Ohia Trail,** which leads to the highest point on Tantalus and the expected magnificent view.

Maunawili Falls Trail

Maunawili Falls is on the other side of Nuuanu Pali, near Maunawili town. This trail offers adventure into Oahu's jungle, with a rewarding pool and falls at the end. At the third red light as you head down the windward side of the Pali Highway, make a right onto Auloa Road. In a few hundred yards, take the left fork onto Maunawili Road and follow it toward the mountains through a residential area. Turn right onto Aloha Oe Drive, follow it to the end, and make a right on Maleko Road that ends in a cul-de-sac. **Warning:** Do not trespass on any private land. There is no public right-of-way! Just before you get to the end of the cul-de-sac look for an open space on the right with a short trail leading down to a culvert. Follow the culvert for about 100 yards, and turn left onto a heavily used jeep trail that soon becomes a walking path. In 400 yards, at three telephone poles, the trail splits into three branches; take the center branch and go straight ahead downhill until you intersect a trail that leads right along the creek. This trail is very muddy, but worth it. Follow it for about 15 minutes until you come to Maunawili Falls—deep enough to dive in. You can also see an upper falls. Above them is an open field perfect for an overnight camp. To the left a path leads past a small banana plantation, along an irrigation ditch

cut into the mountainside, paralleled by a wooden walkway. Very few people venture into this safe but fascinating area.

Maunawili Demonstration Trail

This is one of the most easily accessible, and one of Oahu's newest trails. Soon after passing the Pali Lookout, which is clearly marked along the Pali Highway, you will go through a tunnel. Almost immediately, a sign points to a scenic overlook. Pull off into the parking area and walk back up the highway for about 100 yards where you'll see a break in the guardrail and a sign for Na'ala Hele, the Hawaiian Trail and Access System. The beauty of this trail is that it is reasonably flat with little elevation gain or loss as it winds its way along the windward side of the Koolau Range. The whine of the Pali Highway abates almost immediately and you are suddenly in a brilliant highland tropical forest. You can continue to the end (about three hours one-way) for a full day's hike, or just find a secluded spot after a mile or so for a picnic. The views are spectacular and there are vantage points where you can see the coast all the way from Rabbit Island to Chinaman's Hat. Remember, however, that like all Hawaiian trails, recent rainfall makes for treacherous footing.

Hauula Loop Trails

Built by the Workers Civilian Conservation Corps (WCCC) during the Depression, these manicured trails run up and down two ridges and deep into an interior valley, gaining and losing height as they switchback through the extraordinary jungle canopy. The **Gulch and Papali Trails,** branches of the Hauula Loop Trail, start from the same place. The Hauula Trail is wide with good footing. There're a few stream crossings, but it's not muddy even after a heavy rain, which can shut down the Sacred Falls Trail just a few miles north. The hard-packed trail, covered in a soft carpet of ironwood needles, offers magnificent coastal views once you reach the heights, or you can look inland into verdant gulches and gullies (valleys).

You'll be passing through miniature ecosystems very reminiscent of the fern forests on the Big Island, but on a much smaller scale. The area flora is made up of ironwoods, passion fruit, thimbleberries, ohia, wild orchids, and fiddlehead ferns. To get there, head for Hauula on coastal Rt. 83 (Kamehameha Hwy.), and just past the 7-Eleven store, between mile markers 21 and 22, look inland for Hauula Homestead Road. Take it for a minute until you see the well-marked sign leading to the trails.

Sacred Falls

On coastal Rt. 83, between Hauula and Punaluu (mile markers 22 and 23), an HVB Warrior points you to Sacred Falls. Note that you *cannot* drive to the falls. An old commercial venture put out this misinformation, which persists to this day. The walk is a hardy stroll, so you'll need jogging shoes, not thongs. The area becomes a narrow canyon, and the sun sets early; don't start out past 3 p.m., especially if you want a dip in the stream. The trail was roughed up by Hurricane Ewa, and a sign along it says "Danger. Do not go past this point." Many people ignore this sign; the path is a little more treacherous but is passable.

The area's Hawaiian name was Kaliuwaa ("Canoe Leak"), and although the original name isn't as romantic as the anglicized version, the entire area was indeed considered sacred. En route, you pass into a very narrow valley where the gods might show disfavor by dropping rocks onto your head. Notice many stones wrapped with a ti leaf. This is an appeasement to the gods, so they're not tempted to brain you. Go ahead, wrap a rock; no one will see you! You can hear the falls dropping to the valley floor. Above you the walls are 1,600 feet high, but the falls drop only 90 feet or so. The pool below is ample for a swim, but the water is chilly and often murky. A number of beautiful picnic spots are on the large flat rocks.

North Oahu Treks

Some of the hiking in and around northwest Oahu is quite difficult. However, you should take a hike out to **Kaena Point,** where there is huge surf, sometimes 30 feet high. You have two choices: you can park your car at the end of the road past Dillingham Airfield on the north coast and hike in, or you can park your car at the end of the road past Makua on the Waianae coast and hike in. Both are about the same distance, and both are hardy but not difficult. The trail is only two miles, from each end, and few people come here except some local fishermen.

Peacock Flat is a good family-style trail that offers primitive camping. Follow Rt. 93 toward Dillingham Airfield and just before getting there turn left onto a dirt road leading toward the Kawai-hapi Reservoir. If you want to camp, you need permits from the Division of Forestry and a waiver from the Mokuleia Ranch, tel. (808) 637-4241, which you can get at its office, located at the end of a dirt road just before the one leading to Kawaihapi Reservoir. The ranch will also provide instructions and a key to get through two locked gates before reaching the trailhead, if you decide to go in from that end. Heading through the Mokuleia Forest Reserve, you can camp anywhere along the trail, or at an established but primitive campground in Peacock Flat. This area is heavily used by hunters, who are mostly after wild pig.

Dupont Trail takes you to the summit of Mt. Ka'ala, highest point and by far the most difficult hike on the island. The last mile is downright dangerous, and has you hanging on cliff edges, with the bottom 2,000 feet below! This is not for the average hiker. Follow Rt. 930 to Waialua, make a left at Waialua High School onto a cane road, and follow it to the second gate, about 1.5 miles. Park there. You need a hiking permit from the Division of Forestry and a waiver from the Waialua Sugar Company, tel. (808) 637-3521. Atop Ka'ala, although the views are magnificent, you'll also find a mushroom field of FAA satellite stations.

INFORMATION, EQUIPMENT, AND SAFETY

Hiking Groups and Information

The **Department of Land and Natural Resources,** Division of Forestry and Wildlife, 1151 Punchbowl St., Room 325, Honolulu, HI 96813, tel. (808) 587-0058, is helpful in providing trail maps, accessibility information, hunting and fishing regulations, and general forest rules. The following organizations can provide information on organized hiking trips. **Hawaiian Trail and Mountain Club,** P.O. Box 2238, Honolulu, HI 96804, tel. (808) 262-2845 or 488-1161, meets behind Iolani Palace on Saturday at 9 a.m. and Sunday at 8 a.m.; free for members and $2 for nonmembers. The hikes are announced in the *Honolulu Star Bulletin*'s "Pulse of Paradise" column. For the group's *Hiker's*

Guide, send $1.50 and an SASE to the above address or check its Web site: www.geocities.com /yosemite/trails/3660. **Sierra Club, Hawaii Chapter** P.O. Box 2577, Honolulu, HI 96803, tel. (808) 538-6616, organizes weekly hikes, $1 for members and $3 for nonmembers. Information about the organization and its hikes is listed in its newsletter and on its Web site: www.hi.sierraclub .org. Sierra Club also sells the useful booklet *Hiking Softly in Hawai'i* ($5), which gives general information about hiking in Hawaii; preparation, etiquette, and precautions; a brief chart of major trails on each island, along with their physical characteristics; and other sources of information. Additional information about hiking in Hawaii can be found on the Web site: www2 .edu/~turner/htmc/hi-hike.htm, and about camping at: www.visit.hawaii.org/hokeo/activity/camping.html. The **Hawaii Audubon Society** can be reached at P.O. Box 22832, Honolulu, HI 96822 for information about birdwatching hikes, or call the **Hawaii Nature Center,** tel. (808) 955-0100, for information about hikes.

Since 1997, the ecotour operator **Oahu Nature Tours,** P.O. Box 8059, Honolulu, HI 96830, tel. (808) 924-2473 or (800) 861-6018, Web site: www.OahuNatureTours.com, e-mail: natureguide @OahuNatureTours.com, has offered two daily hiking tours that focus on native birds and plants. The morning tour to the southeast corner of the island runs 7:30-11:30 a.m., and the afternoon tour into the Koolau Mountains lasts 1:30-5:30 p.m.; both run $37.50 apiece. Conducted by owner Michael Walther and with a limit of six participants, each tour is an environmental education experience as well as a fun outing.

For half- or full-day hikes, try **Hike Hawaii,** 91-261 Hanapouli Circle #W, Ewa Beach, HI 96706, tel. (808) 683-3967. Hiking destinations vary from the coast to mountain and rainforest, but there is always information about the flora, fauna, environment, and history of the island. Maximum of six; good for novice hikers to the experienced. Transportation, lunch or snacks, and rain gear are included; $50 half day, $65 for the full day.

Equipment

Like everything else you take to Hawaii, your camping and hiking equipment should be lightweight and durable. Camping equipment size and weight should not cause a problem with baggage requirements on airlines: if it does, it's a tip-off that you're hauling too much. One odd luggage consideration you might make is to bring along a small **styrofoam cooler** packed with equipment. Replace the equipment with food items when you get to Hawaii; if you intend to car camp successfully and keep food prices down, you'll definitely need a cooler. You can also buy one on arrival for only a few dollars.

You'll need a lightweight **tent,** preferably with a rainfly and a sewn-in floor. This will save you from getting wet and miserable, and will keep out mosquitoes, cockroaches, ants, and the few stinging insects on Oahu. **Sleeping bags** are a good idea, although you can get along at sea level with only a blanket. Down-filled bags are necessary for Haleakala, Mauna Kea, Mauna Loa, or any high-elevation-camping—you'll freeze without one. **Campstoves** are needed because there's very little wood in some volcanic areas, it's often wet in the deep forest, and open fires are often prohibited. If you'll be car-camping, take along a multiburner stove, and for trekking, a backpacker's stove is necessary. The grills found only at some campgrounds are popular with many families that go often to the beach parks for an open-air dinner. You can buy a very inexpensive charcoal grill at many variety stores throughout Hawaii.

It's a great idea to take along a **lantern.** This will give added safety for campers. Definitely take a **flashlight,** replacement batteries, and a few small **candles.** A complete **first-aid kit** can be the difference between life and death, and is worth the extra bulk. Hikers, especially those leaving the coastal areas, should take **rain gear,** a plastic ground cloth, utility knife, compass, safety whistle, mess kit, water purification tablets, canteen, nylon twine, waterproof matches, and sunscreen. For the best traction and good ankle support, wear sturdy hiking boots. (For additional suggestions, see the "What to Take" section.)

Camping Gear and Rentals

If you've come without camping gear and wish to rent some try **The Bike Shop,** 1149 S. King St., Honolulu, tel. (808) 596-0588, renting two-person tents and backpacks at $35 each for a weekend or $70 for the week. A $200 deposit, returned when you return the equipment, is required. **Omar the Tentman,** 94-158, Leoole St., Waipahu, tel.

(808) 677-8785, rents a wider variety of equipment and offers prices for one- to three-day or four- to seven-day periods. A dome tent runs $25/30, a six-person tent $52/57, sleeping bags $15/20, backpacks $15/20, stoves $14/18, and lanterns (you supply the fuel) $14/18. No backpacking tents.

Safety
There are two things in Hawaii that you must keep your eye on in order to remain safe: humans and nature. The general rule is, the farther you get away from towns, the safer you'll be from human-induced hassles. If possible, don't hike or camp alone, especially if you're a woman. Don't leave your valuables in your tent, and always carry your money, papers, and camera with you. Don't tempt the locals by being overly friendly or unfriendly, and make yourself scarce if they're drinking. While hiking, remember that many trails are well maintained, but trailhead markers are often missing. The trails themselves can be muddy, which can make them treacherously slippery and often knee-deep. Always bring food because you cannot, in most cases, forage from the land. Water in most streams is biologically polluted and will give you bad stomach problems if you drink it without purifying it first by boiling, filtering, or adding purification tablets. For your part, please don't use the streams as a toilet.

Precautions
Always tell a ranger or official of your hiking intentions. Supply an itinerary and your expected route, then stick to it. Twilight is short in the islands, and night sets in rapidly. In June sunrise and sunset are around 6 a.m. and 7 p.m.; in December these occur at 7 a.m. and 6 p.m. If you become lost at night, stay put, light a fire if possible, and stay as dry as you can. Hawaii is made of volcanic rock which is brittle and crumbly. Never attempt to climb steep *pali* (cliffs). Every year people are stranded and fatalities have occurred on the *pali*.

Heat can cause you to lose water and salt. If you become woozy or weak, rest, take salt, and drink water as you need it. Remember, it takes much more water to restore a dehydrated person than to keep hydrated; take small frequent sips. Be mindful of flash floods. Small creeks can turn into raging torrents with upland rains. Never camp

in a dry creek bed. Fog is only encountered at the 1,500- to 5,000-foot level, but be careful of disorientation. As the weather can change rapidly on the island, be sure to give the National Weather Service a call at (808) 973-4381 for a current weather forecast. Generally, stay within your limits, be careful, and enjoy yourself.

Camping and Hiking Books
Two helpful camping books are *Hawaii: A Camping Guide,* by George Cagala, and Richard McMahon's *Camping Hawaii.*

For a well-written and detailed hiking guide complete with maps, check out *Oahu Trails* (a book for each island is available) by Kathy Morey. Newer and very excellent is *A Hiker's Guide to Oahu,* by Stuart Ball. See also *Hawaiian Hiking Trails,* by Craig Chisholm, and Robert Smith's *Hawaii's Best Hiking Trails,* as well as his *Hiking Oahu, Hiking Maui, Hiking Hawaii,* and *Hiking Kauai.*

Topographical Maps and Nautical Charts
For detailed topographical maps, write **U.S. Geological Survey, Information Services** P.O. Box 25286, Denver, CO 80225, or call (800) USA-MAPS or (703) 648-4888, Web site: www.usgs .gov. In Hawaii, a wide range of topographical maps can be purchased at the **Pacific Map Center,** 560 N. Nimitz Hwy., 206A, Honolulu, HI 96817, tel. (808) 545-3600, or at **Hawaii Geographic Maps and Books,** 49 S. Hotel St., Honolulu, tel. (808) 538-3952. Also useful are the University of Hawaii Press reference maps of each island. For nautical charts, write **National Ocean Service,** Riverdale, MD 20737-1199, tel. (301) 436-6990 or (800) 638-8972.

GOLF

With 37 private, public, and military golf courses scattered around such a relatively small island, it's a wonder that it doesn't rain golf balls. These courses range from modest nine-holers to world-class courses whose tournaments attract the biggest names in golf today. Prices range from $20 a round up to $150. An added attraction of playing Oahu's courses is that you get to walk around on some of the most spectacular and manicured pieces of real estate on the island. Some afford sweeping views of the coast, like the

GOLF COURSES OF OAHU

COURSE	STATUS	PAR	YARDS	FEES†	CART	CLUBS
Ala Wai Golf Course 404 Kapahulu Ave. Honolulu, HI 96851 tel. (808) 733-7387	Municipal	70	5,817	$40	$14	$25
Barbers Point Golf Course NAS, Barbers Point, HI 96862 tel. (808) 682-1911	Military	72	6,394	22/28	10	5
BayView Golf Links 45-285 Kaneohe Bay Dr. Kaneohe, HI 96744 tel. (808) 247-0451	Public	60	3,430	62/73	Incl.	21
Ewa Beach International Golf Club 91-050 Fort Weaver Rd. Ewa Beach, HI 96706 tel. (808) 689-8351	Semiprivate	72	5,998	135	Incl.	35
Ewa Village Golf Course Mango Tree Road Ewa, HI 96706 tel. (808) 681-0220	Municipal	72	7,100	40	14	No
Fort Shaffer Golf Course USAG-HI Golf Bldg. 2104, Schofield Barracks, HI 96857 tel. (808) 438-9587	Military	68	5,800	21	8	6
Hawaii Country Club 94-1211 Kunia Rd. Wahiawa, HI 96786 tel. (808) 621-5654	Public	72	5,916	30/40	Incl.	20
Hawaii Kai Championship Golf Course 8902 Kalanianaole Hwy. Honolulu, HI 96825 tel. (808) 395-2358	Public	72	6,222	100/120	Incl.	30
Hawaii Kai Executive Golf Course 8902 Kalanianaole Hwy. Honolulu, HI 96825 tel. (808) 395-2358	Public	55	2,386	37/42	Incl.	15
Hawaii Prince Golf Club 91-1200 Fort Weaver Rd. Ewa Beach, HI 96706 tel. (808) 689-8361	Resort	36**	6,214	135	Incl.	35
Hickam Mamala Bay Golf Course 625 Worchester Ave.	Military	72	6,412	32	8.50	10

* 9-hole course   ** 27-hole course (par 36 per 9)   † Fees are listed as weekday/weekend

COURSE	STATUS	PAR	YARDS	FEES[†]	CART	CLUBS
Hickam AFB, HI 96853 tel. (808) 449-6490						
Hickam Par Three Golf Course 625 Worchester Ave. Hickam AFB, HI 96853 tel. (808) 449-2093	Military	27*	1,400	$7	$3 (pull)	$3.50
Honolulu Country Club 1690 Ala Puunalu St. Honolulu, HI 96818 tel. (808) 833-4541	Private	71	5,987	41/46	Incl.	25
Kahuku Golf Course P.O. Box 417 Kahuku, HI 96731 tel. (808) 293-5842	Municipal	35*	2,699	20	2 (pull)	10
Kalakaua Golf Course USAG-HI Golf Bldg. 2104, Schofield Barracks HI 96857 tel. (808) 655-9833	Military	72	6,186	25	8	6
Kaneohe Klipper Golf Course MCBH Bldg. 3088 Kaneohe, HI 96863 tel. (808) 254-1745	Military	72	6,216	35	8	10
Kapolei Golf Course 91-701 Farrington Hwy. Kapolei, HI 96707 tel. (808) 674-2227	Semiprivate	72	6,136	70/90	Incl.	30
Ko Olina Golf Club 92-1220 Alii Nui Dr. Kapolei, HI 96707 tel. (808) 676-5300	Resort	72	6,480	145	Incl.	40
Koolau Golf Course 45-550 Kionaole Rd. Kaneohe, HI 96744 tel. (808) 236-4653	Private	72	6,857	90	Incl.	30
Leilehua Golf Course USAG-HI Golf Bldg. 2104 Schofield Barracks HI 96857 tel. (808) 655-4653	Military	72	6,521	31	8	6
Luana Hills Country Club 770 Auloa Rd. Kailua, HI 96734 tel. (808) 262-2139	Semiprivate	72	5,308	80	Incl.	30
Makaha Valley Country Club 84-627 Makaha Valley Rd. Waianae, HI 96792 tel. (808) 695-9578	Private	71	6,091	55/65	Incl.	30

(continues on next page)

GOLF COURSES OF OAHU

(continued)

COURSE	STATUS	PAR	YARDS	FEES†	CART	CLUBS
Mid-Pacific Country Club 266 Kaelepulu Dr. Kailua, HI 96734 tel. (808) 261-9765	Private	72	6,509	$125	Incl.	$25
Mililani Golf Club 95-176 Kualelani Ave. Mililani, HI 96789 tel. (808) 623-2222	Semiprivate	72	6,239	89/95	Incl.	25
Moanalua Golf Club 1250 Ala Aolani St. Honolulu, HI 96819 tel. (808) 839-2411	Semiprivate	36*	2,972	20/25	14	No
Navy-Marine Golf Course 943 Valkenburgh St. Honolulu, HI 96818 tel. (808) 471-0142	Military	72	6,566	40	10	5
Oahu Country Club 150 Country Club Rd. Honolulu, HI 96817 tel. (808) 595-3256	Private	71	5,820	40	Incl.	25
Olomana Golf Links 41-1801 Kalanianaole Hwy. Waimanalo, HI 96795 tel. (808) 259-7926	Private	72	5,887	90	Incl.	25
Pali Golf Course 45-050 Kamehameha Hwy. Kaneohe, HI 96744 tel. (808) 266-7612	Municipal	72	6,494	40	14	30
Pearl Country Club 98-535 Kaonohi St. Aiea, HI 96701 tel. (808) 487-3802	Semiprivate	72	6,232	75/80	Incl.	20
Sheraton Makaha Golf Club 84-626 Makaha Valley Rd. Makaha, HI 96792 tel. (808) 695-9544	Resort	72	6,414	120	Incl.	30
Ted Makalena Golf Course 93-059 Waipio Point Access Rd., Waipahu, HI 96797 tel. (808) 675-6052	Municipal	71	5,946	40	14	No
The Links at Kuilima 57-091 Kamehameha Hwy. Kahuku, HI 96731 tel. (808) 293-8574	Resort	72	6,225	125	Incl.	30

* 9-hole course   ** 27-hole course (par 36 per 9)   † Fees are listed as weekday/weekend

COURSE	STATUS	PAR	YARDS	FEES†	CART	CLUBS
Turtle Bay Country Club 57-091 Kamehameha Hwy. Kahaku, HI 96731 tel. (808) 293-8574	Resort	36*	3,204	$25	Incl.	$25
Waialae Country Club 4997 Kahala Ave. Honolulu, HI 96816 tel. (808) 732-1457	Private	72	7,012	150	Incl.	25
Waikele Golf Club 94-200 Paioa Place Waipahu, HI 96797 tel. (808) 676-9000	Semiprivate	72	6,261	105/110	Incl.	30
West Loch Golf Course 91-1126 Okupe St. Ewa Beach, HI 96706 tel. (808) 675-6076	Municipal	72	5,849	47	Incl.	15

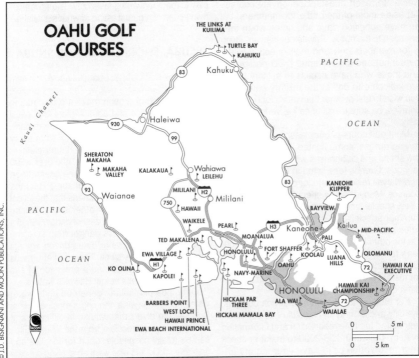

OAHU GOLF COURSES

© J.D. BISIGNANI AND MOON PUBLICATIONS, INC.

Ko Olina Golf Club, while others, like the **Pali Golf Course,** have a lovely mountain backdrop, or, like Waikiki's **Ala Wai Golf Course,** are set virtually in the center of all the downtown action. The Ala Wai Golf Course also must be one of the busiest courses in the country as some 500 rounds of golf are played there daily! In 1994, the PGA rated the **Koolau Golf Course** the toughest course in the United States. Tough or easy, flat or full of definition, Oahu provides ample opportunity and variety for any golfer.

The **Hawaiian Open Invitational Golf Tournament** held in late January or February at the Waialae Country Club brings the world's best golfers. Prize money is close to $1 million, and all three major TV networks cover the event. This is usually the only opportunity the average person gets to set foot on this course.

Municipal and public courses are open to everyone. Resort courses cater to the public as well as to resort guests. Semiprivate courses set aside most of their time for members, but do have specified days and times when they are open to the public. Private courses are strictly for members only and their guests. Military personnel and dependents, DOD personnel, and those who have access to military bases are welcome to golf at the military courses. If you wish to golf at other than municipal or public courses, be sure to call ahead to verify accessibility.

Most golf courses offer lessons. Many have driving ranges, some lighted. Virtually all have pro shops and clubhouses with restaurants and lounges. Greens fees listed in the chart are for non-Hawaii residents and for civilians at military courses. Many courses offer reduced *kama'aina* rates, special time rates, twilight hour rates, and summer specials. Be sure to ask about these rates as they often afford substantial savings. On the other hand, some courses charge higher fees for non-U.S. residents. Military courses charge different greens fees for civilians than for military personnel, and the military fees might differ depending upon rank.

For ease of use for municipal golf courses, the City and County of Honolulu has set up an automated tee time reservation and information system. Call (808) 296-2000 to make or check your reservation or to have your inquiry answered.

TENNIS

Grease up the old elbow because Oahu boasts 181 county-maintained tennis courts, 124 of which are lighted. Most courts also have backboards. Get a complete list of them by writing a letter of inquiry and enclosing an SASE to the Department of Parks and Recreation, Tennis Division, 3908 Paki Ave., Honolulu, HI 96815, or by calling (808) 971-7150. Alternately, you can stop by the Diamond Head Tennis Center at the above address and pick up a copy yourself. No fees are charged for these public courts. Play is on a first-come first-served basis and limited to 45 minutes if there are people waiting. Weekends are often fairly busy, but it's relatively easy to get a court on weekdays. Court rules apply and only soft-sole shoes are allowed. Also, some resort and private courts are open to the public for a fee, though most limit play to members and guests only. The accompanying chart is a partial listing of what's available.

SCUBA, SNORKELING, AND SNUBA

If you think that Oahu is beautiful above the sea, wait until you explore below. The warm tropical waters and coral growth make it a fascinating haven for reef fish and aquatic plant life. You'll soon discover that Hawaiian waters are remarkably clear, with excellent visibility. Fish in every fathomable color parade by. Lavender clusters of coral, red-and-gold coral trees, and over 1,500 different types of shells carpet the ocean floor. In some spots (like Oahu's Hanauma Bay) the fish are so accustomed to humans that they'll eat bread from your hand. In other spots, lurking moray eels add the special zest of danger. Sharks and barracuda pose less danger than scraping your knee on the coral or being driven against the rocks by a heavy swell. There are enormous but harmless sea bass and a profusion of sea turtles. All this awaits below Hawaii's waters.

Oahu has particularly generous underwater vistas open to anyone donning a mask and fins. Snorkel and dive sites, varying in difficulty and challenge, are accessible from the island. Sites can be totally hospitable, good for families and first-time snorkelers who want an exciting but safe frolic; or they can be accessible only to the expe-

TENNIS COURTS OF OAHU

COUNTY COURTS

Under the jurisdiction of the Department of Parks and Recreation Tennis Division, 3908 Paki Ave., Honolulu, HI 96815, tel. (808) 971-7150. Courts listed are in Honolulu, Waikiki, and main towns only.

LOCATION	NAME OF PARK	ADDRESS	NO. OF COURTS	LIGHTED
Aiea	Aiea District Park	99-350 Aiea Heights Dr.	2	Yes
Ewa	Ewa Beach Community Park	91-955 North Rd.	4	Yes
Kahala	Kahala Community Park	4495 Pahoa Ave.	2	No
Kailua	Kailua District Park	21 S. Kainalu Dr.	8	Yes
Kaimuki	Kaimuki Community Park	3521 Waialea Ave.	2	Yes
Kaneohe	Kaneohe District Park	44-660 Keaahala Rd.	6	No
Keehi	Keehi Lagoon Courts	405 Lagoon Dr.	12	Yes
Koko Head	Koko Head District Park	423 Kaumakani St.	6	Yes
Manoa	Manoa Valley District Park	2721 Kaaipu St.	4	Yes
Maunawili	Maunawili Valley Park	962 Maunawili Rd.	2	Yes
Mililani	Mililani District Park	94-1150 Lanikuhana	4	No
Pearl City	Pearl City District Park	785 Hoomaemae St.	2	Yes
Sunset Beach	Sunset Beach Neighborhood Park	59-360 Kam. Hwy.	2	Yes
Wahiawa	Wahiawa District Park	1139-A Kilani Ave.	4	Yes
Waialua	Waialua District Park	67-180 Goodale Rd.	4	Yes
Waianae	Waianae District Park	85-601 Farrington Hwy.	8	Yes
Waikiki	Ala Moana Park	1201 Ala Moana Blvd.	10	Yes
Waikiki	Diamond Head Tennis Center	3908 Paki Ave.	10	No
Waikiki	Kapiolani Tennis Courts	2740 Kalakaua Ave.	4	Yes
Waimanalo	Waimanalo District Park	41-415 Hihimanu St.	4	No
Waipahu	Waipahu District Park	92-230 Paiwa St.	4	Yes

HOTEL AND PRIVATE COURTS THAT ARE OPEN TO THE PUBLIC

LOCATION	RESORT	TEL. (808)	COST
Ainahaina	Honolulu Tennis Academy	373-1282	$20/hr.
Ewa Beach	Hawaii Prince Golf Club	944-4567	8/hr.
Kahuku	Turtle Bay Resort	293-8811	20/hr.
Kopolei	Ihilani Resort	679-0079	24/hr.

rienced diver. All over the island are dive shops from which you can rent or buy all equipment, and where dive boats and instruction on all levels can be arranged. Particular spots are listed under "Beaches and Parks" in the travel sections, but some well-known favorites are Hanauma Bay, Black Point off Diamond Head, the waters around Rabbit Island, Sharks Cove on the North Shore, Maunalua Bay between Koko and Diamond Heads (good for green sea turtles), Magic Island near Ala Moana Beach Park, and some sunken ships and planes just off the Waianae coast.

Scuba

If you're a scuba diver you'll have to show your C Card before local shops will rent you gear, fill

exploring the reefs of
Oahu

J.D. BISIGNANI

your tanks, or take you on a charter dive. Plenty of outstanding scuba instructors will give you lessons towards certification, and they're especially reasonable because of the stiff competition. Prices vary, but you can take a three- to five-day semi-private certification course, including all equipment, for $225-400 (instruction book, dive tables, logbook extra charge). Two-week courses are usually about half that price. More advanced instruction for rescue divers, enriched air diving, and instructors are also available from some shops. Divers unaccustomed to Hawaiian waters should not dive alone regardless of their experience. Most opt for dive tours to special dive grounds guaranteed to please. These vary also, but for an *accompanied* double-tank boat dive expect to spend around $80. Shore dives run about the same and are usually one-tank dives. During the winter months, shore diving is not recommended because of the "mud line" that tends to obscure visibility close to shore. There are special charter dives, night dives, and photography dives. Most companies pick you up at your hotel, take you to the site, and return you home. Basic equipment rental costs $40-50 for the day, and most times you'll only need the top of a wetsuit.

Dive Shops and Rentals

In the Honolulu area, try the following. **Waikiki Diving,** 1734 Kalakaua, tel. (808) 955-5151, closed Sunday, does PADI certification. No snorkeling tours are offered, but snorkeling equipment rents for $8 for 24 hours. A three-day certification course costs $300 plus tax; books are extra and run $35. Open-water, two-tank, two-location boat dives run $75. **South Seas Aquatics,** 2155 Kalakaua Ave., Suite 112, tel. (808) 922-0852, is a full-service dive shop with competitive pricing for certification, tours, and rentals. **Dan's Dive Shop,** 660 Ala Moana Blvd., tel. (808) 536-6181, is open daily and offers several different dive tours. A beginner's tour is $70 for instruction and a one-tank dive, while nonbeginners have two locations and two tanks for $80. Scuba equipment rental is $40, snorkel equipment $10.

Surf and Sea, 62-595 Kamehameha Hwy., tel. (808) 637-9887, is a complete dive shop on the North Shore in Haleiwa offering certification, rentals, charters, and tours. **Aaron's Dive Shop,** 602 Kailua Road, Kailua, tel. (808) 262-2333, or in Pearl City at (808) 487-5533, is a full-service dive shop. A snorkel outfit runs $7 for 24 hours. A four-day scuba certification course costs $390, and a two-week course is $170. Two-tank boat dives run $80-90, and a one-tank dive off the beach is $90. In Kailua, try **Windward Dive Center,** 789 Kailua Road, tel. (808) 263-2311, Web site: www.divehawaii.com, offering various PADI instruction courses. A two-week, open-water dive class is about $120, while a tailor-made short course runs about $300. More advanced courses are also taught here. **Aloha Dive Shop** at Koko Marina (on the way to Hanauma Bay), tel. (808) 395-5922, does it all from snorkeling to boat dives.

Excellent rates, good service. This shop is owned and run by Jackie James, the "First Lady of Diving" in Hawaii, with nearly 30 years of experience.

Snorkeling

Scuba diving takes expensive special equipment, skills, and athletic ability. Snorkeling in comparison is much simpler and enjoyable to anyone who can swim. In about 15 minutes you can be taught the fundamentals of snorkeling—you really don't need formal instructions. Other snorkelers or dive shop attendants can tell you enough to get you started. Because you can breathe without lifting your head, you get great propulsion from the fins and hardly ever need to use your arms. You can go for much greater distances and spend longer periods in the water than if you were swimming. Experienced snorkelers make an art of this sport and you too can see and do amazing things with a mask, snorkel, and flippers. Don't, however, get a false sense of invincibility and exceed your limitations.

Those interested can buy or rent equipment in the dive shops listed below and in department stores. Sometimes condos and hotels have snorkeling equipment free for their guests, but if you have to rent it, don't do it from a hotel or condo, but go to a dive shop where it's much cheaper. Expect to spend $3.50-8 a day for mask, fins, and snorkel. Many charter boats will take you out snorkeling or diving. Prices range from $40 (half day, four hours) to $70 (full day, eight hours). Also, hotels' activities desks can arrange these excursions for no extra charge. Do yourself a favor and wash all the sand off rented equipment. Most shops irritatingly penalize you $1 if you don't. All want a deposit, usually $30, that is put on a credit card slip which is torn up when you return. Underwater camera rentals are now normal at most shops, and go for around $10-12 including film (24-27 shots), but not developing. Happy diving!

Snorkel Rentals

Snorkel Bob's, tel. (808) 735-7944, at the corner of Kapahulu and Mooheau Avenues, has very inexpensive deals on snorkeling. Prices start at $3.50 a day or only $9 per week for full snorkel gear, which you can take to Maui, Kauai, and Big Island locations and return there ($3 extra). The better equipment (still a deal) gets progressively more expensive. Snorkel Bob's also has underwater cameras, boogie boards for $6.50 a day or $26 a week, and wet suits at $15 a week. It's best to stop in and peruse the selection for just what you need. **Hanauma Bay Snorkeling,** tel. (808) 373-5060, rents full equipment for $6.25 a day and underwater cameras for $17. The company offers tours to Hanauma Bay from Waikiki for $18.75, including transportation, equipment, instruction, a fish I.D. chart, and a map of the reef. Also try **Paradise Snorkel Adventures,** tel. (808) 923-7766, which rents top-of-the-line equipment for $6.95 a day and runs a shuttle to Hanauma Bay for $9.95 with equipment. Disposable underwater cameras go for $19.95, and the better ones are $20-25, for 24 or 36 exposures, respectively.

Snuba

No, that's not a typo. **Snuba Tours of Oahu,** tel. (808) 396-6163, offers a hybrid sport that is half snorkeling and half scuba diving. You have a regulator, a weight belt, mask, and flippers, and you're tethered to scuba tanks that float 20 feet above you on a sea-sled. The unofficial motto of Snuba is "secure but free." The idea is that many people become anxious diving under the waves encumbered by tanks and all the scuba apparatus. Snuba frees you. You would think that being tethered to the sled would slow you down, but actually you're sleeker and can make better time than a normal scuba diver. The sled is made from industrial-strength polyethylene and is 2.5 feet wide by 7.5 feet long, consisting of a view window and a belly in the sled for location of the scuba tank. If you get tired, just surface and use it as a raft. Snuba was invented by Mike Stafford of Placerville, California, as an aid to disabled people who wished to scuba. He got the idea from modern gold miners in the Mother Lode area who set a scuba tank on the side of the riverbank and run an air line down to the water to look for gold nuggets wedged under boulders. The first raft came off the assembly line in 1988.

Snuba tours include instruction and transportation, and free swim time runs about 30 minutes. Four times a day, Mon.-Fri., tours are offered to Waikiki Beach for about $70 and to Hanauma Bay for $90. For $80, Mon.-Sat., you can snuba the waters of Maunalua Bay on any of three tours.

REEF FISH

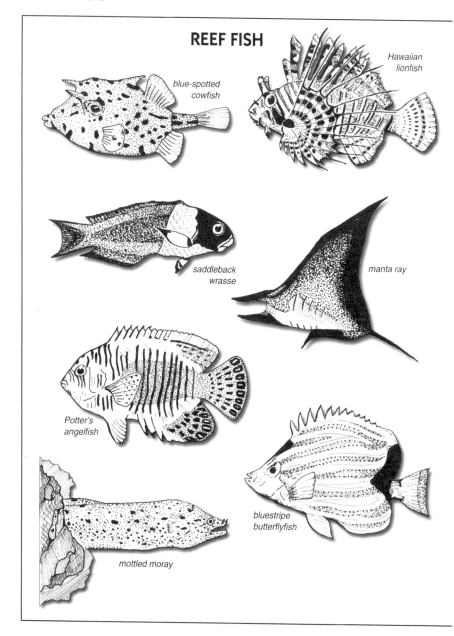

blue-spotted cowfish

Hawaiian lionfish

saddleback wrasse

manta ray

Potter's angelfish

bluestripe butterflyfish

mottled moray

manini

trumpetfish

lagoon humu

moorish idol

threadfin butterflyfish

red-lipped parrotfish

Achilles tang

uhu

LOUISE FOOTE/DIANA LASICH HARPER

SURFING

Surfing is a sport indigenous to Hawaii. When the white man first arrived he was astonished to see natives paddling out to meet the ships on long carved boards, then gracefully riding them into shore on crests of waves. The Hawaiians called surfing *he'enalu* (to "slide on a wave"). The newcomers were fascinated by this sport, recording it on engravings and woodcuts marveled at around the world. Meanwhile, the Polynesians left records of surfing as petroglyphs and in *mele* of surfing exploits of times past. A local Waikiki beachboy by the name of Duke Kahanamoku won a treasure box full of gold medals for swimming at the Olympic Games of 1912, and thereafter he became a celebrity who toured the Mainland and introduced surfing to the modern world. Surfing later became a lifestyle, spread far and wide by the songs of the Beach Boys in the '60s. Now surfing is a sport enjoyed around the world, complete with championships, movies, magazines, and advanced board technology.

It takes years of practice to become good, but with determination, good swimming ability, and a sense of balance you can learn the fundamentals in a short time. At surf shops all around the island you can rent a board for very reasonable prices. The boards of the ancient *ali'i* were up to 20 feet long and weighed over 150 pounds, but today's board is made from ultralight foam plastic covered in fiberglass. They're about six feet long and weigh 12 pounds or so. Innovations occur every day in surfing, but one is the changeable "skeg" or rudder allowing you to surf in variable conditions.

The sport of surfing is still male-dominated, but women champions have been around for years. The most famous surfing beaches in the world are Sunset Beach and the Banzai Pipeline on North Shore Oahu. Every year the nationally televised pro-tour Triple Crown of Surfing is held along

by ship's artist Francis Olmsted, circa 1840

the north shore from late October to early December: the Hawaiian Pro at Haleiwa, the Rip Curl World Cup of Surfing at Sunset Beach, and the Pipe Masters at Bonzai Pipeline. For this round of competition, prize money runs $80,000-100,000. The Backdoor Shootout at Pipeline brings the winner about $50,000. It's only a matter of time before surfing becomes an Olympic sport.

One of the most brilliant books ever written on surfing is *Surfing, The Ultimate Pleasure,* by Leonard Lueras. A copy can be found at almost every surf shop.

All the Hawaiian islands have incredibly good surfing conditions, but Oahu is best. Conditions here are perfect for rank beginners up to the best in the world. Waikiki's surf is predictable, and just right to start on, while the Banzai Pipeline and Waimea Bay on the North Shore have some of the most formidable surfing conditions on earth. Makaha Beach in Waianae is perhaps the best all-around surfing beach, frequented by "living legends" in this most graceful sport.

If there is such a thing as "the perfect wave," Oahu's waters are a good place to look for it. Summertime brings rather flat wave action all around the island, but the winter months are a totally different story, with monster waves on the North Shore, and heavy surf at times even in the relative calm of Waikiki. *Never* surf without asking about local conditions, and remember that "a fool and his surfboard, and maybe his life, are soon parted."

Note: For **surfing conditions,** call (808) 973-4383 or 296-1818, ext. 9800. Heed all warnings!

Surfing Lessons

A number of enterprises in Waikiki offer beach services. Often these concessions are affiliated with hotels, and almost all hotel activities desks can arrange surfing lessons for you. An instructor and board go for about $25 per hour—most guarantee that they will get you standing. A board alone is half the price, but as in skiing, a few

HAWAII STATE ARCHIVES

good lessons to start you off are well worth the time and money. Some reputable surfing lessons along Waikiki are provided by: Outrigger Hotel, 2335 Kalakaua Ave., tel. (808) 923-0711; and Hilton Hawaiian Village, 2005 Kalia Road, tel. (808) 949-4321. Also check near the huge rack of surfboards along Kalakaua Ave., just near Kuhio Beach at the Waikiki Beach Center, where you'll find a number of beachboy enterprises at competitive rates. Also in Honolulu, try **Hans Hedemann Surf,** tel. (808) 591-7778, and **Hawaiian Water Sports,** tel. (808) 255-4352, for instructions and lessons, and in Haleiwa on the North Shore, try **Surf and Sea,** tel. (808) 637-9887.

For rentals, try those place that give lessons or contact **Blue Water Rentals,** tel. (808) 926-1477, or **Local Motion,** tel. (808) 955-7873.

WINDSURFING

The fastest growing water sport, both in Hawaii and around the world, is windsurfing. Technically called sailboarding, most people call this relatively new sport windsurfing, after the name of one of the most famous manufacturers of sailboards. A combination of surfing and sailing, the equipment is a rather large and stable surfboard mounted with a highly maneuverable sail. If it sounds difficult, most people find it slightly easier than surfing because you're mobilized by the wind and not at the mercy of the waves. You don't have to "read" the waves as well as a surfer, and like riding a bicycle, as long as you keep moving, you can hold your balance. Kailua Bay has perfect conditions for this sport, and you can go there any day to see windsurfers skimming the waves with their multihued sails displayed like proud peacocks.

Windsurfing Lessons and Rentals

Far and away the most famous windsurfing beach on Oahu is Kailua Beach Park on the windward coast. Daily, a flotilla of windsurfers glide over its smooth waters, propelled by the always-blowing breezes. Along the shore and in town a number of enterprises build, rent, and sell sailboards. There is also windsurfing along the North Shore. Commercial ventures are allowed to operate along Kailua Beach only on weekdays and weekend

mornings, but weekend afternoons and holidays are *kapu!* Here are some of the best.

Kailua Sailboard Company, with a perfect location only a minute from the beach in Kailua, 130 Kailua Road, tel. (808) 262-2555, open 9 a.m.-5 p.m. daily, is a full-service sailboard and kayak store. Sailboard rentals are $30 per day (24 hours), half day $25; double day and weekly rates are also available. Beginning group lessons are $39 for a three-hour session. During the week equipment is right at the beach so you don't have to have a car to transport it. On weekends a push cart or a roof rack is provided at no additional charge. In addition, boogie boards cost $7.50 per day. Ocean kayaks run $22 a half day, $28 full day, and $120 a week. Double kayak rentals are $29, $39, and $165, respectively. If you're in Waikiki, transportation to and from is included in the rental price—a good deal. If you drive here, owner Aidin Schmer and his Doberman pinschers will watch your car.

Naish Hawaii, 155 A Hamakua Dr., tel. (808) 262-6068 or (800) 767-6068, open 9 a.m.-5:30 p.m. daily, is a very famous maker of custom boards, production boards, sails, hardware, accessories, and repairs. T-shirts, bathing suits, beach accessories, hats, and slippers are also for sale (primarily for men, but plenty of their fashions would be attractive on women as well). Naish is the largest and oldest windsurfing company in Hawaii. The famous Naish Windsurfing School, located at Kailua Beach, gives 90 minutes of personal instruction and an additional hour of board use for $55 including all equipment, $75 for two people.

Also try **Surf and Sea,** tel. (808) 637-9887, on the North Shore in Haleiwa, and **Hawaiian Water Sports,** tel. (808) 255-4352, in Honolulu.

Boogie Boards

If surfing or windsurfing is a bit too much for you, try a boogie board—a foam board about three feet long that you lie on from the waist up. You can get tremendous rides on boogie boards with the help of flippers for maneuverability. You can learn to ride in minutes and it's much faster, easier, and more thrilling than bodysurfing. Boogie boards are for sale all over the island and are relatively cheap. You can rent one from a snorkel, dive, or surf shop for $5-7 a day or about $25 a week, or buy your own for $80-350. The most highly acclaimed boogie-boarding beach on Oahu is Sandy Beach. It also has the dubious distinction of being the most dangerous beach in Hawaii, with more drownings, broken backs, and broken necks than anywhere in the state. Waikiki is tame and excellent for boogie boarding, while Waimanalo Beach is more for the intermediate boarder.

OTHER WATER ACTIVITIES

Kayaks, Jet Skis, Water Skis

Go Bananas Hawaii, 732 Kapapulu, tel. (808) 737-9514, and at 98-406 Kamehameha Hwy., Pearl City, tel. (808) 484-0606, is into kayaks, wave skis, and water toys. Single-person kayaks are $25 per day, $40 for two-person kayaks; $10 extra for 24 hours. Guided tours are offered at $50 for the first person, $40 for the second, and $30 for each additional member. Aside from wave skis, the store sells inflatable kayaks, aqua socks for walking on the reef, books, soaps, sunglasses, and T-shirts.

Located near the beach in Kailua, **Kailua Sailboard Company** (see above) also rents kayaks. It's a good company with a great location and competitive prices. It even provides shuttle service from Waikiki. **Twogood Kayaks Hawaii,** 345 Hahani St., tel. (808) 262-5656, offers kayak rentals, sales, and lessons. Good service, good prices. Full-day rental $32, tandem $42, and the kayak will be dropped off for free at the Kailua Beach Park ($10 delivery fee for other locations in Kailua). Open Mon.-Fri. 9 a.m.-5 p.m., Sat.-Sun. 8 a.m.-5 p.m.

Waikiki Beach Services, tel. (808) 924-4941, rents jet skis along Waikiki. At the Koko Marina Shopping Center, check with both **Fun Island Water Sports,** tel. (808) 395-4386, and **Sea Breeze Water Sports Ltd.,** tel. (808) 396-0100. In Haleiwa, try **Jet Ski Plus,** tel. (808) 637-8006, for jet skis and other watercraft. Expect to pay about $50 for a half hour.

If you like water-skiing, **Suyderhoud Water Ski Center,** tel. (808) 395-3773, at the Koko Marina Shopping center, can provide all your equipment, rentals, and lessons. Rates are $49 each for two people, skis included, for a half-hour session, $98 for an hour. Suyderhoud's is a full pro shop, so you can find all the best equipment and accessories.

Parasailing

For a once-in-a-lifetime treat try **Aloha Parasail,** tel. (808) 521-2446. Strapped into a harness complete with lifejacket, you're towed aloft to glide effortlessly over the waters off Waikiki. Aloha Parasail has free hotel pickup. Others are: **Big Sky Parasail,** tel. (808) 396-0564; **Sea Breeze Water Sports,** tel. (808) 396-0100, at the Koko Marina Shopping Center; and **Hawaii Kai Parasail,** at the Hawaii Kai Shopping Center, tel. (808) 396-9224. At Waikiki, check out **Waikiki Beach Services,** tel. (808) 924-4941. Rides go for $40-50 and last about 10 minutes. Boats usually have up to six riders so you might be on the water for about an hour.

Power Rafts

New to the Honolulu water scene is **Banana Boat Riders of Hawaii,** P.O. Box 8984, Honolulu, HI 96830, tel. (808) 922-5588 or (888) 922-5588, fax (808) 739-2962. The banana boat is a 32-foot inflatable yellow raft powered by twin 225-hp engines. It seats up to 21 and skims and bounces over the waves along the south coast. Riders straddle three inflatable tubes in the center of the craft and hang on to ropes for the safe but wild ride. The one-hour ride leaves throughout the day starting at 9 a.m. and costs $39 for adults and $34 for children 3-11. Pregnant women and those with back problems should not consider riding. This thrill of a ride is sure to please—and get you wet. Wear a swimsuit or clothes that don't need to stay dry, and bring a towel. From January to April, tamer whalewatching rides are also offered for the same cost. Call (808) 922-5588 for information and reservations.

Royal Hawaiian Cruises, tel. (808) 848-6360 or (800) 852-4183, also offers hosted whalewatching tours on cushy, canopied, 49-passenger rafts during the winter months. All run $29 ($21.95 for kids 5-11) and leave early morning, late morning, and early afternoon from Honolulu's Kewalo Basin.

BICYCLING

Pedaling around Oahu can be both fascinating and frustrating. The roads are well paved, but the shoulders are often torn up. Traffic in and around Honolulu is horrifying, and the only way to avoid it is to leave very early in the morning. Many, but not yet all, of the city buses have been equipped with bike racks, so it's easier than before to get your bike from one part of the city to another or out of town. Once you leave the city, traffic, especially on the secondary interior roads, isn't too bad. Unfortunately, all of the coastal roads are heavily trafficked. If you rent a bicycle, you're better off getting a **cruiser** or **mountain bike** (instead of a delicate road bike), which will allow for the sometimes-poor road conditions and open up the possibilities of off-road biking. Even experienced mountain bikers should be careful on Oahu trails, which are often extremely muddy and rutted. Pedaling around Waikiki, although congested, is usually safe, and a fun way of seeing the sights. Always use a helmet, always lock your bike, and always take your bike bag.

You can take your bike with you interisland by plane, but it will cost about $20 one-way. Bikes must be packed in a box or hard case, supplied by the owner. Handlebars must be turned sideways and the pedals removed or turned in. Bikes go space available only—usually not a problem, except, perhaps, during bicycle competitions. In addition, a release of liability for damage must be signed before the airline will accept the bike. There is no fee to transport your bike on the ferry between Maui and Molokai, but between Maui and Lanai the fee is $10 each way. Your bike doesn't need to be packed for the ferries.

For general information on biking in Hawaii, contact **Hawaii Bicycling League,** P.O. Box 4403, Honolulu, HI 96812-4403. This nonprofit organization promotes biking as recreation, sport, and transportation, encourages safe biking practices, conducts biking education, and advocates for biking issues. It publishes a monthly newsletter, *Spoke-n-Words,* filled with news of the organization's business, its bicycle safety program for kids, and rides that are open to the public, as well as current bicycle issues and sponsored bicycle competitions throughout the state. Group rides for all levels of abilities are sponsored almost every weekend, and nonmembers are welcome. If you are a bicycle rider living in the islands or simply want a subscription to the newsletter, write for membership information. For mountain biking and trail information on all the major islands, pick up a copy of *Mountain Biking the Hawaiian Islands,* by John Alford.

For additional information, have a look at the *Bicycle Regulations and Illustrated Safety Tips* booklet put out by the Department of Transportation Services, City and County of Honolulu. Although written for the island of Oahu, the information is applicable to all the islands, except for a few minor details. On Oahu, pick up a copy at city hall or any satellite city hall and most bike shops. From the Neighbor Islands or if coming from outside the state, write or call for a copy: Bicycle Coordinator, City and County of Honolulu, 711 Kapiolani Blvd., Suite 1200, Honolulu, HI 96813, tel. (808) 527-5044. Also very informative for rules of the road and common sense biking tips is the *Rights and Responsibilities for Hawai'i's Bicyclists* booklet. This booklet and the *Bike Oahu* bicycle route map are available free from the State Bicycle/Pedestrian Coordinator, State Department of Transportation, 869 Punchbowl St., Honolulu, HI 96813, tel. (808) 587-2321, and may be available at city halls and tourist offices.

Bike Rental and Bike Shops

For bicycle rentals try: **Big Mountain Rentals,** 2426 Kuhio Ave., tel. (808) 926-1644; **Island Triathlon and Bike,** 569 Kapahulu Ave., tel. (808) 732-7227 (also in Wahiawa and at Hickam A.F.B.); or **Paradise Isle Rentals,** 151 Uluniu Ave., tel. (808) 922-2224. Most rental bikes are mountain bikes or hybrids. Expect to pay about $15-20 a day or $50-70 a week, depending upon the type.

For sales and repairs try: **The Bike Shop,** at 1149 S. King St., tel. (808) 596-0588 (locations also in Aiea and Kaneohe); **Eki Cyclery,** 1603 Dillingham Blvd., tel. (808) 847-2005; **Island Triathlon and Bike,** 569 Kapahulu Ave., tel. (808) 732-7227; **McCully Bicycle,** 2124 S. King St., tel. (808) 955-6329; and **Barnfields Raging Isle Surf and Cycle,** 66-250 Kamehameha Hwy. in Haleiwa, tel. (808) 637-7707.

OTHER SPORTS

Horseback Riding

A different and delightful way to see Oahu is from the back of a horse. The following are a few outfits operating trail rides on different parts of the island. **Kualoa Ranch,** tel. (808) 237-8515, by reservation only, in Kualoa on north windward Oahu, offers picnic rides into Ka'a'awa Valley as part of its all-day adventures. Hotel pickup available. The stable at **Turtle Bay Hilton,** tel. (808) 293-8811, on the North Shore, welcomes nonguests. Guided trail rides through the forest and along the beach are given several times daily; adults $35, children $22 for a 45-minute ride. Ride every day except Monday in the hills above Waimanalo with **Correa Trails Hawaii,** tel. (808) 259-9005, or daily on the North Shore with **Happy Trails Hawaii,** tel. (808) 638-7433.

Hang Gliding
North Shore Hang Gliding, tel. (808) 637-3178, sells hang gliders and can hook you up with a tandem instructor for lessons toward certification. The staff can also give you tips on where to fly on Oahu, if you're already certified.

Spectator Sports
Oahu is home to a number of major sporting events throughout the year. Many are "invitationals" that bring the cream of the crop from both collegiate and professional levels. Here are the major sports happenings on the island.

Football is big in Hawaii. The University of Hawaii's Rainbows play during the normal collegiate season at Aloha Stadium near Pearl Harbor. The December **Aloha Bowl** is a postseason collegiate game. In early January, the **Hula Bowl** brings together two all-star teams from the nation's collegiate ranks. You can hear the pads crack in February, when the NFL sends its best players to the **Pro Bowl.**

Basketball is also big on Oahu. The University of Hawaii's Rainbow Warriors play at the **Neal S. Blaisdell Center** in Honolulu at 777 Ward Street. The **Outrigger Hotels Rainbow Classic** tournament gathers eight heavy-hitting college teams from around the country for holiday sports entertainment. Mid-April sees some of the nation's best collegiate hoopballers make up four teams to compete in the **Aloha Basketball Classic.**

You can watch the Islanders of the Pacific Coast League play **baseball** during the regular season at Aloha Stadium. Baseball goes back well over 100 years in Hawaii, and the Islanders receive extraordinary fan support.

Water sport festivals include surfing events, usually from November through February. The best known are the **Triple Crown of Surfing,**

Hawaiian Pro Surfing Championships, Duke Kahanamoku Classic, Buffalo's Big Board Classic, and the **Haleiwa Sea Spree,** featuring many ancient Hawaiian sports. You can watch some of the Pacific's most magnificent yachts sail into the Ala Wai Yacht Basin in mid-July, completing their run from Los Angeles in the annual **Trans Pacific Yacht Race.**

GONE FISHING

Hawaii has some of the most exciting and productive "blue waters" in all the world. You'll find a statewide sport-fishing fleet made up of skippers and crews who are experienced professional anglers. You can also fish from jetties, piers, rocks, and shore. If rod and reel don't strike your fancy, try the old-fashioned throw net, or take along a spear when you go snorkeling or scuba diving. There's nighttime torch fishing that requires special skills and equipment, and freshwater fishing in public areas. Streams and irrigation ditches yield introduced trout, bass, and catfish. While you're at it, you might want to try crabbing for Kona and Samoan crabs, or working low-tide areas after sundown, hunting octopus, a tantalizing island delicacy.

Deep-Sea Fishing
Most game-fishing boats work the blue waters on the calmer leeward sides of the islands. Some skippers, carrying anglers who are accustomed to the sea, will also work the much rougher windward coasts and island channels where the fish bite just as well. Trolling is the preferred method of deep-sea fishing; this is done usually in depths of 1,000-2,000 fathoms (a fathom is six feet). The skipper will either "area fish," which means running in a crisscrossing pattern over a known productive area, or "ledge fish," which involves trolling over submerged ledges where the game fish are known to feed. The most advanced marine technology, available on many boats, sends sonar bleeps searching for fish. On deck, the crew and anglers scan the horizon in the age-old Hawaiian tradition—searching for clusters of seabirds feeding on baitfish pursued to the surface by the huge and aggressive game fish. "Still fishing," or "bottom fishing" with hand-lines, yields some tremendous fish.

One of the most famous fishing spots in Hawaii is **Penguin Banks** off the west coast of Molokai and the south coast of Oahu. "Chicken Farm" at the southern tip of the Penguin Banks is great trolling waters for marlin and mahimahi. The calm waters off the Waianae coast of Oahu, from Barber's Point to Kaena Point, yield marlin and *ahi.*

The Game Fish

The most thrilling game fish in Hawaiian waters is marlin, generically known as "billfish" or *a'u* to the locals. The king of them is the blue marlin, with record catches well over 1,000 pounds. The mightiest caught in the waters off Oahu was a record breaker at 1,805 pounds. There are also striped marlin and sailfish, which often go over 200 pounds. The best times for marlin are during spring, summer, and fall. The fishing tapers off in January and picks up again by late February. "Blues" can be caught year-round, but, oddly enough, when they stop biting it seems as though the striped marlin pick up. Second to the marlin are tuna. *Ahi* (yellowfin tuna) are caught in Hawaiian waters of depths of 100-1,000 fathoms. They can weigh 300 pounds, but 25-100 pounds is common. There's also *aku* (skipjack tuna) and the delicious *ono,* which average 20-40 pounds.

Mahimahi is another strong, fighting, deepwater game fish abundant in Hawaii. These delicious fish can weigh up to 70 pounds. Shore fishing and baitcasting yield *papio,* a jack tuna. *Akule,* a scad (locally called *halalu*), is a smallish schooling fish that comes close to shore and is great to catch on light tackle. *Ulua* are shore fish and can be found in tidepools. They're excellent eating, average two to three pounds, and are taken at night or with spears.

O'io are bonefish that come close to shore to spawn. They're caught by bait casting and bottom fishing with cut bait. They're bony, but they're a favorite for fish cakes and *poki. Awa* is a schooling fish that loves brackish water. It can get up to three feet long, and is a good fighter. A favorite for throw netters, it's even raised commercially in fishponds. Besides these there are plenty of goatfish, mullet, mackerel, snapper, various sharks, and even salmon.

Charter Boats

The charter boats of Hawaii come in all shapes and sizes, but they are all manned by professional, competent crews and captains intimately knowledgeable of Hawaiian waters. Approximate rates are: private, full day $400-600, half day $250-350; share, full day $125, half day $85. Full days are eight hours, half days four, with three-quarter days and overnighters available too. No licenses are required. All tackle from 30 to 130 pounds is carried on the boats and is part of the service. Oftentimes soft drinks are supplied, but usually you carry your own lunch.

It is customary for the crew to be given any fish that are caught, but naturally this doesn't apply to trophy fish; the crew is also glad to cut off some steaks and fillets for your personal use. Honolulu's Kewalo Basin, only a few minutes from Waikiki, has the largest fleet of charter boats. Pokai Bay also has a fleet, and many charter boats sail out of Kaneohe Bay.

The vast majority of Oahu's fleet moors in **Kewalo Basin,** in Honolulu Harbor along Ala Moana Boulevard next to Fishermen's Wharf. The boat harbor is a sight in itself, and if you're contemplating a fishing trip, it's best to head down there the day before and yarn with the captains and returning fishermen. This way you can get a feel for a charter to suit you best.

For a charter organization try **Island Charters,** tel. (808) 596-2086. Many private boats operating out of Kewalo Basin include: *Sea Verse,* tel. (808) 591-8840; **E.L.O. Sport Fishing,** tel. (808) 947-5208; **Maggie Joe** and **Sea Hawk,** tel. (808) 591-8888; and **The Wild Bunch,** tel. (808) 596-4709.

A few boats operate out of **Pokai Bay,** in Waianae on the northern leeward coast, and there are even a few berthed in Haleiwa on the North Shore.

Coastal Fish

You don't have to hire a boat to catch fish! The coastline is productive too. Catch limits for 21 species of marine fish and eight crustaceans and shellfish are regulated, so check state guidelines.

Freshwater Fishing

Due to Hawaii's unique geology, only a handful of natural lakes and rivers are good for fishing. The state maintains two public freshwater fishing areas on Oahu. The **Wahiawa Public Fishing**

FRESHWATER FISH

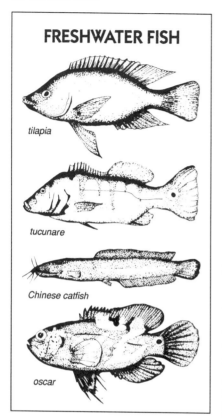

tilapia

tucunare

Chinese catfish

oscar

Area is 300 acres of fishable waters in and around the town of Wahiawa. It's basically an irrigation reservoir used to hold water for cane fields. Species regularly caught here are large and smallmouth bass, sunfish, channel catfish, *tucunare,* oscar, carp, snakehead, and Chinese catfish. The other area is the **Nuuanu Reservoir no. 4,** a 25-acre restricted watershed above Honolulu in the Koolau Mountains. It's open for fishing only three times per year in May, August, and November. Fish caught here are tilapia and Chinese catfish.

Hawaii has only one native freshwater game fish, the *o'opu.* This gobie is an oddball with fused ventral fins. They grow to be 12 inches and are found on all islands, especially Kauai. Introduced species include largemouth and smallmouth bass, bluegills, catfish, *tucunare,* oscar,

carp, and tilapia. The *tucunare* is a tough, fighting, good-tasting game fish introduced from South America, similar to the oscar from the same region. Both have been compared to bass, but are of a different family.

The tilapia is from Africa and has become common in Hawaii's irrigation ditches. It is a "mouth breeder," and the young will take refuge in their parents' protective jaws even a few weeks after hatching. The snakehead is an eel-like fish that inhabits the reservoirs and is a great fighter. The channel catfish can grow to over 20 pounds; it bites best after sundown. Or go for carp—with its broad tail and tremendous strength, it's the poor man's game fish. All of these species are best caught with light spinning tackle, or with a bamboo pole and a trusty old worm. The catch limit of eight species of freshwater fish are regulated.

Fishing Rules

All game fish may be taken year-round, except trout, *ama ama, moi,* and certain crustaceans (check specific regulations). Licenses are needed for freshwater fishing only. A **Freshwater Game Fishing license** is good July 1-June 30. Licenses cost $7.50 for nonresidents, $3.50 for tourists (good for 30 days), $3.75 for residents over age 15 and military personnel and their dependents over age 15, $1.50 for children ages 9-15; they are free to senior citizens as well as to children under age nine when accompanied by an adult with a license. You can pick up a license at most sporting goods stores or at the Division of Aquatic Resources, 1151 Punchbowl St., Honolulu, HI 96813, tel. (808) 587-0100. Be sure to ask for the *Hawaii Fishing Regulations* and *Freshwater Fishing in Hawaii* booklets. Fishing is usually allowed in most State Forest Reserve Areas. Owners' permission must be obtained to fish on private property.

HUNTING

Most people don't think of Hawaii as a place for hunting, but actually it's quite good. Seven species of introduced game mammals and 15 species of game birds are regularly hunted. Not all species of game animals are open on all islands, but every island offers hunting. Game on Oahu includes wild pig and goat, plus a variety of pheasant, francolin, quail, partridge, and dove.

Information

Hunting rules and regulations are always subject to change. Also, environmental considerations often change bag limits and seasons. Make sure to check with the State Division of Forestry and Wildlife for the most current information. Request *Rules Regulating Game Bird Hunting, Rules Regulating Game Mammal Hunting,* and *Hunting in Hawaii.* Direct inquiries to: Department of Land and Natural Resources, Division of Forestry and Wildlife, 1151 Punchbowl St., Honolulu, HI 96813, tel. (808) 587-0166. For recorded hunting information, call (808) 587-0171.

General Hunting Rules

Hunting licenses are mandatory in order to hunt on public, private, or military land anywhere in Hawaii. They're good for one year beginning July 1, and cost $15 residents and servicemen, $95 nonresidents; free to senior citizens. Licenses are available from sporting goods stores and from the various offices of the Division of Forestry and Wildlife. This government organization also sets and enforces the rules, so contact it with any questions. Generally hunting hours are from a half hour before sunrise to a half hour after sunset. Checking stations are maintained, where the hunter must check in before and after hunting.

Rifles must have a muzzle velocity greater than 1,200-foot-pound. Shotguns larger than .20 gauge are allowed, and muzzleloaders must have a .45 caliber bore or larger. Bows must have a minimum draw of 40 pounds for straight bows, 35 pounds for a recurve bow, and 30 pounds for compounds. Arrows must be broadheads. The use of hunting dogs is permitted only for certain species of birds and game, and when dogs are permitted, only smaller caliber rifles and shotguns, and spears and knives, may be used—no big bore guns or shotguns. Hunters must wear orange safety cloth on front and back no smaller than a 12-inch square. Certain big-game species are hunted only by lottery selection; contact the Division of Forestry and Wildlife two months in advance. Guide service is not mandatory, but is advised if you're unfamiliar with hunting in Hawaii. You can hunt on private land only with permission, and you must possess a valid hunting license. Guns and ammunition brought into Hawaii must be registered with the chief of police of the corresponding county within 48 hours of arrival.

Game Animals

All game animals on Hawaii have been introduced. Some are adapting admirably and are becoming well entrenched, while the existence of others is still precarious. **Feral pigs** are escaped domestic pigs that have gone wild and are found on all islands except Lanai. The stock is a mixture of original Polynesian pigs and subsequently introduced species. The pigs are hunted with dogs and usually killed with a spear or long knife—not recommended for the timid or tenderhearted. These beasts' four-inch tusks and fighting spirit make them tough and dangerous. **Feral goats** come in a variety of colors. Found on all islands except Lanai, they have been known to cause erosion and are viewed as a pest in some areas, especially on Haleakala. Openly hunted on all islands, their meat when prepared properly is considered delicious.

Game Birds

A number of game birds are found on most of the islands. Bag limits and hunting seasons vary, so check with the Division of Forestry and Wildlife for details. The **ring-necked pheasant** is one of the best game birds, and found on all the islands. The **kalij pheasant** from Nepal is found only on the Big Island, where the **green pheasant** is also prevalent; some are found on Oahu and Maui. **Francolins,** gray and black, from India and the Sudan, are similar to partridges. They are hunted on all islands with dogs and are great roasted. There are also **chukar** from Tibet, found on the slopes of all islands; a number of **quail,** including the **Japanese** and **California** varieties; **doves;** and the **wild Rio Grande turkey,** which is found on all islands except Kauai and Oahu (although a few of the "featherless variety" have been known to walk the streets of Waikiki).

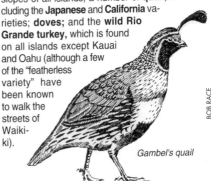

BOB RACE

Gambel's quail

SHOPPING

You can't come to Oahu and *not* shop. Even if the idea of it doesn't thrill you, the lure of almost endless shops offering every imaginable kind of merchandise will sooner or later tempt even the most "big-waste-of-time" mumbler through their doors. So why fight it? And if you're the other type, who feels as though a day without shopping is like being marooned on a deserted island, have no fear of rescue, because everywhere on the horizon is "a sale, a sale!"

You can use "much much more" as either an aspersion or a tribute when describing Oahu, and nowhere does this qualifier fit better than when describing its shopping. Over a dozen major and minor shopping centers and malls are in Honolulu and Waikiki alone! Population centers around the island, including those in the interior, the south shore, windward shore, and North Shore, all have shopping centers in varying degrees—at the very least, a parking lot rimmed with a half dozen shops that can provide immediate necessities.

On the Neighbor Islands, a major shopping mall is usually found only in the island's main city, with mom 'n' pop stores and small superettes taking up the slack. On Oahu, you've got these too, but you're never very far from some serious shopping centers. The tourist trade fosters the sale of art and artifacts, jewelry and fashions, and numerous boutiques selling these are strung around the island like a shell necklace. Food costs, in supermarkets, tend to be reasonable because Oahu is the main distribution center, and with all the competition, prices in general seem to be lower than on the other islands. If your trip to Hawaii includes a stop on Oahu, do most of your shopping here, because of the cutrate prices and much greater availability of goods. When most Hawaiians go on a shopping spree, they head for Oahu. Don't underestimate a simple trip to the grocery store. Often, but not always, you can find uniquely Hawaiian gifts like coffee, macadamia nut liqueur, coconut syrup, and even an assortment of juices much cheaper than in the gift shops. Remember, even thrift and consignment shops may hold some treasures, like older T-shirts, many with distinctive local flavor.

Note: The following are merely general listings; refer to "Shopping" in the travel sections for listings of specific shops, stores, and markets.

SHOPPING CENTERS

Honolulu Shopping Centers
Since it serves as the main terminal for TheBus, you could make a strong case that **Ala Moana Shopping Center** is the heart of shopping on Oahu. At one time billed as the largest shopping center in the country, today it settles for being the largest in the state, with its hundreds of stores covering 50 acres. It's on Ala Moana Blvd., just across from the Ala Moana Beach Park. **The Ward Warehouse** is just a few blocks west of the Ala Moana Center, at 1050 Ala Moana Boulevard. The **Ward Centre,** on Ala Moana across from Ward Warehouse, is a relatively new shopping center that's gaining a reputation for some exclusive shops.

Waikiki Shopping
Shopping in Waikiki is as easy as falling off a surfboard. In two or three blocks of Kuhio and Kalakaua Avenues are no less than seven shopping centers. If that's not enough, there are hundreds of independent shops, plus plenty of street vendors. Main shopping centers include **Royal Hawaiian Shopping Center,** the **Waikiki Shopping Plaza,** and the **International Market Place,** an open-air shopping bazaar across from the Moana Hotel at 2330 Kalakaua Ave., open daily from 9 a.m. until the vendors get tired at night.

The **Hyatt Regency Shopping Center** is located on the first three floors of the Hyatt Regency Hotel, at 2424 Kalakaua Ave. The **King's Village** is at 131 Kaiulani Ave., the **Waikiki Trade Center** is on the corner of Seaside and Kuhio Avenues, and the **Rainbow Bazaar** is a unique mall located at the Hilton Hawaiian Hotel, at 2005 Kalia Road.

Around the Island
Heading east from Waikiki on Rt. 72, the first shopping opportunity is the **Niu Shopping Cen-**

ter on your left, about four miles before Hanauma Bay. The Time Supermarket is known for good prices. Also on the left is the **Koko Marina Shopping Center**, just before Hanauma Bay, with several banks, a few art galleries, sports shops, and Foodland Supermarket. Nearby is the **Hawaii Kai Shopping Center**. Kailua and Kaneohe bedroom communities have shopping malls. Try the **Kaneohe Bay Shopping Center, Windward City Shopping Center,** or **Windward Mall. Kahaluu Sportswear,** along the Kahekili Hwy., about five minutes north of Byodo-In Temple, is a garment factory outlet store with decent prices and the ugliest collection of mannequins in the Pacific. Numerous shops are found along the North Shore from Haleiwa to Waimea, including surf, art, boutiques, and plenty of fast food and restaurants. The **Pearlridge Shopping Center** in Pearl City at the corner of the Kamehameha Hwy. and Waimano Home Road is a full shopping complex with over 150 stores. The **Waianae Mall** at 86-120 Farrington Hwy. serves the Waianae coast with a supermarket, drugstore, fast foods, and sporting goods, and the **Waipahu Town Center** and the **Waikele Factory Stores** in Waikele are good places to start when up in the center of the island.

SUPERMARKETS AND OTHER MARKETS

Around the island plenty of mom 'n' pop grocery stores provide fertile ground for a cultural exchange, but they're expensive. Oahu's large supermarkets include **Times, Safeway, Foodland,** and **Star Markets.** Preference is highly individual, but Times has a good reputation for fresh vegetables and good prices. Japanese **Holiday Mart** has stores around the island. They've got some bargains in their general merchandise departments, but because they try to be everything, their food sections suffer, especially the fruits and vegetables.

Chinatown offers the **People's Open Market** at the Cultural Plaza, located at the corner of Mauna Kea and Beretania Streets. Besides produce, you'll find fresh fish, meats, and poultry; the **Oahu Fish Market** is in the heart of Chinatown along King Street. The shops are run-down but clean, and sell everything from octopus to *kimchi.*

Health Food Stores

Brown rice and tofu eaters can keep that special sparkle in their eyes with no problem on Oahu—there are some excellent health food stores. Most have a snack bar where you can get a delicious and nutritious meal for bargain prices. **Down to Earth,** 2525 S. King St., tel. (808) 947-7678, is an old standby where you can't go wrong; great stuff at great prices. **Kokua Market Natural Foods Co-op,** 2643 S. King St., tel. (808) 941-1922, is a full-service store with organic and fresh produce, cheese, milk, juices, bulk foods, and breads. **Vim and Vigor Foods** has four stores on Oahu, including at the Ala Moana Center, tel. (808) 955-3600. **Celestial Natural Foods,** at the Haleiwa Shopping Plaza on the North Shore, tel. (808) 637-6729, is also top-notch, and **The Source Natural Foods,** tel. (808) 262-5604, at 32 Kainehe in Kailua on the windward side, is open daily.

BOOKSTORES

Oahu has plenty of excellent bookstores. In Honolulu, try the **Honolulu Book Shops,** with four locations: at the Ala Moana Center, tel. (808) 941-2274; in downtown Honolulu at 1001 Bishop St., tel. (808) 537-6224; at the Pearlridge Center, tel. (808) 487-1548; and at the Kailua Shopping Center, tel. (808) 261-1996. **Waldenbooks** has several locations in the city, including at the Pearlridge Center, tel. (808) 488-9488; Kahala Mall, tel. (808) 737-9550; and Waikiki Shopping Plaza, tel. (808) 922-4154. **Borders Books and Music** also has two full-selection stores in Honolulu, one in the Waikele Center, tel. (808) 676-6699, and the other at the Ward Centre, tel. (808) 591-8995. For a fine selection of Hawaiiana try the **Bishop Museum and Planetarium Bookshop** at the Bishop Museum, 1525 Bernice St., tel. (808) 848-4158, and the **Mission Houses Museum** in downtown Honolulu at 553 S. King St., tel. (808) 531-0481. You can find a good selection of books on Hawaiian outdoors, hiking, camping, and recreation, as well as fine maps at the **Hawaii Geographic Maps and Books** shop, tel. (808) 538-3952, at 49 S. Hotel St. in Honolulu. The **East-West Center** bookstore also carries a substantial collection of Hawaiiana as well as books on Asia, many of them published by the center.

SUNDRIES AND PHOTOGRAPHY

ABC has over a dozen minimarts in and around Waikiki. Their prices are generally high, but they do have some good bargains on suntan lotions, sunglasses, and beach mats. The cheapest place to buy **film** is at **Sears, Woolworth's**, or **Longs Drugs**. All have good selections, cheap prices, and stores all over the island. Open seven days a week, **Francis Camera Shop** in the Ala Moana Center is extremely well stocked with accessories. For a large selection of military surplus and camping goods try the **Camouflage Shop Inc.**, 38 Wilikina Dr., in Wahiawa.

If gadgetry fascinates you, head for **Shirokiya Department Store** at the Ala Moana and Pearlridge centers. Besides everything else, they have a wonderful selection of all the gimcracks and doohickeys that Nippon has to offer. The atmosphere is somewhat like a trade fair. Those who can't imagine a tour with anything on their feet but Birkenstock can have their tootsies accommodated, but they won't be entirely happy. If you get a sole blowout, **Birkenstock Footprints**, at Ward Centre, will resole them for $14, but it wants a full week to do it. For one-day service, it'll refer you to a shoemaker, **Joe Pacific**, 1680 Kapiolani Blvd., but he wants a toe-twisting $25 for the service!

FLEA MARKETS AND SWAP MEETS

Amidst the junk, these are the cheapest places to find treasures. Two operate successfully on Oahu and have a regular following. **Aloha Flea Market**, weekends tel. (808) 486-1529, weekdays tel. (808) 732-9611, is at Aloha Stadium every Wednesday, Saturday, and Sunday and most holidays 6 a.m.-3 p.m. It's the biggest flea market on Oahu, selling everything from bric-a-brac to real heirlooms and treasures.

Kam Swap Meet, tel. (808) 483-5933, inside the Kam Drive-In Theater (look for the two big screens), 98-850 Moanalua Road, Pearl City, is open Wednesday, Saturday, and Sunday 5:30 a.m.-1 p.m. Regular stall holders to housewives cleaning out the garage offer great fun and bargains.

ARTS AND CRAFTS

The following are a few of Oahu's many art shops and boutiques, just to get you started. An excellent place to find original arts and crafts at reasonable prices is along **The Fence** surrounding the Honolulu Zoo fronting Kapiolani Park. Island artists come here every weekend 10 a.m.-4 p.m. to display and sell their artwork. The **Honolulu Academy of Arts** is not only great to visit, but has a fine gift shop that specializes in Asian art. The same high-quality and authentic handicrafts are available in both the **Hawaiian Mission Houses Museum** and **Bishop Museum** gift shops. **Ka'ala Art** in Haleiwa is a great one-stop shop for fine arts, pop art, and handicrafts, all by aspiring island artists. The **Punaluu Gallery** is the oldest gallery on the windward coast. It's been there over 30 years and is now operated by candlemaker extraordinaire Scott Bechtol.

ARTS TO BUY

Wild Hawaiian shirts or bright muumuu, especially when worn on the Mainland, have the magical effect of making wearers "feel" like they're in Hawaii, while at the same time eliciting spontaneous smiles from passersby. Maybe it's the colors, or perhaps it's just the "vibe" that signifies "party time" or "hang loose," but nothing says Hawaii like alohawear does. There are more than a dozen fabric houses in Hawaii turning out distinctive patterns, and many dozens of factories creating their own personalized designs. These factories often have attached retail outlets, but in any case you can find hundreds of shops selling alohawear. Aloha shirts were the brilliant idea of a Chinese merchant in Honolulu, who used to hand-tailor them and sell them to the tourists who arrived by ship in the glory days before WW II. They were an instant success. Muumuu or "Mother Hubbards" were the idea of missionaries, who were appalled by Hawaiian women running about au naturel and insisted on covering their new Christian converts from head to foot. Now the roles are reversed, and it's Mainlanders who come to Hawaii and immediately strip down to as little clothing as possible.

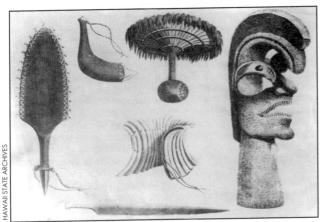

HAWAII STATE ARCHIVES

*carvings and weavings
of old Hawaii*

Alohawear

At one time exclusively made of cotton, or from manmade yet naturally based rayon, these materials were and still are the best for any tropical clothing. Beware, however: Polyester has slowly crept into the market! No material could possibly be worse for the island climate, so when buying your alohawear make sure to check the label for material content. Muumuu now come in various styles and can be worn for the entire spectrum of social occasions in Hawaii. Aloha shirts are basically cut the same as always, but the patterns have undergone changes, and apart from the original flowers and ferns, modern shirts might depict an island scene in the manner of a silkscreen painting. A basic good-quality muumuu or aloha shirt is guaranteed to be worth its price in good times and happy smiles. The connoisseur might want to purchase *The Hawaiian Shirt, Its Art and History,* by R. Thomas Steele. It's illustrated with more than 150 shirts that are now considered works of art by collectors the world over.

Woodcarvings

One Hawaiian art that has not died out is woodcarving. Old Hawaiians almost exclusively used koa because of its density, strength, and natural luster. Koa is becoming increasingly scarce, but many items are still available, though costly. Milo and monkeypod are also excellent woods for carving and have largely replaced koa. You can buy tikis, bowls, and furniture at numerous shops. Countless inexpensive carved items are sold at variety stores, such as little hula girls or salad servers, but most of these are imported from Asia or the Philippines and can be bought at any variety store.

Weaving

The minute you arrive in Hawaii you should shell out $2 for a woven beach mat. This is a necessity, not a frivolous purchase, but it definitely won't have been made in Hawaii. What is made in Hawaii is *lau hala.* This is traditional Hawaiian weaving from the leaves *(lau)* of the pandanus *(hala)* tree. These leaves vary greatly in length, with the largest over six feet, and they have a thorny spine that must be removed before they can be worked. The color ranges from light tan to dark brown. The leaves are cut into strips from one-eighth to one inch wide and are then employed in weaving. Any variety of items can be made or at least covered in *lau hala.* It makes great purses, mats, baskets, and table mats.

Woven into a hat, it's absolutely superb but should not be confused with a palm-frond hat. A *lau hala* hat is amazingly supple and even when squashed will pop back into shape. A good one is expensive ($25) and with proper care will last for years. All *lau hala* should be given a light application of mineral oil on a monthly basis, especially if it's exposed to the sun. For flat items, iron over a damp cloth and keep purses and baskets stuffed with paper when not in use. Palm fronds also are widely used in weaving. They, too, are a great natural raw material, but not as good as *lau hala*. Almost any item, such as a beach bag, woven from palm makes a good authentic yet inexpensive gift or souvenir; a wide variety is available in countless shops.

Gift Items

Jewelry is always an appreciated gift, especially if it's distinctive, and Hawaii has some of the most original. The sea provides the basic raw materials of pink, gold, and black coral that is so beautiful it holds the same fascination as gemstones. Harvesting the coral is very dangerous work. The Lahaina beds off Maui have one of the best black coral lodes in the islands, but unlike reef coral these trees grow at depths bordering the outer limits of a scuba diver's capabilities. Only the best can dive 180 feet after the black coral, and about one diver per year dies in pursuit of it. Conservationists have placed great pressure on the harvesters of these deep corals, and the state of Hawaii has placed strict limits and guidelines on the firms and divers involved.

Pink coral has long been treasured by humans. The Greeks considered it a talisman for good health, and there's even evidence that it has been coveted since the Stone Age. Coral jewelry is on sale at many shops throughout Hawaii, and the value comes from the color of the coral and the workmanship.

Puka shells (with small, naturally occurring holes) and *opihi* shells are also made into jewelry. Many times these items are very inexpensive, yet they are authentic and great purchases for the price. Hanging macramé planters festooned with seashells are usually quite affordable and sold at roadside stands along with shells.

Hawaii produces some unique food items that are appreciated by most people. Various-sized jars of macadamia nuts and butters are great gifts, as are tins of rich, gourmet-quality Kona coffee, the only coffee produced in the United States. Guava, pineapple, passion fruit, and mango are often gift-boxed into assortments of jams, jellies, and spicy chutneys. And for that special person in your life, you can bring home island fragrances in bottles of perfumes and colognes in the exotic odors of gardenia, plumeria, and even ginger. All of the above items are reasonably priced, lightweight, and easy to carry.

FESTIVALS, HOLIDAYS, AND EVENTS

In addition to all the American national holidays, Hawaii celebrates its own festivals, pageants, ethnic fairs, and a multitude of specialized exhibits. They occur throughout the year, some particular to only one island or locality; others, such as the Aloha Festivals and Lei Day, are celebrated on all the islands. Check local newspapers and the free island magazines for dates. Some of the smaller local happenings are semi-spontaneous, so there's no *exact* date when they're held. These are some of the most rewarding, because they provide the best times to have fun with the local people.

The following events and celebrations are either particular to Oahu, or they're celebrated here in a special or different way. This central island has more festivities and events than all the others, and these times provide great social opportunities for meeting people. Everyone is welcomed to join in the fun, and most times the events are either free, or nominally priced. There's no better way to enjoy yourself while vacationing than by joining in with a local party or happening.

JANUARY

January 1: **Hauoli Makahiki Hou.** Start the New Year off right by climbing to the top of Koko Crater on Oahu. A great way to focus on the limitless horizons of the coming year and a great hangover remedy. See the HVB for details. Or continue the party with the **Sunshine Music Festival** rock concert at Diamond Head Crater.

January 2: **Queen Emma Museum Open House.** This is Queen Emma's birthday, and the public is invited to visit her summer home and view a well-preserved collection of her personal belongings; tel. (808) 595-3167.

First Saturday: Watch the old pigskin get booted around in the **Hula Bowl Game,** Aloha Stadium, Honolulu. Annual college all-star football classic. Call Aloha Stadium, tel. (808) 486-9300.

Mid-January to early February: **The Narcissus Festival** in Honolulu's Chinatown starts with the parade and festivities of Chinese New Year, with lion dances in the street, fireworks, a beauty pageant, and a coronation ball; call (808) 533-3181 for locations.

Late January: **Robert Burns Night** at the Ilikai Hotel, Honolulu. Scots from Canada and mainland U.S. celebrate the birthday of Scotland's poet Robert Burns.

The **Cherry Blossom Festival** in Honolulu can begin in late January and last through March. Events include a Japanese cultural and trade show, tea ceremony, flower arranging, queen pageant, and coronation ball. Check newspapers and free tourist magazines for dates and times of various Japanese cultural events; for more information call (808) 949-2255.

FEBRUARY

Early February: **NFL Pro Bowl.** Aloha Stadium, Honolulu. Annual all-star football game offering the best from both conferences. Call (808) 486-9300 for more information.

Punahou School Carnival. Honolulu. Arts, crafts, and a huge rummage sale at one of Hawaii's oldest and most prestigious high schools. Great ethnic foods. You'd be surprised at what Hawaii's oldest and most established families donate to the rummage sale. Call (808) 944-5711 for details.

The Hawaiian Open International Golf Tournament. In Honolulu at Waialae Country Club. Huge prize money lures the best PGA golfers to this tournament, which is beginning its second decade.

Mid-February: **Haleiwa Sea Spree** on Oahu's North Shore. Surfing championships, outrigger canoe races, and ancient Hawaiian sports, topped off by an around-the-island bicycle race. Competitions last four days.

Late February-early March: **Buffalo's Annual Big Board Surfing Classic.** Makaha Beach, Oahu. Features the best of the classic board riders. A real cultural event complete with entertainment, crafts, and food. A two-day event held the last weekend in February and again on the first weekend in March.

MARCH

Remember **Buffalo's Big Board Classic** and the **Carole Kai Bed Race** down Kalakaua Ave. in Waikiki and a free concert at the Waikiki Shell the night before. There's a race and appearances by Hawaii's name entertainers in this fun-filled charity fund-raiser.

Hawaiian Song Festival and Song Composing Contest. Kapiolani Park Bandstand in Waikiki. Determines the year's best Hawaiian song. Presented by top-name entertainers.

Emerald Ball. An elegant affair sponsored by the Society of the Friendly Sons of St. Patrick that features dinner as well as dancing to a big-name band. Also, the Saint Patrick's Day Parade. Kalakaua Ave., Waikiki.

Kamehameha School Annual Song Contest. Blaisdell Center Arena, Honolulu. Competition among secondary-grade students of Hawaiian ancestry. Kamehameha Schools, tel. (808) 842-8211 or 842-8495.

Late March: **Hawaiian Highland Gathering,** Honolulu. A gathering of the clans for Scottish games, competition, Scottish foods, highland dancing, and pipe bands. Great Scotsmen with kilts and lei too. Richardson's Field, Pearl Harbor, tel. (808) 523-5050.

APRIL

Early April: **Easter Sunday.** Sunrise Service at the National Memorial Cemetery of the Pacific, Punchbowl Crater, Honolulu.

Annual Hawaiian Festival of Music. Waikiki Shell, Honolulu. A grand and lively music competition of groups from all over the islands and the Mainland. A music lover's smorgasbord offering everything from symphony to swing and all in between.

April 8: **Wesak or Buddha Day** on the closest Sunday to April 8. Celebrates the birthday of Gautama Buddha. Ornate offerings of tropical flowers at temples throughout Hawaii. Great sunrise ceremonies at Kapiolani Park, Honolulu. Mainly Japanese in their best *kimono*. Flower festival pageant and dance programs in all island temples.

Mid-April: **Aloha Basketball Classic.** Blaisdell Center Arena, Honolulu. Top college seniors are invited to Hawaii to participate in charity games made up of four teams. Blaisdell Center, tel. (808) 527-5400.

Late April or early May: **Pacific Handcrafters Guild Spring Fair,** at Thomas Square Park, Honolulu. An opportunity to see the "state of the arts" in Hawaii. Some of the islands' finest craftsmen in one spot selling their creations; tel. (808) 254-7688.

MAY

May 1: **Lei Day.** May Day to the rest of the world, but in Hawaii red is only one of the colors when everyone wears a lei. Festivities throughout Hawaii with special goings-on at Kapiolani Park, Waikiki.

Late May: **Memorial Day.** Special military services held at Honolulu, National Memorial Cemetery of the Pacific, on the last Monday in May. Call (808) 566-1430.

50th State Fair, at Aloha Stadium, Honolulu. Agricultural exhibits, down-home cooking, entertainment, and produce. Lasts four weekends. Call (808) 488-3389 or 923-1811 for information.

JUNE

Early June: **Mission Houses Museum Fancy Fair** and **Festival of Hawaiian Quilts,** Honolulu. A top-notch collection of Hawaii's best artists and craftsmen for the fair, and Hawaii's best stitchery for the quilt show. A great chance to browse and buy. Also, foods and entertainment; tel. (808) 531-0481.

June 11: **King Kamehameha Day** is a Hawaiian state holiday honoring Kamehameha the Great, Hawaii's first and greatest universal king. Lei-draping ceremony at King Kamehameha statue and parades complete with floats and pageantry featuring a *ho'olaule'a* (street party) in Waikiki. Civic Center, downtown Honolulu.

Mid-June: **Annual King Kamehameha Traditional Hula And Chant Competition.** Blaisdell Center, tel. (808) 536-6540.

Annual Hawaiian Festival of Music, Waikiki Shell, Honolulu. A repeat of the April festivities, but no less of a music lover's delight as local and Mainland bands compete in genres from symphony to swing.

Late June: **Annual Pan-Pacific Festival— Matsuri.** Dances and festivities, parades and performances, music, arts and crafts in Honolulu at Kapiolani Park and other locations. It's a show of Japanese culture in Hawaii. Also, *bon odori,* the Japanese festival of departed souls, which features dances and candle-lighting ceremonies at numerous Buddhist temples throughout the islands. These festivities change yearly and can be held anytime from late June to early August. Call (808) 923-0492 for information.

The annual **Wai'anae Coast Community Cultural Festival** takes place at various spots along the Leeward Coast from mid-June to early August. Events include music and dance, arts and crafts, story telling, foods, and a fishing competition. Call 696-1217 for information.

JULY

Early: **Tin Man Triathlon,** Honolulu. Over 1,000 triathletes gather to swim 800 meters, bike 25 miles, and finish with a 10,000-meter (6.2 miles) run around Diamond Head and back to Kapiolani Park in Waikiki. Call (808) 533-4262.

Trans Pacific Yacht Race, from Los Angeles to Honolulu during odd-numbered years. Yachties arrive throughout the month and converge on the Ala Wai Yacht Basin, where "party" is the password. They head off for Hanalei Bay, Kauai, to begin the year's yachting season.

July 4: **Hawaiian Islands Tall Ships Parade.** Tall-masted ships from throughout the islands parade from Koko Head to Sand Island and back to Diamond Head. A rare treat and taste of days gone by.

Mid-July: **Prince Lot Hula Festival,** Honolulu. A great chance for visitors to see authentic hula from some of the finest *hula halau* in the islands. Moanalua Gardens, tel. (808) 839-5334.

Annual Ukulele Festival, held on the last Sunday of the month 11 a.m.-1:30 p.m. at Kapiolani Park Bandstand, Waikiki. Hundreds of ukulele players from throughout the islands put on a very entertaining show. For information, call (808) 971-2525.

Pacific Handcrafters Guild Summer Fair, Thomas Square Park, Honolulu. A chance to see the "state of the arts" all in one locality. Browse, buy, and eat ethnic foods at various stalls; tel. (808) 254-6788.

HAWAII STATE ARCHIVES

man from the Sandwich Islands dancing

Late July: **International Sailboard Championship Invitational** held at Diamond Head. Watch the amazing "aquabatics" as windsurfers run before the wind on their amazing one-man crafts.

AUGUST

Early August: **Honolulu Zoo Day,** Waikiki. A day of family fun where kids of all ages get a close-up look at the animals and a day of entertainment.

Hula Festival, Kapiolani Park, Waikiki. Recent hula graduates from Honolulu's Summer Fun classes perform hula they have learned. Some amazing bodily gyrations.

Late August: **Hawaiian Open State Tennis Championships,** Honolulu. Held at various courts around town offering substantial prizes. For info call Don Andrews, tel. (808) 971-7150.

Queen Liliuokalani Keiki Hula Competition, Kamehameha Schools, Honolulu. Children ages 5-12 compete in a hula contest. Caution: Terminal Cuteness.

SEPTEMBER

Early September: **Waikiki Rough Water Swim,** Honolulu. A two-mile open-ocean swim from Sans Souci Beach to Duke Kahanamoku Beach. Open to all ages and abilities.

Late September: **Aloha Festivals** celebrate Hawaii's own "intangible quality," *aloha*. There are parades, luau, historical pageants, balls, and various other entertainment on all islands. The spirit of *aloha* is infectious and all are welcomed to join in. Check local papers and tourist literature for happenings near you. Downtown parades attract thousands, and even parking lots do their bit by charging a $1 flat fee during these festival times. The savory smells of ethnic foods fill the air from a multitude of stands, and the Honolulu Symphony performs at the Blaisdell Center, while free concerts are given at the Waikiki Shell. Over 300 planned activities at various locations on all islands; tel. (800) 852-7690.

Molokai to Oahu Canoe Race. Women (men in October) in Hawaiian-style canoes race from a remote beach on Molokai to Fort DeRussy in Honolulu. In transit they must navigate the rough Kaiwi Channel.

Pacific Handcrafters Guild Fall Fair. Thomas Square Park. A fall show of the best works of Handcrafters Guild members. Perfect for early-bird and unique Christmas shopping; tel. (808) 254-6788.

OCTOBER

Makahiki Festival. Waimea Falls Park, Oahu. Features Hawaiian games, crafts, and dances, reminiscent of the great Makahiki celebrations of ancient Hawaii. On an 800-acre tropical preserve.

Molokai to Oahu Canoe Race. Men (women in September) navigate Hawaiian-style canoes across the rough Kaiwi Channel from a remote beach on Molokai to Fort DeRussy, Honolulu.

Oktoberfest. Where else would you expect to find German oom-pah bands, succulent wienerschnitzels, *und* beer, than in Honolulu. At the Budweiser Warehouse, 99-877 Iwaena St., Aiea, noon-10 p.m.

Annual Orchid Plant And Flower Show. Hawaii's copious and glorious flowers are displayed. Blaisdell Center Exhibition Hall, Honolulu. Blaisdell Center, tel. (808) 527-5400.

Late October: **Bishop Museum Festival.** A superb time to visit the world's best museum on Polynesia and Hawaii. Arts, crafts, plants, and tours of the museum and planetarium. A full day for the family, with special "back room" exhibits open to the public which are usually not seen. Bishop Museum, Honolulu, tel. (808) 847-3511.

NOVEMBER

Early November: **Ho'olaule'a in Waianae.** The military lets down its hair and puts on a display accompanied by top entertainers, food, and music in this very ethnic area. All-day event.

November 11: **Veterans Day Parade.** National holiday. A parade from Fort DeRussy to Queen Kapiolani Park, Waikiki. American Legion, tel. (808) 949-1140.

Christmas in November: **Mission Houses Museum Annual Christmas Fair.** Quality items offered by Hawaii's top craftsmen in an open-air bazaar; tel. (808) 531-0481.

Late Oct.-early Dec.: **Triple Crown of Surfing:** Hawaiian Pro, World Cup of Surfing, Pipeline Masters. The best surfers in the world come to the best surfing beaches on Oahu. Wave action determines sites except for the Masters, which is always held at Banzai Pipeline, North Shore, Oahu. Big money and national TV coverage. Call 377-5850 for dates and locations.

Artists of Hawaii Annual Exhibition. The best works of Hawaii's contemporary fine artists. The Honolulu Academy of Arts, tel. (808) 532-8701.

Late Nov.-Dec.: **Hawaii Film Festival.** The best art films from the East, West, and Oceania. Various locations on all islands; tel. (808) 528-3456.

DECEMBER

Christmas celebrations: **Kamehameha Schools Christmas Concert.** Blaisdell Center Concert Hall, Honolulu.

Pacific Handcrafters Guild Winter Fair, Thomas Square, Honolulu. The best by the best, just in time for Christmas. Open air. Pacific Handcrafters, tel. (808) 254-6788.

Mid-December: **Annual Honolulu Marathon.** An institution in marathon races. One of the best-attended and very prestigious races in the country, where top athletes from around the world turn out to compete. Call (808) 734-7200.

Annual Rainbow Classic. Invitational tournament of collegiate basketball teams. Blaisdell Center Arena, Honolulu.

Aloha Bowl Game. Collegiate football. Aloha Stadium, Honolulu.

On **New Year's Eve** hold onto your hat, because they do it up big in Hawaii. The merriment and alcohol flow all over the islands. Firecrackers are illegal, but they go off everywhere. Beware of hangovers and drunken drivers.

ACCOMMODATIONS

The innkeepers of Oahu would be personally embarrassed if you couldn't find adequate lodging on their island. So long as Oahu has to suffer the "slings and arrows" of development gone wild, at least you can find all kinds, qualities, and prices of places in which to spend your vacation. Of the nearly 70,000 rooms available in Hawaii, 36,000 are on Oahu, with 31,000 of them in Waikiki alone! Some accommodations are living landmarks, historical mementos of the days when only millionaires came by ship to Oahu, dallying as if it were their own private hideaway. When the jumbo jets began arriving in the early '60s, Oahu, especially Waikiki, began to build

frantically. The result was hotel skyscrapers that grew faster than bamboo in a rainforest. These monoliths, which offered the "average family" a place to stay, marked a tremendous change in social status of visitors to Oahu. The runaway building continued unabated for two decades, until the city politicians, supported by the hotel keepers themselves, cried "Enough!" and the activity finally slowed down.

Now a great deal of money is put into refurbishing and remodeling what's already built. Visitors can find breathtakingly beautiful hotels that are the best in the land next door to more humble inns that can satisfy most anyone's taste and pocketbook. On Oahu, you may not get your own private beach with swaying palms and hula girls, but it's easy and affordable to visit one of the world's most exotic and premier vacation resorts. The following is merely an overview of the accommodations available on Oahu.

Note: For details and listings of specific accommodations, refer to the "Accommodations" sections in the travel chapters, and the **Accommodations Index** in the back of the book.

The Range

At almost anytime of year, bargains, plenty of them, may be found including **fly/drive/stay deals,** or any combination thereof, designed to attract visitors while keeping the prices down. You won't even have to look hard to find roundtrip airfare, room, and rental car for under $500 a week from the West Coast, based on double occupancy. Rooms on Oahu may be found in all sorts of hotels, condos, and private homes. Some venerable old inns along **Waikiki Beach** were the jewels of the city when only a few palms obscured the views of Diamond Head. However, most of Waikiki's hotels now are relatively new high-rises. In Waikiki's **five-star** hotels, prices for deluxe accommodations, with all the trimmings, may run $200 per night. But a huge inventory of rooms go for half that amount and less. If you don't mind being one block from the beach, you can easily find nice hotels for $50-60. You can even find these prices in hotels on the beach, though most tend to be a bit older and heavily booked by tour agencies. You, too, can get a room in these, but expect the staffs to be only perfunctorily friendly, and the hotels to be a bit worn around the edges. Waikiki's side streets also hold many apartment-hotels that are, in effect, condos. In these you get the benefit of a full kitchen for under $100. Stays of a week or more bring further discounts.

Central Honolulu has few acceptable places to stay except for some no-frills hotels in and around Chinatown. Bad sections of Hotel Street have dives frequented by winos and prostitutes, not worth the hassle for the few dollars saved. Some upscale hotels around Ala Moana put you near the beach, but away from the heavy activity of Waikiki. For those passing through, a few **overnight-style** hotels are near the airport.

The remainder of the island, outside Waikiki, was mostly ignored as far as resort development was concerned. In the interior towns, and along the south and most of the windward coasts, you'll be hard pressed to find a room because there simply aren't any. Even today, only a handful of hotels are found on the leeward coast, mostly around **Makaha,** with the exception of the new and luxurious **Ihilani Resort and Spa.** The area has experienced some recent development with a few condos and some full resorts going up, but it remains mostly undeveloped. **Windward Oahu** does have a few established resorts at Turtle Bay and Punaluu, but most of the lodging there is in rentable beach houses and tiny, basic inns.

To round things off, there is a network of **bed and breakfast** homes, YM/WCAs, youth hostels, elderhostels, and summer sessions complete with room and board at the University of Hawaii. Oahu also offers plenty of spots to pitch a tent at both state and county campgrounds.

HOTELS

Even with the wide variety of other accommodations available, most visitors, at least first-timers, tend to stay in hotels. At one time, hotels were the only places to stay, and characters like Mark Twain were berthed at Kilauea's rude Volcano House, while millionaires and nobility sailed for Waikiki where they stayed in luxury at the Moana Hotel or Royal Hawaiian, which both still stand as vintage reminders of days past. Hotels come in all shapes and sizes, from 10-room, family-run affairs to high-rise giants. A recent trend has turned some into condominiums. Every year more hotels are built and older ones renovated.

Types of Hotel Rooms

Most readily available and least expensive is a bedroom with bath, the latter sometimes shared in the more inexpensive hotels. Some hotels can also offer you a studio, a large sitting room that converts to a bedroom; suites, bedrooms with sitting rooms; or an apartment with full kitchen plus at least one bedroom. Kitchenettes are often available, and contain a refrigerator, sink, and stove usually in a small corner nook or fitted together as one space-saving unit. Kitchenettes cost a bit more, but save you a bundle by allowing you to prepare some of your own meals. To get that vacation feeling while keeping costs down, eat break-

J.D. BISIGNANI

Hilton Hawaiian Village

fast in, pack a lunch for the day, and go out to dinner. If you rent a kitchenette, make sure all the appliances work as soon as you arrive. If they don't, notify the front desk immediately, and if the hotel will not rectify the situation ask to be moved or for a reduced rate. Hawaii has cockroaches, so put all food away.

Amenities

All hotels have some of them, and some hotels have all of them. Air-conditioning is available in most, but under normal circumstances you won't need it. Balmy trade winds provide plenty of breezes, which flow through louvered windows and doors in many hotels. Ceiling fans are better. TVs are often included in the rate, but not always. In-room phones are provided, but a service charge is usually tacked on, even for local calls. Swimming pools are very common, even though the hotel may sit right on the beach. There is always a restaurant of some sort, a coffee shop or two, a bar, a cocktail lounge, and sometimes a sundries shop. Some hotels also offer tennis

courts or golf courses either as part of the premises or affiliated with the hotel; usually an "activities desk" can book you into a variety of daily outings. Plenty of hotels offer laundromats on the premises, and hotel towels can be used at the beach. Bellhops get about $1 per bag, and maid service is free, though maids are customarily tipped $1-2 per day and a bit more if kitchenettes are involved. Waikiki hotels have the very annoying custom of charging for parking above and beyond the room rate! Outside of Waikiki, parking is usually free unless you opt for valet service. Hotels can often arrange special services like baby-sitters, all kinds of lessons, and often special entertainment activities. A few even have bicycles and some snorkeling equipment to lend. They'll receive and send mail for you, cash your traveler's checks, and take messages.

Hotel Rates: Add 10% Room Tax

Every year Hawaiian hotels welcome in the New Year by hiking their rates by about 10%. A room that was $90 this year will be $99 next year, and so on. Hawaii, because of its gigantic tourist flow and tough competition, offers hotel rooms at universally lower rates than those at most developed resort areas around the world; so, even with the 10% room tax (6% transient accommodations tax, plus 4% state excise tax), there are still many reasonable rates to be had. Package deals, especially to Waikiki, almost throw in a week's lodging for the price of an air ticket. The basic **daily rate** is geared toward double occupancy; singles are hit in the pocketbook. Single rates are cheaper than doubles, but never as low as half the double rate; the most you get off is 40%. **Weekly** and **monthly** rates will save you approximately 10% off the daily rate. Make sure to ask because this information won't be volunteered. Many hotels will charge for a double and then add an additional charge ($10-35) for extra persons. Some hotels—not always the budget ones—let you cram in as many as can sleep on the floor with no additional charge, so again, ask. Others have a policy of **minimum stay,** usually three days, but the rates can be cheaper, and **business/corporate rates** are usually offered to anyone who can produce a legitimate business card. Senior citizens are sometimes offered special discount rates of 10-20%. This information will usually not be offered so you must inquire.

Hawaii's **peak season** runs from just before Christmas until after Easter, and then again in early summer. Rooms are at a premium, and peak-season rates are an extra 10% above the normal daily rate. Oftentimes they'll also suspend weekly and monthly rates during peak season. The **off-peak** season is late summer and fall, when rooms are easy to come by and most hotels offer lower rates. Subtract about 10% from the normal rate.

In Hawaiian hotels you always pay more for a good view. Terms vary slightly, but usually "oceanfront" means your room faces the ocean and mostly your view is unimpeded. "Ocean view" is slightly more vague. It could be a decent view, or it could require standing on the dresser and craning your neck to catch a tiny slice of the sea sandwiched between two skyscrapers. Rooms are also designated and priced upward as **standard, superior,** and **deluxe.** As you go up, this could mean larger rooms with more amenities, or can merely signify a better view.

Plenty of hotels offer the **family plan,** which allows children under a certain age to stay in their parents' room free, if they use the existing bedding. If another bed or crib is required, there is an additional charge. Only a limited number of hotels offer the **American plan,** where breakfast and dinner are included with the night's lodging. In many hotels, you're provided with a refrigerator and a heating unit for coffee and tea at no extra charge.

Paying, Deposits, and Reservations

The vast majority of Hawaiian hotels accept foreign and domestic traveler's checks, personal checks preapproved by the management, foreign cash, and most major credit cards. Reservations are always the best policy, and they're easily made through travel agents or directly by contacting the hotel. In all cases, bring documentation of your confirmed reservations with you in case of a mix-up.

Deposits are not always required to make reservations, but they do secure them. Some hotels require the first night's payment in advance. Reservations without a deposit can be legally released if the room is not claimed by 6 p.m. Remember, too, that letters "requesting reservations" are not the same as "confirmed reservations." In letters, include your dates of stay, type of room you

want, and price. Once the hotel answers your letter, *confirm* your reservations with a phone call or follow-up letter and make sure that the hotel sends you a copy of the confirmation. All hotels and resorts have **cancellation requirements** for refunding deposits. The time limit on these can be as little as 24 hours before arrival, to a full 30 days. Some hotels require full **advance payment** for your length of stay, especially during peak season or during times of crowded special events. Be aware of the time required for a cancellation notice *before* making your reservation deposit, especially when dealing with advance payment. If you have confirmed reservations, especially with a deposit, and there is no room for you, or one that doesn't meet prearranged requirements, you should be given the option of accepting alternate accommodations. You are owed the difference in room rates if there is any. If there is no room whatsoever, the hotel is required to find you one at a comparable hotel and to refund your deposit in full.

CONDOMINIUMS

The main qualitative difference between a condo and a hotel is in amenities. At a condo, you're more on your own. You're temporarily renting an apartment, so there won't be any bellhops and rarely a bar, restaurant, or lounge on the premises, though many times you'll find a sundries store. The main lobby, instead of having that grand entrance feel of many hotels, is more like an apartment house entrance, although there might be a front desk. Condos can be efficiencies (one big room), but mostly they are one- or multiple-bedroom affairs with a complete kitchen. Reasonable housekeeping items should be provided: linens, all furniture, and a fully equipped kitchen. Most have TVs and phones, but remember that the furnishings provided are all up to the owner. You can find brand-new furnishings that are top of the line, right down to "garage sale" bargains. Inquire about the furnishings when you make your reservations. Maid service might be included on a limited basis (for example, once weekly), or you might have to pay extra for it.

Condos usually require a minimum stay, although some will rent on a daily basis, like hotels. Minimum stays when applicable are often three days, but seven is also commonplace, and during peak season, two weeks isn't unheard of. Swimming pools are common, and depending on the "theme" of the condo, you can find saunas, weight rooms, jacuzzis, and tennis courts. Rates are about 10-15% higher than at comparable hotels, with hardly any difference between doubles and singles. A nominal extra fee is charged for more than two people; condos can normally accommodate four to six guests. You can find clean, decent condos for as little as $200 per week, all the way up to exclusive apartments for well over $3,000. The method of paying for and reserving a condo is just about the same as for a hotel. However, requirements for deposits, final payments, and cancellation charges are much stiffer than in hotels. Make absolutely sure you fully understand all of these requirements when you make your reservations.

Their real advantage is for families, friends who want to share, and especially long-term stays, for which you will always get a special rate. The kitchen facilities save a great deal on dining costs, and it's common to find units with their own mini-washers and dryers. Parking space is ample for guests, and like hotels, plenty of stay/drive deals are offered.

Hotel/Condominium Information
The best source of hotel/condo information is the **Hawaii Visitors Bureau.** While planning your trip, either visit one nearby or write to one in Hawaii. (Addresses are given in the "Information and Services" section later in this chapter.) Request a copy of the (free) current *Member Accommodation Guide.* This handy booklet lists all the hotel/condo members of the HVB, with addresses, phone numbers, facilities, and rates. General tips are also given.

Hotel/Condo Booking and Reservations
The following is a partial list of booking agents handling a number of properties on Oahu.

Aston Hotels and Resorts, 2250 Kuhio Ave., Honolulu, HI 96815, tel. (808) 931-1400 or (800) 922-7886 Mainland, (800) 445-6633 Canada, or (800) 321-2558 in Hawaii

Go Condo Hawaii, tel. (800) 452-3463, Web site: www.gocondohawaii.com

Hawaii Resort Management, 75-5776 Kuakini Hwy., Suite 105C, Kailua-Kona, HI 96740, tel. (808) 329-9393, fax 326-4136

Homes and Villas in Paradise, 116 Hekili St., Suite 201, Kailua, HI 96734, tel. (808) 262-4663 or (800) 282-2736, Web site: planet-hawaii.com/homes-villas

Marc Resorts Hawaii, 2155 Kalakaua Ave., Honolulu, HI 96815, tel. (808) 926-5900 or (800) 535-0085

BED AND BREAKFASTS

Bed-and-breakfast (B&B) inns are hardly a new idea. The Bible talks of the hospitable hosts who opened the gates of their homes and invited the wayfarer in to spend the night. B&Bs have a long tradition in Europe and were commonplace in 18th-century America. Now, lodging in a private home called a bed and breakfast is becoming increasingly fashionable throughout America, and Hawaii is no exception, hosting about 100,000 guests yearly. Not only can you visit Oahu, you can "live" there for a time with a host family and share an intimate experience of daily life.

Points to Consider
The primary feature of B&B homes is that every one is privately owned, and therefore uniquely different from every other. The range of B&Bs is as wide as the living standards in America. You'll find everything from a semi-mansion in the most fashionable residential area to a little grass shack offered by a down-home fisherman and his family. This means that it's particularly important for the guest to choose a host family with whom his or her lifestyle is compatible.

Unlike at a hotel or a condo, you'll be living *with* a host (usually a family), although your room will be private, with private baths and separate entrances being quite common. You don't just "check in" to a B&B. You make arrangements directly, or you might want to go through an agency (listed below) that acts as a go-between, matching host and guest. Write to request a booklet with a complete description of the B&B, its general location, the fees charged, and a good idea of the lifestyle of your host family. With the reservations application will be included a questionnaire that determines your profile: Are you single? Do you have children? Smoker? etc., as well as arrival and departure dates and all pertinent particulars.

Since B&Bs are run by individual families, the times that they will accept guests can vary according to what's happening in their lives. This makes it imperative to write well in advance: three months is good; earlier is too long and too many things can change. Four weeks is about the minimum time required to make all necessary arrangements. Expect a minimum stay (three days is common) and a maximum stay. B&Bs are not long-term housing, although it's hoped that guest and host will develop a friendship and that future stays can be as long as both desire.

B&B Agencies

A top-notch B&B agency with over 150 homes is **Bed and Breakfast Hawaii,** operated by Evelyn Warner and Al Davis. They've been running this service since 1978, and their reputation is excellent. B&B Hawaii has a membership fee of $10 yearly. For this they mail you their *Directory of Homes,* a periodic "hot sheet" of new listings, and all pertinent guest applications; add $1 for handling. Write Bed and Breakfast Hawaii, P.O. Box 449, Kapaa, HI 96746, tel. (808) 822-7771 or (800) 733-1632, e-mail: bandb@aloha.net; Web site: planet-hawaii.com/bandb.

One of the most experienced agencies is **Bed And Breakfast Honolulu Statewide,** at 3242 Kaohinanai Dr., Honolulu, HI 96817, tel. (808) 595-7533 or (800) 288-4666, fax (808) 595-2030, e-mail: bnbshi@aloha.net, Web site: planet-hawaii.com/bnb-honolulu, owned and operated by Marylee and Gene Bridges, began in 1982. Since then, they've become masters at finding visitors the perfect accommodations to match their desires, needs, and pocketbooks. Their repertoire of guest homes offers more than 350 rooms, with half on Oahu and the other half scattered around the state. When you phone, they'll match your needs to their computerized in-house guidelines.

Other well-known agencies include the following. **Go Native Hawaii** will send you a directory and all needed information if you write to them at 65 Halaulani Place, P.O. Box 11418, Hilo, HI, 96721, tel. (808) 935-4178 or (800) 662-8483. **All Island Bed and Breakfast,** 463 Iliwahi Loop, Kailua, HI 96734, tel. (808) 263-2342 or (800) 542-0344, e-mail: cac@aloha.net, Web site: planet-hawaii.com /all-island, can match your needs up with about 700 homes throughout the state. Run by Susan Campbell, **Hawaii's Best Bed and Breakfast,** P.O. Box 563, Kamuela, HI 96743, tel. (808) 885-4550 or (800) 262-9912, fax (808) 885-0559, e-mail: bestbnb@aloha.net, Web site: www.best-bnb.com, is a smaller business but has listings all over the state. **Pacific Hawaii Bed And Breakfast,** 19 Kai Nanai Place, Kailua, HI 96734, tel./fax (808) 486-8838 or (800) 999-6026, lists perhaps 450 homes throughout the state. **Affordable Paradise,** 570 Wanaao Road, Kailua, HI 96734, tel. (808) 261-1693 or (800) 925-9065, specializes in Oahu B&Bs but can arrange stays on all islands.

Hawaiian Islands Vacation Rentals, 1277 Mokulua Dr., Kailua, HI 96734, tel. (808) 261-7895 or (800) 258-7895, is owned and operated by Rick Maxey, who can arrange stays on all islands and help with interisland flights and car rental. **Babson's Vacation Rentals and Reservation Service,** 3371 Keha Dr., Kihei, HI 96753, tel. (808) 874-1166 or (800) 824-6409, is owned and operated by Ann and Bob Babson, a delightful couple who will try hard to match your stay with your budget.

Agencies specializing in beachfront villas, luxury condominiums, and exclusive estates are **Villas of Hawaii,** 4218 Waialae Ave., Suite 203, Honolulu, HI 96816, tel. (808) 735-9000; and **Vacation Locations Hawaii,** P.O. Box 1689, Kihei, HI 96753, tel. (808) 874-0077.

HOSTELS

Oahu has several very reasonably priced hostels operating currently, five within a Frisbee toss of the beach in Waikiki.

An official American Youth Hostel member, the always-busy **Honolulu International Youth Hostel,** 2323 A Seaview Ave., Honolulu, HI 96822, tel. (808) 946-0591, is located near the University of Hawaii. Bunks, per night, run $12.50 for members and $15.50 for nonmembers. Call ahead for reservations.

In Waikiki, you'll find the **Hale Aloha Youth Hostel,** tel. (808) 926-8313, at 2417 Prince Edward St.; the **Inter-Club Hostel Waikiki,** 2413 Kuhio Ave., tel. (808) 924-2636; **Hawaiian Seaside Hostel,** 419 Seaside, tel. (808) 924-3306; the **Waikiki Beachside Hostel,** 2556 Lemon Road, tel. (808) 923-9566; and the **Polynesian Hostel Beach Club,** 2584 Lemon Road, tel. (808) 922-1340, fax 955-4470. Types of rooms, services, amenities, and restrictions differ among these establishments. Expect to pay $10-16 for a bunk and $30-45 for a room, per night.

The North Shore has two hostels: **Backpacker's Vacation Inn and Hostel,** 59-788 Kamehameha Hwy. in Haleiwa, tel. (808) 638-7838, where rates are $14-16; and **Breck's Hostel,** 59-043 Huelo St., Sunset Beach, tel. (808) 638-7873, where a bunk runs $12.50 and a room $35-40.

HOME EXCHANGES

One other method of staying in Hawaii, open to homeowners, is to offer the use of your home in exchange for the use of a home in Hawaii. This is done by listing your home with an agency that facilitates the exchange and publishes a descriptive directory. To list your home and to find out what is available, contact the following agencies: **Vacation Exchange Club** (Affiliate of Homelink, Int'l), P.O. Box 650, Key West, FL 33041, tel./fax (305) 294-1148 or (800) 638-3841; **Intervac U.S.,** P.O. Box 590504, San Francisco, CA 94159, tel. (415) 535-3497, fax 435-7440; or **Worldwide Home Exchange Club,** 806 Brantford Ave., Silver Springs, MD 20904, tel. (301) 680-8950.

FOOD AND DRINK

Hawaii is a gastronome's Shangri-La, a sumptuous smorgasbord in every sense of the word. The varied ethnic groups that have come to Hawaii in the last 200 years have each brought their own special enthusiasm and culture—and lucky for all, they didn't forget the cook pots, hearty appetites, and exotic taste buds.

The Polynesians who first arrived found a fertile but barren land. Immediately they set about growing taro, coconuts, and bananas, and raising chickens, pigs, fish, and even dogs, though consumption of the latter was reserved for the nobility. The harvests were bountiful and the islanders thanked the gods with the traditional feast called the luau. The underground oven, the *imu,* baked most of the dishes, and participants were encouraged to feast while relaxing on straw mats and enjoying the hula and various entertainments. The luau is as popular as ever, and a treat that's guaranteed to delight anyone with a sense of eating adventure.

The missionaries and sailors came next and their ships' holds carried barrels of ingredients for the puddings, pies, dumplings, gravies, and roasts—the sustaining "American foods" of New England farms. The mid-1800s saw the arrival of boatloads of Chinese and Japanese peasants, who wasted no time making rice instead of bread the staple of the islands. The Chinese added their exotic spices, creating complex Sichuan

dishes as well as worker's basics like chop suey. The Japanese introduced *shoyu* (soy sauce), sashimi, *bento* boxed lunches, delicate tempura, and rich, filling noodle soups. The Portuguese brought their luscious Mediterranean dishes of tomatoes, peppers, and plump, spicy sausages, nutritious bean soups, and mouthwatering sweet treats like *malasadas* (holeless donuts) and *pao dolce* (sweet bread). Koreans carried crocks of zesty *kimchi,* and quickly fired up grills for *pulgogi,* a grilled marinated beef. Filipinos served up their delicious *adobo* stews—fish, meat, or chicken in a rich sauce of vinegar and garlic.

Recently, Thai and Vietnamese restaurants have been offering their irresistible dishes next door to restaurants serving fiery burritos from Mexico and elegant marsala cream sauces from France. The ocean breezes of Hawaii not only cool the skin but waft with them some of the most delectable aromas on earth, to make the taste buds tingle and the spirit soar.

HAWAIIAN CUISINE

Hawaiian cuisine, the oldest in the islands, consists of wholesome, well-prepared, and delicious foods. All you have to do on arrival is notice the size of some of the local boys (and women) to know immediately that food to them is indeed a happy and serious business. An oft-heard island joke is that "local men don't eat until they're full; they eat until they're tired." Many Hawaiian dishes have become standard fare at a variety of restaurants, eaten at one time or another by anyone who spends time in the islands. Hawaiian food in general is called *kaukau,* cooked food is *kapahaki,* and something broiled is called *kaola.* Any of these prefixes on a menu will let you know that Hawaiian food is served. Usually inexpensive, they'll definitely fill you and keep you going.

Traditional Favorites

In old Hawaii, although the sea meant life, many more people were involved in cultivating beautifully tended garden plots of taro, sugarcane, breadfruit, and various sweet potatoes *(uala)* than fishing. They husbanded pigs and barkless dogs *(ilio),* and prized *moa* (chicken) for their feathers and meat, but found eating the eggs repulsive. Their only farming implement was the *o'o,* a sharpened hardwood digging stick. The Hawaiians were the best farmers of Polynesia, and the first thing they planted was taro, a tuberous root that was created by the gods at the same time as humans. This main staple of the old Hawaiians was made into poi. Every luau will have poi, a glutinous purple paste made from pounded taro root. It comes in liquid consistencies referred to as one-, two-, or three-finger poi. The fewer fingers you need to eat it, the thicker it is. Poi is one of the most nutritious carbohydrates known, but people unaccustomed to it find it bland and tasteless. Some of the best, fermented for a day or so, has an acidic bite. Poi is made to be eaten *with* something, but locals who love it pop it in their mouths and smack their lips. Those unaccustomed to it will suffer constipation if they eat too much.

A favorite popular dessert is *haupia,* a custard made from coconut. *Limu* is a generic term for edible seaweed, which many people still gather from the shoreline and eat as a salad, or mix with ground *kukui* nuts and salt as a relish. A favorite Hawaiian snack is *opihi,* small shellfish (limpets) that cling to rocks. People gather them, always leaving some on the rocks for the future. Cut from the shell and eaten raw by all people of Hawaii, they sell for $150 per gallon in Honolulu—a testament to their popularity. A general term that has come to mean hors d'oeuvres in

Hawaii is *pu pu.* Originally the name of a small shellfish, it is now used for any finger food. A traditional liquor made from ti root is *okolehao.* It literally means "iron bottom," reminiscent of the iron blubber pots used to ferment it.

Pacific Rim Specialties (a.k.a. "Hawaiian Regional") Cuisine

At one time the "tourist food" in Hawaii was woeful. Of course, there have always been a handful of fine restaurants, but for the most part the food lacked soul, with even the fine hotels opting to offer secondhand renditions of food more appropriate to large Mainland cities. Surrounded by some of the most fertile, and pristine waters in the Pacific, you could hardly find a restaurant offering fresh fish, and it was at one time a misdirected boast that even the fruits and vegetables laying limp on your table were "imported." Beginning with a handful of extremely creative and visionary chefs in the early 1980s, who took the chance of perhaps offending the perceived simple palates of visitors, a delightfully delicious new cuisine was born. Based upon the finest traditions of Continental cuisine—including, to a high degree, its sauces, pastas, and presentations—the culinary magic of Pacific Rim boldly adds the pungent spices of Asia, the fantastic fresh vegetables, fruits, and fish of Hawaii, and, at times, the earthy cooking methods of the Southwest. The result is a cuisine of fantastic tastes, subtle yet robust, and satiating but health-conscious—the perfect marriage of fresh foods prepared in a fresh way. Now restaurants on every island proudly display menus labeled "Hawaiian Regional." As always, some are better than others, but the general result is that the "tourist food" has been vastly improved and everyone benefits. Many of these exemplary chefs left lucrative and prestigious positions at some of Hawaii's five-diamond hotels, opening signature restaurants of their own to make this fine food much more available and affordable.

Luau

To have fun at a luau you have to get into the swing of things. Basically a huge banquet, you eat and drink until you have trouble moving, somewhat like Thanksgiving on the beach. Entertainment is provided by local performers in what is invariably called a "Polynesian Revue." This includes the tourist's hula, the fast version with swaying hips and dramatic lighting, a few wandering troubadours singing Hawaiian standards, and someone swinging swords or flaming torches. Although individual luau vary, some also offer an *imu* ceremony where the pig is taken from the covered oven, traditional games, arts and crafts, or a *hukilau* (pulling in a fishnet) demonstration. All the Hawaiian standards like poi, *haupia, lomi* salmon, *lau lau,* and *kalua* pig are usually served. If these don't suit your appetite, various Asian dishes, plus chicken, fish, and roast beef might do. If you leave a luau hungry, it's your own fault!

Luau range in price $46-78 per person. The price oftentimes includes admission to the theme parks at which many are now presented. This is the tourist variety—a lot of fun, but definitely a show. The least expensive, most authentic, and best luau are often put on by local churches or community groups. They are not held on a regular basis, so make sure to peruse the free tourist literature where they advertise. If you ask locals "Which is the best?" you won't get two to agree. It's literally a matter of taste.

The following is a listing of the luau available on Oahu at the present time. The **Royal Hawaiian Luau** on the Ocean Lawn of the Royal Hawaiian Hotel, every Monday 6-8:30 p.m., tel. (808) 931-7194, *is* the classic Hawaiian feast, complete with authentic foods, entertainment, and richly spiced with *aloha.* Authenticity is added by lawn seating on traditional *lau hala* mats (table seating too) while the sun sets on Waikiki Beach and the stars dance over Diamond Head. Entertainment is an hour-long Polynesian extravaganza featuring Tahitian and traditional hula, a Samoan fire dance, and bold rhythmic drumming, all done by Tihati. The buffet is a lavish feast of *kalua* pig, salmon, mahimahi, steak, and sides of poi, *haupia,* and a sinful but scrumptious table of desserts like coconut cake, *lilikoi* chiffon pie, banana bread, and guava chiffon pie. You are presented with a fresh-flower lei and welcomed at the open bar for mai tais and other tropical drinks. Cost is $78 adults, $48 for children 5-12.

Germaine's Luau, tel. (808) 941-3338 or (800) 367-5655, often claimed by local people to be *the* best, is held at a private west shore beach Tues.-Sun. 6-9 p.m. The cost for dinner, cocktails, and the Polynesian show runs $46 for adults and $25 for kids 6-12. A free shuttle (reservations required) from Waikiki area hotels can be booked when calling for tickets.

Paradise Cove Luau at the Ko Olina Resort boasts a wonderful dinner with arts and crafts displays on a private beach along the leeward coast. Held 5-8:30 p.m., tickets run $49.50 for adults and $29.50 for kids 6-12. The Royal Ali'i package, at $59.50 adult and $39.50 kids, gives you the standard luau and transportation plus several special extras. Transportation by shuttle bus from Waikiki is included in the price of admission. The shuttle bus departs from various hotels starting at 3:45 p.m. and returns by about 9:30 p.m. Call (808) 973-5828 or (800) 775-2683 for reservations.

In Laie on the windward coast, try the **Ali'I Luau** at the Polynesian Cultural Center. The dinner and show run 5:30-9:30 p.m., and cost is $49 adult and $30 children.

TROPICAL FRUITS AND VEGETABLES

Some of the most memorable taste treats from the islands require no cooking at all: the luscious tropical and exotic fruits and vegetables sold in markets and roadside stands or found just hanging on trees, waiting to be picked. Make sure to experience as many as possible.

The general rule in Hawaii is that you are allowed to pick fruit on public lands, but it should be limited to personal consumption. The following is a sampling of some of Hawaii's best produce.

common banana

Bananas

No tropical island is complete without them. There are over 70 species in Hawaii, with hundreds of variations. Some are for peeling and eating while others are cooked. A "hand" of bananas is great for munching, backpacking, or picnicking. Available everywhere—and cheap.

DIANA LASICH HARPER

Avocados

Brought from South America, avocados were originally cultivated by the Aztecs. They have a buttery consistency and nutty flavor. Hundreds of varieties in all shapes and colors are available fresh year-round. They have the highest fat content of any fruit next to the olive.

Coconuts

What tropical paradise would be complete without coconuts? Indeed, these were some of the first plants brought by the Polynesians. When a child was born, a coconut tree was planted to provide fruit for the child throughout his or her lifetime. Truly tropical fruits, coconuts know no season. Drinking nuts are large and green, and when shaken you can hear the milk inside. You get about a quart of fluid from each. It takes skill to open one, but a machete can handle anything. Cut the stem end flat so that it will stand, then bore a hole into the pointed end and put in a straw or hollow bamboo. Coconut water is slightly acidic and helps to balance alkaline foods. Spoon meat is a custardlike gel on the inside of drinking nuts. Sprouted coconut meat is also an excellent food. Split open a sprouted nut, and inside is the yellow fruit, like a moist sponge cake. "Millionaire's salad" is made from the heart of a coconut palm. At one time an entire tree was cut down to get to the heart, which is just inside the trunk below the fronds and is like an artichoke heart except that it's about the size of a watermelon. In a downed tree, the heart stays good for about two weeks.

Breadfruit

This island staple provides a great deal of carbohydrates, but many people find the baked, boiled, or fried fruit bland. It grows all over the islands and is really thousands of little fruits growing together to form a ball.

Mangoes

These are some of the most delicious fruits known to humans. They grow wild all over the islands; the ones on the leeward sides of the islands ripen April-June, while the ones on the windward sides can last until October. They're found in the wild on trees up to 60 feet tall. The problem is to stop eating them once you start!

Papayas

This truly tropical fruit has no real season, but is mostly available in the summer. Papayas grow on branchless trees and are ready to pick as soon as any yellow appears. Of the many varieties, the "solo papaya," meant to be eaten by one person, is the best. Split it in half, scrape out the seeds, and have at it with a spoon.

Passion Fruit

Known by their island name of *lilikoi*, passion fruit make excellent juice and pies. The small yellow fruit (similar to lemons but smooth-skinned) is mostly available in summer and fall. Many grow wild on vines, waiting to be picked. Slice off the stem end, scoop the seedy pulp out with your tongue, and you'll know why they're called "passion fruit."

Guavas

These small round yellow fruits are abundant in the wild, where they are ripe from early summer to late fall. Considered a pest—so pick all you want. A good source of vitamin C, they're great for juice, jellies, and desserts.

Macadamia Nuts

The king of nuts was brought from Australia in 1892. Now it's the state's fourth-largest agricultural product. Available roasted, candied, or buttered.

Litchis

Called nuts but really small fruits with thin red shells, litchis have a sweet, juicy white flesh when fresh, and appear like nuts when dried.

Potpourri

As well as the above, you'll find pineapples, oranges, limes, kumquats, thimbleberries, and blackberries in Hawaii, as well as carambolas, wild cherry tomatoes, and tamarinds.

FISH AND SEAFOOD

Anyone who loves fresh fish and seafood has come to the right place. Island restaurants specialize in seafood, and it's available everywhere. Pound for pound, seafood is one of the best dining bargains on Oahu. You'll find it served in every kind of restaurant, and often the fresh catch-of-

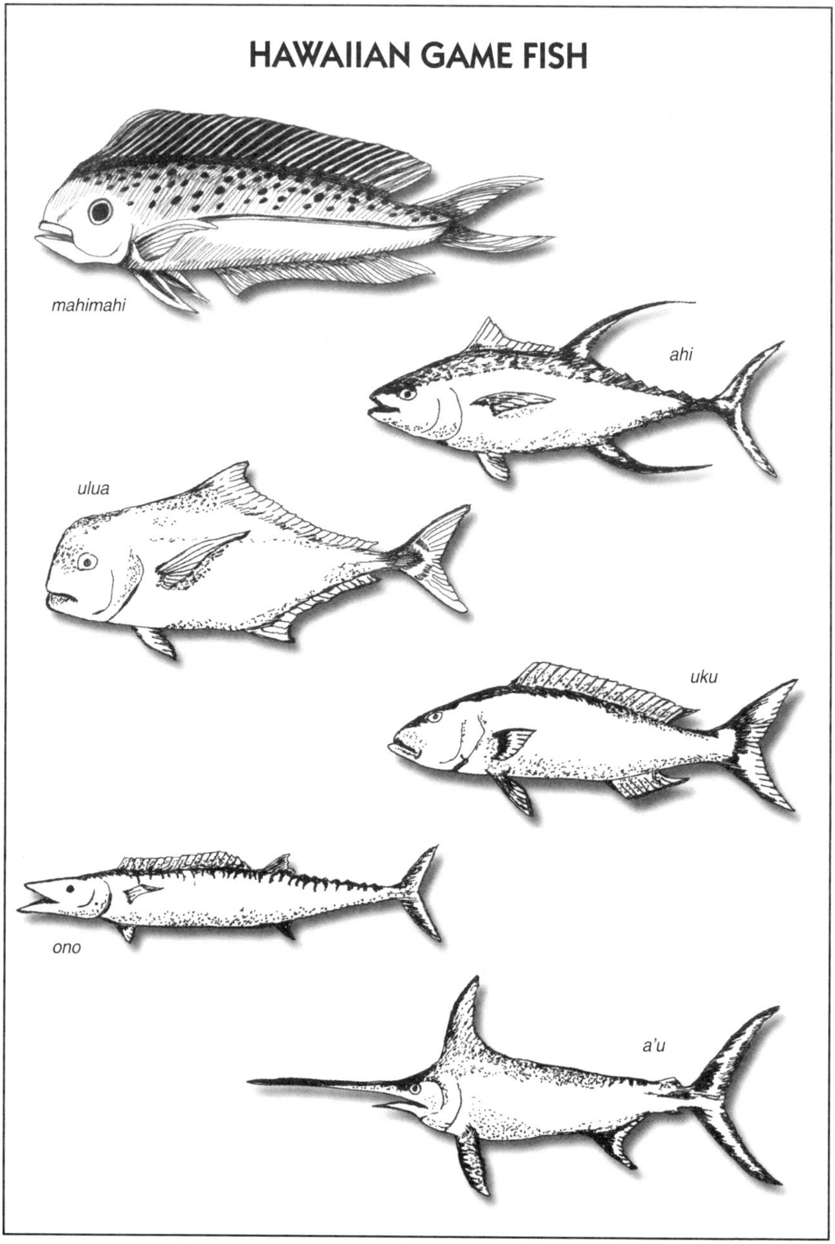

HAWAIIAN GAME FISH

mahimahi

ahi

ulua

uku

ono

a'u

LOUISE FOOTE/DIANA LASICH HARPER

the-day is proudly displayed on ice in a glass case. The following is a sampling of the best.

Mahimahi
This excellent eating fish is one of the most common and least expensive in Hawaii. It's referred to as a "dolphin," but is definitely a fish and not a mammal. Mahimahi can weigh 10-65 pounds; the flesh is light and moist. This fish is broadest at the head. When caught it's a dark olive color, but after a while the skin turns iridescent shades of blue, green, and yellow. It can be served as a main course or as a patty in a fish sandwich.

A'u
This true island delicacy is a broadbill swordfish or marlin. It's expensive even in Hawaii because the damn thing's so hard to catch. The meat is moist and white and truly superb. If it's offered on the menu, order it. It'll cost a bit more, but you won't be disappointed.

Ono
Ono means "delicious" in Hawaiian so that should tip you off to the taste of this wahoo, or king mackerel. *Ono* is regarded as one of the finest eating fishes in the ocean, and its white flakey meat lives up to its name.

Manini
These five-inch fish are some of the most abundant in Hawaii and live in about 10 feet of water. They school and won't bite a hook but are easily taken with spear or net. Not often on a menu, but they're favorites with local people who know best.

Ulua
This member of the crevalle jack family ranges 15-100 pounds. Its flesh is white and has a steaklike texture. Delicious and often found on the menu.

Uku
This gray snapper is a favorite with local people. The meat is light and firm, and grills well.

Ahi
A yellowfin tuna with distinctive pinkish meat. A great favorite cooked, or uncooked in sushi bars.

Moi
This is the Hawaiian word for "king." This fish has large eyes and a sharklike head. Consid-

ered one of the finest eating fishes in Hawaii, it's best during the autumn months.

Seafood Potpourri
Other island seafoods found on menus include *opihi,* a small shellfish (limpet) that clings to rocks and is considered one of the best island delicacies, eaten raw; *aloalo,* similar to tiny lobsters; crawfish, plentiful in taro fields and irrigation ditches; *ahipalaka,* albacore tuna; various octopuses and squids (calamari); and shark of various types.

A'ama are the ubiquitous little black crabs that you'll spot on rocks and around pier areas. They're everywhere. For fun, local fishermen will try to catch them with poles, but the more efficient way is to throw a fish head into a plastic bucket and wait for the crabs to crawl in and trap themselves. The *a'ama* are about as big as two fingers and make delicious eating.

Limu is edible seaweed that has been gathered as a garnish since precontact times and is frequently found on traditional island menus. There's no other seaweed except *limu* in Hawaii. Because of this, the heavy, fishy-ocean smell that people associate with the sea, but which is actually that of seaweed, is absent in Hawaii.

UNIQUE ISLAND DRINKS

To complement the fine dining in the islands, bartenders have been busy creating their own tasty concoctions. The standard range of beers, wines, and well drinks is served in Hawaii, but for a real treat you should try some mixed drinks inspired by the islands. Most look very innocent because they come in pineapples, coconut shells, or tall frosted glasses. They're often garnished with little umbrellas or sparklers, and most have enough fruit in them to give you your vitamins for the day. Rum is used as the basis of many of them; it's been an island favorite since it was introduced by the whalers of last century. Here are some of the most famous: Mai tai, a mixture of light and dark rum, orange curaçao, orange and almond flavoring, and lemon juice; Chi-Chi, a simple concoction of vodka, pineapple juice, and coconut syrup—a real sleeper because it tastes like a milk shake; Blue Hawaii, vodka and blue curaçao; Planter's Punch, of light rum, grenadine, bitters, and lemon juice—great thirst quencher; and Singapore Sling, a sparkling mixture of gin, cherry brandy, and lemon juice (and/or pineapple, lime and orange juices).

Local Brews

A locally brewed beer, **Primo,** manufactured under the auspices of the Joseph Schlitz Brewing Co. of Milwaukee, is a serviceable American brew in the German style, but lacks that full, hearty flavor of the European imports. In the early '70s it enjoyed an estimated 65% of the local market share, the highest in the nation, but after a bad batch was inadvertently released, sales plummeted and the local share fell to 5%, where it has since remained.

In the early '90s two local breweries folded: the Pacific Brewing Company, which produced **Maui Lager,** and the Honolulu Brewing Company, which produced **Koolau Lager,** among others. Both breweries were critically acclaimed, but both geared their beers to the full bodied European taste. Local beer drinkers enjoy a much lighter brew, so sales of the new beers never really took off.

Undaunted, Paula Thompson, a young and energetic ad executive turned *bier meister,* has been brewing small batches of beer in her Kula home for years. A visiting uncle, involved in an Oregon brewery, suggested, after tasting and enjoying one of her beers, that Maui was perfect for a microbrewery of its own. Paula agreed, but to keep start-up costs down, she is brewing her **Whale Ale** and **Aloha Lager** at the Blitz Weinhard Brewery in Portland, Oregon. Once the beer has been established, she hopes to move operations to Maui.

The **Kona Brewing Company** of the Big Island entered the local beer market not too long ago with three basic beers: **Lilikoi Wheat Beer,** a fruity yet hardy beer made with *lilikoi* (passion fruit); **Pacific Golden Ale,** a classic malty ale, light and perfect for sipping at the beach; and **Firerock Pale Ale,** a darker, hoppy beer, perfect with a meal.

More recently, the **Gordon-Biersch Brewery** started brewing beers at the Aloha Tower Marketplace in Honolulu and serving those beers at its pub/restaurant on premises. The brewery offers **GB Export,** a smooth, full-body beer that's similar to a pilsner; **GB Marzen,** a maltier beer with a stronger flavor; and **GB Dunkels,** a dark beer.

Coffee

Kona coffee is the only coffee grown in America. It comes from the Kona District of the Big Island and it is a rich, aromatic, truly fine coffee. If it's offered on the menu, have a cup. Recently, small coffee farms have been started on Maui and Kauai, but so far these are still small-scale operations and have little commercial impact.

Drinking Laws

There are no state-run liquor stores; all kinds of spirits, wines, and beers are available in markets and shops, generally open during normal business hours, seven days a week. The drinking age is 18, and no towns are "dry." Legal hours for serving drinks depend on the type of establishment. Hours generally are: hotels, 6 a.m.-4 a.m.; discos and nightclubs where there is dancing, 10 a.m.-4 a.m.; bars and lounges where there is no dancing, 6 a.m.-2 a.m. Most restaurants serve alcohol, and in many that don't, you can bring your own.

MUNCHIES AND ISLAND TREATS

Certain finger foods, fast foods, and island treats are unique to Hawaii. Some are meals in themselves, others are snacks. Here are some of the best and most popular.

Pu Pu

Pronounced as in "Winnie the Pooh Pooh," these are little finger foods and hors d'oeuvres. They can be anything from crackers to cracked crab. Often, they're given free at lounges and bars and can even include chicken drumettes, fish kabobs, and tempura. With a good display of them you can have a free meal.

Crackseed

A sweet of Chinese origin, crackseed is preserved and seasoned fruits and seeds. Favorites include coconut, watermelon, pumpkin seeds, mango, plum, and papaya. Distinctive in taste, they take some getting used to, but make great trail snacks. Available in all island markets. Also look for dried fish (cuttlefish) on racks, usually near the crackseed. These are nutritious and delicious and make a great snack.

Shave Ice

This real island institution makes the Mainland "snow cone" melt into insignificance. Special machines literally shave ice to a fluffy consistency. It's mounded into a paper cone and your choice of dozens of exotic island syrups is generously poured over it. Given a straw and a spoon, you just slurp away.

Malasadas and *Pao Dolce*

Two sweets from the Portuguese. *Malasadas* are holeless donuts and *pao dolce* is sweet bread. Sold in island bakeries, they're great for breakfast or as treats.

Lomi Lomi Salmon

This salad of salmon, tomatoes, and onions with garnish and seasonings often accompanies "plate lunches" and is featured at buffets and luau.

MONEY-SAVERS

Only one thing is better than a great meal: a great meal at a reasonable price. The following are island institutions and favorites that will help you eat well yet keep prices down.

Kaukau Wagons

These are lunch wagons, but instead of slick, stainless-steel jobs, most are old delivery trucks converted into portable kitchens. Some say they're a remnant of WW II, when workers had to be fed on the job; others say that the meals they serve were inspired by the Japanese *bento*, a boxed lunch. You'll see the wagons parked along beaches, in city parking lots, or on busy streets. Usually a line of local people will be placing their orders, especially at lunchtime—a tip-off that the wagon serves delicious, nutritious island dish for a reasonable price. There might be a few tables, but basically food is served to go. Most of the filling meals are about $3.50, and "plate lunches" are the specialty.

Plate Lunch

One of the best island standards, these lunches give you a sampling of authentic island food and can include teriyaki chicken, mahimahi, *lau lau*,

J.D. BISIGNANI

Those really determined to save money can always try this!

or *lomi* salmon, among others. They're served on paper or Styrofoam plates, are packed to go, and usually cost less than $3.50. Standard with a plate lunch is "two-scoop rice," a generous dollop of macaroni or other salad. Full meals, they're great for keeping down food costs and for instant picnics. Available everywhere from *kaukau* wagons to restaurants.

An innovation on the regular plate lunch is starting to pop up here and there in finer restaurants and even at a few *kaukau* wagons. This is a better quality plate lunch with the freshest ingredients, more health-conscious preparation, and a greater inventiveness in the foods chosen, and they're often served in a classier manner. As would be expected, these meals are not available everywhere yet and cost up to twice as much as the ordinary plate lunch, but they're still a good deal for this variation on a standard Hawaiian tradition.

Saimin

Special "saimin shops," as well as restaurants, serve this hearty Japanese-inspired noodle soup on their menu. Saimin is a word unique to Hawaii. In Japan, these soups would be called *ramen* or *soba,* and it's as if the two were combined into saimin. A large bowl of noodles in broth, stirred with meat, chicken, fish, or vegetables, costs only a few dollars and is big enough for an evening meal. The best place to eat saimin is in a local hole-in-the-wall shop run by a family.

Tips

Even some of the island's best restaurants in the fanciest hotels offer "early bird specials"—the regular-menu dinners offered to diners who come in before the usual dinner hour, which is approximately 6 p.m. You pay as little as half the normal price and can dine in luxury on some of the best foods. The specials are often advertised in the "free" tourist books, which might also include coupons for two-for-one meals or limited dinners at much lower prices. Just clip them out.

GETTING THERE

With the number of visitors each year over six million—and double that number of travelers just passing through—the state of Hawaii is one of the easiest places in the world to get to . . . by plane. About half a dozen large U.S. airlines (and other small ones) fly to and from the islands; about the same number of foreign carriers, mostly from Asia and Oceania, touch down on a daily basis. In 1978 airlines were "deregulated." In 1984, the reign of the Civil Aeronautics Board (CAB), which controlled exactly which airlines flew where and how much they could charge, ended. Routes, prices, and schedules were thrown open to free competition. Airlines that had previously monopolized preferred destinations found competitors prying loose their strangleholds. Thus, Hawaii is now one of the most hotly contested air markets in the world. The competition between carriers is fierce, and this makes for "sweet deals" and a wide choice of fares for the money-wise traveler. It also makes for pricing chaos. It's impossible to quote airline prices that will hold true for more than a month, if that long. But it's comforting to know that flights to Hawaii are cheaper today than they have been in years, and mile for mile are one of the best travel bargains in the industry. Familiarize yourself with the alternatives at your disposal so you can make an informed travel selection. Now more than ever you should work with a sharp travel agent who's on your side.

Almost all travelers to Oahu arrive by air, landing at Honolulu International Airport. A few lucky ones come by private yacht, and the interisland cruise ship SS *Independence* docks at Honolulu.

When to Go

The prime tourist season starts two weeks before Christmas and lasts until Easter. It picks up again with summer vacation in early June and ends once more in late August. Everything is usually booked solid and prices are inflated. Hotel, airline, and car reservations, which are a must, are often hard to coordinate at this time of year. You can save 10-50% and a lot of hassling if you go in the artificially created off season, September to early December, and mid-April (after Easter) until early June. Recently, the decreased number of tourists during the off season has not been nearly as substantial as in years past, indicating the increasing popularity of the islands at this time of year, but you'll still find the prices better, and the beaches, trails, campgrounds, and even restaurants less crowded. The people will be happier to see you, too.

BY AIR

There are two categories of airlines that you can take to Hawaii: **domestic,** meaning American-owned, and **foreign**-owned. An American law, penned at the turn of the century to protect American shipping, says "only" an American carrier can transport you to and from two American cities. In the airline industry, this law is still very much in effect. It means, for example, that if you want a roundtrip between San Francisco and Honolulu, you *must* fly on a domestic carrier, such as Hawaiian or United. If, however, you are flying from San Francisco to Tokyo, you are at liberty to fly a "foreign" airline such as Japan Air Lines, and you may even have a stopover in Hawaii, but you must continue on to Tokyo or some other foreign city and cannot fly JAL back to San Francisco. Canadians have no problem flying Canadian Pacific roundtrip from Toronto to Honolulu because this route does not connect two American cities, and so it is with all foreign travel to and from Hawaii. Travel agents all know this, but if you're planning your own trip be aware of this fact; if you're flying roundtrip it must be on a domestic carrier.

Kinds of Flights
The three kinds of flights are the "milk run," direct, and nonstop. Milk runs are the least convenient. On these, you board a carrier—say in your home town—fly it to a gateway city, change planes and carriers, fly on to the West Coast, change again, and then fly to Hawaii. They're a hassle—your bags have a much better chance of getting lost, you waste time in airports, and to top it off, they're not any cheaper. Avoid them if you can.

On direct flights you fly from point A to point B without changing planes; it doesn't mean that you don't land in between. Direct flights usually do land once to board and deplane passengers, but you sit cozily on the plane along with your luggage and off you go again. Nonstop is just that, but can cost a bit more. You board and when the doors open again you're in Hawaii. All flights from the West Coast gateway cities are nonstop, "God willing," because there is only the Pacific in between!

Travel Agents
At one time people went to a travel agent the same way they went to a barber or beautician, loyally sticking with one. Most agents are reputable professionals who know what they're doing. They should be members of the American Society of Travel Agents (ASTA) and licensed by the Air Traffic Conference (ATC). Most have the inside track on the best deals, and they'll save you countless hours calling 800 numbers and listening to elevator music while on hold. Unless you require them to make very special arrangements, their services are free—they are paid a commission by the airlines and hotels that they book for you.

If you've done business with a travel agent in the past, and were satisfied with the services and prices, by all means stick with him or her. If no such positive rapport exists, then shop around. Ask friends or relatives for recommendations; if you can't get any endorsements go to the Yellow Pages. Call two or three travel agents to compare prices. Make sure to give all of them the same information and to be as precise as possible. Tell them where and when you want to go, how long you want to stay, which class you want to travel, and any special requirements. Write down their information. It's amazing how confusing travel plans can be when you have to keep track of flight numbers, times, prices, and all the preparation information. When you compare, don't look only for the cheapest price. Check for convenience in flights, amenities of hotels, and any other fringe benefits that might be included. Then make your choice of agent; if he or she is willing to give you individualized service, stick with them from this point on.

Agents become accustomed to offering the same deals to many clients because they're familiar with making the arrangements and they worked well in the past. Sometimes these are indeed the best, but if they don't suit you, don't be

J.D. BISIGNANI

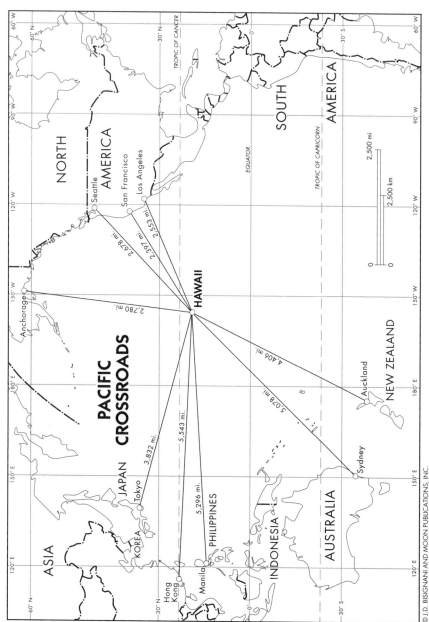

NORTH AMERICA

SOUTH AMERICA

TROPIC OF CANCER

EQUATOR

TROPIC OF CAPRICORN

Seattle

San Francisco

Los Angeles

Anchorage

PACIFIC CROSSROADS

HAWAII

2,780 mi.

2,678 mi.

2,621 mi.

2,553 mi.

4,406 mi.

5,078 mi.

ASIA

JAPAN

Tokyo

KOREA

3,832 mi.

5,543 mi.

5,296 mi.

Hong Kong

Manila

PHILIPPINES

INDONESIA

AUSTRALIA

Sydney

NEW ZEALAND

Auckland

2,500 mi

2,500 km

© J.D. BISIGNANI AND MOON PUBLICATIONS, INC.

railroaded into accepting them. Any good agent will work with you. After all, it's your trip and your money.

Package Tours
For the independent traveler, practical package deals that include only flight, car, and lodging are okay. Agents put these together all the time and they just might be the best, but if they don't suit you, make arrangements separately. A package *tour* is totally different. On these you get your hand held by an escort, eat where they want you to eat, go where they want you to go, and watch Hawaii slide by your bus window. For some people, especially groups, this might be the way to do it, but everyone else should avoid the package tour. You'll see Hawaii best on your own, and if you want a tour you can arrange one there, often more cheaply. Once arrangements have been made with your travel agent, make sure to take all receipts and letters of confirmation (hotel, car) with you to Hawaii. They probably won't be needed, but if they are, nothing will work better in getting results.

Mainland and International Fares
There are many categories of airline fares, but only three apply to the average traveler: first class, coach, and excursion (APEX). Traveling **first class** seats you in the front of the plane, gives you free drinks and movie headsets, a wider choice of meals, more leg room, and access to VIP lounges, if they exist. There are no restrictions, no penalties for advance-booking cancellations or rebooking of return flights, and no minimum-stay requirements.

Coach, the way that most people fly, is totally adequate. You sit in the plane's main compartment behind first class. Your seats are comfortable, but you don't have as much leg room or as wide a choice of meals. Movie headsets and drinks cost you a few dollars, but that's about it. Coach offers many of the same benefits as first class and costs about 30% less. You can buy tickets up until takeoff; you have no restrictions on minimum or maximum stays; you receive liberal stopover privileges, and you can cash in your return ticket or change your return date with no penalties.

Excursion or advance payment excursion (APEX) fares are the cheapest. You are accommodated on the plane exactly the same as if you were flying coach. There are, however, some restrictions. You must book and pay for your ticket in advance (usually 7-14 days). At the same time, you must book your return flight, and under most circumstances you can't change either without paying a penalty. Also, your stopovers are severely limited and you will have a minimum/maximum stay period. Only a limited number of seats on any one plane are set aside for APEX fares, so book as early as you can. Also, if you must change travel plans, you can go to the airport and get on as a standby passenger using a discounted ticket, even if the airline doesn't have an official standby policy. There's always the risk that you won't get on, but you do have a chance, as well as priority over an actual standby customer.

Standby is exactly what its name implies: you go to the airport and wait around to see if any flights going to Hawaii have an empty seat. You can save some money, but cannot have a firm itinerary or limited time. Since Hawaii is such a popular destination, standbys can wait days before catching a plane.

Charters
Charter flights were at one time only for groups or organizations that had memberships in travel clubs. Now they're open to the general public. A charter flight is an entire plane or a "block" of seats purchased at a quantity discount by a charter company and then sold to customers. Because they are bought at wholesale prices, charter fares can be the cheapest available. As in package deals, only take a charter flight if it is a "fly only," or perhaps includes a car. You don't need one that includes a guide and a bus. Most importantly, make sure that the charter company is reputable. It should belong to the same organizations (ASTA and ATC) as most travel agents. If not, check into the company at the local chamber of commerce.

More restrictions apply to charters than to any other flights. You must pay in advance. If you cancel after a designated time, you can be penalized severely or lose your money entirely. You cannot change departure or return dates and times. However, up to 10 days before departure the charter company is legally able to cancel, raise the price by 10%, or change time and dates. It must return your money if cancellation occurs, or if changed arrangements are unacceptable to you. Mostly they are on the up-

and-up and flights go smoothly, but there are horror stories. Be careful. Be wise. Investigate!

Tips

Flights from the West Coast take about five hours; you gain two hours over Pacific standard time when you land in Hawaii. From the East Coast it takes about 11 hours and you gain five hours over Eastern standard time. Flights from Japan take about seven hours and there is five hours difference between the time zones. Travel time between Sydney, Australia, or Auckland, New Zealand, and Hawaii is about nine hours. They are ahead of Hawaii time by 20 and 22 hours, respectively. Try to fly Mon.-Thurs., when flights are cheaper and easier to book. Pay for your ticket as soon as your plans are firm. If prices go up there is no charge added, but merely booking doesn't guarantee the lowest price. Make sure that airlines, hotels, and car agencies get your phone number too—not only your travel agent's—in case any problems with availability arise (travel agents are often closed on weekends). It's not necessary, but it's a good idea to call and reconfirm flights 24-72 hours in advance.

First-row (bulkhead) seats are good for people who need more leg room, but bad for watching the movie. Airlines will give you special meals (vegetarian, kosher, low cal, low salt) often at no extra charge, but you must notify them in advance. If you're "bumped" from an overbooked flight, you're entitled to a comparable flight to your destination within one hour. If more than an hour elapses, you get denied-boarding compensation, which goes up proportionately with the amount of time you're held up. Sometimes this is cash or a voucher for another flight to be used in the future. You don't have to accept what an airline offers on the spot, if you feel it isn't being fair.

Traveling with Children

Fares for children ages 2-12 are 50% of the adult fare; children under two not occupying a seat travel free. If you're traveling with an infant or active toddler, book your flight well in advance and request the bulkhead seat or first row in any section and a bassinet if available. Many carriers have fold-down cribs with restraints for baby's safety and comfort. Toddlers appreciate the extra space provided by the front-row seats. Be sure to reconfirm, and arrive early to ensure this special

seating. On long flights you'll be glad that you took these extra pains.

Although most airlines have coloring books, puppets, etc., to keep your child busy, it's always a good idea to bring your own. These can make the difference between a pleasant flight and a harried ordeal. Also, remember to bring baby bottles, formula, diapers, and other necessities, as many airlines may not be equipped with exactly what you need. Make all inquiries ahead of time so you're not caught unprepared.

Baggage

You are allowed two free pieces of luggage—one large, the other smaller—and a carry-on bag. The two main pieces can weigh up to 70 pounds each; an extra charge is levied for extra weight. The larger bag can have an overall added dimension (height plus width plus length) of 62 inches; the smaller, 55 inches. Your carry-on must fit under your seat or in the overhead storage compartment. Purses and camera bags are not counted as carry-ons and may be taken aboard. Surfboards and bicycles are about $15 extra. Although they make great mementos, remove all previous baggage tags from your luggage; they can confuse handlers. Attach a sturdy holder with your name and address on the handle, or use a stick-on label on the bag itself. Put your name and address inside the bag, and the address where you'll be staying in Hawaii if possible. Carry your cosmetics, identification, money, prescriptions, tickets, reservations, change of underwear, camera equipment, and perhaps a change of shirt or blouse in your carry-on.

Visas

Entering Hawaii is like entering anywhere else in the country. Foreign nationals must have a current passport and proper visa, an ongoing or return air ticket, and sufficient funds for the proposed stay in Hawaii. Canadians do not need a visa or passport, but must have proper identification (such as passport, driver's license, or birth certificate).

Agricultural Inspection

Remember that before you leave Hawaii for the Mainland, all of your bags are subject to an agricultural inspection, a usually painless procedure taking only a minute or two. To facilitate your departure, leave all bags unlocked until after inspection. There are no restrictions on beach sand, coconuts, dried flower arrangements, fresh flower lei, pineapples, certified pest-free plants, seashells, seed lei, and wood roses. However, avocado, litchi, and papaya must be treated before departure. Some other restricted items are berries, fresh gardenias, roses, jade plants, live insects, snails, cotton, plants in soil, soil itself, and sugarcane. For any questions pertaining to plants that you want to take to the Mainland, call the Agricultural Quarantine Inspection office, tel. (808) 586-0844 in Honolulu.

INTERISLAND CARRIERS

The only effective way for most visitors to travel between the Hawaiian islands is by air. Luckily, Hawaii has excellent air transportation that boasts one of the industry's safest flight records. The following airlines have competitive prices, with interisland flights at about $75 each way. You can also save money (about $15) if you **take the first or last daily scheduled flight.** This offer usually applies only to flights to and from Honolulu, but do check because the policy often changes. Another alternative is to **purchase a booklet of six flight vouchers.** You save about $7 per ticket, and they are *transferable*. Just book a flight as normal and present the filled-in voucher to board the plane. Vouchers are perfect for families or groups of friends, and can be purchased at any ticket office or at Honolulu International Airport.

Note: Although every effort has been made for up-to-date accuracy, remember that schedules are constantly changing. The following should be used only as a point of reference. Please call the airlines listed below for their latest schedules.

Hawaiian Airlines

Hawaiian Airlines, tel. (800) 367-5320 nationwide, (800) 882-8811 statewide, Web site: www.hawaiianair.com, offers the most flights. From Honolulu to Kauai, 17 nonstop flights go from 5:30 a.m. to 8 p.m.; flights to Maui begin at 5:30 a.m. with one every 20-30 minutes until 9 p.m., and there are also regularly scheduled flights to Kapalua, West Maui Airport; flights to Hilo and Kona leave about every hour or so from

5:20 a.m. to 7 or 8 p.m. Also, although fewer, daily flights are offered to Lanai and Molokai, and between all the major island airports.

Aloha Airlines

Aloha Airlines, tel. (800) 367-5250, (800) 235-0936 Canada, (808) 484-1111 on Oahu, Web site: www.alohaair.com, connects Honolulu to Kauai, Maui, and both Kona and Hilo on the Big Island of Hawaii. Aloha's routes to Kauai are: from Honolulu, 22 nonstop flights from 5:30 a.m. until 7:50 p.m.; to Maui, about 29 flights daily, with one departing every 20 minutes or so from 5:15 a.m. to 8 p.m.; to Kona, 19 flights daily from 5:25 a.m. to 7:20 p.m.; and to Hilo, 16 flights from 5:25 a.m. to 7 p.m.

A subsidiary of Aloha Airlines, **Aloha Island Air,** tel. (800) 323-3345 nationwide, (800) 652-6541 statewide, offers scheduled flights connecting Honolulu to Molokai, Lanai, and to Kahului and Kapalua on Maui. In addition, there are flights from Hoolehua to Kalaupapa, both on Molokai, and from Kahului to Hana and Lanai. Flights to and from some destinations involve a stopover.

Mahalo Air

Mahalo Air, tel. (808) 833-5555 on Oahu, (800) 277-8333 from the neighbor islands, and (800) 462-4256 from the U.S. and Canada, Web site: www.islander-magazine.com/mahaloschedule.html, is the newest competitor to the market, with flights fanning out from Honolulu. Eight flights throughout the day connect Honolulu to Kona and Lihue, with seven daily flights to Kahului and Molokai, and four a day to Kapalua, Maui.

Trans Air

Trans Air, tel. (800) 634-2094 or (808) 885-5134 in Kamuela, Web site: www.travelocity.com, runs one commuter route between Honolulu and Kamuela (Waimea), aside from their charter services. Flights from Honolulu run daily at 4:30 p.m.; Thursday, Friday, and Saturday at 4:45 p.m.; and Sunday, Monday, and Tuesday at 6 a.m. For each flight, there is a layover of about a half hour in Kamuela before the return to Honolulu.

DOMESTIC CARRIERS

The following are the major domestic carriers to and from Hawaii. The planes used are pri-

INTERISLAND AIR ROUTES

Major Airports With Full Facilities

Secondary Airport

© J.D. BISIGNANI AND MOON PUBLICATIONS, INC.

marily DC-10s and 747s, with a smaller 727 flown now and again. A list of the "gateway cities" from which they fly direct and nonstop flights is given, but "connecting cities" are not. All flights, by all carriers, land at Honolulu International Airport, except for the limited direct flights to Maui and the island of Hawaii. Only the established companies are listed. Entrepreneurial small airlines such as the now-defunct Hawaii Express pop up now and again and specialize in dirt-cheap fares. There is a hectic frenzy to buy their tickets and business is great for a while, but then the established companies lower their fares and the gamblers fold.

Hawaiian Airlines

One of Hawaii's own domestic airlines has entered the Mainland market. It operates a daily flight from Los Angeles, San Francisco, Las Vegas, Portland, and Seattle to Honolulu, with periodic twice-weekly flights from San Francisco and Seattle to Kahului, Maui. The "common fare" ticket price includes an ongoing flight to any of the Neighbor Islands, and if you're leav-

ing Hawaii, a free flight from a Neighbor Island to the link-up in Honolulu. Senior-citizen discounts for people age 60 or older are offered on trans-Pacific and interisland flights. Scheduled flights to the South Pacific run between Honolulu and Pago Pago twice a week, and once a week to Papeete, Tahiti. Hawaiian Airlines offers special discount deals with Dollar Rent A Car and select major-island hotels. Contact Hawaiian Airlines at (800) 367-5320 Mainland, (800) 882-8811 in Hawaii.

United Airlines

Since its first island flight in 1947, United has become top dog in flights to Hawaii. The Mainland routes connect over 100 cities to Honolulu. The main gateway cities of San Francisco, Los Angeles, Chicago, and Vancouver have direct flights to Honolulu; flights from all other cities connect through these. United also offers direct flights to Maui and to Kona on the Big Island from San Francisco and Los Angeles, and from Los Angeles to Kauai. Continuing through Honolulu, United flights go to Tokyo, where connections can be made for other Asian cities. United offers a number of packages, including flight and hotel on Oahu, and flight, hotel, and car on the Neighbor Islands. United interlines with Aloha Airlines and deals with Hertz Rent A Car. It's the "big guy" and intends to stay that way—the packages are hard to beat. Call (800) 241-6522.

American Airlines
American offers direct flights to Honolulu from Los Angeles, San Francisco, Dallas, and Chicago. It also flies from Los Angeles to Maui, with a connection in Honolulu. Call (800) 433-7300.

Continental
Flights from all Mainland cities to Honolulu connect via Los Angeles, San Francisco, Houston, and Newark. Also available are direct flights from Guam to Honolulu. Call (800) 525-0280 or (800) 231-0856 for international information.

Northwest
Northwest flies into Honolulu from Los Angeles, San Francisco, and Seattle. There are onward flights to Tokyo, Osaka, Nagoya, Manila, Guam, Bangkok, Singapore, Hong Kong, Taipei, and Seoul. Call (800) 225-2525.

Delta Airlines
In 1985, Delta entered the Hawaiian market; when it bought out Western Airlines its share became even bigger. It has nonstop flights to Honolulu from Dallas/Ft. Worth, Los Angeles, and Atlanta, and flights to Kahului, Maui, from Los Angeles. Call (800) 221-1212.

FOREIGN CARRIERS

The following carriers operate throughout Asia and Oceania but have no U.S. flying rights. This means that in order for you to vacation in Hawaii using one of these carriers, your flight must originate or terminate in a foreign city. You can have a stopover in Honolulu with a connecting flight to a Neighbor Island. For example, if you've purchased a flight on Japan Air Lines from San Francisco to Tokyo, you can stop in Hawaii, but you must then carry on to Tokyo. Failure to do so will result in a stiff fine, and the balance of your ticket will not be refunded.

Canadian Airlines International
Nonstop flights from Canada to Honolulu originate in Vancouver and Toronto. Call (800) 426-7007 in the U.S. or (800) 665-7530 in Canada.

Air Canada
Air Canada has weekly direct flights from Vancouver to both Honolulu and Maui. Call (800) 776-3000 for information and schedules.

Air New Zealand
Flights link New Zealand, Australia, and numerous South Pacific islands with Los Angeles via Honolulu. Also offered are special APEX fares from Los Angeles to Australia and New Zealand, with stops in Honolulu and up to five other island points. Call (800) 926-7255 or (800) 262-1234 in the U.S. or (800) 663-5494 in Canada for current information.

Japan Air Lines
The Japanese are the second-largest group, next to Americans, to visit Hawaii. JAL flights to Honolulu originate in Tokyo (Narita), Nagoya, Osaka (Kansai), Sendai, and Fukuoka. In addition, there are flights between Tokyo (Narita) and Kona on the Big Island. There are no JAL flights between the Mainland and Hawaii. Call (800) 525-3663.

Philippine Airlines
Philippine Airlines flies between San Francisco and Manila via Honolulu. Connections in Manila are available to most Asian cities. Call (800) 435-9725.

Qantas
Daily flights connect Sydney, Australia, and Auckland, New Zealand, with Honolulu; flights from other cities go through these hubs. Call (800) 227-4500.

China Airlines
Routes from Honolulu with China Airlines are from Taipei direct or through Tokyo, but flights are not available year-round. Connections are available from Taipei to most Asian capitals. Call (800) 227-5118.

Korean Air
Korean Air offers some of the least expensive flights to Asia. All flights to/from Honolulu go di-

rectly to Seoul. Connections to many Asian cities. Call (800) 438-5000.

Asiana Airlines
Direct daily flights are offered from Honolulu to Seoul, with connections to other Asian cities. Call (800) 227-4262.

OAHU FLIGHT ARRIVALS

The old adage of "all roads leading to Rome" applies almost perfectly to Oahu, though instead of being cobblestones, they're sea lanes and air routes. Except for a handful of passenger ships still docking at Honolulu Harbor, and the direct flights to Maui and the Big Island, all other passengers to and from Hawaii are routed through **Honolulu International Airport.** These flights include direct flights to the Neighbor Islands, which means stopping over at Honolulu International and continuing on the same plane, or more likely changing to an interisland carrier whose fare is included in the original price of the flight.

Honolulu International Airport
This international airport is one of the busiest in the entire country, with hundreds of flights to and from cities around the world arriving and departing daily. In a routine year, over 15 million passengers utilize this facility. The two terminals (directions given as you face the main entranceway) are: the main terminal, accommodating all international and Mainland flights, with a small wing at the far left end of the ground floor for a few commuter airlines; and the **interisland terminal** in a separate building at the far right end of the main terminal.

The ground floor of the **main terminal** is mostly for arriving passengers, and contains the baggage claim area, baggage lockers, car rental agencies, and international and domestic arrival doors, which are kept separate. The second floor is for departing passengers, with most activity centered here, including ticket counters, shops, lounges, baggage handlers, the Pacific Aerospace Museum, a business center, and the entrance to most of the gates. From both levels you can board taxis and TheBus to downtown Honolulu and Waikiki.

The **interisland terminal** services flights aboard Hawaii's own interisland carriers. It has its own snack bars, car rental booths, transportation to and from the city, lounges, information windows, and restrooms. It is only a leisurely five minutes stroll between the two terminals, which is fine if you don't have much baggage; if you do, there are plenty of shuttles every few minutes . . . supposedly!

Services, Information, Tips
For general airport information and arrival and departure information, call (808) 836-6431.

The main **information booth,** tel. (808) 836-6413, is located on the ground level just near the central escalators. Besides general information, it has good maps of the airport, Oahu, Honolulu, and Waikiki. Also, inquiry booths lined up along the ground level and at the interisland terminal are friendly and helpful, but not always stocked with as many maps as the main information booth.

The **lost and found** is located on the ground level of the main terminal, and at the interisland terminal; call (808) 836-6547. The **post office** is across the street from the main entranceway toward the interisland terminal.

Storage lockers are located on both levels of the main terminal and at the interisland terminal. Locker rental is for a 24-hour period, with a refundable key deposit. Baggage lockers and a long-term baggage storage facility are located in the parking structure. Prices depend on the size of baggage and length of storage. You *must* have your claim ticket to retrieve your belongings. The service is well run and efficient.

Money can be a hassle at the airport, especially getting change, which is a downright rip-off, and very bad public relations for visitors. Unfortunately, no one will give you change, putting you at the mercy of $1 bill-change machines located throughout the airport. These machines happily dispense 85 cents for every $1 you put in, so if you want to make a phone call, or the like, you're out of luck. The snack bars will only change money for you with a purchase. For a state that prides itself on the *aloha* spirit and depends on good relations with its visitors, this is a ridiculously poor way of greeting people, or giving them a last impression before they return home. The **foreign currency exchange** is on the second floor of the main terminal along the concourse behind the United ticket window. Here, and at a few smaller exchanges on the ground floor, the charge is one percent per transaction on foreign currency, and the same on

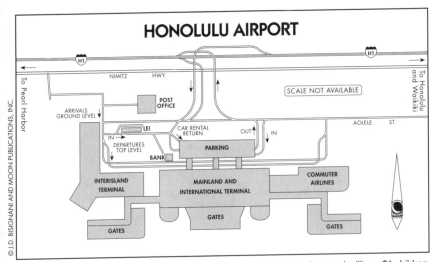

HONOLULU AIRPORT

© J.D. BISIGNANI AND MOON PUBLICATIONS, INC.

traveler's checks, no matter where they're from, with a minimum charge of $1.50.

To refresh and relax, you might visit the **Airport Mini-Hotel,** tel. (808) 836-3044, fax 834-8985, in the main terminal, second level, central lobby, with 19 private, single-bed rooms. You can have a shower for $8.25, which includes soap, towel, shampoo, deodorant, and hairdryer. An eight-hour sleep and a shower runs $33, four hours is $30.25, three hours runs $24.75, and two hours goes for $19.75. If you need a room after 9 p.m. you should make reservations as it probably will be full. Also, **The Shower Tree,** 3085 N. Nimitz Hwy., tel. (808) 833-1411, is only five minutes from the airport with transportation available and luggage storage. This place is a bit like a hostel, with double-bed rooms for $27.25-32.70 and bunk rooms at $39.24 (for two). If the bathroom and TV lounge are down the hall. If these seem a bit pricey, just use the public bathrooms for a quick wash, then choose any one of three small gardens near the central concourse to take a little nap. If you're there just for a short snooze, airport security won't bother you.

Pacific Aerospace Museum

Located in the central lobby on the second floor of the overseas terminal building, this small museum has several interactive aerospace displays and a 27-minute film on the aviation history of Hawaii. Open daily 9 a.m.-6 p.m., entrance is $3 adults,

$2.50 students, seniors, and military, $1 children 6-12; tel. (808) 839-0777. The museum gift shop has a wide variety of items, including hats, books, videos, models, and posters, all relating to aviation and aerospace—perhaps the best selection on the island. Set some time aside to drop by for a look before you get on the plane to leave.

Airport Transportation

The **Wiki Wiki Shuttle** is a free bus that takes you between the main terminal and the interisland terminal. Staffed by courteous drivers, it is efficient—most of the time. When it's not, a nickname could be the "Tricky Tricky Shuttle." Transfer time between the two terminals is only about 10 minutes, which does not include baggage transfer. If you'll be going on to a Neighbor Island make sure the carrier you are using has an interline agreement with the Hawaiian domestic carrier. If not, you must fetch your own bags, place them on the shuttle, and bring them with you to the interisland terminal. Also, if a flight is delayed, it is up to the carrier to notify the Wiki Wiki Shuttle so that adjustments can be made, and they are waiting for you. If your carrier does not contact them, the shuttle bus will follow the normal schedule and may not arrive in time to get you to the interisland terminal. Usually, this is a routine procedure with few problems, but if your connecting schedule is tight, and especially if your carrier has no interline agreement (the airline or your travel agent can tell you), be aware and leave extra time!

Car rental agencies are lined up at booths on the ground floor of both terminals. Many courtesy phones for car rental agencies not at the airport are located in and around the baggage claim area; call for a free van to pick you up and take you to the nearby facility. This procedure even saves the hassle of maneuvering through heavy airport traffic—you usually wait at the island in the middle of the road just outside the baggage claim area. Make sure to specify the number of the area where you'll wait.

If you're driving to the airport to pick up or drop off someone, you should know about **parking.** If you want to park on the second level of the parking garage for departures, you must either take the elevator up to the fourth floor, or down to ground level, and from there cross the pedestrian bridge. There's no way to get across on levels two and three. Parking is $1 for the first half hour, $1 for each additional hour, or $10 for a 24-hour period.

Public transportation to downtown Honolulu, especially Waikiki, is abundant. Moreover, some hotels have courtesy phones near the baggage claim area; if you're staying there, they'll send a van to fetch you. Current charges for taxis, vans, TheBus, and limousine service are posted just outside the baggage claim area, so you won't have to worry about being overcharged.

Only **taxis** that contract with the airport can pick up at the terminal. All others can drop off there but are allowed to pick up only outside the terminal, at a car rental office, for example. From the terminal to Waikiki costs about $21-26, not counting bags. Splitting the fare with other willing passengers can save money. Some companies charge a flat fee of $15 from outside the terminal to Waikiki. A number of vans and motorcoaches leave from the central island in the roadway just outside the baggage claim. They charge about $8, but a wait of up to 45 minutes for one is not out of the ordinary. Moreover, they drop passengers at hotels all over Waikiki, so if you're not one of the first stops by chance, it could be an hour or so after reaching Waikiki before you're finally deposited at your hotel.

Airport Express, tel. (808) 866-7250, charges $8 per person ($4 for children) between the airport and Waikiki, and $13 roundtrip. When going to the airport, you must reserve two days in advance.

You can take **TheBus** (no. 19 or no. 20) to Waikiki via the Ala Moana Terminal, from which you can get buses all over the island. If you're heading north pick up bus no. 20, 51, or 52 just outside the airport. TheBus only costs $1, but you are allowed only one carry-on bag, which must be small enough to be held on your lap. Drivers are sticklers on this point.

TRAVEL BY SHIP

American Hawaii Cruises
This American cruise ship company operates the 800-passenger SS *Independence.* This ship offers a seven-day itinerary that calls at five ports

American Hawaiian Cruises'
SS sIndependence

on the four main islands. For those who want just a taste of a cruise through the islands, three- and four-day trips are also offered. The seven-day fares start at $1,230 per person double occupancy, three- and four-day fares from $670 and $805, respectively. Fares go up from there according to the class and location of your cabin. Children under 18 are often given special rates and cruise free June-Sept. when they share a cabin with their parents. All sailings leave on Saturday from the Aloha Towers in Honolulu. After leaving Honolulu, the seven-day cruise first stops at Nawiliwili on Kauai, followed by Kahului on Maui, then Hilo and Kona on the Big Island, before returning to Honolulu. For the three-day cruise, you board in Honolulu and alight in Kahului. Those on the four-day trip board in Kahului and get off in Honolulu. The ship is a luxury seagoing hotel and gourmet restaurant; swimming pools, health clubs, movies, and nightclubs are all part of the amenities. To enhance the focus on Hawaiian culture, every ship carries a *kumu,* or master teacher, in the capacity of a resource person who conducts activities on board. Onshore excursions are offered at each port of call. Airfare to Hawaii, interisland air flights, rental cars, and accommodation on any island after your cruise can be arranged for you by American Hawaii Cruises. For details contact: American Hawaii Cruises, Robin St. Wharf, 1380 Port of New Orleans Place, New Orleans, LA 70130-1890, tel. (800) 765-7000, fax (504) 585-0690, Web site: www.cruisehawaii.com.

Alternatives

Other companies offering varied cruises include **P&O Lines,** which operates the *Sea Princess* through the South Pacific, making port at Honolulu on its way from the West Coast once a year.

Royal Cruise Line out of Los Angeles, or Auckland alternatively, sails the *Royal Odyssey,* which docks in Honolulu on its South Pacific and Orient cruise, $2,200-4,000.

The **Holland America Line** sails a year-long World Cruise, calling at Honolulu. Call (800) 426-0327.

Society Expeditions offers a 42-day cruise throughout the South Pacific departing from Honolulu. Fares range $3,000-9,000. Call (800) 426-7794.

Information

Most travel agents can provide information on the above cruise lines. If you're especially interested in traveling by freighter, contact: **Freighter Travel Club of America,** P.O. Box 12693, Salem, OR 97309; or **Ford's Freighter Travel Guide,** P.O. Box 505, 22151 Clarendon St., Woodland Hills, CA 91367.

TOUR COMPANIES

Many tour companies advertise packages to Hawaii in large city newspapers every week. They offer very reasonable airfares, car rentals, and accommodations. Without trying, you can get roundtrip airfare from the West Coast and a week in Hawaii for $400-500 using one of these companies. The following companies offer great deals and have excellent reputations. This list is by no means exhaustive.

SunTrips

This California-based tour and charter company sells vacations all over the world. It's primarily a wholesale company but will work with the general public. SunTrips often works with Rich International Air, tel. (305) 871-5113. When you receive your SunTrip tickets, you are given discount vouchers for places to stay that are convenient to the airport of departure. Many of these hotels have complimentary airport pickup service, and will allow you to park your car, free of charge, for up to 14 days, which saves a considerable amount on airport parking fees. SunTrips does not offer assigned seating until you get to the airport. It recommends that you get there two hours in advance, and it ain't kidding! This is the price you pay for getting such inexpensive air travel. SunTrips usually has a deal with a car-rental company. Remember that everyone on your incoming flight is offered the same deal, and all make a beeline for the rental car's shuttle van after landing and securing their baggage. If you have a traveling companion, work together to beat the rush by leaving your companion to fetch the baggage and heading directly for the van as soon as you arrive. Pick your car up, then return for your partner and the bags. Even if you're alone, you could zip over to the car-rental center and then return for your bags without having them sit very long on the carousel. Contact Sun-

Trips, 2350 Paragon Dr., P.O. Box 18505, San Jose, CA 95158, tel. (800) 786-8747 in California, (808) 941-2697 in Honolulu.

Council Travel Services

These full-service, budget-travel specialists are a subsidiary of the nonprofit Council on International Educational Exchange, and the official U.S. representative to the International Student Travel Conference. They'll custom-design trips and programs for everyone from senior citizens to college students. Bona fide students have extra advantages, however, including eligibility for the International Student Identification Card (ISIC), which often gets you discount fares and waived entrance fees. Groups and business travelers are also welcome. For full information, call (800) 226-8624, or write to Council Travel Services at one of these offices: 530 Bush St., San Francisco, CA 94108, tel. (415) 421-3473, or 205 E. 42nd St., New York, NY 10017, tel. (212) 661-1450. Other offices are in Austin, Berkeley, Boston, Davis, Long Beach, Los Angeles, Miami, Portland, San Diego, and Seattle.

Student Travel Network

STA Travel is a full-service travel agency specializing in student travel, regardless of age. Those under 26 do not have to be full-time students to get special fares. Older independent travelers can avail themselves of services, although they are ineligible for student fares. STA works hard to get you discounted or budget rates. STA's central office is at 7202 Melrose Ave., Los Angeles, CA 90046, tel. (213) 934-8722 or (800) 777-0112. STA maintains 39 offices throughout the U.S., Australasia, and Europe, along with **Travel Cuts,** a sister organization operating in Canada. Many tickets issued by STA are flexible, allowing changes with no penalty, and are open-ended for travel up to one year. STA also maintains **Travel Help,** a service available at all offices designed to solve all types of problems that may arise while traveling. STA is a well-established travel agency with an excellent and well-deserved reputation.

Pleasant Hawaiian Holidays

A California-based company specializing in Hawaii, Pleasant Hawaiian Holidays, 2404 Townsgate Road, Westlake Village, CA 91361, tel. (800) 242-9244, makes arrangements for flights, accommodations, and transportation only.

Signature Vacations

Formerly Fiesta West and operating for more than a quarter of a century, this company is Canada's largest complete-package tour operator. Flying mainly from Toronto and Vancouver, but with flights also from Victoria, Calgary, and Edmonton, prepackaged, all-inclusive one-to two-week tours are offered to all the major islands, but to the outer islands only seasonally. Signature Vacations uses Canada 3000 as its main air carrier. All Signature Vacations' bookings are done through travel agents; however, if you need assistance with a purchased tour package, you can call the company's 24-hour worldwide help line, tel. (800) 739-8876, for help, or log on to its Web site: www.signature.ca.

Ocean Voyages

This unique company offers seven- and 10-day itineraries aboard a variety of yachts in the Hawaiian Islands. The yachts, equipped to carry 2-10 passengers, ensure individualized sail training. The vessels sail throughout the islands, exploring hidden bays and coves, and berth at different ports as they go. This opportunity is for anyone who wishes to see the islands in a timeless fashion, thrilling to sights experienced by the first Polynesian settlers and Western explorers. For rates and information contact Ocean Voyages, 1709 Bridgeway, Sausalito, CA 94965, tel. (415) 332-4681.

Travelers with Disabilities

Accessible Vans of Hawaii (formerly Wheelers of Hawaii), 186 Mehani Circle, Kihei, HI 96753, tel. (808) 879-5521, (800) 303-3750 statewide, (888) AVAVANS nationwide, fax (808) 879-0649, is a private company owned and operated by Dave McKown, who has traveled the world with his brother, a paraplegic. Dave knows firsthand the obstacles faced by people with disabilities, and his disabled associate does as well. Accessible Vans of Hawaii provides a full-service travel agency, booking rooms, flights, and activities for the physically disabled. Wheelchair-lift-equipped vans are rented on Oahu, Maui, and the Big Island; $109 a day or $560 a week, plus tax. If a van is needed on Kauai, it must be shipped at the renter's expense. Dave and his associate are good sources of information for any traveler with disabilities.

Ecotours to Hawaii

Sierra Club Trips offers Hawaii trips for nature lovers who are interested in an outdoor experience. Various trips include hikes over Maui's Haleakala and, on Kauai, a kayak trip along the Na Pali Coast and a family camping spree in the Kokee region. All trips are led by experienced guides and are open to Sierra Club members only ($35 per year to join). For information contact the Sierra Club Outing Department, 85 2nd St., 2nd Fl., San Francisco, CA 94104, tel. (415) 775-5500.

Earthwatch allows you to become part of an expeditionary team dedicated to conservation and the study of the natural environment. An expedition in Hawaii might include studying dolphins in Kewalo Basin Marine Mammal Laboratory, humpback whales around the islands, or the living reefs of Maui. Basically, you become an assistant field researcher—your lodgings might be a dorm room at the University of Hawaii, and your meals might come from a remote camp kitchen. Fees vary and are tax deductible, and different projects are offered at various times of the year. If you are interested in this learning experience, contact the nonprofit Earthwatch, 680 Mt. Auburn St., P.O. Box 9104, Watertown, MA 02272, tel. (617) 926-8200 or (800) 776-0188, fax (617) 926-8532, Web site: www.earthwatch.org, e-mail: info@earthwatch.org.

Nature Expeditions International offers quality tours. Trips are nine- or 15-day, four-island, natural-history expeditions, with emphasis on plants, birds, and geology. The guides are experts in their fields and give personable and attentive service. Contact Nature Expeditions International at 6400 E. El Dorado, Suite 200, Tucson, AZ 85714, tel. (520) 721-6712 or (800) 869-0639.

Backroads, 1516 5th St., Suite PR, Berkeley, CA 94710-1800, Web site: www.backroads.com, e-mail: goactive@backroads.com, tel. (510) 527-1555 or (800) 462-2848, fax (510) 527-1444, arranges easy-on-the-environment bicycle and hiking trips to the Big Island and a multisport trip to Maui. Basic tours include: six-day hiking tour $1,795; eight-day bicycle tour $1,895; or a six-day hike/bike/snorkel/kayak tour for $2,595. Prices include accommodations, most meals, and professional guide service. Airfare is not included, and bicycles and sleeping bags can be rented (B.Y.O. okay!) for reasonable rates.

Crane Tours, 22351 Mission Circle, Chatsworth, CA 91311-1257, tel. (818) 773-4601, owned and operated by Bill Crane, has been taking people kayaking and backpacking to the Big Island, Maui, and Kauai since 1976, including tours he leads for the Sierra Club. Although the number of tours he leads yearly has dwindled, he is still offering at least one a year. Prices for these eco-adventures start at about $650 (airfare not included). Call for information on what's available.

GETTING AROUND

Touring Oahu is especially easy, since almost every normal (and not so normal) mode of conveyance is readily available. You can rent anything from a moped to a pedicab, and the competition is very stiff, which helps keep prices down. A few differences separate Oahu from the other islands. To begin with, Oahu has a model public transportation system called TheBus—not only efficient, but very inexpensive. Also, Oahu is the only island that has a true expressway system, though along with it comes rush hour and traffic jams. A large part of Oahu's business is processing people, even if it's only to send them on to another island! The agencies operating these businesses on the island are masters at moving

people down the road. With the huge volume of tourists that visit every year, it's amazing how smoothly it works. The following is a cross section of what's available and should help you to decide how you want to get around. Have fun!

CAR RENTALS

Does Hawaii really have more rental cars than pineapples? Oahu's Yellow Pages have seven pages of listings and ads for car rental agencies. You can rent anything from a 60-passenger Scenic-cruiser to a 60cc moped. Even so, if you visit the islands during a peak tourist frenzy without reserving your wheels in advance, you'll be marooned at the airport.

There's a tremendous field of cars and agencies from which to choose and they're cheaper than anywhere else in America. Special deals come and go like tropical rain showers; swashbuckling price-slashings and come-ons are common all over the rental car market. A little knowledge combined with some shrewd shopping around can save you a bundle. And renting a car is the best way to see the islands if you're going to be there for a limited time. Outside of Oahu, it simply isn't worth hassling with the public transportation system, or relying on your thumb.

Requirements

A variety of requirements are imposed on the renter by car agencies, but the most important clauses are common. Some of the worst practices being challenged are: no rentals to people under 25 and over 70, and no rentals to military personnel or Hawaiian residents! Before renting, check that you fulfill the requirements. Generally, you must be 21, although some agencies rent to 18-year-olds, while others still require you to be 25. You must possess a valid driver's license, with licenses from most countries accepted, but if you are not American, get an International Driver's License to be safe. You should have a major credit card in your name. This is the easiest way to rent a car. Some companies will take a deposit, but it will be very stiff. It could easily be $50 per day on top of your rental fees and sometimes much more. In addition, they may require a credit check on the spot, complete with phone calls to your employer and bank. If you damage the car, charges will be deducted from your deposit, and the car company itself determines the extent of the damages. Some companies *will not* rent you a car without a major credit card in your name, no matter how much of a deposit you are willing to leave.

When to Rent

On this one, you'll have to make up your own mind, because it's a "bet" that you can either win or lose big. But it's always good to know the odds before you plop down your money. You can reserve your car in advance when you book your air ticket, or play the field when you get there. If you book in advance, you'll obviously

have a car waiting for you, but the deal that you made is the deal that you'll get—it may or may not be the best around. On the other hand, if you wait, you can often take advantage of excellent on-the-spot deals. However, you're betting that cars are available. You might be totally disappointed and not be able to rent a car at all, or you might make a honey of a deal.

If you're arriving during the peak seasons of Christmas, Easter, and late summer vacation, *absolutely book your car in advance.* They are all accounted for during this period, and even if you can find a junker from a fly-by-night, it'll price-gouge you mercilessly. If you're going off-peak, you stand a good chance of getting the car you want at the price you want. It's generally best to book ahead, but the majority of car companies have toll-free 800 numbers (p. 132). At least call them for an opinion of your chances of getting a car upon your intended arrival.

Rates

If you pick up a car-rental brochure at a travel agency, notice that the prices for Hawaii rentals are about the lowest in the United States. The two rate options for renting are mileage and flat rate. A third type, mileage/minimum, is generally a bad idea unless you plan to do some heavy-duty driving. Mileage rate costs less per day, but you are charged for every mile driven. Mileage rates are best if you drive less than 30 miles per day—but even on an island that isn't much! The flat rate is best, providing a fixed daily rate and unlimited mileage. With either rate, you buy the gas; don't buy the cheapest because the poor performance from low octane eats up your savings.

Discounts of about 10-15% for weekend, weekly, and monthly rates are available. It's sometimes cheaper to rent a car for the week even if you're only going to use it for five days. Both weekly and monthly rates can be split between Neighbor Islands.

The average price of a subcompact standard shift, without a/c, is $30 per day, $120 per week (add about $8 per day or $50 per week for an automatic), but rates vary widely. Luxury cars are about $10 per day more, with a comparable weekly rate. Most of the car companies, local and national, offer special rates and deals. These deals fluctuate too rapidly to give any hard-and-fast information. They are common, however, so make sure to inquire. Also, peak periods have "blackouts" where normally good deals no longer apply.

Warning: If you keep your car beyond your contract, you'll be charged the highest daily rate unless you notify the rental agency beforehand. *Don't keep your car longer than the contract without notifying the company.* Companies are *quick* to send out their repossession specialists. You might find yourself in a situation with your car gone, a warrant issued for your arrest, and an extra charge on your bill. A simple courtesy call notifying the company of your intentions saves a lot of headaches and hassle.

What Wheels to Rent

The super-cheap rates on the eye-catcher brochures refer to subcompact standard shifts. The price goes up with the size of the car and with an automatic transmission. As with options on a new car, the more luxury, the more you pay. If you can drive a standard shift, get one! They're cheaper to rent and operate and a standard shift gives you greater control. AM/FM radios are good to have for entertainment and for weather and surf conditions. If you have the choice, take a car with cloth seats instead of sticky vinyl.

Insurance

Before signing your car-rental agreement, you'll be offered "insurance" for around $10 per day. Since insurance is already built into the contract (don't expect the rental agency to point this out), what you're really buying is a waiver on the deductible ($500-1,000), in case you crack up the car. If you have insurance at home, you will almost always have coverage on a rental car—including your normal deductible—although not all policies are the same, so check with your agent. Also, if you haven't bought its waiver, and you have a mishap, the rental agency will put a claim against your major credit card on the spot for the amount of deductible, even if you can prove that your insurance will cover. It'll tell you to collect from your insurance company because it doesn't want to be left holding the bag on an across-the-waters claim. If you have a good policy with a small deductible, it's hardly worth paying the extra money for the waiver, but if your own policy is inadequate, buy the insurance. Also, most major credit cards offer complimentary car-rental insurance as an incentive for using their cards to rent the car. Simply call the toll-free number of your credit card company to see if this service is included.

Driving Tips

Protect your children as you would at home with car seats. Their rental prices vary considerably: Alamo offers them free of charge; National charges $3 per day; Hertz needs 48 hours notice; Dollar gives them free but they're not always available at all locations. Almost all the agencies can make arrangements if you give them enough notice. Check before you go and if all else fails, bring one from home.

There are few differences between driving in Hawaii and on the Mainland. Just remember that many people on the roads are tourists and can be confused about where they're going. Since many drivers are from somewhere else, there's hardly a "regular style" of driving in the islands. A farmer from Iowa accustomed to poking along on back roads can be sandwiched between a frenetic New Yorker who's trying to drive over his roof and a super-polite but horribly confused Japanese tourist who normally drives on the left.

In Hawaii, drivers don't honk their horns except to say hello, or in an emergency. It's considered rude, and honking to hurry someone might earn you a knuckle sandwich. Hawaiian drivers reflect the climate: they're relaxed and polite. Oftentimes, they'll brake to let you turn left when they're coming at you. They may assume you'll do the same, so be ready, after a perfunctory turn signal from another driver, for him or her to turn across your lane. The more rural the area, the more apt this is to happen.

It may seem like common sense, but remember to slow down when you enter the little towns strung along the circle-island route. It's easy to bomb along on the highway and flash through these towns, missing some of Hawaii's best scenery. Also, rural children expect *you* to be watchful, and will assume that you are going to stop for them when they dart out into the crosswalks.

The **H-1, H-2, and H-3 freeways** throw many Mainlanders a Polynesian "screwball." Accustomed to driving on super highways, Mainlanders assume that these are the same. They're not. Oahu's super highways are much more twisted, turned, and convoluted than most Mainland counterparts. Subliminally they look like a normal freeway, except that they've been tied into a Hawaiian knot. There are split-offs, crossroads, and exits in the middle of the exits. Stay alert and don't be lulled into familiar complacency.

B.Y.O. Car

If you want to bring your own car, write for information to: Director of Finance, Division of Licenses, 1455 S. Beretania St., Honolulu, HI 96814. However, unless you'll be in Hawaii for a bare minimum of six months and will spend all your time on one island, don't even think about it. It's an expensive proposition and takes time and plenty of arrangements. From California, the cost is at least $600 to Honolulu, and an additional $100 to any other island. To save on rental costs, it would be better to buy and sell a car there, or to lease for an extended period. For information on licensing and insurance on Oahu, contact the County Finance Department, tel. (808) 532-7700.

Car Rental Agencies

When you arrive at any of Hawaii's airports, you'll walk the gauntlet of car rental booths and courtesy phones shoulder to shoulder along the main hallways. Of the two categories of car rental agencies in Hawaii, each has its own advantage. The first category is the big national firms like Dollar, National, Hertz, Avis, and Budget. These big guys are familiar, easy to work with, sometimes offer special fly/drive deals with airlines, and live up to their promises. If you want your rental experience to be hassle-free, they're the ones. Also, don't be prejudiced against them just because they're so well known; sometimes they offer the best deals. Although these companies carry mostly sedans, some now also rent Jeeps, sport-utility vehicles, other 4WD vehicles, trucks, and vans.

Hawaii has spawned a good crop of local entrepreneurial rental agencies. Their deals and cars can range, like rummage-sale treasures, from great finds to pure junk. These companies have the advantage of being able to cut deals on the spot. If nothing is moving from their lot on the day you arrive, you might get a real bargain. Unfortunately, mixed in this category is a hodgepodge of fly-by-nights. Some of these are small, but adequate, while others are a rip-off. Their cars are bad, their service is worse, and they have more hidden costs than a Monopoly board.

National Agencies

All of the following national companies have locations in Waikiki. The local phone numbers given are for the main location at Honolulu International Airport and/or other reservations numbers. Call for more details.

One of the best national firms with an excellent reputation for service and prices is **Dollar Rent A Car,** tel. (808) 831-2330 or 944-1544, (800) 342-7398 statewide, or (800) 800-4000 worldwide, Web site: www.dollarcar.com, which has an excellent reputation and very competitive prices. Dollar rents mostly Chrysler vehicles: sedans, jeeps, convertibles, and 4WDs. Great weekly rates, and all major credit cards accepted.

Alamo, tel. (808) 833-4585 or (800) 327-9633, Web site: www.goalamo.com, has good weekly rates. Mostly GM cars.

National Car Rental, tel. (808) 831-3800 or (800) 227-7368 worldwide, features GM and Nissan cars and accepts all major credit cards. Sometimes you can rent without a credit card if you leave a $100 per day deposit—less if you take full insurance coverage.

Avis, tel. (808) 834-5536, 841-5295, or (800) 321-3712 nationwide, features late-model GM cars as well as most imports and convertibles.

Budget, tel. (808) 537-3600 or (800) 527-0700 worldwide, offers competitive rates on a variety of late-model Ford and Lincoln-Mercury cars and specialty vehicles.

Hertz, tel. (808) 831-3500 or (800) 654-3011 worldwide, Web site: www.hertz.com, is competitively priced with many fly/drive deals. Hertz features Ford vehicles.

Thrifty, tel. (808) 833-0046 or (800) 367-2277 worldwide, Web site: www.thrifty.com, uses Chrysler Corp. vehicles.

Enterprise, tel. (800) 736-8222 in Honolulu or (800) 325-8007 out of town, handles mostly GM cars.

Sears, tel. (808) 599-2205, or (800) 527-0770 elsewhere, accepts Sears credit cards.

Local Agencies

These firms offer bargain rates and older cars. Many of these rent without a major credit card, but they require a stiff deposit. Sometimes they even rent to those under 21, but you'll have to show reservations at a major hotel. Some where you usually make out all right are: **VIP** (Very Inexpensive Prices), tel. (808) 488-6187 or 924-6500; **JN,** tel. (808) 831-2724, which also has trucks and vans; and **Paradise Isle Rentals,** tel. (808) 922-2224, which carries Jeeps, sports cars and convertibles, motorcycles, and mopeds.

Fantasy and Vanity Rentals

The most distinctive and fun-filled cars on Oahu are the sports cars and luxury imports available from **Ferrari Rentals,** tel. (808) 942-8725, in Waikiki at 1879 Kalakaua Ave. This company has a fleet of American and European classic cars, like Viper, Corvette, Ferrari, Porsche, Jaguar, Mercedes, and BMW. The magnificent Lamborghine Diablo goes for the equally magnificent price of $1,300 per day, while they let the lowly Corvette out for the mere pittance of only $260 per day.

ALTERNATE TRAVEL

TheBus

If Dorothy and her mates had TheBus to get them down the Yellow Brick Road, she might have chosen to stay in Oz and forget about Kansas. TheBus, TheBus, ThewonderfulBus is the always-coming, slow-moving, go-everywhere friend of the budget traveler. Operated by Oahu Transit Services, Inc. (OTS), it could serve as a model of efficiency and economy in any city of the world. What makes it more amazing is that it all came together by chance, beginning as an emergency service in 1971. These brown, yellow, and orange coaches go up and down both the windward and leeward coasts, through the interior, while passing through all of the major and most of the minor towns in between, and most often stopping near the best sights.

Route signs are located on the front of the bus and near the bus doors. The **direction** in which TheBus travels is posted after the number and the name of the town. They are designated as EB (eastbound toward Diamond Head) and WB (westbound toward the airport). The **fare** is only $1 adult, 50 cents for students between ages 6-19, while kids under six who can sit on a parent's lap aren't charged at all. The fare is paid in *exact change* upon entering. Even putting a $1 bill for the student fare into the box and not expecting change is unacceptable. Adult **monthly bus passes,** good at any time and on all

routes, are $25, but be aware that they are good only from the first to the last day of every month. If you buy a pass in midmonth, or even later, it's still full price! A student monthly pass is $12.50. Passes for senior citizens and disabled passengers are good for two years and cost $20, or $6 will get you a half-fare discount card good for four years—you need pay only 50 cents for each ride. Seniors (65 or older) must furnish proof of age and will be given the pass within a few minutes of having an ID photo taken. Monthly passes are available at **TheBus Pass Office,** open Mon.-Fri. 7:30 a.m.-3:30 p.m., at 811 Middle St., tel. (808) 848-4500. Route 1, Kalihi Bus stops within a few feet of TheBus Pass Office.

Transfers are free and are issued upon request when entering TheBus, but you can only use them for ongoing travel in the same direction, and on a different line (numbered bus). They are also timed and dated, good for approximately 30 minutes to one hour.

Only baggage that can be placed under the seat or on one's lap is permitted; baby strollers that fold up are allowed. Seeing-eye dogs and other similar service animals can accompany a passenger, but all other animals must be in a carrier that fits under the seat or on the lap. No smoking is allowed, and eating or drinking is not permitted. Please use radios or similar devices with headphones only.

Some buses are now equipped with bike racks, which makes it easier to get around town or out of town without having to jostle with all the traffic. Bike racks carry two bikes only. First, let the bus driver know that you wish to load your bike. Then pull down to unfold the rack, if it isn't down already, and securely set the bike wheels into the slots. Pull up on the securing arm to lock your bike in, then board. When leaving the bus, be sure to let the driver know that you want to unload your bike, or it may go to the next stop without you. For additional instructions, consult the *How to Use the New Bike Rack for Buses* booklet, available from TheBus office.

There are about 75 routes in the system. Get full **route and schedule information** by calling TheBus at (808) 848-5555, 5:30 a.m.-10 p.m., or by visiting the information booth at the Ala Moana Terminal, where you can pick up fliers and maps. For other general information and attractions along the routes call (808) 296-1818 with access code

8287. An excellent, inexpensive little guide is *Hawaii Bus and Travel Guide* by Milly Singletary, available in most bookstores. Recorded information on routes and attractions is available 24 hours a day at (808) 296-1818. TheBus lost and found office can be contacted at (808) 848-4444.

The following are some popular destinations and their bus numbers, all originating from the Ala Moana Terminal: **Aloha Tower,** no. 19, 20, 47; **Airport,** no. 19 or no. 20; *Arizona* **Memorial, Pearl Harbor,** no. 20, 47, 50, or 52 Wahiawa (not no. 52 Kaneohe); **Bishop Museum,** no. 2 School; **Chinatown,** no. 1, 2, 4, 19, 20, 47, 51, or 52 Wahiawa; **Fisherman's Wharf,** no. 19, 20 or 52 Kaneohe; Hanauma Bay, no. 1, 22, or 58, beach bus weekends; **Honolulu (downtown),** no. 1, 2, 3, 4, 9, 11, or 12; **Punchbowl,** no. 15; **Polynesian Cultural Center,** 52 Wahiawa/circle island, 55 Kaneohe/circle island; **Queen Emma Summer Palace,** no. 4; **Sea Life Park,** no. 22, 57, 58; **Waikiki Beach,** no. 2, 4, 8, 14, or 20.

The **Beach Bus,** no. 22, starts on Kuhio Ave. near Kalakaua Ave. and services all of the beach areas, including Hanauma Bay and Sandy Point; Sea Life Park is its terminus. Once a seasonal service, the Beach Bus now operates year-round.

Circling the island by bus is a terrific way to see the sights and meet people along the way. The circle route takes about four hours if you ride the entire loop, but you can use the transfer system to give yourself a reasonable tour of only the sights that strike your fancy. The **circle-is-land** bus is no. 52, but remember that there are two no. 52 buses, going in different directions. The buses are labeled: **no. 52 Wahiawa Kaneohe** goes inland to Wahiawa, north to Haleiwa, along the North Shore, down the windward coast to Kaneohe and back over the *pali* to Honolulu; **no. 52 Kaneohe Wahiawa** follows the same route but in the opposite direction. If you'll be taking this bus to Pearl Harbor, be absolutely sure to take no. 52 Wahiawa Kaneohe, because if you take the other, you'll have to circle the entire island before arriving at Pearl!

Trolley and Shuttles

The **Waikiki Trolley,** tel. (808) 596-2199, an open-air trolley-like bus, will take you on a tour of Waikiki and Honolulu for $18 adults, $8 children. This all-day pass lets you board, exit, and reboard at 20 different stops. Multiday passes for five consecutive days are available for $30 and $10. Starting from the Royal Hawaiian Shopping Center in Waikiki, the trolley runs two routes, a shopping route and sightseeing route, with several overlapping stops. The red line (sightseeing route) operates 8:30 a.m.-6:30 p.m., leaving its last starting point at 4:30 p.m. The yellow line (shopping route) runs from 9 a.m. to about 10 p.m. Pick up a map/brochure from any activity desk or call the number above.

In addition to this trolley, there are several shuttles that run only to specified sites. All leave from various hotels in Waikiki. The **Arizona**

Waikiki Trolley

J.D. BISIGNANI

Memorial Shuttle Bus runs every 90 minutes 7 a.m.-1 p.m. Call (808) 839-0911 for reservations (a must); $3 per person, one-way. The **Hilo Hattie/Dole Cannery Bus** runs daily to those two shopping sites, leaving every 30 minutes 8:30 a.m.-3:30 p.m. No charge. Going to see the marine exhibits? Take the free, daily **Sea Life Park Hawaii Shuttle.** Call (808) 955-3474 for times and pickup points. The **Waimea Valley Shuttle** runs daily at no cost to the North Shore's best known tourist attraction. For a schedule and boarding locations, call (808) 955-8276.

Taxis

The law says that taxis are not allowed to cruise around looking for fares, so you can't hail them. But they do and you can, and most policemen have more important things to do than monitor cabs. Best is to summon one from your hotel or a restaurant. All are radio-dispatched, and they're usually there in a flash. The fares, posted on the taxi doors, are set by law and are fair, but still expensive for the budget traveler. The rates do change, but expect about $2 for the flag fall, and then 25 cents for each additional one-eighth mile. The airport to Waikiki is about $25, though luggage costs extra. Most cab drivers are quite good, but you may pause and consider if your cab sports the bumper sticker "Caution! I drive like you do!"

Of the many taxi companies, some with good reputations are: **SIDA,** a cooperative of owner-drivers, at (808) 836-0011; **Aloha State Taxi,** tel. (808) 847-3566; **Charley's,** tel. (808) 531-1331; **TheCab,** tel. (808) 422-2222, and **City Taxi,** tel. (808) 524-2121. If you need some special attention like a Rolls-Royce limo, try: **Cloud 9 Limousines,** tel. (808) 524-7999. It is one of at least four dozen limo services on the island.

For **travelers with disabilities** and people in wheelchairs, call **Handicabs of the Pacific,** tel. (808) 524-3866.

Motorcycles and Mopeds

Driving a motorcycle can be liberating and exhilarating, yet because they are unprotected, motorcycle drivers are more vulnerable than drivers of cars and trucks. Enjoy your ride, but be very aware of traffic conditions. Drive safely and defensively, and always wear a helmet. Mopeds fall into the same vehicle category as bicycles, so become aware of all appropriate rules and regulations regarding them before you rent and ride.

For rentals, try **Paradise Isle Rentals,** tel. (808) 922-2224, at 151 Uluniu in Waikiki, where you can ride away with the wind in your face on a Nighthawk, Ninja, or Harley-Davidson for $79-99 a day, or scoot away on a 50cc moped for a daily rate of $20. Also look for mopeds in Waikiki at **Adventure Moped Rentals,** 1705 Kalakaua Ave., tel. (808) 941-2222; **Adventure Rentals,** 1946 Ala Moana Blvd., tel. (808) 944-3131; **Big Mountain Rentals,** 2426 Kuhio Ave., tel. (808) 926-1644; or **Big Sky Rentals,** 1920 Ala Moana Ave., tel. (808) 947-0101.

Hitchhiking

Hitchhiking varies from island to island, both in legality and method. On Oahu, hitchhiking is legal, and you use the tried-and-true style of facing traffic and waving your thumb. But, city ordinance specifies that you can only hitchhike from a bus stop! Not many people try so the pickings are reasonably easy. TheBus, however, is only $1 for anywhere you want to go, and the paltry sum that you save in money is lost in "seeing time."

Two things against you: Many of the people are tourists and don't want to bother with hitchhikers, and many locals don't want to bother with nonlocal hitchhikers. When you do get a ride, most of the time it will be from a *haole* who is either a tourist on his own or a recent island resident. If you are just hitchhiking along a well-known beach area, perhaps in your bathing suit and obviously not going far, you can get a ride more easily. Women should exercise caution like everywhere else in the U.S., and avoid hitchhiking alone.

SIGHTSEEING TOURS

Guided land tours are much more of a luxury than a necessity on Oahu. Because of the excellent bus system and relatively cheap rental cars, you spend a lot of money for a narration and to be spared the hassle of driving. If you've come in a group and don't intend on renting a car, they may then be worth it. Sea cruises and air tours are equally luxurious, but provide glimpses of this beautiful island you'd normally miss. The following partial list of tour companies should get you started.

Note: For ocean, bicycling, and hiking tours, refer to the "Sports and Recreation" section above.

Land Tours

If you're going to take a land tour, you must have the right attitude, or it'll be a disaster. Your tour leader, usually driving the van or bus, is part instructor, comedian, and cheerleader. There's enough "corn" in his jokes to impress an Iowa hog. On the tour, you're expected to become part of one big happy family, and most importantly, to be a good sport. Most guides are quite knowledgeable about Oahu and its history, and they honestly try to do a good job. But they've done it a million times before, and their performance can be as stale as week-old bread. The larger the tour vehicle and the shorter the miles covered, the worse it is likely to be. If you still want a tour, take a full-day jaunt in a small van: you get to know the other people and the guide, who'll tend to give you a more in-depth presentation. Tips are cheerfully accepted. Also, be aware that some tours get kickbacks from stores and restaurants they take you to, where you don't always get the best bargains. Most companies offer free hotel pickup and delivery. Lunch or dinner is not included unless specified, but if the tour includes a major tourist spot like Waimea Falls Park or the Polynesian Culture Center, admission is usually included.

About half a dozen different tours offered by most companies are variations on the same theme, and the cost is fairly uniform. One of the more popular is a **circle-island tour,** including numerous stops around Waikiki, the windward coast, North Shore, and center of the island. These usually run about $50, half that for children. An afternoon and evening **Polynesian Cultural Center Tour,** including admission and dinner show, costs close to $60. Tours to **Pearl Harbor and the** *Arizona* **Memorial** and to **Diamond Head** both run around $25.

Some reputable companies include: **Polynesian Adventure Tours,** tel. (808) 833-3000; **Robert's Hawaii Tours,** tel. (808) 539-9400; and **E Noa Tours,** tel. (808) 591-2561. Hotel activities desks and activity centers around Waikiki can also arrange tours for you or point you in the right direction.

Special Walking Tours
The following are special tours that you should seriously consider.

Walking Tour of Chinatown, tel. (808) 533-3181, by the **Chinese Chamber of Commerce,** leaves every Tuesday at 9:30 a.m. from in front of its offices at 42 N. King Street. The cost is $5 for the two-and-a-half-hour tour. The **Hawaiian Heritage Center** offers a similar historical and cultural two-hour tour of Chinatown, leaving from the Ramsey Galleries at 1128 Smith St. every Friday at 9:30 a.m. The cost is $5 per person. Call (808) 521-2749 for reservations.

Walking Tour of Honolulu is a three-hour tour led by a very knowledgeable volunteer from the **Mission Houses Museum,** who is probably a member of the Cousins' Society and a descendant of one of the original Congregationalist missionaries to Hawaii. Starting with a walk through the houses of the museum, you're led on a wonderfully anecdoted walk through the historical buildings of central Honolulu for only $8 (reduced fees for seniors, *kama'aina,* military, and students). Tours are given on Thursday only and start at 9:30 a.m. from the Mission Houses Museum. Reservations are required; call (808) 531-0481.

Honolulu Time Walks, 2634 S. King St., Suite 3, Honolulu, HI 96826, tel. (808) 943-0731, offers fascinating interpretive walking tours focusing on the city's colorful past. The tours, ranging in price $5-40 (most about $10), sometimes including dinner, are thematic and change regularly. Expect topics like A Journey to Old Waikiki, Mysteries of Moiliili, Scandalous Days of Old Honolulu, and the very popular Ghosts of Honolulu. Master storyteller Glen Grant, in costume, hosts many of the tours. Thematic bus and trolley tours are also offered, and several historical shows are performed at the Waikiki Heritage Theater in the International Marketplace. Extremely authentic and painstakingly researched, these tours and shows are immensely educational and entertaining. You can't find better. Reserve!

The **Hawaii Nature Center,** 2131 Makiki Heights Dr., Honolulu, HI, tel. (808) 955-0100, is a nonprofit organization dedicated to environmental education through a hands on approach. Primarily geared toward school-age children, but welcoming the young at heart, the Hawaii Nature Center offers weekend community programs for families and the public to share in the wealth of Hawaii's magnificent natural environment through interpretive hikes, earth care projects, and nature crafts. This is a wonderful opportunity for visitors to explore Hawaii through direct interaction with the environment.

The volunteer organization **Clean Air Team,** 720 South St. #184, Honolulu, HI 96813, tel. (808) 948-3299, hosts a hike up Diamond Head every Saturday 9 a.m.-noon, regardless of weather, leaving from the front entrance of the Honolulu Zoo. There is no cost for this hike, but donations are accepted to further programs of this non-smoker's rights advocacy group.

Kapi'olani Community College offers a non-credit program of walking and bus tours for senior citizens. Both state residents and visitors may participate. Offered at various times throughout the year, these tours focus on sites of local historic and natural interest. Tours are run 8 a.m.-1 p.m. and cost $12. For Information on registration, contact the Office of Continuing Education and Training, Kapi'olani Community College, 4303 Diamond Head Road, Honolulu, HI 96816, tel. (808) 734-9234.

If you don't want to follow the leader, but still desire to get out and stretch your legs while soaking up a bit of the local color, try a **city walking tour.** In order to promote good health and exercise, the Hawaii Department of Health has put together a fun brochure/map briefly outlining 15 different walks in the downtown Honolulu, Waikiki, and Diamond Head areas. To get a copy so you too can go on your own, write to the Physical Activity Promotion Project, Hawaii Department of Health, Room 217, 1250 Punchbowl St., Honolulu, HI 96813, and ask for the *Honolulu Walking Map.* Be sure to include a business-size SASE.

Oahu by Air

When you soar above Oahu, you realize just how beautiful this island actually is, and considering that the better part of a million people live in this relatively small space, it's amazing just how much undeveloped land still exists in the interior and even along the coast. The following are some air tours worth considering. Remember that small one- or two-plane operations come and go as quickly as cloudbursts. They're all licensed and regulated for safety, but if business is bad, the propellers stop spinning.

Novel air tours are offered from Dillingham Airfield, located in the northwest section of Oahu, a few miles down the Farrington Hwy. from Waialua. Once in the air, you can soar silently above the coast with **Glider Rides,** tel. (808) 677-3404, an outfit offering one- or two-passenger piloted rides infinitely more exciting than the company's name. A plane tows you aloft and you circle in a five-mile radius with a view that can encompass 80 miles on a clear day. The rides are available daily 10:30 a.m.-5 p.m. on a first-come, first-served basis. Cost is $60 each if there are two passengers and $100 for a single person; rides last about 20 minutes. Check in with "Mr. Bill."

Also located at the Dillingham Airfield is **Soar Hawaii Sailplanes,** tel. (808) 637-3147. This company offers 20-, 30-, 40-, and 50-minute rides for $120, $140, $150, and $160, respectively, for two persons; aerobatic rides for one passenger (with parachute!) are the same length as the standard rides but $10 less per ride. Open 10 a.m.-6 p.m.; reservations are recommended.

Islands in the Sky is a one-day flying extravaganza, offered by the most reputable island-based airline, **Hawaiian Airlines.** Using regularly scheduled flights, this daily tour goes from Honolulu to Kona on the Big Island, on to Maui, and then back to Oahu for $315 adults or $295 for kids age 2-11. Stops in Kona and on Maui include dinner and transportation, and transport to and from your hotel in Honolulu is also included. Call (808) 838-1555 for reservations.

Eco Air Tours Hawaii, tel. (808) 839-1499, flies out of Honolulu in a nine-passenger Piper Chieftain. Minimum six passengers to fly. Six-island full- and half-day scheduled excursions are offered, starting from $150 per person. A two-hour flight over Oahu, Kauai, and Niihau is also available. All flights include a narration on ecology, culture, and history of the islands. Ground tours are an added option with the six-island flight, and private charters can be scheduled at $400 an hour for the plane. Reservations are necessary at least 24 hours in advance.

Panorama Air Tours, tel. (808) 244-3356 or (800) 428-1231, has tailor-made tours leaving mostly from Maui, although a nine-seater does operate out of Oahu. Most flights will be in the $120-600 range, depending upon the itinerary. Call for options available.

Helicopter companies rev up their choppers to flightsee you around the island, starting at about $70 per person for a short trip over Honolulu/Waikiki. Prices rise up from there to about $170 for a full island tour. Several companies even offer a night flight over Waikiki for a spectacular light show. Usually, transport to and from the heliport is included in the cost. Chopper companies include: **Hawaii Helicopters,** tel. (800) 994-9099, Web site: www.hawaiiheli.com; **Hawaiian Breeze Helicopters,** tel. (808) 223-2404; **Makani Kai Helicopters,** tel. (808) 834-5813; and **Rainbow Pacific Helicopters, tel. (808) 834-1111.**

Sail and Dinner Cruises

If you're taking a tour at all, your best bet is a sail or dinner cruise. They're touristy, but a lot of fun, and actually good value. Many times money-saving coupons for them are found in the free tourist magazines, and plenty of street buskers in Waikiki give special deals. The latter are mostly on the up and up, but make sure that you know exactly what you're getting. Most of these cruises depart around 5:30 p.m. from the Kewalo Basin Marina, near Fisherman's Wharf, or from one of the piers near the Aloha Tower, and cruise Waikiki toward Diamond Head before returning about two hours later. On board is a buffet, an open bar, live entertainment, and dancing. Costs vary but run from $50 on up, per person. **Windjammer Cruises,** tel. (808) 537-1122 or (800) 367-5000, sets sail from pier 7A near the Aloha Tower on a sunset dinner cruise, where all food is cooked on board. There are four options: luau at sea for $39, the standard buffet dinner for $49 per person, a sit-down dinner for $69, and the sit-down steak and lobster dinner for $99; reduced fares for children. All include a couple of complimentary drinks, the hula show, and dancing. As fine as the food and entertainment are, don't think that this is a getaway. The sailing ship *Kulamanu* can carry 1,000 passengers.

High-tech hits the high seas on the **_Navatek I,_** tel. (808) 848-6360 or (800) 852-4183, a unique bi-hulled ship that guarantees the "most stable ride in the islands." Sailing from Pier 6, you have a choice of an early morning Pearl Harbor cruise ($45, $26.50 for children 2-11), midday luncheon cruise ($47, $28.50), the ultimate sunset/dinner cruise ($140, $110) featuring gourmet food and some of the best island entertainers, and the

sailing off Waikiki

late evening skyline dinner cruise ($75 for main deck, $125 for in the upper salon). *Kama'aina* rates available. During the winter, these become whalewatching cruises with naturalists on board. The parent company, Royal Hawaiian Cruises, continues its "policy of donating a percentage of our ticket proceeds to marine mammal research and preservation."

Dream Cruises, tel. (808) 592-5200 or (800) 400-7300, offers a seasonal (April-Dec.) dolphin-watching tour along the leeward coast on board the *Rainbow I* catamaran. Early and late morning two-and-a-half-hour sails leave from Waianae's small boat harbor and include a small breakfast; $45.95 adults, $24.95 for children 17 and under, transportation from Honolulu included. December-April, several daily whalewatching tours leave from Honolulu's Kewalo Basin and cruise off Waikiki and Diamond Head; $19.95 adults and $12.95 for children. The *Lin Wa II,* a craft that resembles a Chinese junk, runs a tame bottom-fishing tour in Honolulu Harbor once in the afternoon ($45.95) and later a sunset fishing and dinner

J.D. BISIGNANI

cruise ($59.95). The crew will cook what you catch on both of these tours. Non-anglers and children have reduced fares. Other offerings include the twice-an-evening dinner/dance cruise off Waikiki ($45.95/$24.95) and a morning Pearl Harbor Coastal Cruise ($19.95/$12.95). The newer midday Pacific Splash tour ($59.95/$29.95) takes you to a mooring spot where you can play with the water toys, swim, and use the two-story waterslide and trampoline. The use of snuba equipment and jet skis, for an additional $40 and $30 prepaid, respectively, are options for this leisurely fun-filled splash cruise.

Paradise Cruises, tel. (808) 983-7827, also does dinner cruise and show combinations on the *Star of Honolulu, Starlet I,* and *Starlet II* ships. They leave out of the Kewalo Basin 5:15-5:30 for two- to three-and-a-half-hour cruises. Prices range from $31 adult for the Sunset Grill to the $199 Five Star, seven-course French dinner cruise with all the extras.

The **Ali'i Kai Catamaran** packs them in for a sunset dinner cruise and live band dance. At $49 adult and $29 for kids 2-11, the ride includes dinner, a Polynesian show, three free cocktails, and dancing. For $65, you can have all that plus the Magic of Polynesia illusion show. Call (808) 539-9400 for reservations.

Captain Bob's Picnic Sail, tel. (808) 942-5077 or (800) 262-8798, tours Kaneohe Bay daily (except Sunday) and features lunch and all the water activities that you can handle on its four-hour sail 10:30 a.m.-2:30 p.m. Prices run $69 adults, $55 for ages 13-17, and $49 for kids 3-12. You can work off lunch snorkeling or playing volleyball on the beach. The food is passable, but the setting offshore with the *pali* in the background is world-class. Transportation from Waikiki is included.

Outrigger Canoe Tour

Perhaps the most culturally sensitive, if not the most unusual, tour that you might try while on Oahu is a daylong outrigger sailing canoe trip with **Hawaiian Experience.** Although the trade winds always blow on this side and help push the canoe along, you too will paddle. The trip starts at Kailua Bay and heads south to Mokapu Point. From there it returns north to Kaneohe Bay for leisurely water activities on the sandbar. A stop at Kualoa Beach is included before the return

to Kailua Bay. Your guides will teach you about the water and marinelife, the flora, fauna, and geology of the coast, and Hawaiian culture. This tour runs $150 per person. For all details, contact Hawaiian Experience, 327-111A Hekili St., Kailua, HI 96734, tel. (808) 261-5751, fax 261-6634. Three- and four-day trips on Oahu and the Big Island are also offered.

Underwater Cruises

As beautiful as Oahu is topside, it can be more exquisite below the waves. **Atlantis Submarines,** tel. (808) 973-9800, (800) 548-6262, costs $89 adult, $39 children 12 and under, and departs daily every hour on the hour 7 a.m.-4 p.m. from the Hilton Hawaiian Village, where you board the Hilton Rainbow Catamaran that ferries you to the waiting sub. Once aboard, you're given a few instructions and then it's "run silent, run deep, run excited" for about one hour. The sub is amazingly comfortable. Seats are arranged so that everyone gets a prime view through the large windows, and the air is amazingly fresh. In early 1994 a brand-new futuristic sub was launched that measures 96 feet and carries 64 passengers (the original sub seats 48). Outfitted with videocams, it allows the passengers to view the undersea world in every direction, while listening to explanations of the varied sea life through a multilanguage audio system. A thrill of a lifetime.

A similar tour is offered by **Voyager Submarine,** tel. (808) 592-7850. Although you can't live in the yellow submarine, it'll escort you to the sea of green. From the comfort of the new sub, you can view the wonders of life below the waves. Captain, captain, full speed ahead.

Ecotourism in Hawaii

Ecotourism is economically, culturally, socially, and environmentally sensitive and sustainable tourism that helps to promote local communities and organizations and work in harmony with nature. Although small potatoes yet in the Hawaiian (and worldwide) tourism economy, ecotourism and its goals are growing in importance and will become a major factor in the economic vitality of tourism in the state. For more information on ecotourism in Hawaii, contact the Hawaii Ecotourism Association, P.O. Box 61435, Honolulu, HI 96839, tel. (808) 956-2866, e-mail: hea@aloha.net, Web site: www.planet-hawaii.com/hea. In addition, the following organizations also can provide related information and contacts: **Ecotourism Society International,** P.O. Box 755, North Bennington, VT 05257, tel. (802) 447-2121, fax 447-2122, e-mail: ecotsocy@iga.apc.org, Web site: www.ecotourism.org; and **Center for Responsible Travel,** P.O. Box 827, San Anselmo, CA 94979, tel. (415) 258-6594.

The following is a partial list of organizations and companies, both public and private, that offer environmentally sound tours and outings on Oahu.

Hawaii Audubon Society, 212 Merchant St., Suite 320, Honolulu, HI 96813, tel. (808) 528-1432 (hiking and birding)

The Nature Conservancy, 1116 Smith St., Suite 201, Honolulu, HI 96817, tel. (808) 537-4508 (hikes)

Sierra Club, 233 Merchant St., 2nd Fl., Honolulu, HI 96803, tel. (808) 538-6616 (hikes and service trips)

Hawaiian Trail and Mountain Club, P.O. Box 2238, Honolulu, HI 96804, tel. (808) 262-2845 or 488-1161 (hikes)

Oahu Nature Tours, P.O. Box 8059, Honolulu, HI 96830, tel. (808) 924-2473 or (800) 861-6018 (nature and birding hikes)

Hawaiian Outdoor Adventures, 44-321 Kaneohe Bay Dr., Kaneohe, HI 96744, tel. (808) 245-3393, fax 254-5999 (multi-activity, multiday tours)

Hike Hawaii, 91-261 Hanapouli Circle #W, Ewa Beach, HI 96706, tel. (808) 683-3967 (hikes)

Hawaiian Experience, 327-111A Hekili St., Kailua, HI 96734, tel. (808) 261-5751, fax 261-6634 (outrigger canoe tours, Hawaiian culture)

SPECIAL NEEDS

Help for the Handicapped
A person with disabilities can have a wonderful time in Hawaii; all that's needed is a little preplanning. The following is general advice that should help.

Commission on Persons with Disabilities
This state commission was designed with the express purpose of aiding handicapped people. It is a source of invaluable information and a distributor of self-help booklets. Any person with

disabilities heading to Hawaii should write first or visit its offices on arrival. For the *Aloha Guide to Accessibility* ($3), write or visit the head office at: Commission on Persons with Disabilities, 919 Ala Moana Blvd., Room 101, Honolulu, HI 96813, tel. (808) 586-8121; on Maui, 54 High St., Wailuku, HI 96793, tel. (808) 243-5441; on Kauai, 3060 Eiwa St. #207, Lihue, HI 96766, tel. (808) 241-3308; on Hawaii, P.O. Box 1641, Hilo, HI 96820, tel. (808) 933-4747.

General Information
The key for a smooth trip is to make as many arrangements ahead of time as possible. Tell the transportation companies and hotels you'll be dealing with the nature of your handicap in advance so that they can make arrangements to accommodate you. Bring your medical records and notify medical establishments of your arrival if you'll be needing their services. Travel with a friend or make arrangements for an aide on arrival. Bring your own wheelchair if possible and let airlines know if it is battery-powered; boarding interisland carriers requires steps. Airlines will board wheelchairs early on special lifts, but they must know that you're coming. Many hotels and restaurants accommodate disabled persons, but always call ahead just to make sure. Also check for accessibility at theaters, shopping centers, tourist attractions, and parks.

Oahu Services
At Honolulu International Airport, parking spaces are on the fourth floor of the parking garage near each pedestrian bridge, and on each level near the elevators at the interisland terminal. Be aware that the Wiki Wiki Bus, all other buses and vans, and taxis to town have steps.

For getting around, the City of Honolulu offers a curb-to-curb service for disabled persons, $1.50 each way; call **Handi-Van,** tel. (808) 456-5555. You must make arrangements at least a day in advance or up to two weeks in advance. A private special taxi company operating all over the island is **Handi-Cabs of the Pacific,** tel. (808) 524-3866 in Honolulu. The cabs take wheelchair-bound persons. Most of the large **rental car companies** can put hand controls (right or left) on their cars, but some restrict these controls to certain size or type vehicles. They generally require prior arrangements, one or two days at least, preferably when making your advanced reservation. Rates are comparable with or the same as for standard rental cars. **Accessible Vans of Hawaii,** tel. (808) 879-5521 or (800) 303-3750, fax (808) 879-0649, rents wheelchair lift-equipped vans on Oahu, Maui, and the Big Island for $109 a day or $560 a week. This is a full-service travel agency and a good source of information on traveling with disabilities. Valid, out-of-state, **handicapped parking placards** may be used throughout the state of Hawaii. To apply for a Hawaii parking permit, contact the Department of Transportation Services, tel. (808) 523-4245, for an application form and all requirements. Passes for disabled but ambulatory persons using **TheBus** cost $20 and are good for two years. Check at TheBus Pass Office at

811 Middle St., tel. (808) 848-4500; open Mon.-Fri. 7:30 a.m.-3:30 p.m.

For **medical equipment rental** see the following establishments for all kinds of apparatus: Honolulu Orthopedic Supply, tel. (808) 847-0099; American Home Care System, tel. (808) 486-4954; C. R. Newton Co., tel. (808) 949-8389; Ali'i Medical Supply, tel. (808) 524-2279; and Center Pharmacy, tel. (808) 622-2773. If you are staying for any length of time on the island, medical help, nurses, and companions might be arranged through Hawaii Centers for Independent Living, tel. (808) 537-1941.

Medical Services are available 24 hours a day from **Doctors on Call Waikiki,** tel. (808) 971-6000. For hospitals and medical care, see "Health Care," below.

HEALTH AND CONDUCT

In a recent survey published by *Science Digest,* Hawaii was cited as the healthiest state in the U.S. in which to live. Indeed, Hawaiian citizens live longer than anywhere else in America: men to 76 years and women to 82. Lifestyle, heredity, and diet help with these figures, but Hawaii is still an oasis in the middle of the ocean, and germs just have a tougher time getting there. There are no cases of malaria, cholera, or yellow fever. Because of a strict quarantine law, rabies is also nonexistent. On the other hand, tooth decay, perhaps because of the wide use of sugar and the enzymes present in certain tropical fruits, is 30% above the national average. With the perfect weather, a multitude of fresh-air activities, soothing negative ionization from the sea, and a generally relaxed and carefree lifestyle, everyone feels better there. Hawaii is just what the doctor ordered: a beautiful natural health spa. That's one of the main drawing cards. The food and water are perfectly safe, and the air quality is the best in the country.

Handling the Sun
Don't become a victim of your own exuberance. People can't wait to strip down and lie on the sand like a beached whale, but the tropical sun will burn you to a cinder if you're silly. The burning rays come through easier in Hawaii because of the sun's angle, and you don't feel them as

much because there's always a cool breeze. The worst part of the day is 11 a.m.-3 p.m. You'll just have to force yourself to go slowly. Don't worry; you'll be able to flaunt your best souvenir, your golden Hawaiian tan, to your green-with-envy friends when you get home. It's better than showing them a boiled lobster body with peeling skin! If your skin is snowflake white, 15 minutes per side on the first day is plenty. Increase by 15-minute intervals every day, which will allow you a full hour per side by the fourth day. Have faith: this is enough to give you a deep golden, uniform tan.

Haole Rot
A peculiar condition caused by the sun is referred to locally as *haole* rot. It's called this because it supposedly affects only white people, but you'll notice some dark-skinned people with the same condition. Basically, the skin becomes mottled with white spots that refuse to tan. You get a blotchy effect, mostly on the shoulders and back. Dermatologists have a fancy name for it, and they'll give you a fancy prescription with a not-so-fancy price tag to cure it. It's common knowledge throughout the islands that Selsun Blue Shampoo has some ingredient that stops the white mottling effect. Just wash your hair with it and then make sure to rub the lather over the affected areas, and it should clear up.

Bugs

Everyone, in varying degrees, has an aversion to vermin and creepy crawlers. Hawaii isn't infested with a wide variety, but it does have its share. Mosquitoes were unknown in the islands until their larvae stowed away in the water barrels of the *Wellington* in 1826 and were introduced at Lahaina. They bred in the tropical climate and rapidly spread to all the islands. They are a particular nuisance in the rainforests. Be prepared, and bring a natural repellent like citronella oil, available in most health stores on the islands, or a commercial product available in all groceries or drugstores. Campers will be happy to have mosquito coils to burn at night as well.

Cockroaches are very democratic insects. They hassle all strata of society equally. They breed well in Hawaii and most hotels are at war with them, trying desperately to keep them from being spotted by guests. One comforting thought is that in Hawaii they aren't a sign of filth or dirty housekeeping. They love the climate like everyone else, and it's a real problem keeping them under control. Many hotels post a little card in each room instructing you to call the desk if you spot a roach; they'll be happy to charge up to your room and annihilate it. Of a number of different roaches in Hawaii, the ones that give most people the jitters are big bombers over two inches long. Roaches are after food crumbs and the like, and very infrequently bother with a human. Be aware of this if you rent a room with a kitchenette or condo. If you are in a modest hotel and see a roach, it might make you feel better to know that the millionaire in the $600-a-night suite probably has them too. Bring your own spray if you wish, call the desk if you see them, or just let them be.

Seasickness

If you get seasick out on the water, try Dramamine or Bonine tablets, although these may make you sleepy or give you a dry mouth. Benadryl also works, but again can cause sleepiness. Some people swear by ginger tablets, and others try an acupressure wristband like Seabands.

WATER SAFETY

Hawaii has one very sad claim to fame: more people drown here than anywhere else in the world. Moreover, there are dozens of yearly swimming victims with broken necks and backs, or with injuries from scuba and snorkeling accidents. These statistics shouldn't keep you out of the sea, because it is indeed beautiful, benevolent in most cases, and a major reason to go to Hawaii. But if you're foolish, the sea will bounce you like a basketball and suck you away for good. The best remedy is to avoid situations you can't handle. Don't let anyone dare you into a situation that makes you uncomfortable. "Macho men" who know nothing about the power of the sea will be tumbled into Cabbage Patch

This "denizen of the deep" is much more afraid of you than you are of him.

HOWARD LINDEMAN

dolls in short order. Ask lifeguards or beach attendants about conditions, and follow their advice. If local people refuse to go in, there's a good reason. Even experts get in trouble in Hawaiian waters. Some beaches, such as Waikiki, are as gentle as a lamb and you would have to tie an anchor around your neck to drown there. Others, especially on the north coasts during the winter months, are frothing giants.

While beachcombing, or especially when walking out on rocks, never turn your back to the sea. Be aware of undertows (the waves drawing back into the sea). They can knock you off your feet. Before entering the water, study it for rocks, breakers, reefs, and riptides. Riptides are powerful currents, like rivers in the sea, that can drag you out. Mostly they peter out not too far from shore, and you can often see their choppy waters on the surface. If caught in a "rip," don't fight to swim directly against it; you'll lose and only exhaust yourself. Swim diagonally across it, while going along with it, and try to stay parallel to the shore. Don't waste all your lung power yelling, and rest by floating.

When bodysurfing, never ride straight in; come to shore at a 45-degree angle. Remember, waves come in sets. Little ones can be followed by giants, so watch the action awhile instead of plunging right in. Standard procedure is to duck under a breaking wave. You can even survive thunderous oceans using this technique. Don't try to swim through a heavy froth and never turn your back and let it smash you. Don't swim alone if possible, and obey all warning signs. Hawaiians want to entertain you and they don't put up signs just to waste money. The first rule is, "If in doubt, stay out."

Yikes!

Sharks live in all the oceans of the world. Most mind their own business and stay away from shore. Hawaiian sharks are well fed—on fish—and don't usually bother with unsavory humans. If you encounter a shark, don't panic! Never thrash around because this will trigger their attack instinct. If they come close, scream loudly.

Portuguese man-of-wars put out long floating tentacles that sting if they touch you. Don't wash the sting off with fresh water, as this will only aggravate it. Hot salt water will take away the sting, as will alcohol, the drinking or rubbing kind, after-shave lotion, or meat tenderizer

(MSG), which can be found in any supermarket or Chinese restaurant.

Coral can give you a nasty cut, and it's known for causing infections because it's a living organism. Wash the cut immediately and apply an antiseptic. Keep it clean and covered, and watch for infection.

Poisonous sea urchins, such as the lacquerblack *wana,* can be beautiful creatures. They are found in shallow tidepools and will hurt you if you step on them. Their spines will break off, enter your foot, and burn like blazes. There are cures. Vinegar and wine poured on the wound will stop the burning. If not available, the Hawaiian method is urine. It might seem ignominious to have someone pee on your foot, but it'll put the fire out. The spines will disintegrate in a few days, and there are generally no long-term effects.

Hawaiian reefs also have their share of moray eels. These creatures are ferocious in appearance, but will never initiate an attack. You'll have to poke around in their holes while snorkeling or scuba diving to get them to attack. Sometimes this is inadvertent on the diver's part, so be careful where you stick your hand while underwater.

HAWAIIAN FOLK MEDICINE AND CURES

Hawaiian folk medicine is well developed, and its cures for common ailments have been used effectively for centuries. Hawaiian *kahuna* were highly regarded for their medicinal skills, and Hawaiians were by far some of the healthiest people in the world until the coming of the Europeans. Many folk remedies and cures are used to this day and, what's more, they work. Many of the common plants and fruits that you'll encounter provide some of the best remedies. When roots and seeds and special exotic plants are used, the preparation of the medicine is as painstaking as in a modern pharmacy. These prescriptions are exact and take an expert to prepare. They should never be prepared or administered by an amateur.

Common Curative Plants

Arrowroot, for diarrhea, is a powerful narcotic used in rituals and medicines. The pepper plant *(Piper methisticum)* is chewed and the juice is

KUKUI (CANDLENUT TREE)

KAREN M^cKINLEY

Reaching heights of 80 feet, the *kukui* (candlenut) was a veritable department store to the Hawaiians, who made use of almost every part of this utilitarian giant. Used as a cure-all, its nuts, bark, or flowers were ground into potions and salves and taken as a general tonic, applied to ulcers and cuts as an effective antibiotic, or administered internally as a cure for constipation or asthma attacks. The bark was mixed with water and the resulting juice was used as a dye in tattooing, tapa-cloth making, and canoe painting, and as a preservative for fishnets. The oily nuts were burned as a light source in stone holders, and ground and eaten as a condiment called *inamona*. Polished nuts took on a beautiful sheen and were strung as lei. Lastly, the wood itself was hollowed into canoes and used as fishnet floats.

spat into a container for fermenting. Used as a medicine for urinary tract infections, rheumatism, and asthma, it also induces sleep and cures headaches. A poultice for wounds is made from the skins of ripe bananas. Peelings have a powerful antibiotic quality and contain vitamins A, B, and C, phosphorous, calcium, and iron. The nectar from the plant was fed to babies as a vitamin juice. Breadfruit sap is used for healing cuts and as a moisturizing lotion. Coconut is used to make moisturizing oil, and the juice was chewed, spat into the hand, and used as a shampoo. Guava is a source of vitamins A, B, and C. Hibiscus has been used as a laxative.

Kukui nut oil is a gargle for sore throats and a laxative, plus the flowers are used to cure diarrhea. *Noni,* an unappetizing hand-grenade-shaped fruit that you wouldn't want to eat unless you had to, reduces tumors, diabetes, and high blood pressure, and the juice is good for diarrhea. Sugarcane sweetens many concoctions, and the juice of toasted cane was a tonic for sick babies. Sweet potato is used as a tonic during pregnancy, and juiced as a gargle for phlegm. Tamarind is a natural laxative, and contains the most acid and sugar of any fruit on earth. Taro has been used for lung infections and thrush, and as suppositories. Yams are good for coughs, vomiting, constipation, and appendicitis.

HEALTH CARE

Full-service hospitals include: **The Queen's Medical Center,** 1301 Punchbowl St., Honolulu, tel. (808) 538-9011; **Kaiser Permanente,** 3288 Moanalua Road, Honolulu, tel. (808) 834-5333; **Castle Medical Center,** 640 Ulukahiki St., Kailua, tel. (808) 263-5500; **St. Francis Medical Center,** 2230 Liliha, Honolulu, tel. (808) 547-6011; **Straub Clinic and Hospital,** 888 S. King St., Honolulu, tel. (808) 522-4000; and **Kuakini Medical Center,** 347 N. Kuakini St., Honolulu, tel. (808) 536-2236.

Medical services and clinics include: **Doctors on Call,** tel. (808) 971-6000 (for Japanese speaking doctors call 923-9966), for emergencies and "house calls" to your hotel, 24 hours a day; **Kuhio Walk-in Medical Clinic,** 2310 Kuhio Ave., Suite 223, in Waikiki, tel. (808) 924-6699; and **Waikiki Health Center,** 277 Ohua Ave., tel. (808) 922-4787, for low-cost care including pregnancy and confidential VD testing, open 9 a.m.-8 p.m. Mon.-Thurs., until 4:30 p.m. Friday, until 2 p.m. Saturday. You can get a free **blood pressure** check at the fire station in Waikiki, corner of Paki and Kapahulu Streets, daily 9 a.m.-5 p.m.

For dental referral call the **Hawaii Dental Association** information hotline, tel. (808) 536-2135, 24-hour service.

There are literally dozens of **pharmacies** around the island, including: **Kuhio Pharmacy,** at the corner of Kuhio and Nahua, tel. (808) 923-4466; **Center Pharmacy,** 302 California Ave., tel. (808) 622-2773; **Longs Drugs,** in Honolulu at the Ala Moana Shopping Center, tel. (808) 941-4433, at the Kaneohe Bay Shopping Center, tel. (808) 235-4511, and at over 20 other locations around the island; **Waianae Drugs,** 85-910 Farrington Hwy., Waianae, tel. (808) 696-6348; and **Waipahu Drug,** 94-748A Hikimoe, tel. (808) 677-0794.

For **alternative health care** try: **Acupuncture Clinic,** 111 N. King St., tel. (808) 545-8080; **Honolulu School of Massage,** 1123 11th Ave., Suite 301, tel. (808) 733-0000. **Ed Hoopai,** 250 Lewers St., second floor of the Outrigger Village Hotel, Suite 1, tel. (808) 926-9045, is an excellent masseur whose motto is "You're in good hands." He deals basically in headaches, neck and shoulders, and lower backs. **Chiropractic Referral Service,** tel. (808) 478-4022, offers free information and referral to qualified chiropractors. For other chiropractors, acupuncturists, and alternative health care providers, please refer to the Yellow Pages.

PROSTITUTION

Though the small towns and villages are as safe as you can find anywhere in America, Hawaii isn't all good clean fun. Wherever there's a constant tourist flow, a huge military presence, and high cost of living, there will be those people that mama warned you about. Most of the heavy night action occurs in Waikiki and Chinatown. Something about the *vibe* exudes sexuality. The land is raw and wild, and the settings are intoxicating. All those glistening bodies under the tropical sun and the carefree lifestyle are super-conducive to most anything you can imagine.

You can go two ways on the "sleaze" scene in Hawaii: ignore it and remain aloof and never see any; or, look for and find it with no trouble. The following is neither a condemnation nor an endorsement of how you should act and what you should do. It's merely the facts and the choice is up to you.

Prostitution—The Way It Was
Ever since the first ship arrived in 1778, Hawaii has known prostitution. At that time, a sailor paid for a woman one night for one iron nail. Funny, today they'll take a plastic card. Prostitution, rampant until the missionaries arrived in 1819, was indeed a major cause of the tragic population decline of the Hawaiian race. The tradition has carried on into this century. Iwilei was a notorious red-light district in Honolulu at the turn of the century. The authorities, many of whom were clientele, not only turned a blind eye to this scene, but semilegalized it. A policeman was stationed inside the "stockade" and police rules were listed on the five entrances. The women were required to have a weekly VD checkup from the Board of Health, and without a current disease-free certificate they couldn't work. Iwilei was even considered by some to be an attraction: when Somerset Maugham passed through the islands in 1916 on his way to Russia as a spy for England, he was taken there as if on a sightseeing tour. The long-established military presence in Hawaii has also helped to keep prostitution a flourishing business. During WW II, troops were entertained by streetwalkers, houses of prostitution, and at dance halls. The consensus of the military commanders is that prostitution is a necessary evil, needed to keep up the morale of the troops.

The Scene Today
Waikiki prostitution is generally geared toward the tourist, while that of Chinatown for servicemen. All sorts of women solicit—whites, blacks, and Asians—but the majority are young white women from the Mainland. They cruise along in the old-fashioned style, meeting your eyes and giving you the nod. As long as they keep walking the police won't roust them.

Most hookers prefer Japanese clientele, followed by the general tourist, and lastly, the always-broke serviceman. In the terse words of one streetwalker queried about the preference for Japanese, she said, "They're small, clean, fast, and they pay a lot."

A Honolulu policeman on his Kuhio Avenue beat said, "I can't do anything if they keep walking. It's a free country. Besides, I'm not here to teach anyone morals. . . . Last week a john "fell" out of an eight-story window and a prostitute was found with her throat slit. . . . I'm just on the front lines fighting herpes and AIDS, man." Unlike the days of Iwilei, there is absolutely no official control or testing for VD.

Then there is Chinatown; it's as rough as guts. The girls are shabby, the bars and strip joints are shabbier, and the vibe is heavy.

Women can find male prostitutes on most of the beaches of Honolulu and Waikiki. Mostly these transactions take place during the day. Although many men make a legitimate living as "beach boys" instructing in surfing and the like, many are really prostitutes. It's always up to the woman to decide how far her "lessons" proceed.

Massage Parlors, Etc.
Besides streetwalkers, Honolulu has its share of massage parlors, escort services, and exotic dance joints; some will even fly their practitioners to the Neighbor Islands if necessary. For massage parlors and "escort services" you can let your fingers do the walking—through 14 pages in the Honolulu Yellow Pages alone. Many legitimate massage practitioners in Hawaii can offer the best therapeutic massages in a variety of disciplines, including *shiatsu, lomi lomi,* and Swedish. Unfortunately, they share the same listings with the other kind of massage parlors. If the Yellow Pages listing reads something like "Fifi's Playthings—We'll rub it day or night, wherever it is," this should tip you off. Usually they offer escort services too, for both men and women.

Honolulu also has a number of exotic dance clubs. Basically, they're strip joints with an extra twist. The dancers themselves are very attractive women who have been brought over from the Mainland. They can easily make $150 per night dancing, and the majority are not prostitutes. Their act lasts for three songs, and gets raunchier as it goes. If you invite a dancer to have a drink, it'll cost you $10, but it will be a real drink. This gets you nothing but conversation. The patron's drinks aren't as inflated as the scene would suggest, and some think it a bargain for the price of one drink to have a naked woman bumping and grinding just five feet away. Working the sexually agitated male crowd are women who can best be described as "lap sitters." They're almost always older Korean women who look as though they've been through the mill. They'll charge you $20 for a fake drink called *niko hana* (nothing), and then try to entice you over to a dark corner table, where they'll chisel $20 more, for all you can manage, or are brave enough to do, in a dark corner of a nightclub. Their chief allies are dim lights and booze.

ILLEGAL DRUGS

The use and availability of illegal, controlled, and recreational drugs are about the same in Hawaii as throughout the rest of America. Cocaine constitutes the fastest-growing recreational drug, and it's available on the streets of the main cities, especially Honolulu. Although most dealers are small-time, the drug is brought in by organized crime. The underworld here is mostly populated by men of Asian descent, and the Japanese *yakuza* is said to be displaying a heightened involvement in Hawaiian organized crime. Cocaine trafficking fans out from Honolulu.

A newer drug menace hitting the Honolulu streets is "ice." Ice is smokable methamphetamine that will wire a user for up to 24 hours. The high lasts longer and is cheaper than cocaine or its derivative, "crack." Users become quickly dependent, despondent, and violent because ice robs them of their sleep as well as their dignity. Its use is particularly prevalent among late-night workers. Many of the violent deaths in Honolulu have been linked to the growing use of ice.

However, the main drug available and commonly used in Hawaii is marijuana, which is locally called *pakalolo.* There are also three varieties of psychoactive mushrooms that contain the hallucinogen psilocybin. They grow wild, but are considered illegal controlled substances.

Pakalolo Growing
About 30 years ago, mostly *haole* hippies from the Mainland began growing pot in the more remote sections of the islands, such as Puna on Hawaii and around Hana on Maui. They discovered what legitimate planters had known for 200 years: plant a broomstick in Hawaii, treat it right, and it'll grow. *Pakalolo,* after all, is a weed, and it grows in Hawaii like wildfire. The locals quickly got into the act when they realized that they, too, could grow a "money tree." As a matter of fact, they began resenting the *haole* usurpers, and a quiet and sometimes dangerous feud has been going on ever since. Much is made of the viciousness of the backcountry "growers" of Hawaii. There are tales of booby traps and armed patrols guarding their plants in the hills, but mostly it's a cat-and-mouse game between the authorities and the growers. If you, as a tourist, are

tramping about in the forest and happen upon someone's "patch," don't touch anything. Just back off and you'll be okay. Pot has the largest monetary turnover of any crop in the islands, and as such, is now considered a major source of agricultural revenue. There are all kinds of local names and varieties of pot in Hawaii, the most potent being "Kona Gold," "Puna Butter," and "Maui Wowie." These names are all becoming passé.

Hawaiian *pakalolo* is sold slightly differently than on the Mainland. The dealers package it in heat-sealed "Seal-a-Meal" plastic bags. The glory days are over, and many deals, especially on the streets, are rip-offs. All passengers leaving Hawaii are subject to a thorough "agricultural inspection," and you can bet they're not only looking for illegal papayas. In 1984 there was an uproar involving a particular post office on the Big Island. It turned out that a staggering 80% of the outgoing packages contained *pakalolo*. The authorities are getting wise.

THEFT AND HASSLES

Theft and minor assaults can be a problem, but they're usually not violent or vicious as in some Mainland cities. Mostly, it's locals with chips on their shoulders and few prospects, who will ransack your car or make off with your camera. A big Hawaiian or local guy will be obliged to flatten your nose if you look for trouble, but mostly it will be sneak thieves out to make a fast buck.

From the minute you sit behind the wheel of your rental car, you'll be warned not to leave valuables unattended and to lock up your car tighter than a drum. Signs warning about theft at most major tourist attractions help to fuel your paranoia. Many hotel rooms offer coin-operated safes so you can lock your valuables away and relax while getting sunburned. Stories abound about purse snatchings and surly locals just itching to give you a hard time. Well, they're all true to a degree, but Hawaii's reputation is much worse than the reality. In Hawaii, you'll have to observe two golden laws: if you look for trouble, you'll find it, and a fool and his camera are soon parted.

Theft
The majority of theft in Hawaii is of the "sneak thief" variety. If you leave your hotel door un-

locked, a camera sitting on the seat of your rental car, or valuables on your beach towel, you'll be inviting a very obliging thief to pad away with your stuff. You have to learn to take precautions, but they won't be anything like those employed in rougher areas like South America or Southeast Asia; just normal American precautions.

If you must walk alone at night, stay on the main streets in well-lit areas. Always lock your hotel door and windows and place valuable jewelry in the hotel safe. When you leave your hotel for the beach, there is absolutely no reason to carry all your traveler's checks and credit cards, or a big wad of money. Just take what you'll need for drinks and lunch. If you're uptight about leaving money in your beach bag, stick it in your bathing suit or bikini. American money is just as negotiable if it is damp. Don't leave your camera or portable stereo on the beach unattended. Ask a person nearby to watch them for you while you go for a dip. Most people won't mind at all, and you can repay the favor.

While sightseeing in your shiny new rental car, which immediately brands you as a tourist, again, don't take more than what you'll need for the day. Why people leave a camera sitting on the seat of their car is a mystery! Many people lock valuables in the trunk, but remember that most good car thieves can "jimmy" it open as quickly as you can open it with your key. If you must, for some reason, leave your camera or valuables in your car, lock them in the trunk, stash them under a seat back that's been reclined, or consider putting them under the hood. Thieves usually don't look there, and on most modern cars you can only pop the hood with a lever inside of the car. It's not fail-safe, but it's worth a try.

Campers face special problems because their entire camp is open to thievery. Most campgrounds don't have any real security, but who, after all, wants to fence an old tent or a used sleeping bag? Many tents have zippers that can be secured with a small padlock. If you want to go trekking and are afraid to leave your gear in the campgrounds, take a large green garbage bag with you. Transport your gear down the trail and then walk off through some thick brush. Put your gear in the garbage bag and bury it under leaves and other light camouflage. That's about as safe as you can be. You can also use a variation on this technique instead of leaving your valuables in your rental car.

Hassles

Another self-perpetuating myth about Hawaii is that "the natives are restless." An undeniable animosity exists between locals (especially those with some Hawaiian blood) and *haole*. Fortunately, this prejudice is directed mostly at the group and not at the individual. The locals are resentful of those *haole* who came, took their land, and relegated them to second-class citizenship. They realize that this is not the average tourist and they can tell what you are at a glance. Tourists usually are treated with understanding and are given a type of immunity. Besides, Hawaiians are still among the most friendly, giving, and understanding people on earth.

Haole who live in Hawaii might tell you stories of their children having trouble at school. They could even mention an unhappy situation at some schools called "beat-up-a-*haole*" day, and you might hear that if you're a *haole* it's not a matter of "if" you'll be beaten up, but "when." Truthfully, most of this depends upon your attitude and your sensitivity. The locals feel infringed upon, so don't fuel these feelings. If you're at a beach park and there is a group of local people in one area, don't crowd them. If you go into a local bar and you're the only one of your ethnic group in sight, you shouldn't have to be told to leave. Much of the hassle involves drinking. Booze brings out the worst prejudice on all sides. If you're invited to a beach party, and the local guys start getting drunk, make this your exit call. Don't wait until it's too late.

Most trouble seems to be directed toward white men. White women are mostly immune from being beaten up, but they have to beware of the violence of sexual abuse and rape. Although plenty of local women marry white men, it's not a good idea to try to pick up a local girl. If you're known in the area and have been properly introduced, that's another story. Also, girls out for the night in bars or discos can be approached if they're not in the company of local guys. If you are with your bikini-clad girlfriend, and a bunch of local guys are, say, drinking beer at a beach park, don't go over and try to be friendly and ask, "What's up?" You, and especially your girlfriend, just might find out. Maintain your own dignity and self-respect by treating others with dignity and respect. Most times you'll reap what you sow.

WHAT TO TAKE

It's a snap to pack for a visit to Oahu. Everything is on your side. The weather is moderate and uniform on the whole, and the style of dress is delightfully casual. The rule of thumb is to pack lightly: few items, and light clothing both in color and weight. What you'll need will depend largely on your itinerary and your desires. Are you drawn to the nightlife, the outdoors, or both? If you forget something at home, it won't be a disaster. You can buy everything you'll need in Hawaii. As a matter of fact, Hawaiian clothing, such as muumuu and aloha shirts, is one of the best purchases you can make, both in comfort and style. It's quite feasible to bring only one or two changes of clothing with the express purpose of outfitting yourself while there. Prices on bathing suits, bikinis, and summer wear in general are quite reasonable.

Matters of Taste

A grand conspiracy in Hawaii adhered to by everyone—tourist, traveler, and resident—is to "hang loose" and dress casual. Best of all, alohawear is just about all you'll need for comfort and virtually every occasion. The classic muumuu is large and billowy, and aloha shirts are made to be worn outside the pants. The best of both are made of cool cotton. Rayon is a natural fiber that isn't too bad, but polyester is hot, sticky, and not authentic. Not all muumuu are of the "tent persuasion." Some are very fashionable and form-fitted with peek-a-boo slits up the side, down the front, or around the back. *Holomuu* are muumuu fitted at the waist with a flowing skirt to the ankles. They are not only elegant, but perfect for "stepping out."

In the Cold and Rain

Two occasions for which you'll have to consider dressing warmly are visits to mountaintops and boat rides where wind and ocean sprays are a factor. You can conquer both with a jogging suit (sweat suit) and a featherweight, water-resistant windbreaker. If you're going to camp or trek, you should add another layer, a woolen sweater being one of the best. Wool is the only natural fiber that retains most of its warmth-giving properties even if it gets wet. Several varieties of "fleece" synthetics currently on the market also have this ability. If your hands get cold, put a pair of socks over them. Tropical rain showers can happen at any time so you might consider a fold-up umbrella, but the sun quickly breaks through and the warming winds blow.

Shoes

Dressing your feet is hardly a problem. You'll most often wear zoris (rubber thongs) for going to and from the beach, leather sandals for strolling and dining, and jogging shoes for trekking and sightseeing. A few discos require leather shoes, but it's hardly worth bringing them just for that. If you plan on heavy-duty trekking, you'll definitely want your hiking boots. Lava, especially a'a, is murderous on shoes. Most backcountry trails are rugged and muddy, and you'll need those good old lug soles for traction. If you plan moderate hikes, you might want to consider bringing rubberized ankle supports to complement your jogging shoes. Most drugstores sell them, and the best are a rubberized sock with toe and heel cut out.

Specialty Items

Following is a list of specialty items that you might consider bringing along. They're not necessities but most will definitely come in handy. A pair of binoculars really enhances sightseeing—great for viewing birds and sweeping panoramas, and almost a necessity if you're going whalewatching. A folding, Teflon-bottomed travel iron makes up for cotton's one major shortcoming, wrinkles; you can't always count on hotels to have irons. Nylon twine and miniature clothespins are handy for drying garments, especially bathing suits. Commercial and hotel laundromats abound, but many times you'll get by with hand-washing a few items in the sink. A transistor radio/tape recorder provides news, weather, and entertainment, and can be used to record impressions, island music, and a running commentary for your slide show. Hair dryer: although the wind can be relied upon to dry wet hair, it leaves a bit to be desired in the styling department. An inflatable raft for riding

waves, along with flippers, mask and snorkel, can easily be bought in Hawaii but don't weigh much or take up much space in your luggage. If you'll be camping, trekking, or boating with only seawater available for bathing, take along "Sea Saver Soap," available from good sporting goods stores. This special soap will lather in seawater and rinse away the sticky salt residue with it.

For the Camper

If you don't want to take it with you, all necessary camping gear can be purchased or rented while in Hawaii. Besides the above, you should consider taking the following: framed backpack (but you can't take these on TheBus) or the convertible packs that turn into suitcases, daypack, matches in a waterproof container, all-purpose knife, mess kit, eating utensils, flashlight (remove batteries), candle, nylon cord, and sewing kit (dental floss works as thread). Take a first-aid kit containing Band-Aids, all-purpose antiseptic cream, alcohol swabs, tourniquet string, cotton balls, elastic bandage, razor blade, Telfa pads, and a small mirror for viewing private nooks and crannies. A light sleeping bag is good, although your fleecy jogging suit with a ground pad and light blanket or even your rain poncho will be sufficient. Definitely bring a down bag for mountainous areas. In a film container pack a few nails, safety pins, fishhooks, line, and bendable wire. Nothing else does what these do and they're all handy for a million and one uses.

Basic Necessities

As previously mentioned, you really have to consider only two "modes" of dressing in Hawaii: beachwear and casual clothing. The following is designed for the midrange traveler carrying one suitcase or a backpack. Remember that there are laundromats and that you'll be spending a considerable amount of time in your bathing suit. Consider the following: one or two pairs of light cotton slacks for going out and about, and one pair of jeans for trekking; two or three casual sundresses—muumuu are great; three or four pairs of shorts for beachwear and for sightseeing; four to five short-sleeved shirts or blouses and one long-sleeved; three or four colored and printed T-shirts that can be worn anytime from trekking to strolling; a beach coverup—the short terrycloth type is best; a brimmed hat for rain and sun—the crushable floppy type is great for purse or daypack; two or three pairs of socks are sufficient, nylons you won't need; two bathing suits (nylon ones dry quickest); plastic bags to hold wet bathing suits and laundry; five to six pairs of underwear; towels (optional, because hotels provide them, even for the beach); a first-aid kit, pocket-size is sufficient; suntan lotion and insect repellent; a daypack or large beach purse. And don't forget your windbreaker, perhaps a shawl for the evening, and an all-purpose jogging suit.

Pets and Quarantine

Hawaii has a very rigid pet quarantine policy designed to keep rabies and other mainland disease from reaching the state. *All* domestic pets are subject to a **120-day quarantine** (a 30-day quarantine is allowed by meeting certain pre-arrival and post-arrival requirements—inquire). Unless you are contemplating a move to Hawaii, it is not feasible to take pets. For complete information, contact the Department of Agriculture, Animal Quarantine Division, 99-951 Halawa Valley St., Aiea, HI 96701, tel. (808) 483-7151.

INFORMATION AND SERVICES

HAWAII VISITORS BUREAU OFFICES

The **HVB** is a top-notch organization providing help and information to all of Hawaii's visitors. Anyone contemplating a trip to Hawaii should visit or write the HVB and inquire about any specific information that might be required. Their advice and excellent brochures on virtually every facet of living, visiting, or simply enjoying Hawaii are free. The material offered is too voluminous to list, but for basics, request individual island brochures (including maps) and ask for copies of the *Member Accommodation Guide* and *Member Restaurant Guide.* Allow two to three weeks for requests to be answered. The HVB has two Web sites, www.gohawaii.com and www.gohonolulu.com.

HVB Offices Statewide

Statewide offices include: **HVB Administrative Office,** Waikiki Business Plaza, 2270 Kalakaua Ave., Suite 801, Honolulu, HI, tel. (808) 923-1811; **Oahu HVB,** Royal Hawaiian Shopping Center, 4th Fl., 2201 Kalakaua Ave., Honolulu, HI 96815, tel. (808) 923-0145; **Maui HVB,** 1727 Wili Pa Loop, Wailuku, HI 96793, tel. (808) 244-3530; **Kauai HVB,** 3016 Umi St., Suite 207, Lihue, HI 96766, tel. (808) 245-3971; **HVB Hilo Branch,** 250 Keawe St., Hilo, HI 96720, tel. (808) 961-5797; and **HVB Kona Branch,** 75-5719 W. Ali'i Dr., Kailua-Kona, HI 96740, tel. (808) 329-7787.

North American Offices

HVB New York, Empire State Bldg., 350 5th Ave., Suite 1827, New York, NY 10018, tel. (212) 947-0717

HVB Washington D.C., 3975 University Dr. #335, Fairfax, VA 22030, tel. (703) 691-1800

HVB San Diego, 11835 Carmel Mountain Road #1304-353, San Diego, CA 92128, tel. (619) 485-7278

HVB Canada, c/o Comprehensive Travel, 1260 Hornby St. #104, Vancouver, BC, Canada V6Z 1W2, tel. (604) 669-6691

European Office

HVB United Kingdom, P.O. Box 208, Sunbury on Thames, Middlesex, England, TW165RJ, tel. (181) 941-4009

Asia/Pacific Offices

HVB Japan, Kokusai Bldg., #2F, 1-1, Marunouchi 3-chome, Chiyoda-ku, Tokyo 100, tel. (3) 3201-0430

HVB Korea, c/o Travel Press, Inc., Samwon Bldg., 10th Floor, 112-5, Sokong-dong, Chung-gu, Seoul 100-070, tel. (2) 773-6719

HVB New Zealand, c/o Walshes World, 87 Queen St., 2nd Fl., Dingwall Bldg., Auckland, tel. (9) 379-3708

HVB Taiwan, c/o Federal Transporta-

The "HVB Warrior" is posted alongside the roadway, marking sites of cultural and historic importance.

tion Co., 8th Fl., 61 Nanking E. Road, Section 3, Taipei, tel. (2) 507-8133

HVB China, c/o East West Marketing Corporation, 38 Da Pu Road, Hai Hua Garden, No. 4, Bldg. 27C, Shanghai, China 200023, tel. (21) 6466-1077

Other Tourism-Related Information Source
The **Airport Visitor Information** center, tel. (808) 836-6413, is a good source of information available on arrival.

LOCAL RESOURCES

For **police, fire, and ambulance** anywhere on Oahu, dial **911.**
   Civil Defense: In case of natural disaster such as hurricane or tsunami on Oahu, call (808) 523-4121 or 527-5373.
   Coast Guard Search and Rescue: tel. (808) 541-2450 or (800) 552-6458.
   Life Guard Service: tel. (808) 922-3888.
   Sex Abuse Treatment Center Hotline: Call (808) 524-7273 for cases involving sexual assault or rape crisis.
   Time of day: tel. (808) 983-3211
   The **Aloha Pages,** at the front of the Yellow Pages phone directory, is a font of at-your-fingertip information for visitors to the island. The **Audio Pages** section, tel. (808) 296-1818, is a free 24-hour "talking telephone" information service on a variety of topics including weather, news, sports, community service, and entertainment. For specific information, dial the above number, followed by a four-digit code number as directed, or check your local Hawaiian phone book for a complete listing of available topics.

Weather, Marine, and Surf Reports
For recorded information on **local island weather,** call (808) 973-4381; for **marine conditions,** phone (808) 973-4382; and for the **surf report,** call (808) 973-4383.

Consumer Protection and Tourist Complaints
If you encounter problems with accommodations, bad service, or downright rip-offs, try the following: **The Chamber of Commerce of Hawaii,** tel. (808) 545-4300; **Hawaii Hotel Association,** tel. (808) 923-0407; **Office of Consumer Protection,** tel. (808) 587-3222; or the **Better Business Bureau,**

tel. (808) 941-5222. For general information, or if you have a hassle, try the City Hall's **Office of Information,** tel. (808) 523-4385, or the **Office of Complaint,** tel. (808) 523-4381.

Post Offices
There are over a dozen post offices in Honolulu, and one in each of the major towns on the island. Window service is offered Mon.-Fri. 8:30 a.m.-4 p.m.; some offices are open Saturday 10 a.m.-noon. For all postal information on Oahu, call (800) 275-8777. The main post office in downtown Honolulu is at 3600 Aolele St. In Waikiki, it is at 330 Saratoga Road; in Kailua, at 335 Hahani; in Waianae, at 86-014 Farrington Hwy.; in Haleiwa, at 66-437 Kamehameha Hwy.; and in Wahiawa, at 115 Lehua.

Reading Material
Besides a number of special-interest Chinese, Japanese, Korean, Filipino, and military newspapers, two major dailies are published on Oahu. The *Honolulu Advertiser,* tel. (808) 525-8000, is the morning paper, and the *Honolulu Star Bulletin,* tel. (808) 525-8000, is the evening paper. They combine to make a Sunday paper. The alternative press *Honolulu Weekly,* tel. (808) 528-1475, adds a different perspective to the mix. Aside from feature articles on pertinent local issues, it does a calendar of local arts and events. This free weekly is available throughout Oahu at over 600 locations. A money-saving paper is the *Pennysaver,* tel. (808) 841-4444, featuring classified ads on just about anything. Call for distribution points.
   Don't miss out on the **free tourist literature** available at all major hotels, shopping malls, the airport, and stands along Waikiki's streets. They all contain up-to-the-minute information on what's happening, and a treasure trove of free or reduced-price coupons for various attractions and services. Always featured are events, shopping tips, dining and entertainment, and sightseeing. The main ones are: *This Week Oahu,* the best and most complete; *The Best of Oahu;* and *Spotlight Hawaii,* with good sections on dining and sightseeing. Two free tabloids, *Waikiki Beach Press* and *Island News,* offer entertainment calendars and feature stories of general interest to visitors. *Oahu Drive Guide,* handed out by all the major car rental agencies, has some excellent tips and orientation maps. Especially useful to get you started from the airport.

ARCHIVES AND LIBRARIES

Bishop Museum Library and Archives, 1525 Bernice St., Honolulu, HI 96817, tel. (808) 848-4148. The archives are open Tues.-Fri. 10 a.m.-3 p.m., Saturday 9 a.m.-noon, while the library is open Tues.-Fri. 1-4 p.m. and Saturday 9 a.m.-noon. Extensive historical and cultural collection.

Episcopal Church of Hawaii, 229 Queen Emma Square, Honolulu, HI 96813, tel. (808) 536-7776. Records and photos of church history in Hawaii from 1862.

Hawaii Chinese Historical Center, 111 N. King St. Room 410, Honolulu, HI 96813, tel. (808) 521-5948. Open 12 hours per week; call. Rare books, oral histories, and photos concerning the history of Chinese in Hawaii.

Hawaiian Historical Society, 560 Kawaiahao St., Honolulu, HI 96813, tel. (808) 537-6271. Open Mon.-Fri. 10 a.m.-4 p.m. Extensive collection of 19th-century materials on Hawaiian Islands, including 3,000 photos, 10,000 books, maps, microfilm. Adjacent to Hawaiian Mission Children's Society. Should be seen together. Should not be missed.

Hawaiian State Archives, Iolani Palace Grounds, Honolulu, HI 96813, tel. (808) 586-0329. Open Mon.-Fri. 7:45 a.m.-4:30 p.m. Archives of the government of Hawaii. Private papers of Hawaiian royalty and government officials, photos, illustrations, etchings recording Hawaiian history. For anyone seriously interested in Hawaii. Shouldn't be missed.

Hawaii State Library, Iolani Palace Grounds, Honolulu, tel. (808) 586-3500. Main branch of statewide library system.

Mission Houses Library, 553 S. King St., Honolulu 96813, tel. (808) 531-0481. Open Tues.-Sat. 9 a.m.-4 p.m. Records, personal journals, letters and photos of early 19th-century Congregational missionaries to the Hawaiian Islands; archive of the Congregational Church in the Pacific. Shouldn't be missed.

University of Hawaii Library, 2425 Campus Road, Honolulu, HI 96822, tel. (808) 956-7204. Manoa campus. The Hamilton Library 4th floor holds the Hawaiian/Pacific Collection.

There are 23 public libraries on Oahu, and these include: Hawaii State Library, in Honolulu at 478 S. King St., tel. (808) 586-3500; Kailua Library, 239 Kuulei Road, tel. (808) 266-9911; Library for the Blind and Physically Handicapped, 402 Kapahulu Ave., tel. (808) 733-8444; Waikiki branch next door, at 400 Kapahulu, tel. (808) 733-8488. Library cards are available free for Hawaii state residents and military personnel stationed in Hawaii, $25 for nonresidents, and $10 for up to three months for visitors. The library system offers numerous services, including reference information during library hours at (808) 586-3621 or (800) 390-3611 from the Neighbor Islands, computer access by phone to the library catalog at (808) 831-6888 or (800) 982-4436 from the Neighbor Islands, Internet access from library computers, and statewide access to the entire library collection. Business hours for each individual library differ, so check with the one you want to visit. Brochures listing hours and other general information are available at all libraries.

For bookstores, refer to the "Shopping" section earlier in this chapter.

OTHER INFORMATION

Telephone: All-Hawaii Area Code 808

Local calls from public telephones (anywhere on the same island is a local call) cost 25 cents. Calling between islands is a toll call, and the price depends on when and from where you call and for how long you speak. Emergency calls are always free. Like everywhere else in the U.S., long-distance rates go down at 5 p.m. and again at 11 p.m. until 8 a.m. the next morning. From Friday at 5 p.m. until Monday morning at 8 a.m. rates are cheapest. For directory assistance call: local, 1-411; interisland, 1-555-1212; Mainland, 1-area code-555-1212; toll-free 1-800-555-1212.

Time Zones

There is no daylight saving time in Hawaii. When daylight saving time is not observed on the Mainland, Hawaii is two hours behind the West Coast, four hours behind the Midwest, five hours behind the East Coast, and 11 hours behind Germany. Hawaii, being just east of the international date line, is almost a full day behind most Asian and Oceanic cities. Hours behind these countries and cities are: Japan, 19 hours; Singapore, 18 hours; Sydney, 20 hours; New Zealand, 22 hours; Fiji, 22 hours.

Electricity

The same electrical current is in use in Hawaii as on the U.S. Mainland and is uniform throughout the islands. The system functions on 110 volts, 60 cycles of alternating current (AC). Appliances from Japan will work, but there is some danger of burnout, while those requiring the normal European current of 220 will not work.

Distance, Weights, and Measures

Hawaii, like all of the U.S., employs the "English method" of measuring weights and distances. Basically, dry weights are in ounces and pounds; liquid measures are in ounces, quarts, and gallons; and distances are measured in inches, feet, yards, and miles. The metric system, based on units of 10, is known but is not in general use. The conversion chart at the back of the book should be helpful.

Island Radio

Several dozen radio stations of all stripes broadcast on Oahu. You will find one that you like when you spin the dial. Among those that are popular are: **KCCB** FM 100 playing Hawaiian and reggae 24 hours a day; **KKLV** 98.5 FM for classical rock and roll; **The Edge** 97.5 FM for alternative rock; **KIKI** FM 94, which gives you rap, dance, and modern R&B; and **KIPO** FM 89.3, Hawaii Public Radio.

Island Facts

Oahu's nickname is "The Gathering Place." Its color is yellow, the island flower is the *ilima,* and the island lei is strung from its bold blossoms. At 597 square miles, Oahu follows Hawaii and Maui in size and has nearly the same area as Kauai.

MONEY AND FINANCES

Currency

U.S. currency is among the drabbest in the world. It's all the same size and color; those unfamiliar with it should spend some time getting acquainted so that they don't make costly mistakes. U.S. coinage in use is: one cent (penny), five cents (nickel), 10 cents (dime), 25 cents (quarter), 50 cents (half dollar), and one dollar (uncommon); paper currency is $1, $2 (uncommon), $5, $10, $20, $50, $100. Bills larger than $100 are not in common usage.

Banks

Full-service banks tend to open slightly earlier than Mainland banks, at 8:30 a.m. Mon.-Friday. Closing is at 3 p.m., except for late hours on Friday when most banks remain open until 6 p.m. Of most value to travelers, banks sell and cash traveler's checks, give cash advances on credit cards, exchange and sell foreign currency, and have 24-hour ATMs (automatic teller machines). Major Banks on Oahu are American Savings Bank, Bank of America, Bank of Hawaii, Central Pacific Bank, and First Hawaiian Bank; each has numerous branch offices throughout the island.

Traveler's Checks

Traveler's checks are accepted throughout Hawaii at hotels, restaurants, and car-rental agencies, and in most stores and shops. However, to be readily acceptable they should be in American currency. Some larger hotels that often deal with Japanese and Canadians will accept their currency. Banks accept foreign-currency traveler's checks, but it'll mean an extra trip and inconvenience.

Credit Cards

More and more business is transacted in Hawaii using credit cards. Almost every form of accommodations, shop, restaurant, and amusement accepts them. For renting a car they're almost a must. With "credit card insurance" readily available, they're as safe as traveler's checks and sometimes even more convenient. Don't rely on them completely because there are some establishments that won't accept them, or perhaps won't accept the kind that you carry.

BOB RACE

HONOLULU

Honolulu is *the* most exotic city in America. It's not any one attribute that makes this so; it's a combination of things. Honolulu's like an ancient Hawaiian goddess who can change her form at will. At one moment you see a black-eyed beauty, swaying provocatively to a deep and basic rhythm, and in the next a high-tech scion of the computer age sitting straight-backed behind a polished desk. The city is the terminus of "manifest destiny," the end of America's relentless westward drive, until no more horizons were left. Other Mainland cities are undoubtedly more historic, cultural, and perhaps, to some, more beautiful than Honolulu, but none come close to having all of these features in the same overwhelming combination. The city's face, though blemished by high-rises and pocked by heavy industry, is eternally lovely. The Koolau Mountains form the background tapestry from which the city emerges; the surf gently foams along Waikiki; the sun hisses fire-red as it drops into the sea, and Diamond Head beckons with a promise of tropical romance.

In the center of the city, skyscrapers rise as silent, unshakable witnesses to Honolulu's economic strength. In glass and steel offices, busi-nesspeople wearing conservative three-piece uniforms are clones of any found on Wall Street. Below, a fantasia of people live and work. In nooks and crannies are an amazing array of arts, shops, and cuisines. In a flash of festival the streets become China, Japan, Portugal, New England, old Hawaii, or the Philippines.

New England churches, a royal palace, bandstands, tall-masted ships, and coronation platforms illustrate Honolulu's history. And what a history! You can visit places where in a mere twinkle of time past, red-plumed warriors were driven to their death over an impossibly steep *pali,* or where the skies were alive with screaming Zeros strafing and bombing the only American city threatened by a foreign power since the War of 1812. In hallowed grounds throughout the city lie the bodies of fallen warriors. Some are entombed in a mangled steel sepulchre below the waves, others from three wars rest in a natural bowl of bereavement and silence. And a nearby royal mausoleum holds the remains of those who were "old Hawaii."

Honolulu is the pumping heart of Hawaii. The state government and university are here. So are botanical parks, a fine aquarium and zoo, a float-

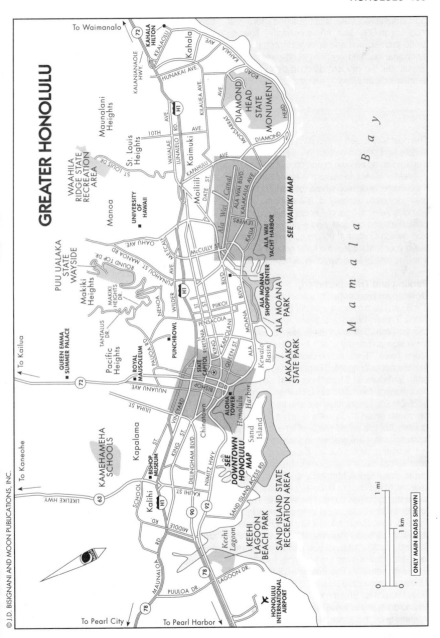

GREATER HONOLULU

To Waimanalo

KAHALA HILTON

KEALAOLU

Kahala

KAHALA AVE.

KALANIANAOLE HWY.

HUNAKAI AVE.

KILAUEA AVE.

AVE.

DIAMOND HEAD STATE MONUMENT

H1

10TH

WAIALAE

AVE.

LUNALILO RD.

ROAD

MONSARRAT

Maunalani Heights

St. Louis Heights

Kaimuki

DIAMOND

HEAD

WAAHILA RIDGE STATE RECREATION AREA

KAPAHULU

DATE ST.

AVE.

Manoa

ST. LOUIS DR.

UNIVERSITY OF HAWAII

Moiliili

Ala Wai Canal

ALA WAI BLVD.

KALAKAUA AVE.

SEE WAIKIKI MAP

PUU UALAKA STATE WAYSIDE

Makiki Heights

ROUND TOP DR.

MANOA RD.

OAHU AVE.

DATE ST.

LEWERS

ALA WAI YACHT HARBOR

MAKIKI HEIGHTS DR.

PUNAHOU ST.

METCALF

McCULLY

M a m a l a   B a y

To Kailua

72

TANTALUS DR.

Pacific Heights

NEHOA

WILDER

ST.

ST.

PIIKOI

BLVD.

ALA MOANA SHOPPING CENTER

ALA MOANA PARK

QUEEN EMMA SUMMER PALACE

PUNCHBOWL

PENSACOLA

BERETANIA

MAKIKI

ALA MOANA

PAUOA RD.

ROYAL MAUSOLEUM

KING

Kewalo Basin

KAKAAKO STATE PARK

NUUANU AVE.

STATE CAPITOL

QUEEN ST.

AIA

LILIHA ST.

BISHOP

ALOHA TOWER

Honolulu Harbor

KAMEHAMEHA SCHOOLS

Chinatown

VINEYARD

Sand Island

To Kaneohe

Kapalama

BISHOP MUSEUM

KING ST.

DILLINGHAM BLVD.

NIMITZ HWY.

SEE DOWNTOWN HONOLULU MAP

SAND ISLAND STATE RECREATION AREA

LIKELIKE HWY.

63

Kalihi

H1

KALIHI ST.

90

92

SCHOOL

SAND ISLAND ACCESS RD.

MAUNALOA

MIDDLE RD.

Keehi Lagoon

KEEHI LAGOON BEACH PARK

78

PUULOA DR.

LAGOON DR.

HONOLULU INTERNATIONAL AIRPORT

78

To Pearl City

To Pearl Harbor

1 mi

1 km

0

0

ONLY MAIN ROADS SHOWN

© J.D. BISIGNANI AND MOON PUBLICATIONS, INC.

ing maritime museum, and the world's foremost museum on Polynesia. Art flourishes like flowers, as do professional and amateur entertainment, extravaganzas, and local and world-class sporting events. But the city isn't all good clean fun. The seedier side includes "girlie" shows, raucous GI bars, street drugs, and street people. But somehow this blending and collision of East and West, this hodgepodge of emotionally charged history, this American city superimposed on a unique Pacific setting works well as Honolulu, the "Sheltered Harbor" of man and his dreams.

SIGHTS

The best way to see Honolulu is to start from the middle and fan out on foot to visit the inner city. You can *do* downtown in one day, but the sights of greater Honolulu require a few days to see. It's a matter of opinion where the center of downtown Honolulu actually is, but the King Kamehameha statue in front of Aliiolani Hale is about as central as you can get, and a perfect landmark from which to start. If you're staying in Waikiki, leave your rental car in the hotel garage and take TheBus (no. 2) for downtown sightseeing.

Parking and Transportation, Downtown Honolulu

If you can't bear to leave your car behind, head for Aloha Tower. When you get to where you can see the Aloha Tower off the S. Nimitz Hwy., look for a sign pointing you left to "Piers 4 and 11, Aloha Tower." Enter to find plenty of parking. The traffic is not as congested here and the large lot is open 24 hours, at $1 per hour, with a four-hour maximum on the meter. Bring change, as none is available. You might have to come back and feed the meter again if you want to go as far as Chinatown, but this will be plenty of time for the local attractions that are well within walking distance.

For various sights outside the downtown area, your rental car is fine. Some shuttles running out to the *Arizona* Memorial are more expensive than TheBus, but so convenient that they're worth the extra few coins. The **Waikiki Trolley,** tel. (808) 596-2199, conducts tours throughout the downtown area. It looks like a trolley but it's a bus that's been ingeniously converted. For $18 adults, $8 children, you can ride it all day long. Multiday passes are available for $30 and $10, respectively. The trolley departs daily at 15-minute intervals 8:30 a.m.-6:30 p.m. from the Royal Hawaiian Shopping Center. You can get off and on at any of the 20 stops along the way or ride along for the entire two-hour trip.

 IOLANI PALACE AREA

The **Statue of King Kamehameha** is at the junction of King and Mililani Streets. Running off at an angle is **Merchant Street,** the oldest thoroughfare in Honolulu, and you might say it's "the beginning of the road to modernity." The statue is much more symbolic of Kamehameha's strength as a ruler and unifier of the Hawaiian Islands than as a replica of the man himself. Of the few drawings of Kamehameha that have been preserved, none is necessarily a good likeness. Kamehameha was a magnificent leader and statesman, but by all accounts not very good-looking. This statue is one of three. The original, lost at sea near the Falkland Islands en route from Paris where it was bronzed, was later recovered, but not before insurance money was used to cast this second one. The original is in the town of Kapaau, in the Kohala District of the Big Island, not far from where Kamehameha was born, but although they supposedly came from the same mold, they somehow seem quite different. The third stands in Washington, D.C., dedicated when Hawaii became a state. The Honolulu statue was dedicated in 1883, as part of King David Kalakaua's coronation ceremony. Its black and gold colors are striking, but it is most magnificent on June 11, King Kamehameha Day, when 18-foot lei are draped around the neck and the outstretched arms.

Behind Kamehameha stands **Aliiolani Hale,** now the State Judiciary Building. This handsome structure, designed by an Australian architect and begun in 1872, was originally commissioned by Kamehameha V as a palace, but was redesigned as a general court building. It looks much more grand than Iolani Palace across the way. Kamehameha V died before it was finished, and it was officially dedicated by King Kalakaua in 1874. Less than 20 years later, on January 17,

Iolani Palace, the only royal residence in America

J.D. BISIGNANI

1893, at this "hall of justice," the first proclamation by the Members of the Committee of Safety was read, stating that the sovereign nation of Hawaii was no more, and that the islands would be ruled by a provisional government.

On the ground floor of this building, the **Judiciary History Center,** tel. (808) 539-4999, offers free exhibits Tues.-Thurs. 10 a.m.-3 p.m.

Next door is the **Old Federal Building,** which is home to several state department offices and the downtown post office station.

Iolani Palace

As you enter the 11-acre parklike palace grounds, notice the emblem of Hawaii in the center of the large iron gates. They're often draped with simple lei of fragrant *maile.* The quiet grounds are a favorite strolling and relaxing place for many government workers, especially in the shade of a huge banyan, purportedly planted by Kalakaua's wife, Kapiolani. The building, with its glass and ironwork imported from San Francisco, and its Corinthian columns, is the only royal palace in America. Iolani ("Royal Hawk") Palace, begun in 1879 under orders of King Kalakaua, was completed in December 1882 at a cost of $350,000. It was the first electrified building in Honolulu, and had a direct phone line to the Royal Boat House, located near where the Aloha Tower stands today.

Non-Hawaiian island residents of the day thought it a frivolous waste of money, but here poignant scenes and profound changes rocked the Hawaiian islands. After nine years as king, Kalakaua built a **Coronation Stand** that temporarily sat in front of the palace (now off to the left). In a belated ceremony, Kalakaua raised a crown to his head and placed one on his queen, Kapiolani. During the ceremony, 8,000 Hawaiians cheered, while Honolulu's foreign, tax-paying businessmen boycotted. On August 12, 1898, after only two Hawaiian monarchs, Kalakaua and Liliuokalani (his sister), had resided in the palace, the American flag was raised up the flagpole following a successful coup that marked Hawaii's official recognition by the U.S. as a territory. During this ceremony, loyal Hawaiian subjects wept bitter tears, while the businessmen of Honolulu cheered wildly.

Kalakaua, later in his rule, was forced to sign a new constitution that greatly reduced his own power to little more than figurehead status. He traveled to San Francisco in 1891, where he died. His body was returned to Honolulu and lay in state in the palace. His sister, Liliuokalani, succeeded him; she attempted to change this constitution and gain the old power of Hawaii's sovereigns, but the businessmen revolted and the monarchy fell. Iolani Palace then became the main executive building for the provisional government, with the House of Representatives meeting in the throne room and the Senate in the dining room. It served in this capacity until 1968. It has since been elevated to a state monument and National Historical Landmark.

Iolani Palace is open to 45-minute **guided tours only,** starting every 15 minutes Tues.-Sat. 9 a.m.-2:15 p.m.; $8 adults, $3 children, with no children under five admitted. The palace is open the same hours on the first Sunday of every month for free admission to *kama'aina;* visitors are charged the regular fees. They're popular so make reservations at least a day in advance. Tickets are sold at a window at the Barracks, open Tues.-Sat. 8:30 a.m.-3:30 p.m. The Palace shop is open Tues.-Sat. 8:30 a.m.-3:30 p.m. For information and reservations call (808) 522-0832.

Palace Grounds

Kalakaua, known as the "Merrie Monarch," was credited with saving the hula. He also hired Henri Burger, first Royal Hawaiian Bandmaster, and together they wrote "Hawaii Pono," the state anthem. Many concerts were given from the Coronation Stand, which became known as the **Royal Bandstand.** Behind it is **Iolani Barracks** (Hale Koa), built in 1870 to house the Royal Household Guards. When the monarchy of Hawaii fell to provisional government forces in 1893, only one of these soldiers was wounded in the nearly bloodless confrontation. The barracks were moved to the present site from nearby land on which the State Capitol was erected.

To the right behind the palace are the **State Archives,** tel. (808) 586-0329. This modern building, dating from 1953, holds records, documents, and vintage photos. A treasure trove to scholars and those tracing their genealogy, it is worth a visit by the general public to view the old photos on display. Open Mon.-Fri. 7:45 a.m.-4:30 p.m.; free. Next door is the **Hawaii State Library,** housing the main branch of this statewide system. As in all Hawaii state libraries, you are entitled to a card on your first visit, and are then eligible to take out books. Library cards are available free for Hawaii state residents and military personnel stationed in Hawaii, $25 for nonresidents, and $10 for up to three months for visitors. The central courtyard is a favorite lunch spot for many of the government workers. Some of the original money to build the library was put up by Andrew Carnegie. For information call (808) 586-3500.

Government Buildings

Liliuokalani was deposed and placed under house arrest in the palace for nine months. Later, after much intrigue that included a visit to Washington, D.C., to plead her case and an aborted counterrevolution, she sadly accepted her fate and moved to nearby **Washington Place.** This solid-looking structure fronts Beretania Street and was originally the home of sea captain John Dominis. It was inherited by his son John Owen Dominis, who married a lovely young Hawaiian aristocrat, Lydia Kapaakea, who became Queen Liliuokalani. She lived in her husband's home, proud but powerless, until her death in 1917. Washington Place is now the official residence of the governor of Hawaii. To the right of Washington Place is the **War Memorial.** Erected in 1974, this memorial replaced an older one and is dedicated to the people who perished in WW II. A courtyard and benches are provided for quiet meditation.

Directly in front of you is the magnificent **Hawaii State Capitol,** built in 1969 for $25 million. The building itself is a metaphor for Hawaii: the pillars surrounding it are palms, the reflecting pool is the sea, and the cone-shaped rooms of the Legislature represent the volcanoes of Hawaii. It's lined with rich koa wood from the Big Island, and is further graced with woven hangings and murals, with two gigantic, four-ton replicas of the State Seal hanging at both entrances. The inner courtyard has a 600,000-tile mosaic, *Aquarius,* rendered by island artist Tadashi Sato, and on one side is a poignant sculpture of *Father Damien of the Lepers.* The State Legislature is in session January to March, and opens with dancing, music, and festivities at 10 a.m. on the third Wednesday in January, public invited. Peek inside, then take the elevator to the fifth floor for outstanding views of the city.

A few steps away, on the corner of Punchbowl and King Streets, stands **Honolulu Hale,** Honolulu City Hall. Built in 1928, with additions in 1951, this office building is open 7:45 a.m.-4:30 p.m. weekdays and houses the office of the mayor, the city council, and a few city departments. It too has a courtyard where music, art, and other public events are held.

St. Andrew's Cathedral

To the left of Washington Place, the governor's residence, is St. Andrew's Cathedral. Construction started in 1867 as an Anglican church, but wasn't really finished until the late 1950s. Many of its stones and ornaments were shipped from England, and its stained glass windows and bell tower are of particular interest. Hawaii's monarchs worshipped here, and the church is still very much in use. Open 8 a.m.-4 p.m. Mon.-Fri.; call (808) 524-2822 for information concerning tours.

MISSION HOUSES MUSEUM

The days when tall ships with tattered sails crewed by rough seamen bore God-fearing missionary families dedicated to Christianizing the savage islands are alive in the halls and buildings of the Mission Houses Museum, 553 S. King St., Honolulu, HI 96813, now a Registered National Historical Landmark. Across from Kawaiahao Church (oldest in Honolulu), the complex includes two main houses, a printing house annex, a library and a fine, inexpensive gift shop, and is operated by the **Hawaiian Mission Children's Society** (or Cousins' Society), whose members serve as guides and hosts. Many are direct descendants, or spouses of descendants, of the Congregationalist missionaries who built these structures. One-hour tours are conducted at various times throughout the day, Tues.-Sat. 9 a.m.-4 p.m.; closed Sunday and Monday. Guided tours of the Frame House, oldest wooden structure in Hawaii are offered 9:30 a.m.-3 p.m. Admission is $6 adults; $5 *kama'aina*, seniors, and military; $3 college students and children ages 4-18. Call (808) 531-0481 for information (see "Special Programs," below).

Construction

If you think that precut modular housing is a new concept, think again. The first structure that you enter is the **Frame House**, the oldest wooden structure in Hawaii. Precut in Boston, it came along with the first missionary packet in 1819. Since the interior frame was left behind and didn't arrive until Christmas Day, 1820, the missionary families lived in thatched huts until it was erected. Finally the Chamberlain family occupied it in 1821. Many missionary families used it over the years, with as many as four households occupying this small structure at the same time. This is where the Christianizing of Hawaii truly began.

The missionaries, being New Englanders, first dug a cellar. The Hawaiians were very suspicious of the strange hole, convinced that the missionaries planned to store guns and arms in this "fort." Though assured to the contrary, King Liholiho, anxious to save face and prove his omnipotence, had a cellar dug near his home twice as deep and large. This satisfied everyone.

Notice the different styles, sizes, and colors of bricks used in the structures. Most of the ships of the day carried bricks as ballast. After unloading cargo, the captains either donated or sold the bricks to the missionaries, who incorporated them into the structures. A common local material was coral stone: pulverized coral was burned with lime to make a rudimentary cement, which was then used to bind cut-coral blocks. The pit that was used for this purpose is still discernible on the grounds.

Kitchen

The natives were intrigued with the missionaries, whom they called "long necks" because of their high collars. The missionaries, on the other hand, were a little more wary of their "charges." The low fence around the complex was symbolic as well as utilitarian. The missionaries were obsessed with keeping their children away from Hawaiian children, who at first ran around naked and played many games with overt sexual overtones. Almost every evening a small cadre of Hawaiians would assemble to peer into the kitchen to watch the women cook, which they found exceedingly strange because their *kapu* said that *men* did the cooking. In the kitchen, actually an attached cookhouse, the woodburning stove kept breaking down. More often than not, the women used the fireplace with its built-in oven. About once a week, they fired up the oven to make traditional New England staples like bread, pies, cakes, and puddings. The missionaries were dependent on the Hawaiians to bring them fresh water. Notice a large porous stone through which they would filter the water to remove dirt, mud, and sometimes brackishness.

The Hawaiians were even more amazed when the entire family sat down to dinner, a tremendous deviation from their beliefs that separated men and women when eating. When the missionaries assembled to dine or meet at the "long table," the Hawaiians silently stood at the open door to watch the evening soap opera. The unnerved missionaries eventually closed the door and cut two windows into the wall, which they could leave opened but draped. The long table took on further significance. The one you see is a replica. When different missionaries left the islands, they, like people today, wanted a souvenir. For some odd reason, they elected to saw a bit off the long table. As years went by, the table got shorter and shorter until it was useless.

Residents

The house was actually a duplex. Although many families lived in it, two of the best known were the Binghams and the Judds. Much of the furniture here was theirs. Judd, a member of the third missionary company, assumed the duties of physician to all the missionaries and islanders. He often prescribed alcohol of different sorts to the missionary families for a wide variety of ailments; many records remain of these prescriptions, but not one record of complaints from his patients. The Binghams and Judds got along very well, and entertained each other and visitors, most often in the Judds' parlor because they were a little better off. The women would often congregate here to do their sewing, which was in great demand, especially by members of the royal household. Until the missionary women taught island girls to sew, providing clothing for Hawaii's royalty was a tiresome and time-consuming obligation.

The missionaries were self-sufficient, and had the unbounded energy of youth, as the average age was only 25. The husbands often built furniture for their families. Reverend Bingham, a good craftsman, was pressed by Queen Kaahumanu to build her a rocking chair after she became enamored of one made for Mrs. Bingham. The queen weighed almost 400 pounds, so building her a suitable chair was no slim feat! Still, the queen could only use it in her later years when she'd lost a considerable amount of weight. After she died, the Binghams asked for it to be returned, and it sits in their section of the house. Compare Bingham's chair to another in the Judds' bedroom, jury-rigged by a young missionary husband from a captain's chair. An understatement, found later in his diary, confirmed that the young man was not a carpenter.

When you enter the Judds' bedroom, note how small it is, and consider that two adults and five children slept here. As soon as the children were old enough, they were sent back to the Mainland for schooling, no doubt to relieve some of the congestion. Also notice that the windows were fixed, in the New England style, and imagine how close it must have been in these rooms.

The Binghams' bedroom is also small, and not as well furnished. Bingham's shaving kit remains, and is inscribed with "The Sandwich Isles." In the bedroom of Mary Ward, a missionary woman who never married, the roof was raised to accommodate her canopy bed.

Another famous family that lived in the complex were the Cookes. When the missionary board withdrew its support, the Cookes petitioned them to buy the duplex, which was granted. Shortly thereafter, Mr. Cooke, who had been a teacher, formed a partnership with one Mr. Castle, and from that time forward Castle and Cooke grew to become one of Hawaii's oldest and most powerful corporations.

The largest building in the compound is the **Chamberlain House.** This barnlike structure was completed in 1831 and used as a warehouse and living quarters for Levi Chamberlain's family. Goods were stored in most of the structure, while the family occupied three modest rooms.

Printing House

The missionaries decided almost immediately that the best way to convert the natives was to speak to them in their own language, and to create a written Hawaiian language which they would teach in school. To this end, they created the **Hawaiian alphabet,** consisting of 12 letters, including the five vowels and seven consonants. In addition, to disseminate the doctrines of Christianity, they needed books, and therefore a printing press. On the grounds still stands the Printing House, built in 1841 but first used as annex bedrooms by the Hall family. The original printing house, built in 1823, no longer exists. In the Printing House is a replica of the Ramage press brought from New England, first operated by Elijah Loomis. He returned to the Mainland when he was 28 and soon died of tuberculosis, but not before he had earned the distinction of being the first printer west of the Rockies. Here were printed biblical tracts, textbooks, or anything that the king or passing captains were willing to pay to have printed. Although it took eight hours of hard work to set up one page to be printed, it is estimated that in the 20 years the press operated under the missionaries, over seven million pages were produced.

Gift Shop

While on the grounds make sure to visit the bookstore and gift shop. It's small but has an excellent collection of Hawaiiana, and some very inexpensive but quality items, such as tapa bookmarks for only 25 cents, and an outstanding collection of Niihau shellwork, considered the finest in Hawaii. The shelves hold tasteful items like woodcarvings, bread boards, hats, weavings, chimes, flags of old Hawaii, and stuffed pillows with classic Hawaiian quilt motifs, as well as a good collection of Hawaiian dolls, for kids and adults. Between the bookstore and the research library are restrooms.

Special Programs
Along with other programs, the museum hosts Hawaii's only **living history program,** with actors who dress in fashions of the period and assume the roles of missionaries in 1830 Honolulu. Feel free to interact and ask questions, but remember that they stay in character, so the answers may surprise you. The living history program is usually offered on the fourth Saturday of the month, 9 a.m.-4 p.m., free admission. Other special programs are also offered like tea with the 19th-century Reverend Hiram and Mrs. Sybil Bingham in their parlor; call (808) 924-1911 for details. Also, consider the walking tour offered by the museum 9:30 a.m.-12:30 p.m. that guides you through the houses of the museum and then on to downtown Honolulu, hitting all the historic sights with an extremely knowledgeable narration by one of the museum's guides. The walking tour is conducted on Thursday only; reserve two days in advance. The cost is $8 for adults; $7 for seniors, military, and *kama'aina;* $5 for college students and other students ages 13-18; $4 for children ages 4-12; and free for children under four.

KAWAIAHAO CHURCH

This church, so instrumental in Hawaii's history, is the most enduring symbol of the original missionary work in the islands. A sign welcomes you and bids the blessing, "Grace and peace to you from God our Father." Hawaiian-language services are given here every Sunday, along with English-language services. The church was constructed from 1836 until 1842 according to plans drawn up by Hiram Bingham, its minister. Before this, at least four grass shacks of increasing size stood here. One was destroyed by a sailor who was reprimanded by Reverend Bingham for attending services while drunk; the old sea dog returned the next day and burned the church to the ground. Kawaiahao ("Water

Kawaiahao Church

of Hao") Church is constructed from over 14,000 coral blocks quarried from offshore reefs. In 1843, following Restoration Day, when the British returned the Hawaiian Islands to sovereignty after a brief period of imperialism by a renegade captain, King Kamehameha III uttered here the profound words in a thanksgiving ceremony that were destined to become Hawaii's motto, *"Ua mau ke ea o ka aina i ka pono"* ("The life of the land is preserved in righteousness").

Other noteworthy ceremonies held at the church were the marriage of King Liholiho and his wife Queen Emma, who bore the last child born to a Hawaiian monarch. Unfortunately, little Prince Albert died at the age of four. On June 19, 1856, Lunalilo, the first king elected to the throne, took his oath of office in the church. A bachelor who died childless, he always felt scorned by living members of the Kamehameha clan, and refused to be buried with them at the Royal Mausoleum in Nuuanu Valley; he is buried in a tomb in the church's cemetery. Buried along with him is his father, Charles Kanaina, and nearby lies the grave of his mother, Miriam Kekauluohi. In the graveyard lies Henri Burger, and many members of the Parker, Green, Brown and Cooke families, early missionaries to the islands. Liliuokalani's body lay in state in the church before it was taken to the Royal Mausoleum. A jubilation service was held in the church when Hawaii became a state in 1959. Kawaiahao holds beautiful Christmas services with a strong Polynesian and Hawaiian flavor. Hidden away in a corner of the grounds is an unobtrusive adobe building, remains of a schoolhouse built in 1835 to educate Hawaiian children.

HONOLULU HARBOR AREA

Maritime Center

The development of this center is a wonderful concept whose time has finally come. It's amazing that a state and former nation, whose discovery and very birth are so intimately tied to the exploration, navigation, and exploitation of the sea, has never had a center dedicated exclusively to these profoundly important aspects of its heritage. Now the Hawaii Maritime Center, at Pier 7, Honolulu Harbor, Honolulu, HI 96813, tel. (808) 536-6373, is exactly that . . . and it needs your support as a visitor. Open since 1989, the center consists of three attractions: the Maritime Center building with displays of Hawaii's past; the classic, and last remaining, fully rigged, four-masted *Falls of Clyde* floating museum; and the reproduction of a Hawaiian sailing canoe, the *Hokule'a,* which recently sailed back in time using ancient navigational methods to retrace the steps of Hawaii's Polynesian explorers. Take bus no. 8 or 20 from Waikiki and you're deposited right in front. Admission for all attractions is $7.50 adults, $4.50 for children 6-17, and free for the younger kids; open 8:30 a.m.-5 p.m. everyday except Christmas.

The main building of the center is the two-story museum. Behind is Pier Seven Restaurant, a seafood restaurant, and an area called Kalakaua Park, a garden and observation area perfect for lunch. Eighty-one steps lead to the "crow's nest" and "widow's walk," with great views of the harbor and city.

Upon entering you find a glass case filled with trophies and memorabilia from the days of King Kalakaua. His words have a sadly prophetic ring. "Remember who you are. Be gracious, but never forget from whence you came for this is where your heart is. This is the cradle of your life." No-

tice the phones installed throughout the capital in 1887, a few years before California had electricity. Kalakaua had previously installed telephones between his boathouse and the palace in 1878, just two years after Bell's invention. The bottom floor of the center recalls ancient fishing methods and the traditional division of land and sea resources among the people.

Another fascinating display traces the development of surfing through the ages, from original boards, more like seagoing canoes at 18 feet long, until the modern debut of the fiberglass board. You can spot a vintage album of *Surfin Safari* by The Beach Boys. Here, too, is a land-surfing sled used for games during the Makahiki Festival. It measures six inches wide and 10-14 feet long. Trails to accommodate it were up to a mile long. Built on steep hills, they were paved in stone, layered with earth and topped with slippery grass. Once launched there was no stopping until the bottom. Yippee!

One corner of the museum is dedicated to tattooing, Polynesian and Western. It shows traditional tattoos worn by both men and women, and then how the Western style became more popular, as Hawaii was a main berth for sailors, who sported these living souvenirs from around the world. **Mail buoys** sounds uninteresting, but these tidbits of old Hawaiiana, still alive today, are fascinating. Fashioned from gaily painted metal cans, passing ships, mainly from Peru and Equador, still radio Honolulu Harbor that they are dropping one. Someone, anyone, who heard the message, would fetch them. Inside are little gifts for the finder, who takes the enclosed mail and sends it on its way.

The second floor is dedicated to the discovery of Hawaii, both by the Polynesians and Westerners. Through ledgers, histories, and artifacts, it traces original discovery, Western discovery, the death of Captain Cook, and the role of the sea otter pelt, which brought the first whalers and traders after sandalwood. The whaling section is dripping with blood and human drama. Look at the old harpoons and vintage film footage. Yes, film footage, and photos. A remarkable display is of scrimshaw from the whaling days. Sailors would be at sea for five to seven years, and would have untold hours to create beauty in what were dismal conditions. Suspended from the ceiling are replicas of dou-

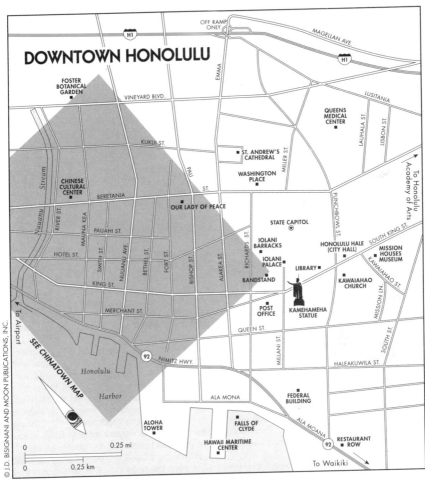

DOWNTOWN HONOLULU

FOSTER BOTANICAL GARDEN

VINEYARD BLVD.

KUKUI ST.

CHINESE CULTURAL CENTER

BERETANIA

Nuuanu Stream

RIVER ST.

MAUNA KEA

PAUAHI ST.

HOTEL ST.

SMITH ST.

NUUANU AVE.

BETHEL ST.

FORT ST.

KING ST.

MERCHANT ST.

SEE CHINATOWN MAP

To Airport

Honolulu Harbor

ALOHA TOWER

0   0.25 mi

0   0.25 km

© J.D. BISIGNANI AND MOON PUBLICATIONS, INC.

OFF RAMP ONLY

H1

MAGELLAN AVE.

H1

EMMA

PALI   ST.

QUEENS MEDICAL CENTER

LUSITANIA

LAUHALA ST.

LISBON ST.

ST. ANDREW'S CATHEDRAL

MILLER ST.

WASHINGTON PLACE

OUR LADY OF PEACE

BISHOP ST.

ALAKEA ST.

RICHARDS ST.

STATE CAPITOL

PUNCHBOWL ST.

SOUTH KING ST.

To Honolulu Academy of Arts

IOLANI BARRACKS

IOLANI PALACE

BANDSTAND

LIBRARY

HONOLULU HALE (CITY HALL)

MISSION HOUSES MUSEUM

KAWAIAHAO CHURCH

KAWAIAHAO ST.

MISSION LN.

KAMEHAMEHA STATUE

POST OFFICE

QUEEN ST.

MILLANI ST.

SOUTH ST.

HALEAKUWILA ST.

92   NIMITZ HWY.

ALA MONA

FEDERAL BUILDING

ALA MOANA

FALLS OF CLYDE

HAWAII MARITIME CENTER

RESTAURANT ROW

92

To Waikiki

ble-hulled sailing canoes, and one of only two fully restored skeletons of the humpback whale (this one is in diving position). One corner is a replica of H. Hackfeld and Co., a whaling supply store of the era. The rear of the second floor shows steamships that cruised between Hawaii, Japan, and the East Coast; a nature exhibit of weather, marinelife, and volcanoes; and an auditorium with a video on the *Hokule'a*.

An free audio tape tour of the center, the kind that plays on a personal cassette player that you listen to with earphones, is available for all who desire a narrated tour. Don't just walk past or save this for the last, as it explains the exhibits and gives insight into what you're seeing. Also, stop in at the gift shop for a collectible of Hawaii's vintage past.

Mac Simpson is the historian/exhibit designer for the Maritime Center. A burly guy with a white beard, he looks the part of an old sea dog. If you have questions about the exhibits, ask him.

Falls of Clyde

This is the last fully rigged, four-masted ship afloat on any of the world's oceans and has recently been designated as a National Historic Landmark. She was saved from being scrapped in 1963 by a Seattle bank that was attempting to recoup some money on a bad debt. The people of Hawaii learned of her fate and spontaneously raised money to have the ship towed back to Honolulu Harbor. The *Falls of Clyde* was always a worker, never a pleasure craft. It served the Matson Navigation Company as a cargo and passenger liner from 1898 until 1920. Built in Glasgow, Scotland, in 1878, she was converted in 1906 to a sail-driven tanker; a motor aboard was used mainly to move the rigging around. After 1920, she was dismantled, towed to Alaska and became little more than a floating oil depot for fishing boats. Since 1968, the *Falls of Clyde* has been a floating museum, sailing the imaginations of children and grownups to times past, and in this capacity has perhaps performed her greatest duty.

Hokule'a

The newest and perhaps most dynamic feature of the center is the *Hokule'a*. This authentic re-creation of a traditional double-hulled sailing canoe captured the attention of the world when in 1976 it made a 6,000-mile roundtrip voyage to Tahiti. Piloted by Mau Piailug, a Caroline Islander, only ancient navigational techniques guided it successfully on its voyage. This attempt to relive these ancient voyages as closely as possible included eating traditional provisions only—poi, coconuts, dried fish, and bananas. Toward the end of the voyage some canned food had to be broken out!

Modern materials such as plywood and fiberglass were used, but by consulting many petroglyphs and old drawings of these original craft, the design and lines were kept as authentic as possible. The sails, made from a heavy cotton, were the distinctive crab-claw type. In trial runs to work out the kinks and choose the crew, she almost sank in the treacherous channel between Oahu and Kauai and had to be towed in by the Coast Guard. But the *Hokule'a* performed admirably during the actual voyage. The experiment was a resounding technical success, but it was marred by bad feelings between members of the crew. Both landlubber and sea dog found it impossible to work as a team on the first voyage, thereby mocking the canoe's name, "Star of Gladness." The tension was compounded by the close quarters of more than a dozen men living on an open deck only nine feet wide by 40 feet long. The remarkable navigator Piailug refused to return to Hawaii with the craft and instead sailed back to his native island. Since then, the *Hokule'a* has made five more voyages, logging over 60,000 miles, with many ethnically mixed crews who have gotten along admirably.

The *Hokule'a*, owned by the Hawaii Maritime Center but sailed by the Polynesian Voyaging Society, makes Pier 7 its home berth when not at sea. This double-hulled canoe, a replica and much older brother of the significantly larger ones that Captain Cook found so remarkable, will fascinate you too.

Aloha Tower

Next door to the Hawaiian Maritime Center, on Pier 9, is the Aloha Tower, a beacon of hospitality welcoming people to Hawaii for six decades. When this endearing and enduring tourist cliche was built in 1926 for $160,000, the 184-foot, 10-story tower was the tallest structure on Oahu. As such, this landmark, with clocks embedded in all four walls, and emblazoned with the greeting and departing word, "Aloha," became the symbol of Hawaii. Before the days of air transport, ocean liners would pull up to the pier to disembark passengers, and on these "Boat Days," festive well-wishers from throughout the city would gather to greet and lei the arriving passengers. The Royal Hawaiian Band would even turn out to welcome the guests ashore.

When you enter the ground floor, you enter what were the huge U.S. Customs rooms that at one time processed droves of passengers coming to find a new life. Today, the crowds come to find a bargain. Only a few harbormasters on the top floor oversee the comings and goings of cargo ships. When you enter the tower a sign claims that you can only get to the observation area on the top floor by elevator. You can walk up to the ninth floor if you want, but to get to the very top does necessitate taking the elevator, which has the dubious distinction of being one of the first elevators in Hawaii. The elevator is a bit like a wheezy old man, huffing and puffing, but it still gets you to the top. Once atop the tower, you get the most remarkable view of the harbor and the city. A high-rise project planned for next door would surely have ruined the view, but due to good sense and citizens with clout, this ill-considered idea has thankfully met a timely end. A remarkable feature of the vista is the reflections of the city and the harbor in many of the neighboring steel and reflective glass high-rises. It's as if a huge mural were painted on them. The tower is open free of charge Mon.-Fri. 9 a.m.-4 p.m., Saturday 9 a.m.-10 p.m., and Sunday 9 a.m.-6 p.m.

PALI HIGHWAY

Cutting across Oahu from Honolulu to Kailua on the windward coast is Rt. 61, better known as the Pali Highway. Before getting to the famous Nuuanu Pali Lookout at the very crest of the Koolau Mountains, you can spend a full and enjoyable day sightseeing. Stop en route at Punchbowl's National Memorial Cemetery, followed by an optional side trip to the summit of Tantalus for a breathtaking view of the city. You can also visit the **Royal Mausoleum State Monument** in the vicinity. Take the H-1 freeway to Vineyard Boulevard (exit 22), cross the Pali Hwy. to Nuuanu Avenue and follow it to the mausoleum. In a minute or two, if you continue up Nuuanu Avenue, it intersects the Pali Hwy., but you'll have passed the Punchbowl turnoff (see following). This small chapel, built in 1865 by Kamehameha IV, holds the bodies of most of the royal family who died after 1825. Their bodies were originally interred elsewhere but were later moved here. The mausoleum at one time held 18 royal bodies but became overcrowded, so they were moved again to little crypts scattered around the three-acre grounds. Of the eight Hawaiian monarchs, only King Kamehameha I and King William Lunalilo are buried elsewhere—King Kamehameha I somewhere on the Big Island and Lunalilo at Kawaiahao Church. Few tourists visit this serene place open weekdays 8 a.m-4 p.m., tel. (808) 536-7602.

Next comes Queen Emma Summer Palace and the Dai Jingu Temple, a Baptist college, and a Catholic church. It almost seems as though these sects were vying to get farther up the hill to be just a little closer to heaven.

A sign, past Queen Emma Summer Palace, points you off to **Nuuanu Pali Drive.** Take it! This few-minutes' jog off the Pali Hwy. (which it rejoins) takes you through some wonderful scenery. Make sure to bear right as soon as you pull off and not up the Old Pali Hwy., which has no outlet. Immediately the road is canopied with trees, and in less than half a mile there's a bubbling little waterfall and a pool. The homes in here are grand, and the entire area has a parklike effect. One of the nicest little roads that you can take while looking around, this side trip wastes no time at all.

Queen Emma Summer Palace

This summer home is more the simple hideaway of a well-to-do family than a grand palace. The 3,000-square-foot interior has only two bedrooms and no facilities for guests. The first person to put a house on the property was John George Lewis. He purchased the land for $800 from a previous owner by the name of Henry Pierce, and then resold it to John Young II. The exterior has a strong New England flavor, and indeed the house was prefabricated in Boston. The simple square home, surrounded by a lanai, was built from 1843 to 1847 by John Young II, Queen Emma's uncle. When he died, she inherited the property and spent many relaxing days here, away from the heat of Honolulu, with her husband King Kamehameha IV. Emma used the home little after 1872, and following her death in 1885 it fell into disrepair.

Rescued from demolition by the Daughters of Hawaii in 1913, it was refurbished and has operated as a museum since 1915. In the '70s, the Summer Palace was added to the National Register of Historic Sites. The palace, at 2913 Pali Hwy., tel. (808) 595-3167, is open daily 9 a.m.-4 p.m., except for major holidays; admission $5, seniors $4, children 16 and under $1. Although it's just off the Pali Highway, the one and only sign comes up quickly, and many visitors pass it by. If you pass the entranceway to the Oahu Country Club just across the road, you've gone too far.

As you enter, notice the tall *kahili*, symbols of noble rank in the entranceway, along with *lau hala* mats on the floor, which at one time were an unsurpassed specialty of Hawaii. Today they must be imported from Fiji or Samoa. The walls are hung with paintings of many of Hawaii's kings and queens, and in every room are distinctive Hawaiian artifacts, such as magnificent feather capes, fans, and tapa hangings.

The furnishings have a very strong British influence. The Hawaiian nobility of the time were enamored with the British. King Kamehameha IV traveled to England when he was 15 years old; he met Queen Victoria, and the two become good friends. Emma and Kamehameha IV had the last child born to a Hawaiian king and queen on May 20, 1858. Named Prince Albert after Queen Victoria's consort, he was much loved but died when he was only four years old on August 27, 1862. His father followed him to the grave in little more than a year. The king's brother, Lot Kamehameha, a bachelor, took the throne but died very shortly thereafter, marking the end of the Kamehameha line; after that, Hawaii elected her kings. Prince Albert's canoe-shaped cradle is here, made in Germany by Wilhelm Fisher from four different kinds of Hawaiian wood. His tiny shirts, pants, and boots are still laid out, and there's a lock of his hair, and one from Queen Emma. In every room there is royal memorabilia. The royal bedroom displays a queen-size bed, covered with an exquisite bedspread or quilt that changes periodically. There's vintage Victorian furniture, and even a piano built in London by Collard and Collard. A royal cabinet made in Berlin holds porcelains, plates, and cups. After Queen Emma died, it stood in Charles R. Bishop's drawing room but was later returned. The grounds are beautifully manicured, and the house is surrounded by shrubbery and trees, many of which date from when the royal couple lived here. Restrooms are around back.

The Daughters of Hawaii have added a gift shop around back, which is open the same hours as the palace. It's small but packed with excellent items like greeting cards, lei, travel guidebooks, beverage trays (reproductions of the early Matson Line menus), little Hawaiian quilt pillows, needlepoint, wraparounds from Tahiti, T-shirts with Queen Emma Summer Palace logo, and Niihau shellwork, the finest in Hawaii.

Walk around back past the basketball court and keep to the right. Soon you'll see a modest little white building. Look for a rather thick and distinctive rope hanging across the entranceway. This is the Shinto temple **Dai Jingu**. It's not nearly as spectacular as the giant trees in this area, but it is authentic and worth a quick look. Shake the bell rope and clap your hands three times as you walk up to the entranceway. For fun, place 25 cents into the *oni kuji* wooden box and out comes a good luck fortune on the back of a small piece of paper. So, for a quarter, find out about love, marriage, business, health, and that sort of thing, and help out the temple at the same time.

Nuuanu Pali Lookout

This is one of those extra-benefit places where you get a magnificent view without any effort at all. Merely drive up the Pali Hwy. to the well-marked turnout and park. Rip-offs happen, so take all valuables. Before you, if the weather is accommodating, an unimpeded view of windward Oahu lies at your feet. Nuuanu Pali ("Cool Heights") lives up to its name; the winds here are chilly, extremely strong, and funnel right through the lookout. You definitely need a jacket or windbreaker. On a particularly windy day just after a good rainfall, various waterfalls tumbling off the *pali* will actually be blown uphill! A number of roads, punched over and through the *pali* over the years, are engineering marvels. The famous "carriage road" built in 1898 by John Wilson, a Honolulu boy, for only $37,500, using 200 laborers and plenty of dynamite, was truly amazing. Droves of people come here, many in huge buses, and they all go to the railing to have a peek. Even so, by walking down the old road built in 1932 that goes off to the right, you actually get private and better views. You'll find the tallest point in the area, a huge needlelike rock. The wind is quieter here.

Nuuanu Pali figures prominently in Hawaii's legend history. It's said, not without academic skepticism, that Kamehameha the Great pursued the last remaining defenders of Oahu to these cliffs in one of the final battles fought to consolidate his power over all of the islands in 1795. If you use your imagination, you can easily feel the utter despair and courage of these vanquished warriors as they were driven ever closer to the edge. Mercy was not shown nor expected. Some jumped to their deaths rather than surrender, while others fought until they were pushed over. The estimated number of casualties varies considerably, from a few hundred to a few thousand, while some believe that the battle never happened at all. Compounding the controversy are stories of the warriors' families, who searched the cliffs below for years, and supposedly found bones of their kinsmen, which they buried. The Pali Lookout is romantic at night, with the lights of Kailua and Kaneohe in the distance, but the best nighttime view is from Tantalus Drive, where all of Honolulu lies at your feet.

PUNCHBOWL, NATIONAL CEMETERY OF THE PACIFIC

One sure sign that you have entered a place of honor is the hushed and quiet nature that everyone adopts without having to be told. This is the way it is the moment that you enter this shrine. The Hawaiian name, Puowaina ("Hill of Sacrifice"), couldn't have been more prophetic. Punchbowl is the almost perfectly round crater of an extinct volcano that holds the bodies of over 33,000 men and women who fell fighting for the United States, from World War II to Vietnam, and a few notable individuals who have served the country in other ways. At one time, Punchbowl was a bastion of heavy cannon and artillery trained on Honolulu Harbor to defend it from hostile naval forces. In 1943 Hawaii bequeathed it to the federal government as a memorial; it was dedicated in 1949, when the remains of an unknown serviceman killed during the attack on Pearl Harbor were the first interred. One of the more recent to be buried here was astronaut Ellison Onizuka, who died in 1986 aboard the *Challenger* space shuttle. To attest to its sacredness and the importance of those who lie buried here, more than five million visitors stop here yearly to pay their respects, making this the most visited site in the state. In addition, the annual Easter sunrise service held here draws thousands.

As you enter the main gate, a flagpole with the Stars and Stripes unfurled is framed in the center of a long sweeping lawn. A roadway lined with monkeypod trees adds three-dimensional depth to the impressionistic scene, as it leads to the steps of a marble, altarlike monument in the distance. The eye has a continuous sweep of the field, as there are no elevated tombstones, just simple marble slabs lying flat on the ground. The field is dotted with trees, including eight banyans, a special tree and symbolic number for the many Buddhists buried here. Brightening the scene are plumeria and rainbow shower trees, often planted in Hawaiian graveyards because they produce flowers year-round as perennial offerings from the living to the dead when they can't personally attend the grave. All are equal here: the famous, like Ernie Pyle, the stalwart who earned the Congressional Medal of Honor, and the unknown who died alone and unheralded on muddy battlefields in godforsaken jungles. To the right just after you enter is the office, tel. (808) 566-1430, with brochures and restrooms. The cemetery is open free of charge 8 a.m.-5:30 p.m. Sept. 30-March 1 and until 6:30 p.m. March 2-Sept. 29, except for Memorial Day when the grounds are open 7

Punchbowl
Cemetery

J.D. BISIGNANI

a.m.-7 p.m. Guided walking tours are conducted by the American Legion at 11 a.m. Mon.-Fri. These two-hour tours cost $15 per person and reservations must be made by calling (808) 946-6383. Tour buses, taxis, and limousines line up at the front. Don't leave valuables in your car.

To get to Punchbowl take the H-1 freeway to Rt. 61, the Pali Hwy., and exit at 21B. Immediately get to the right, where a sign points you to Punchbowl. You'll make some fancy zigzags through a residential area, but it's well marked and you'll come to Puowaina Street, which leads you to the main gate. Make sure to notice landmarks going in, because as odd as it sounds, no signs lead you back out and it's easy to get lost.

The Monument

Like a pilgrim, you climb the steps to the monument, where on both sides marble slabs seem to whisper the names of 28,778 servicemen, all MIAs whose bodies were never found or those who were buried at sea, but whose spirits are honored here. The first slabs on the right are for the victims of Vietnam, on the left are those from WW II, and you can see that time is already weathering the marble. Their names stand together, as they fought and died . . . men, boys, lieutenants, captains, private soldiers, infantrymen, sailors . . . from everywhere in America. "In proud memory . . . this memorial has been erected by the United States of America."

At the monument itself, built in 1966, is a chapel, and in the middle is a statue of a woman, a woman of peace, a heroic woman of liberty. Around her on the walls are etched maps and battles of the Pacific War whose names still evoke passion: Pearl Harbor, Wake, Coral Sea, Midway, Iwo Jima, the Gilbert Islands, Okinawa. Many of the visitors are Japanese. Many of Hawaii's war dead are also Japanese. Four decades ago we battled each other with hatred and malice. Today, on bright afternoons we come together with saddened hearts to pay reverence to the dead.

UNIVERSITY OF HAWAII

You don't have to be a student to head for the University of Hawaii, Manoa Campus. For one, it houses the **East-West Center,** which was in-

corporated in 1975 and officially separated from the university; here nations from Asia and the Pacific present fascinating displays of their homelands. Also, Manoa Valley itself is one of the loveliest residential areas on Oahu. To get to the main campus follow the H-1 freeway to exit 24B (University Avenue). Don't make the mistake of exiting at the University's Makai Campus. Follow University Avenue to the second red light, Dole Avenue, and make a right onto campus. Stop immediately at one of the parking lots and get a parking map! Parking restrictions are strictly enforced, and this map not only helps to get you around, but saves you from fines or having your car towed away. Parking is 50 cents an hour, even for visitors, so think about taking TheBus, which services this area quite well.

Two six-week summer sessions beginning late May and in early July are offered to bona fide students of accredited universities at the University of Hawaii at Manoa. Reasonable rates are available in residence halls (mandatory meals) and in apartments on campus; special courses have an emphasis on Polynesian and Asian culture and languages, including China and Japan. Unbeatably priced tours and outings to points throughout the islands for students and the general public can be arranged at the Summer Session Activities Office. For information, catalog, and enrollment, write Summer Session Office, University of Hawaii, 2500 Dole St., Krauss Hall 101, Honolulu, HI 96822, tel. (808) 956-6894.

Student Center

Make this your first stop. As you mount the steps, notice the idealized mural of old Hawaii: smiling faces of contented natives all doing interesting things. Inside is the **Information Center,** which dispenses info not only about the campus, but also about what's happening socially and culturally around town. Stop here for a campus map and self-guided tour brochure. It even has lists of cheap restaurants, discos, and student hangouts. The food in the cafeteria is institutional but cheap, and has a Hawaiian twist. The best place to eat is **Manoa Gardens** in the Hemenway Center, where you can get a tasty stir-fry or good vegetarian dishes for $3.50 and up.

The **University Bookstore** is excellent, open Mon.-Fri. 8:15 a.m.-4:15 p.m., Saturday 8:15-11:45 a.m. The bookstore is worth coming to for its excellent range of specialty items, like language tapes, and its extensive assortment of travel guidebooks. The **University Art Gallery** is on the third floor, and is worth a look. Free! The exhibits change regularly. Next to the gallery is a lounge filled with overstuffed chairs and big pillows, where you can kick back and even take a quick snooze. This is not a very social campus. By 4:30 or 5 p.m. the place is shut up and no one is around. Don't expect students gathered in a common reading room, or the activity of social and cultural events. When school lets out at the end of the day, people simply go home.

East-West Center

Follow Dole Avenue to East-West Road and make a left. Free tours, Wednesdays only at 1:30 p.m., originate from Imin Center-Jefferson Hall opposite Kennedy Theater. For more info contact the Friends of the East-West Center, 1777 East-West Road, Honolulu, HI 96848, tel. (808) 944-7691. The center's 21 acres were dedicated in 1960 by the U.S. Congress to promote better relations between the countries of Asia and the Pacific with the United States. Many nations, as well as private companies and individuals, fund this institution of cooperative study and research. The center's staff, with help from University of Hawaii students and scholars and professionals from throughout the region, focus on four broad but interconnected issues: regional security, social and cultural changes, the changing domestic political scene in nations of the region, and regional economic growth and its resultant consequences. John Burns Hall's main lobby dispenses information on what's happening, along with self-guiding maps. Imin Center-Jefferson Hall, fronted by Chinese lions, has a serene and relaxing Japanese garden behind, complete with a little rivulet and a teahouse named Jakuan, "Cottage of Tranquility." The murals inside are excellent, and it also contains a large reading room with relaxing couches. While here, check out the bookstore, which carries an impressive selection of Hawaiiana and books on Asia.

The impressive Thai Pavilion was a gift from the king of Thailand, where it was built and sent to Hawaii to be reconstructed. This 23-ton, solid teak sala is a common sight in Thailand. The Center for Korean Studies (not part of the East-West Center) is also outstanding. A joint venture of Korean and Hawaiian architects, its inspiration was taken from the classic lines of Kyongbok Palace in Seoul. Most of the buildings are adorned with fine artworks: tapa hangings, murals, calligraphy, paintings, and sculpture. The entire center is tranquil, and along with the John F. Kennedy Theater of Performing Arts just across the road, is indeed fulfilling its dedication as a place of sharing and learning, culture and art.

MANOA VALLEY

Manoa Valley, a tropical palette of green ablaze with daubs of iridescent color, has a unique designation most aptly described as "urban rainforest." Although not technically true, the valley receiving more than 100 inches of rainfall per year is exceptionally verdant even by Hawaiian standards. However, it wasn't always so. In the late 1800s, the overpopulated valley was almost denuded of trees, only to be reforested by Dr. Lyon, the founder of Lyon Arboretum, who planted trees gathered from around the world. A literal backwater, the runoff from Manoa would flood the relatively dry Waikiki until the Ala Wai Canal was built in the 1920s as a catchment for its torrential flash floods. Only a short drive from arid Waikiki, Manoa was the first place in Hawaii where coffee was grown and where pineapple was cultivated. The great Queen Kaahumanu, who died here in 1832, favored the cool hills of the valley as a vacation spot to escape the summer heat. Manoa, favored by royalty ever since, has maintained itself as one of the most fashionable residential areas in Hawaii, even boasting its own country club at the turn of the century which is yet memorialized by the Manoa Cup held yearly at the Oahu Country Club. In 1893, just before annexation, a bewildered and beaten group of royalists came to Manoa to hide out. They were subsequently captured by a contingency of pursuing U.S. Marines and imprisoned in an area called The Pen, located on the grounds of the now defunct Paradise Park.

Taking Manoa Road past the University of Hawaii you pass **Punahou School,** one of the oldest and most prestigious high schools in Hawaii. Built in 1841 from lava rock, children of the missionary families of wealthy San Franciscans attended, getting the best possible education west of the Rockies.

THE LEGENDS OF MANOA VALLEY

Kahala-o-puna, known for her exceptional beauty, was betrothed to Kauhi, a young chief who was driven mad by unfounded jealousy. He falsely accused his lovely wife of faithlessness and killed her five times, only to have her resurrected each time by her sympathetic guardian *amakua*. Finally, left for dead, Kahala-o-puna was found by a young prince who fell in love with her. Beseeching his animal spirits, he brought her to life one last time, and through them turned the jealous Kauhi into a shark. Kahala-o-puna, warned never to go into the ocean, disobeyed, and was seized in the massive jaws of Kauhi, who fatally crushed the life from her, never to be rekindled. The warm misty rains of Manoa are the tears of the mother of Kahala-o-puna, and the gentle winds are the soft sobs of her bereaved father, who together forever lament the loss of their beloved daughter.

Another legend sings of the spring, Wai-a-ke-akua, created spontaneously by the great gods Kane and Kaneloa, who came to visit this valley. While overindulging in *awa* they became intoxicated and decided that they would dawdle in the lovely valley. Lying down, the gods could hear water running underground, so Kane took his great staff and struck the earth, causing Wai-a-ke-akua to appear. Because of the spring's divine origin, it became known as "water of the gods," making it *kapu* to all but the highest *ali'i*. When Kamehameha conquered Oahu, only he could drink from the spring, which flows with cool sweet water to this day.

Manoa Road eventually crosses Oahu Avenue. Follow it to **Waioli Tea Room,** 3016 Oahu Ave., owned and operated by the Salvation Army, a small park with a snack bar that features fresh-baked pastries and serves lunch daily. Also featured here is the **Little Grass Shack** supposedly lived in by Robert Louis Stevenson when he was a resident of Waikiki. Visit the chapel with its distinctive stained-glass windows. Waioli Tea Room is open daily except Monday, 8 a.m.-3:30 p.m.

Paradise Park, 3737 Manoa Road (at the very end), closed in late 1993, is 13 acres of lush tropical plants founded by James Wong

about 25 years ago. Magnificent blooms compete with the wild plumage of 50 species of exotic birds. However, the Treetop (literally) Restaurant, located here and offering very good food and superlative views, is still operating.

The **Lyon Arboretum,** tel. (808) 988-3177 or 988-7378, is situated on 194 acres at the upper end of Manoa Road. Open to the public, it's principally a research facility and academic institution of the University of Hawaii. You can visit on your own Mon.-Sat. 9 a.m.-3 p.m., but guided tours are also offered on the first Friday and third Wednesday of the month at 1 p.m. and on the third Saturday at 10 a.m. Walking tour maps are available.

 BISHOP MUSEUM

Otherwise known as the Museum of Natural and Cultural History, this group of stalwart stone buildings holds the greatest collection of historical relics and scholarly works on Hawaii and the Pacific in the world. Referring to itself as a "museum to instruct and delight," in one afternoon walking through its halls you can educate yourself about Hawaii's history and people and enrich your trip to the islands tenfold.

Officially named Bernice Pauahi Bishop Museum, its founding was directly connected to the last three royal women of the Kamehameha dynasty. Princess Bernice married Charles Reed Bishop, a New Englander who became a citizen of the then-independent monarchy in the 1840s. The princess was a wealthy woman in her own right, with lands and an extensive collection of "things Hawaiian." Her cousin, Princess Ruta Keeikolani, died in 1883 and bequeathed Princess Bernice all of her lands and Hawaiian artifacts. Together, this meant that Princess Bernice owned about 12% of all Hawaii! Princess Bernice died less than two years later, and left all of her landholdings to the **Bernice Pauahi Bishop Estate,** which founded and supported the Kamehameha School, dedicated to the education of Hawaiian children. (Though this organization is often confused with the Bishop Museum, they are totally separate. The school shared the same grounds with the museum, but none of the funds from this organization were, or are, used for the museum.) Bernice left her personal property, with all of its priceless Hawaiian artifacts, to her husband, Charles. Then, when Queen Emma, her other cousin, died the following year, she too desired Charles Bishop to combine her Hawaiian artifacts with the already formidable collection and establish a Hawaiian museum.

True to the wishes of these women, he began construction of the museum's main building on December 18, 1889, and within a few years the museum was opened. In 1894, after 50 years in Hawaii, Bishop moved to San Francisco, where he died in 1915. He is still regarded as one of Hawaii's most generous philanthropists. In 1961, a science wing and planetarium were added, and two dormitory buildings are still used from when the Kamehameha School for Boys occupied the same site.

Getting There

To get there, take exit 20A off the H-1 freeway, which puts you on Rt. 63, the Likelike Highway. Immediately get into the far right lane. In only a few hundred yards, turn onto Bernice Street, where you'll find the entrance. Or, exit H-1 onto Hofftailing Street, Rt. 61, exit 20B. Keep your eyes peeled for a clearly marked but small sign directing you to the museum. TheBus no. 2 (School-Middle Street) runs from Waikiki to Kapalama Street, from which you walk two blocks.

Admission and Information

The museum is located at 1525 Bernice St., Honolulu, HI 96817, tel. (808) 847-3511, Web site: www .bishop.hawaii.org, and is open seven days a week 9 a.m.-5 p.m. Admission is $14.95 adults, $11.95 for those ages 6-17 and for seniors; kids five and younger and museum members are free, but some exhibits and the planetarium are closed to children under six. *Kama'aina,* military, and other discounts are available but you must ask. It's sometimes best to visit on weekends because many weekdays bring teachers and young students who have more enthusiasm for running

HAWAII STATE ARCHIVES

Princess Bernice

around than checking out the exhibits. Food, beverages, smoking, and flash photography are all strictly prohibited in the museum. The natural light in the museum is dim, so if you're into photography you'll need super-fast film (400 ASA performs only marginally). Daily tours of the Hawaiian Hall are given at 10 a.m. and noon. Throughout the week, the hall offers demonstrations in various Hawaiian crafts like lei-making, featherwork, and quilting 9 a.m.-2 p.m. Before leaving the grounds make sure to visit **Hawaiian Halau,** where a hula is performed Mon.-Fri. at 11 a.m. and 2 p.m. The **planetarium** opens up its skies daily at 11:30 a.m., 1:30 p.m., and 3:30 p.m., and Fri.-Sat. evenings at 7 p.m. by reservation; call (808) 848-4136. Both the library and archives are open to the public, the library on Tues.-Fri. 1-4 p.m. and the archives Tues.-Fri. 10 a.m.-3 p.m., while both open Sat. 9 a.m.-noon. For library reference services, call (808) 848-4148. The snack shop has reasonable prices, and **Shop Pacifica,** the museum bookstore and boutique, has a fine selection of materials on Hawaii and the Pacific, and some authentic and inexpensive souvenirs. Although it has a limited menu, try the **museum cafe** for a snack.

Exhibits

It's easy to become overwhelmed at the museum, so just take it slowly. The number of exhibits is staggering: over 180,000 artifacts; about 20 million(!) specimens of insects, shells, fish, birds, and mammals; an extensive research library; a photograph collection; and a fine series of maps. The main gallery is highlighted by the rich tones of koa, the showpiece being a magnificent staircase. Get a map at the front desk that lists all of the halls, along with a description of what theme is found in each, and a suggested route to follow. Guided tours are given Mon-Fri. at 10 a.m. and noon. The following is just a small potpourri of the highlights that you'll discover.

Bishop Museum

J.D. BISIGNANI

To the right of the main entranceway is a fascinating exhibit of the old Hawaiian gods. Most are just called "wooden image" and date from the early 19th century. Among them are: Kamehameha's war-god, Ku; the tallest Hawaiian sculpture ever found, from Kauai; an image of a god from a temple of human sacrifice; and lesser gods, personal *amakua* that controlled the lives of Hawaiians from birth until death. You wouldn't want to meet any of them in a dark alley! Outside, in what's called the **Hawaiian Courtyard,** are implements used by the Hawaiians in everyday life, as well as a collection of plants that are all identified. The first floor of the main hall is perhaps the most interesting because it deals with old Hawaii. Here are magnificent examples of *kahili,* feathered capes, plumed helmets . . . all the insignia and regalia of the *ali'i.* A commoner sits in a grass shack, a replica of what Captain Cook might have seen.

Don't look up! Over your head is a 55-foot sperm whale hanging from the ceiling. It weighed over 44,000 pounds alive. You'll learn about the ukulele, and how vaudevillians spread its music around the world. Hula-skirted damsels from the 1870s peer provocatively from old photos, barebreasted and with plenty of "cheesecake." Tourists bought these photos even then, although the grass skirts they're wearing were never a part of old Hawaii but were brought by Gilbert Islanders. See authentic hula instruments like a "lover's whistle," a flute played through the nose, and a musical bow, the only stringed pre-European Hawaiian instrument.

Don't miss the koa wood collection. This accomplished artform produced medicine bowls, handsome calabashes, some simple home bowls, and others reputed to be the earthly home of the wind goddess, which had to be refitted for display in Christianized Iolani Palace. A model *heiau* tells of the old religion, and the many strange *kapu* that governed every aspect of life. Clubs used to bash in the brains of *kapu*-breakers are next to benevolent little stone gods, the size and shape of footballs, that protected humble fishermen from the sea. As you ascend to the upper floors, the time period represented becomes increasingly closer to the present. The missionaries, whalers, merchants, laborers, and Westernized monarchs have arrived. Yankee whalers from New Bedford, New London, Nantucket, and Sag Harbor appear determined and grim-faced as they scour the seas, harpoons at the ready. Great blubber pots, harpoons, and figureheads are preserved from this perilous and unglamorous life. Bibles, thrones, the regalia of power and of the new god are all here.

OTHER MUSEUMS AND GALLERIES

Honolulu Academy of Arts

Enjoy the magnificent grounds of this perfectly designed building, a combination of East and West with a Hawaiian roof and thick white stucco walls reminiscent of the American Southwest, created by architect Bertram Goodhue and benefactor Mrs. Charles Montague-Cooke expressly as a museum. The museum, at 900 S. Beretania St. (TheBus no. 2) opposite Thomas Square, tel. (808) 532-8700, Web site: www.honoluluacademy.org, is open Tues.-Sat. 10 a.m.-4:30 p.m., Sunday 1-5 p.m., closed Monday. Admission fees are $5 general and $3 for seniors, students, and military personnel. Members and children under 12 are free, as is everyone on the first Wednesday of the month. Guided docent tours are conducted daily at 11 a.m. The academy houses a brilliant collection of classic and modern art, strongly emphasizing Asian artwork.

James Michener's outstanding collection of Japanese *ukiyo-e* is here. The story goes that an unfriendly New York cop hassled him on his way to donate it to a New York City museum, while a Honolulu officer was the epitome of *aloha* when Michener was passing through, so he decided that his collection should reside here. This collection is rotated frequently and displayed in a specially designed gallery to highlight and protect the prints. Magnificent Korean ceramics, Chinese furniture, and Japanese prints, along with Western masterworks from the Greeks to Picasso, make the academy one of the most well-rounded art museums in America. Some collections are permanent while others change, so the museum remains dynamic no matter how many times you visit.

Enter through the foyer and pass to the courtyard that gets you away from the hustle and bustle of downtown. Great for a little respite from noise. Pass through double French doors to the thick white-walled galleries that create a perfect atmosphere for displaying fine works of art. Discover delights like Paul Gauguin's *Two Nudes on a Tahitian Beach,* James Whistler's *Arrangement in Black No. 5,* John Singer Sargent's *Portrait of Mrs. Thomas Lincoln Hansen Jr.* An entire wing is dedicated to religious art, while another holds furniture from medieval Europe. The courtyards are resplendent with statuary from the 6th century A.D. and a standing figure from Egypt, circa 2500 B.C. The Hawaiian climate is perfect for preserving artwork. In addition to the art exhibitions, educational programs, films, and concerts are supported by the museum.

Stop at the **Academy Shop,** specializing in art books, museum repros, Hawaii out-of-prints, jewelry, notebooks, and postcards. The **Garden Cafe** is open Tues.-Sat. 11 a.m.-2:30 p.m. It has a light but terrific menu, and besides, a trip to the academy demands a luncheon in the cafe.

Honolulu Art Center

Catty-corner from the Academy of Arts, and affiliated with it, is the Honolulu Art Center. Built in 1908 as McKinley High School, and later used as Lincoln (Line Kona) Elementary School, it is now on both the national and state registers of historic places. The building was renovated and reopened in 1990 as a place where art students can do and display their artwork. As the displays change periodically, what you'll get is potluck, but prints and quilts seem to be prominent. As it's a functioning art center, it's a good place to see what kind of artwork young, contemporary Hawaiian artists are doing. Works are displayed in a large, wooden-floored room with a high vaulted ceiling, perhaps the old school gymnasium, where banks of windows provide plenty of natural light.

The Contemporary Museum

Under the direction of Georgiana Lagoria, at 2411 Makiki Heights Dr., tel. (808) 526-1322, the museum welcomes you with two copper-green gates that are sculptures themselves. This open and elegant structure, the former Spalding House, has yielded seven galleries, a shop, and an excellent gourmet restaurant, the Contemporary Cafe. Acquired through the generosity of the *Honolulu Advertiser's* stockholders, the building was donated to the museum as a permanent home in 1988. The focus is on exhibitions, not collections, although works by David Hockney are on permanent display. Always-changing exhibits reflect different themes in contemporary art. Open Tues.-Sat. 10 a.m.-4 p.m., Sunday noon-4 p.m., closed Monday and major holidays; admission $5 general, $3 students and seniors, except on the third Thursday of the month when admission is free. The museum also has a ritzy little restaurant, so you don't have to step out for a bite to eat.

Surrounding the building are three magnificent acres sculpted into gardens perfect for strolling and gazing at the sprawl of Honolulu far below. Led by museum volunteers, a 45-minute tour of the gardens is offered by appointment only. Call the museum for details at least a week in advance.

Aside from the main galleries, works are displayed at the museum cafe; at the museum galleries at the *Honolulu Advertiser,* 605 Kapiolani Blvd.; and at the First Hawaiian Center, 999 Bishop Street. The cafe hours are Tues.-Sat. 10 a.m.-3 p.m. and Sunday noon-3 p.m. The museum gallery hours at the *Honolulu Advertiser* are Mon.-Fri. 8:30 a.m.-5 p.m. For the First Hawaiian Center gallery, the gallery is open Mon.-Thurs. 8:30 a.m.-3 p.m. and Friday until 6 p.m. Admission is free at both the *Honolulu Advertiser* and First Hawaiian Center galleries.

Tennent Art Foundation Gallery

At 201-203 Prospect St., on the *ewa* slope of Punchbowl, the foundation is open Tues.-Sat. 10 a.m.-noon, Sunday 2-4 p.m., tel. (808) 531-1987. Free. There is a library and the walls hold the paintings of Madge Tennent, one of Hawaii's foremost artists, as well as many other contemporary works. It's beautiful, quiet, and worth a visit. Head up Ward Avenue until it meets Prospect Street. Turn left and proceed until Prospect Street veers off to the right. From there it's not far. Look for the salmon-colored wall and gate. The gallery now sits behind a condo.

GARDENS, GUIDED TOURS, ETC.

Foster Botanical Garden

Many of these 13.5 acres of exotic trees have been growing in this manicured garden for over 100 years. It was at one time the private estate of Dr. Hillebrand, physician to the royal court; he brought many of the seedlings from Asia. Two dozen of these trees enjoy lifetime protection by the state. Located at 50 N. Vineyard Blvd., tel. (808) 522-7065, open daily except Christmas and New Year's Day 9 a.m.-4 p.m. Admission is $5 for nonresidents, $3 for residents, $1 for children 6-12, and free for those under age six; a self-guiding brochure sells for $1. Guided tours are given Mon.-Fri. at 1 p.m.; call (808) 522-7066 for reservations. Bring insect repellent. Many nature hikes on Oahu are sponsored by the gardens. Along with four others on the island, these gardens are administered by the Honolulu Botanical Gardens. Before leaving,

stop in for a look at the Foster Garden Gallery and Bookstore for books, postcards, tapa cloth, T-shirts, and other such gift items. The closest stops on TheBus are no. 4 from Waikiki, no. 2 and no.13 to Chinatown.

A stone's throw to the north and set along the Nuuanu Stream on the opposite side of the freeway are the 7.5 acres of the **Lili'uokalani Botanical Garden.** Once the private garden of the last Hawaiian monarch, it's now part of the Honolulu Botanical Garden system. Unlike the imported magnificence of the Foster Botanical Garden, this garden features native Hawaiian plants.

Moanalua Gardens

The private gardens of the Damon Estate, at 1352 Pineapple Place, tel. (808) 833-1944, were given to the original owner by Princess Bernice Bishop in 1884. Just off the Moanalua Freeway, and open to the public, these gardens are not heavily touristed, a welcome respite from the hustle and bustle of the city. Some magnificent old trees include a Buddha tree from Ceylon and a monkeypod called "the most beautifully shaped tree" in the world by *Ripley's Believe It or Not.* The Moanalua Foundation also sponsors walks deep into Moanalua Valley for viewing the foliage of "natural Hawaii." You can walk on your own through the garden, but only after making arrangements at the number above. Free guided walks begin at 9 a.m. usually on weekends; make arrangements, preferably a week in advance, by calling (808) 839-5334.

HONOLULU BEACHES AND PARKS

The beaches and parks listed here are found in and around Honolulu's city limits. World-famous Waikiki has its own entire section (see the Waikiki chapter). The good thing about having Waikiki so close is that it lures most bathers away from other city beaches, which makes them less congested. The following list contains most of Honolulu's beaches, ending at Fort DeRussy Beach Park, just a few hundred yards from where the string of Waikiki's beaches begins.

Sand Island State Recreation Area

You enter this park by way of the Sand Island Access Road, clearly marked off the Nimitz Highway. On the way, you pass through some ugly real estate—scrapyards, petrochemical tanks, and other such beauties. Don't get discouraged, keep going! Once you cross the metal bridge, a favorite fishing spot for local people, and then pass the entrance to the U.S. Coast Guard base, you enter the actual park, 14 acres landscaped with picnic and playground facilities. Follow the road into the park; you pass two observation towers that have been built in the middle of a grassy field, from where you can get an impressive view of Honolulu, with Diamond Head making a remarkable counterpoint. The park is excellently maintained, with pavilions, cold-water showers, walkways, and restrooms, all for day use only; the park closes at 6:30 p.m. However, the camping area is usually empty (state permit required). The sites are out in the open, but a few trees provide some shade.

Unfortunately, you're under one of the main glide paths for Honolulu International Airport. Many local people come to fish, and the surfing is good, but the beaches for snorkeling and swimming are fair at best. Some of the beach area is horrible, piled with broken stone, rubble, and pieces of coral. However, follow the road past the tower and park in the next lot; turn right and follow the shore up to a sandy beach. The currents and wave action aren't dangerous, but remember that this part of the harbor receives more than its share of pollutants. For delicious and inexpensive plate lunches, make sure to stop at Penny's Lunch Wagon, next door to Dancers strip joint, on your way down the access road.

La Mariana Yacht Sailing Club

This small marina at 50 Sand Island Access Road is a love song in the middle of an industrialized area. The marina is Annette La Mariana Nahinua's labor of love that has remained true since 1955. You can read her fantastic story on the menu of the marina's **Hideaway Restaurant,** which is the only real restaurant on Sand Island. In 1955 this area was forgotten, forsaken, and unkempt. Ms. Nahinua, against the forces of nature, and the even more unpredictable and devastating forces of bureaucracy, took this land and turned it into a yacht harbor. The main tools were indefatigable determination, God listening to her prayers, and a shovel and rake. It's one of the last enclaves of old Hawaii, a place to come

for dinner, a drink, or just to look at the boats. The nighttime bartender, Mr. Lee, is friendly but stoic after decades of seeing and hearing it all. Annette, the founder, is now a little gray-haired woman, a motherly type in Birkenstocks, who lives right here above the Hideaway. In the daytime she wanders around spreading her magic while talking to old salts or new arrivals.

The marina is adjacent to an open waterway, which means that you don't have to pay for anchorage. It comes under the old "rights of sailors" to find a free port in which to berth. This unique setup has created an atmosphere in which a subculture of people have built subsistence shacks on the little islands that dot the bay. Some also live on old scows, shipshape yachts, or on very imaginative homemade crafts, afloat and semi-afloat on this tranquil bay. Many are disillusioned and disenfranchised Vietnam vets who have become misanthropes. You'll see the Stars and Stripes flying from their island hooches. Others are yachties who disdain being landlubbers, while others are poor souls who have fallen through the social net. La Mariana is a unique statement of personal freedom in a city where unique statements are generally not tolerated.

Keehi Lagoon Beach Park

Located at the eastern end of Honolulu International Airport, at the northern tip of Keehi Lagoon, this park is just past the **Pacific War Memorial** on Rt. 92 (the Nimitz Highway). Here are restrooms, picnic facilities, and a pay phone. This park is polluted, but some people do swim here. Mostly, local people use the area for pole fishing and crabbing.

Kakaako ("Point Panic") Waterfront Park

This small facility was carved out of a piece of land donated by the University of Hawaii's Biomedical Research Center. Next to Kewalo Basin Harbor, follow Ahui Street, off Ala Moana Boulevard. You'll come to some landscaped grounds with a cold-water shower and a path leading to the bathing area. Kewalo Basin, developed in the '20s to hold Honolulu's tuna fleet, is home to many charter boats. If you're lucky, you may even spot a manta ray, which are known to frequent these waters. This area is poor for swimming, known for sharks, but great for fishing and bodysurfing. Unfortunately, novices will quickly find out why it's called Point Panic. A long sea-wall with a sharp dropoff runs the entire length of the area. The wave action is perfect for riding, but all wash against the wall. Beginners stay out! The best reason to come here is for the magnificent and unobstructed view of the Waikiki skyline and Diamond Head.

Ala Moana Beach Park

Ala Moana ("Path to the Sea") Beach County Park is by far Honolulu's best. Most visitors congregate just around the bend at Waikiki, but residents head for Ala Moana, the place to soak up the local color. During the week, this beautifully curving white-sand beach has plenty of elbow room. Weekends bring families that come for every water sport Oahu offers. The swimming is great, with manageable wave action, plenty of lifeguards, and even good snorkeling along the reef. Board riders have their favorite spots, and bodysurfing is excellent. The huge area has a number of restrooms, food concessions, tennis courts, softball fields, a bowling green, and parking for 500 cars. Many Oahu out-rigger canoe clubs practice in this area, especially in the evening; it's great to come and watch them glide along. A huge banyan grove provides shade and strolling if you don't fancy the beach, or you can bring a kite to fly aloft with the trade winds. Ala Moana Park stretches along Ala Moana Blvd., between the Ala Wai and Kewalo Basin boat harbors. It's across from the Ala Moana Shopping Center, so you can rush right over if your credit cards start melting from the sun.

Aina Moana ("Land from the Sea") State Recreation Area used to be called Magic Island because it was reclaimed land. It is actually the point of land stretching out from the eastern edge of Ala Moana, and is contiguous with it. All the beach activities are great here, too. Jutting out from the western end of Ala Moana, making one arm of land that creates Kewalo Basin Marina, is the much smaller **Kewalo Basin State Park.**

If you're here in the early morning hours, check out the Honolulu Fish Auction at Kewalo Basin. Your dinner might be coming off one of these boats.

ACCOMMODATIONS

The vast majority of Oahu's hotels are strung along the boulevards of Waikiki. Most are neatly clustered, bound by the Ala Wai Canal, and run eastward to Diamond Head. These hotels will be discussed in the Waikiki section. The remainder of greater Honolulu has few hotels, but those that do exist are some of Oahu's cheapest. Most are clean, no-frills establishments, with a few others at the airport, or just off the beaten track.

INEXPENSIVE ROOMS

Oahu has a number of YM/WCAs from which to choose, and the only official youth hostel in the state. The Ys vary as far as private rooms and baths are concerned, facilities offered, and prices. Expect to pay $25-30 single with a shared bath, and more for a double with a private bath.

The **YMCA Central Branch** (men only) at 401 Atkinson Dr., Honolulu, HI 96814, tel. (808) 941-3344, is the most centrally located and closest to Waikiki. You can call ahead, but there are no reservations, no curfew, no visitors after 10 p.m.; it has an outside pool, singles, doubles, and private baths. Rates are $29 a night with a $10 key deposit. This Y is located just across from the eastern end of Ala Moana Park, only a 10-minute walk to Waikiki.

YMCA Nuuanu (men only), 1441 Pali Hwy., Honolulu, HI 96813, tel. (808) 536-3556, just near the intersection of S. Vineyard Blvd., is a few minutes' walk from downtown Honolulu. You'll find a modern, sterile facility with a pool, shared and single rooms, and communal bathroom; $25 a night, $143 a week, with a $5 key deposit.

YMCA Atherton Branch, 1810 University Ave., Honolulu, tel. (808) 946-0253, is near the University of Hawaii. Men and women students are given long-term residence here during the school year. Dormitory style, no recreational facilities. Only during the summertime can you rent a room here. It's the cheapest in town, but there's a three-night minimum and a one-time membership fee of $5.

YWCA Fernhurst (women only), 1566 Wilder Ave., Honolulu, HI 96822, tel. (808) 941-2231, fax 949-0266, e-mail: fernywca@gte.net, just off

Manoa Road, across from the historical Punahou School, offers singles and doubles with shared bath. Daily rates are $30 single or $25 shared. Breakfast and dinner included Mon.-Friday. Long-term stays are paid weekly. Security is 24 hours. Women can stay for up to one year, and many women from around the world add an international flavor. Reserve by phone, fax, or e-mail.

The **Honolulu International Youth Hostel,** 2323 A Seaview Ave., Honolulu, HI 96822, tel. (808) 946-0591, is located near the University of Hawaii. As an official American Youth Hostel, AYH members with identity cards are given priority, but nonmembers are accepted on a space-available day-by-day basis. A bed in a bunk room runs $12.50 a night for members and $15.50 for nonmembers. There are no couples' rooms. The office is open 8 a.m.-noon and again 4 p.m.-midnight. This YH is always busy, but will take reservations by phone with a credit card. For information and noncredit card reservations write to the manager, and include an SASE. For information about AYH and membership cards write American Youth Hostels, 1332 I St. NW, Suite 895, Washington, D.C. 20005.

HOTELS

The **Town Inn** (formerly, Kobayashi Hotel) at 250 N. Beretania St., Honolulu, HI 96817, tel. (808) 536-2377, is in Chinatown, and it's an old standby as an inexpensive but clean hotel. It's away from all the Waikiki action, and the spartan, linoleumed rooms rent for under $41.80 or $46.20 for air-conditioning single or double. Plenty of travelers pass through here, and the hotel's restaurant serves authentic Japanese food at moderate prices.

The **Nakamura Hotel** is a little bit more "uptown" both price- and location-wise. It's at 1140 S. King St., Honolulu, HI 96814, tel. (808) 593-9951. The rooms are well-appointed, carpeted, and have large bathrooms. Some a/c rooms face busy King Street; the *mauka* side rooms are quieter, with plenty of breezes to keep you cool. Often you can find a room at this meticulously clean hotel when others are booked up, only because it's out of the mainstream. Rates are $43 single and $48 double.

The **Pagoda Hotel,** 1525 Rycroft St., Honolulu, HI 96814, tel. (800) 367-6060, on Oahu (808) 941-6611, is behind Ala Moana Park between

Kapiolani Blvd. and S. King Street. Because this hotel is away from the "action," you get very good value for your money. Rooms with kitchenettes start at about $85, with two-bedroom suites at around $120. Substantial discounts are given to residents. All rooms have TV, a/c, and parking, and there's a swimming pool as well as access to the well-known **Pagoda Restaurant.**

Another in the same category is the **Holiday Inn Waikiki,** at 1830 Ala Moana Blvd., tel. (808) 955-1111. Rooms here are clean, decent, away from the action, and reasonably priced at $93-130.

The **Ala Moana Hotel,** 410 Atkinson Dr., Honolulu, HI 96814, tel. (800) 228-3278, on Oahu (808) 955-4811, is another hotel where you're just off the Waikiki strip. It's located just behind Ala Moana Park between Ala Moana and Kapiolani Boulevards, with a walking ramp connecting it directly with the Ala Moana Shopping Center. Rooms start at $120 and go up to around $345 for a two-bedroom suite (six people). There's a/c, TV, swimming pools, an all-night coffee shop, nightclub, and the **Summit Supper Club** on the top of this 36-story, 1,200-room hotel.

BED AND BREAKFAST

The **Manoa Valley Inn,** at 2001 Vancouver Dr., Honolulu, HI 96822, tel. (808) 947-6019 or (800) 634-5115, fax (808) 946-6168, offers a magnificent opportunity to lodge in early-century elegance. Formerly the John Guild Inn, this "country inn" is listed on the national and state registers of historic places. Built in 1915 by Milton Moore, an Iowa lumberman, the original structure was a very modest, two-story, boxlike home. It was situated on seven acres, but the demand for land by growing Honolulu has whittled it down to the present half acre or so. Moore sold the house to John Guild in 1919. Guild, a secretary to Alexander and Baldwin, added the third floor and back porch, basically creating the structure that you see today. The home went through several owners and even did a stint as a fraternity house. It ended up as low-priced apartment units until it was rescued and renovated in 1982 by Rick Ralston, the owner of Crazy Shirts and one of Hawaii's successful self-made men, a patron of arts and antiques. He outfitted the house from his warehouse of antiques with furnishings not original to the house, but true to the period. It was sold again in 1990, at which time it went through another refurbishing and landscaping, and is now operated by Marc Resorts.

Rooms with double beds and a shared bath run a reasonable $99-120, while the larger rooms with private baths and queen- or king-size beds are $140. One suite with a king bed goes for $190, and the detached cottage with its double bed runs $165. A continental breakfast, evening wine and cheese service, and local phone calls are all included in the room charge. Free off-street parking is provided. Check-in is at 3 p.m. and checkout at 11 a.m.

The exemplary continental breakfasts are prepared on the premises. In the morning, the aroma of fresh-brewed coffee wafts up the stairs. The breakfast selections are bran muffins, croissants, little sticky buns, fresh fruit of the season, and hand-squeezed juices. The daily and Sunday newspapers are available. Pick one and sink into the billowy cushions of a wicker chair on the lava-rock-colonnaded back porch. Both inside and out, you'll find coffee tables surrounded by overstuffed chairs and, nearby, decanters of port and sherry and dishes filled with chocolates. Every evening, wine and gourmet cheese, along with crackers and fresh fruits, are presented.

FOOD

The restaurants mentioned below are outside of the Waikiki area, although many are close, even within walking distance. Others are located near Ala Moana, Chinatown, downtown, and the less touristed areas of greater Honolulu. Some are first-class restaurants; others, among the best, are just roadside stands where you can get a satisfying plate lunch. The restaurants are listed according to price range and location, with differing cuisines mixed in each range. Besides the sun and surf, it's the amazing array of food found on Oahu that makes the island extraordinary.

SHOPPING CENTER DINING

Ala Moana Shopping Center

The following are all located at the Ala Moana Shopping Center along Ala Moana Boulevard. Most are located in the **Makai Food Court,** a huge central area where you can inexpensively dine on dishes from San Francisco to Tokyo—most for under $10. Counter-style restaurants serve island favorites, reflecting the multiethnic culinary traditions from around the Pacific. You take your dish to a nearby communal dining area, which is great for people-watching. The **China House,** tel. (808) 949-6622, is open daily for lunch and dinner. This enormous dining hall offers the usual selection of Chinese dishes, but is famous for its dim sum (served 11 a.m.-2 p.m.); you pick and choose bite-sized morsels from carts.

Patti's Chinese Kitchen, tel. (808) 946-5002, first floor facing the sea, has all the ambience you'd expect from a cafeteria-style Chinese fast-food joint, plus lines about a block long. But don't let either discourage you. The lines move incredibly quickly, and you won't get gourmet food, but it's tasty, plentiful, and cheap. The Princess-Queen Special is steamed rice, fried rice or noodles, a chow mein, plus two entrees like sweet and sour pork or a chicken dish—for around $3. The Queen is the same, but add an entree—under $4. You can even have four entrees, which fills two large paper plates. The princesses who eat this much food aren't tiny-waisted damsels waiting for a rescuing prince—they can flatten anyone who hassles them on their own.

Plate lunches, noodle soups, pizza, and a variety of munchies can be ordered from the **Ala Moana Poi Bowl.** The **Aloha Grill** has hot dogs, chili dogs, etc.

Ward Warehouse

This shopping center, located at 1050 Ala Moana Blvd., has a range of restaurants, from practical to semi-chic, all reasonably priced. **Benkei,** tel. (808) 591-8713, is a Japanese restaurant that's beautifully appointed with a rock garden at the entranceway that continues to the inside. It's bright and airy, neo-Japanese traditional. Prices are reasonable, with set menu dishes like *unagi kabayaki* for $12.95, miso-fried fish at $9.25, combination dinners for around $14, and plate lunches for about $6. It has a wide

lunch wagon

selection of *don buri*, yakitori, and tempura for around $6. Open Mon.-Sat. 11 a.m.-2 p.m. for lunch, and for dinner from 5 p.m. Nearby is the opposite side of the coin. A small lunch stand sells saimin and yakitori for under $4. Mostly you stand and eat, but there are a few tables in the common mall area. Also, you'll find **Korean Barbecue Express** and **L&L Drive-In** for a quick bite to eat.

The Old Spaghetti Factory, tel. (808) 591-2513, is a huge place that feels a bit like you might imagine a San Francisco eatery at the turn of the century—almost Victorian. It serves a wide variety of pasta not quite like Mama makes, but passable, and at a reasonable price. Try chicken parmigiana for $7.95, spinach and cheese ravioli for $6.50, or meatballs, Italian sausage, and spaghetti with meat sauce for $7.45. Following your meal, linger over an Italian soda, coffee, tea, draft beer, or house wine. Open Mon.-Fri. for lunch, daily for dinner.

More modern, upscale, and expensive is **Kincaid's Fish Chop & Steak House,** tel. (808) 591-2005, with such items on the dinner menu as sirloin steak for $16.95, pasta and roast chicken Dijon for $11.95, and grilled mixed seafood at $18.95. The lunch menu includes many sandwiches in the $7.95-9.95 range, Korean kalbi ribs for $9.95, Sonora pork chops with garlic plum sauce for $10.95, and grilled northern Pacific salmon for $13.95. Soups and salads are à la carte, and a few desserts round out the list.

For those into health foods **Aloha Health Food,** primarily a vitamin and mineral store, has some prepared food and drinks in a cooler. Right across is **Coffee Works,** specializing in gourmet coffee and tea. It has a bakery and sandwiches for under $5, croissants $1.50. So take your vitamins on one side and get jazzed on the other. For any number of fresh fruit juices and smoothies try the **Juice Stop.**

Orson's Restaurant, tel. (808) 591-8681, is a seafood house on the second floor. It's actually quite elegant considering the location, with a prize-winning sunset view of the small boat harbor at Kewalo Basin across the way. The inside, too, is richly appointed in wood and glass. Prices are $12-15 for fresh catch of the day complemented by an extensive wine list.

The **Chowder House,** tel. (808) 596-7944, on the ground floor has fresh-grilled *ahi,* snow crab salad, Manhattan clam chowder, bay shrimp cocktail, deep-fried shrimp, daily specials, and an all-you-can-eat crab night on Thursday.

Ward Centre

This upscale shopping center is directly across the street from Ala Moana Park and next door to the Ward Warehouse. The following are some of its restaurants and eateries, where you can enjoy not only class, but quality as well.

R. Field Wine Co. is not really a restaurant, but a purveyor of exquisite food, fine wines, crackers, cookies, cheeses, imported pastas, and caviar. Most of the wines are top shelf Californian like Kiestler, Dominus, Opus I, and Robert Mondavi, with a nice variety of their reserve wines going back to 1968. Older French wines, as well as German wines, are also available, and while you're there peruse the humidor for a fine cigar. Most recent has been the addition of local organic produce and other Hawaiian food products. Look here for something for that special evening.

Chocoholics would rather visit the **Honolulu Chocolate Company** than go to heaven. Mousse truffles, Grand Marnier truffles, chocolate eggs with pistachio or English walnut all will send you into eye-rolling rapture. If you enter, forget any resolve about watching your weight. You're a goner!

For a quick lunch try **Mocha Java Cafe,** a yuppie, upscale, counter-service-type place with a few tables. It has a selection of sandwiches with an emphasis on vegetarian. If you want a designer lunch, that's the place to go.

The premier, or at least best-known, restaurant in the complex is **Keo's Thai Cuisine,** tel. (808) 596-0020, known for its mouthwatering Thai dishes and for its beautiful decor. The menu is extensive, with plenty of dishes for non-meat-eaters. Prices can be quite reasonable for Thai noodles, chicken, shrimp, or vegetarian ($6.95-8.95), house salad ($4.95), green papaya salad ($4.95), spring rolls (four for $4.95), and tofu, shrimp, or chicken satay for under $9. Try the delicious soups like spicy lemongrass or Thai ginger for $3.75 per serving. Entrees like the Evil Jungle Prince have quite a spicy reputation, or tame down with Asian watercress stir-fried with garlic, yellow bean sauce, and beef, shrimp, or veggies ($6.95-8.95). Keo's has another location, 625 Kapahulu, tel. (808) 737-8240, and operates the **Mekong I and II,** simpler and less expensive restaurants, located at 1295 S. Beretania and 1726 S. King St., respectively. Keo's is known for its beautiful flower displays of torch ginger, orchids, or plumeria on every table, and you may eat inside or outside.

The **Yum Yum Tree,** tel. (808) 592-3580, is an affordable American standard restaurant that features pies and cakes from its bakery, along with homestyle fresh pasta. It has an extensive dining area, quite cheerful with dark wood floors, ferns, hanging greenery, and an open-beam ceiling. Breakfast is 7 a.m.-noon, lunch 11 a.m.-5 p.m., dinner 5 p.m. to midnight, cocktails 7 a.m.-closing.

Compadres Mexican Bar and Grill, tel. (808) 591-8307, open Mon.-Fri. 11 a.m.-1 a.m., Sat.-Sun. noon-1 a.m., serves from a smaller, late menu 10 p.m.-1 a.m. Although part of a small chain with restaurants in Maui, Palo Alto, and Napa Valley, Compadres offers made-to-order health-conscious Mexican cuisine that was voted as the Best on Oahu by the small but discerning local Mexican population. The open-beamed dining room overlooking Ala Moana park is a mixture of South Seas and south of the border with plenty of ferns and foliage, round-topped wooden tables, bent-backed chairs upholstered in primary reds and greens, with Mexican masks, bronze parrots and ceramic macaws hanging from the walls and ceilings. The huge menu, featuring handmade tortillas made either from white flour, whole wheat, blue corn, or regular old yellow corn, along with homemade chips and salsa, uses no lard in any of the dishes except carnitas, which are pork anyway. The most unique offerings are the **Quesadillas Internacionales,** priced $7.95-9.95. Flavors vary but include Baja with shrimp, spinach, and Monterey jack cheese; and Texas with chicken or steak and fiery sauce. Joining the international festival are the big, double-handed burritos for $5.95, which include Thai with spicy chicken breast, sprouts, carrots, green onions, cilantro, chili peanut paste, rice, and black beans; Baja with barbecued shrimp, whole beans, fiesta rice, jack cheese, and salsa fresca; and Hawaiian with teriyaki chicken thighs, whole beans, fiesta rice, and pineapple salsa. Besides quesadillas, there are standard burritos, tacos, and plenty of vegetarian selections like the Joy Enchilada which will make you giggle all the way to Tijuana, or Compadres Tostada filled with beans, avocado, fresh salsa, and chopped olives. No dish is over $16.50. The bar complements the meal with a full selection of domestic and imported beer, a selection of microbrewery beers like Samuel Adams and Sierra Nevada, 10 different kinds of tequila, margaritas by the glass or pitcher, and island exotic drinks for under $5. Compadres is an excellent choice for a "budget gourmet" meal in a hospitable atmosphere where the prices are right and the service excellent. There's even live music offered now and again. You can't go wrong!

Ryan's Grill, tel. (808) 591-9132, open daily 11:15 a.m.-1:45 a.m., is an ultramodern yet comfortable establishment appointed with black leather chairs, chrome railings, marble-topped tables, and a hardwood floor, which are all dominated by a huge bar and open kitchen. The menu offers standards along with nouveau cuisine and includes onion soup ($4.95), sesame chicken salad ($8.95), and tossed fettuccini with sliced breast of chicken and Cajun sauce ($11.95). Sandwiches are everything from hot Dungeness crab to a grilled chicken club, all for about $10. More substantial meals from the grill include Cajun seafood jambalaya ($11.95). The bar prepares all of the usual exotic drinks and has plenty of draft beer selections from which to choose. Most menu items along with plenty of munchies and *pu pu* are served until 1 a.m., so Ryan's Grill makes a perfect late night stop!

Offering pizza, pasta, and (as they say) pizzazz, **Scoozees a Go Go Bakery and Deli,** tel. (808) 597-1777, is a modern and tasteful restaurant and deli. Imported pastas, prosciutto, cheese, stromboli, and fresh baked goods are available from the counter. Menu items include Italian sausage and pepper sandwich or marinated chicken breast grilled with orange macadamia nut pesto for $8.50, and a multitude of pastas and pizzas for around $8-10. Italian desserts, soft drink, coffees, and smoothies round out what's available. Hours are Sun.-Thurs. 11 a.m.-10 p.m., Fri.-Sat. 11 a.m.-11 p.m.

Sushi Masa, tel. (808) 593-2007, serves reasonable Japanese food like tempura, shrimp, and vegetables for $9.50, chicken teriyaki for $7.75, and tanuki udon for $6.50. You can get a sashini combination plate for $22 or a sushi special for $16.50-18.50.

Aloha Tower Marketplace

A few years ago, a law was passed in Hawaii allowing beer to be sold at the place at which it was made. This allowed breweries to open pubs on premises. **Gordon-Biersch Brewery & Restaurant,** tel. (808) 599-4877, open Sun.-Wed. 11 a.m.-10 p.m., Thurs.-Sat. until 11 p.m., has taken advantage of this opportunity and opened a fine establishment at the Aloha Tower Marketplace. Three beers are brewed here: GB Export, a smooth, medium hop, full-bodied beer similar to a pilsner but less bitter; GB Marzen, an Oktoberfest beer with a little extra oomph from a combination of malts; and GB Dunkles, a dark beer, the house specialty, served unfiltered in the old Bavarian tradition. Aside from these beers, there is a selection of wines, coffees, soft drinks, milk, and juices, but no tropical mixed drinks. A short brewery tour is given free every Saturday at noon. Plan to stay for lunch. The lunch and dinner menus are similar, aside from the sandwiches offered at lunch, but lunch prices are about 25% less. Appetizers include garlic fries for $3.95 and sashimi for $12.95, and the small pizzas run $8.95-9.95. These and the various salads are just preparation for the main courses. Try the risotto with grilled vegetables, Italian sausage, Japanese eggplant, and rosemary and black olive brochetta for $14.95; the guava-glazed roast duck with scallions, noodle cake, and braised greens for $16.95; or the pan-seared ahi tuna on a bed of linguini tossed with anchovies, capers, oregano, and arugula for $18.95. An assortment of wonderful desserts tops off the meal. Dine inside or out. Inside, with its leather booths, is more elegant and quieter for conversation. In the more casual alfresco portico, sit at stout wooden tables under canvas umbrellas and watch the tugboats shuttle ships through the harbor as the lights of the city sparkle across the water. The inside bar is good for a quiet drink, while you can boogie at the outside bar, where different bands come to play every night—never a cover.

Restaurant Row

This new-age complex at 500 Ala Moana Blvd. (across from the Federal Building) points the way to "people-friendly" development in Honolulu's future. It houses shops and businesses, but mostly restaurants, all grouped together around a central courtyard and strolling area. Some restaurants are elegant and excellent, while others are passable and plain. But they are all in a congenial setting, and you can pick your palate and style preference as easily as you'd pick offerings at a buffet. Start at the central fountain area with its multicolored modernistic Lego-inspired tower. Every Saturday at 8 p.m. jazz is offered here overlooking the waterfront.

The **Sunset Grill,** tel. (808) 521-4409, is on the corner. With wraparound windows, a long and open bar, and comfortable maple chairs, it lives up to its name. This is the place to come for a quiet evening drink in the downtown area. The food is prepared in full view on a *kiawe*-fired grill, wood-roasting oven, and Italian rotisserie. Choices include a variety of pasta, gourmet salads, calamari, fresh fish, oysters, chicken, veal, and lamb. Lunch is a wide variety of plump juicy sandwiches of turkey, sausage, beef, fish, or chicken. The chefs at the Sunset aren't afraid to blend East with West in a wide variety of creations. Open daily 11 a.m.-11 p.m., Fri.-Sat. 11 a.m.-midnight, and Sunday 9:30 a.m.-10 p.m.

In the middle of the complex is **The Row,** an outdoor bar with finger food. The **Honolulu Chocolate Co.** is next. Like a smug little devil, it tempts with chocolate truffles, mocha clusters, and fancy nut rolls. So sin! You're on vacation. The **Paradise Bakery Cafe** is a simple counter restaurant with pie, coffee, and donuts.

Prima Trattoria offers very special Italian dishes from the Abruzzi, a coastal and mountainous region along the Adriatic known for its hearty cooking. Choose an antipasto from Italian cold cuts to clams in red wine sauce for $7 and under. Assorted soups and salads range from $3 to $6 for *insalata calamari.* Select your favorite pasta, and then cover it with one of 201 delectable sauces, most under $10. Chicken, veal, and steak are grilled, simmered in wine sauce, or made into parmigiana, or choose a traditional lasagna, *gnocchi,* or a good old pizza. The interior is sharp with neon strips and black marble tables and chairs.

A few others in the Row include **Jamaican Cuisine Bar and Grill,** **Kin Chan Sushi,** and the **Payao Thai Restaurant.**

INEXPENSIVE DINING AROUND TOWN

The following restaurants are located in and around the greater Honolulu area.

In central Honolulu, mostly along Bishop Street's financial district, you'll find excellent and inexpensive restaurants that cater to the district's lunch crowd.

At the corner of Pali Hwy. and Vineyard is **People's Cafe,** tel. (808) 536-5789. Run by Newton and Adelle Oshiro, two going on three generations of the same Japanese family have been serving the full range of excellent and inexpensive Hawaiian food at this down-home restaurant. Plate lunches and other lunches run about $5.50. Combination lunches like the Laulau plate, which is lomi salmon, pipikaula,

chicken luau or chicken long rice, poi or rice, are $9-9.50 and served on sectioned trays. While there's no decor to speak of, the place is clean and the people are very friendly. If you want a real Hawaiian meal at a reasonable price, this is the place to come. It's not fancy, but the food is good and the surroundings clean. The People's Cafe is open Mon-Sat. 10:30 a.m.-7:30 p.m.

Down to Earth Natural Foods and Deli, tel. (808) 947-7678, open Mon.-Sat. 10 a.m.-8:30 p.m., Sunday 10 a.m.-6 p.m., at 2525 S. King St., is a kind of "museum of health food stores" serving filling, nutritious health food dishes for very reasonable prices. Sandwiches, like a whopping avocado, tofu, and cheese, are under $5. Daily full-meal specials, like veggie stroganoff, eggplant parmigiana, and lasagna are around $4, including salad. There are plenty of items on the menu that will fill you up for under $3. Healthwise, you can't go wrong!

Kokua Market, tel. (808) 941-1922, at the corner of S. Beretania and Isenberg, is open to the public Mon.-Sat. 9 a.m-8:30 p.m. It's a full-service store with organic and fresh produce, cheese, milk, juices, bulk foods, breads, and a deli case full of sandwiches and other prepared foods.

Suehiro's at 1824 S. King, tel. (808) 949-4584, open daily for lunch and dinner, with takeout service, gets the nod from local Japanese people. The menu here is authentic, the decor strictly Americana, and the food well prepared and moderately priced.

Another of the same is the **Hungry Lion Coffee Shop,** tel. (808) 536-1188, at 1613 Nuuanu Avenue. Open 24 hours, it serves everything from Asian food to steaks. Many local people come here after a night out. Nothing special, but decent wholesome food on formica tables.

At the Hawaii Maritime Center you'll find the seafood establishment **Pier Seven Restaurant** tucked away in the rear overlooking Honolulu Harbor. More interesting and definitely more local is **Pier Eight Restaurant** sandwiched under the huge elevated pier area just nearby the Maritime Center. Basic, Chinese, fast food to go, open daily 10 a.m.-5 p.m.

The **University of Hawaii,** Manoa Campus, hosts a number of restaurants, ranging from an inexpensive cafeteria to international cuisine at the East-West Center. Inexpensive to moderate restaurants include: **Manoa Gardens,** salad and snacks; **Campus Center Dining Room,** for full meals; and the **International Garden,** at Jefferson Hall in the East-West Center.

Sekiya's Restaurant and Deli at 2746 Kaimuki Ave. tel. (808) 732-1656, looks like a set from a 1940s tough-guy movie. The food is well prepared and the strictly local clientele will be amazed that you even know about the place. Closed Monday.

Hale Vietnam, 1140 12th Ave. in Kaimuki, tel. (808) 735-7581, is building an excellent reputation for authentic and savory dishes at very moderate prices. It gets the highest praise from local people, who choose it again and again for an inexpensive evening of delicious dining. Hours are daily 11 a.m.-9:45 p.m.

Penny's Lunch Wagon, tel. (808) 845-6503, on the Sand Island Access Road, is one of the least expensive and most authentic Hawaiian plate-lunch stands you can find. The most expensive lunch is *lau lau,* pork and butterfish wrapped in a ti leaf, at around $4. You can also try baseball-sized *manapua* for around 60 cents. Penny's is out of the way, but definitely worth a stop.

You can't get much cheaper than free, and that's what the **International Society for Krishna Consciousness** offers every Sunday at 5:30 p.m. for its vegetarian smorgasbord. Their two-acre compound is just off the Pali Hwy. at 51 Coelho Way, tel. (808) 595-5339. Of course there're a few chants for dessert. *Hare Krishna!*

For **shave ice** try the **Waiola Store,** on the corner of Paani and Waiola. You can get it in Waikiki, but for the real stuff in all its syrupy glory come here.

Art and the Sandwich

In Honolulu there are a few opportunities to feed your mind and soul along with satiating your appetite.

The **Garden Cafe,** at the Honolulu Academy of Arts, 900 S. Beretania, tel. (808) 532-8734, is a classy place for lunch. Open Tues.-Sat. 11 a.m.-2:30 p.m. The cafe has grown from a volunteer operation to serving a full luncheon under professional management. Dine inside or out; it's a fine place to get away from the hustle and bustle of the city. Menu items include a chilled tomato and avocado soup with coriander garnish for $3.75, soup or salad and half sandwich for $7.35, and a

turkey sandwich for $8.25. An assortment of desserts, beverages, and drinks can also be ordered. The food is delicious, but be aware that the portions are not for the hungry, being designed primarily for patrons of the arts who seem to be wealthy matrons from the fashionable sections of Honolulu who are all watching their waistlines.

Don't let the Porsches, Mercedeses, and BMWs parked vanity plate to vanity plate in the parking lot discourage you from enjoying the **Contemporary Cafe,** tel. (808) 523-3362 (reservations recommended), at the Contemporary Museum, 2411 Makiki Heights Drive. The small but superb menu is as inspired as the art in the museum, and the prices are astonishingly inexpensive. Dine inside or out, or perch on the porch. Appetizers are sautéed mushrooms, fruit, or smoked salmon for under $10. Salads include home-smoked mahimahi and papaya vinaigrette salad, Malaysian shrimp salad, Greek salad, or chicken salad for under $11. Sandwiches are a fine selection including smoked breast of turkey or *ahi* Caesar for under $10. Desserts run from cheesecake to flourless chocolate roulade, and beverages include homemade lemonade and cappuccino. For a wonderful cultural outing combined with a memorable lunch, come to the Contemporary Cafe. Open Tues.-Sat 11 a.m.-2 p.m. for the main menu, and 2-3 p.m. for drinks and desserts only. Sunday hours are noon-3 p.m. It's just so . . . contemporary! When in downtown Honolulu, check out the branch Contemporary Cafe at the First Hawaiian Center near Bishop and Market Streets.

HAWAIIAN REGIONAL CUISINE

As large a city as Honolulu is, it's able to support many innovative restaurants where locally grown foods are combined with preparation techniques from around the world to produce new and intriguing flavors. The following are restaurants where something new is always on the menu and the combination of ingredients, textures, and tastes is sure to please. Reservations are recommended.

Located in the semi-industrial area of Iwilei, **Sam Choy's Breakfast, Lunch, and Crab,** tel. (808) 732-8645, is as popular as every other Sam Choy restaurant in the islands. The Kona poke and beef stew omelettes are much-requested breakfast items, while various crab entrees appear for dinner depending on the season. Always generous portions at reasonable prices.

Indigo, 1121 Nuuanu Ave. in Chinatown, tel. (808) 521-2900, serves what some classify as Eurasian cuisine. Chef Glenn Chu offers such savory items as Chinese steamed buns filled with eggplant and sun-dried tomatoes, crispy goat cheese wonton filled with fruit sauce, fresh corn polenta, or grilled Atlantic salmon with tomato salsa and shiitake mushroom pepper relish. Some vegan items available.

Located at the Ward Center is **A Pacific Cafe,** tel. (808) 593-0035, where Chef Jean Marie Josselin creates tasty treats like spinach and wild mushroom cannelloni, Australian salmon with Moroccan spice and lentils, and opakapaka crusted with porcini and fresh herbs with fennel and sun-dried tomato Israeli couscous.

For two years running, **Alan Wong's** has been awarded Best Restaurant of the Year by the *Honolulu Magazine.* Here you can try such delicacies as shredded *kalua* pig wrapped in taro pancake on poi vinaigrette with lomi tomato relish, grilled lamb chops with coconut macadamia nut crust, or a vegetarian entree consisting of mashed potatoes, black bean salsa, grilled asparagus, and roasted shiitake mushrooms. Yum! Alan Wong's is located just north of Waikiki at 1857 S. King St., tel. (808) 949-2526.

At 3660 Waialea Ave. near where the road crests the hill in Kaimuki is **3660 On The Rise,** tel. (808) 737-1177, a casually elegant place where you can watch the cooks create behind the glass wall of the kitchen. While the menu changes somewhat every night, Chef Russel Siu's "first flavors" include frizzled shrimp wrapped in shredded phyllo pastry or potato crusted crab cakes, while "second flavors" are soups and salads. "Feature presentations" might be shichimi seared breast of chicken with shiitake mushrooms and soy citrus butter sauce or Chinese steamed fillet of opakapaka lightly seared and simmered in a Chinese black bean broth. Round out your meal with one of the "sweet endings": harlequin crème brûlée or mile-high Wailea pie, perhaps, or indulge in a cup of coffee or glass of cognac or port. Delightful presentation and attentive service. Open Sunday, Tuesday, Wednesday, and Thursday 5:30-9:30 p.m., Friday and Saturday until 10 p.m.—closed Monday.

MODERATE DINING AROUND TOWN

The following listings are for restaurants where two can dine for around $40. This does not include drinks.

Fisherman's Wharf, tel. (808) 538-3808, at 1009 Ala Moana Blvd. on the Kewalo Basin, is a Honolulu institution. This restaurant has been here since 1952, when it took over from Felix's Italian Garden Restaurant, which had been on this spot since the '40s. The restaurant's design gives you the feel of being aboard ship. Its theme is nautical, displaying a collection of ship's accessories, riggings, and figurines, and trophy catches from the sea. Even a few unique museum-quality items adorn the walls. The place exudes the feel of a Honolulu of days past, and you can sit and watch through the windows as fishing boats and cruise ships arrive and depart as they have done for decades, or look out past Waikiki to Diamond Head. Upon entering the first floor Seafood Grotto, you pass a live lobster tank. For lunch, start with shrimp cocktail or oysters on the half shell for under $9. Follow this with Boston-style clam chowder at $3.50 a bowl and a Caesar salad for $4.95. Sandwiches range $5.95-11.95, or choose fresh fish done in a variety of ways at market price, mahimahi strips for $7.95, batter-fried mahi, shrimp, scallops, and clam strips for $11.95, or one of the special entrees from chicken stir-fry to seafood medley $13.95-29.75. The dinner menu is similar, but without the sandwiches and with the addition of pastas and other special entrees. Some additional dinner dishes are seafood parmesan, shrimp curry, combination filet mignon with king crab or shrimp, seafood medley, and lobster for $15.25-27.95. Upstairs, the Captain's Bridge is like a cabaret club that serves light meals, soups, and salads, with a full range of drinks. Friday and Saturday nights there's karaoke, so come up and dance.

The Hideaway Restaurant, at La Mariana Yacht Sailing Club, 50 Sand Island Access Road, is the only real restaurant on Sand Island. Henry, for many years a ship's cook, can cook everything well—maybe not great, but well. If a Chinese person came here and wanted chop suey Henry could do it. If a guy wanted steak and potatoes, you got it! Pasta? Here it is! The Hideaway serves appetizers like sashimi, lumpia, and sautéed mushroom buttons. From the broiler come steaks, pork chops, and burgers with all the fixings; the most expensive is $14.95. From the sea, seafood brochette, shrimp scampi served over linguini, or *ahi* Cajun style fill your plate. Chicken, lobster, and nightly specials fill out the menu. The lunch menu is simpler, with soups, salads, hot and cold sandwiches, and a handful of fish and stir-fry selections. Henry is also known for his onion rings. They're not on the menu; you have to know about them. Now you know.

While the decor has recently been upgraded, it's still very Polynesian and nautical in essence. Inside hang Japanese glass floats that at night are diffused with different colors, providing mood lighting for the cozy black booths and wooden tables with wicker chairs, tiki posts, and decorations scavenged from defunct former restaurants in town. The Hideaway is an out-of-the-way place, local, and real Hawaiiana. Located at a working marina, this is where all the yachties come. Half hidden behind a stand of trees, there is only one small sign at the entrance to point the way. The restaurant serves food Mon.-Fri. 11:30 a.m.-2 p.m. and 5-9 p.m. and Sat.-Sun. noon-5 p.m. From 9 p.m.-midnight on Friday and Saturday, Ron Miyashiro and Singers croon the night away to piano music so stop by for a drink at the bar and enjoy.

Shiruhachi, at 1901 Kapiolani Blvd., tel. (808) 947-4680, is a completely authentic Japanese sushi bar operated by Hiroshi Suzuki. As a matter of fact, until recently 90% of the clientele was Japanese, either visiting businessmen or locals in the know, and the menu was only in Japanese. However, everyone is more than welcome. With a beer, you get free *otsumami* (nibbles), with a wide selection of sushi and other finger foods like yakitori at about $2 for two skewers. A separate section of the restaurant turns into a cocktail lounge, somewhat like an *akachochin,* a neighborhood Japanese bar where people go to relax. There's taped music and a dance floor. If you're into authentic Japanese, this is a great one.

Auntie Pasto's, at 1099 S. Beretania and the corner of Pensacola, tel. (808) 523-8855, is open Mon.-Thurs. 11 a.m.-2:30 p.m., Friday 11 a.m.-11 p.m., Saturday 4-11 p.m., and Sunday and holidays 4-10:30 p.m. The vibe is upbeat pizza parlor, where you can even bring your own wine. Most of the Italian menu entrees are $8.50-

12, and these include eggplant parmesan for $8.50, calamari steak for $9.25, and veal marsala for $11.95. Soups come by the cup, $1.95, or bowl, $2.50; the large salads range from a $2.95 garden salad to a chicken Caesar for $6.95. Antipasto plates, sides, and desserts run $3-6. No reservations necessary, quiet, comfortable.

Wo Fat's, at 115 N. Hotel St., tel. (808) 533-6393, has had a little experience satisfying customers—the oldest eatery in Chinatown, it's been at the same location for over 80 years, and open for business for 100! Besides serving delicious food from a menu with hundreds of Cantonese dishes, the building itself is monumentally ornate. You're entertained just checking out the decor of lanterns, dragons, gilt work, and screens. Most dishes are reasonably priced and start at around $5. This restaurant is highly respected by the people of Chinatown and is part of the Chinatown tour offered by the chamber of commerce.

EXPENSIVE DINING AROUND TOWN

Sometimes only the best will do, and Honolulu can match any city for its fine restaurants. For more fine dining see the Waikiki chapter.

Won Kee Seafood Restaurant, tel. (808) 524-6877, 100 N. Beretania, is a splurge joint where you get delicious seafood. Free parking on Maunakea Street. This is the place for Honolulu's in-the-know crowd. Tasteful and elegant surroundings.

Right next door to the Won Kee is the **Forum Restaurant,** tel. (808) 599-5022. Open daily 11 a.m.-2:30 p.m. and 5-11 p.m., this too is a classy joint with everything from the usual rice dishes to braised imperial shark fin soup for $38 per person.

The **Legend Seafood Restaurant,** tel. (808) 532-1868, two doors down from the Won Kee, emphasizes fish and seafood, but also serves Hong Kong-style dim sum for $1.50, $2.40, $3.25, and $4.25 for small, medium, large, and super size plates, respectively.

The Chart House, at 1765 Ala Moana Blvd. near Ala Wai Yacht Harbor, is open daily 4 p.m. (Sunday 5 p.m.) till 2 a.m., tel. (808) 941-6660. It offers a happy hour until 7 p.m., *pu pu* until midnight, and nightly entertainment. Shellfish specialties start at $15, with chicken and beef dishes a few dollars cheaper.

India House, 2632 S. King St., is open daily for lunch and dinner, tel. (808) 955-7552. Extraordinary Indian dishes prepared by chef Ram Arora. A wide selection of curries, vegetarian dishes, special *naan* bread, kabobs, and fish *tikka*. Specialty desserts include homemade ice cream and toppings.

Keo's Thai Cuisine, 625 Kapahulu, open nightly 5:30-11 p.m., tel. (808) 737-8240, has become an institution. It serves great Thai food at expensive prices. They pride themselves on the freshest ingredients and spices tuned up or down to suit the customer, and Keo's recipes are taught to each chef personally. There's always a line, with a few benches in the parking lot for waiting customers, but no reservations are taken. The eight-page menu offers most of Thailand's delectables, and vegetarians are also catered to. You can save money and still have the same quality food at **Mekong I** and **Mekong II.** Owned by Keo's, it's not as fancy.

ENTERTAINMENT

Dancing, Disco, and Lounge Acts

Anna Bannana's, at 2440 S. Beretania, tel. (808) 946-5190, is the "top banana" for letting your hair down and boogying the night away. It's out by the university just across from Star Market. This dance joint has a laid-back atmosphere, reasonable beer prices, a small cover which goes to the band, no dress code, and a friendly student crowd. Dancing is upstairs, light dining downstairs, and a backyard to cool off between sets. Great place, great fun!

The **Club Jubilation,** at 1007 Dillingham Blvd., tel. (808) 845-1568, sways with Hawaiian music every night but Monday. Listen to hula tunes on traditional and quickly fading slack-key guitar. People from the audience, when moved by the music, will take to the dance floor or the stage for an impromptu performance. What they lack in polish they make up for in sincerity. Everybody's welcome. Beer around $3, with plenty of *pu pu,* like watercress with mayonnaise and soy sauce, along with regular island munchies.

Ocean Club (formerly Studebaker's) at Restaurant Row, 500 Ala Moana, tel. (808) 526-9888, is Honolulu's newest hot spot. Open from late afternoon to early morning, except Sunday and Monday.

Rumours Nightclub, in the Ala Moana Hotel, 410 Atkinson St., tel. (808) 955-4811, is an established disco that cranks up around 9 p.m. and features the newest in dance and rock videos.

classic hula troupe

HAWAII STATE ARCHIVES

Also along Restaurant Row is **Blue Zebra,** a popular disco nightclub with a good dance floor, a fine selection of music, and a reasonable dress code. Blue Zebra is open seven nights a week until the wee hours of the morning.

Nearby, find the **World Cafe** nightclub. The dance floor and pool tables draw a blend of locals and tourists.

The **Fast Zone** at the Fort Street Mall generally draws a younger crowd, many of them students from Hawaii Pacific University. There's no dancing, but it's a place to have a beer and conversation and listen to the strains of hard core alternative music.

TGI Fridays, 950 Ward Ave., tel. (808) 523-5841, is a lively night spot. Good food, large portions, reasonable prices, and music.

Pecos River Cafe, at 99-016 Kamehameha Hwy., tel. (808) 487-7980, has country music by local country bands. On Wednesday evening instructors teach country line dancing and square dancing. Have a few lessons so you can dance to the live band with confidence.

The **Pier Bar** at the Aloha Tower Marketplace has an elevated stage with live acts throughout the week, ranging from Hawaiian to contemporary rock to R&B. The music is potluck, but you're right on the harbor, so you can watch the sunset and always have a great time.

Note: Also see "Entertainment" in the Waikiki chapter.

Girlie Bars and Strip Joints
You'll have no excuse if your maiden Aunt Matilda or local chapter of Fed Up Feminists Inc. ever catches you going into one of these joints, sonny boy! There's not even a hint of a redeeming social value here, and the only reason they're listed is to let you know where *not to go*. Many of these "lounges," as they're called, are strung along the 1600 and 1700 blocks of Kapiolani Blvd., and in the little alleys running off it. Mostly, tough-looking Asian men own or operate them, and they open and shut quicker than a streetwalker's heart. Inside are two types of women: the dancers and the lap sitters, and there's definitely a pecking order in these henhouses. Most patrons are local men or GI types, with only a smattering of tourists. Personal safety is usually not a problem, but a fool and his money are soon parted in these bars.

Chinatown's **Hotel Street** has hookers, both male and female, walking the heels off their shoes. They cruise during the day, but the area really comes alive at night. Mostly, these people are down-and-outers who can't make it against the stiff competition along the main areas of Waikiki. The clientele is usually servicemen and hard-core locals. A few clubs in this area offer strippers. Always be prepared for fights and bad vibes in any of these joints.

Freebies
At **Centerstage,** Ala Moana Center, various shows are presented—mostly music (rock, gospel, jazz, Hawaiian) and hula. Performances usually start at noon. The **Young People's Hula Show,** every Sunday at 9:30 a.m., is fast becoming an institution. Here, hula is being kept alive, with many first-time performers interpreting the ancient movements that they study in their *halau.*

The **Royal Hawaiian Band,** founded over 150 years ago, performs Friday at noon on the Iolani Palace Bandstand, and on Sunday at 12:45 p.m. and 2 p.m. at the Kapiolani Bandstand. Call (808) 527-5666 for other band performance locations.

Everyone is invited to enjoy the **Friday noontime music** at Tamarind Park, on the corner of King and Bishop Streets, where anything from pop to traditional may be performed.

Honolulu Hale (City Hall) presents periodic free musical concerts in the central courtyard and art exhibitions in the central courtyard, Lane Gallery, or Third Floor Gallery. All are welcome.

Various **hula and other cultural programs** are performed around dusk on Saturday and Sunday at the Kuhio Beach Banyan Tree Park.

Sometimes the University has free noontime shows at the student center and evening musical concerts at the Manoa Gardens restaurant. Call the information center, tel. (808) 956-7235, for current happenings.

Hilo Hattie, 700 Nimitz Highway, the largest manufacturer of alohawear in the state, conducts free tours of the factory, complete with complimentary shuttle ride from Waikiki (the shuttle also passes Dole Cannery Square). Up to 40,000 garments are on display in the showroom, plus countless gifts and souvenirs. It's hard to resist spending: prices and craftsmanship are good, and designs are the most contemporary. Open daily 7 a.m.-6 p.m., tel. (808) 537-2926 or (800) 272-5282.

SHOPPING

If you don't watch the time, you'll spend half your vacation moving from one fascinating store to the next. Luckily, in greater Honolulu the majority of shopping is clustered in malls, with specialty shops scattered around the city, especially in the nooks and crannies of Chinatown. For a general overview of what the island has for sale, along with listings for bookstores, food outlets, flea markets, sundries, and art shops, see "Shopping" in the Out and About chapter above.

Ala Moana Shopping Center

This is the largest shopping center in the state, and if you want to get all of your souvenir hunting and special shopping done in one shot, this is the place. It's on Ala Moana Blvd. just across from the Ala Moana Beach Park, open weekdays 9:30 a.m.-9 p.m., Saturday 9:30 a.m.-5:30 p.m., Sunday 10 a.m.-5 p.m., tel. (808) 946-2811. Recently, the Ala Moana Shopping Center has taken off its comfortable Hawaiian shirt and shorts and donned designer fashions by Christian Dior and Charles Jordan. Local people are irritated, and they have a point, to a point. The center has plenty of down-home shopping left, but it now caters as much to the penthouse as it does to the one-room efficiency. It used to be where the *people* shopped, but now portions are being aimed at the affluent tourist, especially the affluent Japanese tourists who flaunt designer labels like politicians flaunt pretty secretaries. If anything, the shopping has gotten better, but you'll have to look around a bit more for bargains.

Plenty of competition keeps prices down, with more than enough of an array to suit any taste and budget. There are about 200 stores including all of Hawaii's major department stores like **Sears, JCPenney's,** and **Liberty House.** Utilitarian shops like shoe makers, eateries, banks, and boutiques feature everything from flowers to swim fins. It's also a great place to see a cross-section of Hawaiian society. Another pleasantry is a free hula show every Sunday at 9:30 a.m. on the Centerstage. The **Hawaii Visitors Bureau** maintains an information kiosk just near Centerstage. The following is a mere sampling of what you'll find.

The restaurants in the **Makai Food Court** are exceptional, if not for taste, at least for price, and are unbelievable for the variety of cuisines represented. In a huge open area you'll find dishes from Bangkok to Acapulco, from Tokyo to San Francisco. Most of these restaurants have only counters for ordering, with tables in a common dining area. Great for people-watching, too!

A good one-stop store with plenty of souvenir-quality items at affordable prices is good old **Woolworth's.** It has all of the same sundries as Mainland stores, but plenty of Hawaiian and Oriental baubles fill the shelves, too. The film prices are some of the best.

House of Music, tel. (808) 949-1051, sells records and tapes. On the ground floor, this is a good store to shop for those island sounds that'll immediately conjure up images of Hawaii whenever they're played.

The Honolulu Book Shop, tel. (808) 941-2274, has the one of the largest selection of books in the state, especially in the Hawaiiana section. Books make inexpensive, easy-to-transport, and long-lasting mementos of your trip to Hawaii. Ground level near Centerstage.

Francis Camera Shop, tel. (808) 973-4480, is a well-stocked camera store with a fine selection of merchandise sure to please the most avid camera buff. If you need something out of the ordinary for your camera bag, this is a good place to come. The staff is friendly and will spend time giving you advice. However, the best place to buy film is at **Sears** (no credit cards). **Woolworth's** and **Longs Drugs** also have good prices, but for cheap and fast developing try **Fromex One Hour Photo,** tel. (808) 955-4797, street level, ocean side.

The Crack Seed Center, tel. (808) 949-7200, offers the best array of crackseed (spiced nuts, seeds, and fruits) that have been treats for island children for years. There're also dried and spiced scallops at $68 per pound and cuttlefish at $2.50 per pound—such a deal! Prices are inflated here, but the selection can't be beat, and you can educate yourself about these same products in smaller stores around the island. Crackseed is not to everyone's liking, but it does make a unique souvenir. Spirolina hunters can get their organic fix at **Vim and Vigor,** featuring vitamins, supplements, and minerals.

Shirokiya is a Japanese-owned department store between JCPenney's and Liberty House on the mountain side of the complex. It has a fascinating assortment of gadgetry, knickknacks, handy items, and nifty stuff that Nippon is so famous for. It's fun just to look around, and the prices are reasonable. Japanese products are also available at **S.M. Iida Limited,** tel. (808) 973-0320, a local store dating back to the turn of the century, featuring garden ornaments and flower-arrangement sets.

Specialty shops in the center include **Hawaii Too** and **Irene's Hawaiian Gifts,** selling a wide assortment of island-made goods and souvenirs, from cheap to exquisite; **Tahiti Imports,** with bikinis, muumuu, and a wide selection of handicrafts from throughout Polynesia; and **Jeans Warehouse** for you aloha buckaroos.

Ward Warehouse

Located just a few blocks west of Ala Moana Center, at 1050 Ala Moana Blvd., open weekdays 10 a.m.-9 p.m., Saturday 10 a.m.-5 p.m., Sunday 11 a.m.-4 p.m., tel. (808) 591-8411, this modern two-story complex lives up to its name as a warehouse, with a motif from bygone days when stout wooden beams were used instead of steel. The wide array of over 75 shops here includes a number of inexpensive restaurants, but the emphasis is on arts and crafts.

Give the tots their first lesson in impulse buying at **Hello Kiddie's,** a toy store, or show them how a pro does it by wandering into **Blue Ginger** for men's and women's fashionable alohawear.

Repent past gluttonies at **Aloha Health Food,** primarily a vitamin and mineral store. Or dress your feet at **Thongs 'n Things,** with everything from spiked golfing thongs to Teva sandals, the best all-around footwear for the island.

Other shops include **Runners Route,** selling jogging shoes, shorts, and some backpacks; **Island Sunspot** and **Villa Roma** for ladies' fashions; and **Beyond the Beach,** which stocks men's and women's alohawear, casual clothing, and sunglasses.

Perhaps the premier shop in the Warehouse is **Nohea Gallery** (*nohea* means beautiful or handsome in Hawaiian), tel. (808) 596-0074, owned and operated by Gail and Lorie Baron, who personally choose for display works by over 500 local artists and craftspeople. Some of the finest works are created by over 100 island woodworkers who make everything from rocking chairs and rolltop desks to traditional canoe paddles using rich grained woods like koa, mango, and rosewood. One of the most acclaimed woodworkers on display is **Kelly Dunn,** who, from his shop in Hawi on the Big Island, turns out bowls from Norfolk Island pine that are so thin you can actually see through them. Other artists displaying their talents include: **Kurt McVay,** who creates masterpieces in glass primarily in cobalt blues and emerald greens highlighted with daubs of oranges and yellows; **Diana Lehr,** who uses oils and pastels to capture the dramatic skyscapes and colors of Hawaii's sunsets and sunrises; **Fabienne Blanc,** who works in ultravibrant watercolors creating surrealistic close-up images of plants and foliage; **Russell Lowrey,** Fabienne's husband, who watercolors and pastels, creating soft, feminine images of the islands; a very talented local couple, under the name of **Ulana O Kukui,** make beautiful jewelry such as rings of gold and silver that they fashion like traditional *lau hala* weaving along with fused and blown glass, and woven baskets of all natural materials; and **Rick Mills,** a University of Hawaii professor, another glass artist who favors cobalt blue. Distinctive and affordable treasures include backgammon games, jewelry boxes, bowls, all kinds of jewelry, prints, and even distinctive postcards. Nohea Gallery is where you can see the "heart of Hawaii" through the eyes of its artists. Have a look!

The **Ward Farmer's Market** is just across the street, at 1020 Auahi, where you can pick up fresh produce and flowers. Down the street at 1116 Auahi Street is **Ward Village Shops,** and more shops are located nearby in **Ward Gateway Center** at 333 Ward Avenue.

Ward Centre

Across the street from the Ward Warehouse, this relatively new shopping center is gaining a reputation for some exclusive shops. The Ward Centre, tel. (808) 531-6411, open weekdays 10 a.m.-9 p.m., Saturday 10 a.m.-5 p.m., Sunday 11 a.m.-4 p.m., is appointed in light wood and accentuated by brick floors that give the feeling of an intimate inside mall, although much is outside.

The Colonnade is a cluster of shops inside the Ward Centre. It includes Willowdale Galleries, twinkling with elegant antiques, crystal place settings, chandeliers, and even candelabra for those closet Liberace wannabes. It's like looking into a giant china closet filled with the best place settings and crystal.

Art A La Carte is a 12-member co-op featuring the works of well known island artists including Gail Bakutis, Cindy Conklin, Helen Iaea, and Masao Yamanoha. Hanging on the walls are landscapes, seascapes, and a variety of portraits done in oils, paper, and watercolors, while cases hold the distinctive raku-style ceramics of Carl Fieber.

You can find that just-right gift at Gems of the Pacific, which mainly deals in coral and black onyx jewelry. Size Me Petite is for the smaller women and young girls, and Allure offers designer bikinis and bathing suits.

Vibrating from a remote corner of the mall, where mystics feel more at home, is Sedona, tel. (808) 591-8010, a metaphysical new-age store. Inside, its shelves and cases are stocked with aromatherapy and massage oils, natural crystals, agates, books, jewelry, figurines, carvings, posters, postcards, and consciousness-lifting tapes. Recharge your spiritual batteries with a personal psychic reading done by various practitioners in a private upstairs area.

Borders Books and Music has a full-selection outlet here, with books, music, newspapers and magazines from around the world, and a gallery and coffee shop upstairs. It has a good Hawaiiana section. Open Mon.-Thurs. 9 a.m.-11 p.m., Fri.-Sat. to midnight, and Sunday 9 a.m.-9 p.m. Call (808) 591-8995 for book information, (808) 591-8996 for music, or (800) 591-8995 from the Neighbor Islands.

Aloha Tower Marketplace

Constructed in 1994, the Aloha Tower Marketplace is one of the newest mall/shopping plazas in Honolulu, one frequented not only by tourists but by locals. Surrounding the Aloha Tower and fronting the working harbor of Honolulu where ships from all over the world load and unload their goods, this marketplace is an old warehouse that's been tastefully converted into an upscale group of over 100 shops offering food and beverages, apparel, art, gifts, jewelry, and specialty items. An indoor-outdoor affair, where the sea breezes blow right

through, the center atrium area looks out over the tower. This central courtyard atrium is also the spot for musical entertainment performed free throughout the day. The outside area is called the Boat Days Bazaar, and it's filled with cabaña-type booths selling mostly apparel, gifts, and souvenirs. Inside, find fashions at Daniella and Beyond the Beach, among others. Magnet Five-Oh has all sorts of magnets from floor to ceiling. If you can't find one here, you haven't looked hard enough. The World of Time carries everything from Swatch watches to pocket watches, and Powder Edge has outdoor gear. Then there is Perfumania, and its name says it all. Browse through Hula Prints and Wyland Galleries. Martin & MacArthur carries mostly koa wood furniture and furnishings. Also check out the Endangered Species Store, which stocks nature-inspired gift items. Part of the profits go to protect endangered species of the world. Most of the shops in this complex are locally owned and nonchain outfits. Have a walk through and support the local economy.

After having a look at the shops, sit down for a snack at one of the many food vendors in the building. Try Gordon-Biersch Brewery & Restaurant for lunch and a chilled local brew, or the Rodeo Cantina for other drinks; Villa Pizza for a quick bite; or Belinda's Aloha Kitchen or Big Island Steakhouse for a more substantial meal. If you're at the marketplace for dinner, you can also enjoy the free concert at the main stage.

A vintage-looking, open-air trolley runs between here and Waikiki, charging $2 each direction for adults and $1 for children 3-11. The trolley starts around 9:15 a.m. and runs ever 20 minutes until 10:45 p.m. Pickups are at 10 hotels and landmarks in Waikiki, and it drops you off right in front of the marketplace.

Downtown Shopping

If you're touring the historical sights of downtown Honolulu, take a short stroll over to the corner of Bishop and King Streets, as good a place as any to call the center of the financial district. The names atop the buildings, both vintage and new, trace "big business" in Hawaii. There's good food to be enjoyed in the restaurants in this area along with some shops stuck away in the corners of the big buildings. Longs Drugs is at 1088 Bishop, and almost next door is Woolworth's, for any sundries and necessities.

The full-service **Honolulu Bookshop** is on the corner of Bishop and Hotel, tel. (808) 537-6224. The selections are excellent. **Hawaiian Islands Stamp and Coin,** tel. (808) 531-6251, at 1111 Bishop St., street level in the International Savings Building, displays rare coins, stamps, and paper money of Hawaii, the U.S., and worldwide. **Discount Mutual,** tel. (808) 591-9441, at 1020 Auahi, sells TVs, VCRs, radios, electronic gear, and more. The **Lion Coffee Co.,** at 894 Queen St., tel. (808) 591-1199, offers a great little tour of its roasting facilities and will mail out a colorful little newsletter on request. For classic Hawaiian shirts head for **Bailey's Antique and Aloha Shirts,** 517 Kapahulu, tel. (808) 734-7628, where you will find thousands of the vintage "collectible garments" on display. The best are made from rayon that was manufactured before 1950. Prices can range from $100 to $2,000.

Dole Cannery Square

Look for the giant pineapple rising 200 feet into the air. A landmark of Honolulu, it was built in Chicago and erected here in 1928. It is still used as a reservoir and holds 100,000 gallons of water that's piped throughout the Dole Cannery, whose outer buildings were transformed in 1988 to a minimall located at 650 Iwilei Road. Upon entering the atrium area, look high on the walls to see reproductions of Dole Pineapple can labels. They're pop art, and convey a feeling of simpler times past. Downstairs you can watch a video about Dole and the cannery. Here also is the **Food Court,** providing snacks, salads, sandwiches, and soups for a quick lunch.

On the two levels you'll find a cluster of some 60 shops laid out as traditional storefronts and featuring items made in Hawaii. **Jungle Jerky Shop** has jerky of all sorts and sells stuffed animals, all life-size, as well as cotton cloth flowers. New shops like **Island Princess** have an added elegance with their fashions, or you can take care of your sweet tooth at **Sharyn's Hawaiian Island Cookies.** One of the nicest shops is the **Village Beach Shop.** It's a complete resortwear store with plenty of muumuu, sandals, and even boogie boards to choose from. It has a fine selection of T-shirts with gold designs by Ericka Paeis, a very creative and distinctive designer in the crowded field of Hawaiian T-shirts.

In the factory itself, workers stay busy processing the fruit. Used is the newest generation of the marvelous Ginaca machine, first built in 1913 by Henry Ginaca, a draftsman hired by James Dole to modernize the industry. This whirring wonder can peel, core, cut, slice, and dice 100 fruits per minute. Within 20 minutes of reaching the machine, the canned fruit's ready for the grocer's shelf. Millions of Hawaii's fruits are canned, juiced, and sliced here for shipment around the world. In the summertime, at the height of the harvest, this factory can process over three million cans of fruit per day!

Kahala Mall

A smaller version of the city center malls, although large enough in its own right, is the Kahala Mall. **Liberty House, Longs Drug, Star Market,** and the eight-plex **Kahala Theaters** anchor this mall, surrounded by dozens of apparel outlets, gift shops, and novelty stores. Both **Barnes and Noble** and **Waldenbooks** have shops here. On the east end of the city this is the shopping center of choice.

Bargains and Discounts

For discounts and bargains, try the following. **Crazy Shirts Factory Outlet,** at 99-969 Iwaena St., Aiea, tel. (808) 487-9919, sells seconds and discontinued styles, with a minimum savings of 50%. **Swim Suit Warehouse,** in the Royal Hawaiian Shopping Center, has women's swimsuits under $20, plus shorts and tops. **The Muumuu Factory,** 1423 Kapiolani Blvd., offers great sales—get there early and bring your helmet and shoulder pads to fight off the crowds. **Goodwill Thrift Shop,** at 780 S. Beretania St., displays the same bargains as on the Mainland, but with a wide assortment of alohawear. **Pzazz** at 1419 Kalakaua Ave. has won accolades for being the best designer resale shop in town for moderately priced quality women's clothing.

Miscellaneous

Everyone, sooner or later, needs a good hardware store. You can't beat the selection at **Kilgo's,** 180 Sand Island Road, tel. (808) 832-2200.

CHINATOWN

Chinatown has seen ups and downs in the last 130 years, ever since Chinese laborers were lured from Guangdong Province to work as contract laborers on the pineapple and sugar plantations. They didn't need a fortune cookie to tell them that there was no future in plantation work, so within a decade of their arrival they had established themselves as merchants, mostly in small retail businesses and restaurants. Chinatown is roughly a triangle of downtown Honolulu bordered by Nuuanu Street on the southeast, N. Beretania Street on the northeast, and S. King St. forming the hypotenuse. Twice this area has been flattened by fire, once in 1886 and again in 1900. The 1900 fire was deliberately set to burn out rats that had brought bubonic plague to the city. The fire got out of control and burned down virtually the whole district. Some contended that the fire was allowed to engulf the district in order to decimate the growing economic strength of the Chinese. Chinatown reached its heyday in the 1930s when it thrived with tourists coming and going from the main port at the foot of Nuuanu Street.

Today, Chinatown is a mixed bag of upbeat modernization and run-down sleazy storefronts. Although still strongly Chinese, there are Japanese, Laotians, and Vietnamese, and even an Irish pub, O'Toole's, on Nuuanu Avenue. This is Asia come to life: meat markets with hanging ducks, and Chinese, Korean, Japanese, and Vietnamese food with their strange aromatic spices all in a few blocks. The entire district takes only 10 minutes to walk and is a world apart from "tourist" Oahu. Crates, live chickens, incredible shops, down-and-outers, tattoo parlors, and temples all can be found in this quarter. When Hotel Street meets River Street, with the harbor in the background, it all abruptly ends. This is a different Honolulu, a Pacific port, crusty and exciting.

SIGHTS

Look for the pagoda roof of **Wo Fat's** on the corner of Hotel and Maunakea Streets. This is the oldest chop suey house in Honolulu, started in 1886 by Mr. Wo Fat, a baker. It's a good landmark for starting your tour. The Chinatown landmark (circa 1922), **Hawaii Theater,** has been renovated and once again is open to the public. One-hour tours of this historic building are given on the first Monday of every month at 10 a.m. and 2 p.m., $5 admission. Call (808) 528-0506 for additional information. You can easily do Chinatown on your own, but for another view and some extremely knowledgeable guides try the **Chinese Chamber of Commerce** tour, tel. (808) 533-3181, which has been operating as a community service for almost 30 years. A guide will show you around Chinatown for only $5. This tour is offered Tuesday mornings at 9:30 a.m. only and starts from the chamber office at 42 N. King Street. Or try the **Hawaiian Heritage Center** Chinatown Historical and Cultural Walking Tour, which starts from the Ramsay Galleries at 1128 Smith St., every Friday at 9:30 a.m. The two-hour tours are $5 per person, minimum of three for tours to go; call (808) 521-2749 for reservations, or write to P.O. Box 37520, Honolulu, HI 96837. An excellent source of general information is the **Hawaii Chinese History Center,** 111 N. King St., Honolulu, HI 96817.

If you want to clear your head from the hustle and bustle, visit the **Kuan Yin Temple,** where Buddha is always praised with some sweet-smelling incense, or peek into the **Taoist Temple.** If that's not enough to awaken your spiritual inner self, visit the **Izumo Taisha Jinja,** a Japanese Shinto shrine. All the accoutrements of a shrine are here—roof, thick coiled rope, bell, and prayer box. This one houses a male deity. You can tell by the cross on the top. There's a ferroconcrete example of a *torii* gate. If you've never visited a Japanese Shinto shrine, have a look here but be respectful and follow the rules. **Lum Sai Ho Tong,** across the street from the Shinto shrine on River St., is a basic Chinese Buddhist temple, very small and usually closed after 2 p.m.

For peace and quiet, or to check out some old-timers playing checkers or dominoes, cross the river and enter **Aala Triangle Park,** or treat yourself by walking a few minutes north to **Foster Botanical Garden** at 180 N. Vineyard for a glimpse of rare and exotic flora from around the world.

BOB RACE

SHOPPING

For shopping head to the **Cultural Plaza,** on the corner of Maunakea and Beretania Streets, but note that it has been struggling lately and shops come and go with regularity. It's more fun to look at than to shop. You'll find Dragongate Bookstore, Tak Wah Tong Chinese Herbalist, Excellent Gem and Diamonds, Peninsula Jewelry. The Cultural Plaza Moongate Stage is the centerpiece. Here they perform Chinese dances and plays, and herald in the Chinese New Year. If there is a presentation happening, attend. Out back, in a little parklike area, you'll find local men spending the afternoon chatting or playing dominoes, Go, or other board games.

Nearby and close to the river is an open market, a cooperative of open-air stalls selling just about everything that Chinatown has to offer at competitive prices. Follow your nose to the pungent odors of fresh fish at **Oahu Market** on King Street, where ocean delectables can be had for reasonable prices.

The **Wingon Co.,** at 131 Hotel, has porcelain ware, but the feature is the big crocks of crackseed. If you want it the way it *was* made, this is it.

Pegge Hopper Gallery, tel. (808) 524-1160, is at 1164 Nuuana St., open Mon.-Fri. 11 a.m.-5 p.m. and Saturday 11 a.m.-3 p.m. Ms. Hopper is one of the three most famous working artists in all of Hawaii. Her original works grace the walls of the most elegant hotels and homes in the islands. If you would like to purchase one of her bold and amazing serigraphs, this shop has the best and widest selection.

Cindy's Flower Shop is just next to Wo Fat's, and it has fresh lei at cheap prices. Located right where S. Beretania turns into N. Beretania, at Smith St. across from the Honolulu Towers, is a garland of flower shops like Lita's Lei and Mauna Kea Lei, famous for good products and prices. Also, at the corner of Pauahi and Maunakea look for **Aloha Lei and Flowers,** which is locally famous for its lei, which it can ship to the Mainland. Several other flower shops in the vicinity of Beretania and Maunakea Streets, selling authentic lei and other flowers, are Maunakea Florist, which is right on the corner, Sweetheart's Lei Shop, just down the street, and Lauli'ilani's Lei and Flowers.

Chinese Acupuncturists and Herbalists, Etc.
Ted J. Kaptchuk, O.M.D., in his excellent book *The Web That Has No Weaver* says, "Actually, Chinese medicine is a coherent and independent system of thought that has been developed over two millennia." Chinese practitioners, unlike most of their Western counterparts, look at the entire individual, not just the acute symptom, and try to pinpoint what they refer to as "internal disharmony." Their diagnosis might be "dampness in the liver" or "fire in the kidney," for which they may prescribe a combination of acupuncture, herbs, dietary supplements and even exercise. The practitioners listed below are all licensed to practice Chinese medicine. A visit, where they will check your overall appearance and a number of "pulses," costs about $10. The herbs that they prescribe, usually dispensed from a wall of drawers labled with Chinese characters, will probably cost under $10 depending upon the malady.

Yuan Chai Tong Ltd. Oriental Herbs and **Dr. W.S. Lam,** licensed acupuncturist, occupy a storefront on the corner of River and N. King. Nearby on King St. is **Fook Sau Tong's,** another Chinese herb specialist. Look in the window to see coiled snake skin, a few dried-out snakes, some flat-looking lizards, and who-knows-what. If you need the bounce put back in your step, maybe some tonics or a few needles in the ear are just what the doctor will order. **Kam Sang Chun,** 1121 Nuuanu

Ave., open daily 9 a.m.-noon and again 2-5:30 p.m., Sunday 9 a.m.-noon, is another long established acupuncturist and herbalist.

Down Smith St. is **Kam Mau Co.,** whose shelves are stacked with every conceivable (and inconceivable) Asian food. This is a great place to sample authentic crackseed. If your tummy revolts or if you need a quick tonic head next door to **Lai An Tong's** herb shop where some mashed antelope antler or powdered monkey brain will set you straight again.

FOOD

You can eat delicious ethnic food throughout Chinatown. If not Honolulu's best, the entire district, food-wise, is definitely Honolulu's cheapest. On almost every corner you've got places like **Mini Garden Noodle House** and **Cafe Paradise** for breakfast, lunch, and dinner. They're basic and cheap eateries whose ambience is a mixture of formica-topped tables and linoleum floors. In almost all, the food is authentic, with most featuring Asian food. You can easily get meals here for $3-5. Some eateries appear greasier than the Alaska Pipeline, so you'll have to feel them out. The local people eat in them regularly, and most are clean enough.

Right at the corner of N. Hotel and Maunakea, you'll see **Wo Fat's Restaurant,** tel. (808) 524-1628, the oldest chop suey house in Hawaii, where you're guaranteed an authentic meal at reasonable prices. A visit to Chinatown is incomplete without lunch at Wo Fat's, or at least a tour of this extremely ornate restaurant. The three floors are covered with paintings of dragons, birds, flowers, and a variety of land- and seascapes. Murals, carvings, and hanging lanterns create the mood of "rococo Chinese." The menu is like a small phone book, with literally hundreds of choices of fish, fowl, beef, and vegetarian dishes. It's hard to spend more than $10

per person, with many dishes considerably less.

Rosarina Pizza, at 1111 Maunakea St., tel. (808) 533-6634, is an alternative to the Asian cuisine. They will sell you a slice of pizza for only $1.40, or a whole pie ranging from a small cheese for $8 to a large combo at $15.25. You can also order a 12-inch sublike pastrami and provolone for $4.75, or an à la carte dinner like spaghetti with meat sauce or sausage, cannelloni, or manicotti, all for under $7.

One place that you shouldn't miss is **Shung Chong Yuein,** a Chinese cake shop at 1027 Maunakea. Look in to see yellow sugar cakes, black sugar cakes, shredded coconut with eggs, salted mincemeat, Chinese ham with egg, lotus seeds, and steamed buns.

Chinatown Joe's, at the corner of Hotel and Nuuanu Streets, is a classic tavern complete with dartboard and mugs of draft beer. Laid-back, local, and friendly, it's a good place to stop in for a breather, or to have a classic pastrami or tuna, ham, and Swiss sandwich.

CHINATOWN

© J.D. BISIGNANI AND MOON PUBLICATIONS, INC.

At the Chinatown Cultural Plaza

As with the shops in the plaza, the restaurants also come and go. One to check is **Buddhist Vegetarian Restaurant**, tel. (808) 532-8218. The Buddhist Vegetarian Restaurant is basic and about as antiseptic as a monk's cell, but the food is healthy. The varied menu includes inexpensive dim sum dishes, stir-fry vegetables for $9.50, spicy hot and sour soup for $6.50, and many braised or fried vegetable or tofu dishes for about $7.50. Most are in the under-$10 catagory, but the Buddhist supreme vegetarian plate goes for $23.95. Lunch is served 10:30 a.m.-2 p.m., dinner 5:30-9 p.m.

Doong Kong Lau Seafood Restaurant offers Hakka cuisine and sizzlers. It's on the river side of the Cultural Plaza, tel. (808) 531-8833. Inside it's utilitarian with leatherette seats and formica tables. You come here for the food. Savories include stir-fried squid with broccoli for $5.95, stir-fried scallops with garlic sauce for $7.95, stir-fried oysters with black beans for $6.95, sizzle plates like seafood combo at $7.95, or shark fin with shredded chicken, $16.50. The menu reads, "The chief recommends deep fried shrimp with toast." Who's to argue with the chief! **Won Kee Sea Food Restaurant** is another restaurant in the Cultural Plaza. Locals swear by it, especially the lunch specials for $4.95. At another stall in this complex is the **Royal Kitchen**, tel. (808) 524-4461, a very popular place with local families and businesspeople. It's especially known for its takeout baked *manapua*, soft dough buns stuffed with pork, charsu, or vegetables, and for its Chinese sausage, *lupcheung*. Open very early in the morning. Stuck in the corner is the reasonably priced **Cheuk's Chinese Restaurant**. Open Monday 10:30 a.m.-2:30 p.m., Tues.-Sun. 10:30 a.m.-8:30 p.m., this is a simple, down-home place, with items like soups and pot stickers for $4.50, beef and pork dishes for about $6, and seafood dishes for around $8.

Chinatown's Vietnamese Restaurants

A recent phenomenon is a number of excellent Vietnamese restaurants that have sprung up like bamboo sprouts along Chinatown's streets. The majority are meticulously clean, and the moderately priced food is "family-pride-gourmet." The decor ranges from oilcloth tablecloths topped by a "bouquet" of plastic flowers and a lazy Susan filled with exotic spices and condiments, to "down-to-earth chic" with some mood lighting, candles, and even linen place settings. As a group, they represent the best culinary deals on Oahu today. Many selections, like the grilled seasoned meatballs or marinated pork (under $8), come with noodles, fresh lettuce, mint, cucumber, bean sprouts, and ground peanut sauce that you wrap in layers of rice paper to make your own version of what can best be described as an "oriental taco." Simply moisten a few sheets of the rice paper in the bowl of water provided and wrap away. Great fun, and they'll show you how! There are plenty of savory vegetarian menu choices as well.

Maxime's Vietnamese Restaurant, 1134 Maunakea St., tel. (808) 545-4188, open Tues.-Fri. 9 a.m.-9 p.m., Sat.-Sun. until 10 p.m., Monday till 5 p.m., is as authentic as its name is contrived. To get an idea, ask to use the bathroom. You'll pass through the cramped but meticulously cleaned kitchen filled with boiling pots that are tended by about three generations of the family. In the dining room, it's just formica tables and red Naugahyde chairs, but the people couldn't be more friendly. Try Maxime's special noodles with pork, shrimp, crab, bean sprouts, lettuce, and pork soup on the side for only $6.50, or an order of shrimp rolls—light aromatic rolls with shrimp, pork, and garden vegetables and rice noodles rolled up in rice paper served with sauce for $4, or only $1.50 as an appetizer. The selections of *pho* soup, which can be beef or chicken (*pho ga*) come with rice noodles, onions, Chinese parsley, basil, bean sprouts, and wine. You can either have the meat in the soup or on the side, for only $4.50 or $5 for the jumbo size. Beverages are lemonade, iced coffee with condensed milk, jasmine tea, fresh coconut juice, sweet and sour lemon juice, and soybean milk. Top off your meal with desserts like caramel custard or sweet beans with coconut milk for under $2.

A Little Bit of Saigon, 1160 Maunakea, tel. (808) 528-3663, open daily 10 a.m.-10 p.m., is the fanciest of the lot, although it is still quite basic. Specialties are "roll ups" that include savory beef, pork or chicken, served with lettuce, fresh herbs, vegetables, sweet and sour fish sauce, and peanut or pineapple and anchovy sauce along with thin rice paper that you use to roll-your-own for $5.95-8.95. Good yet inexpensive selections are stir-fried vegetables that you can have either by themselves or with fresh fish, prawns, chicken, beef, tofu, or scallops, all for under $7.95. For the hearty appetite try the seven-course dinner for two at $29.95 that gives a good sample of the menu. Finish with agar served with tapioca and coconut milk for $1.75. **To Chau Vietnamese Restaurant,** at 1007 River, tel. (808) 533-4549, and **Ha Bien,** at 198 N. King St., serve basic Vietnamese fare for under $7 for most dishes. They're around the corner from the action of Hotel Street, and are family-oriented. Ha Bien is open strange hours, Monday 8 a.m.-4 p.m., open the remainder of the week until 6 p.m.

CHINATOWN NIGHTS

Chinatown is relatively safe, especially during the daytime, but at night, particularly along infamous Hotel Street, you have to be careful. When the sun sinks, the neon lights and the area fires up. Transvestites and hookers slide down the street, shaking their wares and letting you know that they're open for business. Purchasing might leave you with a few souvenirs that you'd never care to *share* with the folks back home.

Not many tourists come this way. But walking down Hotel Street is really an adventure in and of itself. If you stay on the main drag, right down the middle, you'll be okay. At Hotel and Nuuanu Streets you'll find the Honolulu Police Department downtown substation.

There are a lot of nondescript places that open to the street like a wound oozing the odor of stale beer and urine. The **Hubba Hubba Club,** with its live nude shows, no cover, and not-too-inflated drinks, is the best of Hotel Street. This is not a place for candy-asses, wimps, or missionaries. Simply put, there are naked women in there doing exotic and bizarre acts. The Hubba Hubba is basically a clip joint on the up and up. Inside are flashing lights, a runway, and $3 beers, with only mild pressure as you sit and watch the act. As you walk down Hotel Street toward the river it gets sleazier. **Elsie's Bar,** at 145 N. Hotel St., open 6 a.m.-2 a.m., looks meaner than a tattooed snake, but it's a safe place. So if you want to have a night of fun and relaxation come in here. It offers Hawaiian music along with fairly decent Hawaiian food. A few doors down are steps leading upstairs to the **Original Bath Palace.** The *original* place where drunken fools were taken to the cleaners.

BOB RACE

GORDY OHLIGER

WAIKIKI

Waikiki ("Spouting Water") is like a fresh young starlet from the sticks who went to Hollywood to make it big, and did, though maybe too fast for her own good. Everyone always knew that she had a double-dip of talent and heart, but the fast lane has its heartaches, and she's been banged around a little by life. Even though her figure's fuller, her makeup's a little askew, and her high heels are worn down, she has plenty of chutzpah left, and when the curtain parts and the lights come up, she'll play her heart out for her audience.

Waikiki is a classic study of contradictions. Above all, it is an example of basic American entrepreneurialism taken to the nth degree. Along the main strip, high-powered businesspeople cut multimillion-dollar deals, but on the sidewalks it's a carnival midway with hucksters, handbillers, and street people selling everything decent and indecent under the tropical sun. To get a true feeling for Waikiki, you must put this amazing strip of land into perspective. The area covers only seven-tenths of a square mile, which at a good pace, you can walk in 15 minutes. On any given day, about 110,000 people crowd its beaches and boulevards, making it one of the most densely populated areas on earth. Sixty thousand of these people are tourists; 30,000 are workers who commute from various towns of Oahu and cater to the tourists, and the remaining 20,000 actually call Waikiki home. The turnover is about 80,000 new tourists per week, and the pace never slackens. To the head shakers, these facts condemn Waikiki as a mega-growth area gone wild. To others, these same figures make Waikiki an energized, fun-filled place to be, where "if you don't have a good time, it's your own fault."

For the naive or the out-of-touch looking for "grass-shack paradise," the closest they'll come to it in Waikiki is painted on a souvenir ashtray. Those drawn to a smorgasbord of activities, who are adept at choosing the best and ignoring the rest, can't go wrong! People and the action are as constant in Waikiki as the ever-rolling surf.

History
The written record of this swampy area began in the late 1790s. The white man, along with his historians, cartographers, artists, and gunpowder, were already an undeniable presence in the islands. Kalanikupule, ranking chief of Oahu, hi-

jacked the *Jackall,* a small ship commanded by Captain Brown, with which he intended to spearhead an attack against Kamehameha I. The chief held the *Jackall* for a while, but the sailors regained control just off Diamond Head and sent the Hawaiians swimming for land. The ship then hastened to Kamehameha to report the treachery, and returned with his armada of double-hulled canoes, which beached along Waikiki. The great king then defeated Kalanikupule at the famous battle of Nuuanu Pali and secured control of the island. Therafter Waikiki, pinpointed by Diamond Head, became a well-known landmark.

Waikiki's interior was low-lying swampland, long known to be good for fishponds, taro, rice, and bananas, but hardly for living. The beach, however, was always blessed with sunshine and perfect waves, especially for surfing, a sport heartily loved by the Hawaiians. The royalty of Hawaii, following Kamehameha, made Honolulu their capital and kept beach houses at Waikiki. They invited many visiting luminaries to visit them at their private beach. All were impressed. In the 1880s, King Kalakaua was famous for his beach house hospitality. One of his favorite guests was Robert Louis Stevenson, who spent many months here writing one of his novels. By the turn of the 20th century Waikiki had become a highly exclusive vacation spot.

In 1901 the Moana Hotel was built, but immediately a protest was heard because it interfered with the view of Diamond Head. In 1906, Lucius Pinkham, then director of Hawaii's Board of Health, called the mosquito-infested area "dangerous and unsanitary," and proposed to drain the swamp with a canal so that "the whole place can be transformed into a place of unique beauty." By the early 1920s, the Ala Wai Canal was built, its dredgings used to reclaim land, and Waikiki was demarcated. By the end of the 1920s, the Royal Hawaiian Hotel, built on the site previously occupied by the royal beach house, was receiving very wealthy guests who arrived by ocean liner, loaded down with steamer trunks. They ensconced themselves at Waikiki, often staying for the duration of the season.

For about 40 years, Waikiki remained the enchanted domain of Hollywood stars, dignitaries, and millionaires. But for the brief and extraordinary days of WW II, which saw Waikiki barricaded and barb-wired, GIs—regular guys from the Mainland—were given a taste of this "reserved paradise" while on R&R. They brought home tantalizing tales of wonderful Waikiki, whetting the appetite of middle America.

Beginning just before statehood and continuing through the '60s to the mid-'70s, hotels and condos popped up like fertilized weeds, and tourism exploded with the advent of the jumbo jet. Discounted package tours began to haul in droves of economy-class tourists. Businesses catering to the tastes of penny-pinchers and first-timers elbowed their way into every nook and cranny. For the first time Waikiki began to be described as tacky and vulgar. For the old-timers, Waikiki was in decline. The upscale and repeat visitors started to snub Waikiki, heading for hidden resorts on the Neighbor Islands. But Waikiki had spirit and soul, and never gave in. In the last few years, its declining hotels started a campaign to regain their illustrious images. Millions upon millions of dollars have been poured into renovations and remodeling. Luxury hotels renting exclusive and expensive rooms have reappeared and are doing a booming business.

Waikiki Today

The Neighbor Islands are pulling more and more tourists away, and depending on your point of view, this is either a boon or a bust for Waikiki. Direct flights to Maui and the Big Island allow more tourists than ever to bypass Oahu, but still a whopping 80% of the people visiting the islands spend at least one night in a Waikiki hotel, which offer the lowest room rates in Hawaii. The sublime and the gaudy are neighbors in Waikiki. Exclusive shops are often flanked by buskers selling plastic hula dolls. Burgers and beer mingle their pedestrian odors with those of Parisian cuisine. Though Waikiki in many ways is unique, it can also come off as "Anytown, U.S.A." But most importantly it somehow works, and works well. You may not find "paradise" on Waikiki's streets, but you will find a willing "dancing partner," and if you pay the fiddler, she'll keep the beat.

Non-Americans, especially Japanese, still flock for dream vacations, mostly staying at Waikiki hotels, 25% of which are owned by Japanese firms. Mainlanders and locals alike are disgruntled when they see the extent to which Waikiki has become a Japanese town. It's one of the only cities in America where you can have trouble ordering a meal or making a purchase if you don't speak Japanese! The visiting Japanese have been soundly warned by the tour operators before they arrive to never talk to strangers, especially someone on the street. Unfortunately for them, this means a vacation in which they never really leave Japan. They're herded into Japanese-owned shops and restaurants where prices are grossly inflated, and from which the tour operators get kickbacks. Local shopkeepers, not on the list, are aggravated. They say that the once-timid Japanese visitor will now show irritation if the shopkeeper doesn't speak Japanese, and will indignantly head for the door if there is no one provided to deal with them in their native tongue. Also, these visitors have been taught to bargain with American shopkeepers, who they are told inflate prices. This makes for some rugged interaction when the price is already fair, but the Japanese visitor won't believe it. While on average the Japanese tourist spends $340 per day, as opposed to a Mainlander who spends $130 per day, the Japanese really don't spread their money around as much as you would think. The money spent in Japanese shops primarily goes back to Japan. It's an incestuous system that operates in Waikiki.

Getting Around

By far and away the best way to get around Waikiki is on foot. For one, it's easily walked from one end to the other in less than 20 minutes, and walking will save you hassling with parking and traffic jams. Also, TheBus and taxis are abundant and, along with rental cars, have been covered in the Out and About chapter under "Getting Around." Those who have opted for a rental car should note that many of the agencies operate Waikiki terminals, which for some can be more convenient than dropping your car at the airport on the day of departure. Check to see if it suits you. The following information is specific to Waikiki, and offers some limited alternatives.

In mid-1987, **pedicabs,** for all intents and purposes, were outlawed in Waikiki. There used to be 150-160 pedicabs that offered short taxi rides. They took people shopping, sightseeing, and between hotels, but basically they were a joyride. Mainstream businesspeople considered them a nuisance, and there were rumors that some drivers dealt drugs, so they were finally outlawed. Now only 10-12 legal pedicabs operate in and around Waikiki. They're not allowed to go along Kalakaua Avenue, pick up or drop off at hotels, or use any of the main drags. They stay on the back streets or in the park, where they are constantly watched by the police. Charges are a hefty $3 per minute. The main customers are Japanese tourists who marvel at being peddled around town by a muscular *gaijin* in a rickshaw-type conveyance never seen in their own homeland any longer.

The **Waikiki Trolley,** tel. (808) 596-2199, offers tours throughout Waikiki and downtown Honolulu on two different routes, both starting at the Royal Hawaiian Shopping Center. A day pass costs $18 adults, $8 children, and you can get on and off as much as you like. The trolley is really an open-air bus, but it's well done and plenty of fun. Pick up a route map at an activity desk, or call the number above for times and stops.

Waikiki does an excellent job of conveying traffic, both auto and pedestrian, along Kalakaua Avenue, the main drag fronting Waikiki. The city has installed very clear yet unattractive combinations of stoplights and street names. These are metal L-shaped beams, painted a dull brown, that straddle the roadways, clearly pinpointing your location. Unfortunately, they match the area about as well as work boots match a hula dancer. To give the feeling of an outdoor strolling mall, sidewalks along Kalakaua have been widened and surfaced with red brick.

The **Kapiolani Park Kiosk** is on the corner of Kapahulu and Kalakaua Avenues. The kiosk uses vintage photos to give a concise history of Kapiolani Park. An overview map shows all the features of the park. Information is available here concerning events at the Aquarium, Zoo, Waikiki Shell, the Kodak Hula Show, the Art Mart (a collection of island artists selling their creations along the Zoo), and the Kapiolani Bandstand, where you're treated to free concerts by top-name bands and orchestras.

Public parking in Waikiki can be a hassle, although there are plenty of parking garages. A good place to park not far from the beach is the strip running parallel to Kapiolani Park at one end and along Saratoga Street at the other. There are plenty of two-hour parking meters available, especially if you arrive before 9 a.m. Also, inexpensive (for Waikiki) parking is available at the ramp adjacent to the Waikiki 3 Theaters along Seaside Road, but only after 5:30 p.m.

SIGHTS

To see Waikiki's attractions, you have to do little more than perch on a bench or loll on a beach towel. Its boulevards and beaches are world-class for people-watching. Some of its strollers and sunbathers are *visions*, while others are real *sights*. And if you keep your ears open, it's not hard to hear every American accent and a dozen foreign languages. Some actual sights are intermingled with the hotels, boutiques, bars, and restaurants. Sometimes, too, these very buildings are the sights. Unbelievably, you can even find plenty of quiet spots—in the gardens of Kapiolani Park, and at churches, temples, tearooms, and ancient Hawaiian special places sitting unnoticed amidst the grandiose structures of the 20th century. Also, both the Honolulu Zoo and Waikiki Aquarium are well worth a visit.

DIAMOND HEAD

If you're not sandwiched in a manmade canyon of skyscrapers, you can look eastward from anywhere in Waikiki and see Diamond Head. Diamond Head *says* Waikiki. Western sailors have used it as a landmark since the earliest days of contact, and the Hawaiians undoubtedly before that. Ships' artists etched and sketched its motif

long before the names of the newfound lands of Hawaii, Waikiki, and Oahu were standardized and appeared on charts as Owyhee, Whytete, and Woohoo. The Hawaiian name was Leahi ("Brow of the Ahi"); legend says it was named by Hi'iaka, Madame Pele's younger sister, because she saw a resemblance in its silhouette to the yellowfin tuna. The name "Diamond Head" comes from a band of sailors who found calcite crystals on its slopes and thought they'd discovered diamonds. Kamehameha I immediately made the mountain *kapu* until his adviser John Young informed him that what the seamen had found, later known as "Pele's tears," were, except as souvenirs, worthless. Diamond Head was considered a power spot by the Hawaiians. Previously, Kamehameha had worshipped at a *heiau* located on the western slopes, offering human sacrifice to his bloodthirsty war-god, Ku.

Geologically, the 760-foot monolith is about 350,000 years old, formed in one enormous explosion when seawater came into contact with lava bubbling out of a fissure. No new volcanic activity has been suspected in the last 200,000 years. The huge rock is now Hawaii's state monument and a national natural landmark. Its crater serves as a Hawaii National Guard depot; various hiking trails to the summit bypass installa-

Diamond Head from Halekulani

J.D. BISIGNANI

tions left over from WW II. Getting there takes only 15 minutes from Waikiki, either by TheBus no. 57 or by car along Diamond Head Road. The southeast *(makai)* face has some of the most exclusive and expensive real estate in the islands. The Kahala Hilton Hotel here is regarded by many to be one of the premier hotels in the world, and nearby is the super-snobbish Waialae Country Club. Many private estates—homes of multimillionaires, Hollywood stars, and high-powered multinational executives—cling to the cliffside, fronting ribbons of beach open to the public by narrow rights-of-way that oftentimes are hemmed in by the walls of the estates.

HONOLULU ZOO

The trumpeting of elephants and chatter of monkeys emanates from the jungle at the Honolulu Zoo, 151 Kapahulu Ave., tel. (808) 971-7171, open daily 9 a.m.-4:30 p.m., with special evening concerts featuring local artists every Wednesday 6-7 p.m. June-August. For the free evening show, the gates reopen at 4:35 p.m. and there is no admission. General admission is $6 for 13 years and older, $4 for locals, children 6-12 with an adult $1, and children under five free; the Honolulu Zoo family pass is $25. As you walk along, you find the expected animals from around the world: monkeys, giraffes, lions, big cats, a hippo, even a sun bear (what else in Hawaii!). The Honolulu Zoo has the only large snake in Hawaii—a male Burmese python named Monty—housed in the Reptile House. (Only the zoo can legally import snakes, geckos, iguanas, and similar reptiles.) Many islanders love this exhibit, because snakes in Hawaii are so exotic! But the zoo is much more than just a collection of animals. It is an up-close escapade through the jungle of Hawaii, with plants, trees, flowers, and vines all named and described. Moreover, the zoo houses Hawaii's indigenous birdlife, which is fast disappearing from the wild: Hawaiian gallinules, coots, hawks, owls, and the *nene,* the state bird, which is doing well in captivity, with breeding pairs being sent to other zoos around the world. The zoo is also famous for its Manchurian cranes, extremely rare birds from East Asia, and for successfully mating the Galapagos turtle. A **petting zoo** of barnyard animals is great for kids. A concession stand serves typical junk food and soft drinks. Before leaving, have a look at the Zootique shop where you can pick up T-shirts, postcards, posters, stuffed animals, books, and other gift items.

WAIKIKI AQUARIUM

The first Waikiki Aquarium was built in 1904, its entranceway framed by a *torii* gate. Rebuilt and restocked in 1954, it has just undergone another face-lift with a new entranceway, "touch tanks," and an opening directly to the sea. The aquarium, located at 2777 Kalakaua Ave., tel. (808) 923-9741, is open daily 9 a.m.-5 p.m. (entrance until 4:30 p.m.), admission $6 adults, $4 seniors, $2.50 youths 13-17, and free to children under 12. An audio tour ("magic wand" device) in English and Japanese is available for a small fee. Walk or take TheBus no. 2.

Although over 300 species of Hawaiian and South Pacific fish, flora, and mammals live in its sparkling waters, the aquarium is much more than just a big fish tank. The floor plan contains four galleries of differing themes, and a seal tank. The **South Seas Marine Life** exhibit shows fish found in waters from Polynesia to Australia. The tanks hold sharks, turtles, eels, rays, clams, a seahorse, and colorful coral displays. Another exhibit, **Micronesia Reef Builders,** is perhaps the most amazing of all. It contains live coral that seem more like extraterrestrial flowers than specimens from our own seas. Some are long strands of spaghetti with bulbous ends like lima beans, others are mutated roses, or tortured camellias, all moving, floating, and waving their iridescent purples, golds, and greens in a watery bouquet.

Watch the antics of the monk seals, shameless hams, from the side of their 85,000 gallon tank, which now has a "variegated coastline" of natural nooks and crannies patterned after sections of Oahu's Pupukea and Kahe Point. Hawaiian monk seals are one of only two species of tropical seals on earth. Endangered, there are only about 1,500 individuals still surviving, and the "performances" are more of a detailed description of the seals day-to-day life in their dwindling environment. The three seals inhabiting the tank are all males, since placing a breeding couple would almost certainly result in the birth of

WAIKIKI

DETAIL

KING'S VILLAGE
WAIKIKI HANA
HYATT REGENCY
SHERATON MOANA SURFRIDER
PRINCE KUHIO BEACH PARK

KEALOHILANI AVE
LILIUOKALANI AVE
KEALOHILANI AVE
EDWARD ST
PRINCE
KOA
KALAKAUA AVE
KAIULANI AVE

Manoa-Palolo Drainage Canal

Ala Wai Canal

McCULLY ST.

KEONIANA ST
ALA MOANA BLVD
ALA WAI BLVD

HAWAIIAN MONARCH
DOUBLETREE ALANA HOTEL
RAINBOW BAZAAR
HILTON HAWAIIAN VILLAGE
WESTON ILIKAI
DUKE KAHANAMOKU BEACH

ENA RD
KALIA RD
MALUHIA RD
PAOA PL.
HOBRON LN
HOLOMOANA ST

Hilton Lagoon

ALA WAI YACHT HARBOR

To Ala Moana Shopping Center → (92)

PAKI AVE
KAPAHULU AVE
KALAKAUA AVE
MONSARRAT AVE

HONOLULU ZOO
KAPIOLANI PARK
WAIKIKI SHELL
KAPIOLANI PARK BANDSTAND
QUEEN KAPIOLANI
THE FENCE (ART)
WAIKIKI AQUARIUM

To Diamond Head →

KUHIO AVE
PAOAKALANI AVE
OHUA AVE
LEMON
WAIKIKI BEACHSIDE
HAWAIIAN REGENT

Kuhio Beach

ST. AUGUSTINE CATHOLIC CHURCH

B a y

SEE DETAIL

KANEKAPOLEI
KOA AVE
KUHIO AVE
KEALOHILANI AVE
LILIUOKALANI AVE

MIRAMAR AT WAIKIKI
PACIFIC MONARCH
BEACHCOMBER
INTERNATIONAL MARKET PLACE
OUTRIGGER REEF
WAIKIKI TOWN CENTER
CORAL REEF
WAIKIKI BUSINESS PLAZA
ROYAL HAWAIIAN SHOPPING CENTER
SURFRIDER
ROYAL HAWAIIAN

WAINA
NAHUA
NOHONANI
ILIMA ASTON
HONOLULU PRINCE

ALOHA DR
SEASIDE
MANUKAI
KAIULANI AVE
KALAIMOKU
LEWERS
NAMAHANA

WAIKIKI TRADE CENTER
WAIKIKI SHOPPING PLAZA
OUTRIGGER CORAL SEAS
OUTRIGGER EDGEWATER
HALEKULANI
SHERATON WAIKIKI

BEACH WALK
HELUMOA
KALIA RD
SARATOGA RD

Waikiki Beach
Gray's Beach

M a m a l a   Bay

POST OFFICE
FORT DERUSSY MILITARY RESERVATION
BREAKERS
U.S. ARMY MUSEUM OF HAWAII

Fort DeRussy Beach

0   0.25 mi
0   0.25 km

NOT ALL HOTELS ARE SHOWN

© J.D. BISIGNANI AND MOON PUBLICATIONS, INC.

a pup. Marine biologists anguished over the decision. It was felt that seals raised in captivity and then released back into the natural environment might introduce a devastating disease to the native population. This was considered too great a danger to risk.

The aquarium contains a bookshop with a tremendous assortment of titles on the flora and fauna of Hawaii. Restrooms are behind the bookshop area as you face the main gate. The University of Hawaii offers seminars and field trips through the aquarium, everything from guided reef walks to mini-courses in marine biology; information is available at the aquarium.

The Waikiki Aquarium is a very special opportunity for fun and education that will be enjoyed by the entire family. Don't miss it!

Just near the aquarium is the **Natatorium,** a saltwater swimming pool built in 1927 as a WW I memorial, which was allowed to decay over the years until it was closed in 1980. Plans are constantly afoot in the House of Representatives calling for either a restoration or its demolition, but no decision has yet been reached about its fate.

U.S. ARMY MUSEUM OF HAWAII

This museum, with the hulks of tanks standing guard, is one long corridor where you feel the strength of the super-thick reinforced walls of this once-active gun emplacement. Located at Battery Randolf in Fort DeRussy, on the corner of Kalia and Saratoga Roads, the U.S. Army Museum of Hawaii, tel. (808) 438-2821, is open Tues.-Sun. 10 a.m.-4:30 p.m., except Christmas and New Year's Day, for self-guiding tours. An optional hour-long audiocassette can be rented for $3.50 that will guide you through the museum. Guided tours can be arranged for large groups by calling several weeks in advance. Battery Randolph once housed two 14-inch coast artillery rifles meant to defend Honolulu and Pearl Harbors. The architecture is typical of the Taft Period forts constructed between 1907 and 1920. The battery is listed in the National Register of Historic Places. As you enter there is a shop dedicated to "things military," flying jackets to wall posters. Walk the halls to learn the military history of Hawaii traced as far back as Kamehameha I. Here are rifles, swords, and

vintage photos of Camp McKinley, a turn-of-the-century military station in the shadow of Diamond Head.

A side room holds models of artillery used to defend Waikiki from times when Battery Randolph was an active installation. One room shows how the guns worked in a method called "disappearing guns." The gun would raise up and fire and then disappear. The recoil of the gun would lock it back in position, and after it was reloaded a 50-ton counterweight would pop it up ready to fire. The explosive sound would rattle the entire neighborhood so they were seldom test-fired.

Exhibits show the fledgling days of Army aviation in Hawaii, when on July 13, 1913, 14 officers began a military flying school. There are beautiful models of military equipment, especially one of an old truck unit. Then comes the ominous exhibit of "Rising Japan" with its headlong thrust into WW II. Hawaii, grossly overconfident, felt immune to attack because of the strong military presence. Photos from the '30s and '40s depict the carefree lifestyle of visiting celebrities like Babe Ruth and Shirley Temple, which ended abruptly on December 7, 1941, in the bombing of Pearl Harbor.

An entire room is dedicated to the Pearl Harbor attack and is filled with models of Japanese planes, aircraft carriers, and real helmets and goggles worn by the Zero pilots. Most interesting are the slice-of-life photos of Hawaii mobilized for war: defense workers, both men and women, sailors, soldiers, entertainers, and street scenes. Pamphlets from the time read, "Know Your Enemies," and there's a macabre photo of people gathered at a stadium to see a demonstration of the devasting effect of flame throwers that would be employed upon the Japanese enemy. Bob Hope is here entertaining the troops, while a 442nd Regimental Battle Flag bears testament to the most decorated unit in American history, comprised mostly of *nisei* Japanese from Hawaii. Then come photos and exhibits from the soul-wrenching conflicts in Korea and Vietnam. Finally a room, like a whispering tomb, tells of the heroics of Hawaiian soldiers who have been awarded the Congressional Medal of Honor, almost all posthumously.

Make sure to go outside to the upper level exhibit where you'll see one of the old guns still pointing out to sea, which seems incongruous with sunbathers just below on the quiet and beautiful stretch of beach. On the upper deck are depth charges, torpedoes, and shells, along with a multimedia slide show. Your eyes will take a few minutes to refocus to the glorious sunshine of Waikiki after the cold gloom of the bunker. Perhaps our hearts and souls could refocus as well.

FREE SIGHTS AND CURIOSITIES

On the beach near the Sheraton Moana Surfrider Hotel are the **kahuna stones,** a lasting remnant of old Hawaii. The Hawaiians believed these stones were imbued with mana by four hermaphroditic priests from Tahiti: Kinohimahu, Kahaloamahu, Kapunimahu, and Kapaemahu (*mahu* in Hawaiian signifies homosexuality). They came to visit this Polynesian outpost in ancient times and left these stones for the people, who have held them in reverence for over 600 years. About 40 years ago, a group of local historians went looking for the stones but couldn't find them. Around that time, there was a bowling alley along the beach, and when it was finally torn down, it was discovered that the stones had been incorporated into the foundation. Today, the vast majority of visitors and islanders alike no longer revere the stones, often using them as a handy spot to scrape sand off their feet. *Kapuna* versed in the old ways say that the mana, once put in and strengthened by reverence, is now dissipating.

Delineating Waikiki from the rest of the city is the nearly two-mile-long **Ala Wai Canal.** Created in the '20s to drain the swamps that filled this flat oceanfront land, it now channels runoff from the mountains to the sea. The banks of the canal are used extensively by walkers, joggers, and runners, particularly shortly after sunrise and again before sunset; many come here to sit, relax, and watch the parade of paddlers practice for outrigger canoe races. It's cheap entertainment for one of Hawaii's favorite sports. Fishermen also make use of the canal, trying their luck near its mouth near the Ala Moana bridge.

Just across the canal from Waikiki proper is the new and impressive **Hawaii Convention Center.** Built to attract more convention business to the state, it's a combination of large and small meeting halls, exhibition rooms, and banquet facilities, with high-tech sound and light capabilities and instantaneous translation services. Appealing to the aesthetic side of anyone who takes the time to look inside are several waterfalls and pools, tall palm trees, numerous artworks, and a glass ceiling that seems to bring the outside in.

Even if you're not a guest at the following hotels, you should at least drop by their lobbies for a quick look. Dramatically different, they serve almost as a visual record of Waikiki's changing history. Those who have a fondness for the elegance of days gone by should take a tour of the **Sheraton Moana Surfrider Hotel** and steep in the history of the hotel, admiring its turn-of-the-century artifacts and memorabilia. The Moana, Waikiki's oldest hotel, dating from 1901, is a permanent reminder of simpler times when its illustrious clientele would dance the night away at an open-air nightclub suspended over the sea. The Moana houses the Banyan Court, named for the enormous banyan tree just outside. From here, "Hawaii Calls" beamed Hawaiian music to the Mainland by shortwave for 40 years beginning in 1935. In its heyday, the show was carried by over 700 stations. The hotel's architecture is a classic example of the now quaint "colonial style." Daily tours start at 11 a.m. from the concierge desk.

Across the street are the giant, modernistic, twin towers of the **Hyatt Regency.** The lobby, like most Hyatts, is wonderful, with a huge waterfall and a jungle of plants, all stepped down the series of floors, making an effect like the Hanging Gardens of Babylon. Even if you're not a guest here, have a look at the Hawaiian craft items displayed at the hotel museum. It's open 9 a.m.-5 p.m. Mon.-Fri., and it's free. The **Pacific Beach Hotel,** at 2490 Kalakaua Ave., is a first-rate hotel and a great place to stay in its own right. But if you don't, definitely visit the lobby, where the Oceanarium Restaurant has an immense three-floor-high aquarium dedicated to holding 280,000 gallons of sea water. The old mafia dons used to send their rivals to "sleep with the fishes"; here, you have an opportunity to dine with the fishes. Usually you go snorkeling to watch the fish eat, but in this particular instance the fish watch you eat.

The **Royal Hawaiian Hotel,** built in 1927 on the site of the old royal beach house, once had fresh pineapple juice running in its fountains. Now surrounded by towering hotels, it's like a guppy in a sea of whales. However, it does stand out with its Spanish-Moorish style, painted in distinctive pink. In the old days, only celebrities and luminaries came to stay—who else could afford $3 per day? Although it's younger than the Moana, many consider it the grande dame of Hawaiian hotels. The entranceway is elegantly old-fashioned, with rounded archways, overstuffed couches, and lowboys. You pass through the lobby on a shocking cerise and green rug. All the rooms are appointed in the trademark pink, with matching towels, sheets, and pillowcases. When you visit the Royal Hawaiian, the most elegant lobby is not where you check in. Rather, turn right from there and follow the long hallway toward the sea. This becomes an open breezeway, with arches and columns in grand style. You'll come to a small circular area in the hotel. Here is the heart, with Diamond Head framed in the distance.

The **Urusenke Teahouse,** tel. (808) 923-3059, is an authentic teahouse donated to Hawaii by the Urusenke Foundation of Kyoto. It is located at 245 Saratoga Road, which lies along the Waikiki side of Fort DeRussy. Every Wednesday and Friday 10 a.m.-noon, tea master Takashi Machita performs the ancient and aesthetic art of *chanoyu* (tea ceremony). The public is invited to watch the ceremony for free, but a donation of $2 is asked of those who want to partake of the frothy *matcha,* a grass-green tea made from the delicate tips of 400-year-old bushes, and the accompanying sweets. To find delight and sanctuary in this centuries-old ritual among the clatter and noise of Waikiki offers a tiny glimpse into the often puzzling duality of the Japanese soul.

As you walk along Kalakaua Avenue, directly across from Waikiki Beach proper is **St. Augustine Catholic Church.** This modernistic building squashed between high-rises is worth a quick look. The interior, serene with the diffused light of stained glass, looks like a series of A-frames. The **Damien Museum** is housed here, displaying photos and other artifacts of Father Damien, the Belgian priest who humanely cared for the lepers of Kalaupapa, Molokai, until his own death from complications of leprosy. The museum is open daily 9 a.m.-3 p.m. and is free, although donations are gratefully accepted as they are the museum's only source of revenue.

Believe it or not, you should pass through the McDonald's at the Royal Hawaiian Shopping Center to see a permanent collection of Hawaiian art on display. Among the exhibits are carvings, paintings, macramé, and featherwork. Many of the works are by Rocky Kaiouliokahihikoloehu Jensen, a famous island artist.

WAIKIKI BEACHES AND PARKS

In the six miles of shoreline from Kahanamoku Beach fronting the Hilton Hawaiian Village at the west end of Waikiki to Wailupe Beach Park in Maunalua Bay just east of the Kahala Hilton, there are at least 17 choice spots for enjoying surf activities. Most of the central Waikiki beaches are so close to each other you can hardly tell where one ends and another begins. All of these are generally gentle, but as you head east the beaches get farther apart and have their own personalities. Sometimes they're rough customers. As always, never take *moana* for granted, especially during periods of high surf. To get information on the presence of lifeguards, call Ocean Safety at (808) 922-3888; people with disabilities can get information on beach and facility accessibility by calling (808) 586-8121. Now that you've finally arrived at a Waikiki beach, the one thing left to do is kick back and R-E-L-A-X.

Waikiki Beach stretches for two miles, broken into separate areas. A multitude of concession stands offer everything from shave ice to canoe rides. It's not news that this beach is crowded. Sometimes when looking at the rows of glistening bodies, it appears that if one person wants to tan his other side, everybody else has to roll over with him. Anyone looking for seclusion here is just being silly. Take heart—a big part of the fun is the other people.

Umbrella stands set up along Waikiki Beach fronting Kalakaua rent boogie boards, surfboards, paddle boats, and snorkel gear. They're convenient, but their prices are much more than many shops offering the same. The guys by the big banyan tree are slightly cheaper than those set up by the breakwater just before Kapiolani Park. However, all offer decent prices for surfing lessons and rides in outrigger canoes, which gets you three waves and about 20 minutes of fun. Bargaining is acceptable. Find other outrigger canoe rides—you help paddle—in front of the big hotels (try the Outrigger Waikiki). They're great fun and a bargain at $5 per person.

Kahanamoku Beach

This stretch of sand in front of the Hilton Hawaiian Village is named after Hawaii's most famous waterman, Duke Kahanamoku. The manmade beach and lagoon were completed in 1956. A system of pumps pushes water into the lagoon to keep it fresh. The swimming is great, and plenty of concessions offer surfboards, beach equipment, and catamaran cruises.

Fort DeRussy Beach

You pass through the right-of-way of Fort DeRussy military area, where you'll find restrooms, picnic facilities, volleyball courts, and food and beverage concessions. Lifeguard service is provided by military personnel—no duty is too rough for our fighting men and women! A controversy has raged for years between the military and developers who covet this valuable piece of land. The government has owned it since the turn of the century, and has developed what once was wasteland into the last stretch of non-cement, non-high-rise piece of real estate left along Waikiki. Since the public has access to the beach, and since Congress voted a few years back that the lands cannot be sold, it'll remain under the jurisdiction of the military.

Gray's Beach

This section's name comes from Gray's-by-the-Sea, a small inn once located here. The narrow white-sand beach lies in front of the Halekulani Hotel, which replaced Gray's. Take Lewers Street off Kalakaua Avenue and park along Kalia Road; a right-of-way is between the Reef and Halekulani hotels. The sea is generally mild here and the swimming is always good, with shallow waters and a sandy bottom. Offshore is a good break called **No. 3's,** a favorite with surfers.

Next door is **Royal Moana Beach,** lying between Waikiki's oldest manmade landmarks, the Moana and Royal Hawaiian hotels. Access is unlimited off Kalakaua Avenue. The inshore waters here are gentle and the bottom is sandy and generally free from coral. Offshore are three popular

surfing areas, **Popular's, Queen's,** and **Canoes.** Many novices have learned to surf here because of the predictability of the waves, but with so many rookies in the water, and beach activities going on all around, you have to remain alert for runaway boards and speeding canoes.

Waikiki Beach Center
and Prince Kuhio Beach Center

When people say "Waikiki Beach," this is the section to which they're referring. Both beaches front Kalakaua Avenue, and a long sand retaining wall called Slippery Wall fronts both beaches, creating a semienclosed saltwater pool. Here, you'll find surfing, canoeing, snorkeling, and safe year-round swimming along the gently sloping, sandy-bottomed shoreline. There are comfort stations, concession stands, and lifeguards. Be careful of the rough coral bottom at the Diamond Head end of Kuhio Beach. Covered with a coating of slick seaweed, Slippery Wall definitely lives up to its name. Though local youngsters play on the wall, the footing is poor and many knees have been scraped and heads cracked after spills from this ill-advised play. The surf on the seaward side of the wall churns up the bottom and creates deep holes that come up unexpectedly, along with an occasional rip current.

Kapiolani Regional Park

In the shadow of Diamond Head is Kapiolani Park, a quiet 140-acre oasis of greenery, just a coconut's roll away from the gray cement and flashing lights of Waikiki. It has proved to be one of the best gifts ever received by the people of Honolulu, ever since King Kalakaua donated this section of crown lands to them in 1877, requesting that it be named after his wife, Queen Kapiolani. In times past, it was the site of horse and car races, polo matches, and Hawaii's unique pa'u riders, fashionable ladies in long flowing skirts riding horses decked out with lei. The park was even the site of Camp McKinley, the U.S. Army headquarters in the islands from 1898 to 1907.

It remains a wonderful place for people to relax and exercise away from the hustle of Waikiki. The park is a mecca for jogging and aerobics, with many groups and classes meeting here throughout the day. It also serves as the starting point for the yearly **Honolulu Marathon,** one of the most prestigious races in the world.

J.D. BISIGNANI

Kapiolani Regional Park

Its **Waikiki Shell,** an open-air amphitheater, hosts many visiting musical groups, especially during Aloha Week. The Honolulu Symphony is a regular here, providing free concerts, especially on summer evenings. Nearby, the **Kapiolani Bandstand** hosts the Royal Hawaiian Band on Sunday afternoons. Also, under the shade of the trees toward Waikiki Beach, plenty of street entertainers, including clowns, acrobats, and jugglers, congregate daily to work out their routines to the beat of conga drums and other improvised music supplied by wandering musicians. Families and large groups come here to picnic, barbecue, and play softball. The park grounds are also home to the free **Kodak Hula Show,** Elks Club, prestigious Outrigger Canoe Club founded at the turn of the century, Waikiki Aquarium, and 45-acre Honolulu Zoo.

Just in front of the zoo, by the big banyan, are hundreds and hundreds of pigeons, the "white phantoms of Waikiki." In the morning they are especially beautiful darting through the sunshine like white spirits. Go to the Stop N Go or the ABC Store at the corner of Kapahulu and Kapiolani and buy birdseed. Take a few handfuls and stand among the pigeons. They will perch on your arms, shoulders, and head and peck away. If you're not wearing toe-covering shoes be advised that if you drop seed between your toes, you'll get an instant and free pedicure by the hungry birds. This is great fun and free!

The Kapiolani Beach Park section is the only spot along Waikiki with facilities for barbecueing and picnicking. Although it's only a short stroll down the beach from Waikiki central, it gets much less use. This is where local families and those in the know come to get away from the crowds, just a few beach-blanket lengths away. In the park and along the beach are restrooms, volleyball courts, picnic tables, lifeguard towers, a bath house, and a concession stand. Activities include surfing, fishing, snorkeling, and year-round safe swimming. Just be careful of the rocky bottom that pops up unexpectedly here and there. **Kapiolani Park Center** is the beach closest to Waikiki. The swimming is good here, with the best part at the Waikiki end. The beach is at its widest, and the bottom is gently sloping sand. The area called **The Wall** has been designated as a special bodysurfing area. Supposedly, board riders are restricted from this area, but if the surf is good they're guaranteed to break the rules. Experts can handle it, but novices, especially with runaway boards, are a hazard. Kapiolani Park incorporates **Sans Souci Beach** at the eastern end. Many families with small children come to Sans Souci because it is so gentle. This beach, in front of the Colony Surf and New Otani Kaimana hotels, has unlimited access. Changing facilities are found at the deteriorating Natatorium, a saltwater pool built in the '20s. Unless something has been done to the Natatorium by the time you arrive, avoid its murky waters and be careful of the rocky areas to the front of its stone enclosure.

Around Diamond Head
Kaluahole Beach is located at the Waikiki side of Diamond Head. The water conditions are safe all year-round, but the beach is small and lies along a seawall. Once a large beach, it was paved over for building purposes. It has one public right-of-way, poorly marked and sandwiched between private homes. It's almost at the end at 3837 Kalakaua Avenue. The surfing in this area is generally good, and the breaks are known as "Tongg's," named after a local family that lived along this shore.

Diamond Head Beach Park is an unlimited access area along Beach Road (marked). It covers almost two acres of undeveloped shoreline. Unfortunately, the beach is very narrow and surrounded by unfriendly rock and coral. The waters, however, are quite protected and generally safe, except in periods of high surf. This area is good for fishing and finding quiet moments.

Kuilei Cliffs Beach Park lies below Diamond Head Road, with access available from three lookout areas along the road. You must walk down the cliff trails to the beaches below. Here are plenty of secluded pockets of sand for sunbathing, but poor swimming. The surf is generally rough, and the area is always frequented by surfers. When the winds are right, windsurfers also come. Offshore is hazardous with submerged rocks, but this makes it excellent for diving and snorkeling—for experts only! Currents can be fierce, and you can be dashed against the rocks. Whales can sometimes be spotted passing this point, and to add to the mystique, the area is considered a breeding ground for sharks. Most visitors just peer down at the surfers from Diamond Head Road, or choose a spot of beach for peace and quiet.

Farther east is **Kaalawai Beach.** The swimming is good here and generally safe because of a protecting reef. Many locals come to this area to fish, and it is good for bodysurfing and snorkeling. The waters outside the reef are excellent for surfing, and produce some of the biggest waves on this side of the island. Access is by public right-of-way, marked off Kulumanu Place, or a small side road running off Kahala Avenue, or by walking along the shoreline from Kuilei Beach.

Kahala Beach, lying along Kahala Avenue, can be reached by a number of marked rights-of-way located between the high fences of estates in the area. The swimming is not particularly good, but there are plenty of pockets of sand and protected areas where you can swim and snorkel. Local people come to fish, and the surfing is good beyond the reef. The Kahala Hilton is located along this beach at the eastern end. The public can use "their" beach by walking from Kahala Beach. The swimming here is always safe and good because the hotel has dredged the area to make it deeper. Concession stands and lifeguards are provided by the hotel.

Wailupe Beach Park lies on the Waikiki side of Wailupe Peninsula in Maunalua Bay, and is the last beach covered by this chapter. This beach park, clearly marked off the Kalaniana'ole Highway, provides restrooms and picnic facilities. Swimming is officially not recommended. Be careful of the boat channel surrounding the area because the deep dropoff is very abrupt.

ACCOMMODATIONS

Waikiki is loaded with places to stay: 120 properties holding 31,000 rooms jammed into one square mile. And they come in all categories of hotels and condos, from deluxe to dingy. Your problem won't be finding a place to stay, but choosing from the enormous selection. During peak season (Christmas to Easter and again in summer) you'd better have reservations, or you could easily be left out in the *warm*. The good news is that, room for room, Waikiki is the cheapest place to stay in the state. Hotels along the beach tend to be slightly more expensive than their counterparts on a side street or back lane. The beachfront hotels have the surf at the doorstep, but those a block away have a little more peace and quiet. The following listings are not exhaustive. They couldn't be! Here are just some from all categories which you can use as a barometer to measure what's available.

INEXPENSIVE

Youth Hostels

Hale Aloha Youth Hostel, a member of the American Youth Hostel Association, is located in Waikiki at 2417 Prince Edward St., Honolulu, HI 96815, tel. (808) 926-8313. Walk down Kalakaua until you see the Hyatt Regency. Two streets directly behind is Prince Edward. Directions are also available at the airport information counter. A dorm room bunk is $16 for YH members and $19 for those who are not International Youth Hostel Association members. Dorm rooms are not sexually integrated, and you must be at least age 18 to stay unaccompanied by an adult. Couples can rent a studio for $40 members and $46 nonmembers. It's recommended that reservations be made at least two weeks in advance, particularly during peak season. Credit cards can be used for reservations; the business office is open 24 hours a day. The hostel closes at 11 p.m. and all must leave daily 11 a.m.-5 p.m. The maximum three-day stay, especially during peak seasons, can sometimes be extended at the discretion of the manager. Requests must be made before 10 p.m. the previous day. Baggage may be left for the day for $2. Key deposits will not be returned if keys are not returned by 11 a.m., checkout time. Visitors are not allowed at any time, and neither alcohol nor smoking is permitted. Chores are required. Lockers—small, gym locker-types not big enough for a backpack but adaquate for valuables—are available, but you must provide your own lock. The hostel gets visitors from around the world. It's clean and safe. The common area, kitchen, and bathrooms are shared by all.

Inter-Club Hostel Waikiki, at 2413 Kuhio Ave., Honolulu, HI 96815, tel. (808) 924-2636, has self-service laundry facilities, a relaxed island-style TV lounge, and a game room with ping pong and pool tables. Unlike some hostels, it's all right to drink beer on premises. You must be an international traveler or an American with an onward-going ticket to bunk here. Most rooms are dorm style (five to seven beds in each), $16.35 per night, but couples rooms run $32.70 and private rooms $49 for two, with $10 for an extra person; $10 key deposit. Rooms are usually segregated according to gender, but may not be if they are full. Reservations are accepted and are most often necessary; a credit card helps with reservations but is not necessary. The kitchen is used by the staff only. A continental breakfast is served 8-11 a.m. daily; dinner is served only on Monday, Wednesday, Friday, and Saturday for $3.50-4. Large lockers, big enough for a backpack, are $1; small lockers are 50 cents. Safe deposit boxes are also available for your most valuable possessions. Phone cards are sold here, and boogie boards, snorkels, and other water equipment are free for the use with a deposit.

Hawaiian Seaside Hostel, 419 Seaside and Kuhio, Honolulu, HI 96815, tel. (808) 924-3306, is a private hostel for international travelers, who must show a passport and an onward-going ticket. United States citizens are welcomed if they are travelers bound for a foreign destination (onward-going ticket necessary). Rates are $9.75 for the first night, plus a $10 deposit which is returnable upon checkout. After the first night, the rate goes up to $14.30 per night. Reservations are not required but can be accepted with a credit card. Accommodations are in nine mixed dorms, each with bunks and double beds. Bedding is provided. Each dorm has a refrigerator, a bathroom, air-conditioning, and a locker for each bed. Other helpful amenities include free safe deposits, free long-term storage, laundry facilities, a lounge with a wide-screen TV, free videos, and a lanai. The hostel has a common communal kitchen. Semiprivate rooms for two go for $16.50. Weekly rates give you seven nights for the price of six. One private room goes for $40 a night. The hostel, located on a cul-de-sac across from the Honolulu Zoo, is quiet for being so close to the action. It's the closest hostel to the beach. Most of the international travelers that you will find there are Australians, Brits, Germans, and Swedes. Beach mats, boogie boards, surfboards, and snorkeling equipment can be borrowed for your enjoyment on the beach. A hostel van makes a run to various spots of the North Shore three times a week—Monday, Wednesday, and Saturday; $5 for the roundtrip ride. Also, on Wednesday and Saturday, parties are thrown to facilitate socializing, so you can party hearty with new friends. A weekly barbecue at 3 p.m. on Sunday goes for $5.

The management also runs the nearby **Waikiki Beachside Hostel** at 2556 Lemon Road, tel. (808) 923-9566. Rates start at $15 per person for a bunk bed and increase to $35 for a semiprivate room in a unit. A full unit with kitchen goes for $66 a night.

Just down the road at 2584 Lemon Road, tel. (808) 922-1340, fax 955-4470, is the **Polynesian Hostel Beach Club.** Dorm rooms run $12-15, single/double rooms with a shared bath are $30-40, and a studio with bath and kitchen is $45. The hostel has a common room for reading and TV watching, a communal kitchen, storage lockers for valuables, free use of some water equipment, frequent in-hostel activities, and inexpensive excursions. It is only one block from the beach. The management here also runs the Northshore Inn in Wailiku on Maui.

On the other end of Waikiki at 1946 Ala Moana Blvd., located inside the Hawaiian Colony Building across from Fort DeRussy, is **Island Hostel,** tel. (808) 942-8748. Each hostel room has a bathroom, small refrigerator, and a/c. Bunks run $16.50 per person, and private rooms cost $45 a night. A communal kitchen is located in the office, the lounge is open for community activities, and laundry facilities, lockers, and telephones are available.

When the YHs are full try the **Waikiki Prince** just next door to Hale Aloha YH, at 2431 Prince Edward St., tel. (808) 922-1544. Listed as a hotel, it is about the cheapest in Waikiki at $25-35 per night during low season.

Honolulu's YM/WCAs and AYH hostel near the university are near, but not technically in Waikiki. Find a complete list in the Honolulu chapter's "Accommodations" section.

Inexpensive Hotels and Condos

The **Waikiki Hana Hotel** at 2424 Koa Ave., Honolulu HI 96815, tel. (808) 926-8841 or (800) 367-5004, sits just behind the massive Hyatt Regency on a quiet side street. The hotel has just 73 rooms, so you won't get lost in the shuffle, and the friendly staff go out of their way to make you feel welcome. The Waikiki Hana is surrounded by high-rise hotels, so there's no view, but the peace and quiet just one block from the heavy action more than makes up for it. Rooms start at a very reasonable $79 and go to $119 for a superior with kitchenette. All rooms have telephones, a/c, color TV, in-room safes, and are gaily appointed with bright bedspreads and drapes. The **Super Chef Restaurant,** on the ground floor of the hotel, is one of the best in Waikiki for atmosphere, food, and very rea-

sonable prices. On-site parking is another good feature in crowded Waikiki, but the charge is $10 a day. For a quiet, decent, but basic hotel in the heart of Waikiki, the Waikiki Hana can't be beat!

The **Waikiki Beachside Apartment Hotel,** at 2556 Lemon Road, Honolulu, HI 96815, tel. (808) 923-9566, is owned and operated by Mr. and Mrs. Wong, who keep a close eye on who they admit, as they run a very "decent" clean hotel. They rent weekly, charging from $385; off season may be cheaper. Per diem rooms are available during the winter rush at $66 a room, $35 for a semiprivate room, or $16.50 for a dorm bed. Furnished units have full kitchens and baths with twin beds and a convertible sofa and accommodate up to three people at no extra charge. There are laundry facilities, but no maid service is available. Reservations are reluctantly accepted (they like to see you first), and parking is extra. Mrs. Wong says that they are going to renovate the hotel because it has become run-down. There are no firm plans for completion, but when and if they are carried out, the rates will go up. Be advised!

The **Outrigger Coral Seas Hotel,** at 250 Lewers St., Honolulu, HI 96815, tel. (808) 923-3881 or (800) 367-5170, is an old standby for budget travelers. This is the epitome of the economy tourist hotel and houses **Perry's Smorgasbord.** It's one of the Outrigger Hotels, and seems to get all the hand-me-downs from the others in the chain. There's a restaurant, cocktail lounge, TV, pool, and parking. Rates are an economical $75-85, extra person $15, and $130 for a kitchenette. Not to everyone's taste, but with plenty of action and the beach only a few steps away.

The **Royal Grove Hotel,** at 151 Uluniu Ave., Honolulu, HI 96815, tel. (808) 923-7691, built in 1951 and run by the Fong family since 1970, gives you a lot for your money. You can't miss its "paint-sale pink" exterior, but inside it's much more tasteful. Rooms in the older and cheaper wing run $42.50-75 for two, $10 for an extra person; the newer upgraded wing with a/c is $57-75. Most are studios and one-bedroom apartments with full facilities. A tiny pool in the central courtyard offers some peace and quiet away from the street. The Royal Grove passes the basic tests of friendliness and cleanliness. It's used but not abused. During low season it offers reduced weekly and monthly rates.

Hale Pua Nui, at 228 Beachwalk, Honolulu, HI 96815, tel. (808) 923-9693 or 921-4398, offers very reasonable accommodations only a few minutes' walk from Waikiki Beach. A studio apartment with a kitchenette is only $45 off season and $55 during peak season, $269 a week, and $880 a month. The on-site parking is $5 a night. Hale Pua Nui, clean and adequate, is a touch above spartan, with ceiling fans but no a/c, cable TV, phone, and fully equipped kitchen. Unfortunately, the "House of the Big Flower" is a bit wilted. The hotel is geared to repeat clientele, mostly from Canada, who book a year in advance, and not really open to new clientele, especially those who just drop in. If you want a room, call well in advance, and it will send you a form with the house rules (plenty). Remember, too, that there is no elevator, so you must carry your bags to the upper floors.

A two-minute walk puts you on Waikiki Beach when you stay at the **Waikiki Malihini Hotel,** 217 Saratoga Road, Honolulu, HI 96815, tel. (808) 923-9644 or 923-3095, which bills itself as a "small, plain hotel with no extra frills. Just a place to stay in an excellent location." And, that's just what it is! In a semi-quiet area just across from Fort DeRussy, the hotel's 30 units have kitchenettes, daily maid service, fans (no a/c in most units), rental TV, and convenient but not complimentary parking next door. The management, not unfriendly but not overly congenial either, "strongly requests" that you contact them and fill out a card that will inform them of your dates-of-stay, number-in-party, etc., *before* they will make reservations. A well-laid lava rock wall in front provides some privacy for a small picnic area complete with tables and charcoal grills. Rates are studios $40-50, family suites $70-80 (some have a/c). There's a three-day minimum stay during peak season, and payment is by cash only!

MODERATE

The **Queen Kapiolani Hotel** is at 150 Kapahulu Ave., Honolulu, HI 96815, tel. (808) 922-1941 or (800) 367-5004. With its off-the-strip location and magnificent views of Diamond Head, this is perhaps the best, and definitely the quietest, hotel for the money in Waikiki. You're only seconds from the beach, and the hotel provides a spacious lobby, parking, a restaurant, TV, a/c, shops, and a swimming pool. Rates begin at $107 standard to $127 for a superior and go up to $165 with kitchenettes. Suites with kitchenettes run $250-380 a night. The main lobby has been rejuvenated with a $2 million face-lift. The stately marble columns have been redone, new wallpaper has been applied, and the shopping area has been upgraded. The overall effect is open and airy with the living mural of Diamond Head in the background. Select rooms have been made first-class with new carpeting, draperies, furnishing, and amenities. Most boast a spectacular view of Diamond Head. An excellent choice for the money. Also featured, in the **Peacock Dining Room,** is one of the best buffets in Waikiki.

You can't beat the value at the **Pacific Monarch Hotel/Condo** located directly behind the Hyatt Regency at 142 Uluniu Ave., Honolulu, HI 96815, tel. (808) 923-9805. It offers some great features for a moderately priced hotel. Fully furnished studios begin at $125 and go up to $145; one-bedroom condo apartments cost $160-190, all a/c, with on-site parking ($9 a night). The rooms are bright and cheery with full baths, living/dining areas, and cable TV. End units of each floor are larger, so request one for a large or shared party. The swimming pool, with a relaxing jacuzzi, perches high over Waikiki on the 34th floor of the hotel, offering one of the best cityscapes in Honolulu. The lobby is sufficient but small. It's accented with a lava fountain and two giant brass doors. A security key allows guests through the main door to the elevators. Save money and have a great family experience by setting up temporary housekeeping at the Pacific Monarch.

The **Outrigger Hotels** chain has 20 locations in and around Waikiki offering thousands of rooms. Many of the hotels are on quiet side streets, others are on the main drags, while still more perch on Waikiki Beach. Although most are not luxurious, they do offer good accommodations and all have pools, restaurants, a/c, TV, and parking. Several have recently been renovated. Rates vary from hotel to hotel; their cheapest rates are $85 and from there run up to $660 for a two-bedroom ocean suite at the Prince Kuhio; $15 additional person. Special discounts of 20% are offered to travelers over 50 years old. For information and reservations call (800) 668-7444 or check the

Outrigger Web site: at www.outrigger.com. Three of the chain's best hotels in Waikiki are the **Outrigger Reef, Outrigger Waikiki** (both on the beach), and the **Outrigger Prince Kuhio.** Others include the **Outrigger Waikiki Tower, Outrigger Royal Islander, Outrigger Edgewater,** and the **Outrigger Coral Seas.**

The **Outrigger Edgewater Hotel,** at 2168 Kalia Road, Honolulu, HI 96815, tel. (808) 922-6424, is an old standby in the palpitating heart of Waikiki. Rates begin at a reasonable $90, rising to $145 for a kitchenette suite, $15 extra person. Kitchenettes run $100. Facilities include a swimming pool, a good Italian restaurant (open for dinner only), limited parking ($8 for 24 hours), TV, and maid service.

You can capitalize on the off-beach location of the **Aston Honolulu Prince,** at 415 Nahua St., Honolulu, HI 96815, tel. (808) 922-1616 or (800) 922-7866, where you'll find a hotel/condo offering remarkably good value for your money. The hotel/condo invites you into its fully furnished one- and two-bedroom suites. All offer a/c, color cable TV, fully equipped kitchens, and daily maid service. Prices begin at $90 for a standard room and $105 for superior, $135 one bedroom, and $155 two bedroom, with substantial discounts during low season. The apartments are oversized, with a huge sitting area that includes a sofa bed for extra guests. The Honolulu Prince is not fancy, but it is clean, decent, and family-oriented. A fine choice for a memorable vacation at affordable prices.

The **Breakers Hotel,** 250 Beach Walk, Honolulu, HI 96815, tel. (808) 923-3181 or (800) 426-0494, is a very friendly family-style hotel, where if you're a repeat visitor, the staff remembers your name. Only minutes from the beach, this little gem of a hotel somehow keeps the hustle and bustle far away. Every room has a kitchenette and overlooks the shaded courtyard of coconut and banana trees. The rates for studios are $88-95 s, $91-97 d, additional person $8. The garden suites, which are equipped for up to four people, are $120-146. All units have a full kitchenette, a/c, color TV, a safe, and limited parking. There is also a swimming pool, and the **Hotel Cafe Terrace** where you can have a snack or light meal.

At 1956 Ala Moana Blvd. is the refined **Doubletree Alana Waikiki Hotel,** tel. (808) 941-7275 or (800) 367-6070, fax (808) 951-3114. Calling itself an "intimate boutique hotel," it pro-vides all needed amenities in a casual and relaxed atmosphere. All rooms are comfortably outfitted and have a/c, TV, computer hookups, lanai, and Italian marble entryways and baths. Rooms run $160-200, suites $240-550, and the Royal Amethyst Suite (a combined three-suite unit with boardroom) goes for $2,000. Artworks adorn the walls and works by local artists hang in the hotel's gallery. A full-service business center is available for those on working assignments, and everyone can enjoy the fitness center and swimming pool. The fine-dining **Harlequin** restaurant serves breakfast and "Pacific Northwest Rim cuisine" for dinner, while the more casual **Cafe Picasso** is a little easier going and combines dinner with entertainment. In the Doubletree tradition, every guest is welcomed to the hotel with freshly baked chocolate chip cookies.

Sometimes you just hit it lucky and find yourself in a situation where you get more for your money than you expected, and delightfully so. The **Waikiki Beachcomber Hotel,** 2300 Kalakaua Ave., Honolulu, HI 96815, tel. (808) 922-4646, (800) 622-4646 Mainland, or (800) 338-6233 Canada, Web site: www.dps.net/~beachcomber, is definitely one of those *sometimes* things. The Beachcomber, living up to its name, is just a minute from the beach, and with a professional and amiable staff, knows exactly what you want and how to deliver it. Newly renovated to the tune of $5 million, the 500 guest rooms, outfitted in new furniture and carpet, and painted in soothing tropical tones, all feature a private lanai, a/c, TV, phone, room safe, and convenient refrigerator. On the property is a pool, the **Beachcomber Restaurant,** long famous for its live KCCN Aloha Friday Luncheon Buffet, boutique shops, and a lounge for evening relaxation. Offered through the summer months, the Beachcomber Kids program can entertain and feed children while their parents are off doing other activities.Every evening at 7 p.m., except Friday and Saturday, enjoy the voice and humor of one of Hawaii's consummate entertainers, Don Ho, as he presents his musical extravaganza as he has done in Waikiki for years. To add to its image as an entertainment center, the Beachcomber also presents the Magic of Polynesia Show. The rates for guest rooms range from $150 to $285 for a suite with $15 for an additional person, children under 17 free in their parents' room. A bargain special at only $130 puts you in a city view room with a rental car included or a breakfast buffet for two. To stay within budget, while having a quality experience, the Beachcomber is a sure bet! (Website: www.beachcomber.com .

The **Ilima Hotel,** 445 Nohonani St., Honolulu, HI 96815, tel. (808) 923-1877 or (800) 367-5172, is two streets back from the Ala Wai Canal and overlooks the Ala Wai Golf Course. This condo-style hotel is a few blocks from the beach—quiet atmosphere and budget rates. Studio units begin at a reasonable $109, $10 extra persons, one bedroom $144, two bedroom $187. All units have full kitchens, a/c, and TV, along with a pool, parking, and maid service. Discounts are given for those over age 55. **Sergio's Italian Restaurant,** on premises, is open for dinner. Good value.

Miramar at Waikiki, 2345 Kuhio Ave., Honolulu, HI 96815, tel. (808) 922-2077 or (800) 367-2303, is in the heart of Waikiki. The hotel offers generous-size rooms, with lanai, a pool, a restaurant, a/c, TV, and parking ($7 for 24 hours). Rates range $120-140, $20 extra per person.

All you have to do is literally roll out of bed, walk out your door, and pick a spot on Waikiki Beach when you stay at the **Aston Waikiki Shores Condominium,** at 2161 Kalia Road, Honolulu, HI 96815, tel. (808) 926-4733 or (800) 367-2353. Individually owned, the decor in each unit differs, but most are tasteful with island-style furnishings, and all are immense. Typical is a one-bedroom laid out with a sitting area, living room, dining area, two baths with dressing rooms, and a kitchen complete with microwave, dishwasher, coffee maker, and garbage disposal. To make your stay more pleasant, there's daily maid service, private lanai, cable TV, in-room washers and dryers, beach towels, and limited parking, and children stay free with their parents. Rates, especially for what you get, are very reasonable, and start at $180 for a studio with deluxe ocean view, $260 for a one-bedroom unit, and up to $495 for a two-bedroom deluxe ocean front (10% off-season discount—ask!).

A reasonably priced accommodation is the **Coconut Plaza Hotel,** at 450 Lewers St., tel. (808) 923-8828. Rates are $110-125 for a double during peak season. Off season is cheaper, with special day rates for bona fide business travelers on a space available basis. A complimentary continental breakfast is offered daily in the lobby. All rooms are fully air-conditioned, and there is a hotel pool.

Just off Lewers St. at 2233 Helumoa Road is the modern but casual **Waikiki Parc Hotel,** tel. (808) 921-7272. The beach is just a stroll away. The entranceway is done in marble, carpet, and subdued lighting, and coolness seems to permeate the entire property. Rooms are not spacious, but efficient, some with lanai and others with balconies. On the ocean-view side, you look down on the distinctive orchid pool at the Halekulani Hotel. Depending upon location in the building, rooms run $170-255 a night. Open for breakfast, lunch, and dinner are the **Parc Cafe,** the hotel's main dining room, and the Japanese restaurant **Kacho.** The Parc Cafe features buffets at all meals, but the specialty is the weekend evening seafood buffet. The hotel pool is on the eighth floor, and there too you can get light meals and refreshments.

Twinkling lights descending the residential valleys of the Koolaus with Diamond Head framed in perfect symmetry are an integral part of the natural room decor of the **Aston Waikiki Sunset Hotel,** 229 Paoakalani St., Honolulu, HI 96815, tel. (808) 922-0511, (800) 922-7866 Mainland, or (800) 321-2558 Hawaii, one of Waikiki's newest suite-hotels. Charmingly refurbished from head to toe in 1991, the Waikiki Sunset, although *feeling* like a condominium, offers all of the comfort and convenience of a hotel including 24-hour front desk service, daily maid service, and amenities like a swimming pool, sauna, tennis court, travel desk, minimart, and even a restaurant. The entrance, cooled by Casablanca fans whirring over marble floors, sets the mood for this charming hotel tucked away only one block from the Waikiki strip. Units range $245-280. All feature full kitchens outfitted with a large refrigerator, coffee maker, electric stove and oven, disposal, and complete utensils for in-room cooking and dining. All suites feature a private lanai and entertainment center with remote-control color TV, and a tiled bath with a Japanese-style *ofuro,* a soaking tub perfect for the start of a cozy evening. The larger suites have a sitting area, modern and chic with rattan furniture, a bar/breakfast nook, and separate master bedroom. The **Manbow Inn,** on the sixth floor, open 7:30 a.m.-9 p.m., serves breakfast, lunch, and dinner at reasonable prices. The minimart, open 7 a.m.-11 p.m., provides everything from suntan lotion to takeout pizza.

Here, too, you can rent sporting equipment like snorkel sets and boogie boards, with a 10% discount offered to hotel guests.

Varying shades of Italian Trabertine marble covered with pink floral carpets, filigreed mirrors, tables of black lacquer bearing Chinese porcelains, and ornate Louis XV chests under cut crystal chandeliers are the signature touches of the chinoiserie decor (combination of Chinese and European) at the **Aston Waikiki Beachside Hotel,** 2452 Kalakaua Ave., Honolulu, HI 96815, tel. (808) 931-2100, (800) 922-7866 Mainland, (800) 445-6633 Canada, or (800) 321-2558 Hawaii, another of Aston's boutique hotels. A Chinese lord and his concubine sit under an umbrella in a hand-painted silk portrait, while two bronze lions guard the marble staircase leading to a formal parlor on the second floor. Here, white silk couches with puffy pillows, a magnificent Chinese folding screen depicting courtly life, and an 18th-century Chinese secretary in red and black lacquer especially made for the "British market" are the decor. Outside, a tiny courtyard serenaded by a bubbling Italian fountain is set with wooden tables protected by canvas umbrellas. Mornings are perfect here with complimentary coffee and croissants. In the 12 floors above, only 77 luxurious rooms await, ranging in price from $105 for a superior to $290 for a VIP oceanfront (ask for discounted specials). Small, but space-consciously designed, the rooms are vibrant with melba peach carpet and wallpaper with a counterpoint of black. Amenities include air-conditioning, or functional windows to catch the Waikiki breeze, an entertainment center with remote-control color TV and VCR, a mini-fridge stocked with a selection of complimentary soft drinks, and a voice mail message system. Your stay is made even more relaxing with twice daily maid service and turndown service with a special treat left on your pillow, a free morning newspaper, and concierge service for all activities and travel plans. Tastefully decorated, the rooms are appointed with Chinese vases, folding screens painted with birds and flowers, jewelry boxes, and goosedown pillows imported from London. The bathrooms are done in Italian marble and feature glass shower stalls (no baths), floor-to-ceiling mirrors, pedestal sinks with black fixtures from Germany, his-and-her *yukata* (robes), a make-up mirror, a hair dryer, and bath products including shampoo, moisturizer, and French-milled soaps. Ocean view rooms have their own lanai, but be aware that some inside rooms are windowless.

A tunnel of white thumbergia tumbling from a welcoming arbor leads to the entrance of the **Aston Waikiki Beach Tower Hotel,** 2470 Kalakaua Ave. Honolulu, HI 96815, tel. (808) 926-6400, (800) 922-7866 Mainland, or (800) 321-2558 Hawaii, one of Waikiki's newest mini-luxury condo hotels. A lustrous patina shines from brown on tan marble floors while glass-topped tables of black and gold lacquer hold magnificent displays of exotic blooms, and fancy French mirrors and cut glass chandeliers brighten the small but intimate reception area. Enter your suite through a vestibule of brown marble and glass onto a white carpet leading to a combination dining/living room. This common area, accented with contemporary paintings and highlighted by koa trim, offers a full wet bar, drum and glass tables, high-backed chairs, a pastel rainbow couch, and an entertainment center with remote-control TV. The ultramodern kitchen is complete with standard-sized refrigerator with ice maker, a rice cooker, a blender, a coffee maker, a microwave, a four-burner stove and oven, a dishwasher, a double sink, and koa cabinets. The master bedroom has its own entertainment center and private lanai from which you can overlook Waikiki. The bathroom has a double sink, commode, and shower, and a huge walk-in closet holding a complimentary safe, steam iron and board, and a washer and dryer. Rates range $450-680. Special amenities include twice daily maid service, turndown service, concierge desk, valet parking, a paddle tennis court, a swimming pool, spa and sauna, and also meeting rooms and a family plan.

Upon arrival, step onto a path of white tile leading through a tiny but robust garden to a translucent dome sheltering the outdoor reception area of the **Aston Waikiki Joy Hotel,** a lotus flower that blooms in the heart of Waikiki, at 320 Lewers St., Honolulu, HI 96815, tel. (808) 923-2300, (800) 922-7866 Mainland, or (800) 321-2558 Hawaii. Blocks of glass, veined marbles in pinks, whites, and grays, and polished chrome are part of its petals. Immediately, marble steps rise to a veranda, where every morning a complimentary continental breakfast is served accompanied by the soft background chanting of a tiny fountain. The hotel, with only 94 rooms, is divided into two towers, the Hibiscus and the Gardenia. It's intimate enough to make everyone feel like an honored guest. Typical rooms, $170-195, are amazingly spacious. You enter through a vestibule to find an ultramodern room of slate blue and pastel pink contrasted with the embossed effect of a tan Berber carpet. Two accommodating wicker chairs wait to hug you with their overstuffed pillow arms. At the foot of each bed is an ottoman, great for perching on while dressing, and a dresser built in as part of the wall. The hotel rooms each feature a refrigerator and writing desk, which has a believable rendition of Miss Muffet's tuffet as its chair. A king-size bed with a slanted headboard perfectly designed for propping pillows is the "nerve center" of the room. Here, in easy reach, is a dimmer switch for all lighting, a temperature control, and a phone featuring a personalized voice message system. In front of the bed is an entertainment center with remote-control color TV and a stereo system with tape deck. The bathroom, done in pastel barber stripes, is a sanctuary of relaxation where you can slide every evening into a large and bubbling jacuzzi tub. The suites in the Gardenia Tower feature a bedroom and attendant sitting area complete with couch, and a large private lanai. Suite kitchens have a standard-sized refrigerator, two-burner stove, double sink, microwave, toaster, and coffee maker. Here too, the bathrooms feature the wonderful jacuzzi tub. The Waikiki Joy is also very special with a 15-room karaoke studio, the largest and most modern in Waikiki (reservations recommended). The karaoke studio also features a lounge at the entrance, open weekdays 5 p.m.-2 a.m., weekends until 4 a.m., where you can order exotic drinks, standard cocktails, assorted iced teas, and island inspired *pu pu* from tofu to breaded calamari sticks. The hotel restaurant is **Cappucino's,** a European-style bistro featuring live entertainment on the weekends. The Waikiki Joy, aptly named, is the epitome of the adage that "wonderful things come in small packages," but in this case, the wonderful thing *is* the package!

Hale Koa, tel. (808) 955-0555, Web site: www.halekoa.com, is located on the beach in Fort DeRussy; it is maintained especially for active-duty U.S. military personnel, Department of Defense civilians, and a few other categories of former military and defense-related personnel. This well-run and well-maintained hotel has all

the dining facilities, entertainment options, and other amenities of other large hotels in Waikiki. Depending upon military rank or government status, there is a bewildering array of rates for the eight categories of rooms. Call for specifics.

DELUXE

Hilton Hawaiian Village

This glorious first-rate hotel, an oasis of tranquility, sits in its own quiet corner of Waikiki. The Hilton, at 2005 Kalia Road, Honolulu, HI 96815, tel. (808) 949-4321 or (800) 445-8667, is at the far western end of Waikiki, just below Fort DeRussy. Enter along 200 yards of the private hotel driveway, passing the village, a small mall with exclusive shopping and dining. Facing you are the Hilton's "towers," the Tapa, the Diamond Head, the Rainbow, and the prestigious Alii Tower. Rainbow Tower, so called because of the huge multistoried rainbow on the entire side of this building, is, according to the *Guinness Book of World Records,* the tallest ceramic-tile mosaic in the world. All the rooms are deluxe with magnificent views. Amenities include color TV, a/c, self-service bar, refrigerator, 24-hour room service, voice mail, and a safe for personal belongings. Children will also be delighted with the **Rainbow Express,** a year-round program that entertains and educates with everything from hula lessons to a trip to the Honolulu Zoo ($17 half day, $32 full lunch included).

The Alii Tower pampers you even more with a private pool with nightly gourmet *pu pu,* turndown service, fresh flowers, fruit baskets, concierge service, flowers, a fitness center, a sauna, and bath accessories. Rates are $240-310 throughout the Village and $229-340 in the Alii Tower.

The towers form a semicircle fronting the beach, not a private beach because none can be private, but about as private a public beach as you can get. Few come here unless they're staying at the Hilton. It's dotted with palms—tall royal palms for elegance, shorter palms for shade. The property has three pools. The main pool, surrounded by luxuriant tropical growth, is the largest in Waikiki. The lagoon area creates the music of water in bubbling rivulets, tiny waterfalls, and reflecting pools. Torches of fire, and ginger, banana trees, palms, ferns, and rock gardens are the grounds. The concierge can arrange a guided tour of the grounds (free) by a groundskeeper, who will explain the habitat, life cycle, and characteristics of each plant.

The *action* of Waikiki is out there, of course, just down the driveway, but you don't feel it unless you want to. Relax and enjoy the sunset accompanied by music at any one of 10 lounges like the **Shell Bar,** or in the main foyer where another small casual bar swings to the tunes of a piano stylist. Exotic and gourmet dining from throughout the Pacific rim is available at the Village's 10 restaurants, especially the hotel's signature **Bali by the Sea** and **Golden Dragon** restaurants.

As you pull into the driveway there's a geodesic dome, like a giant stereo speaker, where headliner John Hirokawa stars in the **Magic of Polynesia,** a magic show and Polynesian extravaganza performed twice nightly. A miniature golf course has been added to the grounds and an entertainment center, with karaoke and video games, is now located in Joy Square. The hotel has everything to keep its "villagers" contented and happy. As a complete destination resort where you can play, relax, shop, dine, dance, and retreat, the Hilton Hawaiian Village knows what it's about and has found its center.

Halekulani

The Halekulani Hotel, in mid-Waikiki at 2199 Kalia Road, Honolulu, HI 96815, tel. (808) 923-2311 or (800) 367-2343, Web site: www.halekulani.com, was an experiment of impeccable taste that paid off. Some years ago the hotel was completely rebuilt and refurnished with the belief that Waikiki could attract the luxury-class visitor, and that belief has proven accurate. Since opening, the hotel has gained international recognition and has been named as a member of the prestigious Leading Hotels of the World, and Preferred Hotels and Resorts Worldwide. It is one of four AAA five-diamond hotels in Hawaii and the only one on Oahu. In addition, its signature restaurant, La Mer, has also been given a five-diamond rating, making the Halekulani one of the best.

The soothing serenade of the Halekulani begins from the moment you enter the porte cochere where an impressive floral display of protea, anthuriums, orchids, and ferns arranged in the *sogetsu* style of *ikebana* by Kanemoto-san awaits to welcome you. The property was first developed in 1907 by Robert Lewers as a residential grouping of bungalows, none of which survive. However, still preserved is the **Main Building,** dating from the 1930s when the hotel became a fashionable resort owned by Juliet and Clifford Kimball. The Main Building, a plantation-style mansion, houses the hotel's award-winning **La Mer Restaurant,** along with the **Orchids Dining Room,** serving breakfast, lunch, and dinner; **Lewer's Lounge** for an intimate cocktail and nightly entertainment; the very genteel **Living Room,** where you can enjoy refreshments and watercress sandwiches; and the veranda where the afternoon tea is held. Notice the Main Building's distinctive "Dickey Roof," patterned after a Polynesian longhouse, perfectly sloped in such as way as to catch island breezes while repelling a sudden rain squall.

Wander the grounds to be pleasantly surprised that a full 50% is given to open space accented with trimmed lawn, reflecting pools, and bubbling fountains. The heated **Orchid Pool,** with its signature mosaic orchid, is always inviting and within earshot of the foaming surf. Close by is **House Without a Key,** an indoor/outdoor buffet restaurant also serving light snacks and perhaps the best locale in all of Waikiki for a sunset cocktail. Upon arrival, you are escorted directly to the privacy of your own guest room where you register. Awaiting is a platter of fine china bearing a display of fresh fruit and complimentary "Bakeshop" chocolates. Each evening, with turndown service, a dainty orchid and delicate shell are left upon your pillow, along with a once-per-week recipe card from one of the fine hotel restaurants. Enter the guest room through a solid teak door into an antechamber that opens into a room, done in seven shades of white. The floors are covered in rich Berber carpet while the king-sized beds are dressed with soft white quilts. For ultimate relaxation and added convenience, all of the rooms feature a writing desk, small couch, reclining chair, and marble-topped accessory tables softly lit by Oriental-style lamps. A remote-controlled entertainment center, mini-fridge, three telephones, an in-room safe, and a collection of wooden and satin covered hangers complete the amenities. Sliding louvered doors lead to a tiled lanai, private and perfect for in-room dining. The bathroom, with floor to ceiling tile, features a deep soaking tub, a shower stall, two sinks, a separate commode, and a hairdryer. The louvered and glass doors can be opened so that you have a view from your tub directly past the lanai to Diamond Head in the distance. Prices are $295-520 for guest rooms, $700-1,400 for suites, with the President Suite at $4,000 and Royal Suite at $4,500 a night. A third-person charge for over 18 years of age is $125 or $30 for a child if a roll-away bed is needed. Additional amenities include swimming pool, beach service, daily newspapers, free local telephone calls, and a full-service fitness center where you can sign up to go on a fun run with world-class marathon runner Max Telford on Monday, Wednesday, or Friday, or attend an aerobics class on Tuesday, Thursday, and Saturday. The Halekulani awaits to show you its version of classic island charm. You won't be disappointed.

Sheraton Moana Surfrider

The Moana, at 2365 Kalakaua Ave., Honolulu, HI 96815, tel. (808) 922-3111 or (800) 325-3535, fax (808) 923-0308, is the oldest and most venerable hotel in Waikiki. More than just recapturing turn-of-the-century grandeur, the Moana has surpassed itself by integrating all of the modern conveniences. The original Italian Renaissance style is the main architectural theme, but like a fine opera, it joins a variety of architectural themes that blend into a soul-satisfying finale. The restoration has connected the three main buildings, the Moana, Ocean Lanai, and Surfrider, to form an elegant complex of luxury accommodations, gourmet dining, and distinctive shopping. The renovated Moana, filled with memories of times past, is magical. It's as if you stood spellbound before the portrait of a beautiful princess of long ago, when suddenly her radiant granddaughter, an exact image, dazzling in jewels and grace, walked into the room.

You arrive under the grand columns of a porte cochere, where you are greeted by doormen in crisp white uniforms and hostesses bearing lei and chilled pineapple juice. The lobby is a series of genteel parlor arrangements conducive to very civilized relaxation. Art, urns, chandeliers, sofas, koa tables, flowers, vases, and pedestaled glass-topped tables wait in attendance. An elevator takes you to the second floor, where a room filled with 80 years of memorabilia whispers names and dates of the Moana's grand past. After a fresh chilled glass of pineapple juice, you are escorted to check-in.

Upstairs, the rooms are simple elegance. Queen-size beds in the Banyan Wing, rattan chairs, and fat fluffy pillows and bedspreads extend their waiting arms. All rooms have a/c, and the Banyan Wing features a remote-control master keyboard for TV, lights, and music. But this is the Moana! Sachet-scented closets hold *yukata* (robes), terry slippers, and satin hangers. Bathrooms are tile and marble appointed with huge towels and stocked with fine soaps, shampoos, creams, makeup mirrors, and a bathroom scale, which you can hide under the bed.

Being the first hotel built in Waikiki, it sits right on the beach with one of the best views of Diamond Head along the strip. A swimming pool with sundeck is staffed with attentive personnel, and the activities center can book you on a host of activities, including a classic outrigger canoe ride or a sunset sail on a catamaran. Four restaurants, a grand ballroom, a snack bar, and three lounges take care of all your dining needs. Rooms in the Moana wing overlook Banyan Court, scene of a nightly entertainment that can be chamber music provided by a pianist or harpist. Open the windows, allowing the breezes to billow the curtains while the waves of Waikiki join with the music below in a heavenly serenade. Rooms are $250-485, with suites priced from $900. The Sheraton Moana Surfrider is a superb hotel offering exemplary old-fashioned service. Whether you're a guest here or not, feel free to join one of the guided tours of the hotel's restored and refurnished original section, offered twice daily at 11 a.m. and 5 p.m.

Sheraton Waikiki

Dominating the center of Waikiki are the 30 floors and 1,852 rooms of the Sheraton Waikiki Hotel, 2255 Kalakaua Ave., Honolulu, HI 96815, tel. (808) 922-4422, fax 923-8785. Built in 1971 as one of the area's first convention centers, it has a perfect location on the beach. Think of it as a miniature global village where 7,000-8,000 people come and go every day. Over the next few years, the Sheraton company will put several million dollars into refurbishing this complex, bringing the spirit of the sea into the hotel. In conjunction, the *honu* (green sea turtle), which has come back from the brink of extinction and feeds in the evening in the waters of Waikiki, has been incorporated into the hotel logo. Rooms are either ocean view or city view, and all have full amenities, including air-conditioning, TV and movies, mini-refrigerators, and in-room safes. Ocean view rooms run $315-430, city and mountain view rooms $195-300, suites from $600. The hotel has a clutch of shops for apparel, jewelry, gifts, camera needs, and sundries; two freshwater pools; its own nightclub; three cocktail lounges; and three restaurants, including the **Hanohano Room** (its signature restaurant on the 30th floor) the **Ciao!** Italian restaurant, and the more casual **Ocean Terrace Restaurant.** Free to guests are fun runs Mon.-Sat. at 7 a.m. with marathoner Max Telford, aerobic fitness training Mon.-Fri. at 5 p.m., tai chi on Tuesday and Thursday at 4 p.m., and a leisurely guided historical tour along the beach at 9 a.m. every Wednesday. The Keiki Aloha Club can keep your kids (ages 5-12) busy with age-appropriate, supervised activities 9 a.m.-9 p.m. from mid-June through mid-August and 9 a.m.-5 p.m. the rest of the year. Baby-sitting services are also available. Golfers can easily schedule tee times at the Sheraton Makaha Golf Club through the dining and activities desk, while guests who have early arrivals or late-night departures can make use of the lockers, showers, restrooms, and lounge in the Hospitality Center 6:30 a.m.-9:30 p.m.

Royal Hawaiian Hotel

The Royal Hawaiian, second oldest hotel built along Waikiki, at 2255 Kalakaua Ave., Honolulu, HI 96815, tel. (808) 923-7311 or (800) 325-3535, fax (808) 924-7098, provides an ongoing contemporary experience in turn-of-the-century charm. The Royal Hawaiian has also recently completed a $25 million restoration, which has recaptured the grand elegance of days past. Doors first opened in 1927, at a cost of $4 million, an unprecedented amount of money in those days for a hotel. The Depression brought a crushing reduction to Hawaiian tourism, bringing the yearly total down from a whopping 22,000 to under 10,000 (today more visitors arrive in one day), and the Royal became a financial loss. During WW II, with Waikiki barb-wired, the Royal was leased to the Navy as an R&R hotel for sailors from the Pacific Fleet. After the war, the hotel reverted to Matson Lines, the original owner, and reopened in 1947 after a $2 million renovation. Sheraton Hotels purchased the Royal in 1959, built the Royal Tower Wing in 1969, sold the hotel in 1975, but continued to remain as operating manager.

Original double doors featured one solid door backed by a louvered door so you could catch the ocean breezes and still have privacy. Today, the hotel is fully air-conditioned, so the old doors have been removed and new solid rosewood doors carved in the Philippines have replaced them. Rooms might have four-poster beds, canopies, twins, or kings, depending upon your preference. All rooms have remote-control TV, refrigerators, electronic safes, and computer hookups on telephones for lap-top computers. Furniture is French provincial, with bathrooms fully tiled. Completely renovated rooms in the original section have kept the famous pink motif, but are slightly more pastel. They have a marble tile bathroom, a brass butler, louvered drawers, and a huge bed. The tall ceilings are even more elegant with molded plaster cornices. Guests are treated to banana bread on arrival, a daily newspaper, and turndown service with a complimentary late-night sweet treat. Preferential tee-off times at the Makaha Resort are also offered. Each floor of the original Royal has a pool elevator, so guests in beachwear don't clash with the early evening black-tie set. A Hospitality Suite is provided for early morning check-ins or late checkouts and offers complimentary shower facilities, maid service six times during the day, coffee-making facilities, and a sitting and lounging area.

Some of the prestige suites are truly luxurious and feature huge balconies with tiled floors, where a party of 25 could easily be entertained. The tastefully carpeted bedrooms boast a quilt-covered bed heaped with a half dozen pillows. The huge bathrooms overlook the beach and have a small built-in jacuzzi. In the massive Governor's Suite is a formal dining room, two huge bedrooms, two magnificent sitting areas—one a formal parlor, the other an "informal" rec room. The Royal Towers, an addition dating from 1969, are preferred by many guests because every room has an ocean view. From the balcony of most, you look down onto the swimming pool, the beach, palm trees, and Diamond Head in the distance. Not as large as its neighbors, the Royal Hawaiian has 527 rooms, 49 of which are suites. A basic guest room is $290-540, with suites ranging from $475 to over $1,600.

If you stay at the Royal Hawaiian, you can dine and sign at the Moana Surfrider, Sheraton Waikiki, or Princess Kaiulani, all operated by Sheraton Hotels. One of the best features of the

J.D. BISIGNANI

Royal Hawaiian Hotel

Royal, open to guest and nonguest, is the remarkable luau every Monday night and the extraordinary food and entertainment provided Tues.-Sat. by the Brothers Cazimero in the hotel's famous and elegant **Monarch Dining Room.** The Royal Hawaiian, a Waikiki classic, is worth a visit even if you don't stay there.

Hawaiian Regent Hotel

The Hawaiian Regent, at 2552 Kalakaua Ave., Honolulu, HI 96815, tel. (808) 922-6611 or (800) 367-5370, has a long history of treating guests like royalty. The hotel now stands on what was the original site of Queen Liliuokalani's summer cottage. The Regent was the first major Hawaiian project of master designer Chris Hemmeter, famed for his magnificent Westin Kauai and Hyatt Regency Waikaloa hotels. The grand tradition of the hotel is reflected in the open sweeping style that marks a Hemmeter project. After two decades, the Regent appears extremely modern because its design was so visionary when it was built. With almost 1,400 units, the hotel ranks as the third-largest hotel in Hawaii after the Hilton Hawaiian

Village and the Sheraton Waikiki. Rates are $165-270 for a standard room up to $1,000 for a deluxe suite. Children are especially taken care of with the "Kid Quest," a summer program, and honeymooners can choose a junior suite with special amenities for a reduced price. All rooms are oversized and include cable TV, a/c, nightly turndown service, and in-room safes. You can step across the street to mingle with the fun-seekers on Waikiki Beach, or relax at one of the hotel's two pools. A championship Laykold tennis court is open from sunrise to sunset, with lessons and rackets available. The hotel offers a variety of exclusive shops in an off-lobby mall area like Shirokiya and Sandcastles for alohawear and evening wear. An on-site beauty shop and Japanese acupressure/massage service are there to revitalize you after a hard day of having fun in the sun. The Regent is renowned for its fine dining, entertainment, and late-night disco. The **Lobby Bar** is a perfect spot to perch while listening to relaxing Hawaiian music. The **Cafe Regent,** an open-air restaurant just off the main lobby, is open for breakfast, buffet, and lunch selections 6 a.m.-2:30 p.m. The **Tiffany Restaurant,** dinner only, has casual dining in an elegant atmosphere, with a stained-glass ceiling and shuttered windows. The **Ocean Terrace,** designed for kicking back and watching life go by, is a poolside bar serving sandwiches and hamburgers at very good prices. The premier restaurant of the hotel, and one of Waikiki's consistently best, is the award-winning **The Secret,** previously known as the Third Floor, where you can not only dine in Polynesian splendor, but be treated to a magnificent selection of wines collected by Richard Dean, one of only two sommeliers in all of Hawaii.

Enjoy a daily international buffet or spectacular Sunday brunch at **The Summery,** or a traditional Japanese meal at the **Regent Marushin.** You won't be told to hush while you dance or relax to the sounds of live music in **The Library.** And, if you have "dancing feet" take them to **The Point After,** one of Waikiki's swingingest high-tech discos, which will rock you until the wee hours. If you're after peace and quiet, head for the **Garden Courtyard,** a multipurpose area in the center of the hotel. Sit among flowers and full-grown coconut and bamboo trees. Every Monday, Wednesday, and Friday 10 a.m.-noon learn lei-making, hula, or even Hawaiian checkers from *kapuna* who come just to share their *aloha.* The Hawaiian Regent is a first-class hotel that really knows how to make you feel like a visiting monarch. Rule with joy!

Hawaii Prince Hotel

The dynamic seascape of the tall masted ships anchored in the Ala Wai Yacht Harbor reflects in the shimmering pink-tinted glass towers of the Hawaii Prince Hotel, at 100 Holomoana St., Honolulu, HI 96815, tel. (808) 956-1111 or (800) 321-6248, the city's newest luxury hotel. This hotel is also represented by Westin Resorts, tel. (800) 228-3000. The twin towers, Diamond Head and Ala Moana, are scaled by a glass elevator affording wide-angled vistas of the Honolulu skyline. Decorated in green and tan with light burnished maple, the rooms, all ocean view, feature a marble-topped desk with full mirror, a/c, functional windows, and a full entertainment center with remote-control color TV and VCR. Each room has its own refrigerator, walk-in closet with complimentary safe and terry cloth robes, and a king-size bed with fluffy down pillows. The marble bathrooms have separate shower stalls, tubs, and commodes with a full set of toiletries, lighted makeup mirrors, and hair dryers. Room rates are from $250 for an Oceanfront Marina to $410 for an Oceanfront Top (floors 30-33), while suites range up to $2,500; $45 per extra person. Special business rates are offered (ask when booking), and a special golf package is available for $275. Ride the elevator to the fifth floor, where you will find a keyhole-shaped pool and canvas shade umbrellas overlooking the harbor below. Here as well is the **Promenade Deck Snack Shop** serving coffee, jumbo hamburgers, and other munchies beginning at 11 a.m. The business center on the 29th floor gives you access to a secretary, computers, fax machines, modems for e-mail, and a conference room. Fees vary according to services rendered. Other amenities include three excellent restaurants, the **Takanawa, Prince Court,** and **Hakone;** a lobby lounge; a full fitness center; turndown service upon request; valet parking; and a Waikiki/Ala Moana Shuttle. The Hawaii Prince boasts its own golf course, the **Hawaii Prince Golf Club,** the only one of its kind belonging to a Waikiki hotel. Located at Ewa Beach, 35 minutes away by complimentary shuttle, the Arnold Palmer-designed 27-hole championship course includes a fully equipped golf shop, practice range, putting greens, chipping greens, locker and shower facilities, club-

house dining, and tennis courts. The Hawaii Prince, located at the "gateway to Waikiki" is away from the action of the frenetic Waikiki strip, but close enough to make it easily accessible.

Kahala Mandarin Oriental

Cast-up treasures of sand-tumbled glass is the theme captured in the distinctive multihued chandeliers that hang from the 30-foot vaulted ceilings of the grand hallway, the entrance to the Kahala Mandarin. Long considered a standard-setter for Hawaiian deluxe hotels, the Kahala Mandarin, 5000 Kahala Ave., Honolulu, HI 96816, tel. (808) 739-8888, fax 739-8800, or (800) 367-2525, is not technically in Waikiki, but in Kahala, an exclusive residential area just east of Diamond Head. The hotel, built 30 years ago and refurbished in '96-97 to a tune of $80 million, is proud that most of its key employees have been there from the first days and that they have formed lasting friendships with guests who happily return year after year. Surrounded by the exclusive Waialae Country Club (not even hotel guests are welcome unless they are members), the hotel gives a true sense of peace and seclusion and rightly boasts a "Neighbor Island Experience" only minutes from bustling Waikiki. A grand staircase fashioned from lava rock wears a living lei of green ferns and purple orchids, as it descends to **Hoku,** the hotel's formal restaurant, open for lunch and dinner and specializing in Pacific Rim cuisine with a Hawaiian twist. The hotel's informal **Plumeria Beach Cafe,** open 6:30 a.m.-11 p.m., is famous for its impossible-to-resist pastries. Entertainment at the hotel is offered in the evening at the **Plumeria Bar** at beachside and at the lobby lounge. A beach shack offers all kinds of pool-side snacks and boasts the best hamburgers on Oahu.

The hotel, fronting the sheltered Mauna Lua Bay, features a perfect crescent beach, swimming pool, and beach cabana with all watersports gear available including kayaks, rafts, boogie boards, and snorkel gear. Behind, a waterfall cascading from a free-form stone wall forms a rivulet that leads to a dolphin lagoon (feeding daily at noon, 2 p.m., and 4 p.m.) and a series of saltwater ponds teeming with reef fish. A daily 30-45-minute dolphin experience is offered by lottery and runs $90 per adult and $50 for kids 7-12 years old. Other offerings are its arcade shops, scheduled shuttle service to

Waikiki and major shopping malls, its new fitness and executive business centers, and its Hawaiian cultural program.

Average rooms are extra-large and have in-room safes and small refrigerators. Rates are $295 for a garden view room, $340 for a mountain view room, and up to $440 for an ocean view room; the 29 suites are more yet. The Kahala Hilton isn't for everyone, but there's no doubt that you get all that you pay for.

FOOD

The streets of Waikiki are an international banquet, with over a dozen cuisines spreading their tables for your enjoyment. Because of the culinary competition, you can choose restaurants in the same way that you peruse a smorgasbord, for both quantity and quality. Within a few hundred yards are all-you-can-gorge buffets, luau, dinner shows, fast foods, ice cream, and jacket-and-tie restaurants. The free tourist literature runs coupons, and placards advertise specials for breakfast, lunch, and dinner. Bars and lounges often give free *pu pu* and finger foods that can easily make a light supper. As with everything in Waikiki, its restaurants are a close-quartered combination of the best and the worst, but with only a little effort it's easy to find great food, great atmosphere, and mouthwatering satisfaction.

Note: At many of the moderately priced restaurants listed below and at all of the expensive restaurants *reservations are highly recommended.* It's much easier to make a two-minute phone call than it is to have your evening spoiled, so please call ahead. Also, many of the restaurants along the congested Waikiki strip provide valet parking (usually at no charge), or will offer validated parking at a nearby lot. So check when you call to reserve. Attire at most Hawaiian restaurants is casual, but at the better restaurants it is dressy casual, which means close-toed shoes, trousers, and a collared shirt for men, and a simple but stylish dress for women. At some of the very best restaurants you won't feel out of place with a jacket, but ties are not usually worn.

INEXPENSIVE

Eggs And Things, at 1911 Kalakaua Ave., just where it meets McCully, tel. (808) 949-0820, is a late-night institution open from 11 p.m. until 2 p.m. the following afternoon. A number of discos are just around the corner, so the clientele in the wee hours is a mix of revelers, hotel workers, boat captains, and even a hooker or two. The decor is wooden floors and formica tables, but the waitresses are top-notch and friendly. The food is absolutely excellent and it's hard to spend over $10. Daily specials are offered 1-2 a.m., while the morning special 5-8 a.m. gets you three pancakes and two fresh eggs cooked as you like for just a few dollars. Waffles and pancakes are scrumptious with fresh fruit or homemade coconut syrup. Besides the eggs and omelettes the most popular item is fresh fish, which is usually caught by the owner himself, Mr. Jerry Fukunaga, who goes out almost every day on his own boat. It's prepared Cajun-style, or sautéed in garlic and butter, with two fresh eggs and a choice of pancakes, rice, or home-fried potatoes. Prices vary according to market price. Casual attire is acceptable, and B.Y.O. wine or beer is okay.

Around the corner is **The Dynasty Restaurant,** tel. (808) 947-3771, at 1778 Ala Moana Blvd., in Discovery Bay across from the Ilikai Hotel. It has an enormous menu of various Chinese cuisines that is acceptable but not memorable. The servers are friendly and courteous, and it's open daily 10 a.m.-6 a.m. For a very late night repast after "doing the town," the food definitely hits the spot!

Almost across the street and tucked into a nook close to the Hilton Hawaiian Village is the **Saigon Cafe,** at 1831 Ala Moana Blvd., tel. (808) 955-4009, open daily 6:30 a.m.-10 p.m. The Saigon Cafe is a friendly, meticulously clean, unpretentious, family-run affair that definitely offers "budget gourmet" food. Order tureens of soup for two, spiced with lemongrass, hot garlic sauce, and floating with dollops of seafood, chicken, beef, tofu, or pork for under $7. Roll your own spring rolls, which come with slices of meat, fresh vegetables, mint, dipping sauces, and transparently thin rice paper that you dip in water to soften before rolling away. Noodle dishes are large and hearty, while breakfast brings an assortment of eggs, pancakes, and waffles. It's hard to spend more than $10 on a meal that is not only delicious, but fresh, made to order, and healthy as well. Great choice!

Right across from the Hilton Hawaiian Village, downstairs below the California Pizza kitchen is the tastefully arranged **Singha Thai Cuisine.** Lunch is served Mon.-Fri. 11 a.m.-4 p.m., and dinner is served nightly 4-11 p.m. Thai dancers perform every night 6:45-9 p.m. Vegetarian spring rolls for $5.95 and chicken or shrimp sauté for $7.95 are two of the appetizers on the menu; soups run about $6.95. Entrees include a Thai-style spicy eggplant dish for $7.95 lunch or $11.95 dinner, barbecued chicken for $8.95 lunch or $11.95 dinner, grilled jumbo black tiger prawn curry for $17.95, seafood noodles for $14.95, and vegetarian fried rice for $8.95. Ranging $15-25 are the most expensive entrees like fresh local fish, grilled rack of lamb, and lobster with pineapple and yellow curry. This is an upscale place, but authentic Thai.

Right next to the reasonable Royal Grove Hotel, at 151 Uluniu St., tel. (808) 926-9717, is **Na's Barbecue,** serving Korean food. Open 7 a.m.-10 p.m. daily, it's a tiny place, with plastic chairs and one formica table inside and a small courtyard outside, but the people are friendly, the food well-prepared, and the prices are good. Try a plate of *kalbi,* which is marinated and grilled beef short ribs, for $6.99, charbroiled chicken for $6, *mandu,* or fried stuffed dumplings, for $5.99, or various soups for $8-9. Hawaiianized Korean dishes are also on the menu.

Da Smokehouse, 470 Ena Road, tel. (808) 946-0233, open daily 11:30 a.m.-midnight, is one of those places where the food is excellent, but you wouldn't want to eat there. Why? Because it is primarily a takeout restaurant with only a few booths stuck in the back where *da* smoke and *da* grease from *da* wood-fired smoker is *da* decor. Actually, owner Shirley Jones has recently moved *da* wood-fired smoker out back and added a few new tables. *Da* decor is now compromised. Next will come color-coordinated tableware. God forbid! Your choices are smoked beef, pork, chicken, and ham all served picnic style, with two choices of sides including homemade potato salad, baked beans, rice, cole slaw, or french fries. Price ranges are $5.95 for a quarter barbecued chicken, $8.95 for a half bar-

becued chicken, $9.95 for barbecued ham, $11.95 for barbecued pork or beef ribs. The combo plate of all of the above, which can easily feed two, is only $20.95. Desserts for $2.50 include lilikoi pie, cheesecake, mud pie, and sorbet. No liquor, so B.Y.O. A small delivery charge of $1.35 makes Da Smokehouse a perfect alternative to inflated room service prices at surrounding hotels, or for a home-cooked dinner in your condo. You'll love it!

LNT Spaghetti Hale, tel. (808) 949-3216, at 474-A Ena Road, is a tiny family-run place with only a handful of tables—takeout available. The food is Italian, the cooks Asian; a good mix with wonderful results, yet nothing fancy. Some available items are seafood and vegetables for $9.49, and spaghetti with various sauces from $4.99 to $7.

Ena Restaurant, 432 Ena Road, tel. (808) 951-0818, open daily 10 a.m.-11:30 p.m., is a small Chinese restaurant with little atmosphere, but with good food at good prices. Appetizers and soups include crispy won ton $2.95, chicken salad $5.95, and scallop soup for $2.95. Lunch specials like lemon chicken or beef with vegetables are $4.75, while entrees like mixed seafood and vegetables, fillet of fish in hot red sauce, roast duck, twice-cooked Sichuan-style pork, or Hunan-style tofu are from $5.95 to $8.95. The Ena Restaurant, away from the hustle and bustle, is a good choice for a basic meal with no frills.

Ruffage Natural Foods, at 2442 Kuhio, tel. (808) 922-2042, is one of a very few natural food restaurants in Waikiki. It serves a wide assortment of tofu sandwiches, burritos, natural salads, tofu burgers, fresh island fruits, and smoothies for lunch and dinner. Everything is homemade, and the restaurant tries to avoid, as much as possible, processed foods. Just about everything on the menu is less than $6. Aside from the menu items, food supplements, minerals, vitamins, and things of that nature are also available. It's a small hole-in-the-wall type eatery that's easy to miss. A few wooden tables outside under a portico are the ambience.

Ezogiku is a chain of Japanese restaurants. Open till the wee hours, these no-atmosphere restaurants serve inexpensive hearty bowls of Sapporo *ramen* (renowned as the best), curry rice, and *gyoza.* It has multiple locations in and around Waikiki at 2083 Kuhio Ave., 2420 Koa Ave., 2546 Lemon Road, and 2141 Kalakaua Avenue. Ezogiku is a no-frills kind of place. Small, smoky, counter seating, and totally authentic. It's so authentic that on the dishes they spell *ramen* as *larmen*. You not only eat inexpensively, but you get a very authentic example of what it's like to eat in Japan . . . cheaply. Eat heartily for around $6.

The Jolly Roger, 150 Kaiulani, is an American standard restaurant with a Hawaiian flair. If you're after good old-fashioned tuna salad sandwiches, hot roast beef, a tostada even, or just plain soup and salad, this would be your best bet in Waikiki. The Jolly Roger borders on tasteful with a dark green decor accented with bronze, pleasant booth seating, and a profusion of ferns and hanging plants. Open 6:30 a.m.-1 a.m.; breakfast fare includes waffles, pancakes, omelettes, and meats, but try the orange bread as standard or French toast. A lunch special is hamburger steak, $4.95, with dinners well under $10. Happy hour is 6 a.m.-6 p.m., when exotics are poured for $1.75, draft beer $1.50. Free *pu pu* is available 4-6 p.m.

Man Lee's Chinese Restaurant, 124 Kapahulu, tel. (808) 922-6005, is a basic Chinese restaurant that offers daily lunch and dinner specials, for $4.25 and $6, respectively. The atmosphere is quiet since it's around the corner from most of the action, and the food is acceptable but not memorable. A belly-filler only, it's open 11 a.m.-2 p.m. and then again 5-9 p.m.

Wong and Wong, at 1023 Maunakea, tel. (808) 521-4492, is a simple and basic Chinese restaurant where you can have a good and filling meal at a reasonable price. Many people who live and work in and around Waikiki choose to go here for Chinese food.

Perry's Smorgy, at 2380 Kuhio Ave., tel. (808) 926-0184, and at the Coral Seas Hotel, 250 Lewers St., tel. (808) 922-8814, is the epitome of the budget travelers' "line 'em up, fill 'em up, and head 'em out" kind of restaurant. There is no question that you'll waddle away stuffed, but forget about any kind of memorable dining experience. When you arrive, don't be put off by the long lines. They move! First, you run a gauntlet of salads, breads, and potatoes, in the hopes that you'll fill your plate. Try to restrain yourself. Next comes the meat, fish, and chicken. The guys serving up the roast beef are masters of a whole lot of movement and very little action. The carving knife whips around in the air, but does very little damage to the joint of beef. A paper-thin slice

is finally cut off and put on your plate with aplomb. The carver then looks at you as if you were Oliver Twist asking for more. Added pressure comes from the long line of tourists behind, who act as if they have just escaped from a Nazi labor camp. The breakfast buffet is actually very good, with all the standard eggs, meats, juices, and rolls, and the food in general, considering the price, is more than acceptable. You can't complain. The all-you-can-eat dinner is $8.99.

The Shorebird, open for breakfast, lunch, and dinner (from 5 p.m.), is on the beach behind the Outrigger Reef Hotel at 2169 Kalia Road, tel. (808) 922-2887, giving this budget restaurant the best gourmet location in all of Waikiki. Here you'll find a limited but adequate menu of cook-your-own selections for under $15 (discount tickets save you more). Walk through the lobby to the beach for a remarkable sunset while dining. Included is a good, fresh salad bar of vegetables and fruits. Beverages are included, the setting is wonderful, and the value excellent, but you do pay extra for bread. Karaoke is offered nightly for all those Don Ho "wannabes."

The Islander Coffee House, on Lewers St., tel. (808) 923-3233, in the Reef Towers Hotel, open daily 6 a.m.-midnight, has inexpensive breakfasts of two pancakes, eggs, and bacon for $2.69. It also offers steak and eggs Benedict for $4.29, chef salad ($6), hamburgers under $5, and specials every day for inexpensive prices. No dining experience whatsoever, but down-home prices in the heart of Waikiki.

The **Beach Street Cafe,** in the Outrigger Reef Hotel, 2169 Kalia Road, open daily 7 a.m.-9 p.m., is literally on the beach. Breakfast, 7-11 a.m., starts at $2.99 for a scrambled-egg platter, and just $1.95 for cereal and yogurt. Other munchies like burgers and plate lunches are under $4. Cafeteria-style, the cafe has no decor except for a huge open window that frames the living sculpture of Waikiki.

Kapahulu Avenue

Once Kapahulu Avenue crosses Ala Wai Boulevard, it passes excellent inexpensive to moderately priced restaurants, strung one after the other. Kapahulu was the area in which the displaced Chinese community resettled after the great Chinatown fire at the turn of the century. Kapahulu basically means "poor soil," and unlike most areas of Hawaii could barely support vegetables and plants. Undaunted, the Chinese brought in soil with wagons and wheelbarrows, turning the area productive and verdant.

The first eatery is **Rainbow Drive-In,** at the corner of Kanaaina Avenue. It's strictly local, with a kids' hangout feel, but the plate lunches are hearty and well-done for under $4. Another of the same, **K C Drive-In,** just up the road a few blocks at 1029 Kapahulu, specializes in waffledogs and shakes, and even has carhops. Both are excellent stops to pick up plate lunches on your way out of Waikiki heading for the H-1 freeway.

The first sit-down restaurant on the strip is **Irifune Japanese Restaurant,** at 563 Kapahulu, tel. (808) 737-1141, open for lunch Tues.-Fri. 11:30 a.m.-1:30 p.m., for dinner Tues.-Sun. 5-9 p.m., directly across from **Zippy's,** a fast-food joint. Irifune serves authentic, well-prepared Japanese standards in its small dining room. Most meals begin at $8, with a nightly special for around $10. One item that Irifune has become especially known for is its garlic ahi, which goes for $11. You're also given a card that is punched every time you eat there; after 20 meals, you get one free. Irifune is a great deal for Japanese food, and is much cheaper and easily as good as most other Japanese restaurants on the Waikiki strip. Known more for its food than its decor, it's a winner! Get there early; it's a popular place.

The next restaurant in line is **Ono Hawaiian Foods,** 726 Kapahulu, tel. (808) 737-2275, open Mon.-Sat. 11 a.m.-7:30 p.m., an institution in down-home Hawaiian cooking. This is the kind of place that a taxi driver takes you when you ask for "the real thing." It's clean and basic, with the decor being photos of local performers—all satisfied customers—hung on the wall. If you want to try *lomi lomi* salmon, poi, or *kalua* pig, this is *da kine place, brah!* Prices are cheap; the most expensive, a combination plate, is only $9.50. And, if you have a sweet tooth, try **Leonard's Bakery,** which specializes in *malasadas* and *pao dolce.*

The **Rama Thai Restaurant,** on the corner of Kapahulu and Winam Streets, open daily for dinner 5-10 p.m., tel. (808) 735-2789, is *uptown* with some track lighting and linen tablecloths, but the prices and food are still *downtown* Bangkok. A wonderful choice is Thai crisp noodles for $5.50, Rama chicken wings at $8.75, chicken and ginger soup in a coconut-milk spicy broth at $7.50, or

Thai curried beef, chicken, or shrimp for $7.95. Almost half of the menu is vegetarian; each of the veggie items is $5.95. All items are à la carte, so it's not that cheap; a complete meal costs around $15. The fish-ball soup is out of this world, with plenty for two. The tofu in coconut milk is also a great choice. Try the Wednesday evening buffet for $13.95 to get a sampling of food so you can come back and know what to order.

New to this row is **Sam Choy's Diamondhead Restaurant,** 449 Kapahulu Ave., tel. (808) 732-8645. Open Mon.-Thurs. for dinner 5:30-9:30 p.m. and Fri.-Sun. 5-10 p.m. Reservations are accepted, and there is complimentary validated parking. Island chef Sam Choy prepares food using mostly local produce and meat, and fish from Hawaiian waters, mixing and embellishing the varied ethnic cuisine traditions of the islands. There are set and daily special menus. Soups run $6.95-9.95 while entrees range $18.95-29.95. Various soups and salads are also on the menu. The restaurant also has a full bar and wine selection. The decorations are as soothing as the food is delicious.

Also relatively new is the **Internet Cafe,** 559 Kapahulu Ave., tel. (808) 735-5282, Web site: www.aloha-cafe.com. Food, drinks, and Internet connections are available 24 hours a day, seven days a week. Try a focaccia sandwich for $2.95, a personal pizza à la Wolfgang Puck for $6.75, or cheesecake for $3.95 to go along with your coffee, tea, or Italian soda. Power Macs with printers and full Internet access are also served up for $1.50 for 15 minutes or $6 an hour if you didn't bring your computer with you. Internet or chat classes are held here Monday and Wednesday evenings 6-8 p.m. and Saturday morning 11 a.m.-1 p.m. Your basic cinderblock affair, it's clean and friendly.

The Pyramids, 758-B Kapahulu Ave., tel. (808) 737-2900, is the place to head for Greek and Mediterranean cuisine. Open Mon.-Fri. 11 a.m.-2 p.m. for lunch and daily 5:30-10 p.m. for dinner. Being here, you might imagine yourself to be inside King Tut's tomb with hieroglyphics and painted stone blocks on the walls. Live music and belly dancing accompany the meal every evening at 7:15 p.m. and again at 8:30 p.m. Lunch appetizers include tabouli at $4.95, hummus for $4.25, and spanakopeta for $3.95. Try a chicken salad for $6.95 to accompany a sandwich of ground beef and lamb, parsley, and onions, charbroiled and topped with tahini sauce at $5.85. Select from entrees like shish kabob at $12.25 or moussaka for $10.95. Dinner appetizers and entrees are roughly the same items but run about $1 more.

Fast Foods and Snacks

There are enough formica-tabled, orange-colored, golden-arched, belly-up-to-the-window places selling perfected, injected, and inspected ground cow, chicken, and fish to feed an army . . . and a navy, and marine corps too. Those needing a pre-fab meal can choose from the royal **Burger King** and **Dairy Queen, Jack-in-his-Box, Ronnie McDonald, Pizza Hut-2-3-4, Wendy's,** and dippy **Zippy's Drive-In.** Zippy's is a local chain and has much more than the usual hamburger and fries. Fast food addicts easily find pushers throughout Waikiki!

You can't miss the pink, white, and magenta of **J.R.'s Fast Food Plate Lunch Restaurant,** at the corner of Lewers and Helumoa, where $6 or less will get you a hefty plate of rice, macaroni salad, and a slice of teriyaki beef, roast pork, or mahimahi. The food is fair, the portions hefty, and with a touch of local color is far superior to the nondescript national fast food chain restaurants in the area. Upstairs is a dining veranda where you can perch above the endless crowd.

Fatty's Chinese Fast Food, 2345 Kuhio, tel. (808) 922-9600, is very inexpensive. For about $3.50 you get a giant plate of Chinese fast food. A belly-filler only, but not bad.

MODERATE

Roberto and Laura Magni, a couple from Milano, one day discussed moving to Hawaii. With Italian spontaneity and gusto, they looked at each other and simultaneously said "perche no!" **Caffelatte,** at 339 Saratoga Road (across from the P.O.), tel. (808) 924-1414, open daily 5:30 p.m.-1 a.m., on the second floor of a clapboard "New England-Hawaiian style" house encircled by a veranda, is the result of their impetuousness. The cosmopolitan interior, simple and basic, is white on green with wrought-iron tables set with starched white linens. Hardwood floors, framed paintings both traditional and modern, a horseshoe bar, and subdued globed lighting complete the casual but stylish effect. The Mediterranean-inspired service is slow, but very friendly, and very professional. Each waitperson is intimately familiar with the menu and will be happy to recommend and describe each dish. The menu features homemade pasta ranging in price $11.50-20 with offerings like Spaghetti Paradiso with tomato sauce, or *daglia talle*, a flat thin pasta with Italian sausage for $12.50. Traditional favorites are sure to please with lasagna Leonardo da Vinci at $15, various polenta smothered in everything from a simple calamari to brosola, a rolled and herb-stuffed steak, gnocchi for $14.50, and ricotta and spinach ravioli at $17. Top off dinner with Italian desserts like peaches and strawberries in wine, or oranges and bananas in Russian vodka. The bar serves Italian wine by the bottle or glass, along with bubbling spumante and various champagnes. Italy in Hawaii? . . .*Perche no?*

The **Super Chef Restaurant,** tel. (808) 926-7199, at the Waikiki Hana Hotel, 2424 Koa Ave., is a sleeper. It is definitely one of *the* best moderately inexpensive restaurants in Waikiki, where you can get an *almost* gourmet meal for a terrific price. Being in a small hotel on a side street keeps the crowds away, so the quality of the food and service never suffers. The restaurant decor is not spectacular, but it is classy with small linen-covered tables and drum-seat chairs in a open and cheery room. The staff is very friendly, and the chefs prepare each meal individually behind a tile counter. Breakfast is served 6:30-10:30 a.m., when they feature buttermilk pancakes, bacon and ham, or Portuguese sausage with a large juice for just $2.25; or choose a *wiki wiki* breakfast of pastry, juice, and Kona coffee for only $1.75. No lunch menu, but dinner is served 5-10 p.m. One special is a complete dinner of steak with two lobster tails for only $11.95, or rack of lamb for $8.95. The portions are moderate but definitely not minuscule, and on top of it the cooking is just a half step below excellent. Definitely worth a try.

The **Peacock Dining Room,** at the Queen Kapiolani Hotel, 150 Kapahulu, tel. (808) 922-1941, open 5:30-9 p.m., offers one of the most outstanding buffets in Waikiki for both price and quality. Different nights feature different cuisines. All are special but the Japanese buffet on

Beat the crowds inside the Cafe Princess.

so go "south of the border" for burrito madness ($8.50), complete flautas dinner ($9.95), or selections from the lava-rock grill like marinated chicken breast ($12.95), or baby-back ribs (full slab, $15.95). You can also pick Mexican favorites like tacos, enchiladas, and fajitas, all served with rice, beans, and Mexican salad. Nothing on the Mexican side is more than $12.95, with most around $9. Eat, *hombre!*

Eating at **Caffe Guccinni,** at 2139 Kuhio Ave., tel. (808) 922-5287, open daily 5-10:30 p.m., is like following a Venetian gondolier to his favorite restaurant. It's not fancy but the food is good and plentiful, and the pasta is made fresh daily. The staff is usually a cook and a waiter who seats you at one of a dozen tables, most outdoors. It's easy to miss because it's stuck back off the street, which means a nice, quiet area. For a light meal choose garlic bread and Caesar salad, or for a full meal try one of the house specialties (with soup or salad), like eggplant parmigiana, pasta contesto, spaghetti and meatballs, or manicotti; most are under $14. The cappuccino and espresso are freshly brewed and extraordinarily good. For dessert have *cannoli,* a flaky pastry stuffed with ricotta and smothered with slivers of almond and chocolate—excellent! Other desserts include carrot cake, chocolate torte, New York cheesecake, amaretto cheesecake, and crème brûlée; all are $3.50. The owner, Jocelyn Batista, started with a pastry shop and was rightfully proud of her desserts, so give one a try.

Hernando's Hideaway, at 2139 Kuhio, tel. (808) 922-7758, open daily 10:30 a.m.-2 a.m., sits well off the street and is a very casual Mexican restaurant where the emphasis is on plenty of good food and having a good time. Tables are mostly outside under an awning, and every day a special drink is featured. Some of the best offerings are chicken enchilada dinner for $6.75, or an overstuffed calzone for $5.75. Every night, 6-7 p.m. is "power hour," when all well drinks are $1, followed by "pizza hour" 7-8 p.m., when pizza is only $1 per slice. All this activity attracts a younger crowd of both resort workers and vacationers. You can eat until you're as stuffed as a burrito for under $10.

La Provence, 2139 Kuhio, tel. (808) 924-6696, is open Tues.-Sun. 5ish-10:30 p.m., with a full fancy French menu at reasonable prices. Start

Wednesday and Thursday and the seafood buffet on Friday are extraordinary. All range from $12.95 to $15.95. The room itself is tasteful with white tablecloths and full service. Every time you return to the buffet just leave your empty plate and it will be taken away for you. Help yourself from an amazing array of entrees that are expertly prepared. The salad bar is extremely varied, and the desserts will make you wish that you saved room. Excellent value.

Carlos Castaneda wouldn't even notice as he walked past two psychedelic green cactuses into **Pepper's,** at 150 Kaiulani Ave., tel. (808) 926-4374, open daily for lunch 11:30 a.m.-4 p.m., dinner 4 p.m.-1:30 a.m. The interior is Yuppie-Mex with a wraparound rectangular bar with a fat wooden rail, and low ceilings done in a Mexican-style stucco. The specialties of the house are prepared in a wood-fired oven for that hearty outdoor flavor in the heart of "Rancho Waikiki." Light meals are chicken taco salad for $9.95, the Pepper club ($6.95), and tuna melt ($5.95), with a good selection of salads. But you can get these anywhere with an hors d'oeuvre like escargot for $6 or tabouli à la menthe fraiche for $5.50. Move on to a ratatouille at $9.50, giant prawns sautéed with thyme and served with saffron and rice for $15, or a traditional beef stew smoldered in orange zest and herbed red wine sauce served with new potatoes at $12.50. A few more expensive specialty dishes must be ordered 24 hours in advance. The motif is blue on blue, and if you're in a blue mood, eating here will surely raise your spirits.

Pieces of Eight is in the Coral Seas Hotel, tel. (808) 923-6646, open daily 5-11 p.m., happy hour 4-6 p.m., piano bar nightly. This steak and seafood house has managed to create a comfortable and relaxed atmosphere where it serves up excellent steaks and very good fish dishes at a moderate price. The decor is dark wood and burnished brass in a romantically lit main room. A piano stylist tickles the ivories in the background. It's the perfect combination of restaurant that will match itself to your mood. Come for that special night out or just a casual evening meal. "Early birders" 5-7 p.m. can pick selections like garlic chicken or fish 'n' chips with salad bar for $6.95. Entrees are 10-ounce top sirloin ($13.95), ground beef sirloin ($8.95), filet mignon ($15.95), and mahimahi amandine ($11.95). All dinners include choice of potato, rice, or bread, and salad bar is $3.50 extra. A great choice for good food and a pleasant setting at affordable prices. The **Cellar Bar** open from noon to the wee hours serves exotic drinks and light meals like a simple pizza, hamburger, or fish bake combination. If you are out on the town, it is a good choice to munch while enjoying a video game or a game of pool.

The House of Hong, 260 Lewers St., tel. (808) 923-0202, open daily 11 a.m.-10:30 p.m., Sunday from 4 p.m., is a standard, no surprises Chinese restaurant with a flair. The decor borders on tasteful with some tables outfitted in starchy white tablecloths accented by inlaid wall murals and painted ceilings of China scenes. The Cantonese lunch special is weekdays 11 a.m.-3 p.m. for $5.95, with "early bird specials" 4-6 p.m.— dishes like egg flower soup, chicken chow mein, sweet and sour pork, crispy wonton, fried rice, fortune cookie, and Chinese tea for $9.95. Not great, but no complaints either.

The **Oceanarium** at the Pacific Beach Hotel, 2490 Kalakaua Ave., tel. (808) 922-1233, offers a full breakfast, lunch, and dinner menu. For lunch,

try the tropical fruit plate at $7.50, or an entree such as Cajun five-spice chicken for $7.50. Dinner appetizers like Cajun calimari begin at $4.95, while entrees like New York peppercorn steak are $19.95, and specials like live Maine lobster are $21.95. Also featured are fresh island catches at market prices. The Oceanarium is done in elegant muted colors as if you were under water.

Trattoria, in the Edgewater Hotel, 2168 Kalia Road, tel. (808) 923-8415, serves savory dishes from northern Italy. Particularly good are the veal plates with an appropriate bottle of Italian wine. The interior is upscale with bent-wood chairs and white linen tablecloths set with crystal. Antipasti selections include escargot ($8.25) and spinach salad ($7.75). Combine these with pasta dishes like spaghetti puttanesca, a savory dish of fillet of anchovy and melted butter cooked in a hot sauce with tomatoes and black olives ($10.75). Complete dinners, ranging in price $17.95-24.95, include choice of minestrone soup or dinner salad, and lasagna, eggplant or tortellini. Trattoria is a good choice for a moderate restaurant with a pleasant atmosphere and better-than-average cooking. Dinner only.

Benihana, at the Hilton Rainbow Bazaar, 2005 Kalia Road, open daily for lunch 11:30 a.m.-2 p.m., and for dinner 5:30-10:30 p.m., tel. (808) 955-5955, is a medium-priced Japanese restaurant for those who are jittery about the food and prices. Meals are designed to fit *gaijin* taste, and cooks flash their knives and spatulas at your table—as much a floor show as a dining experience. Good, basic Japanese food, *teppan*-style.

Mandarin Palace, at the Miramar Hotel, 2345 Kuhio Ave., tel. (808) 926-1110, is open for lunch and dinner. Highly rated for its Asian cuisine in a full-blown Chinese atmosphere.

White and pink canvas umbrellas shade the outdoor tables of the **Cafe Princess Garden,** just next to its sister restaurant the **Cafe Princess** (indoor restaurant with full table service), both set in a carved garden grotto surrounded by the Royal Hawaiian and Sheraton hotels. Here, in the heart of Waikiki, but buffered from the crowds, you can enjoy a reasonably priced breakfast special of two scrambled eggs, link sausage, and a croissant for $3.50, or lunch specials, served 11:30 a.m.-5 p.m., like soup and a sandwich for $6.50 or a plate lunch for $5.75. Dinner specials served 5-10 p.m. in the

Princess Garden feature steak and lobster for $18.95, while those opting for the inside Cafe Princess can choose jumbo prawns or charbroiled steak for $16.95, or roast prime rib for $11.95. The outdoor Cafe Princess Garden is an excellent people-watching perch from which to enjoy happy hour drinks, 11:30 a.m.-6 p.m., and 10 p.m. until closing, when mai tais are $2.25, pitchers of Bud are $5.50, and frothy chi-chis are only $3.

Duke's Canoe Club, tel. (808) 922-2268, at the Outrigger Waikiki Hotel, has an unbeatable location fronting Waikiki beach. Basically a steak and seafood restaurant, it's a happening place, with plenty of Duke Kahanamoku and surfing memorabilia on the wall, and cocktails and music in the evening.

CASUAL GOURMET

The following restaurant is unique in that it serves inspired gourmet food in a lovely setting for very reasonable prices. Though technically not in Waikiki, but located in Hawaii Kai about 20 minutes away, it is definitely worth the trip.

The word "genius" is oftentimes overused and misapplied, causing it to loose its oomph, but when it comes to creativity with food, Roy Yamaguchi is a genius, par excellence! **Roy's Restaurant,** 6600 Kalanianaole Hwy. and Keahole Dr., tel. (808) 396-7697, in Hawaii Kai Corporate Plaza, open Sun.-Thurs. 5:30-9:30 p.m., until 10:30 p.m. Fri.-Sat., from 5 p.m. Saturday and Sunday, presents Euro-Asian cuisine (Pacific Rim) at its very best. The young master chef, through experimentation and an unfailing sense of taste, has created dishes using the diverse and distinctive flavors of French, Italian, Chinese, Japanese, Thai, and Hawaiian cuisine and blended them into a heady array of culinary delights that destroy the adage that "east is east and west is west." The twain have definitely met, and with a resounding success. Roy's dining room is "elegant casual" much like the food, featuring an open kitchen, and although pleasant enough with a superb view, it is not designed for a lengthy romantic evening. Roy's dining philosophy seems to be the serving of truly superb dishes posthaste with the focus on the "food as the dining experience," not the surroundings. The presentation of every dish, under the direc-

tion of executive chef Gordon Hopkins, who has been with Roy's since its inception, is flawless, and as pleasing to the eye as it is titillating to the palate. The mastery is in "the blend," which can take you to heights of satiation rarely experienced before. Start with the charred ahi and opakapaka pot stickers, hibachi-style salmon with Maui onions, grilled shrimp risotto with fresh mushrooms, herbs, and lobster essence, or even an individual *imu*-oven pizza smothered with grilled chicken, feta cheese, olives, and pesto, most for under $8. Salads feature island-grown greens and vegetables and include such wonderful concoctions as crispy calamari with baby romaine at $7.95, and Chinese chicken with candied pecans and soy ginger dressing at $7.95. Entrees are wonders like grilled loin of lamb with rosemary, crabmeat, and risotto sauce at $17.95, Thai stuffed chicken for $14.95, or a nightly special such as lemongrass encrusted mahimahi with crispy duck cakes in *lilikoi* mustard sauce. Part of the menu changes every night, but there is always fish, which might be garlic-seared red tombo ahi with crispy bacon parmesan aioli for $22.95. Desserts by pastry chef Rick Chang are also superb, and include individually prepared (order at beginning of dinner) fresh fruit cobbler in sauce anglaise, or a richer than rich chocolate souffle. Although Roy's has only been open since 1988, it is *the* trendsetter in new and inspired cuisine, receiving the praise and adulation of other fine chefs throughout the islands who try to mimic and match Roy's flair and style.

CLASSY DINING

Halekulani Dining

Softly the soprano sea sings, while the baritone breeze whispers in melodious melancholy, as you float ephemerally above the waves at **La Mer,** the open-air signature dinner restaurant at the Halekulani Hotel. Splendid in its appointment, the walls, filigreed panels of teak covered in Chinese silkscreen, are predominantly browns and whites, the traditional colors of Hawaiian tapa. Seating is in high-backed upholstered chairs with armrests, and every table is either illuminated by flickering candles or by recessed ceiling lamps that seem to drip the soft gold light of the melting sun upon the table. The superb

Continental French menu, with its numerous selections of seafood, is bolstered by a huge wine list and a platter of select cheeses to end the meal. La Mer sets the standard, and if you were to choose one restaurant for a night of culinary bliss, this is a perfect choice.

The House Without a Key, open for breakfast 7-10 a.m. buffet, lunch 11 a.m.-5 p.m., and dinner 5-9 p.m., is a casual outdoor-indoor restaurant in a magnificent oceanside setting. Named after the first novel written about Charlie Chan, Honolulu's famous fictional detective, the restaurant offers unsurpassed views in every direction, and is perhaps the best spot on the island to enjoy a sunset cocktail. Although casual, the seating is very comfortable with padded chairs at simple wood-trimmed tables. The breakfast buffet, including fresh omelettes, is $18.50. Lunch offers main course salads like Oriental chicken salad, grilled beef fajita salad, or a pasta dish like seafood penne or spaghetti bolognese all for under $15. Sandwiches range from a classic triple-decker club sandwich at $12, to grilled mahimahi on nori bread for $15, while entrees are New York steak at $21 or grilled salmon at $19. Dinner starts with cocktail *pu pu*, including chilled jumbo shrimp at $13.50 or scallops wrapped in bacon for $10.50, with the sandwiches, salads and entrees about the same as the lunch menu. Desserts, designed to soothe your palate as the setting sun soothes your soul, include chocolate macadamia-nut creme pie, Toblerone chocolate mousse, or *lilikoi* cheesecake all priced at $6. Entertainment, nightly 5-8 p.m., performed by **The Islanders** or the **Hiram Olsen Trio,** is great for dancing under the stars. In addition, Mon.-Sat. evenings be entranced by the graceful beauty of the hula dances done by former Miss Hawaii, Konoe Miller; on Sunday, Debbie Nakanelua, another former Miss Hawaii, does the honor of performing the hula. Remember, the door is never locked at House Without a Key.

White, purple, and yellow orchids tumble from trellises, cascade from clay planters, and always grace your table at **Orchids Dining Room,** also at the Halekulani, open daily 7:30-11 a.m. breakfast, 11:30 a.m.-2 p.m. lunch, and 6-10 p.m. dinner, and is another seaside, indoor-outdoor restaurant. Specializing in contemporary American cuisine, Orchids is also famous for its fabulous Sunday brunch at $29.50 adults, $18.50 children.

Chefs Keith Hirata and Shawn Smith make freshness a priority, buying ingredients as locally as possible . . . vegetables, beef, prawns, and especially fish. Beautifully appointed with teak wood and Hawaiian eucalyptus flooring, the setting is casual-elegant with white starched linen tablecloths, captain-style chairs with blue and white pillows, and of course heavy silver and crystal. Arranged with a tri-level central dining area that spreads out to a covered veranda, all tables enjoy a panoramic view of the sea with Diamond Head in the distance. Start the day with a continental breakfast including fresh fruit juice, pastry basket, and beverage at $12.50, or an American breakfast with all of the above plus eggs and a breakfast meat at $16.50, or try Japanese style with grilled fish, steamed rice, pickles, miso soup, seaweed, and green tea, at $19.50. There are also whole wheat pancakes with macadamia nuts and coconut syrup at $9, or just a basket of pastries and coffee for $6.75. The daily brunch is served 8:30-10 a.m., at $20.75. Start your engine with a mimosa, Bloody Mary, screwdriver, or tropical fruit, along with eggs Benedict, frittata, smoked salmon and cream cheese, and various pastries. Lunch begins with an assortment of delicious appetizers like seared *ahi* with mustard shoyu for $15, or a simple salad of mixed greens with various dressings for $6. Soups, all priced at $5, include Portuguese bean and chilled tropical fruit soup. Special dishes are an assortment of pasta under $15, curry including lamb, Thai chicken for around $18, and broiled Hawaiian fish with herbs at $18. A full-course table d'hôte is $25, and all desserts are $6.50. Dinner entrees are luscious seafood platters of charbroiled *a'u* with kula tomato and herbed pasta at $27, pepper crusted opakapaka at $29.50 or rack of lamb Provençale at $33. A taster's menu at $54 is a full five-course meal.

Hilton Hawaiian Village Dining

The Hilton Hawaiian Village, at 2005 Kalia Road, is one of the finest destination resorts in Hawaii. Its two signature restaurants, both *Travel Holiday* award winners, complement the resort perfectly. **Bali by the Sea,** tel. (808) 941-2254, open daily for dinner 6-10 p.m., may sound like Indonesian cuisine, but it's more continental than anything else. The setting couldn't be more brilliant. Sit by the open windows so that the sea breezes fan you as you overlook the gorgeous Hilton beach with Diamond Head off to your left. The room is outfitted in a tropical green paisley carpet, high-backed, armrest-type chairs, white tablecloths, and classical place settings with silver service. Upon ordering, you are presented with a complimentary platter of hors d'oeuvres. Choose appetizers like Hawaiian pot stickers with lemongrass and Thai peanut sauce, or fresh lobster tartare flavored with coriander and cucumber. Soups include the Kona crab chowder flavored with sweet mixed peppers and laced with brandy, or Maui onion soup glazed with Gruyère cheese. Entrees are a magnificent selection of fish from Hawaiian waters baked, sautéed, or broiled and then covered in a variety of sauces. Meat entrees are breast of chicken and lobster, or medallions of veal with honey. The meal ends with a fine presentation of desserts, or a complimentary "steaming chocolate Diamond Head." Bali by the Sea is a superb choice for an elegant evening of fine dining.

The **Golden Dragon,** tel. (808) 946-5336, open nightly for dinner 6-10 p.m., would tempt any knight errant to drop his sword and pick up chopsticks. This too is a fine restaurant where the walls are decorated with portraits of emperors, and the plates carry the Golden Dragon motif. The interior color scheme is a striking vermilion and black, with the chairs and tables shining with a lacquerware type of patina. The floor is dark koa. Outside, the terrace has pagoda-style canopies under which you may dine. Obviously the Golden Dragon isn't your average chop suey house, but the menu has all of the standard Chinese fare from lemon chicken to . . . well, chop suey, but it doesn't end there. The food is expertly prepared, and two fine choices are the exotic Imperial Beggar's Chicken, feeding two for $39.50, which is a chicken wrapped in lotus leaves, encased in clay, and baked (requires 24 hours notice to prepare); and Chef Chang's Signature Selection (for two), which includes seafood and vegetable egg rolls, crispy wontons, island pork charsu, hot and sour soup, stir-fry chicken, wok-seared scallops, beef with vegetables, lobster and shrimp, and pepper and duck fried rice, with litchi ice cream for $31 per person. For a first-class restaurant with impeccable food and service, the prices at the Golden Dragon are very, very reasonable.

Sheraton Waikiki Dining

The signature restaurant at the Sheraton Waiki-

ki is the **Hanohano Room,** located atop the building on its 30th floor. From here, the vista before you sweeps from Pearl Harbor to Diamond Head, and behind you, the city of Honolulu runs up into the hills. While noteworthy during the day, the view at night is stunning with the twinkle of city lights below. Aside from the usual breakfast fare, the Hanohano room serves a breakfast buffet that seems to have endless options. Along with breakfast Saturday morning, the room hosts the ever-popular Parry and Price live radio show on KSSK. The 10 a.m.-1 p.m. Sunday champagne brunch buffet is an outstanding feed, but pricey. In the evening, the restaurant features Pacific Island cuisine. Start with an hors d'oeuvre like Scottish smoked salmon for $9.95 or fresh island ahi sashimi with shredded radish and wasabi for $12.95. Move on to essence of shiitake mushroom soup at $7.95 and chilled asparagus and prawns salad for $7.95. Make your selection of entrees from such items as chicken stuffed with lobster meat to filet mignon and lobster tail, ranging $26.95-48.95. If all the choices are too difficult, try one of the four select menu combinations, $53-75. A wonderful meal may be even more romantic here when a local trio called Stardust plays contemporary jazz and top 40 tunes; the dance floor is always open.

On the first floor, near the hotel entrance, is the **Ciao!** Italian restaurant. More moderate in price, Ciao! offers a pasta buffet every night along with its menu selections. Items from the menu include appetizers for under $9, pizza for $11.50-16, pasta marinara for $11.50, and open face lasagna with shrimp and scallops for $17.95. Filet mignon, rib-eye, and New York steaks come from the broiler for $21-37.50, a grilled and marinated boneless chicken breast with mixed greens and roasted potatoes is $15.50, and the live Maine lobster, steamed or broiled, runs $32.50. Of course, there is a good selection of Italian and California wines to accompany any meal.

The **Ocean Terrace Restaurant** is more casual. Although you can order off the menu for such items as bacon and cheese over hash browns with coffee or tea at $8.95 for breakfast, mahimahi burger with tartar sauce and curly fries at $10.95 for lunch, or stir-fry tender beef and vegetables with firecracker fried rice at $15.75 for supper, the Ocean Terrace is known for its buffets. The ordinary breakfast buffet is

$18.85, while the continental breakfast buffet runs $13.85. Buffet lunch goes for $19.25 and the dinner buffet is $28.75. Dinner buffets vary nightly among international cuisines. Enjoy any meal here with the Great Moana herself as the backdrop, while every night brings different local entertainers to the restaurant stage.

If you don't want to leave your place on the beach or loose your spot at the shell-shaped pool, and still require a midafternoon snack, try the **Kau Kau Express.** Here you can order a Japanese bento box lunch, fresh fruit, health-conscious sandwich, or pizza, and a full range of drinks. The **Sand Bar** serves up poolside drinks.

Hawaii Prince Hotel Dining

The Hawaii Prince Hotel at 100 Holomoana St., tel. (808) 956-1111, features three distinctive restaurants. **Takanawa,** with posts of *sugi* pine, floor-to-ceiling windows, and a koi pond in the center of a Japanese garden, is the hotel's sushi bar. In addition, a buffet of Japanese food is served here for $16.50 every evening.

The Prince Court, the main dining room, offers breakfast, lunch, and dinner. Breakfast, served 5:30-10:30 a.m., starts with juices and fruits ($4-7), seasonal berries and cream ($6), continental breakfast ($10.50), and a buffet breakfast ($15). On Sunday, there's an additional full American breakfast for $30. Lunches start with appetizers like grilled fresh mozzarella ($6.50), barbecued Pacific oysters and fried onions ($9.50), and Cobb salad with Dungeness crab ($9.50). Sandwiches like sliced avocado, tomato, sprouts, and cucumber in pocket bread start at $6.50, while pasta selections are $9-13.50. Dinner offers entrees like the fresh fish of the day, cooked five possible ways including being baked in a cornbread crust or sautéed with angel hair pasta for a reasonable $17.50, or a mixed grill of local slipper lobster, *kahuku* shrimp, and sea scallops for $24.

Hakone, the hotel's fine Japanese restaurant, is appointed with shoji screens and wooden tables with high-backed chairs in front of a glass wall that frames the still life of the Ala Wai Yacht Harbor. Dishes are typical, with set menus *(teishoku)* of chicken teriyaki ($23), katsura steak ($29.50), and the Kaiseki Hakone, a full seven course meal for $60. A Japanese lunch buffet is also served.

Around Waikiki

One of the most laudable achievements in the restaurant business is to create an excellent reputation and then to keep it. **Nick's Fishmarket** at the Waikiki Gateway Hotel, 2070 Kalakaua, tel. (808) 955-6333, open nightly for dinner 6-11:30 p.m., has done just that . . . and keeps doing it. Many gourmets consider Nick's *the* best dining in Waikiki, and it's great fun to find out if they know what they're talking about. Owner Randy Schoch pays personal attention to every detail at Nick's, while executive chef Mariano Lalica creates the culinary magic. Lalica placed first in the "Seafood Olympics" recently held in Hawaii, and is a marvel at preparing fresh fish, which he accents with Thai peanut sauce and balsamic vinegar, rock shrimp sauce with stone ground mustard and macadamia nuts, or roasted garlic and sun-dried tomato vinaigrette. Adventurous and highly skilled, Chef Lalica, like the master of an old sailing ship, will take you to culinary ports of call rarely, if ever, visited. Highly professional waiters, knowledgeable about every dish, are friendly and efficient, and always at hand to suggest just the right wine from the extensive list to perfectly complement your choice of dish. Start with fresh-baked clams casino ($9.95), smoked salmon ($10.50), or, if you're in the mood, how about beluga caviar (don't ask). For soup order the Fish Market Chowder, while the Caesar salad prepared at your table has long won honors as the best available west of California! Although Nick's is primarily renowned for its fish, don't overlook the veal, steaks, and chicken with sides of pasta. An excellent choice is one of Nick's complete dinners featuring entree, soup or salad, vegetables, and hot drink. Other great choices are veal picatta, succulent rack of lamb with a Hawaiian mango chutney, and perfectly prepared abalone imported from the cold waters of the California coast. The sinless along with those expecting salvation "tomorrow" will enjoy the dessert menu, which features Nick's vanbanna pie, a tempting concoction of banana mousse and almond vanilla ice cream dripping with a caramel sauce, New York inspired cheesecake, or a lighter tropical sorbet. A Cafe Menu has recently been added from which you can order until the wee hours while listening to live entertainment in the lounge area. Lobster fried rice, crispy calamari, pasta à la Hawaii, or plump tacos can all be enjoyed, and are all very reasonably priced under $10. Dancing to live music is featured nightly along with special events such as winetasting evenings scheduled throughout the year. The bar prepares a host of exotic island drinks along with a fine cup of cappuccino, and is known for its extensive microbrewery beer selections. If you had only one evening in Waikiki and you wanted to make it memorable, you'd have a hard time doing better than Nick's Fishmarket.

Sergio's, at the Ilima Hotel, 445 Nohonani, open daily for dinner 5:30-11:30 p.m., tel. (808) 926-3388, is one of the finest Italian restaurants in Honolulu. The interior is romantic, subtle, and simple with a combination of booths and tables. Sergio prepares foods from all regions of Italy, blending and matching hearty peasant soups, fresh salads, and antipasti garnished with aromatic cheeses and spicy prepared meats, pasta dishes, entrees, and desserts. The more than a dozen choices of pasta come with sauces of savory meat, or delicate vegetables, and seafood. Entrees of chicken, beef, and fresh fish make your taste buds rise and shout "Bravo! Sergio! Bravo!"

Michel's, at the Colony Surf Hotel, 2895 Kalakaua Ave., tel. (808) 923-6552, open daily for dinner only, is literally on the beach, so your appetite is piqued not only by sumptuous morsels, but by magnificent views of the Waikiki skyline boldly facing the Pacific. The interior is "neo-French elegant," with the dining rooms appointed in soft pastels, velour chairs with armrests, white tablecloths, crystal chandeliers, heavy silver service, and tasteful paintings. The bar is serpentine and of polished koa. Food is French Continental and dinner is *magnifique* with such entrees as fresh Maine lobster on ice, delicate baby coho salmon garnished with shrimp served in its own sauce, or tournedos rossini, a center cut of tenderloin with goose liver and truffles. The dining experience at Michel's is completely satisfying with outstanding food and outstanding service, all in an outstanding setting.

Also located at the Colony Surf is **David Paul's Diamond Head Grill.** Following the success of his award-winning restaurant in Lahaina, Maui, Chef David Paul Johnson hopes to create as big a splash here in the big city. He is one of a new breed of young chefs serving innovative local foods created with Hawaiian, Asian, American and/or European preparation techniques. Kalua duck and tequila shrimp with firecracker rice are only two of the entrees which are certain to please.

Matteo's, in the Marine Surf Hotel, 364 Seaside, tel. (808) 922-5551, open 6 p.m.-2 a.m., is a wonderfully romantic Italian restaurant that sets the mood even outside by welcoming you with a red canopy and brass rail that leads to a carved door of koa and crystal. Inside is dark and stylish, with high-backed booths, white tablecloths, and marble-top tables. On each is a rose, Matteo's signature. Dinners begin with hot antipasti priced $7-14, such as stuffed mushrooms à la Matteo, seafood combo or cold antipasto for two. Light fare of *ensalada e zuppa* (salad and soup), hearts of romaine lettuce, or clam soup matched with garlic bread or pizza bread make an inexpensive but tasty meal. Entree suggestions are chicken *rollatini,* veal *rollatini* (rolled veal stuffed with bell peppers, mushrooms, onions, spinach, and mozzarella), or *bragiola* (rolled beef with mozzarella cheese, garlic, fresh basil, and baked with marinara sauce), all under $20. Complete dinners come with Matteo's special salad, pasta, vegetables, and coffee or tea and include mahimahi Veronica (sautéed fish in lemon sauce and seedless grapes) or veal parmigiana and are priced under $28. Pastas are very reasonable and besides the usual linguine dishes include gnocchi and manicotti à la Matteo. An extensive wine list complements the food. If you are out for a special evening of fine dining and romance, Matteo's will set the mood, and the rest is up to you.

The **Surf Room** is in the Royal Hawaiian Hotel, 2259 Kalakaua Ave., tel. (808) 931-7194. The menu is solid but uninspired. However, the setting couldn't be lovelier, and the buffet is staggeringly huge.

Hy's Steak House, 2440 Kuhio Ave., tel. (808) 922-5555, is one of those rare restaurants that is not only absolutely beautiful, but serves great food as well. Decorated like a Victorian sitting room, its menu offers things other than steaks and chops, but these are the specialties and worth the stiff-upper-lipped price.

Restaurant Suntory, Royal Hawaiian Shopping Center, tel. (808) 922-5511, is a very handsome restaurant with different rooms specializing in particular styles like *shabu shabu, teppanyaki,* and sushi. The prices used to be worse, but they're still expensive. However, the food preparation and presentation are excellent, and the staff is very attentive. Open for lunch and dinner.

Furusato Sushi, right next to the Hyatt Regency at 2424 Kalakaua Ave., tel. (808) 922-4991, and **Furusato Tokyo Steak,** downstairs, are both expensive but top-notch Japanese restaurants. The food and service are authentic, but they are geared toward the Japanese tourist who expects, and almost demands, to pay high prices. In the steakhouse, expect steak since very little else is on the menu. Upstairs is sushi.

Free valet parking is great for this congested part of Waikiki.

Three other exceptional restaurants worth visiting for authentic Japanese food are **Miyako** at the New Otani Beach Hotel, tel. (808) 921-7077; **Kacho** at the Waikiki Parc Hotel, tel. (808) 924-3535; and the **Kyo-ya** at 2057 Kalakaua Ave., tel. (808) 947-3911.

For a variety of Mediterranean cuisine with a Hawaiian twist visit **Cascada** restaurant at the Royal Garden Hotel, tel. (808) 945-0270. Open for breakfast, lunch, and dinner.

ENTERTAINMENT

Waikiki swings, beats, bumps, grinds, sways, laughs, and gets down. If Waikiki has to bear being called a carnival town, it might as well strut its stuff. Dancing (disco and ballroom), happy hours, cocktail shows, cruises, lounge acts, Polynesian extravaganzas, and the street scene provide an endless choice of entertainment. Small-name Hawaiian trios, soloists, pianists, and sultry singers featured in innumerable bars and restaurants woo you in and keep you coming back. Big-name island entertainers and visiting international stars play the big rooms. Free entertainment includes hula shows, ukulele music, street musicians, jugglers, artists, and streetwalkers. For a good time, nowhere in Hawaii matches Waikiki. Also see "Entertainment" in the Honolulu chapter for other listings.

Bars and Lounge Acts

Brother Noland is a local talent who appears here and there around town. He's the cutting edge for ethnic Hawaiian groups playing hot reggae, originals, and plenty of Stevie Wonder, solo or with a group, and shouldn't be missed.

Theresa Bright is an excellent Hawaiian musician. Her sound is a melodious mixture of traditional and contemporary. An accomplished musician with a beautiful voice, she often appears at various venues around town.

In the Park Shore Hotel, 2586 Kalakaua Ave., **The Bar** is a quiet, relaxing place to have a drink. Sometimes, a guest pianist plays.

The **Irish Rose Saloon,** at 227 Lewers, presents live entertainment nightly with dancing till 4 a.m. and features sporting events on its big-

screen TV. Happy hour is 3-8 p.m. It's right across the street from the Outrigger Coral Seas Hotel, just at the entrance of the Al Herrington Show.

A great little bar, the **Brass Rail,** serves up cold draft beer and deli sandwiches (until 4 p.m.). It's into sports and especially Monday Night Football, which usually begins in Hawaii at 7:30 p.m. Located on the ground floor of the Outrigger Waikiki Hotel, at 2335 Kalakaua.

The **Rose and Crown Pub** in King's Village has a pianist playing sing-along favorites in what is a very close rendition of an English-style pub. It has daily specials; for example, on Saturday if you wear your Rose and Crown hat you have happy hour prices all night long. So drink hearty, and hold on to your hat! The crowd is intent on swilling beer and partying. Noisy, raucous, and fun.

Jolly Roger Restaurant, at 150 Kaiulani, presents a changing mixture of live music nightly in its lounge, open until 2 a.m. A good spot for listening to music and enjoying conversation around the bar.

In the International Market Place, **Coconut Willy's** offers free entertainment, with no minimum or cover.

Baron's Studio, Waikiki Plaza Hotel, tel. (808) 946-0277, is open nightly. Quiet drinks, fine background tunes.

The **Paradise Lounge** at the Hilton Hawaiian Village, tel. (808) 949-4321, has entertainment Wednesday, Friday, and Saturday evenings; no cover.

A tradition at the **Lobby Bar** at the Hawaiian Regent is its no-cover entertainment by well-respected Waikiki's musicians.

Visit the **Hanohano** room on the 30th floor of the Sheraton Waikiki Hotel for jazz and contemporary music of Stardust.

The five-diamond Halekulani hotel offers superb nightly entertainment. There is no lovelier location for a sunset cocktail than **House Without a Key,** where The Islanders or The Hiram Olsen Trio perform contemporary tunes nightly 5-8:30 p.m. Gracing the stage are two former Miss Hawaiis, Konoe Miller and Debbie Nakanelua, who perform their inspired hula (Debbie on Sunday, Kanoe the rest of the week). Sunday brunch at the hotel's **Orchids Dining Room** is made even more genteel with the musical strains of harpist Susanne Hussong, accompanied by flutist Susan Gillespie, who perform the hit songs of Broadway musicals. Most nights 9 p.m.-12:30 a.m, from the wood-paneled **Lewers Lounge** flows the liquid sweetness of jazz vocalist Loretta Ables, accompanied by Jim Howard on keyboard and Bruce Hamada on bass.

Enjoy a free steel guitar and hula show at the **Banyan Court** at the Sheraton Moana Surfrider Hotel.

Discos, Dancing, and Nightclubs

Ballroom dancers will enjoy **Tea Dancing at the Royal** in the Monarch Room of the Royal Hawaiian Hotel, featuring the 14-piece Del Courtney Orchestra, Monday 5:30-8:30 p.m.

Nick's Fishmarket at the Gateway Hotel, 2070 Kalakaua Ave., swings with contemporary dance music until 1:30 a.m. A mixed but mostly mature crowd who have stayed on to dance after a magnificent meal, which Nick's is known for. Music is provided by No Excuse, headliners who make Nick's their home when not on tour.

The **Paradise Lounge** in the Rainbow Tower of the Hilton Hawaiian Village is a jazz nightclub, perfect for a night of relaxing entertainment. It has a pianist nightly and a polished wooden dance floor. Weekends bring a variety of jazz ensembles for your listening and dancing pleasure. Perfect for a romantic evening.

The Wave, 1877 Kalakaua Ave., tel. (808) 941-0424, is a rock 'n' roll and new wave hotspot with live music nightly. Every Tuesday, hear Willie Kay, a popular Hawaiian performer, jam with other hot island musicians. They let it rip. The Wave has become an institution of late-night fun and dancing. The crowd is mixed, and you can either choose to dance, perch upstairs in the balcony behind glass where you can check out the dancers below, or have a few drinks and some conversation. The Wave is a sure bet for a night of fun.

The **Waikiki Hard Rock Café,** the fast food joint of nightspots, has jazzed up its act by putting on live music Friday and Saturday evenings. It's located at Kalakaua Ave. and Kapiolani Boulevard.

The following are disco nightclubs in and around Waikiki. Most have videos, a theme, a dress code of alohawear and shoes, no sandals, and start hopping around 9 p.m. with the energy cutoff around 4 a.m.

The **Cellar,** 205 Lewers St., tel. (808) 923-9952, features mostly rock and roll spun by the DJ. The place jumps till 4 a.m. and has plenty of special nights like Thirsty Tuesdays and Ladies' Night. Put on your dancin' shoes and casual attire.

Lewers Street Annex, at 270 Lewers, is a basic disco dance spot featuring top 40 tunes. The clientele is mostly young visitors and some local workers who stop in for a late-night drink. A special feature is the 12 O'clock High, basically happy hour prices noon-midnight. Standard drinks $1.50, domestic beers $1.50, margaritas and mai tais $1.50. Good for casual drinking, dancing, and meeting people.

Everyone trumpets the mating call at **Moose McGillycuddy's Pub and Cafe,** 310 Lewers in Waikiki, tel. (808) 923-0751, especially every Thursday, which is Ladies Night. Standard but good food and plenty of dancing. Try here to answer the call of the wild.

Across the street from Moose McGillycuddy's is **The Jungle,** so after trumpeting your moose calls, all you apes and apesses can lope across the street and swing until the late hour. You never know if the music will be from the '60s, '70s, '80s, or year 2010—it's a jungle in there.

The Esprit, at the Sheraton Waikiki, presents dance music from the '40s to the present Tues.-Sat. from 8:30 p.m. by a local band. Come casual or dressed to the hilt. Good dance floor, no cover, and it's the only nightclub right on the beach.

Eurasia, 2552 Kalakaua Ave., is a disco that's attracting dancers who once filled other discos in the area that have since closed their doors. Also try **Scruples Beach Club** on Kuhio Ave. for international DJ disco music.

Red Lion Dance Palace, 240 Lewers St., tel. (808) 922-1027, offers live rock 'n' roll Wed.-

J.D. BISIGNANI

the distinctive mural at The Wave

Sat. and high-tech video and disco the remaining nights. Nice dance floor. Beachwear is OK. Open 2 p.m.-4 a.m.

Exotic live dancers, like exotic live plants, need a unique atmosphere in which to bloom. Both seem to crave light, one sunlight, the other a spotlight. Most of the flashy fleshy nightspots of Waikiki used to be a few blocks away along Kapiolani Blvd., but they have been moving ever closer to the heart of Waikiki. Now they are strung along Kuhio Avenue, where they're easily recognizable by their garish neon lights advertising their wares. The Kuhio Avenue exotic dance spots are supposedly a step up in class from their Kapiolani Boulevard counterparts, but when their dancers strip to the buff, the difference is hardly noticeable . . . or very noticeable, depending upon point of view. The names of the strip joints really don't matter, just look for the signs of "exotic dancers." Usually a $10 cover and $5 for a drink.

Dinner Shows and Polynesian Extravaganzas
The **Don Ho Show,** an institution that played at the Hilton Hawaiian Village for years, is no longer. Mr. Ho has moved to the Waikiki Beachcomber at 2300 Kalakaua Ave., tel. (808) 922-4646, where he plays two shows nightly, Thurs.-Sunday. The 7 p.m. dinner show costs $46, and the 9 p.m. cocktail show is $28. Either show is recommended. Gone is the glitz and glamour, just Ho and his organ much in the same way as he performed at Duke Kahanamoku's Club in the 1960s. Don Ho is still a great performer, and

"the godfather of modern Hawaiian music." Professional funster **Frank De Lima** hosts Tropical Madness in the Polynesian Palace nightly except Monday, at 9 p.m. De Lima, supported by a cast of various loonies, is guaranteed to tickle your funny bone, "island style."

The Hilton Dome at the Hilton Hawaiian Village fills with magical vibrations when headliner **John Hirokawa** suddenly appears out of nowhere. The **Magic of Polynesia** is a journey into the realm of enchantment and beauty that the entire family can enjoy. Slight of hand, disappearing maidens, swaying hula dancers, fantastic costumes and audience participation are all part of the magical extravaganza. Two shows nightly: dinner seating at 6:30 p.m., adults $45, children $31; cocktail show at 9 p.m., adults $25, children $17.

Society of Seven, a well-established local ensemble, appears nightly at the Outrigger Main Showroom performing a variety of musical tunes from the last 50 years. In various permutations, this band has been performing locally since the late '60s.

Performing two shows nightly in the Outrigger Polynesian Palace is the **Yes! International Revue,** an absorbing collaboration of magic, dance, illusion, and mime.

If you missed them the first time, here's your chance to see the world's greatest entertainers when unbelievably realistic impersonators perform **Legends in Concert,** a Las Vegas-style spectacular presented nightly at the Aloha Showroom of the Royal Hawaiian Shopping Center.

The Ainahau Showroom at the Sheraton Princess Kaiulani Hotel presents the **Sheraton Spectacular Polynesian Revue** nightly for dinner and cocktail shows at 5:30 and 8 p.m.

Free or Small Fee Entertainment

Check the newspapers and free tourist literature for times to the following events.

The **Royal Hawaiian Band** plays free concerts on Sunday afternoons at 12:45 p.m. and 2 p.m. at the bandstand in Kapiolani Park, oftentimes with singers and hula dancers, and again on Friday at 12:15 p.m. at the Iolani Palace. Formed in 1836, the band plays mostly classical music and Hawaiian traditional tunes. Also in the park, free concerts are periodically given by a variety of local and visiting musicians at the Waikiki Shell.

Every evening at King's Village across the street from the Hyatt Regency, a changing of the guard show is performed by the King's Guards in uniforms from the period of the monarchy to give you a peek into one of the rituals of royal ceremony.

The **Kodak Hula Show** is very popular. The show is held on Tues.-Thurs. at 10 a.m. at the Waikiki Shell in Kapiolani Park, but people start lining up at 8 a.m.; be there by 9 if you want a seat. You sit on bleachers with 3,000 people, while Hawaiian *tutu* bedecked in muumuu, lei, and smiles play ukuleles and sing for the ti-leaf-skirted dancers. You can buy film and even rent a camera, as befits the show's sponsor, the Eastman Kodak Company—snap away with abandon. The performance dates back to 1937, and some of the original dancers, now in their eighties, still participate. At the finale, the dancers line up on stage with red-lettered placards that spell out H-A-W-A-I-I, so you can take your own photo of the most famous Hawaiian postcard. Then the audience is invited down for a free hula lesson. People who are too hip hate it, *kama'aina* shy away from it, but if you're a good sport, you'll walk away like everyone else with a big smile on your face.

A potpourri of contemporary entertainment is also found in Kapiolani Park on weekends. Just across from the zoo, musicians, jugglers, clowns, unicyclists, and acrobats put on a free, impromptu circus. Some of the best are B.J. Patches, Twinkles, and Jingles from a local troupe called Clown Alley.

The **Ukulele Tree Hawaiian Music Show** is held in the Outrigger East Hotel Saturday, Sunday, and Monday 5-7 p.m., for free; local musicians and sometimes well-known guests come to play and be heard. For information call (808) 922-5353.

The **Royal Hawaiian Shopping Center** provides free crafts demonstrations and lessons at various times throughout the week: quilting, *lau hala* weaving, coconut weaving, hula, lei-making, ukulele instruction, and haku (floral wristband) weaving. The Polynesian Cultural Center puts on a torchlighting ceremony with song and dance every Monday, Wednesday, and Friday 6-6:45 p.m., and Tuesday and Thursday 10-11:30 a.m. they perform songs and dances. Tuesday, Thursday, Saturday, and Sunday 6-6:15 p.m. is a mini-torchlighting ceremony. Free musical entertainment is also scheduled daily and throughout the day at the fountain court. For specific times for the crafts, call (808) 922-0588.

A free hula show and fireworks are performed every Friday 6:30-7:30 p.m. at the super pool next to the main lobby at the Hilton Hawaiian Village. Anyone can come and stand for the show, but if you occupy one of the seats you must purchase at least one drink.

Molehu I Waikiki, a torchlighting ceremony complete with authentic hula performed by various *halau,* is offered to the public free of charge at Kuhio Beach Park every Saturday and Sunday at 6:45 p.m.

Every Friday evening 8-10 p.m., Kalakaua Ave. comes alive with the music and dance of hula as the **Strolling Hula on Kalakaua** makes seven stops between Beach Walk Street and the Waikiki Shopping Center.

Sometimes, "free" tickets to some of Waikiki's most popular Polynesian Extravaganzas are handed out by condo time-share outfits stationed in booths along the main drags. For attending their sales presentations, usually 90 minutes, you can get tickets, but they might be the toughest freebies you've ever earned. The presentation is a pressure cooker where hardened sales pros try every imaginable technique to get you to sign . . . "right now, because this is the only time that this deal can be offered." If you're really interested in time-sharing, the deals aren't too bad, but if you're there only for the tickets, what a waste of time!

The **Hawaii IMAX Theater,** 325 Seaside Ave. in Waikiki, screens several shows everyday 11 a.m.- 9 p.m. These exciting documentary films on Hawaiian subjects start every hour on the hour, run about 40 minutes in length, and are scheduled on a rotating basis. Adults $7.50, children 3-11 $5. You can see two or more of the different shows on any one day for a reduced fee. Call for current showings and ticket prices; tel. (808) 923-4629.

Just for the thrill of it (and for the spectacular scenery), ride the outside glass elevators of either the Sheraton Waikiki or Ilikai Hotel.

SHOPPING

The biggest problem concerning shopping in Waikiki is to keep yourself from burning out over the endless array of shops and boutiques. Everywhere you look someone has something for sale, and with the preponderance of street stalls lining the boulevards, much of the merchandise comes out to greet you. The same rule applies to shopping as it does to everything in Waikiki—class next door to junk. Those traveling to the Neighbor Islands should seriously consider a shopping spree in Waikiki, which has the largest selection and most competitive prices in the islands. A great feature about shopping in Waikiki is that most shops are only a minute or two from the beach. This enables your sale-hound companion to hunt while you relax. There's no telling how much money your partner can save you! "Ingrate! This bathing suit could have cost $50, but I got it for $25. See, you saved $25 while you were lying here like a beached whale." Everyone concerned should easily be mollified. Charge!

The Fence

The best place to find an authentic island-made souvenir at a reasonable price is at The Fence, located along the fence of the Honolulu Zoo fronting Kapiolani Park. Also referred to as Artists of Oahu/Sunday Exhibit and Art Mart, some of the island's best artists congregate here to display and sell their works on Tuesdays and weekends 10 a.m.-4 p.m. Individual artists are only allowed to display one day a week. The Fence was the good idea of Honolulu's former mayor, Frank Fasi, who decided that Oahu's rich resource of artists shouldn't go untapped. There are plenty of excellent artists whose works are sure to catch your fancy. Also, about once a month on a Saturday or Sunday, booths are set up on the grassy area closer to the zoo, and an arts and crafts fair is held.

Gifts and Souvenirs

ABC Stores scattered throughout Waikiki were founded by a local man, Sid Kosasa, who learned the retail business from his father. This "everything store" sells groceries, sundries, and souvenirs. Prices are good, especially on specials like lotions and beach mats. Very convenient.

Those who just couldn't return home without a deep Hawaiian tan can be helped by visiting **Waikiki Aloe,** 2168 Kalakaua Ave. It specializes in skin-care products, lotions, and tanning supplies.

The **Waikiki Business Plaza,** 2270 Kalakaua Ave., houses a number of jewelry stores. In one stop you can get a pretty good idea of prices and availability. Look for jewelry boxes laden with jade, gold, turquoise, pearls, coral, and *puka* shells, and eel, snake, and leather goods.

Military Shop of Hawaii, 833 Kalakaua Ave., has an entire wall dedicated to military patches, along with clothes, memorabilia, and collectibles.

Those with good taste but a limited budget should check out **Hawaiian Wear Unlimited,** 205 Lewers St., liquidators of alohawear from most of Hawaii's big manufacturers. Also, **Pzazz** "consignment boutique" sells used designer clothing at 1419 Kalakaua Ave.

Up Kapahulu Ave., along Restaurant Row, is **Bailey's Antiques,** tel. (808) 734-7628, which specializes in vintage Hawaiian shirts. Reproductions of these old wearable artworks are also available, as are clothing, jewelry, lamps, figurines, and the like. Nearby is **Peggy's Picks,** with new and used gifts, treasures, and collectibles from around the world.

For a full range of **photo supplies** at bargain prices try: **Woolworth's,** 2224 Kalakaua Ave.; **Fox Photo** in the Waikiki Town Center and Royal Hawaiian Shopping Center, and at the Hilton Hawaiian Village and Sheraton Moana Surfrider; and **Island Camera and Gift Shops** at Princess Kaiulani, Sheraton Waikiki, Royal Hawaiian, and

Sheraton Moana Surfrider hotels. Handbillers often give money-saving coupons to a variety of photo stores. Also for camera and photo supplies, **Central Camera,** 159 Kaiulani Ave., Suite 109, is a fine store where the salespeople are very helpful. Other photo stores are located here and there along Kalakaua, Kuhio, Kalia, and Lewers Streets.

Duty-free goods are always of interest to international visitors. You can find a duty-free store at the Hilton Hawaiian Village. Also, if you want to see a swarm of Japanese jostling for position in a tiny little store trying to feed a buying frenzy, that's the spot.

Waikiki Shopping Centers

The largest credit card oasis is the **Royal Hawaiian Shopping Center.** This massive complex is three stories of nonstop shopping, running for three blocks in front of the Sheraton and Royal Hawaiian hotels. It's open daily 9 a.m.-10 p.m., till 9 p.m. on Sunday, tel. (808) 922-0588. This complex provides an excellent mixture of small intimate shops and larger department stores. There's a **post office** on the second-floor "B" building. The second and third floors of this shopping center are pretty quiet. It's off the street so not as many tourists find their way here. It's a good place to do some comparative browsing before making your purchases. If jewelry is an interest of yours, head up to the third floor and have a look at the Hawaiian Heirloom Jewelry Factory and the intriguing heirloom jewelry museum next door.

Where the Royal Hawaiian Shopping Plaza ends the **Waikiki Shopping Plaza** begins, but on the other side of the street. Here, you'll find multilevel shopping. The mall's centerpiece is a five-story waterfall, an impressive sculpture of water and plexiglass, while other fountains grace the lower level. Another feature of this mall is Waikiki Calls, a free hula show. Many inexpensive eateries are located on the bottom floor, while fancier Chinese and Japanese restaurants are on the fourth and fifth floors. Clothing and accessory shops seem to predominate. The plaza is open daily 9 a.m.-11 p.m., tel. (808) 923-1191. While here, take a ride to the top floor of the Waikiki Business Plaza next door to the Shopping Plaza, where you'll get a fine overview of the Honolulu Waikiki area. Out behind the plaza is an open-air bazaar called **The Royal Market,** where you can find a few treasures among the lesser quality goods.

The **International Market Place** is an open-air shopping bazaar that feels like Asia. Its natural canopy is a huge banyan, and the entire complex is across from the Moana Hotel at 2330 Kalakaua Ave., open daily from 9 a.m. until the vendors get tired at night, tel. (808) 923-9871. Among some fine merchandise and a treasure or two is great junk! If you're after souvenirs like bamboo products, shellwork, hats, mats, lotions, alohawear, and carvings, you can't do better than the International Market Place. The worst thing is that everything starts to look the same; the best is that the stands will bargain. Make offers and try hard to work your way through the gauntlet of shops without getting scalped. Check out the Elvis Store and Museum, which must be seen to be believed.

Directly behind the marketplace is the **Waikiki Town Center,** 2301 Kuhio Avenue. Basically the same theme with open-air shops: gifts, fashions, food, and handmade artifacts. Enjoy the free Polynesian Show nightly at 7 and 8 p.m. This is a little older, funkier mall, one grade up from what you would find in the International Market Place and Duke's Alley. If you want a low-key place to discover "treaure junk" this mall is good. It's even better than the International Market Place because it's more low-key. There aren't nearly as many people here and the salespeople are not as pushy.

For those who can't stand to waste an opportunity to shop, they can do so while passing through **Duke's Alley,** a shortcut between Kuhio and Kalakaua Avenues. Here you'll find a row of stalls selling basically the same merchandise as in the International Market Place.

The **Hyatt Regency Shopping Center,** also called the **Atrium Shops,** is located on the first three floors of the Hyatt Regency Hotel, 2424 Kalakaua Ave., tel. (808) 922-5522, open daily 9 a.m.-11 p.m. The 70 or so shops are mighty classy: if you're after exclusive fashions or a quality memento, this is the place. There's a continental-style sidewalk cafe, backed by a cascading indoor waterfall. Often free entertainment and fashion shows are put on by the various shops.

Smaller Malls

King's Village, at 131 Kaiulani Ave., just next to the Hyatt Regency, takes its theme from last century, where boardwalks pass 19th-century look-alike shops, complete with a changing-of-the-guard ceremony nightly at 6:15 p.m. This attractive com-

Waikiki Bazaar

plex offers free entertainment and attracts some of the best local street artists, who usually set up their stands at night. The **Waikiki Trade Center** is on the corner of Seaside and Kuhio Avenues with some of Waikiki's most elegant shops, featuring sophisticated fashions, exquisite artwork, and fine dining. The **Rainbow Bazaar** is a unique mall located at the Hilton Hawaiian Village, 2005 Kalia Road. Fun just to walk around, shops feature three main themes: Imperial Japan, Hong Kong Alley, and South Pacific Court.

The newest shopping complex to grace the streets of this already shop-filled town is the **King Kalakaua Plaza** located toward the western end of the strip. Nike Town fills a good portion of this building, as does a Banana Republic store.

Street Artists and Vendors

You don't have to try to find something to buy in Waikiki—in fact, if you're not careful, the merchandise will come after you! This takes place in the form of street vendors, who have been gaining a lot of attention lately. Some view them as a colorful addition to the beach scene, others as a nuisance. These carnival-type salespeople set up their mobile booths mainly along Kalakaua Avenue, with some on Kuhio Avenue and the side streets in between. In dealing with them you can have a positive experience if you remember two things: they have some pretty nifty junk, and you get what you pay for.

Also, street artists set up their palettes along busy thoroughfares, and especially at the entrances to small shopping malls. Most draw caricatures of patrons in a few minutes for a few dollars—fun souvenirs.

Right here under the Waikiki banyan is a gentleman named Coco who makes coconut-frond hats, basically a dying art. Just near the canoe rides, you'll see his hats and baskets. Depending on the hat, you can get one for $15 or so. The baskets, good for holding fruit, incidentals, or whatever, are a real souvenir of Hawaii. With Coco making them right before your very eyes, you can't get more authentic than that. Coco says you can still learn how to weave in the Hawaiian tradition. His dad, Uncle Harry Kuikai, weaves at the Royal Hawaiian Shopping Center every Tuesday and Thursday 9:30-11:30 a.m. He'll teach you the basics of weaving and you can make your own souvenir (free). For longer-term tourists, there's an eight-week weaving class sponsored by the Kamehameha School. Just call the high school and inquire as to time and fees.

As you walk around Waikiki you'll see plenty of street-side booths offering unbelievable prices like "rent a car for $5, a jeep for $15, Pearl Harbor Cruise $5, Don Ho Show $20." Why so cheap? It's basically an advertising firm that signs you up to listen to a 90-minute spiel on a time-share condo. What happens during and after the 90-minute hard pitch is up to you, but you do get the payoff at the end.

Activities and Rentals

Not all activities and sports rentals in Waikiki are done at the umbrella stands set up along Waikiki Beach. For a reputable shop, try **Blue Sky Rentals,**

1920 Ala Moana Blvd., tel. (808) 947-0101. Owner Luis Merino can arrange activities and rent equipment for most of your ground, air, and sea needs. Bicycles and mopeds rent for $15 per half day or $20 a full day. Snorkeling gear is $10 a day, boogie boards $10. Introductory scuba dives start from $75, a full-day deep-sea fishing tour from around $100, a tandem ski diving jump at $225, and a glider ride for $60. You'll find these and many more options at Blue Sky Rentals.

Of the beachside sport rental shops, **Prime Time Sports,** tel. (808) 949-8952, is a good bet. Located at Fort DeRussy Beach in front of the Hale Koa Hotel, it rents all sorts of water equipment and gives scuba, surf, and windsurfing lessons, all at reasonable prices.

DIANA LASICH HARPER

BOB RACE

CENTRAL OAHU

For most uninformed visitors, central Oahu is a colorful blur as they speed past in their rental cars en route to the North Shore. Slow down, there are things to see! For island residents, the suburban towns of Aiea, Pearl City, Waipahu, Mililani, and Wahiawa are home. Both routes heading north from Honolulu meet in **Wahiawa,** the island's most central town. The roads cross just near the entrance to **Schofield Barracks,** a warm-up target for Japanese Zeros as they flew on their devastating bombing run over Pearl Harbor.

AIEA, PEARL CITY, AND VICINITY

The twin cities of Aiea and Pearl City, except for the USS *Arizona* Memorial, USS *Bowfin* Submarine Museum, and perhaps a football game at Aloha Stadium, have little to attract the average tourist. Mainly they are residential areas for greater Honolulu, and for the large numbers of military families throughout this area. Likewise, Waipahu doesn't hold much attraction to the tourist because of its largely agricultural base, but **Hawaii's Plantation Village** is an attempt to interpret the importance of plantation culture for visitors.

PEARL HARBOR:
USS *ARIZONA* MEMORIAL

Even as you approach the pier from which you board a launch to take you to the USS *Arizona,* you know that you're at a shrine. Very few spots in America carry such undeniable emotion so easily passed from one generation to another: here, Valley Forge, Gettysburg, not many more. On that beautiful, cloudless morning of December 7, 1941, at one minute before 8 o'clock, the United States not only entered the war, but lost its innocence forevermore.

The first battle of WW II for the U.S. actually took place about 90 minutes before Pearl Harbor's bombing, when the USS *Ward* sank an unidentified submarine sliding into Honolulu. In Pearl Harbor, dredged about 40 years earlier to allow superships to enter, the heavyweight champions of America's Pacific Fleet were lined up flanking the near side of Ford's Island. The naive deployment of this "Battleship Row" prompted a Japanese admiral to remark that never, even in times of maximum world peace, could he dream that the military might of a nation would have its unprotected chin stuck so far out, just begging for a right cross to the jaw. When it came, it was a roundhouse right, whistling through the air, and what a doozy!

Well before the smoke could clear and the last explosion stopped rumbling through the mountains, 3,581 Americans were dead or wounded, six mighty ships had sunk into the ooze of Pearl, 12 others stumbled around battered and punch-drunk, and 347 warplanes were useless heaps of scrap. The Japanese fighters had hardly broken a sweat, and when their fleet, located 200 miles north of Oahu, steamed away, the "east wind" had indeed "rained." But it was only the first squall of the American hurricane that would follow.

Getting There

There are a few options on how to visit Pearl Harbor and the USS *Arizona* Memorial. If you're driving, the entrance is along Rt. 99, the Kamehameha Highway, about a mile south of Aloha Stadium; well-marked signs direct you to the parking area. If you're on H-1 west, take exit 15A and follow the signs. You can also take TheBus,

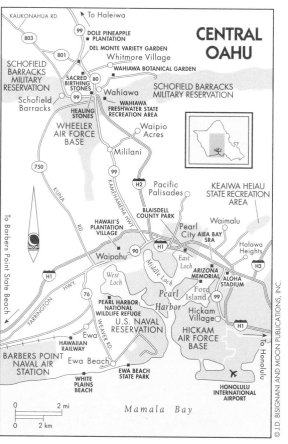

no. 50, or 52 from Ala Moana Center, or no. 20 Airport from Waikiki, and be dropped off within a minute's walk of the entrance. Depending upon stops and traffic, this can take well over an hour.

Arizona Memorial Shuttle Bus, tel. (808) 839-0911, a private operation from Waikiki, takes about 20 minutes and will pick you up at most Waikiki hotels. It charges $3 one-way; reservations are necessary. Returning, no reservations are necessary; just buy a ticket from the lady selling them under the green umbrella in the parking lot.

The **Arizona Memorial Visitor Center** is a joint venture of the U.S. Park Service and the Navy, and is free! The Park Service runs the theater and museum, and the Navy operates the shuttle boats that take you out to the memorial shrine. The complex is open daily 7:30 a.m.-5 p.m., with daily programs 8 a.m.-3 p.m. (closed Thanksgiving, Christmas, New Year's Day), when you can visit the museum and the theater, and take the shuttle boats out to the memorial. If the weather is stormy, or waves rough, they won't sail. For recorded information call (808) 422-0561 or 422-2771. As many as 3,000 people visit per day, and your best time to avoid delays is before 9:30 a.m.

Also, a number of boats operate out of Kewalo Basin doing **Pearl Harbor Cruises.** Costing about $25 for an extensive tour of Pearl Harbor, they are not allowed to drop passengers off at the memorial itself.

Bookstore and Theater
As you enter, you're handed a numbered ticket. Until it's called, you can visit the bookstore/gift shop and museum or, if the wait is long, the USS *Bowfin* moored within walking distance (see following). The bookstore specializes in volumes on WW II and Hawaiiana. The museum is primarily a pictorial history, with a strong emphasis on the involvement of Hawaii's Japanese citizens during the war. There are instructions of behavior to "all persons of Japanese ancestry," from when bigotry and fear prevailed early in the war, as well as documentation of the 442nd Battalion, made up of Japanese soldiers, and their heroic exploits in Europe, especially their rescue of Texas's "lost battalion." Preserved newspapers of the day proclaim the "Day of Infamy" in bold headlines.

When your number is called you proceed to the comfortable theater where a 20-minute film includes actual footage of the attack. The film is historically factual, devoid of an overabundance of flag waving and mom's apple pie. After the film you board the launch: no bare feet, no bikinis or bathing suits, but shorts and shirts are fine. Twenty years ago visitors wore suits and dresses as if going to church!

The Memorial
The launch, a large mostly open-air vessel handled and piloted with professional deft, usually by women Naval personnel, heads for the 184-foot-long alabaster memorial straddling the ship that still lies on the bottom. Some view the memorial as a tombstone; others see it as a symbolic ship, bent by struggle in the middle, but raised at the ends pointing to glory. The USS *Arizona* became the focus of the memorial because her casualties were so severe. When she exploded, the blast was so violent that it lifted entire ships moored nearby clear out of the water. Less than nine minutes later, with infernos raging and huge hunks of steel whizzing through the air, the *Arizona* was

NATIONAL ARCHIVES

Under attack: The Japanese attack on Pearl Harbor set off a chain of events that would make the U.S. the domineering power of the Pacific.

gone. Her crew went with her; nearly 1,100 men were sucked down to the bottom, and only 289 somehow managed to struggle to the surface. To the left and right are a series of black and white moorings bearing the names of the ships that were tied to them on the day of the attack.

The deck of the memorial can hold about 200 people; a small museum holds the ship's bell, and a chapel-like area displays a marble tablet with the names of the dead. Into a hole in the center of the memorial, flowers and wreaths are dropped on special occasions. Part of the superstructure of the ship still rises above the waves, but it is slowly being corroded away by wind and sea water. The flag, waving overhead, is attached to a pole anchored to the deck of the sunken ship. Sometimes, on weekends, survivors from the attack are aboard to give firsthand descriptions of what happened that day. Many visitors are Japanese nationals, who often stop and offer their apologies to these Pearl Harbor survivors, distinguished by special military-style hats. The Navy ordered that any survivor wishing to be buried with his crew members had that right. In 1982 a diver took a stainless-steel container of the ashes of one of the survivors to be laid to rest with his buddies.

USS *Bowfin* Submarine Museum and Park

The **USS *Bowfin,*** a WW II submarine moored within walking distance of the *Arizona* Memorial Center, has been turned into a museum. It's open daily 8 a.m.-5 p.m. except Thanksgiving, Christmas, and New Year's Day; admission is $8 adults or $4 for the museum tour only, $3 children ages 4-12 or $2 for the museum tour only. Children three and under are free for the museum tour but not admitted into the submarine. The rate for *kama'aina,* senior citizens, and active military personnel is $6. Topside are a gift shop, snack bar, and the museum building containing many items once on display at the Pacific Submarine Museum. Here and there across the extensive four-acre grounds lie artillery pieces, torpedoes, missiles, and the conning tower and periscope of the **USS *Parche.*** Guided tours lead you into the sub; the last tour starts at 4:30 p.m. The private, nonprofit organization Pacific Fleet Submarine Memorial Association maintains the park and museum as a memorial and educational exhibit.

Launched one year to the day after the Pearl Harbor attack, the USS *Bowfin* (SS-287) completed nine patrol tours during WW II. Retired in 1979, restored and opened to the public in 1981, it was put on the National Historical Landmark list in 1986. It's a 312-foot-long sausage of steel with a living area only 16 feet in diameter. As you enter the sub, you're handed a telephonelike receiver; a recorded transmitted message explains about different areas on the sub. The deck is made from teak wood, and the deck guns could go fore or aft depending on the skipper's preference. You'll also notice two anchors. As you descend, you feel as if you are integrated with a machine, a part of its gears and workings. In these cramped quarters of brass and stainless steel lived 90 to 100 men, all volunteers. Fresh water was in short supply, and the

USS Bowfin,
WW II submarine

J.D. BISIGNANI

only man allowed to shower was the cook. Officers were given a dipper of water to shave with, but all the other men grew beards. With absolutely no place to be alone, the men slept on tiny stacked shelves, and only the officers could control the light switches. The only man to have a minuscule private room was the captain.

Topside, twin 16-cylinder diesels created unbelievable noise and heat. A vent in the passageway to the engine room sucked air with such strength that if you passed under it, you'd be flattened to your knees. When the sub ran on batteries under water, the quiet became maddening. The main bunk room, not much bigger than an average bedroom, slept 36 men. Another 30 or so ran the ship, while another 30 lounged. There was no night and day, just shifts. Coffee was constantly available, as well as fresh fruit, and the best mess in all the services. Subs of the day had the best radar and electronics available. Aboard were 24 high-powered torpedoes, and ammo for the topside gun. Submariners, chosen for their intelligence and psychological ability to take it, knew that a hit from the enemy meant certain death. The USS *Bowfin* is fascinating and definitely worth a visit.

In the museum building, you're presented with a short pictorial history of man's progress in undersea travel and warfare, from Revolutionary times to the present. Battle flags, recruiting posters, photographs, uniforms, military medals, and a variety of weapons and hardware are displayed, while a cutaway model of the *Bowfin* shows life aboard ship. New to the museum, and the only one displayed for public viewing, is a daunting Poseidon C-3 submarine missile. An ongoing film in the minitheater describes life below the surface for the modern submarine force. For the real aficionado, the museum archives and library of submarine-related literature is open by appointment only.

The museum and park is located at 11 Arizona Memorial Dr., Honolulu, HI 96818, tel. (808) 423-1341, fax 422-5201, Web site: www.aloha.net/~bowfin, e-mail: bowfin@aloha.net. If you are coming by bus, use no. 20 or 47 from Waikiki, or no. 20, 47, 52, or 62 from the Ala Moana Shopping Center.

USS *Missouri*

In 1998, the USS *Missouri* was anchored in the Honolulu harbor after its final journey from the Mainland. Following renovation and the installation of exhibits, it will be opened to public visitation as a floating museum and memorial, at a yet unnamed date. Whereas the destruction of the USS *Arizona* and other ships in the harbor and the incredible loss of life and innocence brought the United States into war with Japan, it was on the deck of the USS *Missouri* that Japan, bruised and bloodied, surrendered to the U.S., ending this most costly of world conflicts.

Visit Ships Program

The Navy holds an **open house** on one of its ships berthed at Pearl Harbor on the first Saturday of each month noon-4 p.m. For information call (808) 471-0281. You must enter through the main Nimitz Gate, and then follow the signs to the ship, which is usually at the Bravo or Mike piers. On your way to the docking area you stop at the Family Services area where you can pick up some snacks or ice cream at the concession. The sailors conducting the tour are polite and knowledgeable, and the tour is free. Those never in the service can always spot the officers—the guys with the white shoes.

BEACHES AND SIGHTS

Keaiwa Heiau State Recreation Area

As you travel up Aiea Heights Road, an exit off H-1, you get a world-class view of Pearl Harbor below. It's not glorious because it is industrialized, but you do ride through suburban sprawl Hawaiian style until you come to the end of the road at **Keaiwa Heiau State Recreation Area**. In the cool heights above Aiea, these ancient grounds have a soothing effect the minute you enter. Overnight tent camping is allowed here (free permit required), with exceptionally large sites; for the few other visitors, the gates open at 7 a.m. and close at 6:45 p.m. As you enter the well-maintained park (a caretaker lives on the premises), tall pines to the left give a feeling of alpine coolness. Below, Pearl Harbor lies open, like the shell of a great oyster.

Keaiwa Heiau was a healing temple, surrounded by gardens of medicinal herbs tended by Hawaii's excellent healers, the *kahuna lapa'au*. From the gardens, roots, twigs, leaves, and barks were ground into potions and mixed liberally with prayers and love. These potions were amazingly successful in healing Hawaiians before the white man brought his diseases.

Walking onto the stone floor of the *heiau,* it's somehow warmer and the winds seem quieter. Toward the center are numerous offerings, simple stones wrapped with a ti leaf. Some are old, while others are quite fresh. Follow the park road to the **Aiea Loop Trail,** which heads back 4.8 miles roundtrip onto one of the ridges descending from the Koolau Mountains. Pass through a forest of tall eucalyptus trees, viewing canyons to the left and right. Notice, too, the softness of the "spongy bark" trees growing where the path begins. Allow three hours for the loop.

Blaisdell County Park

The park's waters, which can be considered part of Pearl Harbor, are too polluted for swimming. It's sad to think that at the turn of the century it was clear and clean enough to support oysters. Pearl Harbor took its name from Waimomi, "Water of Pearls," which were indeed harvested from the oysters and a certain species of clam growing here. Today, sewage and uncountable oil spills have done their devastation. Recently, oysters from the Mainland's East Coast have been introduced and are being harvested from the mudflats. Supposedly, they're fit to eat. Facilities include a pay phone, tables, and restrooms. Access is off Rt. 99 just past Aloha Stadium and before you enter Pearl City.

Hawaii's Plantation Village

The Hawaii's Plantation Village in Waipahu Cultural Park, 94-695 Waipahu St., Waipahu, HI 96797, tel. (808) 677-0110, offers a stroll down memory lane into a once-working plantation village, now an open-air museum. This group of 30 homes, some original and others replicas, and the photos, artifacts, and memorabilia that they contain are a testament to the hard work performed by Hawaii's sugar plantation communities and an insight into the eight ethnic groups represented. Open for guided tours only Mon.-Fri. 9 a.m.-3 p.m. and Saturday 10 a.m.-3 p.m. Tours run about 90 minutes and start every hour. Admission is $5 for adults, $4 for seniors, and $3 for students 5-18.

Hawaiian Railway Line

While there are no commercial passenger train lines operating on the islands, two trains do run for tourists: the Sugar Cane Train on Maui and the Hawaiian Railway train on Oahu. Located in Ewa at 91-1001 Renton Road, tel. (808) 681-5461, the Hawaiian Railway Society gives rides, restores and exhibits engines and train cars, and maintains an open-air train exhibit and gift shop. This organization does more than give tourist rides, however; it provides an educational adventure. The 90-minute roundtrip, fully narrated rides start at 12:30 p.m. and 2:30 p.m. on Sunday only; $8 adults and $5 for seniors and children below 12. On the second Sunday of every month, the Dillingham parlor car is added to the train on both runs. Fares for a seat in the parlor car are $15, with no children under age 13 allowed. Group charter rides can be arranged Mon.-Fri. mornings. The train runs about six miles along narrow-gauge track from the Ewa station at the end of Renton Road west to the leeward coast, just past the Ko Olina Resort. Don't expect a rail burner—this baby moves at a mild 15 miles an hour. All aboard!

At one time, the Oahu Railway and Land Co. (OR&L) railroad totaled 72 miles of track that ran from Honolulu around Pearl Harbor, up the leeward coast, and across the north coast all the way to Kahuku, with another line up from Honolulu to the central island town of Wahiawa. It was a workhorse of a system, hauling people and goods (mostly sugar and molasses), servicing farms and commercial establishments, and, later, transferring troops and bulk items during WW II. After the war, the railroad couldn't compete with the burgeoning bus and trucking firms and the growing importance of the private automobile, so the line was shut down at the end of 1947, after 58 years of service, and most of the track taken up. After much labor was expended restoring a section of the remaining track and some rolling stock, the Hawaiian Railway Society began to offer rides to the public in 1989.

PRACTICALITIES

Accommodations

Except for long-term, accommodations are virtually nonexistent in this area.

The **Pepper Tree Apartment Hotel,** at 98-150 Lipoha Place, Aiea, HI 96701, tel. (808) 488-1993 or (800) 779-8058, offers furnished studios and apartments, all with complete kitchens and baths, TV, and phones. Rooms start at $65 single or $94 double, with a weekly rate of $385, cash only. A laundromat and swimming pool are also available. Many military personnel use this facility as temporary housing. Just down the block, two other places have approximately the same services and rates: **Hawaiian Horizon Apartment Hotel,** tel. (808) 488-4900, and **Harbor Arms Apartment Hotel,** tel. (808) 488-5556.

Luckily a few **bed and breakfast** homes provide some alternatives. One of the most interesting is the home of Corry and Helga Trummel, who reside in Pacific Palisades above Pearl City. What started out as a tract house has become a living museum. Helga has been collecting and inheriting art since she was a little girl in prewar Germany. Every nook and cranny has a curio from Europe, Asia, or Hawaii, and Helga loves to share her artwork and the fascinating stories of her youth. The first floor is completely dedicated to the guests. There's a music room, a library with a fine collection of books on WW II and the western states, two bedrooms, and a separate cottage in the back. Out here too is a small pool, dry sauna, and an observation platform high on the hill. Inside, as you mount the steps to the second floor you're greeted by a wooden statue of a woman with a bowl on her head, original oil paintings, and a grandfather clock, all from the last century. Enter the breakfast nook and suddenly you're in a German hunting lodge. The green and white table and benches painted with flowers are over 100 years old. Gaze around to see a stuffed bear, antique sitar, a mountain goat, stag, stuffed ducks, a collection of beer steins, a white moose head, pronghorn, and a bar. All in what once was a tract house kitchen! The main house is furnished like a very rich German chocolate cake; maybe not to everyone's taste, but definitely more than filling!

Food

Buzz's Steak House, 98-751 Kuahao Place (at the corner of Moana Loa and Kaahumanu), tel. (808) 487-6465, is open for lunch 11 a.m.-2 p.m. and again for dinner 5-10 p.m. It's futuristic, like something a kid would build with an erector set. It'd be perfect if it were down by the sea, where you could see something, but from where it's located you can peer at Pearl Harbor in the distance or have a world-class view of the freeway.

The steakhouse is owned and operated by an old island family whose business grew into a small chain of restaurants from the original location in Kailua. This is one of the remaining two. Buzz's is an institution where islanders go when they want a sure-fire good meal. There's a salad bar and you prepare your own charbroiled steaks and fish. The prices are reasonable.

In the Waimalu Shopping Plaza, try **Stuart Anderson's Cattle Co. Restaurant,** tel. (808) 487-0054, open daily for lunch and dinner. The lounge is open until 2 a.m. weekends, serving huge steaks and all the trimmings.

Across the road is the **Elephant and Castle Restaurant,** at 98-1247 Kaahumanu, tel. (808) 487-5591, open daily for lunch and dinner, breakfast on weekends only. This restaurant has done an excellent job of creating an English-style pub atmosphere. The interior is cool and rich with red velvet, heavy chairs, tapestries, and open beams, with a pool table and dartboards in the pub area. Nightly, it's one of the best places in the area for a beer and a chat. The food is good too. Try English fish 'n' chips, a burger platter, hot sandwiches, or soup and sandwich. Specials on weekends are English prime rib dinner, New York steak, and seafood scampi. Enjoy merry old England Hawaiian style.

Shopping

The main shopping center in Aiea is the **Pearlridge Shopping Center,** tel. (808) 488-0981, open Mon.-Sat. 10 a.m.-9 p.m., Sunday to 5 p.m., with prices geared toward island residents, not tourists, so you have a good chance of coming away with a bargain. Some of the larger stores include Liberty House, JCPenney, Sears, Star Supermarket, Longs, Waldenbooks, and Woolworth's. There are also 16 theaters, two food courts with over 30 restaurants, plus 150 smaller boutiques and specialty shops. The entire complex is air-conditioned and serviced by an in-house monorail for your shopping convenience.

The **Waimalu Shopping Plaza,** located along Kaahumanu St. between the Kamehameha Hwy. (Rt. 99) and the H-1 freeway, has a small cluster of shops and restaurants. There's a **Times Supermarket,** open 24 hours with its pharmacy and deli, and the **Good Health Store,** open 9 a.m.-7 p.m., Saturday 11 a.m.-6 p.m., selling food supplements and minerals.

WAHIAWA AND VICINITY

Wahiawa is like a military jeep: basic, ugly, but indispensable. This is a soldiers' town, with servicemen from Schofield Barracks or nearby Wheeler A.F.B. shuffling along the streets. Most are young, short-haired, short-tempered, and dressed in fatigues. Everywhere you look are cheap bars, burger joints, run-down discos perfumed with sweat and spilled beer, and used-furniture stores. Route 99 turns into Rt. 80 which goes through Wahiawa, crossing California Avenue, the main drag, then rejoins Rt. 99 near the Del Monte Pineapple Variety Garden. Wahiawa has seemingly little to recommend it, and maybe because of its ugliness, when you do find beauty it shines even brighter.

Wahiawa was of extreme cultural and spiritual importance to the early Hawaiians. In town are **healing stones,** whose mystic vibrations were said to cure the maladies of sufferers. In a field not far from town are the **Kukaniloko,** the royal birthing stones, where the ruling *ali'i* labored to give birth to the future nobles of the islands. While in town you can familiarize yourself with Oahu's flora by visiting the **Wahiawa Botanical Garden,** or take a quick look at a serene Japanese temple.

As you gain the heights of the **Leilehua Plateau,** sandwiched between the Waianae and Koolau ranges, a wide expanse of green is planted in cane and pineapple. Just like on supermarket shelves, Del Monte's **Pineapple Variety Garden** competes with Dole's **Pineapple Pavilion,** a minute up the road. As a traveler's way station, central Oahu blends services, amenities, and just enough historical sites to warrant stretching your legs, but not enough to bog you down for the day.

SIGHTS

The Healing Stones

Belief in the healing powers of these stones has been attracting visitors since ancient times. When traveling down Oahi Street (Rt. 80) take a left on California Avenue, and follow it to Kaalalo Place. To glimpse the religion of Hawaii in microcosm, in a few blocks you pass the Riusenji Soto Buddhist

Mission, followed by the healing stones, next door to Olive United Methodist Church. If you've never experienced a Buddhist temple, make sure to visit the grounds of **Riusenji Soto Mission.** Usually no one is around, and even if the front doors are locked you can peer in at an extremely ornate altar graced by Buddha, highlighted in black lacquer and gold. On the grounds look for a stone *jizo,* patron of travelers and children. In Japan he often wears a red woven hat and bib, but here he has on a straw hat and muumuu.

An HVB Warrior marks the stones, just past the Kaalala Elementary School, across the street from a beautiful eucalyptus grove. A humble cinder-block building built in 1947 houses the stones. When you swing open the iron gate it strikes a deep mournful note, as if it were an instrument designed to announce your presence and departure. Inside the building, three stones sit atop rudimentary pedestals. Little scratches mark the stones, and an offertory box is filled with items like oranges, bread, a gin bottle, coins, and candy kisses. A few votive candles flicker before a statue of the Blessed Virgin.

Kukaniloko, the Birthing Stones

Follow Rt. 80 through town for about a mile. At the corner of Whitmore Avenue is a red light: right takes you to Whitmore Village and left puts you on a dirt track that leads to another eucalyptus grove marking the birthing stones. About 40 large boulders are in the middle of a field with a mountain backdrop. One stone looks like the next, but on closer inspection you see that each has a personality. The royal wives would come here, assisted by both men and women of the ruling *ali'i,* to give birth to their exalted offspring. The baby's umbilical cord, a sacred talisman, would be hidden in the cracks and crevices of the stones. Near the largest palm tree is a special stone that appears to be fluted all the way around, with a dip in the middle. It, along with other stones nearby, seem perfectly fitted to accept the torso of a woman in a reclining position. Notice that small fires have been lit in the hollows of these stones, and that they are discolored with soot and ashes.

J.D. BISIGNANI

Schofield Barracks

Wahiawa Botanical Garden

In the midst of town is an oasis of beauty, 27 acres of developed woodlands featuring exotic trees, ferns, and flowers gathered from around the world. Located at 1396 California Ave., tel. (808) 621-7321, it's open daily except Christmas and New Year's, 9 a.m.-4 p.m., admission free. The parking lot is marked by an HVB Warrior; walk through the main entranceway and take a pamphlet from the box for a self-guiding tour. When it rains, the cement walkways are treacherously slippery, especially if you're wearing thongs. The nicer paths have been left natural, but they can be muddy. Inside the grounds are trees from the Philippines, Australia, Africa, and a magnificent multihued Mindanao gum from New Guinea. Your senses will be bombarded with fragrant camphor trees from China and Japan, and the rich aroma of cinnamon. Everywhere are natural bouquets of flowering trees, entangled by vines and highlighted by rich green ferns. Most specimens have been growing for a minimum of 40 years, so they're well established.

Schofield Barracks

Stay on Rt. 99, skirt Wahiawa to the west, and go past the entrance to Schofield Barracks. Schofield Barracks dates from the turn of the century, named after Gen. John Schofield, an early proponent of the strategic importance of Pearl Harbor. A sign tells you that it is still the "Home of the Infantry, Tropic Lightning." Open to the public, the base remains one of the prettiest military in-

stallations in the world. With permission, you can proceed to the Kolekole Pass, from where you get a sweeping view of inland and coastal Oahu. While heading north on 99 as you pass Schofield Barracks, notice a few run-down shops about 50 yards past the entrance. Stop here and look behind the shops at a wonderful still life created by the Wahiawa Reservoir.

On base, you can visit the small **Tropic Lightning Museum** with memorabilia going back to the War of 1812. There are planes from WW II, Chinese rifles from Korea, and deadly *pungi* traps from Vietnam. The museum has lost many of its exhibits in recent years to the U.S. Army Museum at Fort DeRussy in Waikiki, so it remains mostly a portrayal of the history of Schofield Barracks and the 25th Infantry "Tropic Lightning" Division. There is no charge for the museum, which is open 10 a.m.-4 p.m. Tues.-Sat., except federal holidays; tel. (808) 655-0438. Entrance is via the main gate on Kunia Road, and from there you must follow the signs.

Pineapples

A few minutes past the entrance to Schofield Barracks, Rt. 803 bears left to Waialua, while Rt. 99 goes straight ahead and begins passing rows of pineapple. At the intersection of Rt. 80 is the **Del Monte Variety Garden.** You're free to wander about and read the descriptions of the history of pineapple production in Hawaii, and of the genetic progress of the fruit made famous by the islands. This exhibit is much more educational and honest than the **Dole Pineapple Pavilion** just up the road, the one with all the tour buses lined up outside.

While at the Dole Plantation, visit the "World's Largest Maze." Certified by the Guiness Book of World Records, this maze is nearly two acres in area and formed by over 11,000 native Hawaiian bushes and flowering plants. Open 9 a.m.-6 p.m., admission $4.50 adults and $2.50 children.

PRACTICALITIES

Dot's Restaurant, off California Ave. at 130 Mango St., tel. (808) 622-4115, is a homey restaurant specializing in American-Japanese food that gives a good square meal for your money.

The interior is a mixture of Hawaiian/Asian in dark brown tones. Lunch specials include butterfish, teriyaki chicken, pork, or beef plates all for around $4.50. Miso soup is $2, and simple Japanese dishes go for about $3.50. The most expensive item on the menu is steak and lobster for $15. Dot's is nothing to write home about, but you definitely won't go hungry. Open 6 a.m.-9 p.m.

The streets of Wahiawa are lined with stores that cater to residents, not tourists. This means that the prices are right, and if you need supplies or necessities, this would be a good place to stock up. On the corner of California and Oahi Streets is a **Cornet Store,** an old-fashioned five and dime, where you can buy anything from suntan lotion to a crock pot. The **Big Way Supermarket** is at the corner of California and Kilani Avenues.

DIANA LASICH HARPER

BOB RACE

SOUTHEAST OAHU

KOKO HEAD TO WAIMANALO

It's amazing how quickly you can leave the frenzy of Waikiki behind. Once you round the bend past Diamond Head and continue traveling east toward Koko Head, the pace slackens measurably . . . almost by the yard. A minute ago you were in traffic, now you're cruising. It's not that this area is undeveloped; other parts of the island are much more laid-back, but none so close to the action of the city. In the 12 miles you travel from Honolulu to Waimanalo, you pass the natural phenomenon of Koko Crater, a reliable blowhole, the most aquatically active underwater park in the islands, and a string of beaches, each with a different personality.

Man has made his presence felt here, too. The area has some of the most exclusive homes on the island, as well as Hawaii Kai, a less exclusive project developed by the visionary businessman Henry Kaiser, who 20 years ago created this harbinger of things to come. There's Sea Life Park, offering a day's outing of fun for the family, plus shopping centers, the mostly Hawaiian town of Waimanalo, and Bellows Air Force Base, un-

used by the military and now one of the finest camping beaches on the island. Besides camping, few accommodations are found out here, and few restaurants. This lack of development preserves the area as scenic and recreational, prized attributes that should be taken advantage of before this sunny sandbox gets paved over.

SIGHTS, BEACHES, AND PARKS

The drive out this way accounts for half of the 360 degrees of what is called **The Circle Route.** Start by heading over the Pali Highway down to Kailua, hitting the sights on the way, or come this way first along Diamond Head Road to Rt. 72 as you make the loop back to the city. The only consideration is what part of the day you'd rather stop at the southeast beaches for a dip. For the most part, the beaches of this area *are* the sights. The road abounds with scenic points and overlooks. This is the part of Oahu that's absolutely beautiful in its undevelopment. It's hard to find a road on any of the Hawaiian islands that's going to be more scenic than this. At first the countryside is dry because this is the leeward side. But as you approach Waimanalo it gets much more tropical. The road is a serpentine ribbon with one coastal vista after another, a great choice for a joy ride just to soak in the sights. The following listings assume that you follow Rt. 72 east from Waikiki to Waimanalo.

Maunalua Bay

Maunalua ("Two Mountain") Bay is a four-mile stretch of sun and surf between Diamond Head and Koko Head, with a beach park about every half mile. The first is **Waialae Beach County Park** in Kahala. Go straight ahead on Kahala Avenue for one minute instead of going left on Rt. 72 to join H-1 on to Hanauma Bay. This section is the Beverly Hills of Honolulu, as many celebrities like Tom Selleck and Carol Burnett have homes here. The least expensive home in this section easily pushes $1 million asking price. Waialae is a popular windsurfing spot, crowded on weekends. It's a small beach park with basic amenities in a beautiful location where Makapuu Head wraps around and gives the impression that there are two islands off in the distance, but it's just the way Oahu bends at this point.

Next comes **Kawaikui Beach Park.** No lifeguard, but the conditions are safe year-round, and the bottom is shallow, muddy, and overgrown with seaweed. In times past, islanders came to the confluence of a nearby spring to harvest special *limu* that grow only where fresh water meets the ocean. You'll find unlimited access, parking stalls, picnic facilities, and restrooms. Few people use the park, and it's ideal for sunning, but for frolicking in the water, give it a miss.

In quick succession come **Niu and Paiko Beaches,** lying along residential areas. Although there is public access, few people take advantage of them because the swimming, with a coral and mud bottom, is less than ideal. Some residents have built a pier at Niu Beach past the mudflats, but it's restricted to their private use. Paiko Lagoon is a state bird sanctuary; binoculars will help with sightings of a variety of coastal birds.

The residential area in the hills behind **Maunalua Bay Beach Park** is Hawaii Kai, built by Henry Kaiser, the aluminum magnate. The con-

troversial development was often denigrated as "suburban blight." Many felt it was the beginning of Oahu's ruination. The park fronts Kuapa Pond, at one time a huge fishpond, later dredged by Kaiser, who used the dredged material to build the park, which he donated to the city in 1960. Now, most of the land has been reclaimed except for Koko Marina, whose boat launch constitutes the primary attraction of the park.

Except for the boat launch (the only one on this side of the island), the area is of little recreational use because of the mud or coral bottom. However, swimming is possible and safe, but be careful of the sudden drops created by the dredged boat channels. Two undeveloped parks are located at the end of Poipu Drive, **Kokee and Koko Kai Parks.** The currents and beach conditions make both unsuitable for swimming, but they're popular with surfers. Few others come here, but the views of the bay are lovely with glimpses of Molokai floating on the horizon to the south.

Hanauma Bay State Underwater Park

One of the premier beach parks in Hawaii is located in the sea-eroded crater of an extinct volcano just below Koko Head. People flock here to snorkel, scuba, picnic, and swim. During the day, the parking lot at the top of the hill overlooking the crescent bay below looks like a used car lot, jammed with Japanese imports, vans, and tour buses. A shuttle bus runs up and down the hill, and you can rent snorkeling equipment at the concession stand. If you want to avoid the crowds come in the early morning or after 4 p.m. when the sun dips behind the crater and most tourists leave on cue. There's still plenty of daylight, so plan your trip accordingly.

The reef protects the bay and sends a maze of coral fingers right up to the shoreline. A large sandy break in the reef, **Keyhole,** is a choice spot for entering the water and for swimming. The entire bay is alive with tropical fish. Many have become so accustomed to snorkelers that they've lost their fear entirely, and willingly accept food from your fingers—some so rudely you had better be careful of getting your fingers nibbled. The county provides lifeguards, restrooms, showers, picnic facilities, a pavilion, and food concession.

Before you enter the water, do yourself a favor and read the large bulletin board near the pavilion that describes conditions. It divides the bay into three areas ranging from beginner to expert, and warns of sections to avoid. Be especially careful of **Witches Brew**, a turbulent area on the right at the mouth of the bay that can wash you into the Molokai Express, a notoriously dangerous rip current. Follow a path along the lefthand seacliff to **Toilet Bowl**, a natural pool that rises and falls with the tides. If the conditions are right, you can sit in it to float up and down in a phenomenon very similar to a flushing toilet.

Note: Environmental Alert. Because severe overuse was threatening the fragile ecosystem of the bay, tour companies are now banned from dropping people in the park expressly for snorkeling. Tour buses can now only stop at the top of the hill for a 15-minute overview, and then must leave. People wishing to explore the bay may come by rental car, moped, bicycle, or city bus, which has a stop within the park. However, once the parking lot is filled, it is closed! And, the park is closed to all visitors on Wednesday when sorely needed maintenance is performed. Also, please do not feed the fish anything but approved fish food. Peas and bread are only appetizing to large-mouthed fish and severely cut down on the variety of fish that would normally live within the reef. Most importantly, the very reef is being destroyed by people walking upon it. Please do everything you can to avoid this. A few tour companies have tried to continue bringing people into the park and have found ways to violate the *spirit*, if not the *letter* of the restrictions. Please do not patronize them. With care, Hanauma Bay will remain beautiful for all future generations.

One group that you *should* patronize is the volunteers of the **Hanauma Bay Educational Program** (HBEP), a Sea Grant Program out of the University of Hawaii. The HBEP works toward the conservation and preservation of the bay, and the volunteers run a daily (except Wednesday when the bay is closed) educational tour, starting between 8 and 9 a.m. Come join the tour and learn about this important environmental work.

Koko Head Hike

For a sweeping view, hike to the summit of **Koko Head**, not to be confused with Koko Crater, another good hike but farther east on Rt. 72. To start your trek, look for a paved road closed off to vehicles by a white metal fence, on the right be-

fore the road to the parking lot. A 15-minute hike takes you to the 646-foot summit of Koko ("Blood") Head. This was the last place that young, wandering Madame Pele attempted to dig herself a fiery nest on Oahu; as usual, she was flooded out by her jealous sister. From the summit you get an unobstructed view of Molokai 20 miles across the Kaiwi Channel, the bowl of Hanauma Bay at your feet, and a sweeping panorama of Diamond Head and the Koolau Mountains. Below are two small extinct craters, Nono'ula and Ihi'ihilauakea.

Koko Crater

Koko Crater's Hawaiian name is Kohelepelepe ("Fringed Vagina"). Legend says that Pele's sister, Kapo, had a magical "flying vagina" that could fly and that she could send anywhere. Kamapua'a, the pig-god, was intent on raping Pele when Kapo came to her aid. She dispatched her vagina to entice Kamapua'a, and he followed it to Koko Head, where it made the crater and then flew away. Kamapua'a was unsuccessful when taking a flying leap at this illusive vagina.

You can either hike or drive to the crater. To begin the hike, look for the road to the Hawaii Job Corps Training Center just across from Hanauma Bay. Follow the road down past a rifle range and park at the job training building. Behind is an overgrown tramway track. The remaining ties provide a rough but adequate stairway to the top. At the 1,208-foot summit is an abandoned powerhouse and tramway station. The wood is rotted and the floors are weak! The crater itself lies 1,000 feet below. An easier but less exciting route is to follow Rt. 72 for two miles to Wawamalu Beach near the Hawaii Kai Golf Course and then take a left on Kealahou Street. Nearby is a walking path that leads into the crater.

On the floor of Koko Crater is a 60-acre botanical garden that, due to the unique conditions, specializes in succulents, cacti, and other dry land plants. Little developed yet except for one trail through the garden, the garden has no amenities. Free admission.

Halona Cove

As you round a bend on Rt. 72 you come to the natural lookout of Halona Cove, which means "The Peering Place," an excellent vantage point from which to see whales in season. Just before Halona, a sign will point you to the **Honolulu Japanese Casting Club,** with a stone wall and a monument. The monument at one time was of O Jisan, the Japanese god of protection, destroyed by overzealous patriots during WW II. The current monument was erected after the war, and O Jisan was carved into it. Below is a secluded little beach that's perfect for sunbathing. The only way to it is to scramble down the cliff. Swim only on calm days, or the waves can pull you out to sea and then suck you into the chamber of the famous **Halona Blowhole** just around the bend. There's a turnout at the blowhole for parking. The blowhole is a lava tube at the perfect height for the waves to be driven into it. The water compresses, and the pressure sends a spume into the air. Be extremely cautious around the blowhole. Those unfortunate enough to fall in face almost certain death.

Sandy Beach Park

Sandy Beach is one of the best bodysurfing beaches on Oahu, and the most rugged of them all. More necks and backs are broken on this beach than on all the other Oahu beaches combined. But because of the east-breaking waves, and bottom, the swells are absolutely perfect for bodysurfing. The lifeguards use a flag system to inform you about conditions. The **red flag** means "stay out." When checking out Sandy Beach, don't be fooled by bodysurfers who make it appear easy. These are experts, intimately familiar with the area, and even they are injured at times. Local people refer to the beach as "Scene Beach" because this is where young people come to strut their stuff. This is where the boys are because this is where the girls are. There are restrooms, a large parking area, and two lifeguard towers. Rip-offs have happened, so don't leave valuables in your car. *Kaukau* wagons park in the area, selling a variety of refreshments.

As the road skirts the coastline, it passes a string of beaches that look inviting but are extremely dangerous because there is no protecting reef. The best known is **Wawamalu,** where people

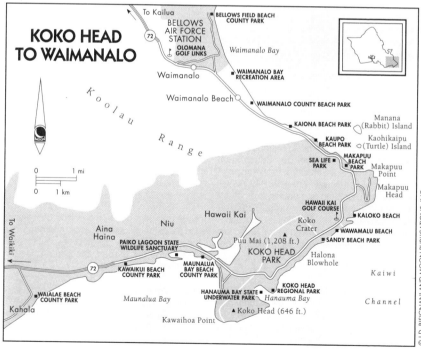

© J.D. BISIGNANI AND MOON PUBLICATIONS, INC.

The lifeguards do a great job at Sandy Beach.

J.D. BISIGNANI

come to sunbathe only. Across the road is **Hawaii Kai Golf Course,** an excellent public course.

Makapuu Beach Park

This beach park is below Makapuu ("Bulging Eye") Point, a projection of land marking Oahu's easternmost point, and a favorite launching pad for hang gliding. Makapuu is *the* most famous bodysurfing beach in the entire state, but it can be extremely rugged; more people are rescued here than at any other beach on Oahu—except Sandy Beach. In winter the conditions are hazardous, with much of the beach eroded away, leaving exposed rocks. With no interfering reef, the surf can reach 12 feet—perfect for bodysurfing, if you're an expert. Board riding is prohibited. In summer, the sandy beach reappears, and the wave action is much gentler, allowing recreational swimming. There are restrooms, lifeguard towers with a flag warning system, and picnic facilities.

Overlooking Makapuu Beach Park is the lighthouse on Makapuu Point. A moderate hike leads to the top. This lighthouse uses prism glass in its lamp and has been functioning for over 100 years. Bunkers near the top were constructed during WW II and referred to by James Jones in his novel *From Here to Eternity*. They were manned during the war to protect the deep-water Makapuu Bay from possible Japanese attack.

Offshore is **Manana ("Rabbit") Island.** Curiously, it does resemble a rabbit, but it's so named because rabbits actually live on it. They were released there in the 1880s by a local rancher who wanted to raise them but who was aware that if they ever got loose on Oahu they could ruin much of the crop lands. During the impotent counterrevolution of 1894, designed to reinstate the Hawaiian monarchy, Manana Island was a cache for arms and ammunition buried on its windward side. Nearby, and closer into shore, is tiny Kaohikaipu ("Turtle") Island, which, along with Manana and several other islands along this coast, is reserved as a seabird sanctuary. Efforts are being made by the National Audubon Society to attract albatross to this island from nearby Kainuio Marine Corps Air Base. Establishing a colony here would keep these ground-nesting animals away from natural predators like mongoose, cats, and dogs.

Sea Life Park Hawaii

Nestled below the lush Koolau Mountains west of Makapuu Point is Sea Life Park Hawaii, tel. (808) 259-7333 or (800) 767-8046, a cluster of tanks holding an amazing display of marine animals that live freely in the ocean just a few hundred yards away. Admission for adults is $19.95, $15.95 for seniors, juniors 4-12 $9.95, under four free. Open daily 9:30 a.m.-5 p.m. On Friday, the park is open until 10 p.m., so there's plenty of time to see the sights and take in the free Hawaiian concert put on at 8:30 p.m. A free shuttle bus runs from major Waikiki hotels (call 808-955-3474 for details), or take TheBus no. 57 from Ala Moana Center, or no. 58, which comes straight up Kuhio Avenue. The park hosts a variety of shows by trained seals, whales, and dolphins, along with the informative Hawaii Ocean Theater. The park's most impressive feature is the **Hawaiian Reef Tank,** a massive 300,000-gallon fish bowl where guests come face to face with over 2,000 specimens of the island's rich marinelife as they descend three fathoms down an exterior ramp. For a more in-depth and intense exposure to the training and care of dolphins, attend **Splash U,** a one-hour interactive dolphin training session where you're behind the scenes and right there with the trainers. These sessions are held four times a day at 10:45 a.m., noon, 1:45 p.m., and 3:15 p.m., and reservations can be made by calling (808) 973-9825. Attendance costs $49.95

per person in addition to the general park entrance. At **Whaler's Cove,** tall tales and legends of old Hawaii are retold while the park's dolphins cavort using the offshore Rabbit Island as a backdrop. The Whaler's Cove has a replica of a whaling ship called the *Essex Nantucket.* Sea lion food is available, and there are public feedings daily at 11:30 a.m., 1:30 p.m., and 3:30 p.m.

Outside the entrance turnstile is a shopping complex and the new **Sea Lion Cafe.** Here too is the **Pacific Whaling Museum,** free admission, housing one of the largest collections of whaling artifacts and memorabilia in the Pacific. Sea Life Park Hawaii is a great learning and entertaining experience for the entire family, or for anyone interested in exploring Hawaii's fascinating marinelife.

Kaupo Beach Park

This is the first park that you come to along the southeast coast that is safe for swimming. It is between Sea Life Park and Waimanalo. The park is undeveloped and has no lifeguards, so you are advised to exercise caution. The shore is lined with a protective reef or rocks, and the swimming is best beyond the reef. Close to shore, the jutting rocks discourage most swimmers. Surfers frequent Kaupo, especially beginners, lured by the ideal yet gentle waves.

Kaiona Beach Park

Just before you enter the ethnically Hawaiian town of Waimanalo, you pass Kaiona Beach Park, which you can spot because of the semi-permanent tents pitched there. Local people are very fond of the area and use it extensively. Look inland to view some remarkable cliffs and mountains that tumble to the sea. The area was at one time called Pahonu, "Turtle Fence," because a local chief who loved turtle meat erected a large enclosure in the sea into which any turtle that was caught by local fishermen had to be deposited. Parts of the pond fence can still be seen. Facilities include restrooms, showers, and a picnic area. Swimming is safe year-round.

SERVICES

Except for the excellent camping in Waimanalo, you're limited when it comes to accommodations in this area. Only a few B&Bs and rental homes are available.

One of the first places to pick up supplies as you head east on Rt. 72 is at the **Times Super Market** in the **Niu Valley Shopping Center,** located about halfway between Diamond Head and Koko Head. Aside from foodstuffs, you can also get your prescription filled here, pick out flowers for your sweetie, or grab a sandwich for your trip down the highway. In the shopping center is **The Swiss Inn,** tel. (808) 377-5447, an authentic Swiss restaurant where the owner/chef pours love and attention into every dish. The food is superb, well prepared, and reasonably priced for the quality; closed Monday and Tuesday. After your meal, have dessert at **Dave's Ice Cream,** also in the center.

A little less ideal for location and a bit closer to Diamond Head, the **Aina Haina Shopping Center** still has many restaurants, a Foodland Supermarket, two banks, a branch post office, and a gas station. Go in on Hind Drive.

Koko Marina Shopping Center

Located along the highway in Hawaii Kai, this center is the largest and easiest access shopping center that you'll find on the way to Hanauma Bay. For photo supplies and sundries, try **Thrifty Drugs, Ben Franklin's, Clic Photo,** and **Surfside Camera.** There are two banks, a **Waldenbooks, The Bike Shop,** and a satellite city hall for camping permits. **Foodland** provides most supplies for picnics and camping, and you can dine at Chuck's Steak House, McDonald's, Magoo's Pizza, Baskin-Robbins Ice Cream, Sizzler, Kentucky Fried Chicken, Zippy's, Marina Grill, or Kozo Sushi.

Note: For Hawaii Kai's outstanding gourmet option, **Roy's Restaurant,** see "Casual Gourmet" in the Waikiki chapter's "Food" section.

The **Aloha Dive Shop** at the Koko Marina is a full-service dive shop. You can rent or buy snorkeling and scuba gear. So, if you haven't picked up rentals from Waikiki and you're heading out to Hanauma Bay, come here. Dives start at $75 for beginners, featuring all-boat diving at Maunalua Bay, Koko Head, and Diamond Head. Open-water, advanced, and search and rescue certification courses are given for $375. This is the shop of Jackie James, first lady of Hawaiian diving. She's been diving here for more than 25 years.

The Japanese own the Koko Marina Center. In the center are thrill-ride (jet skis, parasails, etc.) booking agencies that will take non-Japanese tourists, but are more for the Japanese tourists who come here by the busload and immediately head out on one of these thrill rides. They've already booked from Japan, so it's all set up and off they go.

Big Sky Parasail, tel. (808) 395-2760, can pull you aloft on a wing (and a prayer) for that parasail ride that you've always dreamed about. Upstairs in the center is **Fun Island Water Sports,** tel. (808) 395-4386, which does parasailing, water trampolines, water slides, jet boats, boogie boards, and kayaks, as well as renting snorkeling gear. Fun Island is a floating barge that's towed out into the water where you can splash away to your heart's content. The price is $39 for the basic activities, or $59 including jet boating and $98 with jet boating and parasailing; parasailing alone is $39. Also on the second floor of the center is **Sea Breeze Water Sports Ltd.,** tel. (808) 396-0100. It offers jet-skiing at $49 for 30 minutes, speedboat rides for the same price and time, and a two-tank scuba dive for $49. Sea Breeze advertises that if you can find a better price anywhere, it will match it.

If you prefer to be pulled across the water behind a boat, try **Suyderhoud Water Ski Center,** tel. (808) 395-3773. They'll take out two people for $49 a half hour or $98 an hour, including skis and a short lesson.

Hawaii Kai Corporate Plaza

For those of you who haven't yet had enough shopping, try **Marshall's Store, Payless Shoes, General Nutrition Center,** or **Costco** in this shopping plaza. To fill your stomach, stop at **Andre's** or **Dave's Ice Cream.**

WAIMANALO

This small rural town was at one time the center of a thriving sugar plantation owned by the *hapa* Hawaiian nobleman, John Cummins, who was responsible for introducing rabbits to Manana Island. It has fallen on hard times ever since the plantation closed in the late 1940s, and now it produces much of Honolulu's bananas, papayas, and anthuriums from small plots and farms. The town sits in the center of Waimanalo Bay, which is the longest (three miles) stretch of sand beach on Oahu. To many people, especially those from Oahu, it is also the best. Few but adequate travelers' services are in town.

The **Olomana Golf Links,** a relatively easy public course, is close to town. It's also a good place to go for breakfast. You think you're in Waimanalo when you pass a 7-Eleven Store and McDonald's in a built-up area, but that isn't it. You keep going about a mile or two and then you'll come to the older section of town which is Waimanalo proper.

BEACHES AND PARKS

Waimanalo County Beach Park

This park provides camping with a county permit. The beach is well protected and the swimming is safe year-round. Snorkeling is good, and there are picnic tables, restrooms, and recreational facilities, including a ball park and basketball courts. The park is right in the built-up beach area, and not secluded from the road. Although the facilities are good, the setting could be better.

Waimanalo Bay State Recreation Area

Just up the road is **Waimanalo Bay State Recreation Area,** which remains largely undeveloped, and is much better situated. The access road is hard to spot, but just after McDonald's look for a tall wire fence with the poorly marked entrance in the center. It is good for picnicking and swimming, which can sometimes be rough. The area, surrounded by a dense ironwood grove, is called "Sherwood Forest," due to many rip-offs by thieves who fancy themselves as Robin Hood, plundering the rich and keeping the loot for themselves. Guess who the rich guys are? Fortunately, this problem of breaking into cars is diminishing, but take necessary precautions. This is the best beach on this section of the island.

For those who enjoy the sport of kings, polo matches are held at 2 p.m. on some Sundays of the year at the polo field in Waimanalo across from Waimanalo Bay State Recreation Area.

Bellows Field Beach County Park

Part of this one-time active Air Force base is now one of Oahu's finest beach parks, and there's camping too! As you enter a sign warns that "This military installation is open to the public only on the following days: weekends—noon Friday to 6 a.m. Monday; federal and state holidays—6 a.m. to 6 a.m. the following day. Camping is authorized in this park by permit from the City and County of Honolulu, Parks and Recreation Board, only." They mean it! The water is safe for swimming year-round, but lifeguards are on duty only during the above-stated hours. Bodysurfing and board surfing are also excellent in the park, but snorkeling is mediocre. Surfboards are not allowed in the area between the two lifeguard towers. After entering the main gates, follow the road for about two miles to the beach area. You'll find picnic tables, restrooms, and cold-water showers. The combination of shade trees and adjacent beach make a perfect camping area. The park is marked by two freshwater streams, Waimanalo and Puha, at either end.

FOOD AND SHOPPING

As you enter Waimanalo, look on the right for a sandwich-board sign painted with a bright red chili pepper that marks the **Bueno Nalo Cafe** at 41865 Kalanianaole Hwy. (next door to Bobby's Market), open daily 11:30 a.m.-9 p.m., tel. (808) 259-7186, which offers a very tasty and inexpensive selection of Mexican food à la Hawaiiana. Hearty *menudo* soup covered in melted cheese is only $4.50 while à la carte tacos, tostadas, tamales, and burritos range $2.75-8.25, and combination dinners are priced

at $9.25-10.25. The desserts are real pleasers as well. No drinks are served but you can bring your own. The service is friendly, the atmosphere relaxed, and the food is *muy bueno.*

A short "mile" past Bueno Nalo is **Mel's Market,** where you can pick up almost all camping supplies. Keep going along the Kalanianaole Hwy. for a mile or so to find **Waimanalo Shopping Center** in the middle of town. Here you can do all your business, pick up lunch and supplies, and head on down the road or go to the beach. In the shopping center is also a **visitor information booth, Woolworth's,** and **Waimanalo Fish Market,** where you can also get plate lunches for about $7.50.

Frankie's Drive-In, at the bottom of the hill, is a local favorite plate lunch drive-in, where you can fill up on teriyaki beef or chicken, fried mahimahi, or hamburger steak along with two big scoops of rice and a whack of mac-salad for under $5. Frankie's is great for takeout that can be enjoyed at one of the nearby beaches. Its specialty is a *lilikoi* milkshake, a true island delight!

Pine Grove Village is an open-air bazaar where local people come to sell handmade products and produce. The majority of items are authentic and priced well below similar products found in Honolulu. Participants and times vary, but a group is usually selling daily until 6 p.m. Some excellent buys include local fruits and vegetables, lei, shellwork, hand-dipped candles, bikinis, jewelry, and leather goods. Price haggling is the norm; when the seller stops smiling, that's about the right price.

Bellows Beach

J.D. BISIGNANI

BRIAN BARDWELL

WINDWARD OAHU

Oahu's windward coast never has to turn a shoulder into a harsh and biting wind. The trades do blow, mightily at times, but always tropical warm, perfumed with flowers, balmy and bright. Honolulu is just 12 miles over the hump of the *pali,* but a world apart. When *kama'aina* families talk of going to "the cottage in the country," they're most likely referring to the windward coast. In the southern parts, the suburban towns of **Kailua** and **Kaneohe** are modern in every way, with the lion's share of the services on this side. Kailua has Oahu's best windsurfing beach and a nearby *heiau,* preserved and unvisited, while Kaneohe sits on a huge bay dotted with islands and reef. The coastal **Kamehameha Highway** (Rt. 83) turns inland to the base of the *pali,* passing the **Valley of the Temples,** resplendent with universal houses of worship. At **Kahaluu** starts a string of beaches running north, offering the full range of Oahu's coastal outdoor experience. You can meander side roads into the mountains near the Hawaiian villages of **Waiahole** and **Waikane,** where the normal way of life is ramshackle cottages on small subsistence farms.

The coast bulges at **Ka'a'awa,** where the **Crouching Lion,** a natural stone formation, seems ready to pounce on the ever-present tour buses that disturb its repose. North is **Sacred Falls State Park,** a short hike to a peak at Oahu's beautiful and natural heart (if it isn't muddy). Suddenly, you're in manicured **Laie** where Hawaii's Mormon community has built a university, a temple perfect in its symmetry, and the **Polynesian Cultural Center,** a sanitized replica of life in the South Seas, Disney style. The northern tip at **Kahuku** is the site of one of Oahu's oldest sugar mills. Just outside of town is the **James Campbell National Wildlife Refuge,** and beyond that **Kahuku Point,** where the North Shore begins.

It makes little difference in which direction you travel the windward coast, but the following will be listed from south to north from Kailua to Kahuku. The slight advantage in traveling this direction is that your car is in the right-hand lane, which is better for coastal views. But, as odd as it may seem, this dynamic stretch totally changes its vistas depending upon the direction that you travel. You can come one way and then retrace your steps, easily convincing yourself that you've never seen it before. The road is clearly marked with mile markers. They decrease as you head north from Kaneohe on Rt. 83, the Kamehameha Highway.

Beaches and Parks
Over a dozen beaches line the 24 miles of the windward coast from Kailua to Kahuku. The majority offer a wide range of water sports and camping. A few offshore islands, refuges for Hawaiian water birds, can be visited and explored. You can walk to these islands during low tide, and even camp there.

KAILUA AND VICINITY

The easiest way into Kailua ("Two Seas") is over the Koolau Range on Rt. 61, the Pali Highway. As soon as you pass through a long tunnel just after the Nuuanu Pali Lookout and your eyes adjust to the shocking brilliance of sunshine, look to your right to see Mt. Olomana. Its 1,643-foot peak is believed to be the volcanic origin of Oahu, the first land to emerge from the seas. Below lies Kailua and the Kawainui swamp, perhaps the oldest inhabited area on this side of the island. Kamehameha I, after conquering Oahu in 1795, gave all this land to his chiefs who had fought for him. The area became a favorite of the ruling *ali'i* until the fall of the monarchy at the turn of this century. The Kawainui Canal drains the marsh and runs through Kailua. A good vantage point from which to observe it is along Kalaheo Ave., the main road running along the coast in Kailua. Kailua is developed with shopping centers, a hospital, and the *best* windsurfing beach in the state. Six golf courses surround the town, and a satellite city hall dispenses **camping permits.**

SIGHTS

A good touring loop is to continue straight on Rt. 61 until it comes to the coast. Turn right onto Kalaheo Road, which takes you along the coast to Kailua Beach Park. In the waters offshore will be a spectacle of windsurfers, with their sails puffed out like the proud chests of multicolored birds. To the left of the beach is **Mokapu ("Sacred Area") Peninsula,** home of the Kaneohe Marine Corps Base, closed to civilians except 1-5 p.m. on Sunday when only certain areas are open. Notice that the rock that separates the peninsula creates a large natural archway navigable by sizable boats. Most of the little islands in the bay are bird sanctuaries. The farthest,

Moku Manu, is home to terns and man-o'-wars, birds famous for leading fishermen to schools of fish. Up on the coastal bluffs is a gray house with a flat roof, the residence of a local woman called the "Birdlady of Kailua." The woman has a reputation for taking care of any sick or injured birds that people bring to her. Her entire home is carved from rock, including the chairs and table. Every once in a while tours are offered to the house for a few dollars. They're irregular, so check the local papers, and you may be lucky enough to be there at just the right time.

A'alapapa Drive gains the heights from the beach and takes you through an area of beautiful homes until you come to **Lanikai Beach.** At one time trees came down to the shoreline, but it has steadily eroded away. The Navy attempted to start a retaining reef by dumping barge loads of white bath tile just offshore. Their efforts were not successful, but many homes in town now have sparkling, new, white-tiled bathrooms! As A'alapapa Drive loops back to town, it changes names to Mokulua; a pulloff here affords an expansive panorama of the bay below. By daytime it's enjoyable, but in the evening local kids come here to hang out and drink beer.

Ulupo Heiau State Monument
Ulupo is dedicated to the Ulu line of *ali'i,* who were responsible for setting up *heiau* involving the sacred births of chiefs. Oftentimes the umbilical cord was cut just as a drum was sounded, then the cord *(piko)* was placed in a shallow rock depression at a *heiau.* This temple, supposedly built by the legendary *menehune,* shows remarkable stone craftsmanship, measuring 140 feet wide and 30 feet high. Atop the temple is a pathway that you can follow. Notice small stones wrapped in ti leaves placed as offerings. The *heiau* overlooks Kawainui marsh. To get there, as you approach Kailua on Rt. 61 look for a red light and a 7-Eleven

store. Turn left onto Uluoa Street, following it to Manu Aloha Street, where you turn right. Follow it to the end and park in the YMCA lot.

BEACHES

Along the shoreline of an exclusive residential area, just south of Kailua, sits **Lanikai Beach.** Three clearly marked rights-of-way run off Mokulua Drive, the main thoroughfare. No facilities, but good snorkeling and swimming year-round, with generally mild surf and a long, gently sloping, sandy beach. The beach runs south for almost a mile, broken by a series of seawalls designed to hold back erosion. Many small craft use the sandy-bottomed shore to launch and land. Popular with local people, but not visited much by tourists.

Kailua Beach Park is the main beach in the area. In the last few years, it has become the windsurfing capital of Hawaii. Local people complain that at one time the beach was great for family outings, with safe conditions and fine facilities. Now the wind has attracted a daily flotilla of windsurfers, kayak racers, and jet-skiers. The congested and contested waters can be dangerous for the average swimmer. Many windsurfers are beginners, so if you're a swimmer, be careful of being run over. The conditions are similar to out-of-control skiers found on the slopes of many mountains. The windsurfing area is clearly marked with buoys, which recently

were moved 100 yards northeastward, making the area larger.

The park boasts a pavilion, picnic facilities, restrooms, showers, lifeguards, a boat ramp, and sometimes a food concession (they come and go). The surf is gentle year-round, and the swimming safe. Children should be careful of the sudden drop-offs in the channels formed by the Kaelepulu Canal as it enters the sea in the middle of the beach park. Good surfing and diving are found around Popoi'a Island just offshore. Follow Rt. 61 through Kailua until it meets the coast, and then turn right on S. Kalaheo Street following it to the beach park.

Kalama Beach is reached by making a left onto N. Kalaheo. This beach has no facilities and is inferior to Kailua Beach Park, but the swimming is good, and sections of the beach have been made off-limits to any surf-riding vehicles.

ACCOMMODATIONS

Most options here are cottages, rental homes, and bed and breakfasts.

One of the finest guest homes in Kailua is **Sharon's Serenity,** tel. (808) 262-5621 or (800) 914-2271. This beautiful property sits on a quiet side street fronting the picturesque Kawainui Canal. Sharon goes out of her way to make you feel comfortable and welcome. The coffee is always fresh-perked. Sharon also takes the time to

Kailua Beach, the windsurfing capital of Oahu

J.D. BISIGNANI

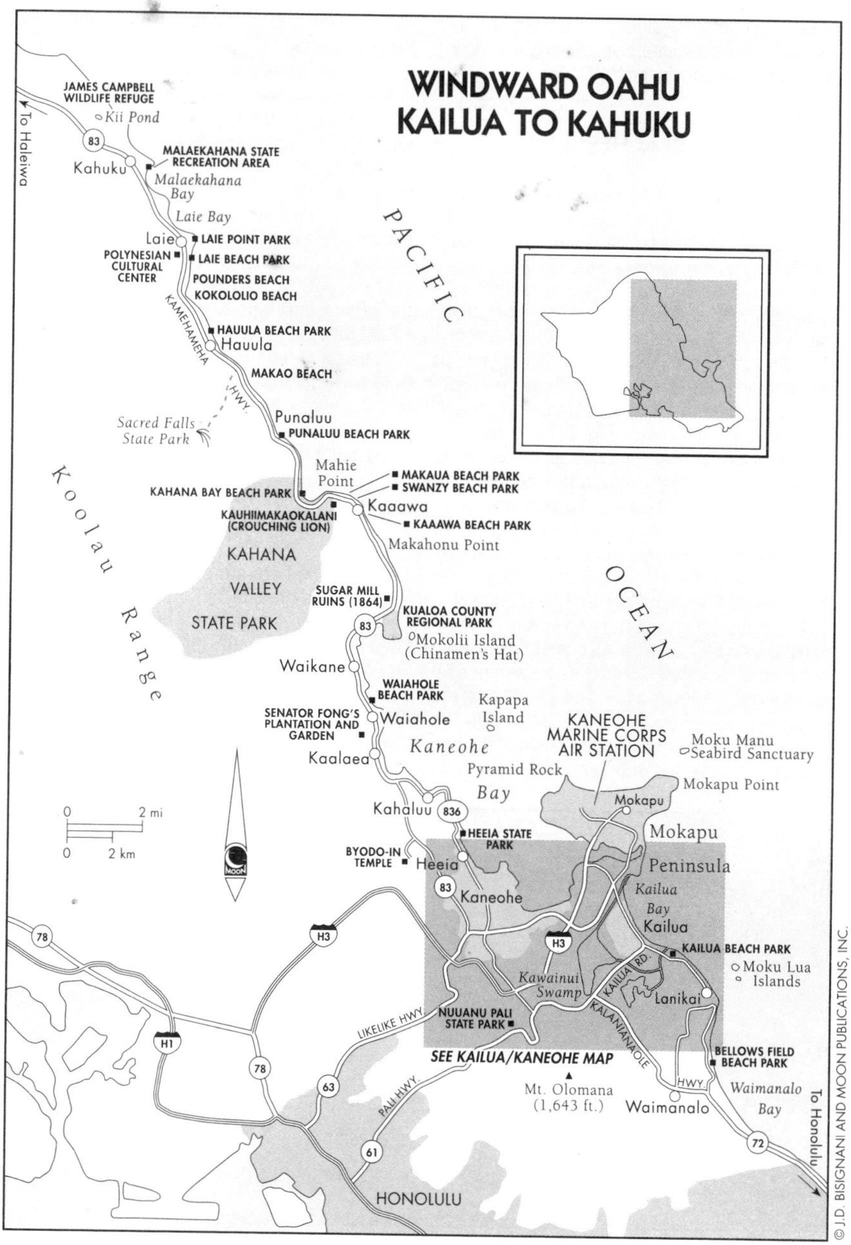

WINDWARD OAHU
KAILUA TO KAHUKU

JAMES CAMPBELL
WILDLIFE REFUGE
Kii Pond
To Haleiwa
Kahuku
MALAEKAHANA STATE
RECREATION AREA
Malaekahana
Bay
Laie Bay
Laie
LAIE POINT PARK
POLYNESIAN
CULTURAL
CENTER
LAIE BEACH PARK
POUNDERS BEACH
KOKOLOLIO BEACH
HAUULA BEACH PARK
Hauula
MAKAO BEACH
Sacred Falls
State Park
Punaluu
PUNALUU BEACH PARK
Mahie
Point
MAKAUA BEACH PARK
SWANZY BEACH PARK
KAHANA BAY BEACH PARK
Kaaawa
KAUHIIMAKAOKALANI
(CROUCHING LION)
KAAAWA BEACH PARK
Makahonu Point
KAHANA
VALLEY
STATE PARK
Koolau Range
SUGAR MILL
RUINS (1864)
KUALOA COUNTY
REGIONAL PARK
Mokolii Island
(Chinamen's Hat)
Waikane
WAIAHOLE
BEACH PARK
SENATOR FONG'S
PLANTATION AND
GARDEN
Waiahole
Kaalaea
Kapapa
Island
Kaneohe
PACIFIC
OCEAN

Moku Manu
Seabird Sanctuary
Mokapu Point
KANEOHE
MARINE CORPS
AIR STATION
Pyramid Rock
Bay
Kahaluu
BYODO-IN
TEMPLE
Heeia
HEEIA STATE
PARK
Mokapu
Mokapu
Peninsula
Kailua
Bay
Kaneohe
Kailua
2 mi
2 km
MOON
78
H3
H1
78
63
61
PALI HWY
LIKELIKE HWY
NUUANU PALI
STATE PARK
Kawainui
Swamp
SEE KAILUA/KANEOHE MAP
HONOLULU
Mt. Olomana
(1,643 ft.)
KAILUA BEACH PARK
Moku Lua
Islands
Lanikai
BELLOWS FIELD
BEACH PARK
Waimanalo
Bay
Waimanalo
72
To Honolulu

© J.D. BISIGNANI AND MOON PUBLICATIONS, INC.

sit with you, giving advice on where to dine, what to see, and a candid description of activities that are worthwhile. She also goes weekly to the People's Market (she'll take you along early Thursday morning) for lovely island blooms including anthuriums, ginger, and heliconia, which she arranges and places throughout the home to add a touch of beauty. The meticulously clean, beautifully appointed home features guest rooms with color TV, Mexican tile throughout, a spacious family room, swimming pool, lanai, and views of the stream, golf course, and mountains beyond. The main guest room has its own attached private bath done in tile and oak cabinetry. In here, the bed is queen-size, and next to it is a comfortable leather recliner with green-shaded reading lamp close at hand. Another bedroom could easily accommodate a family, with a queen-size bed and a twin bed set up like a daybed. It features in-room sliding doors for privacy and its own bath just across the hall. Rates are $55 s, $60-65 d. The price includes a continental breakfast, which Sharon will have waiting in the morning. Sharon's Serenity is an excellent choice for the windward coast, and perfect for getting away from it all.

Kailua Beachside Cottages, tel. (808) 262-4128, fax 261-0893, has 33 separate units in Kailua, ranging in price $60-450 a night. All are fully furnished, and most are close to the water. If you can't find something from this group that meets your needs, you aren't trying.

Pacific Hawaii Bed and Breakfast, tel./fax (808) 486-8838 or (800) 999-6026, or **Affordable Paradise,** tel. (808) 261-1693 or (800) 925-9065, both with offices in Kailua, list private homes in and around town, as well as throughout the state. Rates and homes differ dramatically, but all are guaranteed to be comfortable and accommodating.

FOOD

The **Kailua Shopping Center,** 540 Kailua Road, has a few inexpensive restaurants. One is **Okazu-ya,** just a takeout lunch window, Japanese and Korean style. In the same small complex is **Chef's Grill,** for sandwiches and plate lunches; **Yoshi's,** for Japanese food; and a **Baskin-Robbins** for your sweet tooth.

The **Holiday Food Mart Food Court,** at 345 Hahani Street, has three eateries where you order at a counter and eat outside. **Good Friend**

Chinese Chicken serves plate lunches along with the usual assortment of Chinese dishes. For something a bit heartier, try **Yummy's Korean Barbecue** where you can fill yourself with barbecued short ribs, barbecued chicken, noodle soups, or a combination plate. A good place for a breakfast croissant and a coffee pick-me-up is **Baile,** a French sandwich shop.

Hekili Street Eateries

The 100 block of Hekili Street could be Kailua's mini-version of Honolulu's Restaurant Row. Along this street is **Princess Chop Suey,** your basic chop suey joint. Open Mon.-Sat. 10:30 a.m.-9 p.m., Sunday noon-9 p.m., tel. (808) 839-0575. Naugahyde booths and Formica tables. Everything under $7.95.

Next door is **Sisco's Cantina,** tel. (808) 262-7337, featuring complete Mexican cuisine, open Sun.-Thurs. 11 a.m.-10 p.m., Friday and Saturday 11 a.m.-11 p.m. Tostadas, tacos, burritos, enchiladas, and chiles rellenos are all under $10. More expensive dishes are shrimp Veracruz ($14) and fajitas ($16.25, for two $20.95). All come with Mexican corn, sautéed Tex-Mex mushrooms, and salad. Inside, the south-of-the-border atmosphere is created with hanging piñatas, stucco walls, and blue-tile tables.

A minute down the street is **Detroit Italian Deli,** featuring subs and ice cream.

Around Town

Let the pungent aroma of garlic frying in olive oil lead you to **Assaggio's Ristorante Italiano,** 354 Uluniu St., tel. (808) 261-2772, open Mon.-Fri. for lunch, 11:30 a.m.-2:30 p.m., dinner nightly 5-10 p.m. You are welcomed into a bright and open room done in the striking colors of black, red, teal, and magenta. A wall running down the center of the restaurant separates the bar from the dining room, where tables covered in white linen and black upholstered chairs line the long window area. The typical Italian menu, served with crusty Italian bread, begins with antipasti priced $5.90-9.90, fresh clam scampi at $6.90, and the light and classic prosciutto and melon at $6.90. Soups are pasta fagioli (macaroni and beans, the favorite of Italian contadina), minestrone, tortellini imbrodo (tortellini with ricotta in broth), or vichysoisse served as a cup or bowl, for $1.90 or $2.90. Pasta ranging in price $8-12 includes linguine, fettuccini, and ziti.

Dishes come in two sizes, small (about $2 less) and regular, and are covered in marinara, clam, carbonata, or pesto sauce. Entrees are chicken cacciatore or chicken rolatini, stuffed with ricotta cheese, both at $12.90; baked ziti with eggplant and mozzarella for $9.90; or lasagna for $11.90. Meat dishes are New York steaks, pork chops, or *osso bucco* (veal shanks with onions), all for around $14.90. From the sea comes fresh fish sautéed in garlic oil for $15.90, scallops and shrimp in wine, garlic butter, and snow peas for $17.90, or calamari alla parmigiana at $12.90. Desserts are homemade cheesecake, cannelloni, spumoni, and chocolate mousse all around $4. The full bar serves imported and domestic beers, liquors, coffees, espressos, and plenty of wine varietals.

On a side street near Assaggio's, **Solana** features Mediterranean regional cuisines. Open Mon.-Fri. 5:30-9:30 p.m., until 10:30 Saturday and Sunday; call (808) 263-1227 for reservations. Look for the tiki torches at 30 Aulike Street. Inside are wooden tables, tile floors, and a solarium-like room. To create a feeling of intimacy, you can watch the cook prepare your food in the open kitchen. Try the North African-style seared ahi with white bean and baby artichoke salad and twin pestos as an appetizer for $9.95, or save room for the Moroccan-style osso buco served on a bed of vegetables, with couscous in a tomato and veal sauce with blonde raisins and kalamata olives for $17.50. That's Mediterranean! The grilled, marinated lamb at $24.50 is the most expensive item on the menu, but most entrees are under $18. As wonderful as the main dishes are the appetizers and soups. It's casual gourmet and the service is excellent. Give it a try.

El Charro Avitia, 14 Oneawa St., tel. (808) 263-3943, open daily for lunch and dinner, is a better than average Mexican restaurant. Simple yet tasteful, the south-of-the-border inspired decor is achieved with adobe-like arches, wooden tables, Mexican ceramics placed here and there, and plenty of cacti and hanging plants. The menu features combination dinners of burritos, chili verde, enchiladas, or tacos, all priced under $12. The specialty of the house is the flame-broiled catch of the day at $14.50. Other entrees include fish Veracruzana, as good as you'll find anywhere, carne asada, or *camarones al mojo de ajo* (jumbo shrimp sautéed in butter, garlic, and white wine), all for under $15, and

all served with rice, black beans, fresh vegetables, and a fresh fruit garnish. Less expensive dishes are chimichangas, burritos, taco salad, and Mexican pizza, which is two deep-fried tortillas topped with cheddar cheese, jack cheese, beans, tomatoes, olives, and lettuce, all around $9. Huevos Mexicana, rancheros, and revueltos, served throughout the day, are $8.50. The bar mixes mean margaritas, which come in normal sizes up to a fiesta 40-ounce that will definitely have you yelling *olé!* El Charro Avitia is definitely worth the money!

Just up Oneawa St. is **Ching Lee Chop Suey,** a down-home, inexpensive Chinese restaurant where you can have a complete meal for under $5.

Buzz's Original Steakhouse, at 413 Kawailoa Road, tel. (808) 261-4661, is really *the* original steakhouse of this small island chain owned by the Schneider family. Buzz's is just across the road from Kailua Beach Park, situated along the canal. This restaurant is an institution with local families. It's the kind of place that "if you can't think of where to go, you head for Buzz's." The food is always good, if not extraordinary. It has top sirloin ($14.95), pork chops ($13.95), chicken teri ($11.75), fresh fish (usually about $18), and mahimahi ($12.95). Salad bar is included with all entrees, and separately for $7.95. Everything is charbroiled. Remember, no credit cards.

Saeng's Thai Cuisine, at 315 Hahani, tel. (808) 263-9727, open Sat.-Sun. 5-9:30 p.m., Mon.-Fri. 11 a.m.-2:30 p.m. and again 5-9:30 p.m., offers spicy Thai food with an emphasis on vegetarian meals. Appetizers and starters are Thai crisp noodles ($5.25), sautéed shrimp ($9.95), salads like green papaya salad ($5.25), *yum koong* (shrimp salad, $7.95), and chicken coconut soup ($6.95). Specialties include spicy stuffed calimari $9.95, Thai red curry ($7.95), and à la carte beef, pork, and chicken dishes, all under $8. Vegetarians can pick from mixed veggies with yellow bean paste ($5.95), mixed veggies with oyster sauce ($5.95), or zucchini tofu ($5.95). Saeng Thai is a good change of pace at a decent price.

Harry's Cafe and Deli, tel. (808) 261-2120, 629 Kailua Road, is open Mon.-Sat. 11 a.m.-3 p.m. and 5:30-9 p.m. Owned and operated by Tim Owens, son of songwriter and radio personality Harry Owens, this casual place is decorated with a strong Hawaiian flavor, including some sheet music covers from the '30s, when

Harry penned the famous song "Sweet Leilani." It was Harry, along with Webley Edwards, who inaugurated the radio broadcast Hawaii Calls in 1935, introducing millions of Americans to the sweet sounds of island music during the bleak days of the Depression. The lunch menu strongly favors sandwiches like the club sandwich at $5.50, Reuben at $6.50, and the veggie avocado at $4.50. Also try the soups and salads or the daily special, like the pita pocket filled with curried turkey salad, cucumber slices, sprouts, and onions for $7.50. The dinner menu is a bit more substantial yet very reasonably priced. Choose between such items as fettuccini and sautéed chicken with basil, pesto, and cream for $9.95, or black tiger shrimp for $11.95.

Family-run **Brent's Restaurant and Delicatessen,** next to Harry's, tel. (808) 262-8588, is a slice of New York in paradise. Choose sausage, corned beef, lox, or cheese from the deli case or order a lunch sandwich off the menu. Hearty breakfasts are also served as are à la carte dinners. All items are reasonably priced. Brent's is open daily except Monday 7 a.m.-9 p.m., until 8 p.m. on Sunday.

At the Enchanted Lake Shopping Center is **Yen Yen Chinese Restaurant,** tel. (808) 262-2218, a friendly and inexpensive place to stop for the food, not necessarily for the decor. One of the favorite dishes is prawns with walnuts at $7.50. Vegetarian dishes run $5-6, rice and noodle dishes around $7, and most other main dishes under $10. Appetizers and soups fill out the rest of the menu.

Uluniu Street: Inexpensive Dining

Uluniu Street has inexpensive places to eat, one after the other. After making a left from Kuulei Road (Rt. 61) onto Oneawa, a main thoroughfare, turn right onto Uluniu just at the large Kailua Furniture. First is an authentic but very basic hole-in-the-wall Japanese restaurant, **Kailua Okazuya.** It specializes in *donburi,* a bowl of rice smothered with various savories. Try the *o yakodon buri,* chicken and egg with vegetables over rice for under $4. It serves plate lunches and a sushi special that can't be beat, which includes fresh fish, shrimp, abalone, and octopus for only $5! Next door is **Kolohe Hawaiian Restaurant,** and up the street is the **New Chinese Garden,** a basic Chinese restaurant with decent prices. None of these restaurants is re-markable, but all will fill you up with good enough food for a very reasonable price.

Health Foods

A well-established health food store in Kailua is **The Source,** tel. (808) 262-5604, at 32 Kainehe Street. This place has vitamins and minerals, bulk foods, some organic fresh produce, cosmetics and hygiene products, as well as lots of essences, oils, and natural healing products to help with whatever ails you and to keep you on the straight and narrow. Fresh juices are available from the juice bar, and from the food bar, you can order organic burgers, salads, homemade soups, sushi, smoothies, and the like at very reasonable prices. The food bar is open Mon.-Fri. 10 a.m.-8 p.m., Saturday and Sunday 10 a.m.-4 p.m.

For a little pick-me-up, try **Agnes Bake Shop** across the street for Portuguese-based *malasadas* and *pao dolce,* or soup, salad, cappuccino, or espresso.

SHOPPING

The two towns of Kailua and Kaneohe have the lion's share of shopping on the windward coast. You can pick up basics in the small towns as you head up the coast, but for any unique or hard-to-find items, Kailua/Kaneohe is your only bet. The area offers a few shopping centers. The **Windward Mall,** at 46-056 Kamehameha Hwy., Kaneohe, tel. (808) 235-1143, open weekdays 9:30 a.m.-9 p.m., Saturday to 5:30 p.m., Sunday 10 a.m.-5 p.m., is the premier, full-service mall on the windward coast. Besides department stores like Liberty House and Sears, there are shops selling everything from shoes to health foods.

The **Kaneohe Bay Mall** across from the Windward Mall is a little more down-home, and features a Longs Drugs, especially good for photo supplies. The **Aikahi Park Shopping Center** along Kaneohe Bay Dr., at the corner of Mokapu Blvd., is a limited shopping center whose main shops are a Safeway and a Sizzler Restaurant. The **Kailua Shopping Center,** at 540 Kailua Road, also has limited shopping that includes a **Time's Supermarket,** open till 10 p.m., and a well-stocked **Honolulu Bookshop,** tel. (808) 261-1996, open Mon.-Fri. 9:30-9, Saturday 9:30-5:30, Sunday till 5 p.m., for a full range of reading material. There's also a **Cornet Store** along Kailua Ave. for sundries, lotions, and notions, and a **Longs Drugs.** You never know what kind of treasure lurks at a thrift shop, so have a look at the **Salvation Army Thrift Store** on Uluniu St. to see what kind of bargain you can find.

You'll find just about anything at **Holiday Mart** on Hahani Road., or picnic supplies, beach accessories, or cappuccino at the upgraded landmark **Kalapawai Market,** at the corner of Kailua and Kalaheo roads, which marks the best entrance to Kailua's windsurfing beaches.

Thursday mornings bring a **farmers' market** into town for only one hour, 8:50-9:50 a.m. Those in the know arrive early to get a number at their favorite stalls, which can sell out within minutes of opening. Great for fresh flowers and fruits.

You might pick up an heirloom at **Heritage Antiques,** at the corner of Kailua Road and Amakua St., tel. (808) 261-8700, open daily 10 a.m.-5:30 p.m., which is overflowing with Asian, Hawaiian, and Americana antiques. Here too are **jewelers,** H.W. Roberts and J.K. Phillips, who also specialize as gemologists. **The Hunter Antiques,** across the street from Heritage Antiques, specializes in Depression glass.

Island Treasures, 629 Kailua Road, tel. (808) 261-8131, is a relatively new art gallery in Kailua. Owned and operated by Debbie Costello, who comes from a family of artists, the shop is open daily 10 a.m.-6:30 p.m. Debbie, an artist in her own right, does the beautiful stained glass pieces in the shop. Other artists she represents are John Costello, who does fantasy scenes in acrylics and pastels; Tom Cohen, a master with jewelry, precious stones, and crystals; potters Jerry Meek and Stephen Hatland; Bud Morrison, who works bamboo into objects emanating a Japanese feel; bronze artist Holly Young; Teri Inouye, who renders the flora of Hawaii in colored pencils; and photographer Randy Braun.

SERVICES

Campers can reach the **satellite city hall,** 1090 Keolu Dr., for information and permits by calling (808) 261-8575. A **post office** is at the corner of Kailua and Hahani, just across from the Hawaiian National Bank. Medical aid is available from **Castle Medical Center,** tel. (808) 263-5500.

KANEOHE AND VICINITY

The bedroom community of Kaneohe ("Kane's Bamboo") lies along Kaneohe Bay, protected by a huge barrier reef. Around the edge of the bay lie six of the original 30 fishponds that once graced this fine shore. A lush, fertile land of bountiful farms, Kaneohe was the second most populous area on the island. Through the years, the major crops of this coastal town have shifted from taro to rice, sugarcane, pineapples, and bananas, but today a variety is still grown.

Where Rt. 83 intersects the Likelike Highway on the southern outskirts of Kaneohe, it branches north and changes its name from the Kamehameha Highway to the Kahekili Highway until it hits the coast at Kahaluu. This four-mile traverse passes two exceptionally beautiful valleys: Haiku Valley and the Valley of the Temples. Neither should be missed.

Within the town is **Ho'omaluhia Botanical Garden,** 45-680 Luluku Road, Kaneohe, tel. (808) 233-7323, so large that guided hikes are offered on a daily basis. This garden is one

component of the Hawaiian Botanical Garden system. A 400-acre tract, it includes a 32-acre lake, a dammed reservoir that's part of the flood control for Kaneohe. Day-use and overnight facilities are available, horseback riding is permitted, and walking, jogging, and bicycling are encouraged. Guided nature walks are given 10 a.m. on Saturday, 1 p.m. on Sunday, and Hawaiian plant use walks are run daily 10 a.m.-noon.

Offshore is Moku o' Loe, commonly called **Coconut Island.** It became famous as the opening shot in the TV show "Gilligan's Island," although the series itself was shot in California. In ancient times, it was *kapu* and during WW II served as an R&R camp for B-29 crews. Many of the crews felt the island had bad vibes, and reported having a streak of bad luck. In recent times, Frank Fasi, Honolulu's former mayor, suggested that Hawaii's gate-crashing guests, Ferdinand and Imelda Marcos, should lease Coconut Island. It never happened.

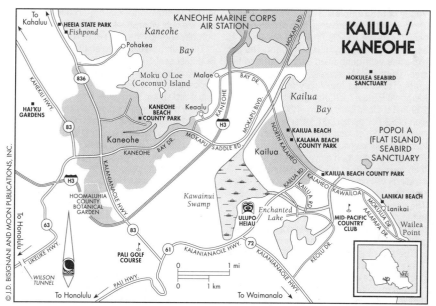

A sandbar has been building in the center of Kaneohe Bay that has made a perfect anchorage for yachts and powerboats. These boat people drop anchor, jump off, and wade to the bar through waist-deep, clear waters. It has become an unofficial playground where you can fling a Frisbee, drink beer, fly a kite, or just float around. Part of the sandbar rises above the water and some barbecue chefs even bring their hibachis and have a bite to eat. Surrounding you is Kaneohe Bay with Chinaman's Hat floating off to your right, and a perfect view of the *pali* straight ahead. The epitome of la dolce vita, Hawaiian style. Fortunately, in recent years, the once crystal-clear bay, which was becoming murky with silt because of development, is clearing again due to conservation efforts.

For a fun-filled day on the water, far from the crowds of Waikiki, try **North Bay Aquatics** located on the grounds of Schrader's Windward Marine Resort, 47-039 Lihikai Dr., Kaneohe, tel. (808) 239-5711. A boat ($10) runs from the resort property to the sandbar on Tuesday and Saturday, where you can swim, snorkel, kayak, or hydrobike to your heart's content. Departure times depend on the tides, so call a day in advance.

Ha'iku Gardens

Ha'iku ("Abrupt Break") Gardens is a lovely section of a commercial area that includes a restaurant and some quiet condominiums. After you pass a community college, Haiku Road is past two red lights. Turn left and proceed for about one-half mile until you see the entrance. The gardens date from the mid-1800s, when Hawaiian *ali'i* deeded 16 acres to an English engineer named Baskerville. He developed the area, creating a series of spring-fed lily ponds, a number of estate homes, and planting flowers, fruits, and ornamental trees. Later a restaurant was built, and the grounds became famous for their beauty, often used for outdoor weddings and special gatherings.

You're welcome to walk through the gardens. Proceed from the restaurant down a grassy area to a pond, where perhaps you'll attract an impromptu entourage of ducks, chickens, and guinea fowl that squawk along looking for handouts. Amidst the lush foliage is a grass shack used for weddings. A path leads around a larger pond whose benches and small pavilions are perfect for contemplation. The path leads under a huge banyan, while a nearby bamboo grove serenades with sonorous music if the wind is blowing.

Valley of the Temples

The concept of this universal faith cemetery is as beautiful as the sculpted *pali* that serves as its backdrop. A rainy day makes it better. The *pali* explodes with rainbowed waterfalls, and the greens turn a richer emerald, sparkling with dewdrops. Don't miss the Valley of the Temples Memorial Park, 47-200 Kahekili Hwy., tel. (808) 239-8811. Open daily 8 a.m.-4:30 p.m.; admission is $2 per person, $1 for seniors and children under 12, or *kama'aina* rates of $5 per carload, but you have to prove you're from Hawaii. Admission is charged only until 4:30 p.m. After that, you can walk in to see the grounds, but the buildings will not be open. High on a hill sits a Christian chapel, an A-frame topped by a cross. The views can be lovely from up here, but unfortunately the large windows of the chapel perfectly frame some nondescript tract housing and a supermarket below. Great planning!

The crown jewel of the valley is **Byodo-In Temple** ("Temple of Equality"), a superbly appointed replica of the 900-year-old Byodo-In of Uji, Japan (depicted on the 10-yen coin). This temple dates from June 7, 1968, 100 years to the day when Japanese immigrants first arrived in Hawaii. It was erected through the combined efforts of an American engineering firm headed by Ronald Kawahara in accordance with a plan designed by Kiichi Sano, a famed Kyoto landscape artist. Remove your shoes before entering the temple. A three-ton brass bell, which you're invited to strike after making an offering, creates the right vibrations for meditation, and symbolically spreads the word of Amida Buddha.

The walls hold distinctive emblems of different Buddhist sects. Upstairs wings are roped off, with no entry permitted. Stand on the gravel path opposite the main temple. You'll see a grating with a circle cut in the middle. Stick your face in to see the perfectly framed contemplative visage of Buddha. Cross a half-moon bridge to the left of the temple and follow the path to a small gazebo. Here a rock, perfectly and artistically placed, separates a stream in two, sending the water to the left and right. The pagoda at the top of the path is called the Meditation House. Go to this superbly manicured area to get a sweeping view of the grounds. In front of the Meditation House is a curious tree; pick up one of the fallen leaves, and feel the natural velvet on the backside.

The grounds are alive with sparrows and peacocks, and from time to time you'll hear a curious-sounding "yip, yip, yip" and clapping hands. Follow it to discover Mr. Henry Oda, who, with crumbs in his fingers, feeds a boiling cauldron of koi in the waters below with mouths agape demanding to be fed. He mostly feeds the fish while Mr. Hisayoshi Hirada, the original "Birdman of Byodo-In," feeds the birds. Mr. Hirada translates his first name into "long live a good man," and he, in his 80s, is living proof. Mr. Hirada began training the birds and carp of Byodo-In after his *first* retirement. He would come daily to feed the fish,

Byodo-In Temple

J.D. BISIGNANI

clapping his hands while he did so. Soon the Pavlovian response took over. Simultaneously, a small and courageous bird, which Hirada-san calls Charlie, began taking crumbs from his fingers. After that, all the birds wanted some. Mr. Oda does a great job of showing visitors around. Mr. Hirada is also there most days, and if you happen to meet him while you're visiting, you have been blessed by the great Buddha of Byodo-In.

A small gift shop selling souvenirs, cards, film, and some refreshments is to the right of the temple. If you wish to photograph the complex, it's best to come before noon, when the sun is at your back as you frame the red and white temple against the deep green of the *pali*.

BEACHES

Kaneohe Bay offers Kaneohe Beach Park, Heeia State Park, and Laenani Beach Park, all accessible off Rt. 836 as it heads northward along the coast. All are better for the views of Kaneohe Bay than for beach activities. They have restrooms and a few picnic tables. The water is safe year-round, but it's murky and lined with mudflats and coral heads. The same conditions hold true for **Waiahole Beach Park** about four miles north, but this area is much less developed, quieter, and good for beachcombing.

Heeia State Park lies along Rt. 836 between Kaneohe and Kahaluu and is designated as an "interpretive park." It sits high on Kealohi Point overlooking Heeia Fishpond below. Kealohi translates as "The Shining," because it was a visible landmark to passing voyagers, but there is a much deeper interpretation. To the Hawaiians this area was a "jumping-off point into the spirit world." It was believed that the souls of the recently departed came to this point and leapt into eternity. The right side, Heeia-kei, was the side of light, while the left side, Heeia-uli, was the domain of darkness. The wise *kahuna* taught that you could actually see the face of God in the brilliant sun as it rises over the point.

On the grounds are a main hall, pavilion, restrooms, and various short walks around the entire area with magnificent views of Kaneohe Bay. The park contains numerous indigenous plants and mature trees, the perfect laboratory for the educational goals set by The Friends of Heeia State Park. As an interpretive park, programs are offered for the community and visitors alike. Bernadette Lono, the Director of Hawaiian Studies, gives personal tours of the area. Her family has been part of this *ahuapua* (ancient land division) for countless generations. Bernadette first acquaints you with the area by asking you to sit Hawaiian style on the grass. The earth or *aina* is fundamental to the Hawaiian belief system, and you should start connected to it. She goes on to explain the symbiotic relationship between inland farmers whose fields stretched to Eolaka, the top of the *pali*, and the fishermen who plied the waters of Mokapu on the other side of the peninsula.

Below, Heeia Fishpond is now privately owned by a Mr. Brooks, who has taken over the management of the pond from the Bishop Estates on a 20-year lease. He will raise mullet *(ama)*, the traditional fish raised by the ancient Hawaiians and *kapu* to all except the *ali'i*.

ACCOMMODATIONS AND FOOD

The **Schrader's Windward Marine Resort** in Kaneohe has been operating for years. It's a hodgepodge of a place, a "cottage hotel," with some fully furnished units and others with kitchenettes. There are some separate units along the bay, while others are quite nondescript. A swimming pool, laundry, and barbecue pit are on the premises, and maid service is offered every third day. Rates run about $50-190, but a room/car/activity package is also an option. For information contact Schrader's Windward Marine Resort, 47-039 Lihikai Dr., Kaneohe, HI 96744, tel. (808) 239-5711 or (800) 735-5711.

On a little simpler scale is **Camp Kokokahi,** located at the pier, at 47-035 Kaneohe Bay Dr., tel. (808) 247-2124, e-mail: kokokahi@gte.net, with private and semiprivate cottages and camping. Rates are $20 single, $15 double or a bunk, and $8 tent. Amenities include barbecue and laundry facilities.

Fortunately, or unfortunately, Kaneohe is a bit of a wasteland as far as tourist services, nightlife, and eating out are concerned. Most people who live here head for the action in Honolulu. There are a few limited choices. **Fuji's Delicatessen,** at 45-270 Wm. Henry Road, tel. (808) 235-3690, is a local favorite known for its down-home Japanese, Korean, and Hawaiian cooking served family style on long communal tables.

The best cheap deal in town is at **Kim Chee One,** at 46-010 Kamehameha Hwy., tel. (808) 235-5560, which has a few sister restaurants scattered around Oahu. The setting is plain, but you'll have trouble finishing the excellent Korean mixed barbecued plate for $6.95, easily enough for two.

The **Chart House at Ha'iku Gardens,** true to its name, sits surrounded by a fragrant garden in a lovely, secluded valley. It's considered one of the most beautiful places on Oahu, and people still come here to be married. The restaurant is part of a small island chain with an excellent reputation for good food. Most entrees are in the $19-25 range, so it's not inexpensive. A variety of appetizers, soups, and salads start the meal, after which you can choose entrees including teriyaki chicken breast for $16.50 and salmon or a combination top sirloin and shrimp for $22.95. The house specialty is a thick cut of prime rib that goes for $21.95. Sit back and relax over a pie, drinks, coffee, or tea while enjoying the lighted evening garden before leaving. On Sunday evening, the local classical and slack key guitar player Ellsworth Simeona provides the entertainment. Open Mon.-Thurs. 5:30-9 p.m., Fri.-Sat. 5-10 p.m., and Sunday 5-9 p.m.; call (808) 247-6671 for reservations.

NORTH KANEOHE BAY

KAHALUU

This town is at the convergence of the Kahekili Highway and the Kamehameha Highway (Rt. 83) heading north. Also, Rt. 836, an extension of the Kamehameha Highway, hugs the coastline heading down to Kailua/Kaneohe. It offers some of the most spectacular views of a decidedly spectacular coast, with very few tourists venturing down this side road. Kahaluu Town is a gas station and a little tourist trap selling junk just in case you didn't get enough in Waikiki. The Hygienic store sells liquor, groceries, soda, and ice, all you'll need for an afternoon lunch. The Waihee Stream, meandering from the *pali,* empties into the bay and deposits fresh water into the ancient **Kahaluu Fish Pond,** a picture-perfect tropical setting. So picture-perfect is the place that it has provided the background scenery to TV and Hollywood productions such as an episode from "Jake and the Fat Man," a setting for *Parent Trap II,* and the famous airport and village scene from *The Karate Kid II.* All of the movie sets have been torn down, but you can still overlook the fishpond by taking a short walk just behind the bank in town.

Senator Fong's Plantation and Gardens

Senator Fong's Plantation and Gardens, 47-285 Pulama Road, Kaneohe, HI 96744 (in Kahaluu), tel. (808) 239-6775, is open daily 10 a.m.-4 p.m.,

except Christmas and New Year's Day. Admission is $10 adults, $8 seniors, and $6 children 5-12. Guided tram tours run at 10:30 a.m., 11:30 a.m., 1 p.m., 2 p.m., and 3 p.m. One of Hawaii's newest attractions, the plantation is a labor of love created by Senator Hiram Fong, who served as state senator 1959-77. Upon retirement he returned to his home and ever since has been beautifying the gardens he started over 40 years ago. The result is 725 acres of natural beauty rising from 80 feet in elevation to 2,600 feet at the ridge of the Koolau Range above. The gardens preserve the native flora and fauna of the land, along with planted flower and fruit gardens, and groves of trees, palms, bushes, and ferns. When you first arrive, there is a large open-air pavilion housing a snack window serving sandwiches, plate lunches, and saimin. Inside is also a small but well-appointed souvenir shop where you can get everything from aloha shirts to postcards. Notice a table set with baskets of flowers where you can make your own keepsake lei for $6.50. **Horseback rides** are also given at $34 an hour; make reservations by calling Aloma Trail Rides at (808) 293-7857.

WAIAHOLE AND WAIKANE

If you want to fall in love with rural, old-time Oahu, go to the northern reaches of Kaneohe Bay around Waiahole and Waikane, a Hawaiian grassroots area that has so far eluded development. Alongside the road are many more fruit stands than in other parts of Oahu. For a glimpse of what's happening look for the Waiahole Elementary School, and turn left up Waiahole Valley Road. The road twists its way into the valley, becoming narrower until it turns into a dirt track. Left and right in homey, ramshackle houses lives down-home Hawaii, complete with taro patches in the back yards. Another road of the same type is about one-half mile up Rt. 83 just before you enter Waikane. If you're staying in Waikiki, compare this area with Kuhio Avenue only 45 minutes away!

Route 83 passes a string of beaches, most with camping. Offshore from Kualoa County Park is Mokolii ("Small Reptile") Island, commonly called **Chinaman's Hat** (between mile marker 30 and 31) due to its obvious resemblance to an Oriental chapeau. Kualoa Park has undergone extensive renovations. There is an expansive parking area, plenty of picnic tables, and a huge grassy area fronting the beach. The road passes through what was once sugarcane country. Most of the businesses failed last century, but you will see the ruins of the Judd Sugar Works a mile or so before reaching Ka'a'awa. The dilapidated mill stands although it was closed more than a century ago. Entering is not advised!

Kualoa County Regional Park
With the *pali* in the background, Chinaman's Hat Island offshore, and a glistening white strand shaded by swaying palms, Kualoa is one of the finest beach parks on windward Oahu. One of the most sacred areas on Oahu, the *ali'i* brought their children here to be reared and educated, and the area is designated in the National Register of Historic Places. It has a full range of facilities and services, including lifeguards, restrooms, and picnic tables. The park is open daily 7 a.m.-7 p.m., with overnight camping allowed with a county permit (mandatory). The swimming is safe year-round along a shoreline dotted with pockets of sand and coral. The snorkeling and fishing are good, but the real treat is walking the 500 yards to Chinaman's Hat at low tide. You need appropriate footgear (old sneakers are fine) because of the sharp coral heads. The island is one of the few around offshore Oahu that is not an official bird sanctuary, although many shorebirds do use the island and should not be molested.

Because of its exposure to winds, Kualoa is sometimes chilly. Although the park is popular, it is not well marked. It lies along Rt. 83, and if you're heading north, look for a red sign to the Kualoa Ranch. Just past it is an HVB Warrior pointing to the park and Chinaman's Hat. Heading south the entrance is just past the HVB Warrior pointing to the Kualoa Sugar Mill ruins.

Kualoa Ranch and Activity Club
The Kualoa Ranch, P.O. Box 650, Ka'a'awa, HI 96730, tel. (808) 237-7321 or (800) 231-7321, offers three organized, pre-packaged, outdoor ac-

J.D. BISIGNANI

Chinaman's Hat

tivity tours. Your choice of activities includes horseback riding, jet ski rides, ATV dune cycle rides, gun range firing, tennis, snorkeling, a helicopter ride, and a trolley ride. Other games, a petting zoo, and Hawaiian exhibits are also available. The Activity Adventure Tour runs $99 for adults, $65 for children 2-11 and includes a full-day pass for up to four activities except the helicopter ride. With the Secret Island and Activity Tour, you get a half day and two activities at the ranch and a half day at the island for water sports. Rates run $79 for adults and $52 for children 2-11. With both these tours, a helicopter ride may be purchased separately for $39 per person. For $69 adult and $45 for children 2-11, the Secret Island and Snorkel Tour gets you a full-day pass at the ranch island for snorkeling and other water activities. For some activities, there are stipulations for the age of participant and adult accompaniment. A balanced, filling buffet lunch and free transportation from various Waikiki hotels are provided with all tours. First pickup is at 7:30 a.m. and tours last eight hours. Kualoa Ranch is open Mon.-Fri. for the ranch activities tours and Mon.-Sat. for the Secret Island and Snorkel tour; closed on national holidays. Call for reservations.

Food and Shopping

Kahaluu Sportswear, at 47-102-A1 Wailehua Road, is a garment factory outlet store that sells inexpensive alohawear. Some is made from unbearable and unwearable polyester, but a great deal are made from cotton or rayon. Prices are about 10-20% cheaper than what you'll find in the malls, or city area.

The **Hygienic Store** along Rt. 83 just past the Valley of the Temples sells groceries and supplies. It's flanked by stalls selling fruits and shellwork at competitive prices. Although they may not always be around, look for little trucks parked along the road near the Hygienic Store selling hot *ono laulau,* which are snacks that come out of the *imu* oven.

Follow the Kahekili Hwy. to Rt. 83 past Waiahole and Waikane, where you'll find some of the best roadside fruit stands on Oahu. One is located just near the Waiahole Elementary School (mile marker 34.5), and another just a few minutes north along Rt. 83 has cold drinking coconuts. Do yourself a favor and have one. Sip the juice, and when it's gone, eat the custardlike contents. A real island treat, nutritious and delicious.

KA'A'AWA TOWN AND VICINITY

SIGHTS AND BEACHES

When you first zip along the highway through town you get the impression that there isn't much, but there's more than you think. The town stretches back toward the *pali* for a couple of streets. On the ocean side is **Ka'a'awa Beach Park,** a primarily local hangout. Across the road is the post office, and the **Ka'a'awa Country Kitchen,** which serves breakfast and plate lunches, where you can easily eat for $5. It has a few tables, but the best bet is to get your plate lunch and take it across the street to the beach park. Next door is a **7-Eleven** with gas and incidentals. Behind the post office is **Pyramid Rock,** obviously named because of its shape.

Oahu's *pali* is unsurpassed anywhere in the islands, and it's particularly beautiful here. Take a walk around. Stroll the dirt roads through the residential areas and keep your eyes peeled for a small white cross on the *pali* just near Pyramid Rock. It marks the spot where a serviceman was killed during the Pearl Harbor invasion. His spirit is still honored by the perpetually maintained bright white cross. While walking you'll be treated to Ka'a'awa's natural choir—wild roosters crowing any time they feel like it, and the din of cheeky parrots high in the trees. A pair of parrots escaped from a nearby home about 10 years ago, and their progeny continue to relish life in the balmy tropics.

As you come around the bend of Mahie Point, staring down at you is a very popular stone formation, the **Crouching Lion.** Undoubtedly a tour bus or two will be sitting in the lot of the Crouching Lion Inn. As with all anatomical rock formations, it helps to have an imagination. Anyway, the inn is much more interesting than the lion. Built by George Larsen in 1928 from rough-hewn lumber from the Pacific Northwest, the huge stones were excavated from the site itself. The inn went public in 1951 and has been serving tourists ever since.

Three beach parks in as many miles lie between Ka'a'awa Point and Kahana Bay. The first heading north is **Ka'a'awa Beach County Park,** a popular beach with restrooms, lifeguards, and picnic facilities. An offshore reef running the entire length of the park makes swimming safe year-round. There's a dangerous rip at the south end of the park at the break in the reef.

Swanzy Beach County Park, two minutes north, has camping with a county permit—weekends only. The sand and rubble beach lies below a long retaining wall, often underwater during high tide. The swimming is safe year-round, but is not favorable because of the poor quality of the beach. Swanzy is one of the best squidding and snorkeling beaches on the windward coast. A break in the offshore reef creates a dangerous rip and should be avoided.

Kahana Bay Beach Park is a full-service park with lifeguards, picnic facilities, restrooms, and the area's only boat launch. Camping is allowed with state permit at the beach. Swimming is good year-round, although the waters can be cloudy at times. A gentle shorebreak makes the area ideal for bodysurfing and beginner board riders. This entire beach area is traditionally excellent for *akule* fishing, with large schools visiting the offshore waters at certain times of year. It once supported a large Hawaiian fishing village; remnants of fishponds can still be seen.

Running up the valley from Kahana Beach is **Kahana Valley State Park.** Few visit here, and it's perfectly situated for a quiet picnic under the coconut trees. Or to stretch your legs, you can follow the trail about five miles along the stream up the valley.

Huilua Fish Pond lies outside the park boundary. Look to the mountainside for Trout Farm Road and immediately to your right, on the ocean side, is the fishpond. Spot a small bridge and a great launching area for a canoe, kayak, or flotation device. Once in, go left under the traffic bridge. Follow Kahana Stream as it gets narrower and narrower (but passable) as it heads inland. You can even use the overhanging ferns to pull yourself along. It's deep so be aware. If you go to the right, you'll reach the bay. It's fairly safe until you come to open ocean. TheBus stop is directly across from the launching area so you can get off here, enjoy the sights, and then continue on.

PRACTICALITIES

Crouching Lion Inn

There was a time when *everyone* passing through Ka'a'awa stopped at the Crouching Lion Inn. Built in 1926, it was the only place *to* stop for many, many years. The inn has seen its ups and downs, and now, fortunately, it is under new management and on the upswing again. The inn, along Rt. 83 in Ka'a'awa, tel. (808) 237-8511, open daily for lunch 11 a.m.-3:30 p.m., and for dinner 5-9 p.m., is beautiful enough to stop at just to have a look, but if you want a reasonably quiet meal, avoid lunchtime and come in the evening when all of the tour buses have long since departed. Sitting high on a verdant green hill, the inn's architectural style is a mixture of English Tudor and country Hawaiian. Inside it is cozy with a few fireplaces as well as open-beamed ceilings, while the view from the veranda is especially grand. Lunch can be a simple order of Portuguese bean soup that comes with a delicious flavored bun at only $3.75 per bowl, or appetizers ($7.25-10.95) like royal shrimp cocktail, sashimi, or honey garlic shrimp. Salad entrees ($9.50-10.25) include Oriental chicken, shrimp parmesan, and fruit of king's salads. The complete salad bar runs $9.95. Regular entrees are chopped steak, chicken macadamia, or *kalua* pork plate all priced under $12. Sandwiches like teriyaki steak and *kalua* pork are $8.25, while various burgers cost $7.50-8.50. Dinner entrees, with fresh-baked rolls, soup or salad, vegetables, and choice of rice, potatoes, or grilled pasta, include Slavonic steak, teriyaki steak, filet mignon, or prime rib for $19.50-24.95. Chicken macadamia and coconut island chicken are $15.75, and kalua pork is $14.95, while seafood selections and vegetarian pleasing stir-fry tempura complete the menu. The inn's famous mile-high coconut pie, macadamia nut cream pie, or double-crusted banana pie, for under $4, are absolutely delicious. To complement your menu selection there is also a full bar serving cocktails, beer, wine, and liquors.

On the premises is the **Livingston Galleries,** open daily 10:30 a.m.-7:30 p.m., tel. (808) 237-7165, which displays original prints, sculptures, and edition prints of both internationally acclaimed and local island artists. The artists displayed include: **Jiang, He Neng,** and **Hede Guang,** all of the Yunnan School of Art that emerged in

China after long years of repression under the Mao regime. Using various media including pastels, watercolors, and chalk the Yunnan artists have created works reminiscent of stained-glass windows that seemingly pre-existed inside their souls waiting for the light to illuminate their beauty. Other artists include **Tony Bennett,** the famous crooner, whose works burst with intense emotion; the fantastic underwater-earth-cosmic paintings of **John Pitre** or **Dana Queen,** his wife and colleague; the foggy coasts and misty *pali*

captured by **Sumner;** bronze sculptures by **Bruce Stanford;** and the terminally cute children rendered by **Mary Koski.** Also displayed is **Beverly Fettig,** an Oahu artist long renowned for her land- and seascapes; **Dennis Morton,** who does landscapes and seascapes in oils; wildlife artist **Daniel Van Zyle;** and one-of-a-kind blown glass by **Tracy and Denise** from North Shore Glass and **Diane Kelley and Bruce Clark.** Some jewelry, kaleidoscopes, and natural flower oil and botanical perfumes are also sold.

PUNALUU AND HAUULA

PUNALUU

Punaluu ("Coral Diving") is a long and narrow ribbon of land between the sea and the *pali,* a favorite place to come for a drive in the "country." Its built-up area is about a mile or so long, but only a hundred yards wide. It has gas, supplies, camping, and some of the cheapest accommodations anywhere on Oahu, along with the **Punaluu Art Gallery,** operated by Scott Bechtol, famous candle artist. On the northern outskirts of town, a sign points to **Sacred Falls,** an excellent hike, weather permitting.

In town is **St. Joachim Church.** There's nothing outstanding about it, merely a one-room church meekly sitting on a plot of ground overlooking the sea. But it's real home-grown, where the people of this district come to worship. Just look and you might understand the simple and basic lifestyle that still persists in this area.

HAUULA

This speck of a town is just past Punaluu between mile markers 21 and 22. The old town center is two soda machines, two gas pumps, and two limited supply stores, Masa's and Ching Jong Leong's. Another store, Segame's, sells cold beer and liquor. At the estuary of a stream is **Aukai Beach Park,** a flat little beach right in the middle of town. A **7-Eleven** and a little church up on the hill with the *pali* as a backdrop add the seemingly mandatory finishing touches. Just near the bus stop on the south end, look for a

local man who is usually there selling lei. The flowers and vines are fresh-picked from the immediate area, and the prices and authenticity are hard to beat.

Outdoor enthusiasts will love the little-used **Hauula Loop Trails.** These ridge trails head up the valleys gaining height along the way. They offer just about everything that you can expect for a Hawaiian trail: the mountains, the valleys, and vistas of the sea. Built by the Civilian Conservation Corps during the Depression, the trails are wide, and the footing is great even in rainy periods that can shut down the nearby **Sacred Falls Trail.**

BEACHES

Right along the highway is **Punaluu Beach County Park.** Punaluu provides shopping, and the beach park has restrooms, cooking facilities, but no lifeguards. The swimming is safe year-round inside the protected reef. Local fishermen, usually older Filipino men who are surf-casting, use this area frequently. They're friendly and a great source of information for anyone trying to land a fish or two. They know the best baits and spots to dunk a line.

Hauula Beach County Park is an improved beach park with picnic facilities, restrooms, pavilion, volleyball court, and camping (permit). Safe swimming year-round inside the coral reef, with good snorkeling; surfing is usually best in the winter months. Rip currents are present at both ends of the beach at breaks in the reef, and deep holes in the floor of a brackish pond are formed where Maakua Stream enters the sea. Across the road are the ruins of the historic **Lanakila Church** (1853), partially dismantled at the turn of the century to build a smaller church near Punaluu.

PRACTICALITIES

Accommodations

Countryside Cabins is a wonderful, inexpensive, and definitely funky place to stay. It's owned and operated by Margaret Naai, still sparkling though nearing 100 years old. The entrance is hard to spot, but it's located *mauka*. Look for the small white sign that says "Cabins." Completely furnished studios are $25 daily, $175 weekly, $475 monthly. Unfurnished rooms are $20 nightly, $140 weekly, $300 monthly. Margaret will reserve a room for you if you send a $10 deposit. She's a peach, but she's getting on in years, so it would be best to send a SASE envelope with your deposit and not count on her to remember. For information and reservations, write Countryside Cabins, 53-224 Kamehameha Hwy., Hauula HI 96717, tel. (808) 237-8169.

Food

An institution along the windward coast, **Pat's at Punaluu**, tel. (808) 293-2624, open daily except Monday 11 a.m.-9 p.m., and breakfast on the weekends only, has an extraordinary view of the coast. The interior is quite tasteful with open beams, ceiling fans, high-backed wicker chairs, and a long polished koa bar. The feeling is warm, peaceful, and very tropical. There's a little bandstand, some fish tanks, and a large lava rock wall that counterpoints the white stucco. Breakfast (weekends only) features three-egg omelettes, bacon or sausage and eggs, or a local artery-clogging "locomoco" for under $6. Lunch includes a variety of appetizers like beer-battered mahimahi, salads, and sandwiches. Full meals are served with salad, potato or rice, rolls, and vegetables, and include a captain's platter of seasonal fish and seafood in a crispy beer-batter tempura at market price, a Hawaiian plate of *kalua* pork, grilled fish, *lomi* salmon and steamed rice, and an order of baby-back ribs. No trip to Pat's is complete without sampling the fresh tarts famous since 1945—your choice of banana,

pineapple, or coconut ladled into an oven-fresh tart shell and mounded with whipped cream. Pat's is also famous for mai tais, made fresh, and so laced with booze that if you intend on driving, it would be good to have a designated driver. Pat's, long renowned as a good, old-fashioned, Hawaiian-style restaurant, has been going through a transition in the last few years. Luckily, it is definitely back on the right track. The previous owners tried to make it a tourist trap complete with mediocre cafeteria to cater to the tour-bus crowd. The new owners have reclaimed Pat's and saved it from a fate worse than deep-fried mahimahi. They're restoring Pat's to its old Island-style tradition, and doing an admirable job. Pat's is back, and is definitely worth a stop.

Don Ho's **Punaluu Cafe**, tel. (808) 237-8020, is basically a easy-going country bar and restaurant; open Mon.-Thurs. 11 a.m.-11 p.m. and Fri.-Sun. 11 a.m.-2 a.m. Lunch is served 11 a.m.-3 p.m., dinner 5-9 p.m. A live band plays Sunday 2-6 p.m., and on other nights they do karaoke, so you can croon for your friends. Lunches include salads, sandwiches, and plate lunches, plus such hearty items as beef stew and baby-back ribs. The dinner menu is similar, with the addition of daily specials. Most entrees are under $13.

Shopping

The **Punaluu Art Gallery**, in Punaluu around mile marker 24, tel. (808) 237-8221, is the oldest art gallery on windward Oahu. Open Thurs.-Mon. 10:30 a.m.-6:30 p.m.; closed Tuesday and Wednesday. Owner and candle artist Scott Bechtol is dedicated to showcasing the works of an assortment of the finest artists that the North Shore has to offer. Scott is well known for his wonderful sculpted candles, all made from the finest beeswax. Some are lanterns shaped like a huge pita bread with the top third cut off. The remainder is sculpted with a scene that glows when the candle is lit. Others are huge tikis, dolphins, or flowers, all inspired by the islands. There's even a 10-foot whale! Some of the larger candles are $70, the man-size tiki is about $800, and Scott's unique "crying tiki" sells for only $20; small tapers go for $5. Scott creates all of this beautiful glowing art with just one precision carving tool . . . a Buck knife! Another artist shown is Bill Cupit, who creates "bananascapes." Bill removes the outer bark from the banana

J.D. BISIGNANI

Scott Bechtol at Punaluu Art Gallery

tree, then he tears and cuts it to make a scene of boats or mountains. The result is a three-dimensional piece. Bill's wife is an artist who specializes in seascapes made with seaweed, while Janet Stewart does watercolors and prints. Other beauty is added by Janet Holiday's silkscreen prints, Peter Hayward's landscapes and seascapes in oil, and the dramatic tropical beauty of the North Shore captured by long-time resident, Edgardo Garcia. The Punaluu Art Gallery is a jewel case of manmade beauty surrounded by natural beauty. They harmonize perfectly.

The **Sacred Falls Bazaar**, seaside on the north end of Punaluu, open daily 9:30 a.m.-6:30 p.m., sells an assortment of neat touristy junk including aloha shirts, shell lei, tie-dyed T-shirts, and fresh island fruit. A minute farther north is the **Jhing Leong Store,** painted shocking pink, where you can pick up a smattering of supplies.

In Hauula look for the **Hauula Kai Center,** a small shopping center with a **post office** and stores for groceries, food, and supplies. Also in Hauula is the **Rainbow Shopping Plaza,** an unabashed tourist trap, classic in its obvious tastelessness. Here you'll find beads and baubles, the **Rainbow Barbecue** for something to eat and the **Rainbow Lounge** where you can have a drink.

LAIE TO KAHUKU

LAIE

The "Saints" came marching into Laie ("Leaf of the Ie Vine") and set about making a perfect Mormon village in paradise. What's more, they succeeded! The town itself is squeaky clean, with well-kept homes and manicured lawns that hint of suburban Midwest America. Dedicated to education, they built a branch of **Brigham Young University** (BYU) that attracts students from all over Polynesia, many of whom work in the nearby Polynesian Cultural Center. The students vow to live a clean life, free of drugs and alcohol, and not to grow beards. In the foyer of the main entrance look for a huge mural depicting Laie's flag-raising ceremony in 1921, which symbolically established the colony. The road leading to and from the university campus is mazelike but easily negotiable.

The first view of the **Mormon Temple,** 55-600 Naniloa Loop, Laie, tel. (808) 293-9297, built in 1919, is very impressive. Square, with simple architectural lines, this house of worship sits pure white against the *pali* and is further dramatized by a reflecting pool and fountains spewing fine mists. The visitor's center of this tranquil, shrinelike church is open daily 9 a.m.-8 p.m., when a slide show telling the history of the Laie colony is presented, along with a guided tour of the grounds. "Smoking is prohibited, and shirts (no halter tops) must be worn to enter." The temple attracts more visitors than any other Mormon site outside of the main temple in Salt Lake City.

Polynesian Cultural Center
The real showcase is the Polynesian Cultural Center. PCC, as it's called by islanders, began as an experiment in 1963. Smart businessmen said

it would never thrive way out in Laie, and tourists didn't come to Hawaii for *culture* anyway. Well, they were wrong, and the PCC now rates as one of Oahu's top tourist attractions, luring about one million visitors annually. Miracles do happen! PCC is a nonprofit organization, with proceeds going to the Laie BYU, and to maintaining the center itself.

Covering 42 acres, the primary attractions are seven model villages including examples from Hawaii, Samoa, the Marquesas, Fiji, New Zealand, Tonga, and Tahiti. Guides lead you through the villages either on a walking tour, or by canoe over artesian-fed waterways. A shuttle tram runs outside the center, and will take you on a guided tour to the BYU campus, the temple, and a short tour of the community (it would be okay except for the missionary hard sell). The villages are primarily staffed with people from the representative island homelands. Remember that most are Mormons, whose dogma colors the attitudes and selected presentations of the staffers. Still, all are genuinely interested in dispensing cultural knowledge about their traditional island ways and beliefs, and almost all are characters who engage in lighthearted bantering with their willing audience. The undeniable family spirit and pride at PCC makes you feel welcome, while providing a clean and wholesome experience, with plenty of attention to detail.

The morning begins with the **Fiafia Festival,** a lei greeting that orients you to the center. Next comes **Music Polynesia,** a historical evolution of island music presented by singers, musicians, and dancers. A brass band plays from 5:30 p.m., touring the different villages, and the **Pageant of Canoes** sails at 2 and 3 p.m. The largest extravaganza occurs during an evening dinner show called **Horizons.** Beginning at 7:30 p.m., the center's amphitheater hosts about 3,000 spectators for this show of music, dance, and historical drama. The costumes and lighting are dramatic and inspired; it's hard to believe that the performers are not professionals. In addition, the **Imax** theater gives you a real sense of what it's like to take a canoe around the shores of Fiji, or to tramp the mountains of New Zealand.

Food is available from a number of snack bars, or you can dine at the **Gateway Buffet Restaurant,** which serves you a buffet dinner as part of a package including the Polynesian extravaganza.

PCC is open daily except Sunday 12:30-6 p.m. for general admission, $27 adult, $16 children, under five free. There are also a variety of packages available including an all-day pass, with dinner and evening show, which lasts until about 9 p.m. The **Ali'i Luau** and dinner show run $49 adults, $30 children. For more information contact PCC at (808) 293-3333 or (800) 367-7060. TheBus no. 52 leaves from Ala Moana to the center and takes about two hours. Most island hotels and tour companies can arrange a package tour to PCC.

Malaekahana Bay State Recreation Area
This state recreation area is the premier camping beach and park along the north section of the windward coast. Separated from the highway by a large stand of shade trees, this 37-acre park offers showers, restrooms, picnic facilities, pavilion, and camping. For camping permits, contact Friends of Malaekahana at P.O. Box 305, Laie, HI 96762, tel. (808) 293-1736; office hours are Mon.-Fri. 10 a.m.-3 p.m. (See the "Camping" section in the Out and About chapter.)

J.D. BISIGNANI

Polynesian Cultural Center

Malaekahana was Pu'uhonua of Laie, a place of refuge, and, according to legend, the only spot on Oahu not conquered by King Kamehameha. The recent restructuring of the recreation area has tried to bring back its traditional role as a healing and gathering place. An alternative learning center erected here is connected to Kahuku High School, where students come to reconnect culturally and spiritually.

Offshore is Moku'auia, better known as **Goat Island.** The island is only a stone's throw from shore. Reef walkers or tennis shoes are advised. You can reach this seabird sanctuary by wading across the reef during low tide. You'll find a beautiful crescent white-sand beach and absolute peace and quiet. Relax and look for seabirds, or try to spot hawksbill or green sea turtles. The swimming inside the reef is good, and it's amazing how little used this area is for such a beautiful spot. Further offshore, about 200-300 yards, is a small island. *You cannot wade to this island. It is too far, and the currents are strong.* Be aware that there are two entrances to the park. The north entrance, closest to Kahuku, puts you in the day-use area of the park, where there are restrooms and showers. The entrance to the camping section is south a minute or two (around mile marker 17) and is marked by a steel gate painted brown and a sign welcoming you to Malaekahana Bay State Recreation Area. Be aware that the gates open at 7 a.m. and close at 7 p.m.

BEACHES

At the southern end of Laie is **Pounder's Beach,** so named by students of BYU because of the pounding surf. The park area is privately owned, open to the public, with few facilities. This beach experiences heavy surf and dangerous conditions in the winter months, but its excellent shoreline break is perfect for bodysurfing. The remains of an old pier at which interisland steamers once stopped is still in evidence.

Laie Beach County Park is an unimproved beach park with no facilities, but a one-mile stretch of beach. The shoreline waters are safe for swimming inside the reef, but wintertime produces heavy and potentially dangerous surf. Good snorkeling, fishing, and throw-netting by local fishermen; get there by following the stream from the bridge near the Laie Shopping Mall.

PRACTICALITIES

Accommodations

The **Rodeway Inn Hukilau Resort,** 55-109 Laniloa St., Laie, HI 96762, tel. (808) 293-9282 or (800) 526-4562, is just outside the Polynesian Cultural Center. Rooms are $84 queen, $89 double, $94 king, with a $5 reduction during off season. The fee includes continental breakfast, free local calls, parking, and 10% off tickets to the Polynesian Cultural Center. All rooms have a/c, TV, refrigerators, and microwaves. It's a cinderblock building, as neat as a pin but basic.

Lora Dunn's House is at 55-161 Kamehameha Hwy., Laie, HI 96762, tel. (808) 293-1000 (between mile markers 19 and 20, ocean side). Lora admits people on a first-come, first-served basis, but will happily take phone reservations for which she requires a deposit. Chances of turning up and finding a vacancy are poor, so at least call from the airport to check availability. A separate studio for two people is $50 a day, while the downstairs self-contained, two-bedroom, full-kitchen unit of her home, which is larger and can accommodate four people, runs $66 per day. There is a two-day minimum. Good value in a quiet, if not spectacular, setting.

Food and Shopping

When you enter Laie you will be greeted by the Stars and Stripes flying over the entrance of the Polynesian Cultural Center. Next door is a whopper of a **McDonald's,** and in keeping with the spirit of Polynesian culture, it looks like a Polynesian longhouse.

On the ocean side of the road is **Masa's Market,** which couldn't be more local with counters stocked with everything from lotus root to lamb. A few minutes south is the **Haaula Kai Shopping Center,** which provides a small variety of dining spots and shopping.

Between Kahuku and Laie is a new **Laie Village Shopping Center,** where you'll find a large and modern **Foodland,** along with a **Bank of America,** a small convenience store, **Lindy's**

Food, The Gallery Restaurant, Laie Chop Suey, Laie Cinemas, and a post office.

KAHUKU

This village, and it is a village, is where the *workers* of the North Shore live. Kahuku is "fo' real," and a lingering slice of what *was* not so long ago. Do yourself a favor, and turn off the highway for a two-minute tour of the dirt roads lined by proudly maintained homes that somehow exude the feeling of Asia.

Practicalities
You can pick up supplies at the **Kahuku Superette,** clearly marked along Rt. 83, or better yet look for a little white *kaukau* wagon that sits across the roadway from the school—most days. It sells great food that they bring from Honolulu's Chinatown fresh every day. Unfortunately, it's here only during school hours, when you can pick up a tasty and inexpensive lunch.

Keep a sharp eye out for a truck and a sign featuring shrimp just along the road. Follow it to **Ahi's Kahuku Restaurant,** operated by Roland Ahi and son, open daily 11 a.m.-9 p.m. The shrimp couldn't be fresher as it comes from local fishermen. The longest that these plump babies have been out of the water is 48 hours, so you are definitely getting *the* best. In this no-frills but super-friendly restaurant, you can have your shrimp cooked to order as scampi, deep-fried, tempura, sautéed, or in a cocktail for $8.25, or $9.50 for a sampler plate. You get about eight shrimp, depending on the size. The shrimp is the pièce de résistance, but basic sandwiches and burgers for under $5.50 are also on the menu, as well as entrees like spaghetti with meat sauce for $6.50 and steak and mahimahi combo for $11.95. Complete meals come with green salad, fresh vegetables, bread, rice or potatoes, and tea. There are plenty of appetizers and side dishes on the menu and a good selection of beer and wine. On Friday and Saturday nights, various local musicians perform until closing. Ahi's serves all of its great food with authentic *aloha.* Stop in! You'll be glad you did!

On the north end of town is the **Mill Shopping Center,** which is really the town's old sugar mill that has been recycled. The interior is dominated by huge gears and machinery, power panels, and crushers that are the backdrop for a string of shops, a restaurant, and the Kahuku Theater. The 10-foot gears and conveyor belts have all been painted with bright colors, and seem like a display of modern art pieces. Outside under a covered area is a little bazaar of shops selling everything from pottery to herbal medicine and fruits and vegetables to aloha shirts. This is the Kahuku Village Association, open daily except Sunday 9 a.m.-5 p.m. Also at the shopping center are a **Circle K** food store and gas station, **Lee's Gifts and Jewelry, Island Snow** for shave ice, and a post office. Located under the veranda behind the gas station at the Mill Shopping Center is the **Country Kitchen,** tel. (808) 293-2110, serving mostly Korean, American standard, and Filipino foods. An indoor-outdoor restaurant with a walk-up window, it is open daily 8 a.m.-6 p.m. for breakfast and lunch. Most dishes are in the under-$10 range.

Just past is the **Tanaka Plantation Store,** at 56-901 Kamehameha Hwy., Kahuku, a refurbished turn-of-the-century company store that now houses a clutch of boutiques and shops. Make sure to visit **The Only Show In Town,** open daily 10:30 a.m.-5:30 p.m., tel. (808) 293-1295. Blown to Oahu's North Shore from Kauai by Hurricane Iniki, Paul Wroblewski has reopened his antiques and collectibles shop and once again jammed it with Hawaiian artifacts, old bottles, costume jewelry, license plates, Japanese glass fishing floats, netsuke, scrimshaw, a collection of Marilyn Monroe memorabilia, and a full line of antique jewelry. Paul's an amiable fellow and is open to any reasonable offer. Remember, he may price according to your attitude. Also, if you have a collectible that you want to sell or get an estimate of value on, ask Paul to take a look.

Next door is **Imua Shop Polynesia,** open daily 10 a.m.-6 p.m., tel. (808) 293-5055, with craft items, carvings, tapa, tiki, aloha shirts, shells, jewelry, Hawaiian quilts, and postcards. If you have any questions on the origin or authenticity of these items, talk to the owner Doris.

Perhaps the most interesting shop in the complex is the **Amazonian Forest Store,** owned and operated by Brazilian world travelers Cesar

Olivera and Katia Ferz. Open daily 11 a.m.-6 p.m.; tel. (808) 293-5053. It specializes in authentic artifacts gathered from the Amazon and other rainforest regions around the world, including Hawaii and Indonesia. Some of the most amazing artifacts are headdresses and paintings by Brazil's Xindu Indians, along with basketry, parasols, coconut purses, string and cotton hammocks, and semiprecious gemstones gathered from throughout South America. If these aren't enough to make you "bug eyed" perhaps a Brazilian string bikini will. They've added a boutique with ladies dresses, sundresses, and beach apparel, and men's casual beachwear.

GEOGRAPHICAL NOTE

The following chapter, The North Shore, begins at the west end in Waialua/Haleiwa and works eastward toward Kahuku. That's because most people visiting the North Shore proceed in this direction, while those heading for "Windward Oahu" start in Kailua/Kaneohe and proceed up the coast. So, the end of this chapter follows geographically with the end of The North Shore chapter. Don't let it throw you.

BOB RACE

THE NORTH SHORE

This shallow bowl of coastline stretches from Kaena Point in the west to Turtle Bay in the east. **Mount Ka'ala,** verdant backdrop to the area, rises 4,020 feet from the Waianae Range, making it the highest peak on Oahu. The entire stretch is a day-tripper's paradise with plenty of sights to keep you entertained. But the North Shore is synonymous with one word: surfing.

Thunderous winter waves, often measuring 25 feet (from the rear!), rumble along the North Shore's world-famous surfing beaches lined up one after the other—**Waimea Bay, Ehukai, Banzai Pipeline, Sunset.** They attract highly accomplished athletes who come to compete in prestigious international surfing competitions. Be aware that *all* North Shore beaches experience very heavy surf conditions with dangerous currents from October through April. The waters, at this time of year, are not for the average swimmer. Please heed all warnings. In summertime *moana* loses her ferocity and lies down, becoming gentle and safe for anyone—leap in!.

The main attractions of the North Shore are its beaches, but interspersed among them are a few sights definitely worth your time and effort. The listings below run from west to east. The most-traveled route to the North Shore is from Honolulu along the H-2 freeway to Wahiawa, and then directly to the coast from there along Rt. 99 or Rt. 803. At Weed Circle or Thompson Corner, where these routes reach the coast, turn left along the Farrington Highway, following it to road's end just before Kaena Point, or turn right along the Kamehameha Highway (Rt. 83), which heads around the coast all the way to Kailua.

Haleiwa is fast becoming the central town along the North Shore. The main street is lined with restaurants, boutiques, art galleries, small shopping malls, and sports equipment stores. **Waialua,** just west, is a "sugar town" with a few quiet condos for relaxation. Farther west is **Dillingham A.F.B.** (inactive), where you can arrange to fly above it all in a small plane or soar silently in a glider. The road ends for vehicles not far from here, and then your feet have to take you to Kaena Point, where *the* largest waves pound the coast. Heading east, you'll pass a famous *heiau* where human flesh molli-

THE NORTH SHORE

OCEAN

PACIFIC

Kuilima
Point

Turtle Bay

Kawela

WAIALEE BEACH COUNTY PARK

KAMEHAMEHA HWY.

To Kailua

Sunset Point

SUNSET BEACH COUNTY PARK

Sunset Beach

EHUKAI BEACH COUNTY PARK

BANZAI PIPELINE

PUPUKEA BEACH PARK

PUU O MAHUKA
HEIAU

Waimea Bay

Waimea (Maunawai)

WAIMEA BAY COUNTY BEACH PARK

Waimea Falls Park

CHUN'S REEF

83

0   2 mi

0   2 km

PAPAILOA BEACH

Kawailoa

HALEIWA BEACH COUNTY PARK

Beach

Kailahulu Bay

HALEIWA ALII BEACH
COUNTY PARK

KAENA POINT
STATE PARK

MOKULEIA
COUNTY BEACH
PARK

MOKULEIA
POLO FIELD

KAIAKA
BEACH PARK

Haleiwa

Kaena
Point

930

DILLINGHAM
AIRFIELD

Waialua

WEED
CIRCLE

KAMEHAMEHA

99

THOMPSON
CORNER

WILIKINA
DR.

803

HWY.

To Wahiawa

To Wahiawa

© J.D. BISIGNANI AND MOON PUBLICATIONS, INC.

fied the gods, a monument to a real local hero, and **Waimea Falls Park,** the premier tourist attraction of the North Shore. Then come the great surfing beaches and their incredible waves. Here and there are tidepools rich with discovery.

Places to stay are quite limited along the North Shore. The best deals are beach homes or rooms rented directly from the owners, but this is a hit-and-miss proposition, with few agencies handling the details. You have to check the local papers. The homes vary greatly in amenities. Some are palaces, others basic rooms or shacks, perfect for surfers or those who consider lodging secondary. Check the bulletin boards outside the Surf and Sea Dive Shop in Haleiwa and Foodland supermarket.

ALONG THE FARRINGTON HIGHWAY

WAIALUA

The first town is Waialua ("Two Waters"). At the turn of the century, Waialua, a stop along the sugar-train railway, was a fashionable beach community complete with hotels and vacation homes. Today, it's hardly ever visited, and it's not uncommon to see as many horses tied up along the main street as it is to see parked cars in this real one-horse town. Sundays can also attract a rumble of bikers who kick up the dust on their two-wheeled steeds.

The sugar mill, an outrageously ugly mechanical monster, is still operating and is central to the town. Quiet Waialua, with its main street divided by trees running down the middle, *is* rural Oahu. There's a general store for supplies, a post office, and snacks at the **Sugar Bar,** a restaurant in the old Bank of Hawaii building that features an international menu—hot dogs from America to bratwurst from Germany. *Magnifique!*

If you're heading to Haleiwa take Haleiwa Road, a back way through residential areas. Look for Paalaa Road on the right and take it past a small Buddhist temple that holds an *o bon* festival honoring the dead, traditionally observed in July.

If polo is your game or if you're just curious, head west of town to the Mokuleia Polo Field and catch a Hawaii Polo Club match, Sundays at 2 p.m.

Beach Areas

Mokuleia Beach County Park is the main public access park along the highway. It provides picnic facilities, restrooms, lifeguards, a playground area, and camping (county permit). In summertime, swimming is possible along a few sandy stretches protected by a broken offshore reef. Mokuleia Army Beach is a wider strand of sand. It's very private, and the only noise interrupting your afternoon slumber might be planes taking off from the airfield. Local people have erected semipermanent tents in this area and guard it as if it were their own. A minute farther toward Kaena is an unofficial area with a wide sand beach. During the week you can expect no more than a half dozen people on this 300-yard beach. Remember that this is the North Shore and the water can be treacherous. Careful!

Camp Harold Erdman is next, one of the best-known camps on Oahu. This YMCA facility is named after a famous Hawaiian polo player killed in the '30s. The facility is used as a summer camp for children, throughout the year for special functions, and as a general retreat area by various organizations. Access is limited to official use.

Five minutes past the airfield, the road ends and a natural area reserve begins. This is a good place to check out giant waves.

Dillingham Airfield

Across the road from Mokuleia Beach Park is **Dillingham Airfield,** small but modern, with restrooms near the hangars and a new parking area.

A public phone is available in hangar G-1. Most days, especially weekends, a few local people sell refreshments from their cars or trucks. The main reason for stopping is to take a small plane or glider ride. **Glider Rides,** tel. (808) 677-3404, takes you on a 20-minute flight. Talk to owner Bill Star, who has been flying from here since 1970. A second company, **Soar Hawaii Sailplanes,** tel. (808) 637-3147, does a variety of rides.

Kaena Point State Park

Kaena Point lies about 2.5 miles down the dirt track after the pavement gives out. Count on three hours for a return hike and remember to bring water. The point can also be reached from road's end above Mahuka on the Waianae (leeward) side of the island. Kaena has *the* largest waves in Hawaii on any given day. In wintertime, these giants can reach above 40 feet, and their power, even when viewed safely from the high ground, is truly amazing. Surfers have actually plotted ways of riding these waves, which include being dropped by helicopter with scuba tanks. Reportedly, one surfer named Ace Cool has already done it. For the rest of us mortals . . . "who wants to have that much fun anyway!" Kaena Point is the site of numerous *heiau.* Due to its exposed position, it, like similar sites around the islands, was a jumping-off point for the "souls of the dead." The spirits were believed to wander here after death, and once all worldly commitments were fulfilled, they made their "leap" from earth to heaven. Hopefully, the daredevil surfers will not revive this tradition!

HALEIWA AND VICINITY

Haleiwa ("Home of the Frigate Birds") has become the premier town of the region, mainly because it straddles the main road and has the majority of shopping, dining, and services along the North Shore. Haleiwa now has a bypass around town. Unless you're really in a rush, follow the brown "Haleiwa Historic Town" sign into town as this is where it's all happening. **Haleiwa Alii Beach Park** is on the western shores of Waialua Bay, which fronts the town. This beach park is improved with restrooms, lifeguard tower, and a small boat launch. Lifeguards staff the tower throughout the summer, on weekends in winter. The shoreline is rocks and coral with pockets of sand, and although portions can be good for swimming, the

park is primarily noted for surfing, in a break simply called "Haleiwa." A little farther to the west, on Kaiaka Point, is **Kaiaka Beach Park.** This is a good swimming and snorkeling beach, and you'll find restrooms and picnic areas here. Camping is allowed with county permit.

Head eastward and cross the **Anahulu River Bridge.** Park for a moment and walk back over the bridge. Look upstream to see homes with tropical character perched on the bank with a bevy of boats tied below. The scene is reminiscent of times gone by.

A much better park is **Haleiwa Beach Park,** clearly marked off the highway on the eastern side of Waialua Bay. Here you'll find pavilions,

typical rural Buddhist temple, on the outskirts of Haleiwa

J.D. BISIGNANI

picnic facilities, lifeguards, restrooms, showers, and food concessions, but no camping. The area is good for fishing, surfing, and most importantly, for swimming year-round! It's about the only safe place for the average person to swim along the entire North Shore during winter.

Kawailoa Beach is the general name given to the area stretching all the way from Haleiwa Beach County Park to Waimea Bay. A string of beaches **(Papailoa, Laniakea,** and **Chun's Reef)** is just off the road. Cars park where the access is good. None of these beaches is suitable for the recreational swimmer. All are surfing beaches, with the most popular being Chun's Reef. One area, about in the center of this line of beaches, is being developed as **Kawailoa Beach Park.**

ACCOMMODATIONS

Located on the back side of Lokoea Pond in town is the **Surfhouse,** 62-202 Lokoea Place, Haleiwa, HI 96712, tel. (808) 637-7146. A budget accommodation, this new white house offers shared and private rooms. The dorm rooms each have six beds and run $15 a night or $95 a week; private rooms are $45 a night or $280 a week. Campers can find a space on the lawn for $9 a night or $56 a week. Laundry service is available and the kitchen can be used for preparing your own meal. Bicycles and water equipment can be rented at inexpensive rates. Make your arrangements with Sofie or Lee.

FOOD

Inexpensive Food

Near Pizza Hut, but a culinary world apart, is **Celestial Natural Foods,** tel. (808) 637-6729, open weekdays 9 a.m.-6:30 p.m., Sunday 10 a.m.-6 p.m. Up front is a complete natural and health food store. In back, and called **Paradise Found,** is a lunch counter that serves vegetarian meals. Some items are nachos for $2.95, couscous at $3.95, pita pockets and chapati wraps for $5.25, and veggie sandwiches at $3.95. Smoothies, fresh juice drinks, teas, sodas, and sweets are also available. The food is healthful and nutritious, but portions are definitely not for the hungry.

Cafe Haleiwa, a hole-in-the-wall eatery on your left just as you enter town, serves one of the best breakfasts on Oahu. Lunch is served too; hours are Mon.-Fri. 6 a.m.-3 p.m., Saturday 7 a.m.-3 p.m., and Sunday 7 a.m.-2 p.m. The "dawn patrol" 6-7 a.m. includes eggs and whole-wheat pancakes for $2.50. Specials of the house are whole-wheat banana pancakes, French toast, spinach and mushroom quiche, and steaming-hot Kona coffee. One of the partners, Jim Sears, is called "the wizard of eggs" and has built up a local following. The cafe attracts many surfers, so it's a great place to find out about conditions.

Another tiny place with great treats is **Kua Aina,** for sandwiches and—some claim—the best burgers on the island.

If you're tired or just need a pick-me-up head for the North Shore Marketplace (after McDonald's, mountain side), where you'll find the **Coffee Gallery,** tel. (808) 637-5571, open daily 6 a.m.-9 p.m., which has the largest selection of fresh roasted gourmet coffees in Hawaii, including Kona coffees and international selections of organically grown coffee from Sumatra, Indonesia, Guatemala, and South America. You can enjoy a steaming cup from its full service espresso bar along with fresh carrot juice, and vegan pastry made without dairy products or eggs. Other more bliss-inducing pastries are blackberry apple crumble pie, super chocolaty brownies, fresh fruit bars, and racks of various cookies and muffins. Every day there is a homemade soup, fresh salad, and a fine selection of deli sandwiches that range from a vegetarian garden burger on a whole wheat bun with lettuce and tomatoes, Maui onion, guacamole, and a side of tortilla chips to pita bread filled with eggplant, pesto, and veggies all priced around $6. It's all vegetarian. Sit outside in the shaded and screened dining area and watch the character-laden "characters" of the North Shore come and go. Coffee Gallery has expanded, with shops now in Honolulu, Wahiawa, and Hawaii Kai.

The **China Chop Suey** restaurant, tel. (808) 637-5281, serves basic Chinese food in a basic place at moderate prices. Most dishes are under $8, but the special dinner for two runs $22. Here also is the **Haleiwa Chinese Restaurant,** tel. (808) 637-3533, open daily 10 a.m.-9 p.m. The interior is nothing special, but the food is very good. The steamed sea bass and *kung pao* chicken are both excellent. A gigantic bowl of tofu soup is $5, while most main courses are under $6. One of the best inexpensive eateries on the North Shore.

For south-of-the-border food, try **Cholo's Homestyle Mexican Restaurant,** tel. (808) 637-3059. Plate items, which include rice and beans, run $4-7.50; dinners include rice, beans, salad, chips, salsa, and a choice of meat and go for $6.25-9.50. Many combinations are also available. The walls are festooned with masks, paintings, prints, and other works of art and crafts.

You can tell by the tour buses parked outside that **Matsumoto's** is a very famous store on the North Shore. What are all those people after? Shave ice. This is one of the best places on Oahu to try this island treat. Not only do the tourists

come here, but local families often take a "Sunday drive" just to get Matsumoto's shave ice. Try the Hawaiian Delight, a mound of ice smothered with banana, pineapple, and mango syrup. If lines are too long here or if you want to frequent the competition, try **Aoki's** shave ice up the way.

Moderate/Expensive Food

Rosie's Cantina, in the Haleiwa Shopping Plaza, open Sun.-Thurs. 7 a.m.-10 p.m., Fri.-Sat. 7 a.m.-11 p.m., prepares hearty Mexican dishes for a good price. The inside is "yuppie Mex" with brass rails, painted overhead steam pipes, and elevated booths. Expect to pay $5 for enchiladas and burritos, while meat dishes are $9-10. Order the enchilada stuffed with crab; add a salad and two could easily make this a lunch. **Pizza Bob's,** also in the plaza, has an excellent local reputation, and its little pub serves up not only delicious pizza, but a variety of salads, lasagna, and sandwiches. People are friendly, there's plenty of food, and the price is right.

Situated in the North Shore Marketplace is **Portofino,** tel. (808) 637-7678, an Italian restaurant that also does a delivery service under the name North Shore Pizza Company; the delivery number is (808) 637-2782. Here they use a wood-fired pizza oven so you know that it's the real McCoy. Aside from pizza, soups, salads, pastas, and fish dishes are also served. Give it a try. It's a friendly place with wholesome food.

Jameson's by the Sea, 62-540 Kamehameha Hwy., tel. (808) 637-4336, is open daily for lunch, dinner, and cocktails. Located at the north end of Haleiwa overlooking the sea, its outdoor deck is perfect for a romantic sunset dinner, while inside the romantic mood is continued with track lighting, shoji screens, cane chairs with stuffed pillows, candles with shades, and tables resplendent with fine linen. Appetizers include a salmon pâté for $7.50, stuffed mushrooms with escargot for $7.50, fresh oysters for $8.95, and a bowl of creamy clam chowder for $4.50. Soups are priced under $5. Try the Yokohama soup, as well as salad with any of the homemade dressings. Main dishes like mahimahi, stuffed shrimp, shrimp curry with mango chutney, and sesame chicken range $18.50-25. For dessert have the lemon macadamia nut chiffon pie for $4.50. The pub downstairs serves lunch from a slightly different menu. It's quiet at night and serves a variety of imported beers; try South Pacific, imported from New Guinea. Breakfast is served Saturday and Sunday 9 a.m.-noon. Reservations highly recommended. Request a window seat for the sunset.

The **Chart House,** at 66-011 Kamehameha Hwy., Haleiwa, tel. (808) 638-8005, open daily for dinner 5-10 p.m., for lunch Thurs.-Sun. 11 a.m.-3 p.m., is part of a small chain known for good food, located in a green cinder-block building on the left before you cross the Anahulu River bridge. Although purely utilitarian on the outside, the inside is modern and tasteful with plenty of tile work, track lighting, bent-back chairs, and ceiling fans. Most appetizers, ranging from artichokes to chowder, are under $8, while the salad bar (included with an entree) is a bit more. Steaks, the specialty of the house, and most entrees are in the $19-25 range. Specials are offered daily, and there's a "wine of the month" chosen to enhance your meal. For dessert try the mud pie or the key lime pie. Although the Chart House is not quite gourmet, the food is good and wholesome, with the price right for what you get.

SHOPPING AND SERVICES

Art Galleries and Shops
Ka'ala Art, open 9 a.m.-6 p.m. daily, tel. (808) 637-7065, as you enter Haleiwa (across from McDonald's), is a perfect place to stop, with some of the best shopping on the North Shore. The brothers Costello, John and Jim, who own and operate the shop, are knowledgeable, longtime residents of the North Shore who don't mind dispensing directions and information. The premier items are John's original artwork, wonderful paintings that are impressionistic and magical, with many of these unique designs silk-screened onto 100% cotton T-shirts or made into inspiring posters. John has also turned his hand to carvings of dolphins and other Hawaiian themes. Also featured are fine carvings from Tonga, Tahiti, and Bali that John has hand-selected on his travels, along with excellent examples of local Hawaiian woodcarvings. Small but wonderful items are tapa cloth made by Sella, a Tongan woman who lives nearby, batiks from Thailand, and jewelry made locally and from Asia. The Costello brothers travel to buy, and they have a keen eye for what's happening and distinctive. Brother Kevin offers a fine selection of imported clothing from Thailand, which is available through the gallery by appointment. A rainbow has spilled in a corner of the shop, where 100% cotton pareu ($18-35) from Hawaii, Tahiti, and Indonesia vibrate in living color. More "art-clothing" includes a rack of beach cover-ups designed by John, tie-dyed and silk-screened using ecologically minded nontoxic colors. There's also a fine postcard selection just to remind the folks back home that you are in Hawaii.

Iwa Gallery, open daily except Tuesday and Wednesday 10:30 a.m.-6:30 p.m., is across the street from the Protestant church, founded in 1892, and next door to Aoki's Shave Ice. This co-op shows the efforts of local artists who have been juried in order to place their artwork on consignment. Featured are the fine candle sculptures of **Scott Bechtol.** Other artists displayed at the gallery include: Angela Kanas, a watercolor artist who does fanciful renditions of Hawaiian gods, goddesses, and traditional folk; Janet Stewart, who depicts island themes like Madame Pele lying with the blood of her hot lava flowing from her body, or a *keiki* hula dancer with a look of concentration on her face, or a kindly *tutu* in a red muumuu; Bill Cupit uses the bark of banana trees to create entire island scenes like ships departing a sheltered harbor. The oil paintings of Peter Hayward, who died at age 87, survive him. Many show translucent waves crashing on lonely shores. Serigraphs and cards by Janet Holiday are often depictions of flowers in bold primary colors; Peggy Pai, born and raised in China, creates silk batik with ephemeral, beautiful, cloudy landscapes; James Rack uses his palette and brush to catch scenes of idyllic Hawaii; and Norman Kelly catches children at play or surfers on towering waves in his fluid watercolors.

Wyland Gallery, across the street from the Haleiwa Shopping Center, is open daily 9 a.m.-6 p.m., tel. (808) 637-7498. Wyland is a famous environmental artist known for his huge whale and marinelife murals, in addition to watercolors and fine oil paintings. The gallery is large, spacious, and well lit. Everything has a Hawaiian or sea theme, and there's even a huge fish tank filled with tropical fish. There're watercolors of Hawaiian maidens by Janet Stewart, lithographs by Roy Tabora of palm trees and cliffs with Michelangelo skies, waterfall paintings by James Coleman, strong and dramatic oils of young Walfrido, and bronze sculptures of the sea by Scott Hanson. You can walk away with a limited-edition lithograph by Wyland with original watercolor mark framed in koa for $1,550. If the original artwork is too expensive, there are posters, mini-prints, and postcards. Wyland's gold jewelry sculpture is also beautiful, distinctive, and affordable.

On the ground floor of Jameson's By the Sea is **Galerie,** tel. (808) 637-8866. Owner-operator Christian Reese Lassen works in oil, acrylic, and watercolor, but in all he displays fantastic seascapes in vibrant brilliant color. Also featured are oil painter William Dechasazo and sculptors Joseph Quillan and Douglas Wylie.

North Shore Marketplace

The North Shore Marketplace, along the Kamehameha Highway between McDonald's and the Haleiwa Shopping Center, is a small complex with some inexpensive and unique shops. The most interesting shop is **Jungle Gem's,** tel. (808) 637-6609, open 10 a.m.-6 p.m., with a metaphysical assortment of crystals, crystal balls, African trading beads, and gems. The shop specializes in locally made jewelry that is reasonably priced and of excellent quality. The owners, Brent Landberg and Kimberely Moore, are knowledgeable gemologists and fine jewelers who do much of the work on display.

Another good shop is **More or Less Beach Wear,** tel. (808) 637-6859, open 9 a.m.-6 p.m. daily, where they make custom bathing suits for women and men and sell hand-painted T-shirts by local artists. The owner and chief designer, Lucinda Vaughen, will take a personal hand in fitting and designing just the right suit for you. Other clothing stores are **Pomegranates In The Sun** and **Patagonia.**

Strong Current North Shore Hawaii, tel. (808) 637-3406, is open daily 9:30 a.m.-6:30 p.m. This is a surf shop that also has beachwear, but it's more than that. It's almost like a museum of surfing with all the collectibles on display. Stop in and reminisce about the '50s and '60s classic era of surfing.

To the left as you drive into the parking lot is **Barnfield's Raging Isle Sports,** tel. (808) 637-7707, a full-service mountain bike and surf shop open daily 10 a.m.-6:30 p.m. Aside from selling and repairing bikes, they rent mountain bikes for $35 a day and lead bike tours. The shop also manufactures surfboards here, the only place on the North Shore legally doing so. Board re-

pairs are also made. Casual clothing and surf wear are stocked, as well as snowboards, bindings, and snow clothing.

Island Inspired is run by the husband and wife team of Michael and Ilona Hemperly. Have a look at the prints done on rice paper, pen and ink drawings, and acrylic washes.

Twelve Tribes International Imports, tel. (808) 637-7634, is a multicultural emporium with items from the global village.

Around back is **North Shore Glass,** tel. (808) 637-4853, where Traci and Dennis produce hand-blown art glass in their open-air studio. Most of what they make goes to the hotels, but they do have a small rack of retail items that they sell in the studio. Check them out to see how the work is done.

Along the Kamehameha Highway

As you move down the Kamehameha Highway you'll pass in rapid succession the **Haleiwa Flower Shop** on the left selling lei and fresh-cut flowers. Next comes **Oogenesis Boutique,** with original fashions for women, and almost next door is **Haleiwa Acupuncture Clinic,** tel. (808) 637-4449, with Richard Himmelmann, in cooperation with Healing Touching Massage by Brenda McKinnon, and chiropractic care by Dr. Edward Bowles, who will make house calls. Nearby is **Haleiwa Family Health Center,** a walk-in clinic, tel. (808) 637-5087, open 8 a.m.-5 p.m. daily, closed Sunday.

Also along the highway is **Haleiwa Shopping Center,** which provides all the necessities in one-stop shopping: boutiques, pharmacy, photo store, and general food and merchandise. For food and picnic supplies try the **Haleiwa IGA.**

Services

The best sources of general **information** for the North Shore are the bulletin boards outside of Surf and Sea and the Foodland supermarket.

As you enter Haleiwa from the west, you'll pass a **Shell** gas station and a full-service **post office.**

Sporting Goods and Rentals

The following shops are all located along the Kamehameha Highway, the main drag through Haleiwa.

Barnfield's Raging Isle Sports, in the North Shore Marketplace, tel. (808) 637-7707, open

10 a.m.-6:30 p.m. daily, is primarily a surf shop and manufacturer of Barnfield's Raging Isle Boards, but it also sells, rents, and repairs bikes.

For surfboards, sailboards, boogie boards, snorkeling equipment, sales and rentals, try

Hawaii Surf and Sail, 66-214 Kamehameha Hwy., tel. (808) 637-5373; **Hawaiian Surf,** tel. (808) 637-8316, 66-250 Kamehameha Hwy.; or **Surf and Sea,** tel. (808) 637-9887, 62-595 Kamehameha Hwy.

WAIMEA BAY AND VICINITY

The two-lane highway along the North Shore is pounded by traffic; be especially careful around Waimea Bay. The highway sweeps around till you see the steeple of **St. Peter and Paul Mission** with the bay below. The steeple is actually the remnants of an old rock-crushing plant on the site. **Waimea Bay Beach County Park** has the largest rideable waves in the world. This is the heart of surfers' paradise. The park is improved with a lifeguard tower, restrooms, and a picnic area.

During a big winter swell, the bay is lined with spectators watching the surfers ride the monumental waves. In summertime, the bay is calm as a lake. People inexperienced with the sea should not even walk along the shorebreak in winter. Unexpected waves come up farther than you'd think, and a murderous rip lurks only a few feet from shore. The area is rife with tales of heroic rescue attempts, many ending in fatalities. A plaque commemorates Eddie Aikau, a local lifeguard credited with making thousands of rescues. In 1978, the *Hokule'a,* the Polynesian Sailing Society's double-hulled canoe, capsized in rough seas about 20 miles offshore. Eddie was aboard and launched his surfboard to swim for help. He never made it, but his selfless courage lives on.

Waimea Valley, Home of Waimea Falls Park
Look for the well-marked entrance to Waimea Falls Park, mountain side from the bay, and then drive for quite a ways into the lush valley before coming to the actual park entrance. Along with the Bishop Museum, the park is the most culturally significant travel destination on Oahu. Although open to the public and more than happy to welcome visitors, Waimea Falls Park has not lost sight of its ancient *aloha* soul, which it honors while providing a wonderful day of excitement and education. Primarily a botanical garden, with a fascinating display of flowers and plants all labeled for your edification, the Waimea Arboretum

collects, grows and preserves extremely rare specimens of Hawaii's endangered flora. If you choose not to walk, an open-air tour bus will take you through, narrating all the way. A thrilling event is the professional diving from the 55-foot rock walls into the pool below Waimea Falls. Culturally enlightening are displays of ancient hula *(kahiko)* performed by very accomplished dancers, a display of Hawaiian games, carving demonstrations, and walks along forest paths that end at fascinating historical sites. On the property is Hale o Lono, one of the island's largest and most ancient *heiau* dedicated to the god Lono.

Waimea Falls Park

J.D. BISIGNANI

Admission is $19.95 adults and $9.95 for juniors age 6-12, open daily 10 a.m.-5:30 p.m.; tel. (808) 638-8511 or (800) 767-8046. Four-wheel drive ATV vehicle and horseback tours are available ($20-75), mountain bikes can be rented (about $50) for use on the park's course, and kayak tours ($20-50) are guided down the river to the sea. The **Proud Peacock** serves dinner until 9 p.m. A free guided moon-viewing tour on the Friday night closest to the full moon used to be offered on a regular basis. This ceased for about a year but plans are to revive it on an intermittent basis. If you're interested, call the park to see if it's happening.

For those coming from Waikiki intending to visit only the park, consider taking the free park shuttle bus. Call (808) 955-8276 for pickup times and locations.

Pupukea Beach Park

A perfect place to experience marinelife is the large tidepool next to Pupukea Beach Park, the first one north of Waimea Bay, across the street from the Shell gas station. A long retaining wall out to sea forms a large and protected pool at low tide. Wear footgear and check out the pools with a mask. Don't be surprised to find large sea bass. A sign warns against spearing fish, but the local people do it all the time. Be careful not to step on sea urchins, and stay away from the pool during rough winter swells, when it can be treacherous. The beach park has restrooms, picnic facilities, and fair swimming in sandy pockets between coral and rock, but only in summertime.

The middle section of the park is called **Shark's Cove,** though no more sharks are here than anywhere else. The area is terrific for snorkeling and scuba in season. Look to the mountains to see **The Mansion** (see following), and next to it the white sculpture of the **World Unity Monument.** If you had to pick a spot from which to view the North Shore sunset, Pupukea Beach Park is hard to beat!

Farther down the road, as you pass mile marker 9 you can't help noticing a mammoth redwood log that has been carved into a giant statue representing an ancient Hawaiian. Peter Wolfe, the sculptor, has done a symbolic sculpture for every state in the union, this being his 50th. This statue is extremely controversial. Some feel that it looks much more like an American Indian than a Hawaiian, and that the log used should have been a native koa instead of an imported redwood from the Pacific Northwest. Others say that its *intention* was to honor the living and the ancient Hawaiians, and that is what's important.

Puu O Mahuka Heiau

Do yourself a favor and drive up the mountain road leading to the *heiau* even if you don't want to visit it. The vast and sweeping views of the coast below are incredible. About one mile past Waimea Bay the highway passes a Foodland on the right. Turn here up Pupukea Road and follow the signs. There is a warning at the beginning of the access road, but the road is well maintained and many people ignore the sign.

Puu O Mahuka Heiau, the largest on Oahu, covers a little over five acres. Designated as a national historical landmark, its floorplan is huge steps, with one area leading to another just below. The *heiau* was the site of human sacrifice. People still come to pray as is evidenced by many stones wrapped in ti leaves placed on small stone piles lying about the grounds. In the upper section is a raised mound surrounded by stone in what appears to be a central altar area. The *heiau's* stonework shows a high degree of craftsmanship throughout, but especially in the pathways. The lower section of the *heiau* appears to be much older, and is not as well maintained.

Drive past the access road leading to the *heiau* and in a minute or so make a left onto Alapio Road. This takes you through an expensive residential area called **Sunset Hills** and past a home locally called **The Mansion**—look

> . . . but a diversion, the most common is upon the water . . . the men lay themselves flat upon an oval piece of plank . . . they wait the time for the greatest swell that sets on shore, and altogether push forward with their arms to keep on its top, it sends them in with a most astonishing velocity. . .
>
> —James King, circa 1779

for the English-style boxwood hedge surrounding it. The home was purported to be Elvis Presley's island hideaway. Almost next door are the grounds of the **Nichiren Buddhist Temple**, resplendent with manicured lawns and gardens. This area is a tremendous vantage point from which to view Fourth of July fireworks lighting up Waimea Bay far below.

The Great Surfing Beaches

Sunset Beach runs for two miles, one of the longest white-sand beach on Oahu. This beach is the site of yearly international surfing competitions. Winter surf erodes the beach, with coral and lava fingers exposed at the shoreline, but in summertime you can expect an uninterrupted beach usually 200-300 feet wide. The entire stretch is technically Sunset Beach, but each world-famous surfing spot warrants its own name though they're not clearly marked and are tough to find . . . exactly. Mainly, look for cars with surfboard racks parked along the road. The beaches are not well maintained either. They're often trashed, and the restrooms, even at Waimea Bay, are atrocious. The reason is politics and money. Efforts all go into Waikiki, where the tourists are. Who cares about a bunch of crazy surfers on the North Shore? They're just a free curiosity for the tourists' enjoyment!

The **Banzai Pipeline** is probably the best-known surfing beach in the world. Its notoriety dates from *Surf Safari*, an early surfer film made in the 1950s, when it was dubbed "Banzai" by Bruce Brown, maker of the film. The famous tubelike effect of the breaking waves comes from a shallow reef just offshore, which forces the waves to rise dramatically and quickly. This forces the crest forward to create "the Pipeline." A lifeguard tower near the south end of the beach is all that you'll find in the way of improvements. Parking is along the roadway. Look for Sunset Beach Elementary School on the left, and the Pipeline is across the road. You can park in the school's lot on non-school days.

Ehukai Beach County Park is the next area north. It has a lifeguard tower and restroom, and provides one of the best vantage points from which to watch the surfing action on the Pipeline and Pupukea, the area to the right.

Don't expect much when you come to **Sunset Beach County Park** itself. Except for a lifeguard

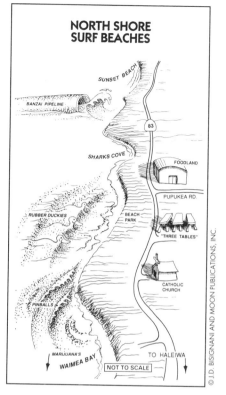

NORTH SHORE SURF BEACHES

SUNSET BEACH
BANZAI PIPELINE
83
SHARKS COVE
FOODLAND
PUPUKEA RD.
RUBBER DUCKIES
BEACH PARK
"THREE TABLES"
CATHOLIC CHURCH
PINBALLS
MARIJUANA'S
TO HALEIWA
WAIMEA BAY
NOT TO SCALE

© J.D. BISIGNANI AND MOON PUBLICATIONS, INC.

tower, there is nothing. Almost as famous as the surfing break is the **Sunset Rip**, a notorious current offshore that grabs people every year. Summertime is generally safe, but never take *moana* for granted.

ACCOMMODATIONS

Resort

The **Turtle Bay Hilton Golf and Tennis Resort** is a first-class resort on Turtle Bay, the northern extremity of the North Shore, P.O. Box 187, 57-091 Kamehameha Hwy., Kahuku, HI 96731, tel. (808) 293-8811 or (800) HILTONS. Once a Hyatt hotel, it was built as a self-contained destination resort and is surrounded by sea and surf on Kuilima

Point, which offers protected swimming year-round. The entrance road to the hotel is lined by blooming hibiscus that outline a formal manicured lawn. In 1993, *Golf Magazine* rated the 27-hole, Arnold Palmer-inspired Links at Kuilima one of the "top 10 best new courses in the U.S., while *Tennis Magazine* rated the hotel's tennis facilities among the top 50 tennis resorts in the entire world! The resort also offers a pool, full water activities including windsurfing and scuba lessons, horseback riding, shopping, and the fanciest dining on the North Shore. Since the hotel is an oasis unto itself, you should *always* call ahead to book any of these activities, even as a guest staying at the hotel, to avoid disappointment. There's very little shopping in this area, so if you're after film, or basic picnic supplies, stop at the hotel's minimall. The resort's newest feature is a seaside **Wedding Chapel**, splendid with open-beamed ceiling, stained glass, and eight-foot beveled windows that can be thrown open to allow the ocean breezes to waft through. All guest rooms are ocean view, but not all are oceanfront. Oceanfront is slightly more expensive, but is worth the price, especially from December to April when humpback whales cavort in the waters off the point. Rooms are furnished with full baths, a mini-fridge, a dressing room, a large vanity, ample closets, a/c, and remote control cable TV. Junior suites come complete with a library, a large bathroom and changing room, two couches, a sitting area, a queen-size bed, and a large enclosed lanai. The Hilton has upgraded and refurbished with new carpets, drapes, bedspreads, wallpaper, and upholstered furniture. Rates are $160-200 for a standard with an ocean, mountain, or bay view; cabanas go for $285; and suites cost $400-1,500; $30 extra person. The Hilton family plan allows children free when they stay in a room with their parents. The Hilton is a first-class destination resort, but because of its fabulous, yet out-of-the-mainstream location, you get much more than what you pay for. The Turtle Bay Hilton is an excellent choice for a vacation with the feel of being on a Neighbor Island.

Condo

Ke Iki Hale is a small condo complex operated by Alice Tracy, 59-579 Ke Iki Road, Waimea, HI 96712, tel. (808) 638-8229. Pass the Foodland supermarket heading north and look for a school

sign. Turn left to the beach to find the condo. The property has 200 feet of private beach with a sandy bottom that goes out about 300 feet (half that in winter). The condo is quiet with a home-away-from-home atmosphere. Rates are: one-bedroom beachfront, $135 per day or $875 per week; two-bedroom beachfront, $185 per day or $1,155 per week; and a two-bedroom compact, $165 per day or $1,106 per week In addition, there is a cottage at $160 a day or $1,050 per week. Streetside units are about 30% less. A one-time cleaning fee is charged, and this ranges $35-65, depending upon the length of stay.

Surfer Rentals

The North Shore of Oahu has long been famous for its world-class surfing. The area attracts enthusiasts from around the world who are much more concerned with the daily surfing report than they are with deluxe accommodations. The Kamehameha Highway is dotted with surfer rentals from Haleiwa to Turtle Bay. Just outside their doors are the famous surfing breaks of Marijuana's, Rubber Duckies, and Pinballs, all famous and known to world-class surfers. Some of these accommodations are terrific, while others are barely livable. Here's a sample of what's offered.

Backpacker's Vacation Inn and Hostel, 59-788 Kamehameha Hwy., Haleiwa, HI 96712, tel. (808) 638-7838 (courtesy phone at airport, no charge), specializes in budget accommodations for surfers, backpackers, and families. Owned and operated by the Foo Family, the main building in this small cluster of buildings is at mile marker 6, the fourth driveway past the church tower coming from Waimea Bay. There are a number of facilities and room styles which could put you on the beach or mountainside, depending on availability and your preference. Basic rates are $14-16 (a little more during high season) for a bunk in the hostel-style rooms, which includes cooking and laundry facilities, and TV in the communal room. Each room has four bunks, microwaves, a shower, and a bath. The feeling is definitely not deluxe, but it is adequate. A complex on the beach, $70 daily, $420 weekly, sleeps four, has a complete kitchen, two double beds, a roll-out couch, a ceiling fan, and a world-class view of the beach from your lanai. The back house, on the mountainside, is farther away from traffic and is among the trees. It's on stilts, and has an open ceiling and rustic common area. Rates are $40 for the main rooms (two people), $25 for a private loft (it gets hot up there), or $14 for a shared bunk. The Vacation Inn has only one rule: use common sense, and clean up after yourself. It provides free boogie boards and snorkeling gear and can arrange whalewatching or sunset sails and scuba and kayak rental. Airport transportation (directly opposite the baggage claim) is free *to* the inn and $5 for the return trip. Everyone's friendly and laid-back. Book ahead. A good choice.

The **Plantation Village** at 59-754 Kamehameha Hwy., tel. (808) 638-7838, operated by Backpacker's, lies across from Three Tables Beach by Shark's Cove, between mile markers 6 and 7. It's on TheBus line and only a five-minute walk from a Foodland store for supplies. The Plantation Village, once a real Filipino working village, has cottages by the sea, secure behind a locked gate, and furnished with cable, stereo, linens, a full kitchen, dishes, washers and dryers, ice machines, and cleaning service. Many of the fruit trees on the grounds provide the guests with complimentary bananas, papayas, breadfruit, or whatever is ripe. Prices are $16 for a shared room and bath with two or three others. The small (300 square feet) private cottages, once the homes of real plantation workers, sleep two and are $40 per night, or $245 per week. A $100 per night deluxe cottage sleeps four, and you get a large front lanai, two couches, wicker furniture in a sitting room, cable TV, a/c, fan, full bath with vanity, and a kitchen fully furnished with microwave, stove, and fridge. The Backpacker's van also services the Plantation Village. During surfing season the place is booked up. Reserve one month in advance, full deposit during high season (Dec.-Feb.), one-half deposit other months. No refund policy in high season.

Located at a quintessential surfing spot along the North Shore is **Breck's Hostel,** 59-043 Huelo St., Sunset Beach, HI 96712, tel. (808) 638-7873, but you don't have to be a surfer to enjoy the ambience. The beach is just across the highway, and nearby are shops, eateries, and the bus. Guests here have free use of the hostel's bodyboards, surfboards, snorkeling equipment, and bicycles, and rides to and from the airport can be arranged. Rates are charged by the day or the week: $12.50 for a basic dorm bed, $15.40 for the

deluxe dorm, $35-45 for a private room or studio, and $16.50 per person in the ocean-view apartment (sleeps eight).

FOOD

Inexpensive/Moderate
East from town, across from Shark's Cove, is **Shark's Shack,** a *usually* open lunch wagon that'll fix you a sandwich or rent you snorkeling gear. Next door is **Pupukea Shave Ice** for an island treat. Farther toward Sunset Beach (around mile marker 9) look for **D'amico's Pizza,** open for breakfast, lunch, and dinner (slow but friendly service). The Sunset Beach store has basic items but is the home of **Ted's Bakery,** where you can get a fine assortment of loaves and pastries. For food supplies, shop **Foodland,** along the highway past Waimea Bay.

The **Proud Peacock,** Waimea Falls Park, tel. (808) 638-8531, is open daily for a lunch buffet and dinner 5-9 p.m. It's fun to dine here even if you don't enter the park. From the dining room, you can look into some of the nicest gardens while feeding crumbs to the peacocks. The beautiful mahogany bar was made in Scotland almost 200 years ago. You can have a light soup and salad, but their seafood *pu pu* platter is hard to beat. Roast pork and roast beef are well-prepared favorites here.

Classy Dining
If you're looking for gourmet dining in an incredibly beautiful setting head for the Turtle Bay Hilton Golf and Tennis Resort. The **Cove Restaurant,** open 6-9:30 p.m. (reservations advised), is the signature restaurant at the resort and welcomes you for an evening of fine dining. Slowly stroll a wooden walkway leading past tiny waterfalls and a profusion of plants to the main room that overlooks the manicured grounds and pool. Start with lobster bisque in a puff pastry shell or a variety of fresh island salads for $6. Move on to filet mignon, veal chops, fresh tiger prawns, and lobster that you choose fresh from the tank. The fresh catch, always an excellent choice, is a very reasonable $19.95. If you really want to treat yourself, order the North Shore potpourri, a silver bowl mounded with ice that cradles *opihi,* shrimp, sashi-

mi, oysters, and fresh fish that come with savory dipping sauces from a basic shoyu and hot mustard to a papaya salsa. Enjoy dessert while gazing through floor-to-ceiling windows that frame the living mosaic of Turtle Bay turned brilliant by a legendary North Shore sunset.

The **Sea Tide Room** is synonymous with Sunday brunch. It enjoys a wonderful reputation, and if friends or family come visiting, islanders take them here to impress. Brunch is buffet style 9 a.m.-2 p.m. and features mounds of fresh fruits and pastries, fresh-squeezed fruit juices, imported cheeses, eggs Florentine and Benedict, fresh fish, seafood, sashimi, shrimp, crab claws, and flowing champagne. Reservations not taken, $25 adults. Expect a wait, which goes quickly as you enjoy the magnificent scenery.

The **Palm Terrace** is the most "ordinary" of the hotel's restaurants, but ordinary par excellence!. Open 6:30 a.m.-10 p.m., the restaurant serves hearty American favorites from all 50 states, supplemented by dishes from around the world. You can dine on smoked Pacific fish, saimin with crispy bread, curried chicken papaya, or a seafood tostada. You will enjoy lunch sandwiches like Portuguese sausage on rye or a clubhouse special. There are hamburgers, of course—the basic burger, right down to a North Shore burger with grilled onions and peppers. For dessert order a cinnamon tulip: macadamia nut ice cream, split bananas, chocolate, and Kahuku watermelon all in a cinnamon tostada pastry shell. The views overlooking Turtle Bay combined with excellent value for the money make the Palm Terrace the best *ordinary* restaurant on the North Shore.

The **Bay View Lounge** is a casual restaurant/nightclub offering a deli-luncheon buffet. It's open 11:30 a.m.-1 a.m. and serves complimentary *pu pu* around sunset, which is a perfect time to drop in. On weekends the Bay View Lounge is the hotspot disco, ID required after 9 p.m.; dress code is collared shirts and close-toed shoes.

GEOGRAPHICAL NOTE

The previous chapter, Windward Oahu, begins in Kailua/Kaneohe and works its way up the coast simply because most people visiting that coast approach it from the south. Those heading for the North Shore usually come from Haleiwa in the west and proceed northeast toward Kahuku. So, the end of this chapter follows geographically with the end of the Windward Oahu chapter. Don't let it throw you.

BOB RACE

THE LEEWARD COAST

The Waianae ("Mullet Waters") coast, the leeward face of Oahu, is separated physically from the rest of the island by the Waianae Range. Spiritually, culturally, and economically, the separation is even more profound. This area is Oahu's last stand for ethnic Hawaiians, and for that phenomenal cultural blending of people called *locals*. The idea of "us against them" permeates the consciousness of the area. Guidebooks, government pamphlets, and word of mouth warn tourists against going to Waianae because "the natives are restless." If you follow this poor advice, you not only miss the last of undeveloped coastal Oahu, but the absolute pleasure of meeting people who will treat you with genuine *aloha*. Along the coast are magnificent beaches long known for their surf, new condos and developments nestled in secure valleys, and prime golfing. Inland, roads will take you to the roof of Oahu. Waianae is the home of small farms, run-down shacks, and families that hold luau on festive occasions, where the food and entertainment are the real article. Anyone lucky enough to be invited into this quickly disappearing world will be blessed with one of the last remaining authentic cultural experiences in Hawaii.

The possibility of hassles shouldn't be minimized because they do happen, but every aggressor needs a victim. The biggest problem is thievery, of the sneak-thief variety. You're marked as a tourist because of your new rental car. If you leave valuables in it, or lying unattended on the beach, they have a good chance of disappearing. But who does silly things like this *anywhere* in the U.S.? You won't be accosted, or held up at gunpoint, but if you bother a bunch of local guys drinking beer, you're asking for trouble. Moreover, the toughness of Waianae is self-perpetuating, and frankly the locals *like* the hard reputation. A few years back a feature writer reported that when he visited Waianae some toughs threw rocks at him. No one had ever reported this before, but after a big stink was made about it, more and more people had rocks thrown at them when they visited here. In recent years *pakalolo* has had a tremendous effect on the area. Local guys began growing and smoking it. This brought some money back into the depressed region, and it changed

MAP: THE LEEWARD COAST

Kaena Point
KAENA POINT STATE PARK
Puu Pueo
(768 ft.)
KAENA POINT
STATE PARK
930
Kauai Channel
Yokohama
Bay
MOKULEIA
BEACH PARK
DILLINGHAM
AIRFIELD
To Haleiwa
Makua
Poohuna Point
Makua
Valley
THE
LEEWARD
COAST
FARRINGTON HWY.
OHIKILOLO BEACH
KEAAU BEACH COUNTY PARK
KEPUHI BEACH
Kepuhi Point
Makaha Valley
MAKAHA BEACH
COUNTY PARK
Makaha
Makaha Stream
MAUNA LAHILAHI
BEACH COUNTY PARK
WAIANAE REGIONAL PARK
POKAI BAY BEACH COUNTY PARK
LUALUALEI BEACH
COUNTY PARK
WAIANAE
Waianae
VALLEY
RD.
Waianae
Range
LUALUALEI NAVAL RD.
LUALUALEI
NAVAL
RESERVATION
93
Maili
MAILI BEACH COUNTY PARK
MAIPALAOA BEACH
ULEHAWA BEACH COUNTY PARK
Maili Point
Lualualei
FARRINGTON HWY.
Nanakuli
NANAKULI BEACH
COUNTY PARK
PACIFIC
KAHE POINT BEACH
COUNTY PARK
0   2 mi
0   2 km
93
KO OLINA RESORT
H1
OCEAN
MALAKOLE
RD.
90
KALAELOA
BLVD.
WAIMANALO RD.
To Honolulu
BARBERS POINT
NAVAL AIR
STATION
BARBERS POINT
BEACH COUNTY PARK

© J.D. BISIGNANI AND MOON PUBLICATIONS, INC.

the outlook of some of the residents. They felt a camaraderie with other counterculture people, many of whom happened to be *haole*. They could relax and not feel so threatened with pursuing an often elusive materialistic path. Many became more content with their laidback lifestyle, and genuinely less interested with the materialistic trip all the way around.

In truth, *we* shouldn't be warned about *them*, but vice versa. The people of Waianae are the ones being infringed upon, and it is they who, in the final analysis, will be hassled, ripped off, and ultimately dispossessed. Recent articles by Oahu's Development Conference strongly state that future development will center on the island's northwestern shore . . . the Waianae coast! A few rocks are poor weapons against developmental progress, which is defined by the big boys with the big dreams and the big bucks to back them up.

When you go through Maili, you'll see what's been happening here since development has come to Waianae. As you drive through town notice a giant outcropping, Maili Point, which meets the sea like a giant fist. It has the same dominant presence as Diamond Head. Pull off at Maili Beach County Park, and to your right are the modest homes of local people. Look up the coast to where the mountains come down to the sea. Out on that headland you can see a giant resort, and on the bending backbone leading up to it, modest homes of the local people.

BEACHES AND SIGHTS

The Waianae coast is very accessible. One road takes you there. Simply follow the H-1 freeway from Honolulu until it joins the Farrington Hwy. (Rt. 93). It runs north, opening up the entire coast. A handful of side roads lead into the interior, and that's about it! A strange recommendation, but sensible on this heavily trafficked road, is to drive north to the end of the line and then stop at the scenic sights on your way back south. This puts you on the ocean side of the highway where you won't have to worry about cutting across two lines of traffic, which can be a steady stream making it tough to navigate. The-Bus no. 51 runs the entire Waianae coast and stops at all of the following beaches.

Note: Four of the beach parks along this coast offer **camping,** but their status periodically changes to **no camping** without notice. Many of the other campers are local people in semipermanent structures; the reason that the status changes quickly is to prevent these people from squatting. Also, remember that this is the leeward coast, which gets plenty of sunshine. Many of the beach parks do not have shade trees, so be prepared. June is the prettiest month because all the flowers are in bloom, but it's one of the worst times for sunburn. The entire coast is great for snorkeling, with plenty of reef fish. However, keep your eyes on the swells, and always stay out during rough seas, when waves can batter you against the rocks. The parks listed below run from south to north.

Barbers Point Beach County Park
The first beach is Barbers Point Beach County Park, at the end of Kalaeloa Boulevard. Turn down it where H-1 and the Farrington Hwy. join. The point was named after Capt. Henry Barber, who was shipwrecked here in 1795. Few people, even island residents, visit this beach park. It's in an industrial area and the shoreline is rocky. One pocket of white-sand beach is open to the public, though it fronts a private residence. The swimming is safe only in summer; snorkeling is better, and you'll find picnic facilities and restrooms.

Kahe Point and Tracks Beach County Parks
Kahe Point and Tracks Beach County Parks are just where the Farrington Hwy. curves north along the coast. They're the first two *real* Waianae beaches, and they're symbolic. You come around the bend to be treated to an absolutely pristine view of the coast with the rolling sea, a white-sand beach, a cove, and the most hideous power plant you've ever seen. Facilities at Kahe Point Beach County Park are restrooms and a phone. The beach is poor except for a section

typical camping beach, leeward coast

J.D. BISIGNANI

just east of the improved park. Swimming is dangerous except on calm summer days, when a lifeguard is present. More often, you'll find people surfing and bodysurfing here. Camping is allowed with a county permit, although periodically this camping area closes temporarily.

The Hawaiian Electric Beach Park, across from the power plant, is known as "Tracks" to island surfers because of the railroad tracks that run along the shore here. Facilities include picnic tables, a pavilion, restrooms, showers, and parking along the highway. The white-sand beach is wide, and the swimming generally safe. The mild waves are perfect for learning how to surf. If you keep your eyes trained out to sea, the area is beautiful. Don't look inland!

Nanakuli Beach County Park

Nanakuli Beach County Park is on the southern outskirts of Nanakuli ("Pretend to be Deaf") town, which is the first real town of the Waianae coast. If you get to the red light you've gone a little too far. The beach park is community-oriented, with recreational buildings, basketball courts, a baseball diamond, and kiddies' play area. Camping is permitted with a county permit. Lifeguards work on a daily basis, and the swimming is generally safe except during periods of high winter surf. The northern end of the beach, called Kalanianaole, is generally calmer than the southern end. They're divided by a housing project, but connected by a walkway. The southern section is fronted by a cliff with a small cove below. During periods of calm surf, the waters are crystal clear and perfect for snorkeling.

Ulehawa Beach County Park

Ulehawa Beach County Park, just north of Nanakuli, offers restrooms, picnic facilities, lifeguards, and sometimes camping. The best swimming is in a sandy pocket near the lifeguard tower. Surf conditions make for good bodysurfing. Most of the park, along a rocky cliff, is undeveloped. Here you'll find unlimited fishing spots. A shallow lagoon is generally safe for swimming year-round. As always, it's best to check with the local people on the beach.

Maili Beach County Park

Maili Beach County Park is at the southern end of Maili ("Many Small Stones") town. It lies between two streams coming down from the mountains. Amenities include restrooms, picnic facilities, and a lifeguard tower. The best swimming is in front of the lifeguard tower. The beach is broken into three parts by a housing development. In wintertime the beach disappears, but it returns wide and sandy for the summer. Most of the park is undeveloped. Plenty of coral pockets offer good snorkeling. Don't just jump in. Ask the locals or swing by the lifeguard tower to make sure that it's safe.

Lualualei Beach County Park

Lualualei Beach County Park has restrooms, picnic facilities, and camping during summer months. The entire park is largely undeveloped and lies along low cliffs and raised coral reef. Swimming is almost impossible. It's primarily good for fishing and looking.

Pokai Beach County Park

Pokai Beach County Park is one of the nicest along the Waianae coast, located just south of Waianae town. It provides restrooms, picnic facilities, lifeguards, and a boat ramp, which brings plenty of small craft into the area. Don't be surprised to see a replica of a double-hulled canoe, often used for publicity purposes. It has appeared in a beer commercial. The park is clean, well maintained, reasonably secure, and family-oriented. There's surfing, snorkeling, and safe swimming year-round. If you're heading for one beach along Waianae, this is a top choice.

Waianae Harbor

To get a look at a small working harbor or to hire a fishing boat, visit Waianae Boat Harbor as you head north from town. Huge installed stones form an impressive manmade harbor, with everything from luxury yachts to aluminum fishing boats. Some cruises and whalewatching tours start from here.

Waianae Valley Road

To head inland take Waianae Valley Road. You quickly gain the heights of the Waianae Range, and eventually come to a sentry box with a soldier inside. From here Kolekole Road is closed to the public, but if you stop and identify yourself, you might be given permission to go to **Kolekole Pass.** The awesome view is well worth the trip.

Makaha Beach County Park

Makaha Beach County Park is famous for surfing, and as you approach, you can't help spotting a dominant headland called **Lahi Lahi,** which was a one-time island. Called "Black Rock" by the local fishermen, and used as a landmark, it still marks Makaha. Surfing competitions have been held here since the Makaha International Surfing Competition began in 1952. In recent years, a local lifeguard named Richard "Buffalo" Keaulana, known to all who've come here, has begun the Annual Buffalo Big Board Riding Championship. Paul Strauch Jr., inventor of the "hang five," comes to Makaha whenever he has a chance, along with Buffalo's sons and other pro surfers, many of whom live in the area. In 1995, Buffalo retired after 36 years as a lifeguard. He has passed the torch on to his son Brian, who now becomes captain of the whole east side. Along with protecting the beach and riding the waves, Brian has a budding acting career as a stunt man for Hollywood. The swimming can be dangerous during high surf, but excellent on calm days. Winter brings some of the biggest surf in Hawaii. Always pay heed to the warnings of the lifeguards.

Makaha

Although Makaha can translate as "water breaking out to sea" because of the area's propensity of damming runoff waters from the mountains behind the beach until enough pressure forces it to "break out," there is another meaning for Makaha that doesn't help its image. The second translation, meaning "Fierce," aptly describes a gang of bandits who long ago lived in the surrounding hills and terrorized the region. They would wait for small bands of people walking the road, then swoop down and relieve them of their earthly goods.

If you follow Makaha Valley Road inland, you pass condos and high-rises clinging to the arid walls of this leeward valley. Surrounded by an artificial oasis of green, this developed resort area provides golfing at the Sheraton Makaha Golf Club and all the amenities of a destination resort. Visit the **Kaneaki Heiau,** a 17th-century temple restored by the resort under the direction of the Bishop Museum. This temple was dedicated to Lono, the benevolent god of harvest and fertility. The grass and thatched huts used as prayer and meditation chambers, along with a spirit tower, have all been replicated.

Once past Makaha, the road gets rugged, with plenty of private places to pull off. This crab claw of land, which ends at Kaena Point, forms a bay. The seascape demands attention but look into the interior. The mountains seem naturally terraced as they form dry, deep valleys. All are micro-habitats, each different from the other. On top of one notice a gigantic golf ball, really a radar tracking station, that lets you know you're coming to the end of the passable road.

Keaau Beach County Park

Keaau Beach County Park has restrooms, picnic facilities, and camping (county permit). The improved part of the park has a sandy beach, but mostly the park is fronted by coral and lava, and is frequented mostly by fishermen and campers. The unimproved section is not good for swimming, but it does attract a few surfers, and is good for snorkeling and scuba but only during calm periods. The improved section is a flat grassy area with picnic tables, shade trees, and pavilions.

Kaena Point State Park

Yokohama Bay is the end of the line; the pavement ends here. If you're headed for Kaena Point or beyond to the north coast you'll have to walk through this windswept coastal park. Yokohama Bay is a long stretch of sandy beach that is mostly unimproved. A lava-rock bathhouse is on the right, just after the entrance. The area was named because of the multitude of Japanese fishermen who came to this lonely site to fish. It's still great for fishing! The swimming can be hazardous because of the strong wave action and rough bottom, but the snorkeling is superb. Lifeguards are on duty during the summer months. Mostly the area is used by surfers and local people, including youngsters who dive off the large lava rocks. This is inadvisable for people unfamiliar with the area. Yokohama is a great place to come if you're after a secluded beach. Weekdays, you'll have it to yourself, with a slightly greater number of people on the weekends. Definitely bring cold drinks, and remember that there are no shade trees, so a hat or beach umbrella is a necessity. Many camp here unofficially.

Kaneana Cave is a few minutes south of Yokohama Bay on your left as you head back down the coast. You probably didn't notice it on your way north because of the peculiar land formation that conceals the mouth in that direction. Legend has it that this cave was the home of Nanue the shark man. Unfortunately, people have come here with spray cans and trashed the cave. If you can overlook that, it's a phenomenon—a big one. You can spot it by looking for three cement blocks, like road dividers, right in front of the entrance. It's at the foot of a 200-foot outcropping of stone. When you see local people defacing the natural beauty like this, it's hard to believe that the Hawaiians had such a spirit bond with the *aina.*

PRACTICALITIES

ACCOMMODATIONS

Condos

Except for camping, there are no inexpensive places to stay along the Waianae coast. Some local people let rooms for a good rate, but there is no way to find this out in advance. Your best bet is to check out the bulletin boards at various stores along the coast. Accommodations range from moderate to expensive, with Makaha Valley being the most developed resort area of Oahu outside of Waikiki. All are condos and require a minimum stay of seven days.

The **Maili Cove,** 87-561 Farrington Hwy., Waianae, HI 96792, tel. (808) 696-4447, rents one-bedroom apartments for $350-450 per week. It has a swimming pool, parking, and TV, along with a few hotel units.

The **Makaha Beach Cabanas,** 84-965 Farrington Hwy., tel. (808) 696-2166, are in Makaha along the beach just past the high school. All units have a lanai overlooking the water. They're not fancy, but are spotlessly clean and serviceable. All units are fully furnished with complete kitchens; from $350 per week.

The **Makaha Shores** are privately owned units that overlook a beautiful white-sand beach and provide great viewing of the surfers challenging the waves below. All units are fully furnished. The least expensive accommodations are at the **Makaha Surfside.** The beach is rocky near the condo, but it makes up for this with two pools and a sauna. All units are individually owned and fully furnished. **Makaha Valley Towers** rise dramatically from Makaha Valley, but they don't fit in. They're either a testament to man's achievement or ignorance, depending on your point of view. In keeping with the idea of security, you drive up to a gate manned by two guards. You're stopped, asked your business, and sent unsmilingly on your way. The condo provides fully furnished units, a/c, TV, and pool. If you're staying in this ill-fitting high-rise, at least try to get a top floor where you can take advantage of the remarkable view. Of the three condos, these have the most expensive units. Rates vary according to property, but generally fall into the $250-450 a week range for studios, $350-550 for one-bedroom units, and up to $750 for two bedrooms per week. Monthly rates are also available, and you get substantial savings for longer rentals. For rental information, contact Hatfield's Realty, tel. (808) 696-8415; Sugar Kane Realty, tel. (808) 696-5833; Waianae Coast Realty, tel. (808) 696-6366; or Sun Estates, tel. (808) 487-0000.

Ihilani Resort and Spa

The courtiers anxiously waited for the grand night when the torches would be lighted and the drums beaten to announce the lovely princess as she was presented to the assembled *ali'i.* Those closest to the young beauty were confident that their years of training had refined the grace and nobility that matched their dignified heritage. She had proven to be an enthusiastic and willing student, endearing herself to all because of her gaiety, sweetness, and loving heart. But to assume her rightful place with the most powerful in the land, she would have to gain the self-possessed assurity that only comes from the wisdom of experience. It is much the same with the Ihilani Resort and Spa, at 92-1001 Olani St., Kopolei, HI 96707, tel. (808) 679-0079, (800) 626-4446, Web site: www.ihilani.com, Oahu's newest luxury resort, which officially opened its doors in December 1993. The hotel, an alabaster specter floating amidst the 640 emerald-green acres of the Ko

Olina Resort, rises above a white-sand beach at the southern end of the Waianae coast. It's about 25 minutes west of the Honolulu airport—simply follow the H-1 expressway to the clearly marked Ko Olina exit. You approach the resort by way of a cobblestone drive that winds its way up to a porte cochere where valets and lei-bearing hostesses wait to greet you. The open breezeway leads to a towering glass-domed atrium brightened by cascading trellised flowers, and ringed by living green ferns. Below, rivulets trickle through a series of free-form ponds, some like glass-reflecting sculptures, others alive and tinkling a natural refrain. The guest rooms, huge at almost 700 square feet, are pleasantly appointed in pastels and white and all feature a/c, ceiling fans, louvered doors, remote-control entertainment centers, in-room safes, minibars, and luxurious cushioned teak furniture including a dining table and lounge awaiting you on your private lanai. A futuristic feature is a bedside master control telephone system from where you can regulate the room's lighting, a/c, and voice mail service at the touch of a finger. Bathrooms, an intricate play of marble and tile, feature double sinks, hair dryers, a basket of fine toiletries, separate commode and shower stalls, and deep oversized tubs. Evening brings turndown service when little gifts of mineral bath gels or soothing facial compresses are left on your pillow, compliments of the spa. Terrace view rooms run $295, the golf-mountain view rooms $325, while the ocean view rooms go for $415 a night. Many spa, golf, and tennis packages are also available, and they save a good deal on room rates. Other amenities are 24-hour room service, concierge service, tennis courts, and a beauty salon. With time and maturity, the Ihilani Resort and Spa, tucked away from the madding crowd, gives every indication of becoming one of Oahu's premier destinations. In fact, for 1998, it received the prestigious AAA Five Diamond Award for excellence in service and accommodations.

Dining at the Ihilani is in the masterful and infinitely creative hands of executive chef, Katsuo Sugiura (Chef Suki), who has created dishes in what he describes as "Tropical Pacific." This fantastic blending of east and west relies heavily on locally grown herbs, vegetables, meats, and most importantly, island seafood. It is a blissful marriage built on Mediterranean, Oriental, and Hawaiian cuisine that can easily be influenced by Scandinavian, Caribbean and Southwestern ingredients. Mostly, Chef Suki is an artist who is constantly experimenting and creating new presentations on a daily basis. Using smoking techniques that he has perfected over the years, Suki not only creates distinctive individual dishes, but he creates them especially for each guest, sealing the recipe and repeating it when you return, if you so desire. The Ihilani's signature restaurant is the dinner-only **Azul,** complemented by a magnificent wine cellar, with breakfast, lunch, and dinner served at the open-air **Naupaka Terrace.** Health-conscious cuisine for breakfast and lunch is offered at the **Spa Cafe,** on the sixth level of the Ihilani Spa. Traditional Japanese fare is offered for dinner only at the **Ushio-tei.** And golfers or those into a more casual setting will enjoy clubhouse dining for lunch at the Ko Olina Golf Course's **Niblick Restaurant.** For snacks during the day, try the **Poolside Grill** or **Hokule'a Bar.**

Located in a separate facility just a short walk across from the main entrance is the **Ihilani Spa,** a magnificently soothing, revitalizing, and uniquely Hawaiian spa experience. This facility is centered around Thalasso water therapy, a computer-controlled water-jet massage utilizing fresh seawater and seaweed. After being immersed in this state-of-the-art tub, you move on to the Vichy Shower, Grand Jet, or Needle Pavilion, where 12 shower heads poke stimulating sprays into every nook and cranny. Next, the superbly trained staff offers hands-on experiences in the form of therapeutic massage including Swedish, *lomi lomi,* or *shiatsu.* You can also opt for a manicure, pedicure, or skin-rejuvenating facial. To keep trim and supple, head for the fitness facility on the third level where you will find a lap pool, jacuzzi, aerobics room, and strengthening equipment.

The green velvet of the **Ko Olina Championship Golf Course,** designed by Ted Robinson, and already named as one of the finest courses in America by *Golf Digest,* fronts the hotel. Open since 1990, the course is fully matured and has already hosted a number of prestigious tournaments. If you'd rather play tennis, the resort's six Kramer-covered tennis courts await your pleasure.

FOOD AND SERVICES

For anyone with an urge to eat a two-scoop plate lunch, no problem. Little drive-in lunch counters are found in almost every Waianae town. Each serves hearty island food such as teriyaki chicken, pork, or mahimahi for under $5. A favorite is the **Makaha Drive-In.**

You also see plenty of fruit sellers parked along the road. Their produce couldn't be fresher, and stopping provides you not only with the perfect complement to a picnic lunch but with a good chance to meet some local people.

For your shopping and dining needs in Nanakuli, try the **Pacific Shopping Mall,** where you'll find Sac and Save Supermarket, the largest in the area. In the complex is **Nanakuli Chop Suey Restaurant,** open 10 a.m.-8:30 p.m., tel. (808) 668-8006, serving standard Chinese fare at local down-home prices. Just behind McDonald's is the **Eden BBQ Lounge,** tel. (808) 668-2722, with sit-down and takeout Korean food at moderate prices; open 10 a.m.-9 p.m. daily.

The **Waianae Mall** is a complete shopping facility. Don't worry about bringing supplies or food if you're on a day excursion. You'll find all that you need at the mall, which includes Red Baron Pizza, Waianae Chop Suey, Subway Sandwiches, Woolworth's, and Longs. Have no fear if you're addicted to fast foods. Some major franchises have decided that your trip to leeward Oahu wouldn't be complete without something processed in a Styrofoam box. If you're looking for ethnic flavor try the **Tamura Superette,** which stocks plenty of ingredients used in ethnic foods. An **L&L Drive-In** is here as well for the plate lunch lovers. For banking needs, try the Bank of America branch office. You'll spot a number of gas stations in the middle of town, along with Circle K and 7-Eleven convenience stores.

Aside from the Drive-In, Makaha has Woolworth's and a shopping basket of neighborhood markets.

Arts and Crafts
The **Waianae Hawaiian Heritage Cultural Center** offers workshops in lei-making, *lau hala* weaving, hula, and the Hawaiian language. The center welcomes people either to observe or participate in the programs. For times and schedules contact the State Foundation on Culture and Arts, tel. (808) 586-0300.

BOOKLIST

ASTRONOMY

Bryan, E.H. *Stars over Hawaii.* Hilo, HI: Petroglyph Press, 1977. Charts featuring the stars filling the night sky in Hawaii.

Rhoads, Samuel. *The Sky Tonight—A Guided Tour of the Stars over Hawaii.* Honolulu: Bishop Museum, 1993. Four pages per month of star charts—one each for the horizon in every cardinal direction. Exceptional!

COOKING

Alexander, Agnes. *How to Use Hawaiian Fruit.* Hilo, HI: Petroglyph Press, 1984. A full range of recipes using delicious and different Hawaiian fruits.

Beeman, Judy, and Martin Beeman. *Joys of Hawaiian Cooking.* Hilo, HI: Petroglyph Press, 1977. A collection of favorite recipes from Big Island chefs.

Choy, Sam. *Cooking From the Heart with Sam Choy.* Honolulu: Mutual Publishing, 1995. This beautiful, handbound cookbook contains many color photos by Douglas Peebles.

Fukuda, Sachi. *Pupus, An Island Tradition.* Honolulu: Bess Press, 1995.

Margah, Irish, and Elvira Monroe. *Hawaii, Cooking with Aloha.* San Carlos, CA: Wide World, 1984. Island recipes including *kalua* pig, *lomi* salmon, and hints on decor.

Rizzuto, Shirley. *Fish Dishes of the Pacific—from the Fishwife.* Honolulu: Hawaii Fishing News, 1986. Features recipes using all the fish commonly caught in Hawaiian waters (husband Jim Rizzuto is the author of *Fishing, Hawaiian Style*).

CULTURE

Hartwell, Jay. *Na Mamo: Hawaiian People Today.* Ai Pohaku Press, 1996. Profiles 12 people practicing Hawaiian traditions in the modern world.

Heyerdahl, Thor. *American Indians in the Pacific.* London: Allen and Unwin Ltd., 1952. Theoretical and anthropological accounts of the influence on Polynesia of the Indians along the Pacific coast of North and South America. Though no longer in print, this book is fascinating reading, presenting unsubstantiated yet intriguing theories.

Kirch, Patrick V. *Feathered Gods and Fishhooks: An Introduction to Hawaiian Archaeology and Prehistory.* Honolulu: University of Hawaii Press, 1985. This scholarly, lavishly illustrated, yet very readable book gives new insight into the development of precontact Hawaiian civilization. It focuses on the sites and major settlements of old Hawaii and chronicles the main cultural developments while weaving in the social climate that contributed to change. A very worthwhile read.

FAUNA

Boom, Robert. *Hawaiian Seashells.* Honolulu: Waikiki Aquarium, 1972. Photos by Jerry Kringle. A collection of 137 seashells found in Hawaiian waters, featuring many found nowhere else on earth. Broken into categories with accompanying text including common and scientific names, physical descriptions, and likely habitats. A must for shell collectors.

Carpenter, Blyth, and Russell Carpenter. *Fish Watching in Hawaii.* San Mateo, CA: Natural World Press, 1981. A color guide to many of the reef fish found in Hawaii and often spotted by snorkelers. If you're interested in the fish that you'll be looking at, this guide will be very helpful.

Fielding, Ann, and Ed Robinson. *An Underwater Guide to Hawaii.* Honolulu: University of Hawaii Press, 1987. If you've ever had a desire to snorkel/scuba the living reef waters of Hawaii and to be familiar with what you're seeing, get this small but fact-packed book. The amazing array of marinelife found throughout the archipelago is captured in glossy photos with accompanying informative text. Both the scientific and common names of specimens are given. This book will enrich your underwater experience and serve as an easily understood reference guide for many years.

Goodson, Gar. *The Many-Splendored Fishes of Hawaii.* Stanford, CA: Stanford University Press, 1985. This small but thorough "fish-watchers" book includes entries on some deep-sea fish.

Hobson, Edmend, and E.H. Chave. *Hawaiian Reef Animals.* Honolulu: University of Hawaii Press, 1987. Colorful photos and descriptions of the fish, invertebrates, turtles, and seals that call Hawaiian reefs their home.

Hosaka, Edward. *Shore Fishing in Hawaii.* Hilo, HI: Petroglyph Press, 1984. Known as the best book on Hawaiian fishing since 1944. This book receives the highest praise because it has born and bred many Hawaiian fishermen.

Kay, Alison, and Olive Schoenberg-Dole. *Shells of Hawaii.* Honolulu: University of Hawaii Press, 1991. Color photos and tips on where to look for certain shells.

Mahaney, Casey. *Hawaiian Reef Fish, The Identification Book.* 1993. A spiral-bound reference work featuring many color photos and descriptions of common reef fish found in Hawaiian waters.

Nickerson, Roy. *Brother Whale, A Pacific Whalewatcher's Log.* San Francisco: Chronicle Books, 1977. Introduces the average person to the life of earth's greatest mammals. Provides historical accounts, photos, and tips on whalewatching. Well-written, descriptive, and the best "first time" book on whales.

Pratt, H.D., P.L. Bruner, and D.G. Berrett. *The Birds of Hawaii and the Tropical Pacific.* Princeton, N.J. Princeton University Press, 1987. Useful field guide for novice and expert birdwatchers, covering Hawaii as well as other Pacific Island groups.

van Riper, Charles, and Sandra van Riper. *A Field Guide to the Mammals of Hawaii.* Honolulu: Oriental Publishing. A guide to the surprising number of mammals introduced into Hawaii. Full-color pages document description, uses, tendencies, and habitat. Small and thin, this book makes a worthwhile addition to any serious trekker's backpack.

FLORA

Kepler, Angela. *Exotic Tropicals of Hawaii.* Honolulu: Mutual Publishing, 1989. This small-format book features many color photos of exotic tropical flowers.

Kuck, Lorraine, and Richard Togg. *Hawaiian Flowers and Flowering Trees.* Rutland, VT: Tuttle, 1960. A classic, though no longer in print, field guide to tropical and subtropical flora illustrated in watercolor. A "to the point" description of Hawaiian plants and flowers with a brief history of their places of origin and their introduction to Hawaii.

Merrill, Elmer. *Plant Life of the Pacific World.* Rutland, VT: Tuttle, 1983. The definitive book for anyone planning a botanical tour to the entire Pacific Basin. Originally published in the 1930s, it remains a tremendous work, worth tracking down through the out-of-print book services.

Miyano, Leland. *Hawaii, A Floral Paradise.* Honolulu: Mutual Publishing, 1995. Photographed by Douglas Peebles, this large-format book is filled with informative text and beautiful color shots of tropical flowers commonly seen in Hawaii.

Sohmer, S.H., and R. Gustafson. *Plants and Flowers of Hawaii.* Honolulu: University of Hawaii Press, 1987. Sohmer and Gustafson cover the vegetation zones of Hawaii, from mountains to coast, introducing you to the wide and varied floral biology of the islands. They give a good introduction to the history and unique evolution of Hawaiian plantlife. Beautiful color plates are accompanied by clear and concise plant descriptions, with the scientific and common Hawaiian names listed.

Teho, Fortunato. *Plants of Hawaii—How to grow them.* Hilo, HI: Petroglyph Press, 1992. A small but useful book for those who want their backyards to bloom into tropical paradises.

HEALTH

McBride, L.R. *Practical Folk Medicine of Hawaii.* Hilo, HI: Petroglyph Press, 1975. An illustrated guide to Hawaii's medicinal plants as used by the *kahuna lapa'au* (medical healers). Includes a thorough section on ailments, diagnosis, and the proper folk remedy. Illustrated by the author, a renowned botanical researcher and former ranger at Volcanoes National Park.

Wilkerson, James A., M.D., ed. *Medicine for Mountaineering and Other Wilderness.* 4th ed. Seattle: The Mountaineers, 1992. Don't let the title fool you. Although the book focuses on specific health problems that may be encountered while mountaineering, it is the best first-aid and general health guide available today. Written by doctors for the layperson to use until help arrives, it is jam-packed with easily understandable techniques and procedures. For those intending extended treks, it is a must.

HISTORY

Apple, Russell A. *Trails: From Steppingstones to Kerbstones.* Honolulu: Bishop Museum Press, 1965. This "Special Publication #53" is a special-interest archaeological survey focusing on trails, roadways, footpaths, and highways and how they were designed and maintained throughout the years. Many "royal highways" from precontact Hawaii are cited.

Ashdown, Inez MacPhee. *Old Lahaina.* Honolulu: Hawaiian Service Inc., 1976. A small pamphlet-

type book listing most of the historical attractions of Lahaina Town, past and present. Ashdown is a life-long resident of Hawaii and gathered her information firsthand by listening to and recording stories told by ethnic Hawaiians and old *kama'aina* families.

——*Ke Alaloa o Maui.* Wailuku, HI: Kama'aina Historians Inc., 1971. A compilation of the history and legends connected to sites on the island of Maui. Ashdown was at one time a "lady in waiting" for Queen Liliuokalani and has since been proclaimed Maui's "Historian Emeritus."

Cameron, Roderick. *The Golden Haze.* New York: World Publishing, 1964. An account of Capt. James Cook's voyages of discovery throughout the South Seas. Uses original diaries and journals for an "on the spot" reconstruction of this great seafaring adventure.

Daws, Gavan. *Shoal of Time, A History of the Hawaiian Islands.* Honolulu: University of Hawaii Press, 1974. A highly readable history of Hawaii dating from its "discovery" by the Western world down to its acceptance as the 50th state. Good insight into the psychological makeup of influential characters who helped form Hawaii's past.

Finney, Ben, and James D. Houston. *Surfing, A History of the Ancient Hawaiian Sport.* Los Angeles: Pomegranate, 1996. Features many early etchings and old photos of Hawaiian surfers practicing their native sport.

Fornander, Abraham. *An Account of the Polynesian Race; Its origins and Migrations, and the Ancient History of the Hawaiian People to the Times of Kamehameha I.* Rutland, VT: C.E. Tuttle Co., 1969. This is a reprint of a three-volume opus originally published 1878-85. It is still one of the best sources of information on Hawaiian myth and legend.

Free, David. *Vignettes of Old Hawaii.* Honolulu: Crossroads Press,1994. A collection of short essays on a variety of subjects.

Fuchs, Lawrence. *Hawaii Pono.* New York: Harcourt, Brace and World, 1961. A detailed, scholarly work presenting an overview of Hawaii's history, based upon psychological and socio-logical interpretations. Encompasses most socio-ethnological groups from native Hawaiians to modern entrepreneurs. A must for social histor-ical background.

Handy, E.S., and Elizabeth Handy. *Native Planters in Old Hawaii*. Honolulu: Bishop Mu-seum Press, 1972. A superbly written, easily understood scholarly work on the intimate rela-tionship of precontact Hawaiians and the *aina* (land). Much more than its title implies, this book should be read by anyone seriously interested in Polynesian Hawaii.

Ii, John Papa. *Fragments of Hawaiian History*. Honolulu: Bishop Museum, 1959. Hawaii's his-tory under Kamehameha I as told by a Hawaiian who actually experienced it.

Joesting, Edward. *Hawaii: An Uncommon His-tory*. New York: W.W. Norton Co., 1978. A truly uncommon history told in a series of vignettes re-lating to the lives and personalities of the first white men in Hawaii, Hawaiian nobility, sea cap-tains, writers, and adventurers. Brings history to life. Absolutely excellent!

Kurisu, Yasushi. *Sugar Town, Hawaiian Plan-tation Days Remembered*. Honolulu: Watermark Publishing, 1995. Reminiscences of life gowing up on sugar plantations on the Hamakua Coast of the Big Island. Features many old photos.

Liliuokalani. *Hawaii's Story By Hawaii's Queen*. 1964. Reprint, Rutland, VT: Tuttle, 1991. A mov-ing personal account of Hawaii's inevitable move from monarchy to U.S. Territory by its last queen, Liliuokalani. The facts can be found in other his-tories, but none provides the emotion or point of view expressed by Hawaii's deposed monarch. A "must-read" to get the whole pic-ture.

McBride, Likeke. *Petroglyphs of Hawaii*. Hilo, HI: Petroglyph Press, 1996. A revised and up-dated guide to petroglyphs found in the Hawaiian Islands.

Nickerson, Roy. *Lahaina, Royal Capital of Hawaii*. Honolulu: Hawaiian Service, 1978. The story of Lahaina from whaling days to present, spiced with ample photographs.

INTRODUCTORY

Cohen, David, and Rick Smolan. *A Day in the Life of Hawaii*. New York: Workman, 1984. On December 2, 1983, 50 of the world's top pho-tojournalists were invited to Hawaii to photo-graph the variety of daily life on the islands. The photos are excellently reproduced, and accom-panied by a minimum of text.

Day, A.G., and C. Stroven. *A Hawaiian Reader*. 1959. Reprint, New York: Appleton, Century, Crofts, 1985. A poignant compilation of essays, diary entries, and fictitious writings that takes you from the death of Captain Cook through the "statehood services."

Department of Geography, University of Hawaii. *Atlas of Hawaii*. 2nd ed. Honolulu: University of Hawaii Press, 1983. Much more than an atlas filled with reference maps, this also contains commentary on the natural environment, cul-ture, and sociology; a gazetteer; and statistical ta-bles. Actually a mini-encyclopedia.

Michener, James A. *Hawaii*. New York: Ran-dom House, 1959. Michener's fictionalized his-torical novel has done more to inform *and* mis-inform readers about Hawaii than any other book ever written. A great tale with plenty of local color and information, but read it for pleasure, not facts.

Piercy, LaRue. *Hawaii This and That*. Honolulu: Mutual Publishing, 1994. Illustrated by Scot Ebanez. A 60-page book filled with one-sen-tence facts and oddities about all manner of things Hawaiian. Informative, amazing, and fun to read.

LANGUAGE

Elbert, Samuel, and Mary Pukui. *Hawaiian Dic-tionary*. Honolulu: University of Hawaii, 1986. The best dictionary available on the Hawaiian language. The *Pocket Hawaiian Dictionary* is a less expensive, condensed version of this dictionary, and adequate for most travelers with a general interest in the language.

Elbert, Samuel. *Spoken Hawaiian*. Honolulu: University of Hawaii Press, 1970. Progressive conversational lessons.

MYTHOLOGY AND LEGENDS

Beckwith, Martha. *Hawaiian Mythology*. 1970. Reprint, Honolulu: University of Hawaii Press, 1977. Nearly 60 years after its original printing in 1940, this work remains the definitive text on Hawaiian mythology. Beckwith compiled this book from many sources, giving exhaustive cross-references to genealogies and legends expressed in the oral tradition. If you are going to read one book on Hawaii's folklore, this should be it.

Colum, Padraic. *Legends of Hawaii*. New Haven: Yale University Press, 1937. Selected legends of old Hawaii, reinterpreted but closely based upon the originals.

Elbert, S., comp. *Hawaiian Antiquities and Folklore*. Honolulu: Univerity of Hawaii Press, 1959. Illustrated by Jean Charlot. A selection of the main legends from Abraham Fornander's great work, *An Account of the Polynesian Race*.

Kalakaua, His Hawaiian Majesty, King David. *The Legends and Myths of Hawaii*. Edited by R.M. Daggett, with a foreword by Glen Grant. Honolulu: Mutual Publishing, 1990. Originally published in 1888, Hawaii's own King Kalakaua draws upon his scholarly and formidable knowledge of the classic oral tradition to bring alive ancient tales from precontact Hawaii. A powerful yet somewhat Victorian voice from Hawaii's past speaks clearly and boldly, especially about the intimate role of pre-Christian religion in the lives of the Hawaiian people.

Melville, Leinanai. *Children of the Rainbow*. Wheaton, IL: Theosophical Publishing, 1969. A book on higher spiritual consciousness attuned to nature, which was the basic belief of pre-Christian Hawaii. The appendix contains illustrations of mystical symbols used by the *kahuna*. An enlightening book in many ways.

Thrum, Thomas. *Hawaiian Folk Tales*. 1907. Reprint, Chicago: McClurg and Co., 1950. A collection of Hawaiian tales from the oral tradition as told to the author from various sources.

Westervelt, W.D. *Hawaiian Legends of Volcanoes*. 1916. Reprint, Boston: Ellis Press, 1991. A small book concerning the volcanic legends of Hawaii and how they related to the fledgling field of volcanism at the turn of the century. The vintage photos alone are worth a look.

NATURAL SCIENCES

Abbott, Agatin, Gordon MacDonald, and Frank Peterson. *Volcanoes in the Sea*. Honolulu: University of Hawaii Press, 1983. A simplified yet comprehensive text covering the geology and volcanism of the Hawaiian Islands. Focuses upon the forces of nature (wind, rain, and surf) that shape the islands.

Carlquist, Sherwin. *Hawaii: A Natural History*, 2nd ed. National Tropical Botany, 1980. Definitive account of Hawaii's natural history.

Hazlett, Richard, and Donald Hyndman. *Roadside Geology of Hawaii*. Missoula, MT: Mountain Press Publishing, 1996. Begins with a general discusion of the geology of the Hawaiian Islands, followed by a road guide to the individual islands offering descriptions of easily seen features.

Hubbard, Douglass, and Gordon MacDonald. *Volcanoes of the National Parks of Hawaii*. 1982. Reprint, Volcanoes, HI: Hawaii Natural History Association, 1989. The volcanology of Hawaii, documenting the major lava flows and their geological effect on the state.

Kay, E. Alison, comp. *A Natural History of the Hawaiian Islands*. Honolulu: University of Hawaii Press, 1994. A selection of concise articles by experts in the fields of volcanism, oceanography, meteorology, and biology. An excellent reference source.

PERIODICALS

Aloha, The Magazine of Hawaii and the Pacific. Davick Publications, P.O. Box 49035, Escondido, CA 92046. This excellent bimonthly magazine is much more than glossy photography. Special features may focus on sports, the arts, history, flora and fauna, or just pure island adventure. *Aloha* is equally useful as a "dream book" for those who wish that they could visit Hawaii, and as a current resource for those actually going. One of the best for an overall view of Hawaii, and well worth the subscription price.

Hawaii Magazine. 1400 Kapiolani Blvd., Suite B, Honolulu, HI 96814. This magazine covers the Hawaiian Islands like a tropical breeze. Feature articles on all aspects of life in the islands, with special departments on travel, events, exhibits, and restaurant reviews. Up-to-the-minute information, and a fine read.

Naturist Society Magazine. P.O. Box 132, Oshkosh, WI 54920. This excellent magazine not only *uncovers* bathing-suit-optional beaches throughout the islands, giving tips for naturalists visiting Hawaii, but also reports on local politics, environment, and conservation measures from the health-conscious nudist point of view. A fine publication.

PICTORIALS

Grant, Glenn. *Hawaii The Big Island.* Honolulu: Mutual Publishing, 1988. Includes the historic, social, and nature photos of many photographers.

La Brucherie, Roger. *Hawaiian World, Hawaiian Heart.* Pine Valley, CA: Imagenes Press, 1989.

POLITICAL SCIENCE

Albertini, Jim, et al. *The Dark Side of Paradise, Hawaii in a Nuclear War.* Honolulu: cAtholic Action of Hawaii. Well-documented research outlining Hawaii's role and vulnerability in a nuclear world. This book presents the antinuclear and antimilitary side of the political issue in Hawaii.

Bell, Roger. *Last Among Equals: Hawaiian Statehood and American Politics.* Honolulu: University of Hawaii, 1984. Documents Hawaii's long and rocky road to statehood, tracing political partisanship, racism, and social change.

SPORTS AND RECREATION

Alford, John. *Mountain Biker's Guide to O'ahu: Mauku Trails of Hawai'i* Honolulu: Ohana Pub. 1995.

Ambrose, Greg. *Surfer's Guide to Hawaii.* Honolulu: Bess Press, 1991. Island-by-island guide to surfing spots.

Ball, Stuart. *Hiker's Guide to Oahu.* Honolulu: University of Hawaii Press, 1993. Very excellent.

Cagala, George. *Hawaii: A Camping Guide.* Hunter Pub., 1994. Detailed descriptions of campsites throughout the Hawaiian islands.

Chisholm, Craig. *Hawaiian Hiking Trails.* Lake Oswego, OR: Ferglen Press, 1989.

Lueras, Leonard. *Surfing, the Ultimate Pleasure.* Honolulu: Emphasis International, 1984. One of the most brilliant books ever written on surfing.

McMahon, Richard. *Camping Hawai'i: A Complete Guide.* Honolulu: University of Hawaii Press, 1997. A helpful handbook.

Morey, Kathy. *Oahu Trails.* Berkeley, CA: Wilderness Press, 1993. Morey's books are specialized, detailed trekker's guides to Hawaii's outdoors. Complete with useful maps, historical references, official procedures, and plants and animals encountered along the way. If you're focused on hiking, these are the best to take along. *Maui Trails, Kauai Trails,* and *Hawaii Trails* are also available.

Rosenberg, Steve. *Diving Hawaii.* Locust Valley, NY: Aqua Quest, 1990. Describes diving locations on the major islands as well as the marinelife divers are likely to see. Includes many color photos.

Smith, Robert. *Hawaii's Best Hiking Trails.* Huntington Beach, CA: Hawaiian Outdoor Adventures, 1991. Other guides by this author include *Hiking Oahu, Hiking Maui, Hiking Hawaii,* and *Hiking Kauai.*

Thorne, Chuck, and Lou Zitnik. *A Divers' Guide to Hawaii.* Kihei, HI: Hawaii's Diver's Guide, 1984. An expanded diver's and snorkeler's guide to the waters of the six main Hawaiian Islands. Complete list of maps with full descriptions, tips, and ability levels. A must for all levels of snorkelers and divers.

Thorne, Chuck. *The Diver's Guide to Maui.* Kahului, HI: Maui Dive Guide, 1984. A no-nonsense snorkeler's and diver's guide to Maui waters. Extensive maps, descriptions, and "straight from the shoulder" advice by one of Maui's best and most experienced divers. A must for all levels of divers and snorkelers.

Wallin, Doug. *Diving & Snorkeling Guide to the Hawaiian Islands,* 2nd ed. Pisces Books, 1991.

A guide offering brief descriptions of diving locations on the four major islands.

TRAVEL

Clark, John. *Beaches of the Big Island.* Honolulu: University of Hawaii Press, 1985. Definitive guide to beaches, including many off the beaten path. Features maps and black-and-white photos.

Riegert, Ray. *Hidden Hawaii.* Berkeley, CA: And/Or Press, 1992. Ray offers a "user-friendly" guide to the islands.

Stanley, David. *South Pacific Handbook.* 6th ed. Chico, CA: Moon Publications, 1995. The model upon which all travel guides should be based. Simply the best book in the world for travel throughout the South Pacific.

Warner, Evie, and Al Davies. *Bed and Breakfast Goes Hawaiian.* Kapa'a, HI: Island Bed and Breakfast, 1990. A combination bed and breakfast directory and guide to sights, activities, events, and restaurants on the six major islands.

GLOSSARY

CAPSULE HAWAIIAN

The list on the following pages gives you a "taste" of Hawaiian and provides a basic vocabulary of words in common usage which you are likely to hear. Becoming familiar with them is not a strict necessity, but they will definitely enhance your experience and make talking with local people more congenial. You'll soon notice that many islanders spice their speech with certain words, especially when they're speaking pidgin, and you too can use them just as soon as you feel comfortable. You might even discover some Hawaiian words that are so perfectly expressive they'll become regular parts of your vocabulary. Many Hawaiian words have been absorbed into the English dictionary.

Also see the **Language** and **Food and Drink** sections in the Introduction for other applicable Hawaiian words and phrases. The definitions given are not exhaustive, but are generally considered the most common.

Words marked with an asterisk (*) are used commonly throughout the islands.

a'a*—rough clinker lava. A'a has become the correct geological term to describe this type of lava found anywhere in the world.

ae—yes

ahupua'a—pie-shaped land divisions running from mountain to sea that were governed by *konohiki,* local *ali'i* who owed their allegiance to a reigning chief

aikane—friend; pal; buddy

aina—land; the binding spirit to all Hawaiians. Love of the land is paramount in traditional Hawaiian beliefs.

akamai—smart; clever; wise

akua—a god, or simply "divine." You'll hear people speak of their family or personal *amakua* (ancestral spirit). Favorites are the shark or the *pueo* (Hawaiian owl).

ali'i*—a Hawaiian chief or noble

aloha*—the most common greeting in the islands; can mean both hello or goodbye, welcome or farewell. It can also mean romantic love, affection, or best wishes.

amakua—a personal or family spirit, usually an ancestral spirit

aole—no

auwe—alas; ouch! When a great chief or loved one died, it was a traditional wail of mourning.

awa, also known as *kava,* a mildly intoxicating traditional drink made from the juice of chewed awa root, spat into a bowl, and used in religious ceremonies

halakahiki—pineapple

hale*—house or building; often combined with other words to name a specific place, such as Haleakala ("House of the Sun"), or Hale Pai ("Printing House")

hana*—work; combined with *pau* means end of work or quitting time

hanai—literally "to feed." Part of the true *aloha* spirit. A *hanai* is a permanent guest, or an adopted family member, usually an old person or a child. This is an enduring cultural phenomenon in Hawaii, in which a child from one family (perhaps that of a brother or sister, and quite often one's grandchild) is raised as one's own without formal adoption.

haole*—a word that at one time meant foreigner, but which now means a white person or Caucasian. Many etymological definitions have been put forth, but none satisfies everyone. Some feel that it signified a person without a background, because the first white men could not chant their genealogies as was common to Hawaiians.

hapa*—half, as in a mixed-blooded person being referred to as *hapa haole*

hapai*—pregnant; used by all ethnic groups when a *keiki* is on the way

haupia*—a coconut custard dessert often served at a luau

heiau*—A platform made of skillfully fitted rocks, upon which temporary structures were built as temples and offerings made to the gods.

holomuu*—an ankle-length dress that is much more fitted than a muumuu, and which is often worn on formal occasions

hono—bay, as in Honolulu ("Sheltered Bay")

honu—green sea turtle (endangered)

ho'oilo—traditional Hawaiian winter that began in November

hoolaulea—any happy event, but especially a family outing or picnic

hoomalimali*—sweet talk; flattery

huhu*—angry; irritated

hui*—a group; meeting; society. Often used to refer to Chinese businesspeople or family members who pool their money to get businesses started.

hukilau—traditional shoreline fish-gathering in which everyone lends a hand to *huki* (pull) the huge net. Anyone taking part shares in the *lau* (food). It is much more like a party than hard work, and if you're lucky you'll be able to take part in one.

hula*—a native Hawaiian dance in which the rhythm of the islands is captured by swaying hips and stories told by lyrically moving hands. A *halau* is a group or school of hula.

huli huli—barbecue, as in *huli huli* chicken

i'a—fish in general. *I'a maka* is raw fish.

imu*—underground oven filled with hot rocks and used for baking. The main cooking method featured at a luau, used to steam-bake pork and other succulent dishes. The tending of the *imu* was traditionally for men only.

ipo—sweetheart; lover; girl- or boyfriend

kahili—a tall pole topped with feathers, resembling a huge feather duster. It was used by an *ali'i* to announce his or her presence.

kahuna*—priest; sorcerer; doctor; skillful person. In old Hawaii *kahuna* had tremendous power, which they used for both good and evil. The *kahuna ana'ana* was a feared individual because he practiced "black magic" and could pray a person to death, while the *kahuna lapa'au* was a medical practitioner bringing aid and comfort to the people.

kai—the sea. Many businesses and hotels employ *kai* as part of their name.

kalua—means roasted underground in an *imu*. A favorite island food is *kalua* pork.

kama'aina*—a child of the land; an old-timer; a longtime island resident of any ethnic background; a resident of Hawaii or native son or daughter. Hotels and airlines often offer discounts called *"kama'aina* rates" to anyone who can prove island residency.

kanaka—man or commoner; later used to distinguish a Hawaiian from other races. Tone of voice can make it a derisive expression.

kane*—means man, but actually used to signify a relationship such as husband or boyfriend. Written on a lavatory door it means "Men's Room."

kaola*—any food that has been broiled or barbecued

kapu*—forbidden; taboo; keep out; do not touch

kapuna—a grandparent or old-timer; usually means someone who has gained wisdom. The statewide school system now invites *kapuna* to talk to the children about the old ways and methods.

kaukau*—slang word meaning food or chow; grub. Some of the best food in Hawaii comes from the *"kaukau* wagons," trucks that sell plate lunches and other morsels.

kauwa—a landless, untouchable caste once confined to living on reservations. Members of this caste were often used as human sacrifices at *heiau*. Calling someone *kauwa* is still considered a grave insult.

kava—also known as *awa*, a mildly intoxicating traditional drink made from the juice of chewed *awa* root, spat into a bowl, and used in religious ceremonies

keiki*—child or children; used by all ethnic groups. "Have you hugged your *keiki* today?"

kiawe—an algaroba tree from South America commonly found in Hawaii along the shore. It grows a nasty long thorn that can easily puncture a tire. Legend has it that the trees were introduced to the islands by a misguided missionary who hoped the thorns would coerce natives into wearing shoes. Actually, they are good for fuel, as fodder for hogs and cattle, and for reforestation, none of which you'll appreciate if you step on one of their thorns or flatten a tire on your rental car!

kokua—help. As in "Your *kokua* is needed to keep Hawaii free from litter."

kona wind*—a muggy subtropical wind that blows from the south and hits the leeward side of the islands. It usually brings sticky hot weather and is one of the few times when air-conditioning will be appreciated.

konane—a traditional Hawaiian game, similar to checkers, played with pebbles on a large flat stone used as a board

koolau—windward side of the island

kukui—a candlenut tree whose pods are polished and then strung together to make a beautiful *lei*. Traditionally the oil-rich nuts were strung on the rib of a coconut leaf and used as a candle.

kuleana—homesite; the old homestead; small farms. Especially used to describe the small spreads on Hawaiian Homes Lands on Molokai.

Kumulipo*—ancient Hawaiian genealogical chant that records the pantheon of gods, creation, and the beginning of humankind

la—the sun. Often combined with other words to be more descriptive, such as Lahaina ("Merciless Sun") or Haleakala ("House of the Sun").

lanai*—veranda or porch. You'll pay more for a hotel room if it has a lanai with an ocean view.

lani—sky or the heavens

lau hala*—traditional Hawaiian weaving of mats, hats, etc., from the prepared fronds of the pandanus (screw pine)

lei*—a traditional garland of flowers or vines. One of Hawaii's most beautiful customs. Given at any auspicious occasion, but especially when arriving or leaving Hawaii.

lele—the stone altar at a *heiau*

limu—edible seaweed of various types. Gathered from the shoreline, it makes an excellent salad. It's used to garnish many island dishes and is a favorite at luau.

lomi lomi—traditional Hawaiian massage; also, raw salmon made into a vinegared salad with chopped onion and spices

lua*—the toilet; the head; the bathroom

luakini—a human-sacrifice temple. Introduced to Hawaii in the 13th century at Waha'ula Heiau on the Big Island.

luau*—a Hawaiian feast featuring poi, *imu*-baked pork, and other traditional foods. Good ones provide some of the best gastronomical delights in the world.

luna—foreman or overseer in the plantation fields. They were often mounted on horseback and were renowned for either their fairness or their cruelty. Representing the middle class , they served as a buffer between plantation workers and white plantation owners.

mahalo*—thank you. *Mahalo nui* means "big thanks" or "thank you very much."

mahele—division. The "Great Mahele" of 1848 changed Hawaii forever when the traditional common lands were broken up into privately owned plots.

mahimahi*—a favorite eating fish. It's often called a dolphin, but a mahimahi is a true fish, not a cetacean.

mahu—a homosexual; often used derisively like "fag" or "queer"

maile—a fragrant vine used in traditional lei. It looks ordinary but smells delightful.

maka'ainana—a commoner; a person "belonging" to the *aina* (land), who supported the *ali'i* by fishing and farming and as a warrior

makai*—toward the sea; used by most islanders when giving directions

make—dead; deceased

malihini*—what you are if you have just arrived: a newcomer; a tenderfoot; a recent arrival

malo—the native Hawaiian loincloth. Never worn anymore except at festivals or pageants.

mana*—power from the spirit world; innate energy of all things animate or inanimate; the grace of god. Mana could be passed on from one person to another, or even stolen. Great care was taken to protect the *ali'i* from having their mana defiled. Commoners were required to lie flat on the ground and cover their faces whenever a great *ali'i* approached. *Kahuna* were often employed in the regaining or transference of mana.

manauahi—free; gratis; extra

manini—stingy; tight; a Hawaiianized word taken from the name of Don Francisco Marin, who was instrumental in bringing many fruits and plants to Hawaii. He was known for never sharing any of the bounty from his substantial gardens on Vineyard Street in Honolulu, therefore his name came to mean "stingy."

mauka*—toward the mountains; used by most islanders when giving directions *mauna*—mountain. Often combined with other words to be more descriptive, such as Mauna Kea ("White Mountain").

mele—a song or chant in the Hawaiian oral tradition that records the history and genealogies of the *ali'i*

menehune—the legendary "little people" of Hawaii. Like leprechauns, they are said to have shunned humans and possess magical powers. Stone walls said to have been completed in one night are often attributed to them. Some historians argue that they actually existed and were the aboriginals of Hawaii, inhabiting the islands before the coming of the Polynesians.

moa—chicken; fowl

moana*—the ocean; the sea. Many businesses and hotels as well as places have *moana* as part of their name.

moe—sleep

moolelo—ancient tales kept alive by the oral tradition and recited only by day

muumuu*—a "Mother Hubbard," an ankle-length dress with a high neckline introduced by the missionaries to cover the nakedness of the Hawaiians. It has become fashionable attire for almost any occasion in Hawaii.

nani—beautiful

nui—big; great; large; as in *mahalo nui* (thank you very much)

ohana—a family; the fundamental social division; extended family. Now used to denote a social organization with grassroots overtones, as in the "Protect Kahoolawe Ohana."

okolehau—literally "iron bottom"; a traditional booze made from ti root. *Okole* means "rear end" and *hau* means "iron," which was descriptive of the huge blubber pots in which *okolehau* was made. Also, if you drink too much it'll surely knock you on your *okole*.

ono*—delicious; delightful; the best. *Ono ono* means "extra or absolutely delicious."

opihi—a shellfish or limpet that clings to rocks and is gathered as one of the islands' favorite *pu pu*. Custom dictates that you never remove all of the *opihi* from a rock; some are always left to grow for future generations.

opu—belly; stomach

pahoehoe*—smooth, ropey lava that looks like burnt pancake batter. It is now the correct geological term used to describe this type of lava found anywhere in the world.

pakalolo—"crazy smoke"; grass; smoke; dope; marijuana

pake—a Chinese person. Can be derisive, depending on tone in which it is used. It is a bastardization of the Chinese word meaning "uncle."

pali*—a cliff; precipice. Hawaii's geology makes them quite common. The most famous are the *pali* of Oahu where a major battle was fought.

paniolo*—a Hawaiian cowboy. Derived from the Spanish *espaniola*. The first cowboys brought to Hawaii during the early 19th century were Mexicans from California.

papale—hat. Except for the feathered helmets of the *ali'i* warriors of old Hawaii, hats were generally not worn. However, once the islanders saw their practical uses and how fashionable they were, they began weaving them from various materials and quickly became experts at manufacture and design.

pa'u—long split skirt often worn by women when horseback riding. Last century, an island treat was *pa'u* riders in their beautiful dresses at Kapiolani Park in Honolulu. The tradition is carried on today at many of Hawaii's rodeos.

pau*—finished; done; completed. Often combined into *pau hana,* which means end of work or quitting time.

pilau—stink; bad smell; stench

pilikia—trouble of any kind, big or small; bad times

poi*—a glutinous paste made from the pounded corm of taro which ferments slightly and has a light sour taste. Purplish in color, it's a staple at luaus, where it is called "one-, two-, or three-finger" poi, depending upon its thickness.

pono—righteous or excellent

pua—flower

puka*—a hole of any size. *Puka* is used by all island residents, whether talking about a pinhole in a rubber boat or a tunnel through a mountain.

punalua—a traditional practice, before the missionaries arrived, of sharing mates. Western seamen took advantage of it, leading to the spread of contagious diseases and eventually to the ultimate demise of the Hawaiian people.

*punee**—bed; narrow couch. Used by all ethnic groups. To recline on a *punee* on a breezy lanai is a true island treat.

*pu pu**—an appetizer; a snack; hors d'oeuvres; can be anything from cheese and crackers to sushi. Oftentimes, bars or nightclubs offer them free.

pupule—crazy; nuts; out of your mind

pu'u—hill, as in Pu'u Ulaula ("Red Hill")

*tapa**—a traditional paper cloth made from beaten bark. Intricate designs were stamped in using beaters, and natural dyes added color. The tradition was lost for many years but is now making a comeback, and provides some of the most beautiful folk art in the islands.

*taro**—the staple of old Hawaii. A plant with a distinctive broad leaf that produces a starchy root. It was brought by the first Polynesians and was grown on magnificently irrigated plantations. According to the oral tradition, the lifegiving properties of taro hold mystical significance for Hawaiians, since it was created by the gods at about the same time as humans.

ti—a broad-leafed plant that was used for many purposes, from plates to hula skirts (never grass). Especially used to wrap religious offerings presented at the *heiau*.

*tutu**—grandmother; granny; older woman. Used by all as a term of respect and endearment.

*ukulele**—*uku* means "flea" and *lele* means "jumping," so literally "jumping flea"—the way the Hawaiians perceived the quick finger movements used on the banjolike Portuguese folk instrument called a *cavaquinho*. The ukulele quickly became synonymous with the islands.

*wahine**—young woman; female; girl; wife. Used by all ethnic groups. When written on a lavatory door it means "Women's Room."

wai—fresh water; drinking water

wela—hot. *Wela kahao* is a "hot time" or "making whoopee."

*wiki**—quickly; fast; in a hurry. Often seen as *wiki wiki* (very fast), as in "Wiki Wiki Messenger Service."

USEFUL PHRASES

Aloha ahiahi—Good evening.
Aloha au ia oe—I love you!
Aloha kakahiaka—Good morning.
Aloha nui loa—much love; fondest regards
Hauoli la hanau—Happy Birthday.

Hauoli makahiki hou—Happy New Year.
Komo mai—please come in; enter; welcome
Mele kalikimaka—Merry Christmas.
Okole maluna—bottoms up; salute; cheers; kampai

ACCOMMODATIONS INDEX

RESTAURANT INDEX

INDEX

BIRDWATCHING

GARDENS

KAMEHAMEHA

MILITARY MEMORIALS AND MUSEUMS

SURFING

T

TEMPLES AND *HEIAU*

UV

ABOUT THE AUTHORS

J.D. BISIGNANI 1947-1997

Joe Bisignani was a fortunate man because he made his living doing the two things that he liked best: traveling and writing. He will be greatly missed.

A mainstay of Moon Publications since 1979, he was best known in the travel world for his wildly successful, five-volume Hawaii Handbook series, of which *Maui Handbook* won the Hawaii Visitors Bureau's Best Guidebook Award in 1991, while *Hawaii Handbook* earned Best Guidebook as well as the Grand Award for Excellence in 1988. His *Japan Handbook* won the Lowell Thomas Travel Journalism Gold Award in 1993. Together with founder Bill Dalton and other writers, "Joe Biz" profoundly influenced the company's success in the travel publishing world.

ROBERT NILSEN

Robert Nilsen was born and raised in Minnesota. His first major excursion from the Midwest was a two-year stint in South Korea with the Peace Corps. Following that eye-opening service, he stayed on in Korea independently, teaching and traveling for another two years. Setting his sights on other lands and other cultures, he made his way through Asia during 1978-80, first heading south from Seoul to Bali and then west as far as the Khyber Pass before returning home to the United States. Over the intervening years, he has had the good fortune to return five times to various countries in Asia and the Pacific. Robert has written *South Korea Handbook* for Moon Publications, revised *Honolulu-Waikiki Handbook, Kauai Handbook, The Big Island of Hawaii Handbook,* and *Maui Handbook,* and contributed to the *Indonesia Handbook.* Since the passing of his good friend J.D. Bisignani, he has shouldered full responsibility for the revision of the Hawaii series of Moon Travel Handbooks, which also includes *Hawaii Handbook.*

www.moon.com

Enjoy our travel information center on the World Wide Web (WWW), loaded with interactive exhibits designed especially for the Internet.

ATTRACTIONS ON MOON'S WEB SITE INCLUDE:

ATLAS
Our award-winning, comprehensive travel guides cover destinations throughout North America and Hawaii, Latin America and the Caribbean, and Asia and the Pacific.

PRACTICAL NOMAD
Extensive excerpts, a unique set of travel links coordinated with the book, and a regular Q & A column by author and Internet travel consultant Edward Hasbrouck.

TRAVEL MATTERS
Our on-line travel zine, featuring articles; author correspondence; a travel library including health information, reading lists, and cultural cues; and our new contest, **Destination X,** offering a chance to win a trip to the mystery destination of your choice.

ROAD TRIP USA
Our best-selling book, ever; don't miss this award-winning Web guide to off-the-interstate itineraries.

Come visit us at: **www.moon.com**

LOSE YOURSELF IN THE EXPERIENCE, NOT THE CROWD

For 25 years, Moon Travel Handbooks have been the guidebooks of choice for adventurous travelers. Our award-winning Handbook series provides focused, comprehensive coverage of distinct destinations all over the world. Each Handbook is like an entire bookcase of cultural insight and introductory information in one portable volume. Our goal at Moon is to give travelers all the background and practical information they'll need for an extraordinary travel experience.

The following pages include a complete list of Handbooks, covering North America and Hawaii, Mexico, Latin America and the Caribbean, and Asia and the Pacific.To purchase Moon Travel Handbooks, check your local bookstore or order by phone: (800) 345-5473 M-F 8 am.-5 p.m. PST or outside the U.S. phone: (530) 345-5473.

"An in-depth dunk into the land, the people and their history, arts, and politics."
—*Student Travels*

"I consider these books to be superior to Lonely Planet. When Moon produces a book it is more humorous, incisive, and off-beat."
—*Toronto Sun*

"Outdoor enthusiasts gravitate to the well-written Moon Travel Handbooks. In addition to politically correct historic and cultural features, the series focuses on flora, fauna and outdoor recreation. Maps and meticulous directions also are a trademark of Moon guides."
—*Houston Chronicle*

"Moon [Travel Handbooks] . . . bring a healthy respect to the places they investigate. Best of all, they provide a host of odd nuggets that give a place texture and prod the wary traveler from the beaten path. The finest are written with such care and insight they deserve listing as literature."
—*American Geographical Society*

"Moon Travel Handbooks offer in-depth historical essays and useful maps, enhanced by a sense of humor and a neat, compact format."
—*Swing*

"Perfect for the more adventurous, these are long on history, sightseeing and nitty-gritty information and very price-specific."
—*Columbus Dispatch*

"Moon guides manage to be comprehensive and countercultural at the same time . . . Handbooks are packed with maps, photographs, drawings, and sidebars that constitute a college-level introduction to each country's history, culture, people, and crafts."
—*National Geographic Traveler*

"Few travel guides do a better job helping travelers create their own itineraries than the Moon Travel Handbook series. The authors have a knack for homing in on the essentials."
—**Colorado Springs** *Gazette Telegraph*

MEXICO

"These books will delight the armchair traveler, aid the undecided person in selecting a destination, and guide the seasoned road warrior looking for lesser-known hideaways."

—*Mexican Meanderings* Newsletter

"From tourist traps to off-the-beaten track hideaways, these guides offer consistent, accurate details without pretension."

—*Foreign Service Journal*

Archaeological Mexico	**$19.95**
Andrew Coe	420 pages, 27 maps
Baja Handbook	**$16.95**
Joe Cummings	540 pages, 46 maps
Cabo Handbook	**$14.95**
Joe Cummings	270 pages, 17 maps
Cancún Handbook	**$14.95**
Chicki Mallan	240 pages, 25 maps
Colonial Mexico	**$18.95**
Chicki Mallan	400 pages, 38 maps
Mexico Handbook	**$21.95**
Joe Cummings and Chicki Mallan	1,200 pages, 201 maps
Northern Mexico Handbook	**$17.95**
Joe Cummings	610 pages, 69 maps
Pacific Mexico Handbook	**$17.95**
Bruce Whipperman	580 pages, 68 maps
Puerto Vallarta Handbook	**$14.95**
Bruce Whipperman	330 pages, 36 maps
Yucatán Handbook	**$16.95**
Chicki Mallan	400 pages, 52 maps

LATIN AMERICA AND THE CARIBBEAN

"Solidly packed with practical information and full of significant cultural asides that will enlighten you on the whys and wherefores of things you might easily see but not easily grasp."

—*Boston Globe*

Belize Handbook	**$15.95**
Chicki Mallan and Patti Lange	390 pages, 45 maps
Caribbean Vacations	**$18.95**
Karl Luntta	910 pages, 64 maps
Costa Rica Handbook	**$19.95**
Christopher P. Baker	780 pages, 73 maps
Cuba Handbook	**$19.95**
Christopher P. Baker	740 pages, 70 maps
Dominican Republic Handbook	**$15.95**
Gaylord Dold	420 pages, 24 maps
Ecuador Handbook	**$16.95**
Julian Smith	450 pages, 43 maps
Honduras Handbook	**$15.95**
Chris Humphrey	330 pages, 40 maps
Jamaica Handbook	**$15.95**
Karl Luntta	330 pages, 17 maps
Virgin Islands Handbook	**$13.95**
Karl Luntta	220 pages, 19 maps

NORTH AMERICA AND HAWAII

"These domestic guides convey the same sense of exoticism that their foreign counterparts do, making home-country travel seem like far-flung adventure."

—*Sierra Magazine*

Alaska-Yukon Handbook	**$17.95**
Deke Castleman and Don Pitcher	530 pages, 92 maps
Alberta and the Northwest Territories Handbook	**$17.95**
Andrew Hempstead and Nadina Purdon	530 pages, 72 maps,
Arizona Traveler's Handbook	**$17.95**
Bill Weir and Robert Blake	512 pages, 54 maps
Atlantic Canada Handbook	**$17.95**
Nan Drosdick and Mark Morris	460 pages, 61 maps
Big Island of Hawaii Handbook	**$15.95**
J.D. Bisignani	390 pages, 23 maps

Boston Handbook	**$13.95**
Jeff Perk	200 pages, 20 maps
British Columbia Handbook	**$16.95**
Jane King and Andrew Hempstead	430 pages, 69 maps
Colorado Handbook	**$18.95**
Stephen Metzger	480 pages, 59 maps
Georgia Handbook	**$17.95**
Kap Stann	370 pages, 50 maps
Hawaii Handbook	**$19.95**
J.D. Bisignani	1,030 pages, 90 maps
Honolulu-Waikiki Handbook	**$14.95**
J.D. Bisignani	400 pages, 20 maps
Idaho Handbook	**$18.95**
Don Root	610 pages, 42 maps
Kauai Handbook	**$15.95**
J.D. Bisignani	320 pages, 23 maps
Maine Handbook	**$18.95**
Kathleen M. Brandes	660 pages, 27 maps
Massachusetts Handbook	**$18.95**
Jeff Perk	600 pages, 23 maps
Maui Handbook	**$15.95**
J.D. Bisignani	420 pages, 35 maps
Michigan Handbook	**$15.95**
Tina Lassen	300 pages, 30 maps
Montana Handbook	**$17.95**
Judy Jewell and W.C. McRae	480 pages, 52 maps
Nevada Handbook	**$18.95**
Deke Castleman	530 pages, 40 maps
New Hampshire Handbook	**$18.95**
Steve Lantos	500 pages, 18 maps
New Mexico Handbook	**$15.95**
Stephen Metzger	360 pages, 47 maps
New York Handbook	**$19.95**
Christiane Bird	780 pages, 95 maps
New York City Handbook	**$13.95**
Christiane Bird	300 pages, 20 maps
North Carolina Handbook	**$14.95**
Rob Hirtz and Jenny Daughtry Hirtz	275 pages, 25 maps
Northern California Handbook	**$19.95**
Kim Weir	800 pages, 50 maps
Oregon Handbook	**$17.95**
Stuart Warren and Ted Long Ishikawa	588 pages, 34 maps
Pennsylvania Handbook	**$18.95**
Joanne Miller	448 pages, 40 maps

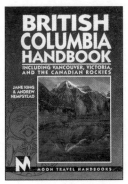

Road Trip USA	**$22.50**
Jamie Jensen	800 pages, 165 maps
Santa Fe-Taos Handbook	**$13.95**
Stephen Metzger	160 pages, 13 maps
Southern California Handbook	**$19.95**
Kim Weir	720 pages, 26 maps
Tennessee Handbook	**$17.95**
Jeff Bradley	530 pages, 44 maps
Texas Handbook	**$18.95**
Joe Cummings	690 pages, 70 maps
Utah Handbook	**$17.95**
Bill Weir and W.C. McRae	490 pages, 40 maps
Virginia Handbook	**$15.95**
Julian Smith	340 pages, 30 maps
Washington Handbook	**$19.95**
Don Pitcher	870 pages, 113 maps
Wisconsin Handbook	**$18.95**
Thomas Huhti	590 pages, 69 maps
Wyoming Handbook	**$17.95**
Don Pitcher	610 pages, 80 maps

ASIA AND THE PACIFIC

"Scores of maps, detailed practical info down to business hours of small-town libraries. You can't beat the Asian titles for sheer heft. (The) series is sort of an American Lonely Planet, with better writing but fewer titles. (The) individual voice of researchers comes through."

—Travel & Leisure

Australia Handbook	**$21.95**
Marael Johnson, Andrew Hempstead,	
and Nadina Purdon	940 pages, 141 maps
Bali Handbook	**$19.95**
Bill Dalton	750 pages, 54 maps
Bangkok Handbook	**$13.95**
Michael Buckley	244 pages, 30 maps
Fiji Islands Handbook	**$14.95**
David Stanley	300 pages, 38 maps
Hong Kong Handbook	**$16.95**
Kerry Moran	378 pages, 49 maps
Indonesia Handbook	**$25.00**
Bill Dalton	1,380 pages, 249 maps

Micronesia Handbook	**$14.95**
Neil M. Levy	340 pages, 70 maps
Nepal Handbook	**$18.95**
Kerry Moran	490 pages, 51 maps
New Zealand Handbook	**$19.95**
Jane King	620 pages, 81 maps
Outback Australia Handbook	**$18.95**
Marael Johnson	450 pages, 57 maps
Philippines Handbook	**$17.95**
Peter Harper and Laurie Fullerton	670 pages, 116 maps
Singapore Handbook	**$15.95**
Carl Parkes	350 pages, 29 maps
South Korea Handbook	**$19.95**
Robert Nilsen	820 pages, 141 maps
South Pacific Handbook	**$22.95**
David Stanley	920 pages, 147 maps
Southeast Asia Handbook	**$21.95**
Carl Parkes	1,080 pages, 204 maps
Tahiti-Polynesia Handbook	**$15.95**
David Stanley	380 pages, 35 maps
Thailand Handbook	**$19.95**
Carl Parkes	860 pages, 142 maps
Vietnam, Cambodia & Laos Handbook	**$18.95**
Michael Buckley	760 pages, 116 maps

OTHER GREAT TITLES FROM MOON

"For hardy wanderers, few guides come more highly
recommended than the Handbooks. They include
good maps, steer clear of fluff and flackery, and offer
plenty of money-saving tips. They also give you the
kind of information that visitors to strange lands—on
any budget—need to survive."

—*US News & World Report*

Moon Handbook	**$10.00**
Carl Koppeschaar	141 pages, 8 maps
The Practical Nomad: How to Travel Around the World	**$17.95**
Edward Hasbrouck	575 pages
Staying Healthy in Asia, Africa, and Latin America	**$11.95**
Dirk Schroeder	230 pages, 4 maps

MOONBELTS

Looking for comfort and a way to keep your most important articles safe while traveling? These were our own concerns and that is why we created the Moonbelt. Made of heavy-duty Cordura nylon, the Moonbelt offers maximum protection for your money and important papers. Designed for all-weather comfort, this pouch slips under your shirt or waistband, rendering it virtually undetectable and inaccessible to pickpockets. It features a one-inch high-test quick-release buckle so there's no fumbling for the strap or repeated adjustments. This handy buckle opens and closes with a touch, but won't come undone until you want it to. Moonbelts accommodate traveler's checks, passport, cash, photos, etc. Measures 5 x 9 inches and fits waists up to 48″.

Available in black only. **US$8.95**
Sales tax (7.25%) for California residents
$1.50 for 1st Class shipping & handling.

To order, call (800) 345-5473
outside the US (530) 345-5473 or fax (530) 345-6751

Make checks or money orders payable to:
MOON TRAVEL HANDBOOKS
PO Box 3040, Chico, CA 95927-3040 U.S.A.
We accept Visa, MasterCard, or Discover.

 MOON TRAVEL HANDBOOKS

ROAD TRIP USA

Cross-Country Adventures on America's Two-Lane Highways

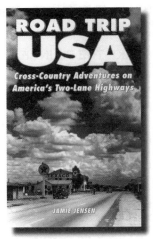

ROAD TRIP USA
Cross-Country Adventures on America's Two-Lane Highways

JAMIE JENSEN

$22.50   800 pages

"For those who feel an adrenaline rush everytime they hear the words 'road trip,' and who understand that getting there is at least half the fun, this is quite simply the best book of its type ever published."

—*Conde Nast Traveler* web site

"Just might be the perfect book about hitting the summoning highway . . . It's impossible not to find something enticing in *Road Trip USA* to add to your next cycling expedition. An encyclopedia of roadside wonders."   **—Harley Davidson *Enthusiast***

"For budding myth collectors, I can't think of a better textbook."

—*Los Angeles Times*

"A terrific guide for those who'd rather swat mosquitoes than take the interstate."

—Colorado Springs *Gazette Telegraph*

"Jensen is well-versed in travel, has an enjoyable yet informative style and will guide you along each mile. Don't leave home without it!"   **—*Mobilia***

"Zany inspiration for a road Gypsie in search of off-the-beaten-path adventure."

—*The Toronto Globe and Mail*

"A historic journey into the heart and soul of America."
—*Route 66 Magazine*

"Jamie Jensen and the 12 intrepid contributors to *Road Trip USA* have been everywhere and seen everything compiling this exhaustive, delightful, destination-anywhere guide to American road-tripping."

—*Citybooks*, Washington D.C.

"Not only a fantastic guide . . . a great companion!"

—*The Herald*, Columbia S.C.

THE PRACTICAL NOMAD

✈ TAKE THE PLUNGE

"The greatest barriers to long-term travel by Americans are the disempowered feelings that leave them afraid to ask for the time off. Just do it."

✈ TAKE NOTHING FOR GRANTED

"Even 'What time is it?' is a highly politicized question in some areas, and the answer may depend on your informant's ethnicity and political allegiance as well as the proximity of the secret police."

✈ TAKE THIS BOOK

$17.95   576 pages

With experience helping thousands of his globetrotting clients plan their trips around the world, travel industry insider Edward Hasbrouck provides the secrets that can save readers money and valuable travel time.
An indispensable complement to destination-specific travel guides,
The Practical Nomad includes:

> **airfare strategies**
>
> **ticket discounts**
>
> **long-term travel considerations**
>
> **travel documents**
>
> **border crossings**
>
> **entry requirements**
>
> **government offices**
>
> **travel publications**
>
> **Internet information resources**

WHERE TO BUY MOON TRAVEL HANDBOOKS

BOOKSTORES AND LIBRARIES: Moon Travel Handbooks are distributed worldwide. Please contact our sales manager for a list of wholesalers and distributors in your area.

TRAVELERS: We would like to have Moon Travel Handbooks available throughout the world. Please ask your bookstore to write or call us for ordering information. If your bookstore will not order our guides for you, please contact us for a free catalog.

Moon Travel Handbooks
P.O. Box 3040
Chico, CA 95927-3040 U.S.A.
tel.: (800) 345-5473, outside the U.S. (530) 345-5473
fax: (530) 345-6751
e-mail: travel@moon.com

IMPORTANT ORDERING INFORMATION

PRICES: All prices are subject to change. We always ship the most current edition. We will let you know if there is a price increase on the book you order.

SHIPPING AND HANDLING OPTIONS: Domestic UPS or USPS first class (allow 10 working days for delivery): $4.50 for the first item, $1.00 for each additional item.

Moonbelt shipping is $1.50 for one, 50 cents for each additional belt.

UPS 2nd Day Air or Printed Airmail requires a special quote.

International Surface Bookrate 8-12 weeks delivery: $4.00 for the first item, $1.00 for each additional item. Note: We cannot guarantee international surface bookrate shipping. We recommend sending international orders via air mail, which requires a special quote.

FOREIGN ORDERS: Orders that originate outside the U.S.A. must be paid for with an international money order, a check in U.S. currency drawn on a major U.S. bank based in the U.S.A., or Visa, MasterCard, or Discover.

TELEPHONE ORDERS: We accept Visa, MasterCard, or Discover payments. Call in your order: (800) 345-5473, 8 a.m.-5 p.m. Pacific standard time. Outside the U.S. the number is (530) 345-5473.

INTERNET ORDERS: Visit our site at: www.moon.com

ORDER FORM

Prices are subject to change without notice. Be sure to call (800) 345-5473,
or (530) 345-5473 from outside the U.S. 8 a.m.–5 p.m. PST for current prices and editions.
(See important ordering information on preceding page.)

Name: _____ Date: _____

Street: _____

City: _____ Daytime Phone: _____

State or Country: _____ Zip Code: _____

QUANTITY	TITLE	PRICE

Taxable Total_____

Sales Tax (7.25%) for California Residents_____

Shipping & Handling_____

TOTAL_____

Ship: ☐ UPS (no P.O. Boxes) ☐ 1st class ☐ International surface mail

Ship to: ☐ address above ☐ other _____

_____

_____

Make checks payable to: **MOON TRAVEL HANDBOOKS**, P.O. Box 3040, Chico, CA 95927-3040
U.S.A. We accept Visa, MasterCard, or Discover. **To Order**: Call in your Visa, MasterCard, or Discover number,
or send a written order with your Visa, MasterCard, or Discover number and expiration date clearly written.

Card Number: ☐ **Visa** ☐ **MasterCard** ☐ **Discover**

☐ ☐ ☐ ☐ ☐ ☐ ☐ ☐ ☐ ☐ ☐ ☐ ☐ ☐ ☐ ☐

Exact Name on Card: _____

Expiration date:_____

Signature: _____

U.S.~METRIC CONVERSION

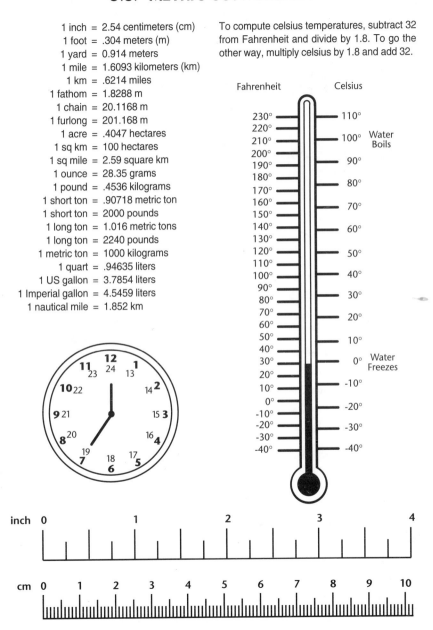

1 inch = 2.54 centimeters (cm)
1 foot = .304 meters (m)
1 yard = 0.914 meters
1 mile = 1.6093 kilometers (km)
1 km = .6214 miles
1 fathom = 1.8288 m
1 chain = 20.1168 m
1 furlong = 201.168 m
1 acre = .4047 hectares
1 sq km = 100 hectares
1 sq mile = 2.59 square km
1 ounce = 28.35 grams
1 pound = .4536 kilograms
1 short ton = .90718 metric ton
1 short ton = 2000 pounds
1 long ton = 1.016 metric tons
1 long ton = 2240 pounds
1 metric ton = 1000 kilograms
1 quart = .94635 liters
1 US gallon = 3.7854 liters
1 Imperial gallon = 4.5459 liters
1 nautical mile = 1.852 km

To compute celsius temperatures, subtract 32 from Fahrenheit and divide by 1.8. To go the other way, multiply celsius by 1.8 and add 32.

Fahrenheit   Celsius

230° — — 110°
220° —
210° — — 100° Water Boils
200° —
190° — — 90°
180° —
170° — — 80°
160° — — 70°
150° —
140° — — 60°
130° —
120° — — 50°
110° —
100° — — 40°
90° —
80° — — 30°
70° —
60° — — 20°
50° —
40° — — 10°
30° —
20° — — 0° Water Freezes
10° —
0° — — -10°
-10° — — -20°
-20° — — -30°
-30° —
-40° — — -40°

inch 0   1   2   3   4

cm 0 1 2 3 4 5 6 7 8 9 10

The Frugal Traveler Says . . .
See Honolulu on a Dollar

Enjoy the tropical breezes when you go topless in your Chrysler Sebring Convertible. There's simply no finer car for: • taking the coastline drive to Oahu's Great North Shore (not part of Canada) • cruising Waikiki like you own the place • zipping along the newly opened super-scenic H-3 Freeway • appearing extremely cool pulling up to valet parking

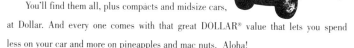

Thrill the kids with an exciting Dodge Caravan. Just because you're on vacation doesn't mean you won't have to cart all their stuff: • space for kid seats and diaper bags • enough room to separate the in-laws • as many cupholders as the law allows

Sport about like a sporty sort in your sporty Jeep® Cherokee. It's the perfect vehicle for carrying sporty gear: • throw your golf clubs in the back seat • let your surfboard ride in style • wear your super-loud aloha shirt with real pride • meet other sporty people

You'll find them all, plus compacts and midsize cars, at Dollar. And every one comes with that great DOLLAR® value that lets you spend less on your car and more on pineapples and mac nuts. Aloha!

Call 944-1544 on Oahu, 1-800-342-7398 from the neighbor islands, and for worldwide reservations call toll free 1-800-800-4000.

D LLAR.
RENT A CAR
DOLLAR MAKES SENSE.®

✿ Dollar features quality products of the Chrysler Corporation and other fine cars. ©1998 Dollar Rent A Car Systems, Inc.